THE
GROWER'S
GUIDE

THE
GROWER'S
GUIDE

CAXTON

This edition specially produced for CEEPI Ltd/Dealerfield Ltd in 1989

ISBN 0 907305 33 4

Printed and bound in Yugoslavia by Mladinska Knjiga.

ACKNOWLEDGEMENTS

A–Z Collection, Bernard Alfieri, Heather Angel, Ardea Photographics,
Ashmer Seeds Ltd, Barnaby's Picture Library, Michael Boys, Pat Brindley,
S. Buczacki, Camera Press, R.J. Corbin, John K.B. Cowley, Crown
Copyright, Michael Davies, Samuel Dobie & Sons, H.L. Edlin, The
Electricity Council, Derek Fell, Monica Fuller, Brian Furner, Stephen
Gardener, Glasshouse Crops Research Institute, Halls, Homes and
Greenhouses, J. Hamilton, Iris Hardwick, Angela Hormack, Angelo
Hornack, Humex Ltd, G.E. Hyde, ICI, IGDA, Leslie Johns, Clay Jones,
Marshall Cavendish, Michael Leale, Elsa Megson, Tania Midgley, Mid-West
Photographic Agency, Ken Muir, Murphy Chemicals Ltd, National
Vegetable Research Station, Nutting & Theodey, Oxford Scientific Films,
PBS, Picture Point, F.M. Procter, Ray Proctor, Rex Rathmore, Richards of
Darlington, Valerie Rose, Shell Photo Service, Donald Smith, Harry Smith,
Peter Stiles, Suttons Seeds, Thompson & Morgan Ltd, University of
Reading, W.J. Unwin Ltd, Michael Warren, Elizabeth Whiting,
D. Wildridge.

CONTENTS

GARDENING UNDER GLASS

A YEARLY PLANNER FOR THE EDIBLE GARDEN   *327*

SUCCESSFUL FRUIT AND VEGETABLE GROWING

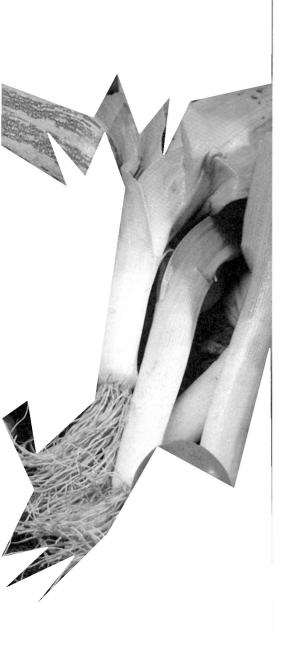

INTRODUCTION

The publication of a book comprising both fruit and vegetables is of particular value and interest to the gardener for, in the past, it has been customary to deal with these two subjects separately. Possibly this was because a collection of top fruit would normally be planted to form an orchard which would be quite separate to the vegetable garden. Nowadays, except for the plantings of commercial growers, the orchard as such is on its way out. The average garden is not large enough to accommodate this luxury.

This does not mean that interest in top fruit has been squeezed out. It would, I feel sure, be true to say that there has never been a time when the value of fresh fruit and vegetables has been so widely accepted or so much appreciated. Continuing high prices (often with no improvement in quality) have prompted many people to grow at least part of their requirements.

At first sight it would seem that smaller gardens and an increasing awareness of the value of fresh fruit and vegetables pose a difficult problem. Fortunately, the plant breeders have not been idle. The old standard and half-standard trees have largely given way to bush trees where a pair of steps give height enough to gather the crop. More recently, the dwarf and semi-dwarf types, which are small enough for the average garden, have been developed. In choosing these, care should be taken that the varieties will cross-pollinate each other; good nurserymen are always willing to give advice on this point. Cordons and espaliers are two other forms which are eminently suited to the smaller garden. These can be used alongside paths or as a dividing screen between different parts of the garden. All these types are fully described in this book.

House walls should not be forgotten, either. Correctly trained and tended trees grown on house walls yield superb fruit. Some of the more delicate fruits such as apricots, peaches and nectarines will flourish on south-facing walls, while a north or east wall will support a Morello cherry. Another good subject for a house wall, or a cool greenhouse, is the vine. The renewed interest in home wine-making has turned attention to vines, and new cultivars have now appeared which can be expected to set and ripen a reasonable crop. Moreover, we have learnt that grapes can be grown much farther north than was at one time thought possible.

Where soft fruits are concerned it has long been the custom to grow strawberries in the vegetable garden and include them in the vegetable cropping plan. A row of raspberries does not take up too much space if it is sited across one end of the garden or alongside a path. They, too, can be used to make a leafy and productive screen. Gooseberries can be grown as cordons to edge a path, and blackberries and loganberries, trained on wires stretched between posts, also make leafy screens or can be used to clothe boundary fences.

In this connection I would make a special plea for the loganberry – a neglected fruit. Picked fresh from the cane they are tart unless they are *fully* ripe, and this may have turned some people against them, but in pies and flans they are excellent. They also make a splendid jam and a superb jelly.

Most housewives will want a few blackcurrant bushes. This fruit, as many people know, is of particular value because of its high vitamin c content. Nowadays, labour costs of picking are so high it is becoming increasingly difficult to find blackcurrants in the shops, and when they are found they are expensive. Redcurrants and whitecurrants are not so well known, but a handful of redcurrants in a mixed fruit pie gives the whole a delightful, piquant flavour, and they make a fine jelly.

Then, too, for those who like to try something a little more difficult and unusual there are fruits like the Chinese gooseberry and the Cape gooseberry.

With both fruit and vegetables the importance of freshness can never be stressed too much. Most people like strawberries, but this delicious fruit can only be tasted to perfection when a sun-ripened fruit is picked and eaten straight from the plant. The Victoria plum is one of the most popular fruits; perfection here is a ripe fruit freshly picked from a tree on a sunny wall. The limp lettuce so often offered in shops or market stalls has very little in common with a Sugar Cos lettuce, cut and washed only a short time before it is eaten. Nor has the flaccid bundle of leaves which so often passes for spring cabbage much resemblance to a well-hearted spring cabbage, with its own distinctive, 'nutty' flavour. Peas and beans are two other subjects where freshness is so important.

Growing one's own fruit and vegetables allows one to choose those varieties which are of first-rate table quality. The commercial grower, understandably enough, concentrates on the varieties that yield heavily, and pack and travel well. These are not always those of the highest quality.

More and more people to-day are setting aside a part of the garden for a vegetable patch, and more and more people are taking an allotment, or joining the queue in the many areas where the supply of plots does not equal the demand. All the basic vegetables, with their cultivation, will be found within these pages, together with some not so well known.

The increase in Continental travel has awakened interest in vegetables such as courgettes, aubergines and sweet peppers. Courgettes (which are really baby marrows), are not difficult to grow. Aubergines and sweet peppers, although more demanding, should prosper in those areas where outdoor tomatoes do well, and the use of frames or cloches will go far to ensure their success.

Frames and cloches are a great asset in the vegetable garden. Protection to growing crops can be given at both ends of the season, and because of the growing time saved it is often possible to sow or plant an extra crop. A small greenhouse, even without heat, can be used for growing lettuce and raising vegetable seedlings, in addition to its more usual role of producing a crop of tomatoes.

The smaller the plot the more essential it is to get maximum results from it. Intensive cultivation is one of the subjects covered in this book. Another is the correct spacing of vegetables and the latest methods by which space can be saved without crowding the crops. This is a field in which research is still going on.

There is valuable information on the different *types* of vegetables, and the importance of choosing the right *varieties* – subjects of special value to those who are new to vegetable gardening. Recommended varieties are given for all fruits and vegetables. Some of these are old favourites, others are new varieties of merit. Gardeners are often accused of being too conservative in their choice of varieties. New varieties of vegetables are always coming along and, by trying several each season, important discoveries can be made. After all, the established varieties were once new introductions!

Common diseases and pests are listed, together with the measures to be taken against them. Regrettably, such information is necessary, but they should not prove too depressing; no gardener is likely to encounter all the pests and diseases mentioned here. Where fruits and vegetables are grown in good conditions, from tested seeds of healthy stock, disease should not be a problem. Prevention is usually better than cure and is certainly less expensive! Pests will be encountered from time to time, and should be dealt with at the first sign of trouble, *not* when they have gained a firm hold.

Garden terms in common use (which may sometimes puzzle the beginner) are explained in brackets in the text and have been gathered together for easy reference in a useful glossary at the end of the book.

Even with careful planning the supply will sometimes exceed the demand, but the fruit and vegetable gardener of to-day has no need to waste any of his precious crops. A surplus of fruit can be jammed or bottled, or put into the deep freeze. Most vegetables freeze well and can be stored in this way for use in lean periods. There can be no doubt that the advent of the deep freeze has given a boost to fruit and vegetable growing. Another important point is that the gardener who grows his own fruit and vegetables can pick and freeze them when they are in the peak of condition.

Young married couples with growing families, in particular, will be anxious to make the fullest use of their gardens, and this book will help them to do just that. Others, perhaps setting up house for the first time, or planning their first garden, will need advice on what fruit and vegetables they can include. Even the older hands, it is hoped, will find much to interest them and something of use.

Gardening is a relaxing hobby. The stresses and strains of modern living can be soothed away in the garden, and with an added bonus of fresh fruit and vegetables, the therapy is all the more valuable and beneficial.

Basic Principles in the Garden

In the simplest of terms, gardening is the care and cultivation of plants. It is a therapeutic activity as it involves gentle, healthy exercise in the open air. However, the enjoyment of gardening is in the success of one's work and in this, insufficient knowledge can lead to failure and frustration. Therefore to enjoy gardening to the full you need to understand certain basic principles.

You need to know how to grow individual varieties respecting their preferences for shade or sun, marshy ground or dry. It is much easier and rewarding to grow a plant where the conditions are to its liking than to try and defy the laws of Nature.

Essentially gardening should be a leisurely pursuit but it can only be so if you carefully pre-plan your activity. A vegetable plot need not be demanding if you co-ordinate the weeding and feeding of your plants. Fruit bushes can be easily controlled if you plant a dwarf or semi-dwarf variety. Flowering shrubs are great time-savers – they require little attention once established and are great weed smotherers. They provide a background of colour throughout the winter, flower in the spring and summer and act as living fences.

In planting perennials, you can choose from a wide range of shapes, sizes and colours and they lead a long life. All that is required is the lifting, dividing and re-planting of the plants once every four to five years.

Biennials and annuals can be grown afresh every year and provide the opportunity for you to ring the changes.

Hardy annuals are of special value to those gardeners without greenhouses. The seeds can be sown in open ground, bloom in the summer and carpet the garden with colour throughout the remainder of the season.

Gardening need not be expensive. If you develop your skills in taking cuttings and offshoots you can benefit from neighbour's plants. Fertilizers too which can be expensive to buy in the shops can be manufactured on your compost heap. By recognising and treating the various pests and diseases which afflict certain plants you can save yourself the expense of replacing them.

Tools are however worth the investment. Good tools together with an understanding of gardening are the basic ingredients to good gardening.

Acid and Alkaline Soils

To grow healthy plants it is vital to provide the right soil conditions. One of the most important tasks is to maintain the correct balance of acidity or alkalinity according to the plants being grown. Some subjects grow better in an alkaline (limey or chalky) soil while others, such as rhododendrons, will grow only in an acid one (free of lime or chalk). The majority of garden plants, however, much prefer a soil that is midway between these two extremes.

Before you prepare your soil for planting it is advisable to carry out a soil test with one of the soil-testing kits that are available from garden centres and good department stores. Such a test will indicate the degree or intensity of acidity or alkalinity. This is measured on a logarithmic scale called the pH scale. On this scale pH 7 is neutral (neither acid nor alkaline) while lower numbers indicate increasing degrees of acidity and higher numbers show increasing degrees of alkalinity. A wide range of commonly-grown plants, including vegetables, fruit, roses, hardy perennials, trees and shrubs, grow best in a slightly acid to neutral soil of pH 6·5 to 7·0.

High acidity or alkalinity

If your soil pH is below 5·5 then many plants may fail to grow. Also the numbers of undesirable organisms increase rapidly.

On the other hand an excessively limey soil; with a pH of over 8·0, can produce many plant disorders. Certain important plant foods, particularly iron and magnesium (but also manganese), are made unavailable to plants if the soil is limey. If a plant cannot absorb sufficient iron then its leaves will turn yellow and it may become stunted and eventually die. This yellowing is known as lime-induced chlorosis. Bushes (particularly fruit bushes, roses and hydrangeas) and fruit trees quickly show symptoms of chlorosis if iron is not available. You can, however, cure this condition with annual drenches of a solution of sequestrene (applied according to maker's instructions); this supplies iron in a readily-available form.

How to make a soil test

When using the soil-testing kit, quarter-fill the test tube (supplied with the kit) with soil and add the lime test solution, following the instructions provided. Then shake the tube to mix the contents thoroughly. Allow the solution to settle. When the soil has settled the clear liquid above will be of a certain colour according to the acidity or alkalinity of the soil. This colour can vary from red (when the soil is very acid) through orange (when only slightly acid) to shades of green (when the soil is neutral or limey). A chart showing the various colours with the appropriate pH number alongside is included in the kit. The liquid in the tube must, of course, be matched as closely as possible with one of these colours in order to ascertain the pH of your soil.

INTERNATIONAL SOIL TESTING AIDS

Colours shown on chart are guides and may not exactly match fluid in test tube

LIME TEST (ACIDITY)

A 7½ pH

B 6½ pH

C 6 pH

D 5¼ pH

E 4½ pH

NITROGEN TEST

The first figure in the NPK formula for commercial fertilizer

A 2%

B 3%

C 4%

D 6%

E 8%

PHOSPHORUS TEST

The second figure in the NPK formula

A 4%

B 5%

C 6%

D 8%

E 10%

POTASH TEST

The third figure in the NPK formula

A 2%

B 4%

C 8%

D 12%

E 16%

Gardening on alkaline soil

Some plants like a reasonably limey soil (pH of up to 8·0). Examples of these are members of the cabbage family (including wallflowers and aubrieta), carnations and pinks, beech, hornbeam, box, yew, clematis, gypsophila, and scabious. Cabbages and wallflowers suffer far less from club root disease (that causes the roots to swell and the plants to become stunted) if grown in a limey soil. Another interesting fact is that hydrangeas produce blue flowers in an acid soil, but pink blooms in alkaline conditions. If the soil is neutral, the blooms will be mauvish.

To lower the pH of a soil (reduce its alkalinity) you can incorporate heavy dressings of peat, leaf mould, well-rotted manure or garden compost each year. Applying flowers of sulphur will also reduce the pH but a heavy application is needed to reduce the pH by even one unit. For example, to reduce it from 8·0 to 7·0 would necessitate a dressing of about 1kg per sq m (2 lb per sq yd).

In chalky or limey areas it is probably inadvisable to use tap water for pot plants as the water will be alkaline and could result in chlorosis. Instead try to use rainwater collected from a greenhouse or garage roof, or the water obtained from defrosting the fridge or freezer, as this will be soft or acid.

Acid soils

To raise the lime content of an acid soil, treat it with a dressing of hydrated lime or ground chalk. Usually this application is made in the winter after you have finished digging over the garden. Allow the lime to lie on the surface over the winter and then fork it in in the spring. Do not apply manure and lime in the same winter as they interact unfavourably.

On heavy or clay soils apply lime more generously – as much as 500g per sq m (1 lb per sq yd) at one time – but less frequently than on light or sandy types; lime helps to open up and flocculate (create a good crumb structure) the heavier type of soil. Sandy soils are best limed fairly lightly, 135–270g per sq m (4–8 oz per sq yd) annually. On such soils lime is easily leached or washed out by heavy rain. Sandy soils are generally more acid than clay soils and peaty soils are often excessively acid.

If the soil is very acid, say a pH of 5·0 or below, it is inadvisable to apply a large quantity of lime in a single application in order to bring the pH value up to slight acidity or neutral. Instead, apply a moderate dressing – about 500g per sq m (1 lb per sq yd) – regularly each winter over a number of years.

Above: our chart is adapted from Sudbury's soil-testing kit; below: colour of hydrangeas varies with soil balance

How to Improve Difficult Soils

The beginning of winter is the time for digging over the garden so that the elements have a chance to work on the soil before cultivation begins again in the spring. It is during this digging that you can do much to improve difficult soils. 'Difficult' means those that may be hard to work with or those that, because of their poor structure, are either too wet or too dry for good plant growth, or lacking in essential humus or organic matter.

Soils can be divided into four main types: clays, sands, chalk soils and loams. Loams come midway between clays and sands. They are usually easy to work and provide ideal conditions for plants. Clay, sand and chalk each have special characteristics that can make them difficult soils and it may take several years to turn them into easily-managed growing mediums.

CLAY

Clay is commonly known as a heavy soil because it is very hard to cultivate – both to dig and to prepare for seed sowing or planting in the spring. Because of its chemical composition it has a very dense or close structure. It is able to hold large amounts of water within the clay particles, causing them to swell. Water is also held on the surface of the particles, and the particles themselves are held together by electrostatic attraction. It is therefore a very wet and sticky soil and takes a long time to dry out and warm up in the spring.

During the autumn and winter, and in wet weather at other times of year, clay may become waterlogged and this will affect the health of plants. When a soil is holding too much water the oxygen supply to the plants' roots is reduced and if this condition continues over too long a period the plants may die. In hot weather during spring and summer, clay soils can become as hard as rock; for as they dry out the clay particles contract, making cultivation almost impossible.

Opening up clay soils

Dig clay soils in early to mid winter (November to mid December) so that frosts can break them down throughout the winter. Frosts will make a heavy soil more crumbly and therefore far easier to cultivate in the spring. You can also make

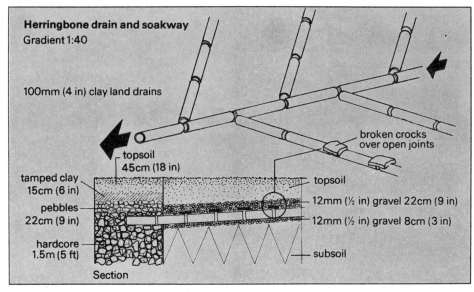

Herringbone drain and soakway
Gradient 1:40

100mm (4 in) clay land drains

broken crocks over open joints

topsoil 45cm (18 in)

tamped clay 15cm (6 in)

pebbles 22cm (9 in)

hardcore 1.5m (5 ft)

Section

topsoil

12mm (½ in) gravel 22cm (9 in)

12mm (½ in) gravel 8cm (3 in)

subsoil

When clay holds too much water, it may be necessary to make a herringbone drain and soakaway before soil is workable

a clay soil more crumbly, and take out most of the stickiness, by applying a top dressing of horticultural gypsum (sulphate of lime) immediately after digging. Let it lie on the surface over the winter, during which time it will be washed into the topsoil by rain. Gypsum can generally be obtained from good gardening shops and centres. Apply it fairly generously each year, at a rate of about 500g–1kg per sq m (1–2 lb per sq yd).

Hydrated lime has a similar effect to gypsum. Again it can be applied as a top dressing after digging. Apply it as evenly as possible. Generally an application every two or three years is adequate for most crops.

It is interesting to note that, though gypsum improves the soil without raising the pH level (increasing alkalinity), hydrated lime raises the pH as well. Both cause flocculation (create a good crumb structure), thus improving the soil texture, drainage and aeration.

During the actual digging, incorporate as much organic matter as possible to 'open up' the soil and to prevent it forming into large clods. This should give better drainage of surplus water and improve aeration. There are various types of organic matter that are suitable, such as well-rotted farmyard or horse manure, garden compost, peat, leaf mould, spent hops, bracken, straw, composted seaweed

and composted sawdust. Try to apply at least one barrowload per square metre or yard. It is best to double dig (see page 21) clay soil as this will enable you to get the organic matter down into the lower soil. When double digging remember to keep the soil in its proper layers; in other words, never mix topsoil with subsoil.

Do not apply lime and manure at the same time, but leave an interval of two or three months between applications. If you are digging in organic material in the autumn, then scatter the lime over the soil surface in early spring.

Spring is also the time to apply a general-purpose fertilizer prior to sowing and planting. It is not much use applying this in the autumn or winter, as most of the plant foods will have been washed too far down in the soil to be of use to the plants when they are needed.

Drainage for clay soils

If clays are constantly waterlogged during wet weather, and none of the other cultural recommendations prove successful, it may be advisable to install a drainage system, although this can be a costly operation and may prove difficult in a small garden.

Basically it involves laying a system of earthenware land drainpipes in the lower soil in a herringbone pattern. The main central pipe, that takes the water from the lateral pipes, should slope gently to a soakaway or ditch at the lowest point of the site. The lateral pipes slope gently to the main pipe.

SAND

Sandy soils are the opposite of clays. They are generally known as 'light' soils because they are easy to work with. Sand has a gritty texture, consisting mostly of grains of silica that are chemically stable. So, unlike clays, the soil particles do not stick together and the soils are very loose in structure.

Because of this loose structure, sandy soils are incapable of holding much water. They warm up quickly in spring but during dry weather they can dry out very rapidly and cause plants to wilt or die through lack of moisture. Again, because of their loose structure and chemical stability, sandy soils cannot hold much plant food and are therefore said to be 'hungry' soils.

Feeding sandy soils

It is not necessary to dig sandy soils as early as heavy clay types, but even so digging should still be completed well before sowing and planting time in the spring. Ordinary single digging to the depth of a spade should be sufficient.

However, in sandy soils an iron pan may form in the lower soil that may be impermeable to air and moisture, and therefore harmful to plants in that it prevents surplus water draining away. An iron pan is a rock-hard layer of soil that, as the name implies, contains a large quantity of iron. Sandy soils naturally contain a large amount of this element that, over the years, is leached (by rain) into the lower soil where it cements sand particles together. If you discover an iron pan, you would do best to break it up by double digging the site. Thereafter you can carry out ordinary single digging as it will probably be many years before a pan forms again.

The main consideration in improving sandy soils is to incorporate as much organic matter as possible to supply humus. Most sandy soils are seriously lacking in humus and so have a very poor structure, the soil being unable to hold water and plant foods. The humus acts as a sponge and ensures adequate moisture during dry periods. Apply plenty of organic matter every year (provided this ties in with the cropping programme) for it quickly disappears in this type of soil. Also apply a general-purpose fertilizer in spring, prior to sowing and planting.

CHALK

In some respects chalk soils are similar to sands. If you have only a thin layer of soil overlying chalk you will often be faced with lack of moisture during dry weather due to the percolation of water down

Dug out trench reveals 'tired' topsoil and subsoil that needs improving with an application of humus

through the chalk out of reach of plant roots. Such a soil will also be lacking in humus and plant foods. An additional problem with chalk soils is high alkalinity that can cause many plants to show symptoms of chlorosis (dwarfing of the plant and yellowing of the leaves). This occurs because the plants are not obtaining sufficient iron from the soil; iron is rendered unavailable to plants in conditions of high alkalinity. Roses, many soft and top fruits, hydrangeas and ericaceous plants (such as rhododendrons, azaleas and heathers, etc.) are prone to chlorosis.

Soils over limestone should be treated as chalk soils; it is often forgotten that chalk is a pure form of limestone.

Improving chalk soils

Chalk soils (especially thin soils overlying solid chalk) need plentiful additions of organic matter; on some types it is almost impossible to apply too much. On such a site you would do best to dig as deeply as possible each year – preferably double digging. This will enable you to get organic matter well down into the soil, so that, over a number of years, you gradually increase the depth of suitable growing soil. Also add organic matter to the topsoil – mix it well in if possible. Any of the kinds of organic matter suggested for clay soils can be used, but very acid materials (such as peat and leaf moulds) are particularly suitable as they help to reduce alkalinity – if only very slightly.

Alkalinity can be reduced by incorporating flowers of sulphur into the soil, but very large applications are necessary to do any good; you would need to use about 500g–1kg per sq m (1–2 lb per sq yd).

As with chalk and sand, apply a general-purpose fertilizer in spring before you begin to sow or plant.

TYPES	PROBLEMS	ADVANTAGES	HOW TO IMPROVE
CLAY Smooth, not gritty, often wet, sticky and slimy in winter and brick-like in summer	The very small particles stick together when wet, making a solid, almost airless mass. Heavy and difficult to dig and break down. Cold – takes a long time to warm up in spring. Dries out slowly, unevenly and in clods. Seeds germinate poorly (because of lack of air) and plant roots have difficulty in growing (because it is so heavy and solid).	Usually rich in plant food. Can hold water well in dry summers. Is receptive to the addition of plant and animal organic matter, which will decompose by physical, chemical and bacterial activity in the soil. This completely decomposed material is called humus. **Humus** is rich in plant foods, gives the soil 'body' and encourages the retention of food, water and air. In particular, it helps to make clay more workable by breaking down the mass.	Unless already alkaline (chalky), spread garden lime – 375g per sq m (12 oz per sq yd) – all over dug soil in autumn and let the weather work it in. Otherwise fork in during February. Lime makes it easier to dig and cultivate. For lasting improvement dig in large quantities of organic (animal and plant) matter in early spring for several years. This will rot down in the soil and gradually improve its structure and colour. Preferably use 'strawy' farmyard manure, otherwise plenty of peat and garden compost. Continue organic treatment every year, liming every 2–3 years. Do not mix lime with other fertilizers; apply 1 month before, or 2–3 months after, other soil conditioners. If clay is very heavy, artificial drainage may be required.
SAND Light and dry, gritty, crumbly and rough to handle	Poor in plant food. Unable to retain moisture; rainwater passes right through, leaching (washing out) plant foods into the subsoil out of reach of plant roots. Can be very acid due to leaching of lime.	Easy to work at any time of year. Warms up quickly after winter so cultivation can begin early in spring. Plenty of air in soil, allowing plant roots to grow strongly and deeply. Excellent for vegetables, especially root crops, when sufficient organic matter is added to retain water.	Manure, peat and compost must be dug in deeply to increase the soil's organic content. This will add plant foods and increase food- and moisture-retaining abilities. Treatment must be repeated yearly. Also add general fertilizer before sowing or planting in spring and autumn. A light sprinkling of lime should be added every other year if soil is acid. Watering with nitrogenous fertilizer is advantageous throughout the growing season. Artificial watering will probably be necessary during dry spring and summer periods.
CHALK OR LIMESTONE Variable, often shallow, topsoil with recognizable lumps of chalk or limestone, especially in lower soil	Lacks humus and plant food. Difficult to work when wet. Tends to dry out quickly in summer. The calcium in chalk or limestone soil inhibits plants from using many plant foods, and deficiencies may result. Chalky soil is alkaline, and not tolerated by most plants.	Generally light, easy to work, free-draining and warms up quickly in spring. Good for rock garden plants.	Add large quantities of farmyard manure, compost or other organic matter, preferably to the top layer of soil, each spring and autumn. This will break down (into humus) in the soil, improving its condition. Give top-dressings of general fertilizers throughout the growing season.
PEAT Dark brown or black, spongy to touch	Usually waterlogged and may need artificial drainage. May be very acid and sour. Often deficient in plant foods.	Contains plenty of organic matter as it consists mainly of organic material nct yet fully decomposed. Easily worked. Too acid for most garden plants but very fertile when drained and limed.	If soil is waterlogged, then a soakaway or drainage pipes may be needed. Liming helps drainage and counteracts acidity. Add lime at 250g per sq m (8 oz per sq yd) every 2–3 years. Add regular, fairly heavy, dressings of general-purpose fertilizers in spring, summer and autumn.
LOAM Dark, crumbly, easy to clean from fingers	Should not be any problem as long as the drainage is satisfactory and the humus and plant food content is maintained.	Ideal garden soil, with a balanced mixture of sand, humus and clay. If humus content is maintained, a well-drained, well-aerated soil rich in plant food will result. Warm enough for early cultivation.	The improvements depend on the proportions of clay and sand in the loam. Sandy loam will require the regular spring and autumn addition of organic matter and fertilizers. Clayey loam may need regular addition of 375g per sq m (12 oz per sq yd) every 2–3 years. Heavy loams will benefit from being roughly dug over in autumn.

Basic Digging

'Single digging' means digging the soil to one spade's depth (one 'spit'); double digging is done to a depth of two spits. The latter was widely practised in private gardens of old, where it was commonly – and more colourfully – called 'bastard trenching'.

If you are unfortunate enough to acquire a garden on a heavy clay soil with poor drainage, then a few years of double digging will help to improve both the soil fertility and the drainage. Otherwise single digging is all you need do.

The object of single digging (which from here on I shall refer to simply as digging) is to turn over the top 20–30cm (9–12 in) of soil; the lower levels are then exposed and aerated. At the same time annual weeds, such as groundsel and chickweed, are turned in and buried so that they will provide valuable humus. Perennial weeds with long tap-roots (like docks and dandelions) will re-emerge if they are buried, so they should be pulled out, left on the path to die, and then placed in the middle of the compost heap. That way every scrap of organic fertilizer that nature provides free is put back into the soil.

Tools for the job

The basic equipment for digging consists of a few layers of warm clothes, stout footwear and a good, strong spade or fork. What you wear on your feet is important. The tendency nowadays is to wear wellingtons but I prefer a robust pair of boots or shoes.

Wellingtons are heavy, tend to chaff the ankles and are inclined to 'sweat'. My gardening boots have thick soles made of some composite material that stands a good deal of rough treatment.

When it comes to the choice of implement you can opt for a spade or a fork. Both are available with two kinds of handle – T-grip and D-grip. I prefer the D-handle because all four fingers of the hand are placed inside the D giving a stronger grip and better leverage.

Whichever you choose it is better to pay a little extra and buy a good-quality tool. A good spade or fork is a sound investment that, properly used and cared for, will last a lifetime. Half- or fully-polished blade or prongs slip more easily into the soil and earth is less inclined to cling to them.

For spring digging you can use either a spade or a fork. If you have a light or sandy soil, or a good loam, a spade will do a better job; but on a very heavy clay, which has lain undisturbed over the winter a fork will make digging easier and the end result will be just as good. So select whichever tool best suits you and your soil.

It is advisable to dig your vegetable plot at least a week or two before you are ready to sow or plant as the soil should have time to settle before you start.

And so to work

For many people the thought of digging is a very off-putting idea. They regard it as a back-breaking slog that must be avoided if possible. But this need not be the case if the job is approached in the right frame of mind. So relax, enjoy it and remember that it takes you out into the open air and that it is a marvellous muscle-toner. Don't set yourself impossible goals and stop before you get exhausted.

First of all dig out a trench one spit deep and about 3–3·5m (10–12 ft) long at one end of the plot. Don't make the trench any longer; it is far better for your morale to finish digging a short strip than to half-finish a longer one. Put the soil from the trench into a wheelbarrow and push it to the other end of the plot (where it will be used to fill in the final trench).

Go back to the start of the row and work your way down the second trench, turning the soil over into the first one. Continue in this manner until you have finished the strip. A word of advice –

*Four steps to successful single digging: **1** marking the spit; **2** placing the spade at the correct digging angle; **3** turning the soil over into the first trench; **4** turning soil from third trench into second one after filling it with manure*

don't try to speed the job up by digging great slices out of the soil. It is much easier, and a lot less tiring, to handle chunks no wider than 15cm (6 in) – at least until you have established a relaxed rhythm. Carry on digging down to the end, fill in the last trench, have a rest and then start on the second strip. Do it this way and you will be surprised how quickly the work gets done.

The newly-turned earth is now an uneven surface of gleaming clods of soil. Leave it like this until the day you are ready to sow and plant, to give it a chance to dry out and settle. Then all you need do on a dry day is shuffle and tramp all over it to break down the lumps before raking it to a fine tilth.

Fertilizers and manures

If you are to get a good, healthy crop fertilizers are absolutely essential. Assuming that none were used in the previous autumn I suggest that a top dressing of general fertilizer, such as Growmore or Fish, blood and bone, or one of the proprietary, concentrated animal manures should be spread over the soil at 70–145g per sq m (2–4 oz per sq yd) before you start digging. Digging the plot puts the fertilizer down into the soil where the plant roots will reach and benefit from it in due course.

I also suggest that you keep some of the fertilizer you use and put a little of it, say about 35g per sq m (1 oz per sq yd) over the whole plot just before you start sowing and planting. This will give the germinating seedlings a boost until their roots reach the main feed below.

Double-digging

Double digging is simply digging the soil two spits deep, that is, to the depth of two spade blades. It should improve the fertility and drainage of a heavy clay soil and is very useful where long-term crops are to be grown or an area is being given over to cultivation for the first time. As in single digging (see page 20), the soil from each succeeding trench is transferred into the one behind it, until finally, the soil from the first trench goes into the last trench.

Digging and filling

The first step is to divide the plot into two and mark out the two sections into 60cm (24 in) wide strips. Starting at the end of the plot dig out the first strip to one spade's depth. The soil should be left next to the adjacent strip in the other half-plot.

Break up the bottom of the trench to the depth of your fork tines and then

1 Double digging the final trench and turning the soil into the one before.
2 Shovelling in the compost and spreading it evenly. **3** Mixing compost in with the broken-up second spit. **4** Filling final trench with soil left over from the first

Above: mechanical cultivator with a rotating head helps to make double digging less back breaking. There are various fork tines for the cultivator head to deal with different types of soil

move onto the second strip. Make sure that each ensuing trench is as near as possible the same width as the one before so that the same quantity of soil is removed and a level surface is maintained. The soil from the second digging goes into the first trench, the bottom of the second trench is broken up and the process goes on until the final trench is filled with the pile of soil

which has been waiting to fill the gap.

Compost and manure

If you want to apply compost or manure, it should be spread over the surface of the whole plot. As each trench is emptied, rake in the manure from the next strip and fork it into the broken-up second spit.

Feeding Plants

Ascophyllum nodosum, *'egg' or knotted wrack, exposed on the rocks at low tide*

Plants, like people, need a regular supply of food if they are to survive and grow well. The main ways of feeding your plants are by applying fertilizers and bulky organic matter (like manure) to the soil. Manure supplies some nutrients, but its most important function is to improve the soil structure by adding organic material. This turns the soil into a healthy medium in which plants can thrive. Fertilizers provide some, or all, of the basic plant foods.

When digging, particularly in late autumn or early winter, it is wise to incorporate in each trench well-rotted farmyard manure, garden compost, seaweed or hop manure. These materials will supply bulky organic matter and a variable amount of plant food. None of them, however, supplies adequate nutrients for the plants to make optimum growth; therefore fertilizers will have to be added at planting time to ensure that the plants have sufficient food.

The organic matter is digested by bacteria in the soil and turned into humus. This humus is like a sponge; it holds water and prevents rapid drying-out of light soils. It also helps to break up sticky clay soils by improving drainage. Organic material is, therefore, essential because it improves the soil's structure.

MANURES

Never apply manure at the same time as lime (calcium). This is because the lime can liberate any available nitrogen in the form of ammonia, which may then be lost through evaporation. Also, never grow root crops on ground where fresh manure has been used, for your vegetables may well produce deformed roots.

Seaweed as manure

If your garden is near the coast, use seaweed as a manure. It is excellent for digging – wet or dried – into the soil in the autumn. Seaweed is one of the oldest manures known and contains many plant foods. It is now possible to obtain specially refined seaweed manures from gardening shops.

Manure for mulching

Rotted manure or garden compost makes a good mulch for established plants such as trees, shrubs, top and soft fruit, vegetables, roses, dahlias and chrysan-themums. Place a layer of mulch, 5–8cm (2–3 in) thick, around the plants in spring. It will then provide some food and humus and help prevent evaporation of moisture from the surface soil.

FERTILIZERS

Bulky organic matter is not capable, by itself, of supplying all the foods the plants will require, so fertilizers must also be added to the soil.

As a general rule, dry fertilizers should be applied to moist soil, or else well watered in after application if the ground is dry. Always apply them evenly, and discard or break up any lumps; these can 'burn' roots. Apply all fertilizers carefully and according to maker's instructions. If you exceed the recommended rate of application you may seriously injure your plants.

Before sowing or planting, the usual procedure is to rake in a dry fertilizer which contains the major plants foods (nitrogen, phosphates and potash). There are many of these 'general-purpose' or compound fertilizers on the market. Probably the best known is National Growmore, which is available under numerous brand names. This is suitable for all vegetables, fruit and flowers. You can also apply it as a top dressing in spring or summer by lightly raking it into the soil surface around any of your established plants.

Special dry fertilizers for specific crops (such as roses and tomatoes) are available. These contain the correct balance of nitrogen, phosphates and potash suited to the particular plant.

Lawn fertilizers

There are several proprietary lawn fertilizers which make the lawn 'green up' quickly and grow well due to the high proportion of nitrogen they contain. Feed your lawn once or twice during spring and summer to ensure a lush, deep-green sward. Autumn lawn fertilizer, which is applied in mid autumn (September), contains more potash; this helps to 'ripen' the grass and make it more resistant to hard winter weather.

'Straight' fertilizers

You can also apply 'straight' fertilizers to plants, especially as a supplement to the ready-mixed, general-purpose kinds applied earlier in the growing season; but you must be aware of specific food requirements of individual plants before trying out these fertilizers. Be sure to handle them carefully and accurately.

Sulphate of ammonia and nitro-chalk supply nitrogen which encourages plants to make lush, leafy growth. They are quick-acting fertilizers and should be used very sparingly. They can be used on lawns and also on green vegetables such as cabbage, kale, broccoli and spinach. Apply them in spring and summer only.

Sulphate of potash and muriate of potash both supply the potash (potassium) essential for the production of fruit and flowers. It also helps to ripen the stems, which is necessary for the successful overwintering of all hardy plants. Potash can be applied in summer or early autumn. Wood ashes contain potassium

and, once they have weathered for 3–6 months, can be dug into the soil during autumn digging or raked into the surface.

Superphosphate of lime supplies phosphate (phosphorus). This is also essential for good root production and all-round growth. It is usually applied in spring and summer at the rate of 3g per litre ($\frac{1}{2}$ oz per gal) of water and applied to the soil around plants about once a week. Avoid getting it on the foliage.

Liquid fertilizers
Use liquid fertilizers in conjunction with powdered or granulated fertilizers – not as a substitute. They should be considered as supplementary feeds to boost the growth of plants. They are generally used in the summer when plants are in full growth. Being liquid, they are quickly absorbed by plants and rapidly stimulate growth.

Dilute liquid fertilizers according to maker's instructions, and apply them to moist soil. Use them as frequently as once a week and on all kinds of plants in the

house, greenhouse and garden. You can apply them most easily with a rosed watering can.

There are many brands of liquid fertilizer on the market, some of which are formulated for specific crops.

Foliar feeding
Foliar feeding is a fairly recent technique of applying liquid fertilizers to plants. The fertilizer is sprayed or watered onto the leaves where it is quickly absorbed by the plants and circulated in the sap stream. The nutrients are made im-

Above: applying chemical fertilizer by spoon in small measured quantities
Above right: sieving leaf mould into a wheelbarrow for use as compost
Right: fertilizer spreaders give even results
Far right: applying lime by hand

mediately available to plants. This makes them particularly useful to transplanted plants before their new roots have become established.

You can buy special foliar feeds from gardening shops. Alternatively you can apply any liquid fertilizer to the foliage and it will be quickly absorbed.

Sulphate of ammonia can be dissolved at the rate of 3g per litre ($\frac{1}{2}$ oz per gal) of water and applied to leaves to promote growth of foliage. Likewise sulphate of potash will encourage fruiting and ripening of growth.

LIME
Lime is another plant food and this is applied on its own, generally in the winter after autumn digging, in the form of dehydrated lime. It is mainly the vegetable plot that will require lime and an application every two or three years will be adequate.

Lime lowers the acidity of the soil, and as many plants (especially vegetables such as brassicas) do not thrive in an acid soil, liming enables you to grow a wider range of plants. But do not lime if you have a naturally alkaline or limy soil with a pH of 7 or above. Hydrated lime is the type generally used.

Effects of Fertilizers on Vegetables

As an aid to understanding the role of fertilizers in vegetable growing it is helpful to consider the basic food requirements of plants in general. These are very simple, since all that is needed are supplies of twelve mineral elements. Each of these elements, however, has its own dominant role in plant nutrition so the balance between them affects the type of growth.

Key elements

All the essential plant foods are available in normal fertile soil but the soil stocks of some elements need to be replenished regularly if fertility is to be maintained. In particular, additional supplies of **nitrogen, phosphorus** (phosphate) and **potassium** (potash) are required. Most general garden fertilizers are therefore based on these three elements, although some specialist fertilizers also contain **magnesium.** In addition most fertilizer mixtures have some content of **sulphur** and **calcium** although these are not mentioned on the pack. Use of complete, or compound, fertilizers thus provides an easy way of maintaining suitable levels of the six major plant foods in the soil.

The remaining six key elements are: **iron, manganese, copper, zinc, boron** and **molybdenum** and generally these do not need to be replenished. These are only used in trace quantities by plants so that soil stocks are normally more than adequate. Deficiencies when they do occur are difficult to remedy by the use of solid fertilizer because of the very low levels involved and because of the risk of plant damage by over-application. The best approach in this situation, therefore, is to use either liquid or foliar feeds containing very low concentrations of all six trace elements.

Effects on plant growth

Although all twelve elements are essential for healthy plant growth, each food has its own special function. Nitrogen stimulates vigorous vegetative growth. Potash, on the other hand, favours flowering and fruiting in addition to giving sturdy growth. Phosphorus, whilst essential for

most growth processes, is of special importance in root growth. The remaining three major elements, namely magnesium, calcium and sulphur play more general roles in plant physiology.

It is less easy to define the roles of the six minor, or trace, elements but all are involved in important growth processes. Certainly a deficiency of any of them can have serious effects causing leaf damage, stunting or malformed growth.

Choice of principal fertilizer

The food value of a fertilizer is measured by the quantity of nitrogen, phosphate and potash that is available to plants. These quantities are expressed as specific percentages of N for nitrogen (N), of P_2O_5 for phosphate (P) and of K_2O for potash (K). A typical example of a complete fertilizer is Growmore, that contains 7 per cent N, 7 per cent P_2O_5 and 7 per cent K_2O. This information, printed on all fertilizer packages, is of value to the gardener. It not only shows the balance of NPK but also gives a good indication of whether the product is good value for money. Some cheap fertilizers may not be, because of their low food content.

The varying nutritional requirements

Above: correct food balance in the soil and an occasional liquid feed give a crisp healthy lettuce crop
Below: values listed on fertilizer packages

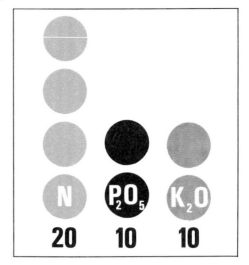

of root crops, brassicas, tomatoes, beans and peas, could be solved by the use of special fertilizer mixtures for each crop. In practice, however, it is simpler and cheaper to use a fairly even balance of NPK as a base dressing and then, where necessary, to vary the feeding by later side dressings or by the use of liquid feeds.

Application of fertilizers

The safe and efficient way of using any fertilizer is to apply it evenly over the growing area at a reasonable rate. For instance Growmore should generally be used at around 140 g per sq m (4 oz per sq yd) just before sowing or planting out. Localized application in seed drills or planting holes must be avoided because of risk of damage to the plant roots. Should later side dressings be needed, these too must be applied evenly over the area. This ensures that the food is available to the whole root system. Rather less care is needed when applying liquid feeds but here it is important to use fairly high volumes. The fertilizer content of liquid feeds is quite low, so plenty of solution is needed to have a worthwhile feeding effect. Generous application of liquid feeds also ensures that the solution penetrates into the root zone.

Fertilizer programmes

In all cases a general NPK fertilizer should be lightly worked into the topsoil before sowing seed or planting out. Proprietary products should be used at the rates recommended by the manufacturers. As a general guide, the rate of application of a product containing 5–7 per cent nitrogen plus phosphate and potash should be about 140g per sq m (4 oz per sq yd).

When using fertilizers with higher or lower nitrogen content the application rate needs to be adjusted accordingly. Subsequent fertilizer treatments vary with the type of crop.

Potatoes Early potatoes should not need any further feeding. In the case of maincrop varieties, however, a second application of NPK fertilizer should be given prior to earthing-up. This ensures adequate supplies of phosphate for root growth and nitrogen for heavy cropping.

Brassicas With these essentially leafy crops the key requirement is to ensure continuity of supplies of nitrogen. So later feeding can be done with straight nitrogen fertilizers. One approach is to use quick-acting sulphate of ammonia (21 per cent N). This fertilizer needs to be applied carefully because of the risk of root damage. Each application therefore should not exceed 35g per sq m (1 oz per sq yd). The first treatment can be given about a month after planting out. A second application can then be made in late summer. An alternative method is to use one of the newer slow-release nitrogen fertilizers. These have an even higher fertilizer content than sulphate of ammonia. So only 35–50g per sq m (1–1½ oz per sq yd) is needed over the whole growing season. A major advantage of these slow-release feeds is that it is safe to apply the whole quantity at one application. This provides a steady supply of nitrogen for several months.

Summer cauliflowers present a special case. With these it is important that growth is continuous since any setback can result in the premature development of small, poor-quality heads. For this reason, regular liquid feeding may be better than the use of solid fertilizer.

Onions and leeks Both these are gross feeders and so benefit from additional feeding. This can be as a single application of sulphate of ammonia or as repeated liquid feeds.

Peas and beans No additional feeding is needed to supplement the base dressing.

Swedes and turnip No additional feeding is needed.

Radish No additional feeding is necessary but regular watering is needed in dry weather to ensure quick growth.

Beetroot A second application of NPK fertilizer should be given when the roots begin to swell to ensure continued growth.

Lettuce This salad crop benefits from liquid feeding.

Outdoor tomatoes With this crop the objective is to encourage flowering and fruit set rather than to stimulate excessive vegetable growth. No further feeding should therefore be given till the first fruits on the bottom truss have set. From then on the plants benefit from regular weekly waterings with a high potash liquid feed. Several good proprietary brands of liquid tomato feeds are available and these should be used in preference to general liquid feeds.

Tomatoes have a special need for magnesium and their leaves tend to yellow if additional quantities of this element are not supplied. One way of remedying this deficiency is to spray the plants at intervals with a solution of Epsom salts using 6g per litre (1 oz per gal). An alternative approach is to use a tomato liquid feed with added magnesium.

Trace element deficiencies These are uncommon in vegetable crops. Boron deficiency may, however, occur if excessive quantities of lime have been applied. This nutrient shortage shows up as dark concentric rings in beetroots, swedes and turnips. It can also cause cracking of celery stalks and hollow stems in brassicas. The remedy is to apply household borax at 17g per sq m (½ oz per sq yd), evenly in solution form, in early to mid spring (February–March).

These easily-recognizable deficiencies – in potassium (above, far left), magnesium (above left) and calcium (left) – can be prevented by using a good liquid feed

Sprayers and Dusters

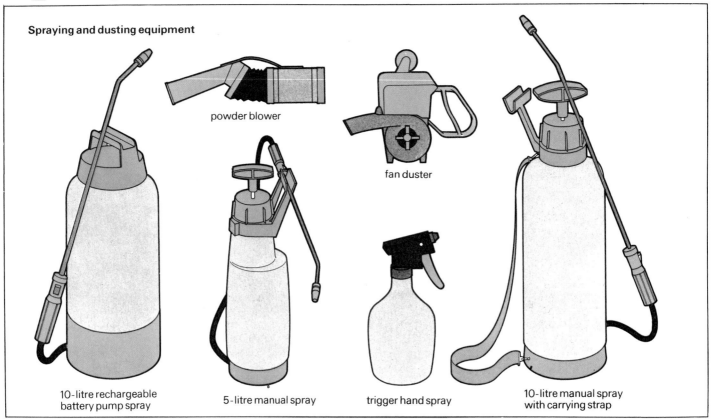

Spraying and dusting equipment

powder blower

fan duster

10-litre rechargeable battery pump spray

5-litre manual spray

trigger hand spray

10-litre manual spray with carrying strap

To keep your plants and crops healthy you have to keep spraying at certain times to prevent—or counteract—the adverse effects of weeds, pests and diseases. It saves you time and trouble if you use the right spray for the job.

Many manufacturers of pesticides (both liquids and dusts) produce their chemicals in a pack which itself is the dispenser.

Dusts are sold in puffer-packs made of opaque polythene, with a small plastic nozzle-type orifice. To spray the dust you simply squeeze the sides of the pack. Other dust packs have pepper-pot tops.

Liquids are sometimes sold in inexpensive transparent plastic bottles with a manually-operated spray mechanism as the closure. It is not advisable to refill.

The most popular pack today is the aerosol can. This system is very effective and convenient to use, but must be stored away from heat.

Both aerosol sprays and dust packs are ideal for small gardens or limited applications, but prove very expensive for large areas or prolonged use.

Permanent sprayers
The capacity range here goes from ½lit (1 pt) to several litres. Sprayers over 5lit (10

pt) capacity can be awkward and heavy to handle when full and are not recommended. On large areas it pays to refill, rather than struggle with a larger sprayer.

Traditionally, spraying equipment was made from metal and proved to be extremely heavy. Today, virtually all sprayers are made from lightweight but strong polythene and plastic with stainless metals in some of the working parts.

Trigger sprayers
The smallest sprayers are suited for use on house plants, greenhouse plants and limited use outdoors. They are appropriately called hand sprayers because they are held in the hand and operated by simply pressing a trigger rather like a pistol. Naturally, the range of these models is limited and the operator has to be close to the plant to be sprayed.

Pump sprayers
These consist of a container, a short length of hose and a lance. They require two hands for operation. The container is held in one hand while the lance is directed towards the target with the other hand. The spray container has a maintenance-free pump fitted through the top. The pump is primed by pushing in and pulling out the handle several times

to build up pressure. Everything is then ready for spraying and all you do is depress a simple trigger fitted to the hand end of the lance.

Spray patterns are basically cone shaped and are altered by rotating the nozzle fitment at the end of the lance.

Many of these sprayers have a useful shoulder strap so they may be carried around the garden with ease; this also allows you a free hand to pull the odd long branch or shoot out of the way. The carrying handle itself is usually dual purpose, enabling the lance to be slotted in when the sprayer is not in use.

Battery-operated sprays are convenient because they avoid the need for pressure-pumping. The batteries are re-chargeable and sealed so they are not affected by wet weather. Life between charges is about 1½ hours. Units are made in 5lit (10 pt) and 10lit (20 pt) sizes.

Dusters
Two types of dusting equipment are made: a cheap bellows type with handle which, when shaken, operates the bellows and expels the dust from the attached canister; and a more sophisticated piece of equipment in which you turn a geared handle to operate a fan and distribute the powder from a hopper.

Staking and Tying Equipment

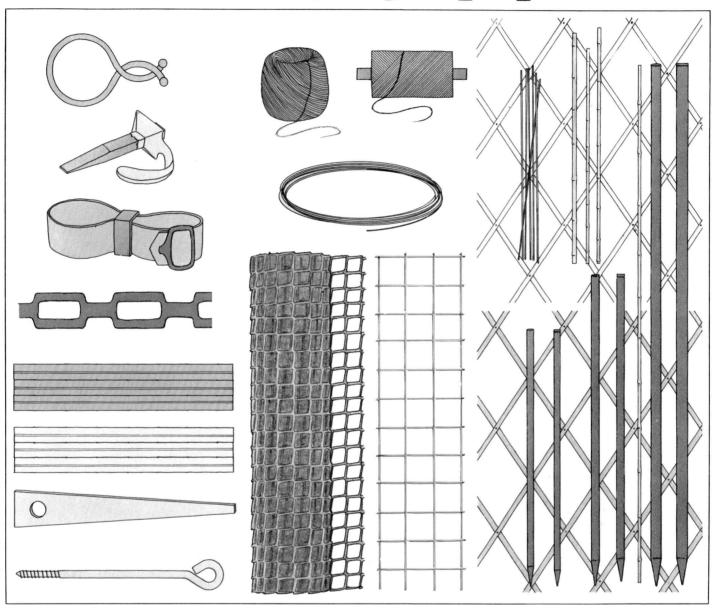

Bamboo and split canes The longer the cane the thicker the diameter. From 30cm–3·6m (1–12 ft) lengths.

Chestnut, cedar or pine stakes Treat with horticultural wood preservative, if not pre-treated.

Plastic buckle ties and buffers Be sure to place the buffer between trunk and stalk to prevent chafing.

Plastic tree or rose ties These can be adjusted each year to allow for increase in girth.

Plastic or wire plant ties Paper-covered wire type only needs the ends twisting together to hold stem to stake; pliable plastic-coated wire type bends around stem and stake.

Plastic clips Ideal for quick support. Long-lasting if stored each winter.

Galvanized, heavy-gauge wire Fixed on a wall, can be used instead of trellis.

Vine eyes Hammer-in or screw-in types, useful for tying in light branches against walls with garden twine or string.

Lead-headed nails Hammer in to wall and bend round flexible arm, or use with garden twine or string.

Garden twine or string Usually green and treated for weather resistance, but can stretch under wet conditions. Tarred garden string is durable, but has an unpleasant smell.

Polypropylene garden string Tough and does not stretch in wet weather.

Raffia Good tying material. Can be torn to any thickness.

Traditional trellis Made of treated cedar, or hardwood for heavier, rustic types. Can be bought ready-made, rigid or expanding, in natural or painted finish. (See Week 6 for fixing details.)

Plastic-coated trellis Rot-proof and long-lasting, rigid or expanding, usually in green or white.

Plastic mesh/nylon netting Convenient but more expensive than chicken wire; easily stored at end of season. Available in different width rolls or packs of specific sizes. Needs stretching between posts or supporting by metal or wood frame structure.

Making a Compost Heap

Waste not organic materials from the house or garden and want not for compost is a maxim worth following. Compost, when rotted down, will improve and maintain your soil by adding humus-forming matter, plant foods and beneficial bacteria.

Compost is not difficult or time-consuming to make. Certain types of plant and household waste can be used to make it. Suitable plant waste includes grass clippings, flower and vegetable stems that are not too tough, light hedge trimmings, wet peat, wet straw and annual weeds. Leaves can be used, but not in great quantities as they are more valuable for use as leaf mould. A separate bin can be kept in the kitchen for such household waste as tea leaves, vegetable trimmings, hair, egg shells and vacuum cleaner dust. Bonfire ashes, animal manure, and sawdust are also suitable.

Not suitable for the compost heap are coarse plant material such as cabbage stems and tree prunings, diseased plants, pernicious weeds like docks, dandelions, and bindweed roots, any dead plants on which weedkiller has been used, and cooked matter, such as meat or fish.

Ideal site

As a compost heap is not particularly sightly, it is best situated in the working part of the garden and screened from the house. It should be protected from hot sun or cold winds, but not be against a wall or hedge. An ideal site is beneath a tree. The shape of the heap can be circular or rectangular, although most people find a rectangular one easier to cope with. The best size to aim for is about 1m (3 ft) wide, 1½–2m (5–6 ft) long, and 1–1½m (3–5 ft) high when completed.

Construction

It pays to construct the site of the heap correctly, rather than tipping the waste straight onto the ground. First dig a shallow pit – about 15cm (6 in) deep. Place the soil on one side as you will need it later. Then put down in the pit an 8cm (3 in) layer of broken bricks or stones mixed with coarse tree prunings, woody cabbage stems, straw and similar tough plant material. These will help essential drainage and allow air penetration.

When the base is prepared, begin to build up the compost heap. This should be done roughly as follows:

Layer 1: about 15cm (6 in) of organic material.

Layer 2: a sprinkling of a proprietary compost accelerator according to the manufacturer's instructions. This should supply the essential bacteria, nitrogen and chalk necessary to break down the raw matter into usable compost.

Layer 3: a 2–3cm (1 in) layer of soil, taken from the dug-out heap.
These three layers are repeated until the heap reaches the required height.

Follow these rules for successful composting:
1 Always be sure that each layer of organic material is well firmed down (but not too tightly compressed) by treading on it or beating it flat with a spade blade.
2 If using grass clippings in large quantities, mix them with other materials or they will form a soggy mass in the heap.
3 Check from time to time to make sure that the heap is moist. If it has dried out, either sprinkle water over it or, preferably, hammer stakes into the heap to make holes and then pour water into the holes.
4 To finish off the heap, level the top and put a 2–5cm (1–2 in) thick layer of soil over the top and around the sides to act as a cover.

A properly made compost heap provides material to be used either for digging into the ground or for mulching. Mulch is a top dressing layer on the surface of the soil around the plants. The compost will be ready to be dug in after about 10–14 weeks in summer or 14–18 weeks in winter. When the compost is ready for use the heap will consist of a brownish black, crumbly, pleasant-smelling and easily handled material. If the heap doesn't seem to be rotting down well in the allotted time, something has gone wrong with the construction. If this happens, it is worth the trouble of digging a second shallow pit alongside and rebuilding the first heap into that,

Slotted wood bin

If you lack the space for a compost heap as described, a bin will also give you good results

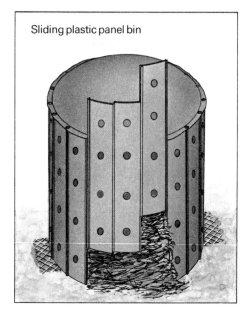

Sliding plastic panel bin

turning the top to bottom and sides to middle and following the sandwich layer principle again. In any case, as one heap is finished, a second one should be started so that there is always a supply of essential humus-forming material ready to add to the soil.

The method of compost-making described here is simple and cheap. If, however, you have a very small garden, it may be easier for you to buy a proprietary bin compost unit, which has its own instructions for use.

28

You can help to improve and control
the climate condition of your garden
by creating 'microclimates' for
particular corners or groups of plants.
Here we analyze the garden microclimate
in the hours of day and night.

The Microclimate in your Garden

Every garden has to endure the general climate of the region in which it is situated, but within that region exposure to sunshine, wind or rain makes weather considerably different from one garden to another. Open hillsides facing south get more sunshine than gardens hemmed in by buildings, hilltops are windier than valleys, and gardens along the banks of rivers or lakes suffer more fog than those quite a short distance away. These inescapable peculiarities combined with cunning contrivance by ourselves create the individual 'microclimate' of a garden or even a corner of a garden.

Heat from the sun

The natural source of all warmth is the sun whose rays warm up any substance they strike. Water is partly transparent to sunshine so that the benefit of heat is spread over a large volume of water, raising its temperature very little in a short period. Glass, when clean, is almost entirely transparent to sunshine and it is objects underneath glass that warm up rather than glass itself. Other solids warm in the sunshine according to the materials of which they are made, and some of the best absorbers of heat in the garden are brick, paving stone and bare soil.

Although the sun is the biggest heat radiator we know, everything on earth is also a radiator in its own small way. On a sunny day, objects no sooner acquire heat from the sun than they re-radiate some for the benefit of anything nearby which hasn't done so well. Hence a south-facing terrace and house wall will be a definite hot spot on a sunny day because of heat radiating from the surfaces. Also vegetables, widely spaced in weed-free soil, will enjoy a warmer microclimate than a crowded flowerbed sited in a lawn.

Heat by conduction and convection

Heat is also distributed by conduction, through brick, downwards into soil and, particularly important, to the air that lies in contact with heated surfaces. Air so warmed becomes lighter and rises upwards to be replaced by colder air from above which then warms in turn. Gradu-

*Above right: distribution of heat in the garden by conduction and convection
Right: wind control can affect a microclimate with noticeable results*

ally warmed air spreads throughout the garden by this convection method, even circulating to areas receiving no direct radiant heat from the sun. On cloudy days, air temperature is pre-determined by its past history and the amount of heating it has received in other parts of the world. Temperatures are similar throughout a garden, except perhaps for special very small areas. A chimney-breast wall can provide a favoured microclimate for a bush whose buds tend to get nipped by late spring frosts. It doesn't hurt so much to lose expensive heat from indoors through brick if you can use it to benefit the garden. But for the best result in creating a warm microclimate at that spot you must trap the heat under a polythene cover or lean-to, otherwise wind – which is only moving air – will whip it away before it accumulates.

The need for water

Wind is a thief of moisture as well as heat. All air contains water vapour, the actual amount depending upon whether its stock has been replenished by journeying across the sea or kept short by travelling across large expanses of land. At any particular temperature air has a maximum possible capacity for vapour and this capacity increases with rising temperature. Moreover, so long as its vapour content is under capacity, air is thirsty for more and drinks from whatever source it can find – washing on the line, soil, or the leaves of plants. Hence rising temperature on a sunny day, or an inherently dry air stream which come from the east, are both likely to denude a garden of moisture and it may be necessary to act the rain-god and alter the microclimate by artificial watering. The same necessity occurs on

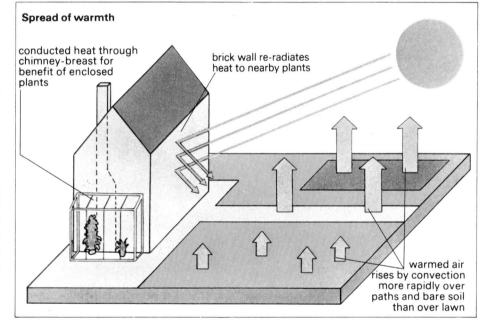

Spread of warmth

conducted heat through chimney-breast for benefit of enclosed plants

brick wall re-radiates heat to nearby plants

warmed air rises by convection more rapidly over paths and bare soil than over lawn

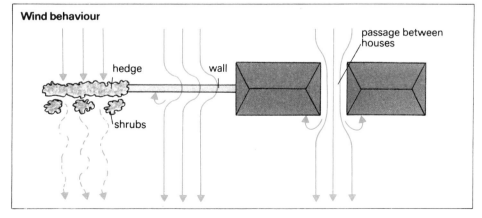

Wind behaviour

passage between houses

hedge

wall

shrubs

even a cloudy day, if a strong wind, damp or dry, is blowing. That merely means that a great deal of air is passing very quickly and taking lots of gulps of moisture in the process. A strong wind is a blessing to dry out soil after a rainy spell, but in drought conditions it makes already bad conditions worse.

Protection against wind
If you add to these characteristics of wind its sheer brute strength and battering power, protection against it can be seen as a major objective in modifying the microclimate of a garden. Secure staking helps, not because it actually makes a garden less windy but because it tricks plants into thinking it is less windy by giving them extra strength to resist! The trouble is that wind cannot be stopped, only diverted. When it comes across a row of houses with passageways between, it funnels into the constriction and comes out of the exit with increased speed, rather like water forced through the nozzle of a hosepipe. If wind encounters a wall, it either goes round the corners or over the top, giving increased speed in those areas because extra air is crowding through. Moreover, wind eddies backwards in the relatively 'empty' space on the leeward side, sometimes with as nasty effect for plants situated there as if they had received the direct blast of air. A hedge or permeable fence gives better wind protection because it allows enough air through to prevent the eddy space behind, yet breaks the initial force of the blast.

Place for a wind barrier
The choice of site for a wind barrier may be obvious, like the end of a passageway which runs in the same direction as the most frequent winds. Or it may involve a difficult choice between incompatible factors. In Britain the coldest winds come from between north and east, the most drying winds from between north-east and south-east, gales come in any season from any direction but mainly from the western half of the compass. Damaging salt-laden winds in coastal gardens come from whichever direction faces the sea. You can't protect a whole garden from every direction unless you risk undue stagnation of damp air in wet seasons. Gardens on the shoreline have little choice and *must* protect against onshore wind, even if this means some deprivation of sunshine in western and southern districts. Gardens in the middle of such coastal towns possibly have enough buildings between them and the sea to act as a preliminary barrier and have too

great a need for sunshine for you to dare erect another barrier except against cold north winds. East coast gardeners in Britain have less heart-searching to make because by protecting against north and east winds they deal with both the cold, the dry and the salt winds without detracting from their quota of sun.

Glass as a barrier
The ultimate cossetting against the wind is to enclose with glass, remembering that if the wind blows in the same direction as a line of cloches the upwind end must be firmly closed to prevent air funnelling through. Moreover, if it is windy and sunny a watchful eye must be kept for the 'greenhouse effect' on air temperature. Air beneath the glass warms on contact with the heating surface of the ground, and if none can escape the same air gets heated over and over again and air temperatures and moisture evaporation rate increase very rapidly. Such excessively hot microclimates have killed children and dogs left in parked cars in the sun and can even more easily cause the collapse of plants. Some ventilation is essential, and perhaps an opaque wash over the glass as well would help the atmosphere in high summer.

Walls for protection
Although it is relatively easy to make the microclimate of a garden wetter than the general weather pattern ensures, there is little that can be done to prevent excess water in a rainy season except by enclosure and substituting artificial watering for rain. But it is helpful to remember that walls give considerable protection against rain unless it is driving straight onto the wall, and therefore beds alongside walls have different microclimates on all sides of a house. A wall facing south-east strikes a happy compromise between adequate sunshine without excessive rain, but the soil beneath may need topping up with water even in a very wet season. North walls are always very dry, though curious things can alter the microclimate even there. For instance, if you have plants under an overflow pipe, they will flourish better than the others because of their built-in 'rainfall'.

Heat stored at night
When the sun sets at night, gardens lose their principal income of heat but continue as effective radiators themselves, expending heat previously put into storage. On cloudy nights heat radiated from the ground is partly absorbed by the cloud and partly reflected back again so

that temperatures on earth do not fall excessively. But on cloudless nights nearly all radiated heat is lost to space and ground temperature falls rapidly. The air near the ground cools in consequence and thereby becomes heavier. But if a strong wind is blowing the cooled air gets whipped away by turbulence before it suffers an undue fall in temperature.

Warmth at the top
With calm conditions, however, the cooled heavy air hangs stolidly over level ground, continuing to cool as the ground beneath gets still colder. Only gradually is the fall in temperature communicated to the layers of air higher above the ground, resulting in an inversion of the usual temperature pattern. The microclimate enjoyed by the tops of trees is warmer than that experienced by the flowerbeds, a fact that saves much fruit blossom in the ground frosts of early spring.

On sloping ground, heavy cooling air obeys gravity and slithers down to the lowest area, thus creating a down-slope wind of its own. Valleys and hollows become receptacles for the coldest air and it helps create a warmer microclimate in a garden if an easy exit can be ensured for this draining cold air. Keep hedge bottoms free of dead leaves and sticks and set fences or gates a little above ground if they are at the bottom of a slope.

Dew-point
When air cools its capacity for water vapour decreases, even though the actual vapour content has been determined by its past travels. Consequently, cooling air eventually reaches a temperature called dew-point at which its *actual* vapour content is the same as the maximum possible. Air is then saturated and if any further cooling occurs, dew forms on the ground where the air is coldest, or, if dew-point is below 0°C (32°F), hoar frost forms. This is a frequent, if intermittent, feature of most British gardens during the winter and so it is not usually considered worthwhile keeping non-hardy plants outdoors. But in spring gambles have to be taken if a garden is ever to get into summer shape, and frost is possible even up to early mid summer (early June) in some inland areas away from the moderating influence of the sea. The most risky occasions are calm, clear nights when the air is also dry. That means that air temperature can fall far, perhaps down to 0°C (32°F) before any condensation occurs. Though some plants can bear a temperature a degree or so below freezing, such knife-edge conditions are obviously worrying.

Fog versus frost

On still, clear nights when the airstream is moist through some considerable depth, perhaps after a long journey across the sea, a blessed frost protection comes in unpleasant disguise – fog. Very little cooling soon reduces damp air to dew-point temperature through quite a considerable thickness, and the resultant fog blanket prevents any further radiation heat loss and fall in air temperature. While it is likely that greenhouses and cloches will be firmly closed against such fog, you must be on guard against rapidly-changing microclimates under glass next day. A spring sun may clear the previous night's fog during mid morning when many gardeners are away from home. The heat trapped under glass will cause a rapid rise in temperature and arrangements must be made for greenhouses and cold frames to be opened by hand if you are not fortunate enough to have automatic ventilation.

Conserving warmth

Brisk wind and damp air are not, however, weather features which an amateur gardener is likely to be able to summon up for the whole garden, though Californian fruit farmers are having considerable success in manufacturing fog with very fine overhead jets of water. The alternative is to cover individual plants on the same principles that we clothe ourselves. Cover them to prevent loss of existing heat and do it in the late afternoon when there is still worthwhile warmth to conserve.

Glass is only adequate on its own for a very short period and serves best with an additional opaque covering of sacking or blinds. Paper hats for small plants like tomatoes may be adequate and even wigwams of twigs are better than nothing because they cut down exposure to the clear sky. Trees and house walls, likewise, protect against radiation heat loss. All artificial covers must enclose the *whole* plant and not just the base.

Soil is a deep storage unit of heat accumulated during the previous season and particularly after a mild winter it may still have some reserve heat left that can be put to good use in counteracting a ground frost. If this mite of heat is insulated from the foliage by a cover over the soil its value is lost – rather like having a hotwater bottle in bed under the blanket and then lying on *top* of the blanket yourself! Cover completely, cover in good time and, since water is a good conductor of heat, keep the soil moist and clear of interference by weeds or mulch. The best you can do to ameliorate the micro-climate of large fruit trees is by initial good choice of a site high up on a slope, then keeping air drainage underneath the trees unimpeded by long grass or bushes.

Methods of protection against short frosts are useless when cold air comes with north or east winds because then air temperature can be below freezing level for days on end at all heights that matter to the garden. The cold air-streams are often accompanied by low cloud so there is no chance of the sun raising temperatures during the day. Frost bites deep into the ground and penetrates cloches, cold frames or single-boarded sheds, and the only way to offer frost-shy plants or stored tubers warmer conditions is to take them into an artificially-heated greenhouse or your home.

Treatment indoors

Warmth alone, however, does not make a healthy microclimate and there are dangerous draughts and droughts indoors that need careful watching. The colder it is outside, the faster will the cold air pour through cracks around doors or windows into the cosy warmth indoors. Colloquially we call such draughts 'howling winds' and that is exactly how they will seem to plants standing nearby on windowsills. If you really want to bestow an advantageous microclimate, double-glaze windows (even with polythene in the greenhouse), or put plants somewhere out of the 'wind'. Then think of moisture requirements. When air is warmed to the extent necessary in very cold weather to make indoor living comfortable, its capacity and thirst for more water increases enormously.

Pot plants provide a ready supply of moisture and it is essential to keep pace with the thieving air by replenishing water. Humidifiers in a centrally-heated room greatly add to the comfort of human beings as well as plants, and you can improve the microclimate of the plants even more by standing them on pebbles almost covered by water in a container of the same depth as the plant pot. The water evaporates steadily into the dry air, enveloping the plant in moist air before it disperses into the room. And as a temporary moist microclimate for wilting cut flowers, try wrapping them in a cylinder of water-soaked newspaper. Half an hour's treatment works wonders on drooping miniature roses.

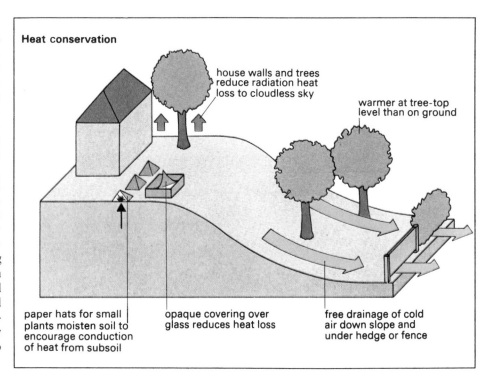

Heat conservation

house walls and trees reduce radiation heat loss to cloudless sky

warmer at tree-top level than on ground

paper hats for small plants moisten soil to encourage conduction of heat from subsoil

opaque covering over glass reduces heat loss

free drainage of cold air down slope and under hedge or fence

Above: some of the methods used to conserve warmth at night-time

Watering in the Garden

Plants need water for many reasons. Seeds will not germinate without water and plants can only use the nutrients in the soil if they are in soluble form. Water gives the plant its shape and stiffness; without it the plant becomes limp. If the water loss becomes too great the stomata (holes) in the surface of the 'skin' close and the basic plant processes come to a halt. You must, therefore, ensure that plants always have enough water for all their needs.

During dry weather you must give your plants the water that nature has failed to provide. Too often, however, the mistake is made of watering irregularly and in insufficient quantity. It is essential to give enough water to penetrate the soil down to the layer where the plant roots are growing. If you only sprinkle the surface, the water will simply evaporate in the heat of the sun.

How much water?
Apply sufficient water to penetrate the soil to a depth of at least 15cm (6 in) – preferably more. This means applying at least 2–3cm (1 in) of water, depending on the soil type. The lighter and more sandy the soil, the deeper this amount of water will penetrate. If you are using a sprinkler, you can measure the amount of water being applied by placing a number of tin cans over the area being watered. When there is 2–3cm (1 in) of water on the bottom of the tins you will know it is time to turn off the sprinkler.

If you water with a hosepipe then you will have to dig down into the soil with a hand trowel to see how far the water has penetrated.

Start watering before the soil dries out to any great depth; a good guide is when the top 2–5cm (1–2 in) is becoming dry. In hot, summer weather you may have to water at least once a week.

It is usually best to apply water in the evening, as then none will be evaporated by the sun and it will penetrate the soil to a good depth.

Many people do not realize that wind is a major drying agent (especially in spring and early summer), so watering will be necessary after windy weather.

Sprinklers and hoses
Applying all this water will be very time-consuming if you have to rely on a hosepipe alone. It is therefore a good idea to attach a sprinkler of some kind to the end and let it distribute the water.

There are many types on the market to suit all pockets. The cheapest are those with no moving parts (mini-sprinklers), but which produce a fine circular spray from a static nozzle. Often the base of these is equipped with a spike which you push into the ground to hold the sprinkler firmly.

Rotating sprinklers are slightly more expensive. They have two adjustable nozzles on an arm which is spun round by water pressure, giving a circular pattern. These are probably the most popular for private gardens.

The more sophisticated oscillating sprinklers apply water in a square or rectangular pattern. A tubular bar with a row of nozzles (non-adjustable) moves backwards and forwards, watering a very large area. It is worked by water pressure. Some can be adjusted to water a small or large area.

Sprinkler hoses are perforated plastic hoses of various kinds which are connected to the main hosepipe and produce a gentle spray of water along their complete length. One of these can be laid along rows of crops, or between plants.

You will, of course, want a good reinforced plastic or PVC hosepipe; a 13mm ($\frac{1}{2}$ in) diameter hose is a suitable size for general use.

Oscillating sprinkler that will deliver an even spray into a corner

A rotary type sprinkler that waters in a regular circular pattern

A perforated hose sprinkler, handy for long borders

Watering vegetables
Most vegetables benefit greatly from regular watering, especially crops like runner, French and broad beans, peas,

marrows, lettuce, radish, cucumbers and tomatoes. Vegetables such as cabbages and other greenstuff, and root crops like potatoes and carrots, can get by without regular watering, although their yields will not be so heavy.

All newly-transplanted vegetables must be well watered in if the ground is dry and then kept moist until established. You can water these individually with a watering can.

Germinating seeds
Seeds must be kept moist to encourage them to germinate. This is especially true of the modern pelleted seeds, which will fail to grow if they lack sufficient moisture.

Fruit trees and bushes
Fruit trees, provided they are well established, will not come to much harm if you do not water during dry spells, but the fruits may be smaller than normal. However, black, red and whitecurrants, raspberries, strawberries, gooseberries, blackberries, loganberries and other hybrid berries really do need watering in dry weather if they are to crop well.

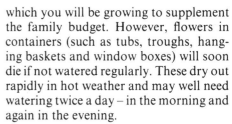

Above: use a fine rose for watering cuttings and seedlings

Flowers in beds and containers
It may not be possible to water everything in the garden, especially in a very dry season when there may be restrictions on the use of sprinklers in the garden. If this is the case, the flower garden must take third place – after fruit and vegetables,

which you will be growing to supplement the family budget. However, flowers in containers (such as tubs, troughs, hanging baskets and window boxes) will soon die if not watered regularly. These dry out rapidly in hot weather and may well need watering twice a day – in the morning and again in the evening.

Watering the lawn
Lawns rapidly turn brown in dry weather, although they will green up again once the rains start. To keep a lawn green in the summer you will need to begin watering before it starts to turn brown and continue at weekly intervals, or more frequently, thereafter. Remember also not to cut a lawn too short in dry weather – so raise the mower blades.

Mulching the soil
There is a method of conserving moisture in the soil which will enable you to cut down on watering. It is known as 'mulching' and consists of placing a 5–8cm (2–3 in) layer of organic matter around and between plants – covering the root area. Use garden compost, well-rotted farmyard manure, leaf mould, spent hops, straw, grass mowings or sawdust.

Another method is to use black polythene sheeting. To anchor it to the ground, bury the edges in 'nicks' made with a spade in the soil; then place a few stones or bricks on top. You can buy rolls of special black mulching polythene.

All plants benefit from being mulched, for moisture is conserved and so they do not dry out so rapidly. If you have to limit mulching, however, then concentrate on your vegetables and fruits, rather than on your flowerbeds.

Left: mulching trees and shrubs with compost will conserve moisture

This unusual design for our colourful Edible Garden is enough to tempt any gardener from a beginner to an experienced enthusiast. It is quite easy to carry the plan through with the help of our instructions

bushes, giving a planting of four black-currants and one redcurrant. In front of the bushes lies a narrow border, which you can edge with low-growing herbs like parsley, chives, thyme and marjoram.

Behind the currants, by the left-hand (south) boundary fence, stands a standard apple tree next to a bed of soft fruits which includes strawberries and raspberries. This bed is protected by a cage to keep off the birds. The cage need not be an elaborate or permanent structure. Four corner poles with additional supports between them and nylon mesh netting

stretched over the whole will prevent the most persistent birds from stealing the fruit. If you feel so inclined, you could make this structure more decorative.

Espalier-trained fruit trees

You will notice that we have tried to make full use of every bit of available space. Even the boundary walls support their quota of plants. Espalier-trained pear and peach trees need little space yet reward the gardener with abundant fruit. All they ask in return is timely pruning and adequate feeding.

Key to the ground plan (below) identifies the various features included in our Edible Garden, which takes up an area of 22 by 7·5 metres (72 by 25 feet)

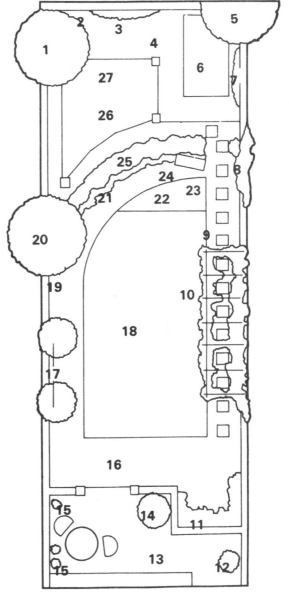

Key to ground plan

1 cooking apple 2 compost
3 espaliered pear tree 4 paved area
5 Kentish cob 6 greenhouse
7 espaliered peach tree 8 nasturtium
9 paving stones set in grass
10 runner beans climbing on pergola
11 herb rock garden 12 tub 13 terrace

14 bay tree 15 hanging basket
16 grass 17 damson 18 food plot
19 water tap (hidden) 20 eating apple
21 herbs 22 seed bed
23 rosemary bush 24 garden seat
25 currant bushes
26 raspberries and strawberries
27 fruit cage

Greenhouses and garden frames

There is always the question of whether or not to invest in a greenhouse. Even a modest structure is an expensive item, but a properly-managed and fully-productive greenhouse will pay for itself in two or three years. In it you can grow upwards of 25kg (50 lb) of tomatoes every year, a cucumber plant, winter lettuce, pot plants and a host of other good things.

If you have a greenhouse, you can garden all the year round, come rain, snow or shine. All owners, no matter what the size of their greenhouse, yearn for something still bigger. Once you've got one it opens up an entirely new world of gardening. You begin with easy things, progress to the more ambitious, and end up growing exotic specimens and proudly showing them off to your envious neighbours. The best attitude is to think big, buy big and grow plenty.

Once you have a greenhouse, then a garden frame is almost a must. If you haven't got one, you won't have anywhere to harden off (adapt from hot to cool conditions) the tender plants raised in the all-embracing warmth of the green-house before you plant them out. In fact it may be a good idea to *start* with the garden frame. If your funds won't yet run to a greenhouse, then you should build your own frame or buy one ready-made. At the very least you will be able to start seeds off in it weeks before you could do so outdoors, and in the summer it will come in handy for growing less hardy crops, such as melons or courgettes.

Statutory compost heap

The remaining area is to a degree flexible. The only thing it must have is a compost heap. These are often thought of as obnoxious mounds that attract flies and offend the neighbours. Properly tended compost heaps do neither and we will be advising you on how to go about maintaining one. They are the natural way to dispose of garden and kitchen waste whilst at the same time producing high-grade soil-conditioning and feeding material at little or no cost.

The average family and garden create a large amount of organic waste which will provide virtually free, natural plant food. So a compost heap you must have.

Optional play area

From now on your choice is determined by family and finance. If you have small children it would be in the common interest to provide them with a sandpit and a portable paddling pool. They love sand and water and as soon as they come to realize that a specific area, however small, is exclusively theirs, it will be much easier to discourage them from jumping up and down on your prized vegetables.

Getting it all together

So this is what our new-style Edible Garden is all about. It is a pleasure to look at, and in return for a reasonable amount of attention it will do much to keep your plates filled and your appetites satisfied from one year's end to the next.

This introduction sets the scene for you, explaining how the various elements of our Edible Garden fit together. As the months go by, we will be trying to give you all the help and advice we can as we take you through the various stages from planning to end-product in greater detail. And with our seasons work in the Edible Garden we will hopefully keep you on the path to successful growing and good eating (see page 327).

Courgettes (top left), carrots (centre left), onions (centre right) and capiscum (peppers) can all be grown successfully if you follow our advice.

TOP FRUIT

APPLES

The apple tree is one of the most adaptable of plants. The main garden types are dwarf and semi-dwarf bushes and cordons. There are also various ornamental forms, but for the gardener who wants to produce a good succession of apples throughout the season by the simplest means, bushes and cordons are the best proposition.

Many of the apple varieties bred over the past few decades do not grow well on their own roots. This means that cuttings rooted may not grow at the required pace or strength. To solve these difficulties, apples are budded (grafted) onto specially developed rootstocks. The rootstocks resemble the original species of *Malus* from which most apple trees are derived. They are usually denoted by numbers and letters which refer to the research stations where they were developed. All apple trees bought from a nursery will be grafted on a selected rootstock.

Always plant bushes and cordons with the graft unions between the rootstock and the chosen variety clear of the soil, and never allow soil to cover them in later years. The union is the swelling at about 15cm (6 in) above the stem base. If the trees are planted to the soil mark on the stem, the unions will be at the correct height above soil level.

Bush trees

The ultimate size of a bush tree depends primarily on the rootstock. Determine the choice of rootstock by the general nature of the soil. The stocks which give dwarf and semi-dwarf trees are M9 and M26 respectively. There is also MM106, which gives trees somewhat bigger than true semi-dwarfs and produces bigger crops, but which is still easily managed from ground level.

Planting and staking

Dwarfs grow well in rich soil, but are often too weak for light, sandy ones. On these soils plant either semi-dwarfs or trees on MM106 stock. On rich soil, dwarfs reach a final overall height of about 1·4m (4½ ft), and at maturity will produce an average annual yield of about 11kg (25 lb) of fruit.

Semi-dwarfs on lighter land will reach about 1·8m (6 ft) at maturity, to give an average of 14kg (30 lb), and trees on MM106 on light land will reach 2·5–3m (8–10 ft) with a cropping range averaging

RECOMMENDED VARIETIES

DESSERT APPLES	WHEN TO EAT
George Cave	early to mid autumn (August–September)
James Grieve	mid autumn (September)
Merton Worcester	mid to late autumn (September–October)
Lord Lambourne	late autumn to early winter (October–November)
Sunset	late autumn to mid winter (October–December)
Chivers Delight	late autumn to late winter (October–January)
Merton Russet	late winter to mid spring (January–March)
Sturmer Pippin	mid spring to early summer (March–May)

CULINARY APPLES	
Arthur Turner	late summer to late autumn (July–October)
Grenadier	mid autumn (September)
George Neal	mid to late autumn (September–October)

All these apples are of excellent quality and are comparatively easy to grow. Although the culinary varieties overlap they are worth planting as a trio, because each has its distinct flavour.
Cox's Orange Pippin is a universal favourite but can be difficult for beginners, so choose Sunset instead.
Some of the listed varieties may be difficult to obtain. Other varieties which are quite good and reasonably easy to grow as dessert apples are:

Discovery	early to mid autumn (August–September)
Ellison's Orange	mid to late autumn (September–October)
Golden Delicious	early to late winter (November–January)
Egremont Russet	late autumn to mid winter (October–December)

16–18kg (35–40 lb). Trees grafted on M26 and MM106 can grow on rich land, when final tree heights will be above those for light soil, and crops therefore bigger.

Bush trees are free-growing. Plant them at minimum distances of 2·5m (8 ft) on M9, 3m (10 ft) on M26 and 3·7m (12 ft) on MM106.

Permanent stakes are needed for dwarfs; semi-dwarfs will need initial staking, but stakes can sometimes be removed later. Trees on MM106 usually do not require stakes.

Shaping bush trees

Except for simple formative pruning, you can leave bush trees for the most part to grow at will. There are some detailed systems of pruning but simple methods give good results, bring the trees into crop at the earliest possible time, and keep them in crop thereafter.

The principle is to have an open, cup-shaped arrangement of four or five main branches (main leaders), each with at least one fork (sub-main leader), to give a final complement of at least eight or ten branches. These provide a more or less permanent basic structure, and should receive little pruning to keep them in shape once the structure has been established. They support the many side shoots (laterals) which carry the fruit.

If you buy a two- or three-year-old tree it should have had the basis of this arrangement already formed in the nursery. However, in the first winter you must tip back each leader to just short of an outward-facing bud, removing 15–25cm (6–9 in) of wood. This will stimulate the growth necessary to build up a rigid framework. You may have to repeat this tipping for the following two or three winters (according to whether the trees were planted as three- or two-year-old specimens). Be sure, also, to cut out any strong inward growths that would cause congestion or compete with leaders. Never allow laterals to rub against leaders. Some young trees may be without sub-main leaders, but these will grow later. When they appear treat them exactly as for the main leaders.

Carry out routine annual pruning of the formed tree in winter. Remove congesting laterals and keep the tree's centre open to air and sunlight. If you do this every year you will find there is not much wood to remove each time.

Top left: James Grieve has an excellent flavour and is frost-resistant. Far left: Merton Russet crops heavily and is crisp and tart. Left: Sturmer Pippin is an excellent early-fruiting variety

Cordons

Cordons are single 'rods' between 1·8m (6 ft) and 2·5m (8 ft) long, clothed throughout most of their length with short fruiting spurs. They are planted 60–90cm (2–3 ft) apart and inclined at 45 degrees, being trained along 2·5m (8 ft) bamboo poles which are fixed to three wires at about 60cm (2 ft), 1·2m (4 ft) and 1·8m (6 ft) from ground level, tightly stretched between strong end posts. These posts should be 2·5m (8 ft) long, buried 60cm (2 ft) and with extra support from wood

Below: first pruning of dwarf bush. Inset shows graft union 8cm (3 in) above soil

inside strainers. Long rows need intermediate posts at 4·5m (15 ft) intervals. A typical garden row of cordons takes up no more room than a row of runner beans. Make alleyways 1·8m (6 ft) wide between the rows to allow easy access.

Pruning cordons

On newly-planted trees cut back all laterals longer than 10cm (4 in) to three buds. Good strong rods seldom need cutting, but tip weaker ones back by 15–25cm (6–9 in). Thereafter lateral pruning is done in summer, but any further rod tip stimulation needed is done only in winter.

Above: an apple bough in blossom. Below: Lord Lambourne flowers early and is a regular and heavy cropper. Below right: Sunset, a good tree for garden cultivation, bearing fine-flavoured apples

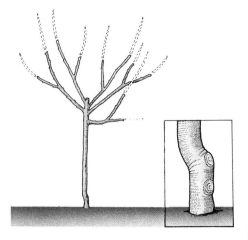

Below: cordon supports. Insets show knot for tying cordon to poles, and graft union

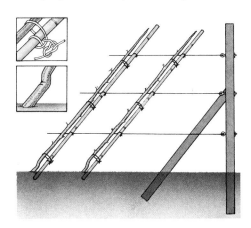

Below: summer pruning of laterals and sub-laterals on cordon apple trees

Lateral pruning aims at fruit spur formation, and a good rule of thumb is: 'laterals to three leaves, sub-laterals to one leaf'. So cut all laterals growing directly from the rods to the third good leaf from the base, and cut all other shoots (sub-laterals) to one good leaf from the base. Cut only when the shoots are mature along the base portion – that is, when the base is woody, the shoot sturdy, and the leaves fully-formed and a dark green colour. As they do not all mature at once, the cutting process goes on over a period from late summer until early autumn (mid July to mid August) according to the area in which you live.

It is absolutely imperative that you don't cut the shoots until they have reached the correct stage of ripeness. Cutting immature wood leads to masses of secondary growth and ruins all attempts to get fruit spurs to form. Even with perfectly-timed pruning some secondary growths may occur from time to time, and these must be removed at their points of origin in mid autumn (September).

Choosing an apple tree

The choice of apple varieties is very wide and it is essential to ensure that the ones you choose will cross-pollinate. Most apples will only produce fully and regularly if their flowers are pollinated by pollen from another variety that blossoms at the same time. There are a few self-pollinating varieties, but even these crop better if cross-pollinated.

If you only have room for one tree, check to see whether any of your neighbours own an apple tree and choose a variety to complement it.

Consider only top quality trees. They cost more than inferior ones, but they will pay over and over again. Cheap trees usually end up on the bonfire. Find a first-class nurseryman, order your trees in good time and take the advice offered in the catalogue.

APRICOTS

The apricot is a truly delicious fruit that deserves a place of honour on a warm wall. It has been grown in Britain for more than 400 years, though not widely until the last century, when not only the great establishments but also the cottage gardens of the countryside had their apricot trees.

There are three primary points to consider in the culture of apricots: the flowers appear early in spring (February) and are therefore susceptible to frost damage; many fruits may fall if the trees are dry at the roots; and fruit set may be sparse unless the flowers are hand-pollinated, because there are few pollinating insects about when the flowers open in early or mid spring (February or March).

Frost protection

Except perhaps during very cold spells apricots grown on south-facing house walls will benefit from some warmth, even if it is only 'domestic' heat from a room that, being south-facing, is probably well lived in. The aim is to conserve this warmth, as far as possible, around the apricot flowers, and also to provide direct protection from frost.

This can be achieved, to a considerable extent, by draping the tree with two or three layers of fish-netting (or net curtaining) each evening when frost is forecast, from the time when the buds first show colour. The material must be clear of the tree, and is best arranged over a temporary frame, that need only be a light construction and can be used again each year. It is a simple matter to attach the upper edge of the netting to a batten forming the top rail of the frame, so that the net can be rolled up and let down as necessary – possibly even until mid summer (June).

Preventing root dryness

Root dryness is a common hazard of wall trees but is easily prevented by watering and mulching. The blossom and fruit-setting period is critical, and so is the time of initial fruit swelling. Throughout these phases, if the weather is dry, water thoroughly till the root area is soaked. As soon as the fruit has set, lay a good mulch over the roots. This will conserve soil moisture for several weeks, thus reducing the need for summer watering.

Right: a fine crop ready for picking

Hand-pollinating and thinning

To effect pollination, touch the flowers lightly with a small, soft brush when the pollen is visible. Do this at midday. If the weather is very dry it is advisable to 'prime' the stigmas by misting the tree with slightly tepid water. Although the pollen grains will be transferred from anthers to stigmas more effectively if the grains are dry, the stigmas may not be fully receptive if they are also dry. Thus the object of misting is to dampen the stigmas so that the pollen grains will adhere more effectively. Mist the tree before noon, and repeat daily for two or three days before the anthers open to shed their pollen. Stop the misting as soon as pollen starts appearing.

Juicy apricots should be the result if the fruit is properly thinned (right)

The fruits should be thinned, at intervals, from when they are nut size until almost full size, so that those left to mature and ripen have about 13cm (5 in) between them.

Choosing and planting trees

Dwarf fan trees are the best for most situations, though even these can reach 2·5m (8 ft) in height and at least 4·5m (15 ft) overall spread. It is extremely important, wherever wall space is limited to an area of about these dimensions, to stipulate the trees on St Julian A rootstock. This is the least vigorous of the stocks commonly used for apricots. Trees on stronger stocks will make far too much growth for garden work, and attempts to keep them within bounds by pruning will almost certainly bring disaster because apricots will not put up with hard pruning.

The best time to plant is late autumn to early winter (October to November). Wall wires will be needed for the training of the main branches. An average spacing for the wires is 25cm (9 in) apart; the final number will depend on the height of the tree. The lowest one starts at about 30cm (12 in) from ground level.

Varieties of apricot

The earliest variety is New Large Early (not to be confused with Large Early) which normally ripens in late summer (mid July). It has large, golden-yellow fruits flushed dark red, with orange-coloured, aromatic flesh and a fine, melting flavour. Large Early matures somewhat later; in spite of its name it does not often ripen before the end of summer (late July). From late summer to early autumn (late July to mid August) there is Breda. This variety is medium-sized and coloured a deep golden-orange with purplish-red spots on the cheek exposed to the sun. The flesh is a rich orange

colour, scented, very juicy and sweet flavoured. The kernel is also sweet, unlike that of other varieties.

Another late summer variety, that continues until early autumn is Moorpark. The fruit is medium-large with greenish-yellow skin having dark, reddish markings. The flesh is orange-coloured, scented and very sweet.

One of the finest-flavoured varieties is Shipley's, also called Shipley's Blenheim. This was raised about 150 years ago by Miss Shipley, a daughter of a gardener to the Duke of Marlborough. It blossoms later than the others mentioned. The fruits are yellow-skinned with an orange flush deepened by red. The flesh is very juicy, aromatic and superbly flavoured.

A good variety for jam-making is Croughton. The fruit is small to medium in size, the skin golden-orange with flesh of a similar general colour but deeper. It

has a sweet flavour, but is slightly coarse in texture and not very juicy. It should be picked from late summer to early autumn (mid July to early August), with special care being taken to gather the fruits as they ripen, because if they are left beyond the correct stage they may be too dry for fine-quality jam.

You may find some variations between your fruit and the description given here of it. This is because apricot seedlings come nearly true to the parents but with slight differences in skin colour; and among the older varieties at least, seedlings have almost undoubtedly been propagated and sold as the varieties from which they arose, though in strict terms they are not true to these.

Soil requirements

The only fertilizers normally needed are bonemeal at 35–100g per sq m (1–3 oz per sq yd) and sulphate of potash at 25–35g per sq m (¾–1 oz per sq yd), both being applied in autumn, though not necessarily every year. The important thing to avoid is lush growth, which is induced by nitrogen fertilizers. Such growth is unfruitful, and the cutting back necessary to keep it within practical bounds will almost certainly lead to trouble, with dieback of many of the shoots being a strong possibility.

Apricots are by nature quite strong growers, but provided the growth is natural and not forced, it will not be too lush. Some lime may be needed to maintain the pH a little above neutral. Good drainage is imperative. Do not attempt to grow apricots on wet, heavy land; to do so would be a waste of time and money.

Shaping and pruning
Formative pruning follows the standard procedure for fan training (as described in the section on Peaches, page 51).

Existing branches on newly-bought trees are tipped back in early spring (February) by some 15–25cm (6–9 in). The resultant extensions are trained in, fanwise, during summer. One good shoot is selected from the upper side of each of the topmost branches, and these two new ones, which should grow from the basal portions of the parent branches, are trained in. They are tipped back early in the following spring (February) and, again, their extensions are trained in during summer. The centre of the fan is thus filled in by leading more shoots off in this way.

Branch tipping thus proceeds until all the branches have reached the desired lengths. Thereafter pruning with knife or secateurs is replaced by pinching with finger and thumb, which is confined to the sideshoots, or laterals, growing from the branches. Here the object is to induce fruiting spurs to form. When the laterals have made some 8cm (3 in) of growth, which will normally be in early summer (May), pinch out their tips. Secondary growth will then arise. Pinch the tips of these above the first leaf as soon as this leaf has fully expanded. Fruit spurs will then form. Laterals start to appear before the fan has been fully formed. For some time, therefore, branch pruning and lateral pinching proceed together, in their respective seasons.

Some laterals may be more vigorous than others; these should be stopped at a correspondingly greater length, say 10–13cm (4–5 in) with their secondary growths being stopped at one leaf. If strong laterals are stopped initially at 8cm

(3 in) and subsequently at one leaf, there might be a further flush from the second stopping. Such a response inhibits fruit spur formation and is an example of the unbalanced growth that it is so important to prevent.

Ripening and picking
Although apricots must have warmth during the growing season, it is natural warmth from the sun that they require,

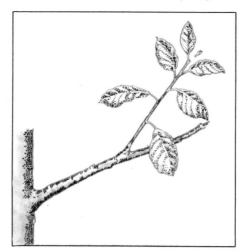

not artificial heat. (The wall warmth mentioned earlier is in a different category, relating to frost prevention.) If you want to grow a greenhouse apricot, the house must be cold. Any artificial heat will cause flower-drop and force out the very type of lush growth that leads to disaster. Even in districts too cold for outdoor apricots this rule still applies.

The fruits must be left to ripen on the tree. The ideal time to pick them is in the

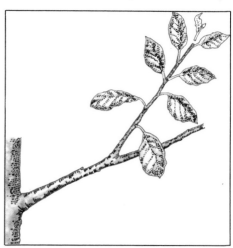

Above left: when laterals are about 8cm (3 in) long, pinch out tips. Above: pinch out tips of secondary growth above first fully-expanded leaf
Left: growing on a south-facing wall that provides warmth gives good results
Below: Moorpark fruits in late summer

early morning when they are literally 'dew fresh', though not many people would be picking and eating apricots at that hour. Nevertheless, that is the time when they are at perfection.

Pests and diseases
The most common enemies of apricots are caterpillars, silver leaf disease and a condition known as dieback.
Caterpillars Certain caterpillars attack the leaves of apricot trees but they are easily controlled either by hand picking or by applying a spray of derris or pyrethrum if their numbers warrant it.
Silver leaf Fungus disease that causes the foliage to appear silvery, and infected shoots and branches die back. Cut off infected wood about 15cm (6 in) below the end of the diseased area. Treat large cuts with a protective paint.
Dieback Condition in which large branches and shoots begin to die back. Caused by bad soil conditions or, more commonly, by a fungus that enters through a wound. Cut out and burn infected wood and paint the cut with a protective paint.

GRAPES

There are several fine grape varieties that will succeed on a sunny wall and in an unheated greenhouse, so do not be put off growing a grape vine on the grounds that greenhouse heating is too expensive for 'luxury' fruits. The main points for successful cultivation are good greenhouse hygiene, simple temperature control, correct humidity and ventilation and attention to watering.

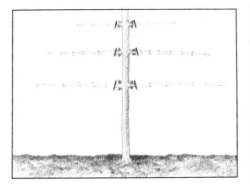

Laterals should be cut back, as indicated, to two buds from the rod

When trusses form, the laterals are cut back to the second leaf beyond each truss

Most old gardening books advise planting preparations for grapes involving the use of chopped turfs and various measures that were all very well in the days of large gardens and plentiful labour, but are hardly applicable nowadays. Neither are they essential, though good ground preparation is necessary.

For greenhouse culture, planting in an indoor border is better than in an outdoor one from which the vine stem is led into the greenhouse (preferably through the foundations). But you may need to use an outdoor border if a large area is to be given over to a vine, for it will then need to produce an extensive root system to

Right: fine-flavoured Black Hamburg
Below: a luxuriant greenhouse crop

promote the required growth. In the small greenhouse, top growth must be more limited, and this means limiting the root area accordingly.

Preparing the soil
The essential factor is good drainage. Vines will flourish in a range of soils, even quite heavy ones, so long as their roots are never dry and never waterlogged. If you think drainage needs improving in heavy soil, dig out a border 60cm (24 in) deep and 90–120cm (3–4 ft) wide, line the base with a layer of packed mortar rubble 25–30cm (9–12 in) deep, mix a barrow-load or two of sharp garden sand with the subsoil (which should be kept separate from the topsoil), return this to the trench and then return the topsoil. The border can be as long as you wish, but should not be less than 1.2m (4 ft). This is obviously quite an undertaking, but remember that the vine may be with you for a lifetime so it will pay to make a really good job of improving drainage where necessary. You can spread the workload over many weeks prior to autumn planting. Time will be needed, anyway, for the heaped border to settle.

For general-purpose preparation, where the soil is well drained and needs no special measures, dig thoroughly over the area that the roots will gradually occupy during the first few years. Mix in some old mortar rubble, a half-dozen or so shovels of bonfire ash, and bonemeal at about 100g per sq m (3 oz per sq yd). There is not much point, at this stage, in applying bonemeal over more than the immediate area into which the roots will grow. To start with a length of 1.8m (6 ft) – 90cm on either side of the planting spot – will suffice. So a 90cm (3 ft) wide border will have an initial area for bonemeal of 1.5 sq m (2 sq yd).

Planting and training
Vines are best planted in the autumn. If your plant arrives in a pot, take it out,

47

spread out its roots and place it in the hole to the depth indicated by the soil mark on the stem. Fill the hole with fine soil, firming in carefully as you go. Water thoroughly (using a rose on the can) and apply a mulch of well-rotted compost.

There are several ways of training vines. You can stretch wires across the roof area of the greenhouse at about 30–38cm (12–15 in) apart – or along one wall. The simplest method, and almost certainly the best for beginners, is to grow the plant as a single rod (stem) from which laterals grow out right and left to be trained along the wires. The main rod is allowed to reach the top wire, which should be 30–38cm (12–15 in) below the roof ridge, so that the vine leaves are not pressed against the glass. Although the length of the laterals is more or less determined each season by the pruning, there may be circumstances (such as when growing outdoors or in a large greenhouse or conservatory) when they can be left uncut. They will then reach their full natural length which can be 1.2–1.8m (4–6 ft), giving an overall spread of 2.5–3.8m (8–12 ft). Make provision for this by planting the vine at the centre point of the greenhouse or the wall, rather than squeezing it in at one end in order to save space. Planting at, or near, one end of the house or wall is possible, but you will have to keep the laterals on that side of the rod short, or even suppressed. This may result in loss of crop, because the yield from the other side of the rod will not necessarily be increased.

Pruning a vine

After planting the vine, cut it back to four buds. The top bud will normally send out an extension in due course. Train this in vertically, to form the rod, and rub out any shoots breaking from the other three buds. If the top bud fails, use the best growth from one of the remaining buds. While the rod is being formed, allow no more than about 60cm (24 in) of each season's extension to remain at the season's end. If much more than 60cm (24 in) is made, cut off the portion above that length (as soon as the leaves have fallen) to ensure a strong rod capable of producing fruiting laterals annually for many years. Thus it will take five summers to form a 3m (10 ft) rod: this is about the average size for the amateur's greenhouse.

The buds on the rod will produce lateral shoots. From each bud, two or more laterals will start into growth in spring. Remove all but the strongest one when they are 2–5cm (1–2 in) long, and train the retained ones along the wires. It

is unlikely that flowers will appear at this early stage, but if any do, cut them off. It is imperative to prevent both premature and excessive cropping. Allow no fruit to form until the third season, and then only one bunch. In the fourth season three bunches will be ample, and in the fifth, six will be enough. Thereafter one bunch per 30cm (12 in) of rod is a useful guide, giving ten bunches from a 2.5m (10 ft) rod, though a well-established vine in good health can safely produce more.

For the first two years, leave the laterals to grow freely during the growing season. As soon as possible after leaf fall, cut them all back to one or two buds close to the rod, and cut the rod back to 60cm (24 in) as already described. Some of the lighter laterals will automatically be removed by cutting back the rod.

Thereafter, the laterals must be cut on a routine spring and summer basis.

In spring reduce the buds to one per lateral. Then allow laterals to grow. Subsequently stop all laterals that have made flower trusses at two leaves beyond the trusses, and all flowerless ones at approximately 75cm (2½ ft). Stop secondary growths (arising from the stoppings) at one leaf.

When the rod has reached the full required height, cut back its tip each autumn to well-ripened wood. This will mean removing only a few centimetres in seasons of good ripening weather unless the vine is extremely vigorous and makes long tip growth. In this case, however, it is better to check its growth in summer when you are doing the lateral cutting. Cut back all laterals again in the autumn. This summer and autumn treatment is given every year.

Left: a good wine grape and a generous cropper, Seyve-Villard; right: Noir Hâtif de Marseilles, an early black variety that does well in the open; below: use vine scissors for thinning and harvesting

Care of growing plants

The year's routine maintenance programme begins after harvesting and pruning. Start by giving the greenhouse a thorough clean, including both sides of the glass. Remove the top few centimetres of soil and replace with a fresh layer mixed with well-rotted compost and bonemeal. If necessary treat the plants for mealy bugs (see Pests and diseases section). Maintain full ventilation from now until early spring (February), the object being to keep the vine dormant during the winter. In early spring adjust the ventilation lights to give about 10°C (50°F) and damp down in sunny weather.

Reduce the young shoots to one bud and train in resulting new growth. Take precautions against powdery mildew if necessary (see Pests and diseases section).

By early summer (May) growth will be rapid. Tie in as necessary, keeping leaves clear of the glass. Hand pollinate the flowers by first tapping the rod smartly to expel the flower caps; then enclose the trusses in your hand and run it lightly downwards. Pollination should be done about midday. The pollen must be dry, so at this period avoid damping down and overhead sprinkling. Close side lights to conserve heat.

Tending fruiting plants
After pollinating, damp the greenhouse down and water the border thoroughly. When the grapes have set, remove any poor bunches and, a little later, remove any of the surplus in accordance with the number to be retained in relation to rod length. Use vine scissors to thin the grapes. You will have to learn by experience how many to remove, but as a general guide one-third of the total per bunch is removed, always taking off lateral fruits and the inward ones on each strig (fruit stem) and leaving the tip ones. If outward grapes are removed, the shape of the bunch at maturity will be spoilt, and this applies particularly to the fruits at the top or 'shoulder' of each bunch.

From now on keep the temperature at around 10°C (50°F) and the atmosphere fairly moist, but never at the expense of ventilation, and never let the vine be 'cooked' on hot days or scorched by fierce sunlight. If the weather is very hot, apply a light limewash (or Coolglass) to the outside of the glass.

After thinning the bunches, apply a standard vine fertilizer (according to maker's instructions), soak the border and mulch with compost. Stop secondary growths from routine pruning.

In late summer (July) the grapes swell visibly and then cease for two or three weeks. This is the stoning period (when the pips swell) after which the grapes will resume growth. When they do, you can apply a second dressing of fertilizer if past experience has shown that one dressing is not enough; but if growth is good and the fruits normally finish well, a second dose of fertilizer will not be needed.

From late summer through early autumn (July to late August) open the lights early in the morning and close them in late afternoon (after damping down thoroughly) but leave a roof light open all night. Ensure that the soil is always moist, but do not flood the border. In early to mid autumn (late August) reduce the humidity by decreasing the amount of damping down. The grapes will nearly be ready for harvesting. Examine them frequently for any that are rotting and remove these immediately. Use vine scissors for harvesting and do not handle the grapes; hold each bunch by its stalk.

Wall-grown grapes
Except for measures obviously referring to a greenhouse, the year's programme outlined here applies equally well to a wall-grown vine outside. Perhaps the main point for special attention with wall culture is watering. Wall plants always dry out at the roots much more quickly than others do because the wall absorbs moisture along its base.

Pests and diseases
Vines in a greenhouse may be afflicted by mealy bugs and powdery mildew. Grape splitting can also be a problem.

Mealy bugs This small, whitish, bug-like creature is often troublesome in the greenhouse. It sucks the sap from the stems and leaves of vines (and other plants), thus greatly weakening them. If you have had trouble from them in the past, then after harvesting and pruning remove loose bark (under which they hide) from the rod and spray with tar oil at 500cc to 10 lit (1 pt to 2½ gal) water.

Powdery mildew Produces greyish-white powdery patches on stems, leaves and grapes. If the vine was seriously affected the previous year, then spray with dino-cap when the shoots are 5–8cm (2–3 in long). This is not a routine treatment but a special measure. Follow it with another spray before flowering, when the laterals are 30–38cm (12–15 in) long. Apply a third spray just before flowering and a final one after fruit set.

If mildew was previously troublesome but not severe, then apply only three sprays, omitting the very early one.

Thinning out non-flowering laterals, to give better air circulation, can also help to reduce the incidence of mildew.

Grape splitting A condition arising when the grapes are 'overcharged' with sap. In this event, leave about one-third of the flowering laterals unstopped in the following year, to absorb sap that would otherwise have gone to the grapes.

RECOMMENDED VARIETIES

Black Hamburg For cold or heated greenhouses and warm walls in mild areas; produces fine-flavoured grapes.
Royal Muscadine For cold or heated greenhouses and warm walls in mild areas; has pale amber-skinned fruit.
Muscat du Samur Fine-flavoured, very early-fruiting variety suitable for wall culture.
Brant Late-fruiting variety; produces heavy crops of small black grapes and beautiful autumn foliage; can be grown outdoors in mild areas.
Noir Hâtif de Marseilles Bears an early crop of black, muscat-flavoured fruit.
Seyve-Villard Excellent white grape for wine-making; crops and ripens well.

PEACHES AND NECTARINES

The melting quality of peaches and nectarines, allied with their delicate skins, gives the impression that these fruits are tender subjects on which infinite care must be lavished. In fact, although they are often grown in heated or unheated greenhouses, fine specimens come from trees growing outdoors in temperate regions.

The nectarine is a smooth-skinned form of the peach. Technically it is a mutation, or bud sport, which arose more than 2,000 years ago. Many people prefer nectarines to peaches, finding they have a more delicate flavour.

As a bush tree, the nectarine has not proved as popular as the peach in northern Europe, and it is said to be somewhat less hardy. It is, however, a fine subject for fan training.

Follow the advice given for the culture of peaches. Pests and diseases that affect peaches also apply to nectarines.

Choosing the site
Far from being tender subjects, peaches are hardy enough to succeed in the open almost anywhere except really cold regions such as northern Britain, provided the trees are sheltered from spring frosts and cold winds. Peach flowers open early, sometimes in a period of sharp frost, so never plant a tree in a hollow or in low-lying land that terminates in a wall, building or dense hedge. These form barriers to the flow of air, and such positions are frost traps.

Shelter from frost really means exposure to air flow; the hollow may look like a well-protected site, but it will be lethal to peach flowers. There is, however, a difference between air flow and blasting winds. These can do as much damage to blossoms as can frost. The ideal site is open and sunny but not windswept.

Soil requirements
Peaches do not need any special soil requirements, but the soil must be up to normal garden fertility, adequately drained but moisture-retentive. The best aid to moisture conservation is a generous mulch of compost laid over the root area each spring.

A tree on a lawn is very attractive, though not everyone likes the idea of a mulched tree in this position. If the soil is rich, the tree may well succeed without a mulch, but on lighter land the competition for water with the lawn may be too much for an unmulched tree. The fruits will be small and lacking in juice.

A peach without juice is a certain sign of insufficient soil moisture. Peach trees need large quantities of 'free water'; this is the term given to water which is present in the root zone of trees and which they can draw on when they need it during the growing season.

Training and pruning bushes
The initial framework of a bush tree comprises five or six main leaders (main branches) which soon produce fruiting laterals (sideshoots). After planting, tip back the main leaders by about 30cm (12 in) to just above a growth bud to encourage further extensions. Repeat this treatment annually for a year or two until the tree head has reached the desired size. Fruit is borne only on two-year-old

Below: nectarine Lord Napier. Right: two peaches – Peregrine (above) and J. H. Hale

wood, thus when laterals have carried a crop they are cut out to make way for maiden (one-year-old) ones. Cut these out when they, in turn, have cropped the following year.

The entire pruning can be compressed into five words: cut out the fruited shoots. Nothing could be simpler.

The only other point needing explanation is that the tree's framework may need modifying from time to time when the main leaders, or parts of them, cease to send out laterals. When this happens, cut the leader back flush with a strong outward-going sideshoot; this sideshoot then becomes a replacement leader. If there is no suitable growth present, remove the old leader completely at its point of origin. On a well-growing bush peach tree there is always an ample supply of maiden laterals to take over from the fruited ones, and always enough strong shoots to replace old leaders. Indeed,

there is often too much growth; in this case the surplus, which will congest the tree if left, must be cut as early as possible in summer. From time to time there may be shoots with dead tips. This is nothing to worry about unduly; simply remove the tips in spring, cutting to two buds or so below the dead portions.

Training and pruning fans
The other tree form is the fan which is grown on southerly-facing walls and fences. Buy trees already partly formed, because fan forming is skilled work. The tree will have foundation branches growing out left and right from a short stem. The centre will be open, but will fill up as the fan becomes established.

The tree should be planted about 25cm (9 in) away from the wall. Erect a supporting system of parallel wires, about 15cm (6 in) apart, tightly strained, and firmly held by wall nails. Autumn is the best time to plant. Tip back the foundation branches by about 25cm (9 in) to stimulate further growth. Repeat the tipping as necessary each year, until the branches have covered their allotted wall space. Shoots will grow out from the basal portions of the upper sides of the foundation branches. Train in one from each of the two highest foundation branches, thus adding to the original complement. Tip back the two new extensions by about 25cm (9 in) in winter. These additional two branches may be enough to complete the basic form, but if more are wanted, repeat the process annually as appropriate, until the fan's centre has been filled in.

Make all these cuts for stimulating new shoot and branch growth down to small,

Below: cut back fruiting laterals after harvest, as indicated. Bottom: Worn-out old leader cut out in favour of new one

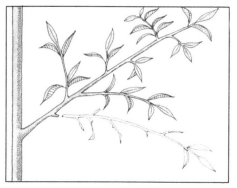

Below: basic shape of 3-year-old fan, and right, wall wires fixed with vine eyes

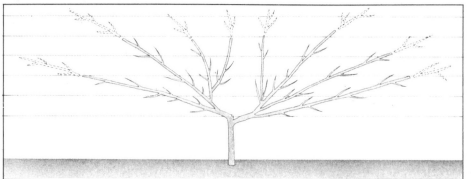

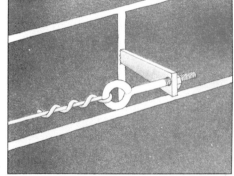

Left: peach Rochester. Above: tree form of Peregrine on Brompton root stock

pointed buds (which produce wood) and not to plump, rounded ones (which produce flowers). You can, however, cut to triple buds; these comprise a growth bud flanked by two flower buds and the former will grow out.

Fruit is carried on the laterals which grow from the foundation branches. As with the bush tree the guiding principle is to cut out the fruited shoots after harvest. There will be plenty of maiden ones for the next year's crop. Tie these in neatly

from time to time during the season. They grow out from both the upper and lower side of branches, and sometimes may be excessive in number, causing congestion. In this event thin them to some 15cm (6 in) apart, either by removing the surplus ones or by cutting them back to two or three leaves.

Ideally, you should not tie the young foundation branches directly to the wires, but train them along thin bamboos. When the branches have become well established, remove the canes and then tie the branches to the wires with soft string.

Thinning the fruit
The peach tree usually sets an enormous number of fruits. Quite a lot will fall naturally within a fortnight, but the number remaining will frequently be far too many. If they are left they will not reach anything like the full size, and quality will be poor. When they have reached the size of small walnuts they must be thinned to about 25cm (9 in) apart. This may seem a shocking waste, but it is absolutely essential if you are to achieve a crop of good-quality fruit instead of dry little specimens.

Pests and diseases
Bush peach trees are not usually attacked by pests to a degree that warrants spraying, but the fungus disease peach leaf curl must be prevented. Fan-trained trees are vulnerable to greenfly and red spider mite.

Peach leaf curl An extremely destructive fungus disease that causes the leaves to become red and distorted. The fungus takes up residence on the tree, overwintering in the bud scales and breaking out again in spring when some of the unfolding leaves may already be red along their edges. Affected foliage is swollen and fleshy, and symptoms are unmistakable. To prevent peach leaf curl, spray in early spring (February) just before the buds burst, using lime sulphur, liquid copper fungicide or captan. Repeat the treatment a fortnight later and once again at leaf fall.

Greenfly These aphides can be serious pests of peaches grown as fans on walls. They curl the leaves, stunt the growth and greatly depress yields. Apply a tar oil wash in mid winter (December) to kill the overwintering eggs. Alternatively, spray in spring using either a systemic insecticide, or liquid derris or malathion, to check greenfly that have hatched.

You must apply spring sprays before the greenfly have curled the leaves. Keep a close watch for early damage and for the appearance of greenfly. There are two main species found on peaches; one is green, the other is blackish-brown. Bush trees are rarely attacked by greenfly.

Red spider mite Causes the leaves to become mottled and bronzed, though not curled. The leaves fall prematurely, and trees can be severely checked. Spray with derris, malathion or a systemic insecticide just before the flowers open and again at petal fall. The timing of these applications is critical; adhere to it strictly, otherwise control will not be effective. Red spider mites are much less of a menace on bush trees than on fan trees.

PEARS

The finest-quality pears are not only delicious fruits, but are one of the supreme tests of the gardener's skill. Yet they are by no means difficult to bring to the picking stage. The secret of perfection lies in picking at the right time, and in good storage of the 'keeping' varieties.

To grow well, pears need a soil that is warm, fairly rich, moisture retentive and well drained. Use a good-quality compost, dug in to a spade's depth when planting and also as a spring mulch. Give new trees a good start by picking off any flowers appearing in the first spring after planting, but leave on all the surrounding leaves. Do this at white bud stage when the blossoms are easily handled.

There are several tree forms you can grow. Pears are ideally suited to the trained systems, which are very attractive, and the normal forms of these are fans, cordons and espaliers.

Pruning bush trees

Bush trees, the easiest form to grow, are planted 3–3·5m (10–12 ft) apart. Their shape is virtually the same as that of the bush apple. They have an open centre and a cup-shaped arrangement of main and sub-main leaders.

The formative pruning work is the same as for apples: cut back the leaders of the newly-planted tree by about 15–25cm (6–9 in) to stimulate further extension growth and repeat the process in subsequent winters until the tree has made a sturdy framework.

Most pears are free flowering. This means that the laterals growing from the main and sub-main leaders (the branches and their forks) will form many fruit-bearing spurs – the fat-looking buds that are seen in winter. On some varieties multiple spurs (or spur clusters) develop from the original buds. The pears will hang from these in bunches. If you cut the laterals too much they will not make fruit spurs, but will make growth instead. So keep lateral pruning on bush trees to the essential minimum to ensure good crops.

You must, however, remove congesting laterals; cut back fruited ones that are past their prime (and are producing poorly or not at all) to growth buds near the base, so that fresh laterals will grow out for future cropping.

One of the signs of a neglected tree is a vast conglomeration of old, unproductive fruit spurs, with few or no young laterals. This condition need never arise if you cut back laterals in winter when they begin to show symptoms of decline.

Some varieties (such as Doyenné du Comice) droop noticeably. This is a natural habit, and it would be wrong to try to prevent it by excessive cutting. Nevertheless, some corrective work may

be needed. Where a badly drooping leader has a strong shoot growing near the bend, cut off the drooping part flush with the point of origin of the upright shoot. The latter will then become a replacement leader. If there is no shoot present, cut back the drooping part to a fruit spur just behind the bend.

It cannot be emphasized too strongly that you must not prune bush pear trees hard or haphazardly. Prune lightly, with a definite purpose for every cut. If you are in doubt, wait until the summer before doing any corrective pruning.

Pruning trained pears

With trained forms the pruning system is entirely different. Whether you are growing fans, cordons or espaliers, comparatively hard summer pruning is essential. The underlying reason is that trained forms are kept to the right shape and size, and encouraged to bear heavy crops by a combination of root and top restriction. This can be achieved only by summer pruning, since this automatically checks growth and stimulates fruit bud formation. Winter pruning has the completely opposite effect.

Prune as for cordon apples, by cutting

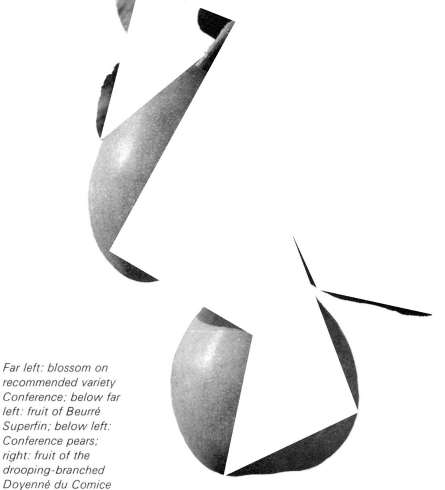

Far left: blossom on recommended variety Conference; below far left: fruit of Beurré Superfin; below left: Conference pears; right: fruit of the drooping-branched Doyenné du Comice

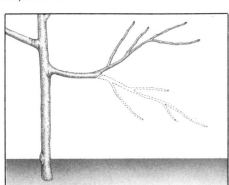

Above: cut back a drooping leader to an upper shoot, which then becomes the replacement leader.
Below: upright cordon showing graft

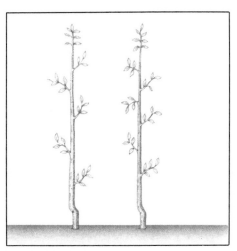

all laterals growing directly from the cordon rods (or from the main branches of fans and espaliers) to the third good leaf from the base; cut all other sideshoots to the first good leaf from the base.

As with apple trees, do not prune pear shoots until they are ripe along their basal portion – that is, when they are clothed in dark green leaves along that portion and resistant to bending. This stage is reached earlier than with apples, occurring throughout early to mid summer (mid June to mid July). In autumn remove any secondary shoots arising from the cuts at their points of origin.

Training cordons

You can grow cordon pears either at an angle or vertically. The latter way is excellent for training up pergolas or arches. Plant the trees 75cm (2½ ft) apart and train them up the two sides of the pergola. Then lead the trees over the top so that each tree meets its opposite number to form a covered arch.

Upright pear cordons are ideal for a sunny wall, especially if it is high and narrow. Bear in mind the balance between the size and shape of your wall and the dimensions of the tree you wish to grow. A wide wall is suited to fans and espaliers, a narrow one to vertical cordons. Do not make the mistake of cramming a fan or espalier onto a short wall as you would need to chop the trees hard in order to make them fit the space.

Training espaliers

Espaliers are horizontal cordons arranged in parallel tiers left and right of a central stem. Several nurseries supply partly-formed specimens, usually of three tiers, that are just right for small or medium-sized gardens. Tip back the branches or 'arms' of the newly-planted espalier by 15–25cm (6–9 in) to encourage further extensions. When they have grown to the length you require, remove the tip growths in early spring (February) to form lateral buds; in due course, these will become the fruiting spurs. Continue winter tipping for two to three seasons.

Espaliers can be grown against walls or fences, either as path edgings or as divisions between different parts of the garden. The overall length at maturity varies somewhat according to type, but on average is about 3·6m (12 ft), that is 1·8m (6 ft) on both sides of the stem. Thus you should estimate 3·6m (12 ft) as the minimum planting distance where more than one tree is wanted. Initially, you will need a supporting system of posts and wires. Train the branches along the wires – the supports can often be removed later once the tree has established its shape. Do not train the trees directly against the wall, as free air circulation behind the trees is imperative; instead, use a temporary structure of light posts.

Training fan trees

Fan pear trees are basically the same shape as the peach fans (see page 51) and are also supplied partly formed. Tip back the leaders or 'ribs' in winter for extension growth; the fruit is carried on short spurs along these. All trained pear trees are, in effect, multiple cordons until they reach their desired length.

Picking and storing

The seasons given under Recommended Varieties are for edibility and not necessarily for picking. It is extremely important to pick at the right time and store properly. Skin colour is not a guide to picking and pears must never be left to ripen on the tree. Instead, use the 'lifting' test; it is not infallible, but it is the safest guide to follow. Lift each pear to a horizontal position; if it parts readily from the spur, then it is ready for picking. If they fall into the hand at a touch, then this usually means they have been left too long; if they fall off untouched then they are definitely past the picking stage, and may go mealy or 'sleepy' in store. If they leave the spur with a snap, then you are probably picking too early, and the pears will shrivel up in storage.

Right: the variety William's Bon Chrétien will cross-pollinate with both Buerré Superfin and Conference
Below: three-tiered espalier, showing the branches trained along the wires

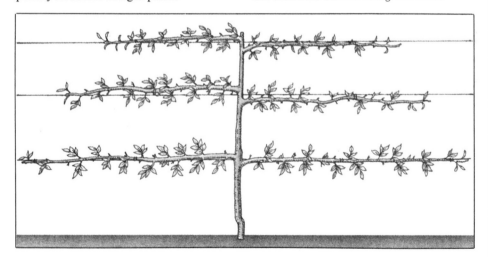

RECOMMENDED VARIETIES	
TYPE	WHEN TO EAT
Doyenné du Comice	early winter (November)
William's Bon Chrétien	mid autumn (September)
Conference	late autumn to early winter (October–November)
Buerré Superfin	mid autumn (October)
Marie Louise	late autumn to early winter (October–November)
Winter Nelis	early to late winter (November–January)

Of course, they will not all reach picking stage together, so you can pick them over a period and allow them to ripen over a similar period.

At the correct stage for harvesting, very few varieties will have their full skin colour; some may have a flush or tinge of colour, others may still be green. The full colour will come later. Most storage pears attain perfection over a period, but once attained it lasts for only a short time – though only the connoisseur would detect a deterioration of quality early on.

Keep storing pears in a fairly dry atmosphere at 4–7°C (40–45°F) and lay them out on shelves or trays. Storage cabinets with pull-out slatted trays are ideal. If you are storing the pears in a shed keep it free from strong smells; oil, fertilizer, paint, binder twine and creosote tend to destroy the flavour and aroma of pears. When the stalk ends yield to very slight pressure, bring the pears into a temperature of about 15°C (60°F). They will then complete their ripening process quite soon.

Choosing for cross-pollination

Provide for cross-pollination by choosing a succession of pears. Choose varieties whose flowering periods overlap sufficiently, but avoid grouping certain varieties that will not cross-pollinate, even though their blossoms do coincide. Almost the only pear that is fully self-fertile is Fertility Improved, but it is not one of outstanding quality. The variety Conference produces some fruits from its own pollen in some seasons, but many of them are seedless and misshapen.

The queen of pears is probably Doyenné du Comice which is in season in early winter (November). Of the many available varieties, any of the others listed under Recommended Varieties would be suitable to go with it. If you only want two trees (the minimum for cross-pollination) select them from Conference, William's Bon Chrétien and Buerré Superfin, or from Doyenné du Comice, Marie Louise and Winter Nelis. William's Bon Chrétien is a dual-purpose variety, being a splendid dessert pear *and* excellent for cooking.

If you only have space for one bush tree, buy the Family Tree which comprises three varieties on one rootstock. Varieties are selected by the nursery for quality, effective cross-pollination and seasonal succession. Naturally, the yield of each type is only one-third of the total, but can still average about 30kg (15 lb) from a well-grown tree. One excellent combination offered is William's Bon Chrétien, Doyenné du Comice and Conference.

PLUMS AND CHERRIES

Plums (including gages) and cherries are both popular fruit and most larger gardens have room for at least one or two of each, especially if there is a suitable large wall for them to be trained against. Some of the finest varieties of plums are self-pollinating and will produce without pollinating partners, though all cherries will require a second pollinating variety.

One of the great advantages of plums is that varieties grown on St Julian rootstock are semi-dwarf, suitable for growing in the open or as fans on walls. In addition, many of them are self-fertile – a useful point if you only have room for one tree. A single bush tree of Victoria plums can give around 18kg (40 lb) annually, from the sixth to the fifteenth year from planting, and often much more in later years. A fully-grown fan tree of a size suitable for the average garden should give about 9kg (20 lb) annually. Many garden trees, however, are undernourished and so fail to reach these yields.

Soil requirements

Plum trees are fairly high nitrogen users, and they also need potash and phosphates. A routine feeding programme for well-cropping bush trees should be 20–35g nitro chalk or sulphate of ammonia per square metre ($\frac{1}{2}$–1 oz per sq yd) of root area in mid spring (March), 20g ($\frac{1}{2}$ oz) sulphate of potash similarly in late winter (January), and 100–140g (1$\frac{1}{2}$–2 oz) superphosphate during every second or third autumn.

The fan uses less nutrients than the bush, though roughly in the same proportions; adjust the application rates to not less than half of the above figures.

Plums prefer either a neutral or a slightly alkaline soil; if acidity is suspected, test the soil and, if necessary, apply lime (according to the instructions) to bring the pH up to 7 or a little above. Most soils will eventually be depleted by heavily-cropping trees, so you must maintain the balance in the 'soil bank'.

Planting the trees

Plant bush trees 3·5m (12 ft) apart, and fans 4·5m (15 ft) apart. For each bush tree, dig a circle approximately 1m (3 ft) in diameter and add half a barrow-load of well-rotted compost. Mulch this area in spring for the first few years. For fans, dig a hole about 1·20m (4 ft) long, and up to 60cm (2 ft) out from the wall. Plant the tree 20cm (9 in) from the wall, allowing 60cm (2 ft) each side of the stem.

Right: the favourite variety Victoria, a self-fertile plum and a good cropper
Below: the ideal sour cherry, Morello

Pruning the trees

Winter formative pruning for plum trees is the same as for the other fruit trees we have mentioned so far (see pages 41, 50 and 54). Because of the risk of silver leaf disease, routine pruning is done only in summer. Silver leaf rarely attacks the thin wood cut during winter formative work, but could infect the thicker wood removed in routine pruning. Prune preferably in early mid summer (early June), otherwise defer it until early autumn (late August).

Plums fruit on both old and new wood, but do not leave the old wood until it has become worn out. As the best quality fruit is carried on young shoots and twigs, try to have as much new wood as possible on the tree.

Routine pruning

Routine pruning consists of eliminating congestion each year, taking out older wood and retaining the young. This will often mean sacrificing a few plums, but the results will be beneficial at harvest time. Prune systematically, retaining the basic shape of the tree, and (as far as possible) leaving the main leaders uncut. On some varieties, notably Victoria, the leaders may droop. In this event cut back as appropriate, removing · the · badly drooping portions, or cut back to upward-growing laterals if these are present.

Caring for fans

When pruning fans, train in the laterals and remove any that are growing into the wall or straight out. In late summer (July) tip back laterals at the fifth to seventh leaf from the base. Remove the older fruited shoots when the crop is finished, retaining the younger ones, and shorten earlier tipped laterals by half.

As the fan settles down to production, establish and maintain a clear pattern of pruning. There will be laterals that have cropped for two years or so, others just starting into crop, and maiden ones not yet in fruit. Keep this rhythm going, but avoid having masses of surplus shoots. Some maiden shoots may have to be suppressed for a year by cutting them back to one or two buds, while others may have to be removed altogether.

Pests and diseases

The main enemies of plums are silver leaf and two types of aphid.

Silver leaf The commonest disease of plums, particularly Victoria, is silver leaf, a fungus infection that invades newly-damaged wood. In its early stages, when only a few leaves are silvered, it can often be controlled by cutting away all the silvered shoots down to clean, unstained wood. A heavily-silvered tree, however, will rarely survive. The silvered leaves are not infectious, but in time the wood bearing them dies, and fungal infections appear on it. These discharge masses of spores that endanger not only plums but other fruit in the garden as well. In the final stage of silvering the leaves are very torn, with brown edges and brown-edged holes.

Branch breakage under heavy crops is a frequent cause of silver leaf. To prevent this, thin the small plums in mid summer (June) to one per cluster. Excessive crops will not produce high-quality fruit, so thinning is often needed anyway. Where branches remain heavily laden even after thinning, prop them up with stout forked sticks, with a pad in the fork to prevent chafing. Never let wall ties bite into the wood of fans, and always allow sufficient room for shoot and branch expansion.

If any branches get damaged, remove them at once and paint the wounds immediately with grafting wax or horticultural bitumen paint. It is useless to take these protective measures long after the damage has occurred; if silver leaf is going to infect it will do so at the time of the damage or very soon afterwards. If treatment is left until too late and the wood is already infected, the disease will be sealed in.

Aphides Two types of aphid can seriously debilitate the trees. One type causes severe leaf curling, particularly of Wyedale. The other infests the undersides of leaves, secreting honeydew on which black, sooty-looking mould forms. Regular attacks of aphides can cause failure with garden plums. A tar oil wash thoroughly applied in mid winter (December) will kill most of the eggs, but if this presents difficulties apply malathion at bud burst (just before the flowers open) and repeat two weeks later.

Damsons

Do not forget damsons, which make lovely pies and jams, and are useful for bottling. They are grown and cared for in the same way as plums.

Cherries

Cultivation of cherries is similar to that of plums, although the sweet varieties do present problems.

The two biggest difficulties of sweet cherries are that, except for a variety now on trial, all sweet cherries must be cross-pollinated (which means that at least two trees are needed to give correct partners), and all varieties produce standard trees

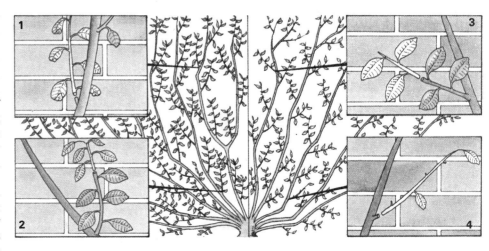

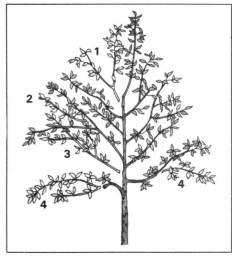

that grow too large for the average garden. They take some years to start bearing fruit, and when they do fruit many cherries are ruined by birds. Those that escape the birds are usually out of reach unless you use long ladders.

These problems may be reduced by a new semi-dwarfing rootstock now on trial and giving good results. However, it will probably be some time before such trees are available to the home gardener. The alternative to this problem of size is to grow sweet cherries as fans against a wall.

Fan trees

A wall space of about 10·5m (35 ft) and 2·5m (8 ft) high is necessary for fan trees. Plant two trees about 5·25m (18 ft) apart. Fan cherries are built up in the same way as fan plums. The routine pruning

Below: self-fertile gage, Denniston's Superb, ideal for use as dessert fruit

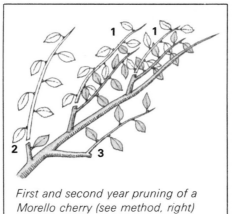

First and second year pruning of a
Morello cherry (see method, right)

shoots in crop and one-year shoots for the
next year's crop.

Fruit is carried only on two-year wood,
so when routine pruning is done either
in mid summer (June) or just after harvest, you should remove the fruited
shoots and retain those of the current
season, **1**. Many of the fruiting shoots
send out new ones from basal growth
buds. If there are too few new shoots in
the tree, cut the fruited ones back to the
basal buds instead of removing them, **2**.
If **2** was carried out in the previous year,
it will look like **3** now (see left).

Pests and diseases

The main enemies of cherries are blackfly,
blossom wilt infection and birds.

Blackfly As for sweet cherries, you can
use winter tar oil to combat blackfly, or
take the alternative measures given for
aphides affecting plums. However, it
should be made clear that Morello
cherries can – and often do – survive and,
indeed, flourish for many years without
ever becoming infested.

Blossom wilt infection which causes
shoots to die back is almost endemic on
Morellos in some areas. Cut out all
affected twigs as soon as they appear.
However, it is far better to prevent severe
infection by spraying with Bordeaux
Mixture or liquid copper fungicide just
pre-flower.

Birds The best protection for Morello
cherries while they are still ripening is
afforded by lightweight netting.

To prune a fan-trained plum tree

*Above left: before fruiting, **1** cut back
laterals growing into wall, and **2** tip
back laterals at fifth to seventh leaf
from the base in late summer (July);
after fruiting, **3** shorten earlier tipped
laterals by half, and **4** remove older
fruiting laterals*

For routine plum pruning

*Left: **1** cut back lateral competing
with main leader; **2** cut back long laterals
running alongside sub-leaders; **3** cut out
old sub-leaders; and **4** cut out drooping
leaders back to an upward-growing
lateral or downward-growing bud
Above: support heavily-laden branches
of plum tree with a forked stick, placing
a protective pad in the fork to avoid
rubbing of branches*

Morello cherries

Morello cherries are classed as sour and
are not dessert fruit, but they are splendid
for cooking and jam-making. Bush trees
are fairly small and easily managed, as are
fans. Fans of sour cherries thrive on any
wall aspect and can be planted in
positions that would be too cold for most
other fruits.

Allow a wall space of about 4·5m (15 ft)
for fans with the stem in the centre. Build
up the fan from its nursery stage exactly
as for plums. Thereafter train in laterals
and remove fruited ones or cut them back
to basal buds as appropriate when the
crop is over. This *must* be done every year,
for if neglected the system will break
down. It is equally important to prune
bush trees each year. With both forms the
annual pattern to maintain is two-year

comprises stopping the laterals at the fifth
or sixth leaf. In early autumn (late
August) shorten these shoots to about
three leaves. The object is to get the tree to
bear fruit on fairly short spurs close to the
main branches. Pruning is virtually the
same as for plums, as fruits are produced on old and new wood. Mulch with
well-rotted compost at fruit set, with
about 20g of sulphate of potash per sq m
($\frac{1}{2}$ oz per sq yd), and 90g ($2\frac{1}{2}$
oz) superphosphate similarly every
second or third year. After a heavy crop
give 25–35g per sq m ($\frac{3}{4}$–1 oz per sq yd) of
nitro chalk or sulphate of ammonia in late
winter (January), but generally 20g ($\frac{1}{2}$ oz)
will be enough.

Pests

The great scourge of sweet cherries is
blackfly, which cripples the tip leaves and
generally makes a mess. Winter tar oil
kills most of the eggs, or the alternative
measures given for aphides affecting
plums can be taken. To protect against
birds, drape the fan with lightweight
netting while the fruit is ripening.

RECOMMENDED VARIETIES

PLUMS AND GAGES

Coe's Golden Drop Grows well on sunny walls. Has superbly-flavoured golden or amber
fruits and is pollinated by Denniston's Superb or Victoria.
Denniston's Superb Self-fertile gage that provides fine dessert fruit.
Jefferson's Gage Must be pollinated by Denniston's Superb; also produces dessert fruit,
golden yellow with red spots.
Laxton's Delicious Bright red dessert plum of good quality that can be planted with
Wyedale.
Quetsche Richest-flavoured stewing plum; self-fertile. From specialist fruit nurseries.
Victoria The favourite variety and ideal choice if only one tree desired. Self-fertile, the fruit
is ideal for dessert, cooking and jam.
Wyedale Excellent English jam-making plum, pollinated by Laxton's Delicious.

DAMSONS

Merryweather Heavy cropper, with large fruits excellent for bottling.
Shropshire Prune The finest damson, with fruit that makes lovely pies and jam. Like
Merryweather, is self-fertile.

SWEET CHERRIES

Merton Favourite Fruits mid to late summer (June to July), producing richly-flavoured
black cherries. Cross-pollinates with **Bigarreau Napoleon,** a variety producing red or
yellow fruits in late summer.

SOUR CHERRIES

Morello The ideal sour cherry, splendid for cooking and jam. Trees are self-fertile, so only
one tree is needed.

PESTS AND DISEASES
of stone fruit

Peaches, cherries, plums and damsons – and the infestations that can affect them – are our subject here. As well as describing the symptoms to look out for, we also advise on what remedial action should be taken.

Stone fruit suffer from only a limited number of pests and diseases. Consequently, effective control is achieved with the minimum of spray treatments.

Plum pests
The following pests also affect damsons, but whether it be damsons or plums, the steps outlined for the control of these pests are the same.

Aphides Three species of aphid attack plums and damsons, and all overwinter as eggs on the bark. These eggs hatch out at bud-burst, and the young greenfly move on to the new growth. All three species interfere with extension growth, the leaf-curling aphid particularly so.

Caterpillars Winter moth and other caterpillars feed on developing foliage.

Red spider mite Damsons, and some varieties of plum – Czar, for example – are prone to attack by this pest. Red spiders pass the winter as bright red eggs on the bark, and hatch out in early summer (May). The small, reddish-coloured mites feed on the undersides of the leaves, causing them to become speckled and sometimes bronzed. In certain cases, the leaves may fall prematurely.

Plum fruit moth Adult moths lay their eggs at the base of the fruit stalk from late summer to early autumn (mid July to early August). The developing caterpillars eat their way to the fruit stone, where they mature, and then – in early to mid autumn (late August) – they depart to complete their development. When mature the caterpillars are reddish in colour, hence their name of red plum maggots.

Plum sawfly The adults lay eggs on the flowers during blossoming, and the creamy white caterpillars then live on the fruits till they are mature, when they drop to the ground to pupate.

Control of plum pests
Winter washes are some help against aphides and red spider mite, but a simpler, easier approach is to rely on spring and summer sprays. Normally all that is needed for the effective control of

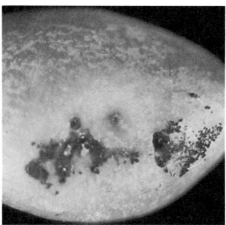

Prominent among plum pests are aphides, that swarm over new foliage (top) and caterpillars, that burrow through to the fruit stone (above)
Right: spotted underside to plum leaves points to infestation of rust disease
Pests affecting peaches include red spider mite (centre right) and aphides, that cause leaves to curl (far right)
Above right: blackfly on cherry leaf

aphides and caterpillars is a routine spray at white-bud stage with a good garden insecticide such as malathion, fenitrothion or dimethoate. Ideally, the spray should show some systemic activity in order to control leaf-curling aphides.

If plum sawfly is a problem, then you will have to give a second spray at petal fall, but in most cases this will be enough. However, if red spider mite appears, it will also be necessary to spray in mid summer (early June), and again two or three weeks later.

Finally, an attack by plum fruit moth will mean further sprays in late summer and again in early autumn (late July and mid August).

Plum diseases

The following diseases also affect damsons; treatment is the same as for plums.

Blossom wilt and brown rot This over-winters in cankers and in mummified fruits. These infection centres then produce spores in spring that infect the blossoms, causing them to wilt. The same disease is responsible, later in the season, for a brown rot of the fruits.

Plum rust Small brown spots on the underside of the leaves and a speckling of the upper leaf surfaces are the indications of this disease. Severely-infected leaves fall prematurely.

Silver leaf A fungus enters the wood through a wound, causing a silvering of the leaves and die-back of the shoots.

Control of plum diseases

Cutting out cankered wood – painting the wounds with a sealing paint – and collecting and burning mummified fruits is the best way to deal with blossom wilt and brown rot. Should plum rust develop, however, protective sprays with thiram or zineb should be applied to reduce the spread of the disease.

In the case of silver leaf, cut out infected shoots and burn them, and paint the wounds with protective paint.

Cherry pests

Most people think of birds as being the main pests of cherries, but the following insects can also be a great nuisance.

Aphides Cherry blackfly, that overwinters in the egg stage and hatches at about the time of bud-burst, can be very damaging to cherry trees. Infected leaves curl up and the new growth is severely checked.

Caterpillars Winter moth and related caterpillars sometimes attack cherries as the flower-buds open.

Cherry fruit moth The caterpillars of this moth bore into the flower-buds and feed on the flowers and young fruitlets.

Control of cherry pests

As with plums and damsons, winter washes give some control of the main pests, but it is easier to rely on a general insecticide, such as malathion, fenitrothion or dimethoate, applied at white-bud stage. Ideally, the selected product should have some systemic activity to control the leaf-curling cherry blackfly.

Cherry diseases

Always cut out diseased wood of the cherry in the summer, thus lessening any risk of further infection.

Bacterial canker This bacterial disease can be very damaging, as it kills whole branches and can lead to the complete die-back of the tree. Infection occurs during autumn, and the disease then progresses during the winter months. Leaves on infected branches turn yellow and brown.

Control of cherry diseases

The recommended method of control for bacterial blight is to give three applications of a copper fungicide – Bordeaux mixture, for example – at two-week intervals, starting in early to mid autumn (end of August). It is also desirable to cut away any badly infected branches.

Peach pests

The following pests also affect nectarines and apricots, when the controls are the same as for peaches.

Aphides Several species of greenfly and blackfly attack peach trees at bud-burst or shortly after, causing severe leaf curl.

Red spider mite These small, reddish mites feed on the undersides of the leaves, causing a speckling of the foliage. In severe cases, the leaves may fall early.

Control of peach pests

Since winter washes are liable to damage some varieties, it is better to rely on spring and summer sprays. A routine spray with a systemic greenfly killer such as malathion, dimethoate or fenitrothion should therefore be applied at the end of the blossom period to deal with greenfly and blackfly. If red spider mite is present, spray against it before flowers open.

Peach diseases

The following diseases also affect nectarines and apricots, and the same controls apply as for peaches.

Leaf curl This extremely widespread and common disease causes the leaves to thicken and become distorted. Infected leaves also fall prematurely, so the disease has serious effects on the cropping and general vigour of the trees.

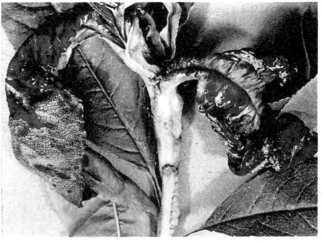

Above: powdery growth on skin of peaches indicates presence of powdery mildew
Left: leaf curl causes peach leaves to swell and distort, and also to redden

Powdery mildew This overwinters in the buds, causing them to produce stunted growth covered with a thick coating of powdery spores that are capable of infecting healthy leaves.

Control of peach diseases

The standard recommendation for the control of leaf curl is to spray the trees in early spring (end of February) with either a copper fungicide or lime sulphur. A second spray should be applied in autumn just before, leaf fall. An alternative approach is to spray with thiram at fortnightly intervals, starting when the first diseased leaves appear.

Thiram sprays will also help to control powdery mildew, as will a series of sulphur sprays, applied every 14 days, starting when the disease is first noticed.

SOFT FRUIT

BLACKBERRIES AND HYBRIDS

Blackberries are a versatile fruit. They can be used for making a variety of desserts, jams and wine, and they also keep well in the freezer. A certain amount of training and some pruning is necessary for a good crop, but otherwise the plants are easy to cultivate.

BLACKBERRIES

One of the earliest articles on cultivated blackberries appeared in 'The Gardeners' Assistant' in 1859, when ten types were listed under the name bramble. This fruit belongs to the genus *Rubus* and was originally given the name *Rubus frucoticosus*. Botanists later recognized much variation in wild blackberries and they were divided into more than 150 species.

Everyone who has picked the wild fruits will know that some are large, juicy and well flavoured, while others are small, woody and poorly flavoured. Seasonal conditions play a part, but the main reason for the difference in quality is the difference in species. Added to this is the fact that seedlings arise, of which some may be superior or inferior to the species from which they sprang.

Cultivated varieties

The best of the wild types have been selected for cultivation or used in breeding programmes for raising improved forms, and the list has now been reduced in the last thirty years from sixteen or so to about half a dozen. The most widely-known is probably Himalaya Giant, that was introduced to this country at the end of the last century by a Hamburg nurseryman, Theodor Reimers, who gave it his own name in Germany. It was known as Himalaya in Great Britain because it was thought that it arose from seed collected from the Himalayas but it is now known to be a species, probably a form of *R. procerus*, which grows throughout much of western Europe.

Himalaya is very vigorous, producing canes up to 3m (10 ft) long, which are heavily thorned. The jet-black berries are large (hence the 'Giant' part of the name), juicy and impressive looking, but can be disappointing in some seasons, with little discernible 'bramble' flavour, though this does come out well when the berries are used with apples to make jam. The variety is a prodigious cropper, sometimes giving 14kg (30 lb) per plant, and it rarely fails. It is in season from mid to late autumn (mid August to October). Its main drawback is the difficulty of handling the canes.

The earliest variety, starting to crop at the end of the summer and continuing for about a month (late July to late August) is Bedford Giant. This is said to be a seedling of the Veitchberry, which is a raspberry-blackberry hybrid. Bedford Giant is another vigorous, prickly grower producing abundant crops of large berries. The flavour is sweet and superior to that of the Himalaya. Bedford Giant is rather susceptible to the bacterial infection crown gall; galls, that can be quite

Above: early-fruiting Bedford Giant
Right: popular Oregon Thornless

large, appear on the canes – sometimes at the crown and sometimes farther up. These are unsightly but, as far as research work has established, they do not unduly affect growth and cropping. Occasionally, however, a gall may completely girdle a cane; and then the cane will die above that point.

A fine variety for early to mid autumn (August to September) is John Innes, raised at the John Innes Horticultural Institution in England. This is juicy, sweetly-flavoured and crops heavily from canes up to 2·6m (8 ft) long.

Thornless varieties

However good the thorned varieties are there is little doubt that the thornless ones are preferable for the garden. Oregon Thornless, one of the most popular varieties, tends to be a lighter cropper than the thorned varieties, but it can yield well in a good year. It is a wild plant, native to Oregon, and was taken up there for domestic culture around the first quarter of the century, but it was introduced into Britain only recently. Growth is moderate, with canes reaching some 1·8m (6 ft). The berries are fairly large, sweet and with a good 'bramble' flavour. The parsley-leaved foliage is attractive, lending the plant a decorative aspect, and making it an ideal subject for a dividing screen between the flower and vegetable gardens. It crops from mid to late autumn (September to October).

Another excellent thornless type from the United States is Smoothstem, – resulting from a cross between Merton Thornless and the American variety Eldorado. It is in crop from the end of

early autumn until late autumn (late August to October), producing very heavy yields of large berries.

HYBRIDS

The list of blackberry hybrids has shrunk considerably over the last four decades, perhaps because there was not a great deal to choose between most of them. The three main types now offered are those with deep red berries, represented primarily by the loganberry (described on page 56), those with purplish-black berries of which the chief example is the boysenberry, and the raspberry-blackberry hybrid – the Veitchberry.

Boysenberry This originated in California, and the first type seen in Britain was thorned. This type is still available but is likely to become superseded by the thornless variety now on sale. The berries are large, have a fine flavour, and ripen from late summer to early autumn (July to August). A yield of approximately 3·5–4·5kg (8–10 lb) is given per plant. The canes are up to 2–4m (8 ft) long. The berries make delicious jam. A useful feature of boysenberries is that they are good drought-resisters and will thrive on soils that might normally be too light for maximum production of blackberries.

Veitchberry This is a cross between the

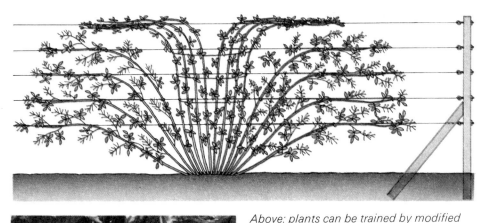

Above: plants can be trained by modified open fan method (as used for loganberries)
Left: thornless boysenberry, good for jam

raspberry, November Abundance, and a large-fruited blackberry. It fills the gap between the summer-fruiting raspberries and the blackberries. The berries are borne on vigorous canes and are finely-flavoured. This hybrid was raised at the famous English nursery of James Veitch.

Planting blackberries and hybrids

In practice any reasonably good soil will suit blackberries and their hybrids. They will always benefit from organic treatment, with compost being dug in before planting, at the usual rate for soft fruit of one barrowload per 10sq m (12 sq yd) or so, and thereafter used as a spring mulch over the root area. Plants given a good start and then well tended, will crop for ten to fifteen years, often longer; a planting distance of 2·5m (8 ft) apart is about right for John Innes, Oregon and Smoothstem; the others will need about 3–3·6m (10–12 ft).

Training the plants

Support the plants with posts and wires; ideally you should have four wires spaced at 90cm, 1·2m, 1·5m and 1·8m (3 ft, 4 ft, 5 ft and 6 ft) from ground level. The end posts should be 2·5m (8 ft) long, buried to 60cm (2 ft). Treat the bottom 75cm (2½ ft) with a standard preservative. Provide additional support by using inside strainer posts or outside wire struts, firmly anchored. Struts do, of course,

take up extra room and can be effective trip wires for people not watching their step, or for children in a hurry.

The same training systems are used as for loganberries (see page 86). Thus you can train the canes on the open fan principle, with fruiting ones spread out fanwise left and right of centre along the first three wires, with a gap in the centre up which the current season's canes are led to a temporary position on the top wire. Alternatively, the fruiting canes can be led off along the wires in one direction, and the current season's ones in the opposite direction (the rope or arch method). These are arranged each year to ensure that where there are two or more plants, the fruiting canes of one plant meet the fruiting canes of its neighbour, while non-fruiting (i.e. current season's) meet similar ones.

Autumn and winter pruning

Prune all fruited wood as soon as possible after harvest. If you are using the open fan system, release the new season's canes from the top wire and tie them fanwise ready for fruiting the following year. With the rope or arch method the new canes are already in position. Remove the fruited ones; the space they occupy will, in due course, be taken over by the current growths of the following year.

With John Innes and Himalaya some

once-fruited canes can be left for a further season if desired, since these varieties will make a second year's flush of fruiting laterals from the previous season's canes, thus boosting the crop. In these cases, cut back (in winter) all laterals to basal buds on any canes to be left; new ones will grow out and fruit in the next summer. Often, however, there are enough new canes, especially with Himalaya, to fill the allotted space without worrying about retaining any of the fruited ones, and in any case it is a mistake to retain wood for two seasons if this means congestion.

Pests and diseases

Blackberries and their hybrids are fairly sturdy plants but are prone to one or two ailments.

Blackberry mite A condition that frequently mystifies gardeners, particularly when the season is ideal for ripening, is failure of the berries to ripen fully. Many of the drupels (the small globules of which the berries are composed, and that contain the seeds) remain red. Himalaya is probably the most widely affected. This trouble is caused by the blackberry mite, sometimes called red berry mite, a microscopic species that feeds on the berries, preventing the drupels from ripening, and often causing distortion. Complete control is difficult to achieve but the mites can be substantially reduced by burning canes carrying infested berries immediately after harvest, and following this up next season with a spray of lime sulphur in early summer (mid May) at 500ml to 10 litres (1 pt to 2½ gal) water; or a solution of wettable sulphur in water at 50g to 10 litres (2 oz per 2½ gal) water just before flowering. Lime sulphur may cause some leaf scorch, but this is not usually enough to do serious damage. Wettable sulphur is not the same as sulphur dust; the latter is not formulated for use as a spray.

Virus diseases (such as stunt) affect blackberries and hybrid berries. They are spread by leaf hoppers and aphides. Burn affected plants, and only propagate from healthy specimens.

RECOMMENDED VARIETIES

BLACKBERRIES

Himalaya Giant	fruiting in early to late autumn (mid August to October)
Bedford Giant	fruiting in late summer to mid autumn (late July to late August)
John Innes	fruiting in early to mid autumn (August to September)
Oregon Thornless	fruiting in mid to late autumn (September to October)
Smoothstem	fruiting in mid to late autumn (late August to October)

HYBRIDS

Boysenberry	fruiting in late summer to early autumn (July)
Veitchberry	fruiting in late summer (July)

BLACKCURRANTS

Blackcurrants are the richest source of vitamin C of all the garden fruits. Here we give full details on how to plant and care for your bushes, so that they crop regularly and heavily, and also explain how you can raise new plants from cuttings.

Blackcurrants thrive in organically rich soil. They can hardly have too much good quality, well-rotted compost. Dig it in before planting, at the rate of one full barrowload per 8–10 sq m (10–12 sq yd), and use it as a mulch every spring just after fruit set. If there is enough compost, cover the pathways as well as the plant rows. Use a depth of 8cm (3 in) if it can be spared. This will not only cut out hoeing, thereby leaving the near-surface root mass undisturbed, but it will ensure the greatest possible degree of summer moisture retention, and encourage each bush to make a really large root system. Abundant roots mean abundant top growth; the fruits are borne on shoots made the previous year, so the more two-year shoots, the bigger the crop.

Compost alone often will not boost growth and crops to the maximum. It may have to be supplemented with a proprietary fertilizer high in nitrogen in early or mid spring (February or March) at 25–35g per sq m ($\frac{3}{4}$–1 oz per sq yd).

Planting the bushes

It is imperative to get the plot really clean before planting. If such weeds as couch grass, bindweed and creeping buttercup are left, it will be almost impossible to eradicate them later from around the bushes without disturbing the roots.

Planting holes must be wide enough to take the roots comfortably and, more important, deep enough to ensure that the crotch of the bush is about 10cm (4 in) below soil level. New shoots are needed not only above ground but also below. The latter are 'stool' shoots, and can provide a significant portion of the crop.

Plant the bushes a minimum of 1·5m (5 ft) apart. Cut back newly-planted bushes to buds just above soil level. Do not crop them in their first summer as they must be given every chance to build up strongly. They will then crop well in the second summer and onward.

Below left: plant bush in 10cm (4 in) deep hole and cut back shoots; below: plant cut-off shoots 15cm (6 in) apart

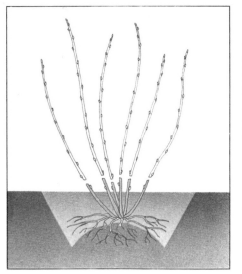

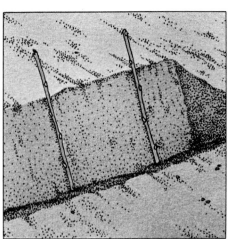

Raising from shoots

Use some of the cut-off shoots to raise more bushes. Trim them to 20–23cm (8–9 in), removing tip portions. Plant them 15cm (6 in) deep and 15cm (6 in) apart, with all buds intact, into a well-prepared nursery strip. The maiden bushes will be ready for planting out during the following winter.

Caring for growing bushes

Blackcurrant bushes have no permanent framework, but they send out many shoots from old wood. The aim in pruning is to have good supplies of maiden shoots each year for cropping the following year. Fruited shoots can be cut out when the fruit is picked, and this is often sufficient pruning. The other time to prune is in winter, leaving maiden branches, but cutting out fruited shoots. The two are easily distinguished; cropped shoots are darker than maiden ones, and carry the dried remains of the fruit strings.

Many fruited shoots will have maiden ones growing from them, and maiden tip extensions. Where a fruited shoot is supporting a maiden one, cut off the upper fruited part at the junction with the new shoot, and leave the latter intact. The

Below left: juicy fruits ripening and picked ready to eat (above)

basal portion of the old piece will then become a temporary support.

Where fruited shoots have no maiden side growths but do have good maiden extensions, leave them in. Such extensions can produce useful fruiting trusses. But where the extensions are very short and puny, cut out the shoots at the base. Cut out entirely any fruited shoots bare of maiden side growths and tip extensions.

Below: cut out fruited shoots at harvest time and, if necessary, in the winter

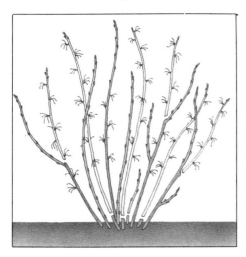

There may be weak maiden shoots deep within the centre of the bush. Their poor growth is due to lack of sunlight. Remove them as they are useless for cropping.

Protection from the wind
One of the commonest causes of crop failure is 'running off', when the flowers either shrivel or set fruit that falls soon after. This is the result of imperfect pollination due to strong, cold winds at blossom time. The winds not only damage the flowers but discourage pollinating insects, without whose help pollination is rarely satisfactory. If the garden is windswept, plant the bushes in the lee of any existing shelter from the east round to the north-west. The best shelter is an evergreen hedge. A temporary screen of sacking stitched to strong hazel rods is not as effective as the windbreak hedge, because it shelters only the bushes and not the surrounding area. If the area remains windblown, it will not attract pollinating insects.

Pests and diseases
The main pests infesting blackcurrants are aphides and gall mites ('big bud' mites).

Aphides These insects can do great damage to the leaves by sucking the sap and distorting them. The familiar sooty mould forms after an attack of aphides, often on the berries. The most practical control is a winter tar oil spray, thoroughly applied to kill the eggs. Alternatively, spray with derris, malathion, or a systemic in the spring as soon as aphides are seen on the undersurface of the leaves.

Gall mites These live and breed inside the buds, causing them to swell to several times the normal winter size. The buds are killed by the mites, which then infect new buds in the spring. The mites also transmit a virus disease called reversion, which does not kill but renders the bushes incapable of fruiting. Never use cuttings from infested bushes for propagation.

A limited measure of control may be achieved by picking off and burning swollen buds. The standard control is a spray of lime sulphur according to the maker's recommendation at the grape stage: that is, when the unopened flower buds hang like bunches of tiny grapes.

Some buds infested with gall mites may become detached from the plant and carried by the wind to nearby bushes, causing 'big buds' to appear on previously clean bushes. The mites may also be transported by various flying insects (particularly aphides) to which they cling. It is therefore a sound policy to spray with lime sulphur every year as an insurance against infection from any blackcurrant bushes in the vicinity.

The only variety of blackcurrant in present cultivation that has some degree of immunity to gall mites is Seabrook's Black. It is not completely immune, but may go for several years without an infestation.

RECOMMENDED VARIETIES
Tor Cross Early season variety fruiting mid to late summer (late June–mid July)
Laxton's Giant Early season variety fruiting mid to late summer (late June–early July). Good alternative to Tor Cross. Crops heavily, with very large, sweet fruit.
Seabrook's Black Early–mid season variety fruiting mid to late summer (late June–mid July). Only variety resistant to gall mite. Good crops of large fruit.
Wellington XXX Mid season variety fruiting late summer (July). Very heavy cropper, producing large fruits on long, spreading branches.
Baldwin Mid to late season variety fruiting late summer to early autumn (mid July–August). Produces heavy crops of well-flavoured fruit very rich in vitamin C.
Amos Black Very late season variety fruiting early to mid autumn (August–September). Flowers late enough in most areas to miss frosts.

DECORATIVE BERRIES
from blueberries to wineberries

There are several bush fruits that are edible and also sufficiently attractive to warrant a place in the garden as ornamental shrubs. We shall now look at several of these dual-purpose plants.

BLUEBERRIES

These berries grow in wild and cultivated forms in Canada and the northern regions of the United States of America. The British wild type *Vaccinium myrtillus* (known as whortleberry, whinberry, bilberry and blaeberry) is related to them. It grows on acid moorlands and produces small fruits that, although palatable, are inferior to garden forms.

The fruiting season for cultivated varieties is from late summer to late autumn (mid July to early October).

Species of cultivated blueberry

The species most grown for its fruits is *Vaccinium corymbosum*, known as the highbush blueberry; this has also been a recognized ornamental garden plant for a considerable time. Several named varieties with improved fruits have been raised from it.

The general habit of the species is dense, rounded and twiggy with a height of 1·5–2·2m (5–7 ft) according to variety. The leaves vary in size from about 2–9cm (1–3½ in) long. They are bright green in summer, turning gradually to red in the autumn. Clusters of six or more small, white or pale pink flowers appear in early summer (May) before the leaves are fully expanded. The black, blue-bloomed berries also appear in clusters and ripen during early and mid autumn (August and September). They make delicious pies and other desserts, and are sweet enough for eating fresh.

The other main type is the lowbush blueberry *V. angustifolium*, a compact, dwarf shrub with leaves that become richly coloured in autumn. The flowers and berries are very similar to those of the highbush. Another dwarf species, *V. deliciosum*, produces solitary flowers and sweet black berries.

An evergreen, red-berried form is *V. floribundum*. As its name implies, this produces an abundance of flowers. The densely-clustered, rosy-tinted flowers appear in mid summer (June) and the fruit follows in early autumn (August). This is a most attractive species; the young shoots are red, and the leaves change from purplish-red to dark green. It is probably not sufficiently winter-hardy for cooler regions (since it is tropical in origin) but it will thrive in mild areas.

Soil requirements

Blueberries need an acid soil with a pH of 4·5. If your soil grows good azaleas or rhododendrons it will usually suit blueberries. They also require a good supply of moisture. The native British blueberries grow not only on moorland in high rainfall areas, but also on sandy heathlands where rainfall is much higher, and the species *V. corymbosum* is known in North America as the swamp blueberry, a name that clearly indicates its need for abundant moisture.

Blueberries will not grow in chalk or limestone soils so in these conditions you will have to prepare special beds or planting holes for them. One way is to dig holes 30cm (12 in) deep and 45cm (18 in) square, and to fill them with a mixture of moist peat and 25 per cent sharp sand. The sand is included to improve drainage; blueberries need plenty of moisture but they will not stand being waterlogged. Peat and sand do not, of course, provide the plants with much nourishment; so apply sulphate of ammonia at 35g per sq m (1 oz per sq yd) in early spring (March), and sulphate of potash at 17g per sq m (½ oz per sq yd) in winter. Alternatively, apply a general NPK (nitrogen, phosphate and potash) fertilizer in spring.

Another way of cultivating the plants

Two varieties of the highbush blueberry – Blue Ray (top) and Jersey (above)

where the soil is alkaline is to grow a bush in a tub, using the peat and sand mixture.

Planting and tending
In the garden, set the plants 1·2–1·8m (4–6 ft) apart, with the crowns about 10cm (4 in) below soil level to encourage the growth of new shoots from the base. Give them a good mulch of peat or compost annually to help conserve moisture.

Adequate summer moisture is essential and, since watering may become prohibited in some regions if drought sets in, this is all the more reason why soil water must be conserved. If the plants establish themselves quickly they should make some 30–45cm (12–18 in) of growth during the first season.

Don't prune newly-planted bushes and confine routine pruning to the removal of some of the old shoots from time to time.

Pests and diseases are practically non-existent, so no routine spraying is required, but netting is advisable to protect the fruit from birds.

CRANBERRIES
Vaccinium oxycoccus, the small cranberries, are natives of the northern hemisphere. They are very small evergreens with a spreading habit, bearing red, somewhat acid berries that make delicious tarts, pies and jellies. The leaves are small and silvery on the underside, and the tiny delicate flowers are pink-petalled. There is an American form, *V. macrocarpum*, with much larger oval berries, but it is not very readily available in Britain.

Planting and tending
The cultivation and soil requirement of cranberries are very similar to those of blueberries except that the bushes, being

Above: small cranberry in fruit; top: the Worcesterberry, a gooseberry hybrid

smaller, may be planted close together; 60–90cm (2–3 ft) apart is suitable. Birds can soon eat up much of a cranberry harvest so, as with blueberries, you would be wise to protect the berries with netting.

WORCESTERBERRIES
Confusion over the history of Worcesterberries has existed for many years. The myth that the berry arose as a blackcurrant-gooseberry hybrid has been around for over half a century. Some versions even gave its parents as Boskoop Giant blackcurrant and Whinham's Industry gooseberry. Hybrids between currants and gooseberries have long been known but they are completely sterile and also thornless, whereas Worcesterberries are very fertile and thorned.

Science, however, has established that it is a hybrid between two gooseberry species; technically it is an inter-specific gooseberry hybrid, known as *Ribes divaricatum*, this being the name of one of the two species from which it is thought to have arisen. It is sometimes listed as an American wild gooseberry.

The reddish-purple berries are roughly midway in size between blackcurrants and gooseberries. They have a pleasant flavour when eaten fresh, and may be used for jam and in cooked dishes.

Planting and tending
The Worcesterberry makes a hardy, free-growing bush with strong branches reaching about 1·2–1·5m (4–5 ft) in height and arching over at the tips.

To accommodate the arching habit, and to see it at its best, bushes should be planted 1·8m (6 ft) apart – if more than one bush is wanted.

The soil should be well-drained and loamy, with a good organic content, and the bushes will always benefit from mulching. Although gooseberries in general need fairly heavy supplies of potash (without which they are liable to show marginal leaf scorch) Worcesterberries do not seem so prone to potash deficiency. If leaf scorch does appear, apply sulphate of potash at 17–25g per sq m ($\frac{1}{2}$–$\frac{3}{4}$ oz per sq yd) of root area in autumn.

Pruning is much the same as for blueberries. In addition, keep the growths thinned out enough to make picking among the thorns less hazardous.

RECOMMENDED VARIETIES

BLUEBERRIES
Early Blue (or Earliblue) Early season.
Pemberton Early season.
Burlington Early to mid season.
Rubel Early to mid season.
Grover Mid season.
Goldtraube Mid season.
Jersey Late season.

CRANBERRIES
Vaccinium macrocarpum **Early Black.**
Vaccinium oxycoccus (red cranberry) No named varieties.

WORCESTERBERRIES
Ribes divaricatum No named varieties.

Many members of the bramble family are ornamental as well as producing fine-flavoured fruit. These include the Chinese raspberry, the Japanese wineberry and one with no common name, *Rubus leucodermis*. Two other unusual fruits are Cape gooseberry and Chinese gooseberry – neither of which is related to the gooseberry family, or to each other.

CAPE GOOSEBERRY

Salads made from fruit as well as vegetables are a pleasant change from the conventional lettuce and cucumber mixture, and one of the best fruits to add is the Cape gooseberry. This fruit, *Physalis (edulis) peruviana*, originated in South America. It can be eaten fresh and is also excellent for making preserves, or stewed.

Many gardeners will know its decorative relation, *P. alkekengi* (Chinese lantern plant). This has rounded, veined, downward-hanging husks containing the fruit. The berries are of indifferent dessert quality and so are used mainly for other culinary purposes.

The fruit of *P. peruviana* is a deep golden colour and roughly cherry sized. The flavour is very good and the fruit has a high vitamin value. It will keep in first-class condition within the husk for several months if dried carefully before storage and kept in a cool dry and airy place. The husks are considerably larger than the fruits; they are very attractive (as are the small, pale yellow 'starry' flowers) but are partially hidden by the large leaves.

Right and below: Physalis alkekengi
(Chinese lantern plant)
Bottom: Physalis peruviana
(Cape gooseberry)

How and where to plant

Grow the plants in the open garden, under glass or in pots. For outdoor culture they require no special soil, and should not be given rich treatment. They will make good growth in any normal garden soil without additional feeding provided they are kept sufficiently watered. Give them a mulch (such as peat) to conserve water but do not use a growth-promoting type like animal manure.

Set the plants 60–90cm (2–3 ft) apart in mid spring (March) and keep them under cloches or in frames to protect them from late frosts or cold, drying winds. Such winds can check the plants severely, or even shrivel them up. If you cannot supply this protection put the plants temporarily in small pots and keep them indoors in a sunny position until early to mid summer (late May). Then transfer them to 25cm (9 in) pots for outdoor cultivation.

In colder regions pot culture is preferable anyway, because the plants can be brought indoors to avoid the autumn frosts and will then ripen their fruits in safety. Use medium-sized pots and J.I. No 3 or a peat-based compost.

Actinidia chinensis *(Chinese gooseberry)*

Providing support

The growth habit is not unlike that of tomatoes, and so the plants need to be supported by canes. They reach a height of about 60cm (24 in) on average, but can exceed 90cm (3 ft). If you want to restrict the plants to a certain height, simply pinch out the stem at the highest side-shoot. If sideshoots are growing at the expense of stem height, stop some of them when about 30cm (12 in) or so long, and pinch out new ones as they arise. Do not, however, adopt any form of regular stopping and pinching; as long as growth is within the required limits, let it proceed.

After fruiting

The fruits are ready for gathering in the autumn when the husks part easily. Make sure that the husks are perfectly dry if you are going to store them. Apart from that no special storing measures are necessary.

When the fruit has been gathered, cut the plants back to soil level and, with outdoor culture, give the stools winter protection under straw or a thick layer of garden litter.

Pests and diseases

Inspect the plants weekly for aphides, especially the tips of the shoots and at the stalk ends of the 'lanterns'. If you find any, spray with derris or malathion.

CHINESE GOOSEBERRY

Another ornamental and edible fruit is the Chinese gooseberry *Actinidia chinensis*. It is believed to have come to the West in the 19th century. 'The London Journal of Botany', in 1847, described specimens sent to the Royal Horticultural Society by the famous plant hunter Robert Fortune. The plant was also found in Japan by another of the Society's plant hunters who wrote about it in 'The Garden' in 1882.

It is a hardy climber with very large, handsome leaves, and clusters of bright yellow flowers 2–4cm (1–1½ in) across, bearing many stamens. The fruit is about the size of a walnut. It is covered with gooseberry-like hairs, and also tastes rather like a ripe gooseberry. It may be eaten fresh or stewed.

How and where to plant

This plant is a rapid grower suitable for covering walls, fences and trellises in sunny positions in mild areas. It grows to a considerable length, and the recommended minimum planting distance is 5·5m (18 ft). You will need at least one male and one female plant for pollination; it is said that one male will pollinate eight females.

No special soil is needed for outdoor growing, but good supplies of organic matter should be dug in, and mulching will always help. Garden soil of good fertility will suffice for pot culture, together with a feed of liquid manure at regular intervals during summer. For greenhouse cultivation, artificial heating is not necessary.

Providing support

Chinese gooseberries, being climbers, need a support structure of canes or wires. You can also grow the plants individually in 30cm (12 in) pots; train them up bamboo canes and stop them according to the vertical space available. A good method for pot culture is to stand the plants in a greenhouse with their lower stem portions trained up bamboos, and the higher portions supported by wires.

Pollination and pruning

Hand pollination of the flowers is advisable for greenhouse culture; this is a simple matter of transferring the pollen from the anthers of the male flowers to the stigmas of the female, using a pollinating (camel hair) brush.

Routine pruning consists of cutting off, in mid to late winter (December to January), the stem above the last bud that bore fruit during the preceding year. In spring a new branch will grow and bear a number of grown fruits.

CHINESE RASPBERRY

The Chinese raspberry is an ornamental bramble with yellow, edible fruits. There are some related forms, one of which is probably better than the type species since it bears more heavily (though it does not seem to be so easy to come by). The type species is *Rubus biflorus*, and the heavier-cropping form is *R. biflorus quinqueflorus* which crops more heavily because it produces more flowers.

The Chinese raspberry is not widely grown and you may have difficulty in obtaining it from nurseries or garden centres. But you may well find some canes growing in a friend's or neighbour's garden and be able to take a cutting.

This raspberry has strong, spiny stems completely covered in a coating of white wax. These 'whitewashed' canes are most striking, particularly in winter. The leaves are composed of three to five leaflets, dark green above and white beneath. The habit of *R. biflorus* is semi-erect, giving a strong, medium-sized shrub; that of *R. b. quinqueflorus* is erect or semi-erect with a definite arching over of the canes. In this form the canes can reach 3m (10 ft) and will touch the ground and tip root if allowed to do so. For propagating purposes this is very useful; the newly-grown canes can be dug up in autumn or winter and planted out. But, unless you want new canes for propagation, discourage tip rooting as the new canes produced in this way will be in addition to those growing seasonally from the stools, and you will soon have a miniature forest.

Another point worth noting is that the growth habit of *R. b. quinqueflorus* is far from orderly. So if you want more erect, more manageable (though not so productive) plants you would do better with *R. biflorus*.

Planting and tending

Allow 60cm (24 in) or so between canes when planting and dig in a good quantity of compost. The object is not only to get fruit but also to encourage stout canes, because the stouter they are, the whiter is

the waxy covering. After the crop is gathered, cut out the fruited canes in exactly the same way as for summer fruiting raspberries.

JAPANESE WINEBERRY

Perhaps the most ornamental of all the decorative berries is the Japanese wineberry *Rubus phoenicolasius*. This was discovered growing wild in the mountains of Japan, and is recorded as having been introduced to British gardens in 1876.

The canes are vigorous, semi-erect and can reach 1·8m (6 ft) in good soil. They are covered in soft, red bristles, and the leaves are large, pale green above and covered with a whitish down underneath. The berries are golden-yellow (or sometimes bright orange) and are enclosed in an attractive hairy calyx. They are rather small but very pleasantly flavoured, and may be eaten fresh or used for cooking. Each spray ripens its berries evenly.

Rubus phoenicolasius (Japanese wineberry) is a particularly decorative plant, as well as having delicious berries

Planting and pruning

Any good soil will suit this fruit. Plant 1·2m (4 ft) apart to give the bush-like growth enough room to flourish. Prune out the fruited canes at soil level as soon as the crop is finished for the year. No training system is required.

RUBUS LEUCODERMIS

A distinctive variation on the theme of ornamental brambles is provided by the blue-bloomed stems and purplish-black fruits of *Rubus leucodermis*. It was introduced into Britain nearly 150 years ago. Partly erect and partly spreading in habit, it fruits in mid summer (June).

Its leaves have three to five coarsely-toothed leaflets and a white, felt-textured underside.

GOOSEBERRIES

In Britain, the traditional time for the first gooseberries is Whit Sunday, which usually falls towards mid summer (June). An early-fruiting variety will certainly give enough small green berries by this time to make a pie. And if you have planned your gooseberry bed, it will herald the start of a three-month season of this versatile fruit that is equally good whether eaten raw, cooked in pies or turned into jam.

For an early crop of gooseberries, try a variety such as Keepsake, whose berries make rapid growth from the time the fruits set to maturity. The main crop comes in mid season and is heavy, with medium-sized, pale green, slightly hairy berries.

Another good variety for an early pick, followed by a mid season main crop, is Careless. When fully ripe the berries are large, milky-white and practically hair-less, with a transparent or semi-transparent skin. But avoid this variety if your soil is on the poor side, because it will not make much headway and the berries will be small. Improve the soil first and plant Careless later, when conditions are better. Good soil is necessary for all gooseberries but Keepsake is a more vigorous grower than Careless, and is a better choice if your soil is below par.

A fine mid season, deep red berry with a rich flavour is Lancashire Lad, which makes delicious jam. You can also pick it while still green, for cooking. The queen of the yellow-green varieties is the large-fruited Leveller, which also ripens in mid season and is ideal for showing. But, like all the highest-quality fruit, it does need the best conditions. On light soils that drain too freely it will be stunted, often with the greyish, brittle leaf margins that denote potash deficiency. And you will get the same results on heavy soils with impeded drainage.

If your soil is heavy but nevertheless well drained, a good choice would be the mid season, dark red Whinham's Industry. This is one of the best flavoured of all. The sweetest-flavoured mid to late season green variety is probably Lancer, which has translucent, thin-skinned, pale green berries tinged with yellow.

There are several other varieties available, but those given here will provide first-rate fruits for cooking and dessert.

Preparation and cultivation

Gooseberries need a fertile, well-prepared soil, but not one that is too rich or overcharged with nitrogen; excessive richness will help to encourage American gooseberry mildew. Whatever your soil type, dig in thoroughly plenty of well-rotted compost before planting. A free root run and adequate drainage combined with a summer moisture reserve are the essentials for a good crop. The only fertilizer likely to be needed on any sort of routine basis, provided you maintain a good organic content, is sulphate of potash. The standard dressing is 25g per sq m (¾ oz per sq yd) in early spring (February). However, if the leaves are a healthy green and show no signs of marginal scorch, not even this is necessary. But it must be applied if signs of potash deficiency appear.

Gooseberries detest the hoe. They make a massive, absorbing root system in the top few centimetres of soil, and like these roots to be left in peace. Annual mulching in spring (March–April) just after the fruits set will suppress weeds, maintain a moisture reserve and eliminate hoeing. If you cannot manage this every year, then as far as possible get the weeds out by hand in the root area of the bushes, and restrict the hoe to a narrow strip along the centre of the alleyways.

In any event there will not be many weeds from the mulched area, even if you treat it on a two-year basis, provided the compost is properly made and free of weed seeds. Remember that although hoeing cleans the soil initially, it stirs up the weed seeds that otherwise might have died, remained dormant, or had their new growth smothered by a mulch.

Gooseberries can be grown as cordons 30cm (12 in) apart, or as bushes 1·2–1·5m (4–5 ft) apart. Bushes must be grown on a short stem, while cordons should be free of suckers from below soil level, so plant

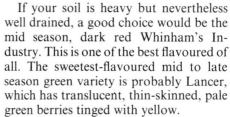

Left: top-quality large-fruited Leveller

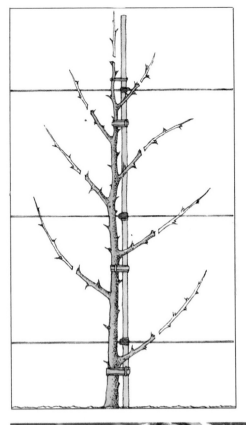

both types no deeper than the soil mark on the newly-purchased plant. Spread the roots out to their fullest extent, cover them with friable soil, then tread in lightly. Add more soil and tread in firmly. Finish off with an untrodden surface. You do not want depressions round the stems collecting pools of winter rain.

Training cordons

Cordons are usually grown vertically, though you can train them obliquely if you prefer. Using light end posts, 1·2m (4 ft) long and sunk to a depth of 30cm (12 in) or 45cm (18 in) to be on the safe side, strain three wires between them at 30cm (12 in) intervals. Then fix bamboo canes about 1 m (3 ft) long to the wires, allowing one cane for each plant.

Cordons make neat path edgings, but remember in this case to allow the stems about 30–38cm (12–15 in) of soil width on each side so that the roots can forage well, and mulch this strip each spring. One of the objects of the system is to get quality berries, and an organic root covering is a definite aid to this.

Tip back the newly-planted cordons by some 15cm (6 in) and repeat in subsequent winters if necessary. Some varieties will reach the top wire with little tipping. At the same time, cut back sideshoots to three buds. Thereafter cut back all sideshoots to the fifth leaf from the base in mid to late summer (late June or early July) and to three buds each winter. The result will be fine berries growing from induced fruiting spurs along the cordons.

Pruning bushes

You can prune bushes in exactly the same way. In this case each branch is really a cordon, the only difference being that it grows naturally from the bush and is not trained. Tip back each branch of a newly-planted bush by half, and repeat the operation in subsequent winters as it becomes necessary.

Some varieties droop considerably. If this habit becomes too pronounced, prune back in winter to an upward bud just below the bend. Remove any weak or congesting shoots to maintain an airy atmosphere in the bushes.

Light pruning method

The method described above is the conventional one that has been used for

Top, far left: prune a cordon by cutting back sideshoots to three buds.
Top left: on a bush, cut back sideshoots to five leaves in summer.
Left: dark red Whinham's Industry

many years, but light pruning (which was advocated by William Forsyth, gardener to King George III) can give just as good results and brings the bushes into crop earlier. In trials with Careless and Leveller, planted in mid spring (March) of one year and pruned lightly, they produced some 2kg (4 lb) of fruit per bush the following year.

With light pruning, the branches are not built up over successive winters and there is no sideshoot cutting. All the growths are left, except for poor or congesting shoots. Berries soon form on the uncut ones, usually in singles or perhaps doubles, from individual buds rather than in spur clusters. Each growth is cropped for a year or two, and is then removed in favour of a new one. Not all fruiting growths are removed in any one year; a pattern evolves in which there are always some shoots still in fruit and some maiden ones ready to fruit in their second summer. The only danger is overcrowding, so to prevent this, work on a basis of allowing at least one full hand's span between all adjacent growths. Be very strict over this.

Pests and diseases

There is one serious disease liable to attack your gooseberries and at least three fairly common pests.

American gooseberry mildew This shows first as thick, white, powdery patches on leaves and fruit while in the final phase there is a brownish, felty covering on the berries. It is essential to stop this fungus early, as soon as you see the first white patches on the young leaves and shoots. Apply a systemic fungicide at once and repeat at 10–14 day intervals if necessary.

Sawfly caterpillar These green caterpillars with black spots are very common pests on young bushes. They can strip a bush of every leaf. There are three generations annually, so if the first is not controlled there will be trouble at intervals throughout the season. The first batch of eggs is laid in late spring and early summer (April and May) on the undersides of leaves in the centre of the bush near ground level. They hatch about 2–3 weeks later. Look for the tiny, newly-hatched caterpillars and give them a few squirts of derris while they are still bunched in the centre of the bush. At this stage they are a sitting target and easily killed.

Magpie moth caterpillar These pests also eat the leaves, and are frequently confused with sawfly caterpillars. The magpie moth caterpillars are 'loopers', drawing themselves into a loop each time they move forward, and have black and white markings with a yellow stripe along each

Top: immature aphides on the underside of a gooseberry leaf; these pests overwinter on the plant in the egg stage

Above left: early-cropping variety Keepsake is a vigorous grower. Above: later-fruiting dessert variety Lancer

side. They start feeding before flowering time, but often go undetected at this stage. A derris spray immediately before flowering will kill them, but if you miss this out, then apply derris after the fruits have set as soon as the caterpillars are seen.

Aphides These are the other main pests, curling the leaves and distorting young shoots. One species, the lettuce aphid, flies from gooseberries to lettuces, so there is a double reason for controlling it. The second sort flies to certain types of willow herb. Both overwinter on gooseberries in the egg stage, and can be eradicated with a tar oil spray. The alternative is a spray of malathion or a systemic insecticide just before, or immediately after, the flowering period.

RECOMMENDED VARIETIES	
EARLY AND MID SEASON	
Keepsake	pale green
Careless	milky-white
MID SEASON	
Lancashire Lad	deep red
Leveller	yellow-green
Whinham's Industry	dark red
MID AND LATE SEASON	
Lancer	pale green

MEDLARS, QUINCES AND MULBERRIES

Medlars, quinces and mulberries make attractive trees and produce fruits that have many culinary uses – particularly for jellies and jams. Many people also enjoy mulberries and medlars as fresh fruit.

Medlars and quinces both belong to the rose family but mulberries are unrelated. All share a liking for moist loam, and the quince nearly always does best by the side of water, though such a site is by no means essential. On light, freely-drained soil, however, quince trees will not make a great deal of headway unless the root area receives generous amounts of well-rotted compost – initially before planting and thereafter as an annual mulch.

MEDLARS

Medlar trees (*Mespilus germanica*) reach on average about 4·5m (15 ft) in height, and their habit (form of growth) is spreading. The leaves are long (oblong-lanceolate, in botanical terms) and downy, with dark green on the upper

Medlars are an unusual fruit to include in your harvest, while their trees make an attractive addition to the garden. Top right: the single flowers. Right: autumn tints of the leaves. Below: recommended variety Dutch, almost ready for picking

surface and lighter green on the lower. In autumn they become russet coloured. The young twigs are also downy, and eventually turn black. The bark of the stem and branches tends to peel. The flowers are borne singly and have white- or pink-tinted petals, and are up to 4cm (1½ in) across. The fruits are mainly round with a reddish-brown, rather leathery and rough skin. At the top the fruit is indented and retains a hairy calyx and leaf-like segments. The trees are virtually free of pests and disease.

Shaping and pruning

The trees appear to have a rather mazy branch system that, particularly in winter, may look untidy or congested at first sight; but this is actually a distinctive feature of its growth and you should not try to correct it by too much branch pruning, though any laterals that are cluttering up the tree should be removed. The regular cutting away of worn-out shoots and fruit spurs is, however, very important. Although medlar trees will crop year after year without being pruned, they will become heavily congested if not kept tidy, and a major thinning operation will then be necessary. It is much better to remove potential congestion when the shoots are young, and to do this annually between mid winter and mid spring (November and March).

Picking and storing

Medlars are not edible in their raw state until the flesh has become very soft. Pick them from late autumn to early winter (October to early November), preferably after a sharp frost, and store them in a single layer, eye downwards. You can store them on a shelf in a cool shed, but the best method is to lay them on a bed of silver sand. Let them become thoroughly ripe ('bletted'); this is the stage at which they are ready for eating, and is normally reached within two or three weeks.

Medlars are normally free of pests and diseases but the stored fruit is rather susceptible to a mould that starts on the stalks. If you dip the stalks in a cup of water into which two tablespoons of salt have been thoroughly mixed, this will usually give protection.

How to use

Medlar jelly is very good, and beautifully coloured. Some recipes use fruits taken straight from the trees, still firm and only just ripe. But there are old recipes that recommend using the ripe fruit, and some of these, especially those that include apples, make very fine jelly.

QUINCES

Quince trees do not often reach more than about 4·5m (15 ft) in height as standards, and are only about shrub size in bush form. They are a lovely sight when the pale green, downy leaves are expanding in spring against the dark-coloured wood. The habit is rather drooping. The flowers are sweet-smelling and very beautiful, with five large, pinkish petals of delicate hue. The autumn leaf-colour is a rich yellow. The common quince *Cydonia oblonga*, the type with edible fruits, is quite distinct from the ornamental Japanese ones. The ornamental types have fruits of varying shape and size, and flowers of different shades of red, white and orange. They have been known by various botanical names, *Cydonia japonica* being one, but are now classed separately from the common quince in the genus Chaenomeles.

Training and pruning

The tree habit of the common quince is very twisted, though the branches are relatively thin. Do not attempt corrective pruning; just let the tree grow at will, but remove obvious congestion in winter. This removal is important; without it you will find, fairly soon, a considerable mass of thicket-like growth in the tree. This will inhibit free air circulation and sunlight penetration, so increasing the likelihood of leaf blight. The growth habit of the tree is not suited to wall training.

Picking and storing

The fruit is pear-shaped, has a golden-yellow, slightly downy skin, and is aromatic. It remains hard long after picking time, which is probably a reason why it can be stored for a considerable period. Unlike medlars, quinces do not benefit from frost, and although the end of autumn (late October) is often given as the harvest time, it sometimes happens that a frost has struck by then. The fruits will usually come away from the spurs in late autumn (mid October). Pick them when they are quite dry and store them in a cool, frost-proof shed away from apples and pears. The aroma during storage is strong, and can spoil other stored fruit. The quinces are ready for use after two or three months.

How to use

Slices of quince are excellent for adding a touch of extra flavour to stewed apples – they are much more subtle as a flavouring than cloves. Quince jelly is very pleasant, and a lovely amber colour. The jam is ruby coloured and slightly sharp with a rather odd smell.

Pests and diseases

Quince trees may suffer from leaf blight. This causes reddish-brown spots on the foliage, often resulting in severe leaf drop, and the fruits can be affected. Prevent it by spraying with liquid-copper fungicide just after blossom and, in winter, by cutting out and burning any twigs and fruit spurs showing reddish-brown, mainly circular, areas with dark margins.

Left and below left: Cydonia oblonga, the edible common quince. Below: the purely ornamental Japanese quince

MULBERRIES

The habit of mulberry trees is rather similar to that of medlars, but unless your garden is spacious enough to take a standard tree, a bush is better since standards can reach 9m (30 ft) or more at maturity (though it will be quite a long time before this height is attained). They can also be grown on walls, and a fan on a southerly wall is usually advised for colder regions.

The roots, though fleshy, are brittle, and if you damage them at planting time (or if you cut them) they bleed. To avoid this, make sure your planting holes are large enough to take uncut roots.

Edible species

Two main types of mulberry are grown for their fruit: the black *Morus nigra* and the white *M. alba*. *M. nigra* has heart-shaped leaves that are rough on the upper surface and downy on the lower. The fruits are blackish-red at maturity, and look much like loganberries. They have a pleasant, somewhat acid taste. The leaves of the white mulberry are smooth on the upper surface and downy below. The fruits are a much lighter red at maturity, sweetish and about half the size of the black type. The flowers of both species are small, borne on spikes, and not a very decorative feature.

Of several less common forms, *M. australis* and *M. cathayana* are valuable fruiting species for small gardens, as they

Mulberries are best grown in bush form. Below: the flowers, and below right, the fruit, of the black Morus nigra

RECOMMENDED VARIETIES	
MEDLARS	
Nottingham	Small, richly-flavoured, russet-brown fruits; erect habit.
Dutch	Large, russet-brown fruits, spreading habit.
QUINCES	
Bereczki	Heavy cropper with large, fine-flavoured, pear-shaped fruits; sometimes listed as Vranja – an almost identical variety.
Meech's Prolific	Very large flowers; starts to crop at an early age; fruits are pear shaped and medium sized.
Champion	Large, apple-shaped fruits with golden-yellow flesh.
MULBERRIES	
Morus nigra	Reddish-black fruits with a pleasant, rather acid flavour.
M. alba	Lighter red, sweetish fruits.
M. australis	Dark red, sweet fruits; shrub-sized tree.
M. cathayana	Fruits vary in colour from light red to black; shrub-sized tree.

make trees of little more than shrub size. The fruits of *M. australis* are dark red but sweet. Those of *M. cathayana* are variable in colour from black to light red. For wine, tarts and jam, mulberries are among the choicest of fruits, particularly those of the black species.

Training and pruning

Mulberries can be grown as pyramid-shaped trees. It is generally recommended that laterals be cut to six leaves from the base in late summer (July), but that leaders be left uncut unless they are too vigorous, in which case their tops should be cut back.

With wall trees, train in the main leaders fan-wise at some 38cm (15 in) apart; they usually cover the wall space without having to be stimulated by pruning. Train sideshoots of wall trees to six leaves from the base in late summer (July). Free-growing trees require little pruning other than the winter removal of congestion, but if the spur formation is sparse, cut back some maiden laterals to four or five buds.

When to pick

Fruit for eating fresh comes off at a touch when fully ripe, or can be left to fall – preferably onto closely-shaven grass, which is the best setting for a mulberry tree. For culinary use the fruits are best gathered when slightly under-ripe.

Pests and diseases

Mulberry trees are virtually disease-free, but they do occasionally suffer from twig canker. Affected shoots, carrying brownish waxy pustules, should be cut out and burnt as soon as you spot them.

RASPBERRIES AND LOGANBERRIES

Raspberries and loganberries are most rewarding soft fruits and are comparatively easy to grow. Many people, however, are unfamiliar with loganberries. These are larger than raspberries and their colour, when fully ripe, is a deep wine-red.

Raspberries and loganberries thrive on most garden soils which retain summer moisture but do not become waterlogged in winter. The only basic soil type on which they will usually fail is the highly alkaline. If their roots are in chalk or limestone where the pH is above 7, iron deficiency will be a problem. The higher the alkalinity, the greater this problem will be. In theory you can overcome it by adding a proprietary iron compound, but this method can be expensive and might have to be adopted annually.

Some acidity, however, is safe; cane fruits will be happy in a soil with a pH of 6, which is slightly acid, or in one of 7, which is neutral, and they will tolerate acidity down to a pH of 5, but not below. You can always check acidity with a soil-testing kit, and apply lime as appropriate. The amount recommended by the manufacturers should be scattered evenly and forked in, preferably a few weeks before planting.

Preparing the ground
The best foundation is good quality compost dug deeply into the top 30cm (12 in) of soil at the rate of about a bucket – 9 litre (2 gallon) size – to a trench 60cm (2 ft) wide and 1·5m (5 ft) long, following the complete removal of all perennial weeds and their roots.

Prepare the ground in late summer or early autumn (July or August), ready for planting either when plants become available from the nurseries – usually from late autumn (October) onwards – or in the spring. Do not skimp on the compost at this stage because the plants will rapidly produce masses of shallow roots, making it impossible to dig in compost later without damaging them.

This base dressing of compost can be supplemented by laying a mulch each spring along the raspberry rows in a continuous strip some 45cm (18 in) wide and 2–5cm (1–2 in) deep, and – if you have enough to spare – round the root area of loganberry plants as a circular mat about 45cm (18 in) in diameter. To be fully effective as a conserver of soil moisture and to suppress weeds, which are two of the prime functions of a mulch, the material must be generously applied. Some perennial weeds, like dock, may still appear, but the roots are easily pulled out by hand from the friable soil which results from efficient mulching.

Choosing the site
The main factor in choice of site is shelter from cold winds. At blossom time these can ruin the flowers, and at any period in the growing season they may cause leaf damage, sometimes to a severe degree. Every effort should be made to plant in a spot sheltered from northerly and easterly winds.

Westerly winds, on the other hand, cause little or no leaf scorch. However, if you have no choice but to plant in the path of any prevailing wind – and this is sometimes the case in country gardens – be sure the rows run along the wind rather than across it. Rows planted broadside could be badly blown about.

Spring frosts are seldom damaging because cane fruits come into flower when the frost hazard has passed.

How to plant raspberries
Plant your raspberries 45–60cm (18–24 in) apart, the latter distance being advisable for varieties making many canes (main stems), leaving a gap of 1·75–2m (6–6½ ft) between the rows. The roots should be covered to a depth of 7–8cm (3 in).

The simplest way is to take out a wedge of soil to the required depth and about a spade's width, and then, with someone holding the cane in position, replace the soil. Firm planting is essential; press home the soil (by treading it down) and then finish off the surface lightly. After planting, cut back the canes to 25–30cm (9–12 in) above soil level, so that the plants do not fruit the following summer, but spend the first year building strong roots and canes.

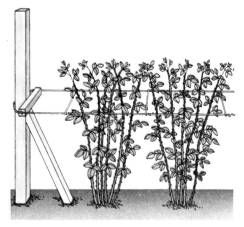

Training raspberries by the box system

The best method of training raspberries is the box system. With a post at each end of the row, firmly staple two parallel wires at about 60cm (24 in) above ground level to each one and fit with cross wires twisted around them to separate the canes of each stool (the root or stump from which the stems grow) from those of its neighbour. If necessary the wiring can be repeated at about 1·25m (4 ft) above the ground to accommodate the tall-growing varieties. To hold the parallel wires at the right distance apart, nail or screw 15cm (6 in) distance pieces (battens) to the end posts, and to intermediate posts where the rows are long. The battens, which should be about 4cm (1½ in) in

Malling Promise, a strong and upright variety producing heavy crops of firm fruit, provided the stock from which the excellent Malling Exploit was derived

diameter, can be grooved to take the wires, or the wires can be stapled to un-grooved surfaces. You don't have to tie in the canes, and the cross wires are easily adjustable to accommodate new ones. In this way every stool with its canes is enclosed within its own 'box', which greatly facilitates the pruning out of old canes, and allows a good air flow between the canes. This is an important point: adequate air movement to dry the canes, leaves and berries quickly after rain is a necessary factor in the prevention of fungus diseases.

End posts need not be particularly heavy, since they take little strain, serving mainly to hold the wires taut: 5–6cm (2 in) in diameter and 2m (6 ft) long is usually adequate. Sink them 45cm (18 in) and strengthen them with wood strainers. The bottom 60cm (24 in) should be thoroughly treated with a standard proprietary preservative. Creosote in this case is not suitable because it gives surface protection only and can be harmful to plants.

Pruning the canes

Routine pruning (for all except autumn fruiting varieties) consists of removing all fruited canes after harvest, and all weak new ones, leaving about 6–8 of the best per stool. Tip back (cut the tops off) new canes in early spring (February) at 1·5m (5 ft) or so (or just below the point where they have bent over) to encourage fruiting. Autumn-fruiting raspberries are left unpruned until early spring (February) when old canes are cut back to just above ground level.

Pests and virus diseases

Although there may be occasional outbreaks of pests and diseases, routine detailed spraying will not be necessary. The virus diseases are, in principle, the only really severe threat, but the Malling raspberries recommended here are tolerant of virus infection in varying degrees. This means that if they do become infected they will not suffer to any marked extent, and often no leaf symptoms will appear.

The Glen Clova variety is, however, showing itself to be intolerant, and susceptible to cross-infection, so it would be unwise to plant it with a tolerant variety. For example, if Malling Jewel and Glen Clova were neighbours, the former might become infected (without showing any symptoms of the disease) and pass the infection to Glen Clova, which could then suffer. Planted on its own, however, Glen Clova has so far shown virtually no virus infection.

Virus diseases are transmitted by certain greenfly species. The most common form of virus is probably mosaic. If the virus-transmitting greenfly feed on an infected plant and then (within 24 hours) feed on an uninfected one, they will transmit mosaic to the latter. It is almost impossible to keep down greenfly completely, but if you are growing a virus-intolerant raspberry it pays to apply an annual winter wash of tar oil against the over-wintering greenfly eggs.

The nastiest pest is the grub of the raspberry beetle. A spray with a derris pesticide after full bloom and again 10 days later is the answer.

Deficiency diseases

The chief nutritional element which may be lacking from time to time is potash; deficiency in this will show as greyish or brownish leaf margins which become dead and brittle. To correct this, apply 15–25g per sq m ($\frac{1}{2}$–$\frac{3}{4}$ oz per sq yd) of sulphate of potash in the autumn.

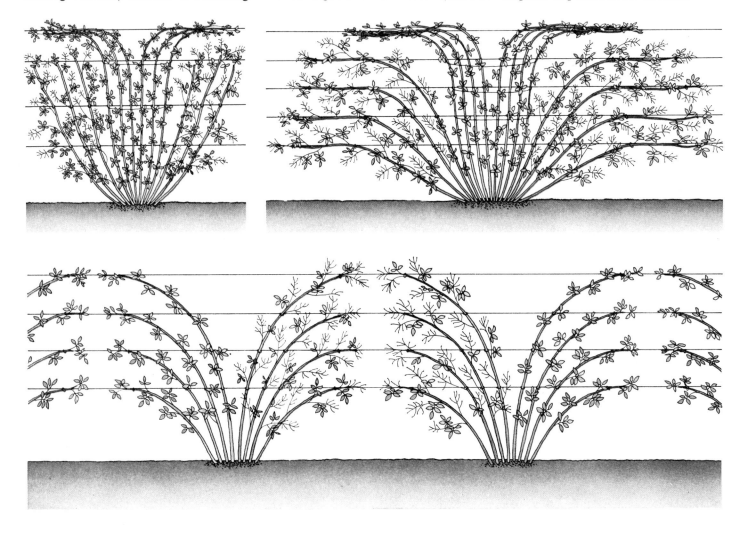

LOGANBERRIES

Loganberries are usually planted about 3·75m (12 ft) apart and are cut back as for raspberries. The main training systems are the open fan, the 'modified open fan' and the 'rope' or 'arch' method. The two latter systems make use of practically all cane growth whereas half of this may have to be sacrificed with the open fan – resulting in much crop loss. But the open fan method is more convenient where space is limited, as the plants can be put in much nearer together only 2·5–3m (8–10 ft) apart.

Open fan Fix wires at about 60cm (2 ft), 1m (3½ ft), 1·5m (5 ft) and 2m (6 ft) from ground level to stout end and middle posts 2·5m (8 ft) long, which have been sunk 60cm (2 ft) into the ground. Arrange the fruiting canes fan-wise on the first wires, with a gap in the centre. Lead the new canes up through this gap and tie temporarily to the top wire. After harvesting cut the fruited canes right out at the base and tie the new ones in to replace them.

Modified open fan Fix wires at 60cm (2 ft), 90cm (3 ft), 1·25m (4 ft), 1·5m (5 ft) and 2m (6 ft) from ground level. Train the fruiting canes to more or less their full length, left and right of centre along the first four wires, while the top wire again takes the new ones.

Rope or arch Train all fruiting canes in one direction, and all new ones in the opposite direction. When more than one stool is planted, arrange the training so that the fruiting canes of one stool always meet the fruiting canes of its neighbour.

Separation of fruiting from non-fruiting wood makes picking and pruning much easier and reduces the risk of cane spot fungus, the spores of which are washed from old to new canes. (All methods of training provide for this separation.) Other pests and virus diseases are covered opposite.

Modern loganberry plants can produce a dozen or more canes each season, all of which you can tie in practically full length with the rope and modified open fan systems, thereby ensuring the maximum crop – which may be 4·5–5kg (10–12 lb) per plant when the plants are fully established. In all cases you need to sink stout posts 2·5m (8 ft) long, to a depth of 60cm (2 ft).

Above right: ripe loganberries
Previous page: systems of loganberry training .Open fan, for use in limited space (far left, above), modified open fan (above left) and rope or arch (left)

RECOMMENDED VARIETIES

Skilful selection from among the modern varieties of raspberries and loganberries means that the gardener can enjoy the benefits of an extended picking season.

RASPBERRIES

The modern range of raspberries in Britain is composed chiefly of those raised at the East Malling Research station in Kent. In order of ripening the following are the best of those available.

Malling Exploit Early season variety fruiting in late summer (July). Canes abundant and vigorous; fruit large, bright red, firm and well-flavoured. Crops heavily and picks easily. Generally acknowledged to be superior to the earlier-raised Malling Promise from which it was derived.

Malling Jewel Early to mid season variety fruiting in late summer to early autumn (July–August). Cane growth strong but not abundant; fruit fairly large, medium to dark red, good flavour; picks easily and berries do not crumble. A reliable variety cropping well and regularly.

Malling Enterprise Mid to late season variety fruiting in early to late autumn (August–October). Canes strong but not usually abundant; fruit very large, medium red, firm, with excellent flavour; picks easily and does not crumble. Crops well, and tolerates heavier soil than other varieties provided drainage is adequate.

There are several more East Malling varieties, such as **Orion, Admiral** and **Delight,** on trial or being tested. Some are extremely heavy croppers producing fine quality berries, and will no doubt be released for general culture in due course. Two more outstanding varieties now available are **Glen Clova** from Scotland and **Zeva** from Switzerland. The former is an exceptionally heavy producer of top quality berries which are first-rate for eating and processing. The canes give a heavy mid season (early autumn) crop and a small mid autumn pick. Zeva starts to fruit in late summer and continues until mid to late autumn, though the summer crop is not abundant, and autumn is the period of heaviest cropping. The berries can be huge, sometimes 2–3cm (1 in or more) long, and the flavour is very fine. A distinct advantage of Zeva is that it needs no supporting system. It makes bush-like growth and can be grown as a single bush (where space is too limited for raspberry rows) even in a large tub or container. Finally, the autumn fruiting variety **September** is a splendid choice for those who want mid to late autumn raspberries, and the old favourite **Lloyd George** is still a winner if the improved New Zealand strain is bought. This latter is stocked by most leading fruit nurseries.

LOGANBERRIES

The best loganberry is the **Thornless**; it arose as a mutant or bud 'sport' of the thorned type which means it is identical to the original loganberry in all respects – except for having no thorns. Any natural plant variation is called a 'sport'.

REDCURRANTS AND WHITECURRANTS

Redcurrants eaten straight from the bush are among the most refreshing of soft fruit and are a delicious addition to fruit salads. They also make fine jelly and mix well with other fruit (especially raspberries) in jams, juices and desserts.
Whitecurrants are sweeter and are usually eaten as fresh dessert fruit.

Although redcurrants and whitecurrants will grow on a wide range of soils, they prefer a medium loam that is well drained but able to hold summer moisture, and is slightly acid or neutral (though they will stand some degree of alkalinity).

They do, however, react adversely to waterlogged roots and lack of potash. These often go together for, although potash is not necessarily absent in such soils, waterlogged roots cannot use it. Dry roots cannot make use of potash either, so if the soil is too light it will need good supplies of well-rotted organic matter to build up a moisture-conserving medium, and if it is too heavy it will need the same treatment to open up the soil and improve its drainage.

Bushes, cordons and espaliers

Both redcurrants and whitecurrants can be grown in bush form or as cordons and espaliers, and you can plant them in partial shade or in full sun. Redcurrant cordons can be trained against a north-facing wall if necessary, where they will do quite well, though their ripening period will be somewhat delayed. If possible choose a fairly sheltered spot for planting, to avoid wind damage.

The planting distances are 1·5m (5 ft) apart for bushes, 38cm (15 in) for cordons and 1·2–1·5m (4–5 ft) for espaliers.

You may want no more than one heavy-cropping bush. The variety called Earliest of Fourlands, for example, can produce about 5kg (11 lb) of redcurrants per bush in its fourth summer from planting, though average yields of all varieties could be some way below those of bumper years.

Bushes have a short stem from which the branches grow out to give an open centre bush. Plant to the soil mark at the base of the stem.

Each bush should have about eight cropping branches. Since the pruning of cordons and espaliers is the same as for

Above: Jonkheer van Tets — one of the best varieties for garden culture, it produces fine crops early in the season

Below: Red Lake is an American variety Overleaf: White Versailles has sweet berries in very long bunches

bushes, a single cordon can be expected to produce one eighth of a bush crop, and a three-tier espalier (which would have six horizontal branches) would give about three-quarters of a bush crop.

Summer and winter pruning

Newly-bought bushes will not usually have eight branches, but they may have four, and these can easily be doubled by pruning.

After planting, cut back each branch by about half to an outward-pointing bud. During the next year extensions will grow, and generally each branch will send out a strong shoot from just below the extension, thus doubling the original number of branches. Tip these secondary shoots back by about half in the following winter and tip the leading extensions back by about one-third. Repeat as necessary in future winters, cutting all extensions back by one-third until the branches have reached the desired length. Some varieties grow strongly and quickly; with these, two (or at most three) winter cuttings are often enough.

Fruit is borne in clusters from short spurs along the branches; these are induced by summer and winter pruning. Summer pruning is done when the side shoots are mature along their basal portion, a stage that normally coincides with an increase in colour of the berries, about mid to late summer (late June). Cut the shoots back to within about 10cm (4 in), of the fourth or fifth leaf from the base. The branches are not cut. In winter cut the sideshoots again, to one or two buds from the base, leaving them as short spurs 13–20mm ($\frac{1}{2}$–$\frac{3}{4}$ in) long.

From time to time remove older branches to make way for new ones, maintaining a total of about eight branches.

The sideshoots of cordons and espaliers are treated in the same way, and the cordon rods and espalier branches are tipped as necessary in winter to stimulate extensions.

Feeding the plants

Red and whitecurrants do not need a great deal of feeding, but remember that heavy crops take their toll of soil foods. So keep the plants steadily supplied with moderate dressings of a combined organic fertilizer – applied annually or biennially as you think fit. Generally the lowest rate given in the maker's instructions will suffice; if they recommend, say, 70–100g per sq m (2–3 oz per sq yd), then use 70g (2 oz). Look out, however, for early stages of marginal leaf scorch, denoting potash deficiency. If this ap-

pears do not step up the routine dressing of combined fertilizer, but apply a separate dressing of sulphate of potash in autumn at about 17g per sq m ($\frac{1}{2}$ oz per sq yd). Do not use muriate of potash on currant bushes. Mulching, either in autumn or directly after fruit set, will help to conserve soil moisture.

Pest control

Aphides are the only serious pests. These can cause severe leaf damage. Distorted foliage with red blisters is a common sight on unsprayed bushes. Use a winter wash of tar oil to destroy the eggs. Alternatively you can spray the young aphides in spring with insecticides (such as derris or one of the systemics), but you must apply them

as soon as the pests appear. As hatching occurs over a period, it may be necessary to apply two sprays (especially of derris). With tar oil, however, only one application is needed.

Choosing varieties

Some varieties have a lax habit; the form of the bush is loose and droopy, and shoots can easily be broken by the wind. Avoid varieties that grow in this way and also those that make 'blind' buds – ones that fail to grow. The recommended varieties given here are all strong, heavy-cropping bushes with no blind buds and little or no tendency to loose, open growth. All of them will give good-sized, high-quality currants.

RECOMMENDED VARIETIES

REDCURRANTS

Jonkheer van Tets Very early season variety ripening in mid summer (mid to late June); vigorous, upright growth; good cropper producing large fruit.

Earliest of Fourlands Early season variety ripening in mid to late summer (late June to early July); large bushes of erect habit producing firm, bright red fruit.

Laxton's No 1 Early season variety ripening in mid to late summer (late June to early July); produces heavy crops of good-sized fruit.

Red Lake Mid to late season variety ripening in late summer (mid July); an American variety producing long trusses of large, fine-flavoured fruit.

Wilson's Long Bunch Late season variety ripening in late summer (late July); produces large crops of medium-sized, light red fruit on very long branches.

WHITECURRANTS

White Versailles Mid season variety ripening in late summer (early July); strong-growing, fertile bushes producing large, pale yellow, richly-flavoured currants.

STRAWBERRIES

Strawberries will flourish in the open garden, under frames, cloches or polythene
tunnels, in the greenhouse and in practically any properly-drained container –
from an old wooden wheelbarrow to the modern, highly ornamental tower pots.
If you give them the right soil conditions and are careful about watering,
they will grow in hanging baskets, and be decorative as well as productive.

The main requirement of strawberries is a well-drained, moisture-retentive soil enriched with organic matter. The modern varieties are largely free of pests and diseases and produce crops of finely-flavoured, brightly-coloured berries, varying in size from medium to very large.

Summer fruiters and perpetuals

There are two types of strawberries: the summer fruiters, that produce berries from mid to late summer (June to July), and the perpetuals that fruit in relays from mid summer to mid or late autumn (June to September or October) – if the plants are kept under cloches during the summer.

The summer fruiters will generally crop for three seasons, though the third season's yield will usually be light. The perpetuals are more or less finished after one season, except for the variety Gento that can give quite a good yield in its second year.

Although the total crop from perpetuals is heavy, the number of berries gathered at each picking is often small. One variety may give a total of 500g (1 lb) per plant, but from perhaps 15 or more pickings spread over eight or nine weeks. Other varieties, of which Gento is an example, can produce some huge berries. So if you want the weight to be made up in berry numbers as well as in size, you must buy an appropriate number of plants, say a dozen for a family of four, to give each person a worthwhile share of the pickings.

Soil requirements

Strawberries are essentially a rotation crop. The summer fruiters occupy their plot for two or three seasons, and new plants are put in elsewhere. The perpetuals remain for one season, or at the most two seasons, and again a fresh site is chosen for new plants. If you are growing plants in containers, use fresh soil for each new planting. Never plant into soil if the crop previously occupying it was infected with verticillium wilt – a fungus infection which affects strawberries. Potatoes and tomatoes are susceptible to this disease, and so are the weeds groundsel, thistles and plantains.

Rotate strawberries with crops needing and receiving good organic manuring – like peas and beans. These have nitrogen-fixing nodules on their roots, so cut off the spent tops and leave the roots behind to supply nitrogen to the strawberries. Additional nitrogen-supplying fertilizers are not often required; an excess leads to leaf growth at the expense of berries, and this in turn hinders air circulation and

sunlight penetration. These conditions invite grey mould (botrytis) that thrives in cool, damp conditions.

Strawberries like acidity, so do not add any lime to the strawberry bed. However, should you have limed the vegetable garden for a previous crop, this will not usually cause any trouble. One variety, Gento, does not appear to mind a limy soil, which makes it a good perpetual to choose for chalky districts.

On soils rich in humus you can achieve excellent results without using any fertilizers, but on less fertile land apply a general fertilizer (according to maker's instructions), that includes strawberries among plants for which it is formulated.

When to plant

Early autumn (August) is the best time to plant summer fruiters. You can then allow the plants to crop freely in the following summer. If you plant summer fruiters in the spring, remove all blossoms that appear, allowing the plants to build up strength for cropping the following year. Whether you plant in autumn or spring, remove the flowers appearing in early summer (May), but leave sub-

sequent ones. Thereafter (with perpetuals that fruit again in the second year) leave all flowers intact.

How to plant

To prepare the soil, trench to about 15cm (6 in) to facilitate the placing of compost in the root zone. One barrowload per 8–10 sq m (10–12 sq yd) is a satisfactory dressing. A standard spacing is 45cm (18 in) between plants and 60–90cm (2–3 ft) between rows (depending on varieties). The summer fruiting variety Elista, however, can be planted with only 25cm (9 in) between plants. Plants must be set with their crowns level with the soil surface. If they are too high the new roots, that spring from the crown bases, will fail to contact the soil quickly enough and will perish; if too deep the crowns may rot, especially in wet summers.

Many nurseries sell pot-grown plants. These may arrive either in composition-type pots that are planted directly into the soil, when they soon rot to provide free root growth, or else with their roots enclosed in a fibrous net (that also rots). In both instances the tops of the containers should be at soil level. Make sure,

when buying plants, that they are certified as being from virus-free stock; most reputable nurseries now supply these.

Propagation by runners

Summer fruiters should have their runners removed in the first summer. These grow out from the parent plants and in due course form 'runner plants' that root on contact with the soil. In the second season you can leave them to grow on and use them to provide new plants for setting out in early autumn (August). They will then crop the following summer, thus giving you a continuation of summer harvests, and save the expense of buying new stock every third year.

Propagation is simple. Separate the plants from their parents by cutting the runners. Avoid cutting too close to the plantlet. Then lift them carefully and plant them out. Runners normally root readily in friable soil (or in a pot sunk in the soil). To make certain of rooting, however, peg the runners down with stones when the first leaves have appeared.

Allow no more than three runner plants (and preferably only two) to grow from each parent plant, using only the

first to form on each runner. Never propagate from plants that are doing poorly; runner stock from poor parents will rarely succeed, and may well harbour disease.

Alternatively, keep two or so healthy plants just for runner production. Plant them away from the main strawberry bed and keep them 'de-blossomed'. If you choose this method, then remove and destroy runners from fruiting plants.

Some perpetuals do not make runners. Leave the runners on those that do, since the plantlets produce fruit in addition to that on the parents, thus increasing the total crop by up to about 25 per cent.

Mud and frost protection

When the first fruits have started to weigh down the stems, the plants can have a mat of straw laid round them to protect the berries from being splashed by mud. Another method is to lay strips of polythene sheeting, anchored by stones, along the rows. See that the soil is moist before laying down sheeting and that plants sit on a slight mound so that water does not collect around them. Black polythene sheeting is often recommended

Far left, above left and left: Tamella, Pantagruella and Baron Solemacher Below: for best flavour, pick and eat strawberries when they are 'dew fresh'

because it suppresses weeds. However, clear sheeting has been shown to give bigger crops in recent experiments.

Tunnel and cloche cultivation

Polythene sheeting tunnels are the latest means of getting an early pick from the summer fruiters. This is useful if you want early strawberries for a special occasion; otherwise you may not find the extra attention they need worth the end results. There are various patterns of tunnel. The best is the type which has a bar running along the length of its ridge. The sides can then be rolled up and fixed to this bar at flowering time to allow pollinating insects free play. Without their help many flowers may fail to set or may produce small or malformed berries.

An advantage of tunnels is that they reduce the need for watering. Loss of water by evaporation through the leaves is greatly reduced – but, of course, the water must be there in the first place. This means giving the plants a thorough watering just before the tunnels are fitted, usually in early to mid spring (late February to mid March) for a first pick in early summer (the third week of May) in the south of England. After a wet winter, however, there will probably be enough moisture in the ground to make this initial watering unnecessary. Roll up the tunnels in any unseasonably hot weather. If you are using cloches or Dutch lights, take off

alternate cloches at flowering time, and open Dutch lights fully. With all types of culture the coverings must be in position overnight for early berries. If frost is forecast it is wise to cover Dutch lights, cloches and tunnels with light sacking or something similar, removing this the following morning.

Protect plants in the open from frost in flowering time – early summer (May) – by covering them with newspaper or straw at night; remove it in the morning. Never put down a straw mulch under the plants until the frost has gone, the mulch can worsen frost damage to blossoms by insulating them from ground warmth.

Pests on strawberries
Strawberries fall prey to many pests, but most of them are easily controlled.
Slugs Mostly a problem on soils with a high content of organic matter. Put down metaldehyde pellets at fruiting time.
Red spider mite Mostly found on plants grown under cloches or polythene tunnels. It causes a mottling of the foliage, and plant growth is weakened. Spray with malathion before flowering, or make several applications of derris.
Aphides These pests cause a curling of the foliage, and sap the strength of the plant. More seriously they are carriers of virus disease. The variety Royal Sovereign is particularly susceptible to aphides. Spray well into the centre of the plant with derris, malathion or pyrethrum.
Squirrels and birds Both these animals are fond of strawberries. The best protection is netting.

Virus diseases
There are several types of virus diseases that attack strawberries. The superficial symptoms of these diseases are very similar – stunting of the plant and discoloration of the leaves.
Green petal, **arabis mosaic**, **yellow edge and crinkle** These are spread by eelworms in the soil and by aphides and leaf hoppers. To help control the spread of the diseases, spray with derris or malathion. Remove all weak and unhealthy plants and burn them. Buy certificated stock plants, and propagate only from healthy plants – and from these only for four or five years.

Fungus diseases
Leaf spot, red core, mildew and grey mould (botrytis) are fungus diseases which may attack strawberries.
Leaf spot Pick off and burn any leaves with greyish-red spots.
Red core This is only likely to occur in areas where drainage is poor. Gradually

all plants infected will appear stunted and die. If you cut into the roots, they will appear red in the centre. Spores of the fungus can live in the soil for twelve years or more. See that the ground is properly drained (by correct soil preparation) before planting. If plants become infected, burn them; strawberries should not be planted on the infected land again.
Mildew A dry-weather disease which shows as a white powdery mould. To control it, spray with dinocap, benomyl or wettable sulphur. Royal Sovereign is particularly prone to mildew. Although this variety is a fine summer fruiter it is much more prone to disease than the modern types, and therefore not recommended for beginners.
Grey mould (botrytis) This attacks mainly in wet summers. The fungus first appears in early summer (May), though it is invisible then, because only the spores are present. To defeat it at the outset, apply an appropriate fungicide. Several are available to gardeners, and are either protective formulations based on captan or thiram (don't spray during the three weeks before picking because of taint), or systemics based on benomyl. They are sold under brand names, complete with full instructions.

Tending the plants
The main jobs are weeding (best done with a hoe), removing or attending to the runners and watering in dry weather – especially important from first flower until just before harvesting. If you are using strips of polythene sheeting these will conserve root moisture and reduce watering, but they will prevent the

penetration of rain. So, as with tunnels, a thorough watering must be given before the strips are laid.

As soon as the final harvest has been gathered, the old leaves should be cut off plants that are to be left for a further year. Old foliage produces substances that inhibit the maximum development of flower-buds for the next season. The simplest way is to clip over with shears, taking great care not to cut the crowns or any young leaves surrounding them. The cut-off foliage is then gathered up and burnt. Prick over the surrounding ground lightly with a fork, and lay a light dressing of compost.

The exception to this treatment is Cambridge Favourite. With this variety, the removal of the leaves would result in a reduced crop the following year.

Straw protects berries from mud; as shown here with Cambridge Favourite variety

RECOMMENDED VARIETIES

SUMMER FRUITING	In season from mid to late summer (June to July)
Pantagruella	Early season; acid-sweet in flavour.
Cambridge Rival	Early to second early; medium to medium-large berries; shiny, darkish crimson at maturity; flesh pinkish, sweet and rich; moderate cropper.
Cambridge Vigour	Mid season; first berries medium-large, then smaller; scarlet at maturity; heavy yielder in maiden year.
Domanil	Mid to late; high proportion of large berries; heavy cropper.
Grandee	Mid season; produces some giant berries; heavy second-year cropper; a show bench variety.
Tamella	Mid to late; very heavy cropper; an outstanding strawberry for all purposes – highly recommended.
PERPETUALS	In season from mid summer to mid autumn (June to September)
Gento	The supreme variety to date; crops heavily on parent plants and runners; gives some very large, shining, scarlet berries.
Trelissa	Medium to large berries in abundance on parents and runners; can be trained against trellis work for decoration.
Baron Solemacher	A fine old favourite of the alpine type, producing masses of small berries of the best quality for making jam; does not make runners; a fine decorative plant for shady borders.

BRASSICAS

BROCCOLI

The term broccoli – a plural form of the Italian 'broccolo', or cabbage-top – covers two types of vegetables – the heading broccoli, which is closely akin to the cauliflower, and the sprouting broccoli. The latter, instead of producing a large curd, forms many leafy shoots each of which bears its own curd. There are both white and purple varieties and, in addition, a green kind that is known as calabrese or Italian sprouting broccoli.

Above: shoot of white sprouting broccoli

Nowadays it is customary to find the heading varieties of broccoli listed in the catalogues as 'winter cauliflower'. This is reasonable enough, but it should be noted that there are differences between the cauliflower and the heading broccoli. The broccoli is not quite so white and often a little coarser in texture than the true cauliflower, and it is ready for harvest at a different time of year.

Of the two, broccoli is easier to grow. It is much hardier and less demanding in its soil requirements, and will do well in most soils if they are in a good, fertile condition. It does not need freshly-manured soil – in fact it does better without it. With broccoli, as with spring cabbage, the aim is to produce a plant that is large enough and hardy enough to stand through the winter. Lush, sappy growth should be avoided.

Preparing the soil
As the plants do not need to be planted out until mid or late summer (June or July) they make a good follow-on crop to the first broad beans, peas or potatoes. If the ground was manured for the previous crop, simply prick over the top few centimetres of soil with a fork. A top dressing of superphosphate of lime, at 70g per sq m (2 oz per sq yd), is a beneficial addition. Remember, also, that broccoli, like all the brassicas, likes firm ground.

Sowing times
Seeds can be sown from mid spring to early summer (March to May) according to variety. The harvest season (except for calabrese) extends roughly from late winter to mid summer (January to early June). Those that mature in late winter and early spring (January and February) will be mainly confined to the milder, frost-free districts. In colder areas choose varieties to harvest from mid spring (March) onwards.

If you are growing more than one row, then use several varieties; that way you will have a succession of curds.

Sow the early varieties of both heading and sprouting broccoli in mid or late spring (March or April), and the later varieties in late spring (April) except for those which do not mature until early or mid summer (May or June): these need not be sown until early summer (May). Sow the seeds thinly in a seedbed, in drills 13mm ($\frac{1}{2}$ in) deep and 25cm (9 in) apart. Make sure that each variety is labelled before the rows are raked in. Sprinkle calomel dust along each seed drill as a precaution against club root and where cabbage-root fly is a problem, use either a bromophos or diazinon insecticide according to maker's instructions.

Thinning and transplanting
As soon as the plants are large enough to handle, thin them to 5cm (2 in) apart. This thinning (which is too often neglected) makes for good, straight plants.

The move into their final quarters can be made when the plants are about 15cm (6 in) high. Dull, showery weather is the best time to move the plants, but it is not always possible to wait for these conditions. If the ground is dry and hard, water the plants well a few hours before moving them.

To transplant, first ease the plants with a fork and lift them carefully. Keep as much soil on the roots as possible and plant them in their new quarters straight away. Allow 60cm (24 in) between plants and rows; if space is a problem you can reduce this to 50cm (20 in). Plant firmly so that the lower leaves of each plant are just clear of the soil, and then water them in. If your plants are strong and well-grown, and if you move as much soil with them as possible, the check from transplanting will be minimal.

Buying ready-grown plants
If you were unable to sow seeds, plants are usually available from garden centres and market stalls. Always find out the variety and when it is likely to mature. Do not choose plants which are weak and spindly. Ensure the plants are sturdy and about 13–15cm (5–6 in) high. Providing the rootball is not too badly damaged they should settle down quickly in their new positions.

Perennial broccoli and calabrese
An unusual member of the broccoli family is the perennial broccoli, usually listed as Nine Star Perennial. This plant produces from six to nine heads instead of the usual one. They are smaller than the normal heading types, but much larger than the heads of sprouting broccoli. The plant will continue to produce heads for several years providing you do not allow it to seed. The plants need extra room in which to develop, so allow 90cm (3 ft) between plants. They are best put out alongside a path or fence where they can be left undisturbed. After their first flowering, top-dress the plants each spring with some well-rotted manure or compost.

The green Italian sprouting broccoli, more commonly known as calabrese, deserves a special mention. Large quantities of this are now grown commercially and used in the frozen vegetable trade. It is becoming increasingly popular with housewives and is as easy to grow as the sprouting broccoli. Some varieties have a large, central green head which is followed by a limited number of sideshoots; other varieties have a smaller head and more spears. The shoots are tender and of first-rate flavour.

Sowing and cultivation are the same as for sprouting broccoli, but the plants mature in autumn and early winter, not in the spring. Their main season is mid to late autumn (September to October) but in an open autumn they will continue to produce their shoots into early or mid winter (November or December).

Above right: purple sprouting broccoli
Right: white sprouting broccoli

RECOMMENDED VARIETIES

Type	Variety	When to sow	When to transplant	When to cut
	*St Agnes	mid to late spring	mid to late summer	early to mid spring
	*Snow-white	mid to late spring	mid to late summer	mid spring
	Veitch's Self-protecting	mid spring	mid summer	mid winter
	St George	late spring	mid to late summer	late spring
	Walcheren Winter	mid spring	mid summer	late spring to early summer
	Late Queen	early summer	late summer	early to mid summer
	Mirado	early summer	late summer	mid summer
	*Not completely hardy – for mild areas only			
Sprouting broccoli	Early White	mid spring	mid to late summer	early to mid spring
	Early Purple	mid spring	mid to late summer	early to mid spring
	Late White	late spring	late summer	mid to late spring
	Late Purple	late spring	late summer	mid to late spring
Perennial broccoli	Nine Star Perennial	late spring	mid summer	mid spring
Calabrese	Express Corona (F.1 hybrid)	mid to late spring	mid summer	early to mid autumn
	Autumn Spear	late spring	late summer	late autumn to early winter

Key to seasons

early spring (February)	early summer (May)	early autumn (August)	early winter (November)
mid spring (March)	mid summer (June)	mid autumn (September)	mid winter (December)
late spring (April)	late summer (July)	late autumn (October)	late winter (January)

Harvesting broccoli

Like cauliflowers, heading broccoli tend to mature quickly if the weather conditions are suitable. Cut them as soon as they are at their best, when the edges of the curd are just beginning to open; the head is then usually 15–20cm (6–8 in) in diameter.

The sprouting broccoli are ready for picking when they look like miniature cauliflowers about 15cm (6 in) in length. It is not necessary to wait until the curds can be seen. The plants will produce further small curds over several weeks.

Pests and diseases

Although this is a relatively easy crop to grow, there are a few pests and diseases which you may encounter.

Club root Often known as 'finger and toe', this attacks the root system and causes swellings which deform the roots. This, in turn, causes the plant to wilt and look stunted. There is, as yet, no cure but the disease can be prevented. Club root is always worst on acid soils, so if your soil is acid give a dressing of 100–135g per sq m (3–4 oz per sq yd) of garden lime prior to planting and sprinkle calomel dust along the seed drills. When transplanting, make a paste from calomel dust and dip the roots in it.

Below: picking off shoots of broccoli

Cabbage-root fly This insect lays its eggs against the plant stems. From the eggs little white grubs hatch out and burrow down into the soil where they attack the roots. It is always advisable to give the ground a routine dressing of bromophos or diazinon to prevent this pest.

Cabbage whitefly This pest is particularly bad on all members of the cabbage family and can make many vegetables almost unusable. Spray at the first sign of an attack with a pesticide based on resmethrin.

Cabbage white butterfly During the summer and autumn, keep a close watch for the cabbage white butterfly. The caterpillars which hatch out from the eggs have a voracious appetite and, if they are not dealt with quickly, the plants will soon look like lace curtains. Do not wait for this stage, but as soon as a butterfly is seen spray the plants with derris or trichlorphon or malathion and repeat the spray whenever necessary.

Flea beetle This pest can be a problem after germination. Spray or dust with a BHC compound as a precaution.

BRUSSELS SPROUTS

It is not surprising that the brussels sprout should be among the most popular members of the brassica family. With its ability to grow in most soils, its hardiness and its long period of use it is one of the most valuable of winter vegetables.

You can choose from tall, half-tall and dwarf varieties of sprouts. The dwarf and half-tall types are especially useful for small gardens and exposed sites. There are now a number of F.1 hybrids that give uniform sprouts of medium size and these are specially recommended for freezing.

Plants are readily available from market stalls or garden centres; choose plants that are a healthy green and not too large.

Preparing the site
Choose an open site where the soil is 'in good heart'. Sprouts need plenty of nourishment and will not do well in poor soils. A medium to heavy loam is the best choice, but they will do quite well in lighter soils providing the site has been prepared several months in advance.

This early preparation is all-important. Dig in as much manure or compost as you can spare. Farmyard manure is still the best, but is often difficult to come by. Useful alternatives are spent mushroom compost, deep litter from poultry houses, or garden compost. It does not matter if the compost is not fully rotted as the process of decomposition will be continued in the soil. Try to complete the manuring and digging by the end of the year and leave the soil rough.

If garden lime has not been used recently, apply it during early or mid spring (February or March) at about 135g per sq m (4 oz per sq yd); but do not apply it within 3–4 months of manuring. In mid spring (March) break down the soil with a cultivator.

One of the disadvantages of growing sprouts is that ground must be reserved for them; unlike cabbages or cauliflowers they cannot be used for double cropping as the planting period is too early. Planting should be completed before late summer (the end of June) and preferably a couple of weeks earlier.

However, by careful planning, the ground can be cropped until the sprouts are quite well grown. Lettuce, radishes, spring onions and summer spinach, or turnips, beetroot and carrots for pulling young, may be sown in rows 60–75cm (2–2½ ft) apart. It is then a simple matter to plant out the sprouts between the rows of the earlier crops. These will be cleared by the time the sprouts need the space.

When and how to sow
When you sow depends on when you want to harvest. For a very early crop – in

Left: good, even-sized sprouts. Below: recommended variety Irish Elegance

mid autumn (September) – sow in an unheated greenhouse in late winter (January). When the seedlings are big enough to handle, prick them off, 5–8cm (2–3 in) apart, into trays about 15cm (6 in) deep. Alternatively, sow outdoors in early or mid autumn (August or September) and then cover the young plants with cloches later. Four rows, 10cm (4 in) apart, can be accommodated under a barn cloche.

There is, however, little point in having brussels sprouts while there is still a selection of autumn vegetables available. Many gardeners consider that sprouts taste much better after the first frost. For a mid season picking from late autumn to mid winter (October through December), sow outdoors in early to mid spring (late February or March). Where this early sowing is likely to present problems (as in cold areas or on heavy soils), place cloches in position a few weeks in advance of sowing to warm up the soil.

For a late picking from the middle of winter (late December) onwards, sow in mid to late spring (March or the first week or two in April). Plants from these sowings should be ready for moving in early or mid summer (May or June). Sow the seeds thinly in short rows 13mm (½ in) deep, and when the seedlings are big

enough to handle, thin them to 5cm (2 in) apart. This gives straighter and stronger plants. Dust the seedlings with derris to protect them from flea beetle.

How to transplant
When the plants are about 20cm (8 in) high they are ready for transplanting. Ease them out with a fork, then separate them carefully and move them with as much soil as possible. A showery period is the best time for transplanting but this cannot always be arranged! In dry periods water the seedbed well a few hours before transplanting.

To protect the young plants from cabbage-root fly, either dip the roots of each plant in a paste made from calomel dust or sprinkle a small teaspoonful of the dust around each plant.

It is important to plant firmly, with the lower leaves just clear of the soil. A dibber or trowel is needed for this work; a trowel is better as it makes a bigger hole and avoids cramping the roots. A simple test for firmness is to pull gently at the topmost leaf of a plant. If the plant 'gives' it is not firm enough; if the end of the leaf tears, all is well.

The planting distances for sprouts are 68–75cm (2¼–2½ ft), all ways, for taller

varieties and 60cm (2 ft) for the dwarf varieties. These should be regarded as minimum distances, for sprouts need room in which to mature.

Tending growing plants
Unless your site is a sheltered one, you may need to stake taller plants. Where the plants are grown in a block it will be the corner plants that are most at risk, particularly those facing the prevailing wind. With the approach of autumn, draw a little soil up to the plants to give them better anchorage. Feeding should not be necessary if you prepared the ground well in the first place, but sprouts do respond to foliar feeding, and this is an extra boost that can be given at about fortnightly intervals during the peak growing period of late summer and early autumn (July and August).

Snap off any lower leaves that go yellow during the late summer and put them on the compost heap. If you leave them on the plants they may cause the lower sprouts to go mouldy or rotten.

'Blown' sprouts are those which remain open and refuse to button up into solid sprouts. Loose soil is often the cause and this is one reason why you should prepare the site early, particularly on light soils.

Above: early-maturing crops like lettuce can be grown between rows of sprouts
Below: transplant when sprouts have 4 leaves; test for firmness by pulling a leaf

Above: bend buttons sharply down to pick
Below: stake corner plants to avoid damage

Overfeeding with nitrogenous fertilizer is another cause of 'blown' sprouts.

One method of building up the sprouts is to pinch out the growing point of the plant when its optimum size has been reached – usually in late autumn (October). This practice is known as 'cocking'. Remove only a small piece, about as big as a walnut, but don't confuse this with the practice of removing the whole top of the plants.

Below: red sprouts taste like red cabbage
Below right: recommended variety Peer
Gynt is a half-tall early cropper
Bottom: a fine crop ready for picking

These cabbage-like heads do make an excellent vegetable and are preferred by some people to the sprouts – but do not remove them too early. The outer leaves of the plant, and its head, are there to protect the sprouts from the winter weather. If you remove them too soon this protection will be lost. It is better to leave them in place until mid spring (March), when the worst of the winter is over, and then make use of them. The topmost sprouts will then fill out.

One of the advantages of sprouts is that they yield their crop over a period. You can remove a few sprouts from each plant as they become ready, and leave those higher up the stem to grow up to size.

To gather the sprouts, hold the plant with one hand, take off the leaves as far up the plant as you intend to remove the sprouts, and then snap the buttons off with a downward pressure of the thumb. If, as sometimes happens, the buttons are so tight and close together that removal is difficult, use a sharp knife. Whatever method you use, take the sprouts off cleanly so that no portion is left to go mouldy or rotten. In late spring (April) any sprouts or tops that have not been used will burst open and throw up seed stems. Do not allow these to flower, for it is at this stage that the plants are taking most nourishment from the soil. Chop off all the green leaves and stems and dig them in. The roots should be forked out and burnt on your next bonfire. The greenstuff will eventually rot down into humus and will, in the meantime, help to keep the soil open. Late spring (April) is the time for planting potatoes, which like a loose soil, and there is no better crop than potatoes to follow brussels sprouts.

Pests and diseases

Brussels sprouts are vulnerable to the pests and diseases that commonly attack the brassica family.

Cabbage-root fly The transplanting period is the time when precautions should be taken against this pest that lays its eggs against the stems of the plants. The maggots that hatch from the eggs burrow into the soil and attack the stems below soil level. Affected plants wilt in sunshine and will eventually collapse. Sprinkle a small teaspoonful of calomel dust around each plant or dip the roots and stems of the seedlings in a paste made from the dust prior to planting out.

Club root A fungus disease that causes swollen and deformed roots. There is (as yet) no cure, but it can be controlled if lime is used as recommended in the section on preparing the site. Calomel dust will also give some control.

RECOMMENDED VARIETIES

Early Half Tall Produces a very early crop of large, good-quality sprouts.
Bedford Filbasket Mid season variety with large, tightly-packed sprouts.
Irish Elegance Tall, mid season variety.
Cambridge No. 5 Tall, late variety.
Peer Gynt (F.1 hybrid) Early, half-tall variety with medium-sized sprouts; recommended for freezing.
Citadel (F.1 hybrid) Mid season variety, recommended for freezing.
Red Produces sprouts that look and taste like miniature red cabbages.

CABBAGE

The cabbage, despite its rather unglamourous reputation, is a useful vegetable which no garden should be without. Not only is it a valuable food source, containing calcium and vitamins A and C, but it is available all year round and is easier to grow than most brassicas.

Cabbages can be divided into five main groups: spring, summer, winter, savoy and red. There is also Chinese cabbage.

Preparing the soil

Like all brassicas, cabbage does best in a firm and preferably alkaline soil. A light to medium soil is ideal, but it will grow quite happily in all soils, providing they are well drained.

In many cases cabbages will be planted as a follow-on crop to other vegetables. If the ground was manured for the previous crop a further manuring is not necessary, but you could usefully apply a general fertilizer at 70g per sq m (2 oz per sq yd).

Sowing and transplanting

Cabbages are easily raised from seeds sown in a seedbed. Most of the summer varieties can be sown for succession and it is better to make several small sowings rather than one large one. As with broccoli (see page 64), sprinkle calomel dust along each seed drill as a precaution against club root, and where cabbage-root fly is a problem, use either a bromophos or diazinon insecticide, according to the maker's instructions.

When the seedlings are large enough to handle, thin to 5cm (2 in) apart. This gives them room to make good, sturdy plants.

The move into their final quarters should take place when the plants are about 15cm (6 in) high. Ease the plants up with a fork and separate them carefully. Leave as much soil on the roots as possible and plant them at once. A dibber can be used but a trowel makes a bigger hole and gives the roots more room. Plant so that the lower leaves are just clear of the soil, firm around the roots and water the plants well in. Then keep the plants free from weeds and see they do not lack water during dry periods.

Spring cabbage

Spring cabbage have a distinct 'nutty' flavour of their own, as well as having much else to commend them. They mature in spring when vegetables are scarce; there is usually no caterpillar

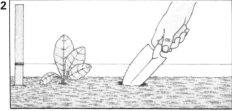
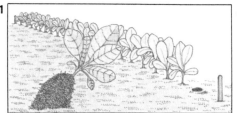

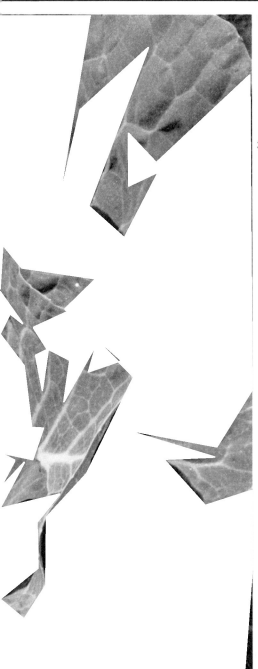

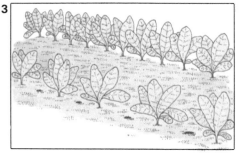

1 Cabbage seedling ready to transplant
2 Transplanting to final growing position
3 Thinning out for use as spring greens
4 Earthing-up with a swan-necked hoe

Left and above: summer cabbage Golden Acre Baseball and winter Avon Coronet

problem; being late they often miss the cabbage-root fly and they are seldom attacked by club root, which is not active during the winter months.

Sow in late summer or early autumn (July or August) and transplant during mid or late autumn (September or October). It is as well to make two sowings, about three weeks apart, and take the best plants from each. If the weather is dry at sowing time, water the seed drills well a few hours beforehand.

Spring cabbage usually follow one of the summer crops. They are ideal for following potatoes, and in this case the soil will only need lightly forking over before the plants are put out. Do not give them any manure, and use no fertilizers until the spring. The aim is to grow a strong plant to withstand the winter.

One mistake often made with spring cabbage is to give them too much room. Planted closer together they protect one another. For the smaller varieties, allow 38cm (15 in) between the rows and for the larger ones 50cm (20 in). Small cabbages can go as close as 30cm (12 in) between plants, but the larger ones will need 45cm (18 in). If enough plants are available it is a good plan to halve the distance between the plants and then take out every other plant in mid or late spring (March or April) for use as 'spring greens'.

In mid spring (March) a top dressing of a high nitrogen fertilizer will give the plants a useful boost. Hoe it into the soil and let the rain wash it in.

The main enemy of spring cabbage is not the weather but wood pigeon. In severe weather they will be desperate enough to attack plants in home gardens. Cover them with cloches – large barn cloches will cover two rows – to protect them from attack and produce an earlier crop. The thin, plastic strawberry netting also gives good protection. Make sure, though, that it hangs well clear of the plants.

Summer cabbage

The season for summer cabbage is late summer to late autumn (July to October). You can make a first sowing of an early variety in early spring (February) if you have a frame or cloches. During mid and

Winter cabbage

Sow winter cabbage in late spring or early summer (April or May) for harvesting from late autumn to early spring (October to February). Winter cabbage comprise the Dutch-type white cabbages like Winter White, the Christmas Drumheads selection and one outstanding variety known as January King. They are noted for their ability to stand several weeks without cracking open. Use them to bridge the gap between the summer cabbages and the savoys, and as a follow-on crop if planted out in late summer (July). If the variety Winter White is dug up by the roots and hung head downwards in a shed or cellar it will keep well for weeks.

Savoy cabbage

The leaves of the savoy cabbage are dark green and heavily crimped, and they will survive even a severe winter. Sow in late

late spring (late March or April) make successional outdoor sowings, with a final sowing (again of an early variety) in early summer (May).

They will be ready for planting out from early to late summer (May to July). Those that you leave till later in the summer (late June or July) can make use of ground vacated by the first potatoes, peas or broad beans. You may also be able to do some intercropping by planting early summer cabbage between rows of peas or dwarf beans. In the first instance the peas will be cleared by the time the cabbages need more room, and in the second the cabbages will have been cut by the time the beans are at their peak.

Above: hardy savoy cabbage Lincoln Late
Right: hardy, slow-growing red cabbage

spring or early summer (April or May) to harvest from mid winter to late spring (December to April). There are early and late varieties. You can even plant out the late varieties in early autumn (August), making a useful follow-on crop.

Red cabbage

Although red cabbage is mostly used for pickling, it also makes quite a good table vegetable. As it needs a long period of growth, sow not later than mid spring (March). An early spring (February) sowing under cloches is better. The finest red cabbage of all comes from a sowing

RECOMMENDED VARIETIES

Type	Variety (P) pointed hearts (others are round)	Siz
Spring cabbage	April (P)	sma
	Durham Early (P)	me
	First Early market (P)	lar
Summer cabbage	Greyhound (P)	sma
	Golden Acre	me
	Winnigstadt (P)	larg
	Hispi (P)	sma
Winter cabbage	Winter White	larg
	Christmas Drumhead	me
	January King	me
Savoy cabbage	Savoy King	me
	Ormskirk Rearguard	me
Red cabbage	Large Blood Red	larg
	Niggerhead	me
Chinese cabbage	Pe-tsai	
	Nagaoka (F.1 hybrid)	

Key to seasons
early spring (February)   early summer (May)
mid spring (March)   mid summer (June)
late spring (April)   late summer (July)

ing distance plants		When to sow	When to transplant	When to harvest
(15 in)	30cm (12 in)	mid to late summer	mid to late autumn	late spring to mid summer
(18 in)	38cm (15 in)	mid to late summer	mid to late autumn	late spring to mid summer
(21 in)	45cm (18 in)	mid to late summer	mid to late autumn	late spring to mid summer
(15 in)	30cm (12 in)	early spring to early summer	early to late summer	late summer to mid autumn
(18 in)	45cm (18 in)	late spring	mid to late summer	mid to late autumn
(21 in)	45cm (18 in)	late spring to early summer	mid to late summer	mid to late autumn
(15 in)	30cm (12 in)	mid spring to autumn	early summer to late autumn	late summer, autumn and spring
(21 in)	53cm (21 in)	late spring	late summer	early to mid winter
(21 in)	45cm (18 in)	late spring	late summer	early to mid winter
(21 in)	53cm (21 in)	late spring	late summer	mid winter to early spring
(24 in)	53cm (21 in)	late spring to early summer	late summer	mid winter to early spring
(24 in)	53cm (21 in)	late spring to early summer	late summer to early autumn	late winter to late spring
(24 in)	60cm (24 in)	early to mid spring or late summer to early autumn	early to mid summer	mid to late autumn
(21 in)	53cm (21 in)	early to mid spring or late summer to early autumn	mid to late spring	mid to late autumn
(30 in)	20cm (8 in)	late summer	do not transplant	mid to late autumn
(30 in)	20cm (8 in)	late summer	do not transplant	mid to late autumn

tumn (August)   early winter (November)
umn (September)   mid winter (December)
umn (October)   late winter (January)

attacks the root system and causes swellings which deform the roots. This, in turn, causes the plant to wilt and look stunted. There is, as yet, no cure – but the disease can be prevented. Club root is always worst on acid soils, so if your soil is acid, give it a dressing of garden lime at 100–135g per sq m (3–4 oz per sq yd) prior to planting, and sprinkle calomel dust along the seed drills. When transplanting, make a paste from calomel dust and dip the roots in it.

Cabbage-root fly This insect lays its eggs against the plant stems. From the eggs little white grubs hatch out and burrow down into the soil where they attack the roots. It is always advisable to give the ground a routine dressing of bromophos or diazinon to prevent this pest.

Cabbage whitefly This pest is particularly

Below: lettuce-like Chinese cabbage

made at the same time as spring cabbage in late summer or early autumn (July or August). The plants grow more slowly than spring cabbage and, as they are perfectly hardy, can be left in the seedbed until mid or late spring (March or April).

Chinese cabbage

Although described as a cabbage, this vegetable closely resembles a large cos lettuce. Its crisp, delicately-flavoured head can be boiled like cabbage or used in salads.

The plants are easily grown from seed but should not be transplanted. A good, medium-to-heavy loam suits them best; on poor, light, hungry soils they tend to go to seed quickly.

Because of this tendency towards seeding, it is better to delay sowing until late summer (July), and this means that they are useful for following earlier vegetables. A good site is in the lee of a taller crop that will give the plants some shade for part of the day. Sow the seeds in drills 6mm ($\frac{1}{4}$ in) deep and 75cm ($2\frac{1}{2}$ ft) apart. The easiest and most economical way is to sow a few seeds every 30–38cm (12–15 in) and then thin to the strongest.

Beyond keeping them free from weeds, the plants need no special attention, but see that they never lack water.

Pests and diseases

Some pests and diseases affect cabbages badly. Watch out for signs of trouble.

Club root (known as 'finger and toe')

bad on all members of the cabbage family and renders many vegetables almost unusable. Spray at the first sign of attack with a pesticide based on resmethrin.

Cabbage white butterfly During the summer and autumn, keep a close watch for the cabbage white butterfly. The caterpillars which hatch out from the eggs have voracious appetites and, if they are not dealt with quickly, the plants will soon look like lace curtains. Do not wait for this stage, but as soon as a butterfly is seen spray the plants with derris or trichlorphon or malathion and repeat the spray whenever necessary.

Flea beetle This pest can be a problem when the seedlings have germinated. Spray or dust with a BHC compound.

CAULIFLOWERS

The cauliflower is one of the most popular of the brassicas, though not one of the easiest to grow well. The name actually covers two types – the summer and autumn cauliflowers, and the cauliflower broccoli which is in season in late autumn and spring. This section deals with the true cauliflower – the summer and autumn varieties.

Cauliflower seeds are expensive (but not, of course, as expensive as cauliflowers themselves) and you may not wish to buy several new packets every year. But fortunately the seeds remain viable for several years and there is no reason why a packet should not be spread over two seasons. A better method is to buy new seeds each year and share them – and the expense – with another gardener.

Preparing the ground

Cauliflowers are gross feeders and like a rich, deep loam. They will not thrive on heavy, badly-drained clays, on very light loams which dry out in the summer, or on poor, hungry soils. If you plant them in these conditions they tend to retaliate by forming only small heads (a process known as 'buttoning') which open quickly and shoot up to form seed.

Choose, if possible, a site in full sun and with some shelter from cold winds. Dig this over during the autumn, working in as much compost or manure as can be spared. If you have not limed the ground recently spread a dressing over the soil surface at 135g per sq m (4oz per sq yd) and let the rain wash it in.

Sowing for all seasons

There are different varieties for different periods, so you can plan for a succession of harvests.

Cauliflowers for cutting in mid and late summer (June and July) should be sown in mid autumn (September) and over-wintered under glass. Those for heading in early and mid autumn (August and September) are sown in mid or late spring (March or April), and those for maturing in late autumn and early winter (October and November) should not be sown until early summer (May).

There are several ways of raising plants of the early varieties. You can, for instance, sow the seeds outdoors in mid autumn (September) and then prick off the plants into trays of potting compost as soon as they are big enough to handle. Keep the plants in a cold frame or a cold greenhouse throughout the winter. Or you can thin the plants where they stand and cover them with cloches. In either case leave about 8cm (3 in) between the plants; this will give them room to make strong, healthy growth. Transplant them, with a good soil ball, in the spring.

If you miss the mid autumn (September) sowing you can sow in a warm greenhouse in late winter (January) or in a cold one in early spring (February). Sow two or three seeds at 8cm (3 in) intervals in one of the soilless composts, as these encourage the formation of a good rootball. Thin to the strongest plant. Although the plants need protection during the winter you should ventilate them during the daylight hours whenever possible. Begin to harden them off in mid spring (March) so that they can be put out into their final positions during late spring (the second half of April).

Maincrop sowings are made outdoors in late spring (April). Thin the plants, as soon as you can handle them, to stand 4–8cm (2–3 in) apart. Don't leave the rows overcrowded; bent, spindly plants will be the result.

One of the drawbacks to growing cauliflowers in the past has been the fact that so many of them mature together, giving a glut one week and none the next. You can offset this to some extent by making two sowings – with a fortnight between – instead of one. If you have a deep-freeze the problem of coping with a surplus becomes less important as the summer varieties can be frozen for future use at your convenience.

Buying plants

Although plants can be bought from market stalls and garden centres you would do far better to raise your own. Some of the soil is bound to be knocked off the roots of bought plants in transit and very few of them are named. If, for any reason, it becomes necessary to buy plants, choose those with a good colour and straight stems. Avoid plants that are too big; one of about 15cm (6 in) will tolerate the move better and establish itself more quickly than a larger plant.

How to transplant

The importance of transplanting healthy plants with a good rootball cannot be stressed too much. Any check to the growth of cauliflowers is liable to cause

buttoning, and transplanting is one of the danger periods. The best method is to ease up the plants with a fork, then lift them out with as much soil as possible and put them straight into their final positions. Plant firmly, with the lower leaves just clear of the soil, and water them well in.

Plants of the early varieties should be spaced 45cm (18 in) apart all ways. The summer varieties will need 55cm (22 in) and the later ones 60cm (24 in).

As the later varieties are not ready for transplanting until late summer (July) you can use them as a follow-on crop to peas or early potatoes. There is no need to dig the plot over; simply prick over the top few centimetres with a fork, apply a general fertilizer at 70g·per sq m (2 oz per sq yd) and rake level.

Tending and harvesting
In periods of drought give the plants as much water as possible in order to keep them growing, for drought can check growth and cause premature heading, ruining your crop.

When the plants are growing strongly they will appreciate doses of liquid manure at weekly or fortnightly intervals. Use either a proprietary liquid manure or a home-made solution, made by suspending an old sack containing several fork-loads of manure in a tub or tank and leaving it for a few days. Dilute the manure water until it has the appearance of weak tea. Young children should be kept well away from it.

Keep a close watch on the crop once the curds (florets) begin to form as they come quite quickly, especially during the summer months. Bright sunlight turns the curds yellow; to prevent this, snap the stems of a few of the outer leaves and fold them down over the developing curd to shut out the light. The same protection can be given to the late varieties if frost threatens. However, the modern strains of late cauliflowers are mostly 'self-protecting' – the inner leaves fold over the curd naturally and therefore give good protection.

Fresh cauliflowers will keep in good condition for about a week if you dig them up by the roots and hang them, head downwards, in a cool, dark place. If the soil is at all dry, water them well an hour or two before lifting.

This firm-headed cauliflower with crisp white curd has been carefully tended in rich, well-prepared soil, given plenty of water in the growing season, shielded from frost and bright sunlight and protected from pests and diseases

Pests and diseases

Cauliflowers, unfortunately, are subject to quite a variety of pests and diseases.

Birds The tender young leaves of newly-transplanted plants may be attacked by birds. Use black cotton, or flashing strips of foil to keep them off.

Rabbits On open allotments, and sometimes even in home gardens, rabbits can be terribly destructive. The only really effective remedy is to surround the whole brassica plot with 90cm (3 ft) high chicken-wire. Although this is expensive initially, you can use it over and over again. You can also try spraying or dusting with an animal repellent – quite harmless to pets.

Cabbage-root fly A more subtle, but no less dangerous, enemy that lays its eggs at the base of the plant. When the maggots hatch they burrow into the soil and attack the stem below ground. The first sign of trouble is when the leaves begin to flag. Later, the leaves turn yellow and the whole plant collapses. At this stage the maggots can often be found in the stem. You must then dig up and burn affected plants.

If the fly can be deterred from laying, or killed, there will be no eggs and no maggots. So as soon as the leaves have straightened up after transplanting sprinkle calomel dust around the plants – a small teaspoonful to each plant. As an alternative method, mix some of the powder in water to form a paste, and then

Above: Flora Blanca type cauliflowers with large, solid, very white curds

Right: club root disease turns the fine roots into thick, swollen 'fingers'

Below: protect from sun or frost by snapping leaves over the curd

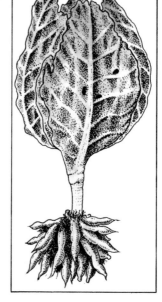

dip the roots and stems in the paste as you are transplanting.

If, in spite of this treatment (or due to lack of it), you find that cabbage-root fly has taken hold do not write the crop off. If the attack is not too severe you can encourage the plants to overcome it by forming new roots. They will do this if earth is drawn up under the lower leaves so that the stems are covered. Providing that you never allow them to dry out, these new roots will be enough to carry the crop through.

Caterpillars Summer varieties are especially vulnerable to the caterpillars of cabbage-white butterflies. The best remedy is to pick them off by hand, but this is time-consuming and not for the squeamish. A spray or dust with derris is effective, but you may need several applications. Derris has the advantage of being safe to use right up to the time of heading. Do not wait for trouble – at the first sign of any cabbage-white butterflies spray at once.

Club root (known in some areas as 'finger and toe'). This is the disease that you have most to fear from when growing any of the brassicas. Affected plants are stunted and sickly and the roots are swollen and deformed.

There is, as yet, no cure for club root but it can be controlled. Adequate liming of the soil helps to discourage it. Calomel dust is another good method of control; sprinkle in the drills before sowing and use it again (as described above) at transplanting time. You can 'starve out' the disease by ceasing to grow brassicas on the diseased soil but this takes a long time. Where incidence is severe it is wise to omit brassicas from the cropping plan for a few years. Remember that turnips and swedes are also members of the brassica family and are liable to be attacked.

RECOMMENDED VARIETIES

EARLY SOWINGS under glass for summer cutting:
Snowball; Mechelse Delta; Dominant.

MAINCROP SOWINGS – late spring (April) for summer cutting:
All the Year Round; Flora Blanca; Kangaroo.

MAINCROP SOWINGS for late autumn to early winter (October to December) cutting:
South Pacific; Flora Blanca No 2 (formerly Veitch's Autumn Giant); **Igea** (also known as Snow White).

SUCCESSIONAL SOWINGS
All the Year Round

KALE

The kales may well be described as the Cinderellas of the brassica family. Over the years they have acquired the reputation of being 'stop-gap' vegetables and lacking in flavour. This does not do them justice and has arisen largely through errors in picking. The leaves and shoots of kale should always be gathered while still young and small; it is the large leaves that are unpalatable.

On the credit side the kales are easy to grow and exceptionally hardy. Even a severe winter does not usually harm them. In addition, they are not exacting in their soil requirements and are more resistant to club root disease than the other brassicas.

Types of kale

In most seed catalogues this vegetable is listed as Borecole or Curly Kale. This is something of a misnomer, as not all kales are curly. They fall mainly into two groups – the curly and the plain-leaved. The curly kales are also often referred to as 'Scotch' kales. The dwarf form of the curly kale is of special value in open allotments or in exposed gardens, as it is much less subject to wind damage. Of the plain-leaved forms the best known are Cottager's kale and Thousand-headed kale; cut the centre out of these and they will produce tender young shoots. A new hybrid called Pentland Brig is a cross between the curly kale and plain-leaved kale and is gaining an excellent reputation for hardiness and heavy cropping.

Right: Dwarf Curled kale at RHS Wisley
Below: detail of Dwarf Curled variety

Two other type
Asparagus and Ru
is not quite so
mentioned, while
opposite. This unu
and has fine, d
Unfortunately nei
widely distributec
seedsmen still list

There is anothe
kale, that needs
ment. This is the l
kales and picking
summer (June). U
not transplant wel
in situ (where it is
not present any dif
not be sown until
early autumn (July

Sow the seeds in
and 45cm (18 in) a
plants to stand 30c
useful vegetable f
spring when fresh

Soil requirements
Most soils will sup
there is good drain
mind a heavy soi
waterlogged. A ric

BROAD BEANS

Young, fresh broad beans make a dish fit for a king. They must, however, be picked while the pods are still green and before the skins of the seeds begin to get tough.

A medium to heavy loam gives the heaviest crops, but broad beans can be grown in any well-drained soil. They are lime-lovers and if their patch hasn't been recently limed, give it a dressing at 70g per sq m (2 oz per sq yd), before sowing.

When to sow
The two sowing periods are early to mid winter (November to December) for an early crop; early to late spring (February to April) for a maincrop harvest.

An early winter sowing is debatable, for though reasonably hardy, broad beans are not immune to frost. Fortunately cloches give the plants adequate protection. Outdoor crops may succeed in warmer areas, but cloches are probably necessary until late spring (end of March) in colder northern regions.

Don't sow cloche crops until early winter (mid November), or the plants may reach the glass roof before it is safe to de-cloche.

Broad beans are usually grown in a double row 25cm (10 in) apart and 20cm (8 in) between the seeds, which are spaced out in a drill 5cm (2 in) deep. Sow the seeds in staggered positions along the rows. If you intend growing more than one double row allow 60cm (24 in) between each pair. Single rows should also be set 60cm (24 in) apart.

First unprotected sowings can be made from early spring to early summer (late February to May), with the heaviest crops coming from the earlier sowings. If outdoor conditions are unfavourable, begin sowing in early spring (February) in a cold greenhouse. Fill a 10cm (4 in) seed tray with compost and put the seeds in 2·5cm (1 in) deep and 8cm (3 in) apart. Transplant in late spring (April).

Care of growing plants
Tall varieties can grow to about 1·2m (4 ft) high and staking is usually necessary. Insert bamboo poles on each side of the rows and firmly wind garden wire or tough string from cane to cane.

Blackfly is the greatest pest menace to the broad bean, particularly later sowings; a severe infestation can cripple a whole crop. They attack the soft-growing points of the plant; once the first flowers have set, cut out the damaged tips.

In early summer (May) spray the plants with derris or a reliable aphicide and continue spraying until the pests have been eliminated.

Mice are broad bean nibblers and can quickly cause havoc to your crop. Set traps or spray a strong repellent around the base of the plants.

Chocolate spot disease is prevalent in heavy rainfall areas. It appears as dark brown blotches on leaves, stems and pods, and a severe attack can drastically reduce your crop. Check it in the early stages by spraying with Bordeaux mixture fungicide.

Choose Aquadulce Claudia for an early-season crop. It has white flowers (above) and fine, long pods (below)

RECOMMENDED VARIETIES

The two main types are the Longpod and the Windsor. The latter is less hardy but is considered by many to be the better flavoured.

A lesser-known broad bean is the Dwarf type. This breaks (makes side shoots) to form several stems. The seeds are sown 30cm (12 in) apart with 40cm (15 in) between each row. They crop heavily over several weeks and have a good flavour.

LONGPOD: **Aquadulce Claudia** (autumn sowing); **Dreadnought** (winter sowing); **Bunyard's Exhibition** (winter sowing); **Imperial White** (winter sowing); **Imperial Green** (winter sowing).

WINDSOR: **Giant Green** (spring sowing); **Giant White** (spring sowing).

DWARF: **The Sutton** (successional sowing).

RUNNER BEANS

Few vegetables give a better return for the time and money spent on them than runner beans. From the time the plants begin to flower until the first frosts cut them down, they will continue to produce their pods, and only a little of those pods is lost when they are prepared for cooking. They can also be ornamental.

Runner beans will grow in most soils. On heavy soils which warm up slowly do not sow too early, and on very light soils you may find it difficult to keep the plants sufficiently well watered. These are the extremes, however, and in between them the runner bean requires no special consideration. If lime has not been given recently, apply it at about 135g per sq m (4 oz per sq yd) when the site is prepared.

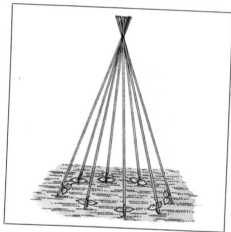

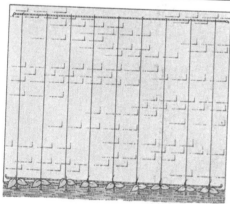

Top: staking runner beans by a wigwam of poles drawn together and fastened at the top. Above: beans can be grown up a wall by erecting a 'fence' of strings for them to cling to. Right: the most common way of staking is to use bean poles made of larch wood or heavy-grade bamboo

Preparing a trench

For best results dig out a trench 90cm (3 ft) wide and a spade's depth. Shovel out the loose soil and then break up the subsoil with a fork. As the soil is put back, mix in some compost or well-rotted manure. Leave a shallow depression at the top of the trench to help with watering later on. The trench should be prepared well in advance of sowing time – mid spring (March) is a good period.

Some gardeners line the bottom of the trench with thick layers of newspaper which are then thoroughly soaked with water. The newspapers hold some of the moisture and give it up when the plant roots need it.

If manure or compost cannot be spared for the runners, open up the trench in the autumn. Keep every scrap of kitchen waste in an old bucket, well covered. When the bucket is full, empty it into the trench and cover the waste with an inch or two of soil. Continue this process, with an occasional sprinkling of lime, until the trench is full. Although in good, fertile soil the beans will grow without any

The pods of the French (or kidney) bean are smaller than those of the runner bean and have a distinctive flavour of their own.

Normally the pods are eaten like runner beans, but some varieties can be grown for the seeds, that are usually dried for winter use and are then called haricots.

FRENCH BEANS

Some varieties of French bean are flat-podded; others are round. The round varieties are sometimes called 'snap' beans – the test for quality and freshness being that the pods break cleanly when they are snapped in half.

Most varieties of French bean are dwarf, the plants forming a little bush 30–38cm (12–15 in) tall, but there are also climbing varieties that will grow to a height of 1·5–1·8m (5 or 6 ft). These give a heavier crop and are especially useful where you have a trellis or boundary fence to support them.

French beans will grow in most soils provided the drainage is good. Light to medium soils are preferable as they warm up more quickly than cold, heavy soils in which the seeds tend to rot. A soil that was manured for the previous crop will suit them, and if lime has not been applied recently, work in a dressing at 100g per sq m (3 oz per sq yd) a few weeks before you start sowing.

Sowing under glass

Unfortunately, French beans are tender subjects and cannot be planted outside while frosts are expected. But you can get an early crop by sowing the seeds in a cool greenhouse in mid spring (mid March), using 9cm (3½ in) pots. When the plants have made their first pair of true leaves they can be planted in the greenhouse border, or under cloches outside.

An alternative, where staging is used, is to grow the plants in 25cm (10 in) pots and keep them on the staging. Sow six or eight seeds in a 25cm (10 in) pot and then select three of the best for growing on. When the flowers begin to appear, syringe the plants night and morning with clear water to ensure good fertilization.

Sowing outdoors

For outdoor crops a sowing can be made *in situ* under cloches in late spring (April) or without protection from early summer (mid May). A late sowing in mid to late summer (the second half of June) will give pickings until the first frosts, and if this sowing is cloched in mid autumn (September) the period of cropping will be extended for a few more weeks.

FRENCH BEANS AND HARICOTS

Sow the seeds in drills 5cm (2 in) deep, spacing them 15cm (6 in) apart. Sow two seeds at each spacing and if both germinate pull one seedling out. Put in a few extra seeds at the end of each row for filling up any gaps that may occur. If the plants are to be grown in single rows, allow 53–60cm (21–24 in) between the rows. Another method is to grow the plants in double rows. If it is necessary to move any plants to fill up gaps, do this with a trowel, taking as much soil as possible with each plant.

Tending, staking and picking

The French bean stands drought better than the runner, but if watering becomes necessary give the plants a good soaking and then mulch them with good compost, lawn mowings (not too thickly) or moist peat.

Some kind of support is essential for the climbing varieties. If a trellis or wire fence is not available then tall brush-wood, as used for tall peas, is ideal. Large-mesh netting is a good alternative.

Above: bamboo canes and string provide ample support for dwarf types
Overleaf: climbing French bean in flower with (below) Romano, a good variety

For the dwarf varieties all that is needed is something to keep them upright. If they keel over, the lower pods will touch the ground and slug damage may result. Twiggy sticks, pushed in among the plants, is one way of supporting them. Another good method is to push in bamboo canes at intervals down each side of the row, and then run string from cane to cane about 15cm (6 in) above ground.

Begin picking as soon as the pods are large enough to use. It is better to pick on the young side than to let the pods go past their best and get tough. Pick several times a week, and take off all the pods that are ready whether they are needed or not. Any surplus can be frozen or salted.

Pests and diseases

The two pests most likely to be encountered are slugs and blackfly.

Harvesting Streamline runner beans. This variety produces vigorous plants and crops over a long period. The long, fine-flavoured pods are borne in clusters

Making a wigwam

Another method of growing runner beans is to grow the plants in circles or 'wigwams'. Mark out a rough circle 1·2–1·8m (4–6 ft) in diameter, and put the poles in round the circumference. Draw all the poles inwards towards the centre and fasten them at the top. Then put the plants or seeds in against the poles in the usual way. The circles take up less room than a straight row and can often be fitted into odd corners, and as they do not present a straight surface to the wind they are far less likely to blow down.

Growing along a fence

A third method of growing is to sow or plant a single row at the foot of a fence and let them climb up it. A temporary fence can be made with a few stakes, horizontal strands of garden wire at the top and bottom, and lengths of string stretched vertically between the two wires. The plants will climb the strings without difficulty.

Once the runners have twined round the poles they will soon begin to climb. When they have reached the top, pinch out the growing points to keep the row uniform and make the plants bush out. Where they are climbing up a fence they can be left to fall over and cover the other side. Keep the rows free from weeds and in dry weather give them plenty of water.

Growing without stakes

It is also possible to grow runners without stakes. In this method the seeds are sown 20cm (8 in) apart in single rows 90cm (3 ft) apart. The plants run along the ground and form a continuous row. If the runners reach out too far and threaten to become entangled in the next row, pinch out the growing points. To pick, lift up the foliage on each side of the row in turn.

The obvious advantage of this method is that it is easy because no stakes are required. In hot weather the pods, being mostly under the leaves, do not become old so quickly. The disadvantages are that in wet weather some slug damage is likely, and that where the pods touch the ground they no longer grow straight. But for the gardener who has little time to spare and is not short of space in his vegetable plot, this method has its points.

Dwarf varieties reaching a height of only about 75cm (18 in) need little or no staking. A few twiggy sticks pushed in amongst the plants keeps them upright.

Ailments and pests

There are a few problems that may affect your growing plants, so take precautions. **Bud-dropping** The flowers do not open properly and fall off without being fertilized. This can be caused by cold winds, rapid changes of temperature, or dryness of the root system. Spraying with clear water night and morning may be of some benefit, but it does not take the place of a good watering around the roots. During a very hot summer, it shows clearly that beans which are watered regularly bear far more pods than plants left to fend for themselves.

Blackfly (aphides) can sometimes be a nuisance, especially if they have already infested broad beans in the vicinity. These aphides will gather round the tender tips of the shoots, inhibit flowering and make the plants unpleasant to handle. Do not let them reach this stage. Keep an eye open for them and at the first sign of trouble spray with derris or malathion.

If the attack comes late, when pods have already formed, use only derris as malathion is poisonous for a few days after application. Repeat the spraying until the plants are clear.

Frost warning

The runner bean is not a hardy plant and cannot be put out while the danger of frost is present. If a late frost threatens after the plants are through the soil, or just after they have been transplanted, cover them with newspaper, plant-pots, straw, leaves or anything else that will protect them. Plants which are only touched but not killed by frost will shoot again, but the crop will be later.

Picking the beans

When cropping begins, look over the plants every few days. Pick the pods while still young, before the beans have started to form in them, as old pods will be 'stringy'. If pods are missed and have become too old at the next picking never leave them on the plants. Pull them off and put them on the compost heap. Do not be tempted to leave them for seed, for as soon as the plants are permitted to form seed the production of young beans rapidly falls off.

If it is intended to save seed, leave one or two plants at the end of a row and do not pick any pods from them. When the pods have become dry and papery pull them off, shell out the beans, and store them in a dry, cool place.

RECOMMENDED VARIETIES

DWARF
Gina New white-flowered dwarf bean with a distinct runner bean flavour.

TALL
Streamline, Enorma, Crusader, Achievement, Kelvedon Marvel, and **Fry** (F.1 hybrid).

PEAS

Garden peas have to be home-grown to be fully appreciated. No bought peas can equal a dish of those picked in their prime, and shelled and cooked soon after.

There are tall, medium and dwarf varieties of peas. The choice will to some extent depend on what time and staking materials are available, and whether the site is sheltered or exposed.

A row of tall peas generally gives the best return but, on the other hand, rows of dwarfs can be grown closer together.

Peas prefer a deep, moisture-retentive soil in which their tap roots can thrust well down. They do not thrive on cold, sticky clay soils; nor do they like light, gravelly ones. Fresh manure, while not harmful, is not recommended because peas do not occupy a site long enough to make use of it; a strip that was manured for a previous crop is more suitable.

Sowing time

A sowing can be made in early winter (November) for picking in early summer (May). In favoured districts on a sunny, sheltered border the crop could come through winter without protection; in other areas it is wise to use cloches.

Round-seeded varieties are hardier than the wrinkled-seeded and should be used for an autumn sowing. For summer picking, seeds can be sown from early spring to early summer (February to May). Use round-seeded peas for an early spring (February) sowing, then move on to a wrinkled-seeded variety.

Tall peas are also sown in late spring and early summer (April and May) and take about 14 weeks to mature (about two weeks longer than dwarf types).

For sowing from mid to late summer (June to July) turn to the wrinkled-seeded varieties.

How to sow

Peas can be sown in a broad drill 15cm (6 in) wide and 5cm (2 in) deep, containing three rows of seeds, or in a narrow drill of only one row. A broad drill is better for tall peas. Space the seeds about 5 cm (2 in) apart. The distance between each row is the same as the height of the plants.

To save space tall peas can be sown alongside a path. Trenching will get the best results from here, but it needs to be done well in advance of sowing. Dig out a trench 60cm (2 ft) wide and a

Fat, ripe pea pods ready for harvesting, the result of careful cultivation

spade's depth. Shovel out the loose soil and break up the subsoil with a fork. Add good compost or well-rotted manure before returning the soil.

Other types of peas

There are several less common types that are well worth growing.

Sugar pea (mangetout) When the peas can be felt in the pods, but before they have filled out, is the time to cook them whole for eating pod and all. Sow in late spring to early summer (April to May).

Petits pois These are smaller than the ordinary pea but many consider them to be of better flavour. Sow from mid spring to mid summer (March to June). Staking is advisable.

Asparagus pea (winged pea) This type has reddish flowers that are followed by small three-sided pods. The flavour is supposed to resemble that of asparagus, hence the name. It is not as hardy as an ordinary pea and should not be sown before late spring or early summer (April or May).

Sow the seeds 10cm (4 in) apart in drills 2–3cm (1 in) deep and 60cm (2 ft) apart. The plants grow up to 60cm (2 ft) and some twiggy support is advisable. Gather the pods when they are about 4cm (1½ in) long.

Care of growing plants

Peas must be hand-weeded, especially when they are in a broad row, and it is best to do it when the plants are 15–23cm (6–9 in) high. If left too long, the weeds cannot be pulled out without disturbing the peas. Keep the hoe going between the

115

RECOMMENDED VARIETIES

Dwarf (round-seeded)
Feltham First, 60cm (2 ft) early winter sowing.

Dwarf (wrinkled-seeded)
Kelvedon Wonder, 60cm (2 ft) and Early Onward, 75cm (2½ ft), mid and late spring sowings; Onward, 75cm (2½ ft) and Hurst Green Shaft 75cm (2½ ft), late spring and early summer sowings (the latter has mildew resistance); Little Marvel, 45cm (18 in), mid to late summer sowing.

Tall-growing
Alderman, 1·50m (5 ft), Lord Chancellor, 1m (3½ ft) and Miracle 1·20m (4 ft), late spring and summer sowings.

Other types of peas
Sugar pea (mangetout) – tall-growing Carouby de Maussane, 1·50m (5 ft); **dwarf** Sweetgreen, 45cm (18 in) and Grace, 75cm (2½ ft).
Petits pois – tall-growing Gullivert, 1–1·5m (3–3½ ft).
Asparagus pea (winged pea) – dwarf, 45cm (1½ ft).

rows for as long as possible.

When peas are about 15cm (6 in) high they can be sprinkled with super-phosphate of lime at about 30g per metre run (1 oz per yard), along each side of the rows. Keep it an inch or two away from the plants and hoe it in.

Peas have root nodules which contain a nitrifying bacteria so they require little, if any, additional nitrogenous fertilizer.

Watering can pose a problem because peas are deep-rooting. During a drought this is an asset, providing you water them thoroughly. A mere sprinkling from a watering can, however, will do more harm than good.

Mulching with compost, lawn-mowings, old mushroom-manure or peat, will help to conserve moisture. Spread the mulch along each side of the rows, but not touching the plants; leave about 5cm (2 in) of bare soil either side so that rain can get through. The mulch should

Two rows of netting such as this give maximum support (below left); hold bine as well as pod when picking (below)

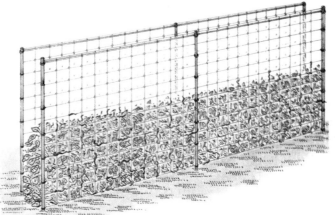
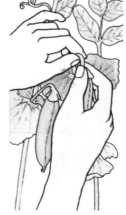

be 5cm (2 in) deep and put on when the soil is moist – *never* when it is dry.

Methods of support
Tall peas need staking and, although dwarfs are not supposed to need it, you will find that anything more than 45cm (18 in) tall will do better if staked. Twiggy sticks are ideal, though often difficult to come by. If you grow raspberries, you can use the prunings from the raspberry canes. Trim them and then push them into the soil on each side of the peas, leaning them inwards, so that they come together at the top.

Cord or plastic netting is used for tall-growing crops. You will find the thin 15cm (6 in) plastic-mesh type satisfactory, but it must be firmly erected and kept taut. The weight of a row of tall peas at peak harvesting time is considerable and

once blown down it cannot be put back. A strong stake should be driven in at each end of the row and tall canes inserted at 2m (6 ft) intervals.

It is best to put netting up each side of a row and let the peas grow in between. Modern varieties do not climb as readily as the old kinds and are easily blown away from a single row of netting.

How to harvest
A good row should give at least three pickings, starting with the lower pods which fill out first. When picking hold the pea bine (haulm or stem) in one hand and pull off the pod with the other. This prevents damage to the bine; if it gets bent or bruised the top pods will not fill.

When the crop is finished cut off the bines at soil level and leave the roots in the ground so that the nitrogen from the root nodules can be released into the soil. This will benefit any plants that may follow.

Pests and diseases
Mice Always guard against mice, especially with autumn sowings; it is advisable to set one or two traps after sowing.
Sparrows These birds have a liking for the first tender leaves and can create havoc with a crop. Pea-guards, made from wire netting fixed over a wooden frame, helps keep the birds at bay, but when the leaves eventually grow through the netting the guards have to be removed.
Pea weevil This tiny, beetle-like creature eats holes in the leaves of young plants and inhibits their growth. As soon as the seedlings are through, dust with derris and re-apply if rain washes it off. When the plants are 10–15cm (4–6 in) high, the danger period is over.
Grubs The pea moth makes its appearance when flowering begins and the grubs may be found inside the pods. Spray the flowers with a reliable insecticide as they open, and again 10 days later.
Thrips (thunder flies) Sometimes appearing in large numbers, thrips make silvery streaks on the leaves and flowering may be affected. Control these pests by spraying with an insecticide such as BHC or liquid malathion.
Mildew A common disease among peas, the powdery form of mildew covers leaves and stems with a white dust. It can be kept in check by spraying with dinocap. Unlike downy mildew, which appears as a grey fungus on the undersides of young leaves, it is more prevalent during a dry season. Late sowings suffer most from it and the best safeguard is to ensure that the peas have an open, sunny position with a good circulation of air.

Asparagus pea pods are eaten whole. Pick the pods young, before they get stringy

CUCURBITS

MARROWS AND COURGETTES

During the last few years the image of the marrow has come a long way from those unappetizing slabs of boiled vegetable, covered with white sauce, that were the usual offerings. Nowadays, few people want a really large marrow unless it is to win a prize at a village show. Newer varieties of marrow have been developed, giving smaller fruits which are ideal for stuffing. Courgettes (baby marrows), can be cooked whole, sliced and fried, or used in salads, and their popularity is rapidly increasing.

As well as ordinary marrows and courgettes, there are the custard marrows which are flat in shape and have scalloped edges. They are considered by many people to have a better flavour than the ordinary marrows. There is also the newer and curious vegetable spaghetti marrow. This is boiled whole, and when it is cut in half the inside can be forked out like spaghetti.

With the marrow enjoying a new following, it is fortunate that it is neither demanding in its soil requirements nor difficult to grow. Marrows will grow in any good soil, but they prefer a loam which does not dry out too quickly, and a sunny position. There are two types of plants, the trailing marrows and the bush. The trailing type sends out long runners or vines on which the fruits form, while the bush type is contained in a rough circle. The bush type is better for the small garden as it takes up less space.

If trailing marrows are chosen, some thought should be given to siting them. They are not suitable neighbours for crops such as lettuce, carrots or onions, where the rows are close together. They may be allowed to wander into the greens or potatoes, or be sited next to peas or some other early crop which will be cleared before the marrows need more room. One suitable method is to leave out a couple of tubers at the end of a potato row and plant a marrow instead.

Preparing the stations
As the trailing marrows need 1·8m (6 ft) between plants and the bush marrows 1m (3 ft), the most economical way of manuring for them is to prepare a special station for each plant. Dig out a hole 60cm (24 in) square and about 45cm (18 in) deep, and half fill it with well-rotted manure or good compost. If this is not available, fresh lawn-mowings are better than nothing and will generate a little heat as they rot. Prepare the sites several weeks in advance of sowing or planting so that the soil has time to settle down again.

Sowing under glass
For an early crop raise the plants in a cold greenhouse or frame from mid spring (March) onwards. Fill some 9cm ($3\frac{1}{2}$ in) pots with a good potting compost or one of the soilless composts. Plant one seed in each pot, edgeways, burying the seed about 13mm ($\frac{1}{2}$ in) deep. Fill several extra pots in case some seeds do not germinate. Alternatively plant two seeds in each pot and pull one out if both grow.

Keep the plants in a good light so that they do not become drawn (too tall and spindly), and then, during early summer (mid May) begin to harden them off ready for planting outdoors. If single cloches are available to cover the plants for a few more weeks they can go straight out into the prepared stations.

Below: the yellow custard marrow.
Right: Long Green Trailing produces a heavy crop of large fruit and is excellent for winter storage

Planting out

The marrow is not frost-hardy, and it cannot be planted out until all danger of frost is past. This usually means towards the end of early summer (late May in the south of England and one or two weeks later farther north).

Marrows are not the easiest plants to transplant and care should always be taken when moving them. If the plants have been raised in pots made of clay or plastic, water them well a few hours before transplanting so that the rootball will slip easily out of its pot. Peat or fibre pots have an advantage as they can be planted out intact. If using these, keep the soil moist until the pot disintegrates, for if it dries out the roots will be constricted. To give the roots additional freedom, tear off the bottom of the pot and slit it up one side before planting.

Sowing into the ground

Another method of growing is to sow directly into the ground in late early summer (mid to late May). To make sure of a plant at each prepared site, push three seeds into the soil, spacing them in a triangle about 15cm (6 in) apart. Thin bush marrows to a single plant, but with trailing marrows two plants can be left at each position and trained to go in different directions. Train the vines early as they resent being disturbed once they have taken hold of the soil. If a trailing marrow just wanders on and on without forming fruits, pinch out the growing point. This will encourage it to produce side-shoots.

Care of growing plants

Once the young plants are growing strongly see that they do not lack water. A mulch of peat or lawn-mowings will help to conserve moisture. Liquid manure or diluted soot water (see Carrots, page 143) can be given at intervals.

Trailing marrows are also climbers. Planted at the foot of a wire fence the vines will naturally climb up the wire. Some tying in of the vines is advised, and once the fruits begin to swell they will need some support to prevent large fruits from pulling the vines down again. Choose the smaller-fruiting varieties for this method, which is particularly useful in small gardens.

Fertilization of the female flowers is generally done quite adequately by insects. If, however, the flowers fail to set, strip off the petals from a male flower and push it gently but firmly into the heart of a female flower. The two are easy to distinguish as females have a tiny marrow behind the flower.

Top: Long White Trailing has large creamy-white fruits that make excellent jam

Above: constant cutting ensures a heavy crop with these Golden Zucchinis

yellow and die. Unfortunately there is no cure for this disease.

Picking and storing the fruits

As the fruits ripen they change colour and the skin hardens. White fruits turn yellow and green ones, if striped, show a darker tinge in the stripes. The neck (where the fruit joins the stem) also hardens and is more difficult to cut. Leave the fruits on the plants until the first frost threatens; then cut the remaining ones and take them indoors. This will normally be about mid to late autumn (late September or early October).

If the fruits come faster than they can be used, leave some of them to ripen for winter use. It must be remembered, however, that once the fruits are permitted to ripen on the plant, the production of new fruits will slow down. Choose fruits of good shape for storing. Never select any that are pointed at the butt end (the end away from the stalk) as these usually go bad.

The ripe fruits can be used throughout the winter months and will keep perfectly well if stored properly. Damp outhouses, and garden sheds which are not frost-proof, are not suitable. A dry room with a fairly even temperature of 10°–15°C (50°–60°F) is ideal. Handle the fruits carefully at all times and never store them on top of one another. Stored marrows should not touch each other. Years ago, in the days of the oak-beamed ceilings, it was the custom to put them in nets or broad bands of cloth and hang them from the ceiling. This method is still the best.

An extra bonus from the ripe marrows is the seeds, which can be extracted from the pith, dried on a sheet of paper in front of a fire, and then stored for future sowings the following year.

Top: vegetable spaghetti is an unusual and delicious vegetable borne on trailing plants. It is easy to grow and yields a large number of medium-sized fruit. Above: Table Dainty matures early and produces a good crop of fairly small marrows

Sometimes the fruits fall off while still small. This can be caused by lack of water, a poor soil or inadequate fertilization.

Do not spray the plants with insect-icides, or give fertilizers to plants at the fruiting stage, as they encourage the production of seeds.

The only pest which may trouble them is red spider mite, but these almost invisible creatures are not a serious pest outdoors. Attacked leaves have a rusty, shrivelled appearance and should be cut off and burned. Spraying with clear water night and morning will discourage the pest as it prefers dry conditions. Occasionally, cucumber mosaic virus will attack marrows; the plants gradually turn

PUMPKINS, SQUASHES AND MELONS

Pumpkins and squashes are closely related to the marrow and are cultivated in much the same way. They need a site in full sun and a good fertile soil, but otherwise are not difficult vegetables to grow in your garden. Cantaloupe melons can also be grown outside, but only in regions with mild winters and hot summers; otherwise use a cool greenhouse.

PUMPKINS AND SQUASHES

As squashes need to be 90–120cm (3–4 ft) and pumpkins 1·8m (6 ft) apart, you can make more economical use of your compost or manure by preparing 'stations' for the seeds. Do this some weeks in advance, taking out a hole about 60cm (24 in) square and about 45cm (18 in) deep, and half-filling it with well-rotted manure or compost. Prepare the stations in mid to late spring (the beginning of April) so that the soil, when returned, has time to settle down before planting. Leave the station in the form of a slight mound.

Sowing and raising plants

Raise the plants in a greenhouse, frame or even in a sunny window by sowing individual seeds in 9cm (3½ in) pots of J.I. No 1 or a soilless compost. Push each seed (on edge) down about 13mm (½ in) into the soil. The end of spring (second half of April) is early enough for this sowing as the plants are not frost-hardy and cannot

go outdoors until there is no risk of frost.

Bear in mind, however, that neither squashes nor pumpkins move easily and that transplanting, if done, must be carried out with as little disturbance to the roots as possible. For this reason the expendable cardboard pots or soil blocks are to be preferred to ordinary pots.

Where cloches are available it is much easier to sow *in situ* in late spring to early summer (the last week in April or the first week in May) and then cover each prepared station with a single cloche, de-cloching in mid summer (the middle of June) when the risk of frost is over. Sow three or four seeds at each station, some 8cm (3 in) apart and 13mm (½ in) deep. If more than one seed germinates, thin to the strongest plant. If protection cannot be given, delay the sowing until early to mid summer (the second half of May).

In dry periods see that the plants do not lack water. A mulch of lawn mowings, compost or peat can be spread around the plants (but not right up to the stems). This helps to keep the root-run moist.

Generally, pollination is done naturally by insects. Hand pollination can be done by taking the petals off a male flower and pushing it firmly into the centre of a female flower. This is best done at midday

Right: Butternut squash, a sweet variety
Below: two trailing pumpkins, (left)
orange-skinned Mammoth (and right)
fine-flavoured Hundredweight

when it is warmest. Female flowers are easily identified: they have a swelling behind the flower which is the immature squash or pumpkin.

Ripening, harvesting and storing

Some varieties of squash are classed as 'summer' squashes and others as 'winter' squashes. The summer squashes are cut in an immature state for use during the summer months. The winter squashes are left to ripen and are stored for winter use.

In the case of pumpkins, limit the number of fruits to two or three per plant. For culinary use it is better to have two or three fruits of medium size than one monster specimen. But should you want a

larger one, it is not a difficult matter. Let several fruits set on a plant and then choose the best one. Cut the others off and prevent the plant from setting any more by pinching off each female flower as it appears. When the fruit is swelling, feed the plant at fortnightly intervals with weak liquid manure or soot water. Before the fruit becomes too big, lift it carefully and slip a flat tile or piece of board under it. This will help to keep it clean and prevent possible slug damage.

As they ripen, the fruits of squashes and pumpkins turn a deeper colour. Leave them on the plant until the first frosts are expected, then cut them from the plant with stem still attached. Store in a light, dry, cool and frost-free place.

OUTDOOR MELONS

Outdoor melons (cantaloupes) are not difficult to raise in a cool greenhouse, frame or sunny window. Sow two seeds on edge in a 9cm (3½ in) pot, 13mm (½ in) deep. Make the sowing in late spring (middle of April); if both seeds germinate in each pot, pull out the weaker. Keep the seedlings in full light and transplant them into their permanent positions in early summer (middle of May).

For best results make up a soilbed in the frame by putting down some well-rotted manure or good compost and covering it with 15cm (6 in) of sifted soil. A frame 1·2m (4 ft) long and 75–90cm (2½–3 ft) wide will take one plant. For growing under cloches prepare stations as

Left: small and round Ogen melon raised on flower-pot to avoid slug damage
Below: much larger Burpee Hybrid has firm, orange flesh

described for pumpkins and squashes, and allow 90cm (3 ft) between plants.

Tending and harvesting

When a plant has made five leaves, pinch out the growing point. Two sideshoots will break from each stop. For cloche cultivation these sideshoots are trained in opposite directions along the cloche run. In frames stop the sideshoots again after the fourth leaf so that they also produce two shoots (making four in all) and train one shoot into each corner of the frame.

To prevent the cloches or frames becoming a mass of leaves as further sideshoots are made, some judicious stopping and thinning of surplus shoots is usually necessary. Allow three or four fruits to each plant and when these have set, pinch back the fruit-bearing shoot at the second leaf beyond the fruit.

Fertilization is usually a natural process, but if the fruits are slow in setting, pollinate by hand – as described for pumpkins and squashes.

Melons like sunshine, and shading should be needed only during the hottest part of the day. Ventilate freely in warm weather and water regularly. Spraying the plants with clear water night and morning helps to keep the red spider mite away.

To tell when a melon is ripe for cutting, press the fruit gently at the end opposite the stem; if the fruit 'gives' to this pressure it is ripe.

Some varieties crack slightly against the stalk and give off a delicious smell.

RECOMMENDED VARIETIES

PUMPKINS
Mammoth (trailing) Orange-skinned with yellow flesh.
Hundredweight (trailing) Very large orange pumpkin; good flavour.

SQUASHES – SUMMER
Butternut (trailing) Sweet with bright orange flesh.
Baby Crookneck (bush) Bright yellow fruits.

SQUASHES – WINTER
Hubbard Squash Golden (trailing) Excellent variety for winter storing.

OUTDOOR MELONS (CANTALOUPES)
Sweetheart (F.1 hybrid) Pale green with firm, salmon-pink flesh; tolerant of low temperatures.
Ogen Small, round, deliciously-sweet fruit.
Dutch Net (F.1 hybrid) Orange flesh of fine quality and flavour.
Burpee Hybrid (F.1 hybrid) Large, round golden fruits with orange flesh; firm and juicy.

ONIONS

GARLIC AND LEEKS

There is a widespread belief that garlic is difficult to grow. This may come from its association with warmer climates, and the fact that the standard variety is listed as Best Italian. Whatever the cause, the belief is a mistaken one, as garlic is quite hardy and easy to cultivate.

Leeks are also very easy to grow, and few vegetables are more accommodating. The leek can be used as a follow-on crop to early vegetables; it is not much troubled by pests or diseases; it is perfectly hardy; and it matures during winter and early spring when a change of vegetable is welcome.

GARLIC

The best soil for garlic is a light to medium loam, well supplied with humus. Prepare the site, which must be in full sun, in mid autumn (September) by digging in some well-rotted manure or compost. The bulbs can be planted as early as late autumn (October), but early to mid spring (February to March) is preferable as they make little growth in the winter.

Planting the bulbs

Each bulb of garlic is made up of a number of segments or cloves. Bulbs can be planted whole to give larger bulbs, but it is more economical to plant the best cloves separately. Insert them 2–3cm (1 in) deep and 25cm (9 in) apart, in rows 30cm (12 in) apart. Buy bulbs from a leading seedsman; you can, however, use those bought for the kitchen. After the first year select some of the best quality bulbs for the next planting.

Garlic requires no special cultivation beyond keeping the weeds at bay. The

Left: garlic bulbs hanging up to dry
Below: when dry, remove loose skin and dead foliage from bulbs, and store

plants are usually free from pests and diseases. Watering is not necessary, except in very dry seasons. Pinch out flower-heads if they appear.

Lifting, drying and storing
In late summer or early autumn (July or August), according to the time of planting, the foliage begins to yellow, starting at the leaf tips. This is the signal to lift the bulbs and spread them out to dry. Put the bulbs in an empty frame with the lid raised to admit air, or in a cloche or two with the ends left open, or simply tie them in bunches and hang them on a sunny wall. When the bulbs are thoroughly dry, rub off any loose skin and dead foliage, and store them in a dry, light and frost-proof place.

LEEKS
Leeks will grow in most soils, but they do best where the soil's pH is 6–6·5. If it is lower than this, apply hydrated lime according to maker's instructions. As the plants are not put out until late summer or early autumn (July or August), they usually follow an earlier crop, and if manure was used for this crop the soil will be in good condition. If the site was not manured earlier, dig in some good compost if available. As leeks are deep rooting, the compost must be put down where it will retain moisture and the roots can take hold of it.

Sowing from seed
The plants are easily raised from seeds, which should be sown in mid to late spring (March or early April) in shallow drills 6mm ($\frac{1}{4}$ in) deep. If onions are being grown from seed, sow leeks at the same time alongside the onions. If the seeds are sown thinly, no further thinning out will be necessary. Gardeners who miss this sowing can obtain plants from markets or garden centres during the transplanting period.

Planting out
Where only a few leeks are required, an excellent way of obtaining the best results is to dig out a trench 60cm (24 in) wide and a spade's depth. Shovel out the loose soil, break up the subsoil with a fork, and then put in a layer of well-rotted manure or compost. Return about half the topsoil and mark the site of the trench with sticks. Do this a few weeks before planting so that the soil has time to settle. The trench will take two rows of plants 38cm (15 in) apart. Allow 20cm (8 in) between the leeks, and stagger the two rows.

Right: mid-season leek, Musselburgh

Top: composition of trench suitable for planting out a few leek seedlings
Above: before planting leek seedlings, cut back roots and trim leaves as shown

For harvesting in midwinter, plants will need to go out in late summer (July). An early autumn (August) planting will give leeks from late winter (January) onward. As there is usually no shortage of other vegetables before this time, there is little point in planting out too early.

To transplant from the seed row, first ease the plants with a fork, then pull them up and separate them carefully. Throw out any plants that are bent or very short in the stem – these will never make good leeks – and take off any loose skin. Cut back the roots to about 4cm (1½ in) from the stem, and shorten the tops by about half. This does not harm the plants, which soon form fresh roots, but it does make transplanting much easier. The plants are ready for moving when they are about 15–20cm (6–8 in) long, usually about 10–15 weeks old.

A dibber is the best tool for planting but a trowel can be used. Make a hole deep enough to take the plant up to its lowest leaves, drop it in, trickle a little soil over the roots and pour some water into the hole. It is unnecessary to fill the hole in, as this will be done during subsequent cultivation.

When the plants are put out in the open ground, allow 20cm (8 in) between them and a minimum of 30cm (12 in) between the rows; 38cm (15 in) is better, and if you are intending to earth the plants up a little, 45cm (18 in) will be required.

To transplant leeks: **1** *draw drill with hoe;* **2** *make planting holes with a dibber;* **3** *drop plantlets into holes;* **4** *trickle soil over roots, and pour in water, but don't fill in hole*

Care of growing plants

Take care when hoeing that the stems of the leeks are not nicked with the hoe, as any wound is an entry point for pests and diseases. Being deep-rooting, the plants do not suffer too quickly from drought, but if it becomes very dry they will appreciate a good soaking of water. An occasional application of liquid manure or soot water will also be beneficial.

The edible part of the leek is the blanched stem, and this area can be increased if a little soil is drawn up the stems. Do this only when the soil is dry and friable and will run through the hoe; to plaster wet soil against the plants will do more harm than good. A dry day in late autumn or early winter (late October or November) is the time to choose. With a draw hoe, carefully pull up the soil to each plant and take care that soil does not fall into the heart of the plant. Where the plants are being grown in a trench the remainder of the dug-out soil is returned to the trench as the plants grow.

Pot leeks

The pot leek differs from the ordinary leek in having a shorter but much thicker stem. Its culture is the same as that of ordinary leeks, but its popularity is limited and mainly confined to certain northern areas of Britain.

Pests and diseases

As a rule leeks are trouble-free, but they may be attacked by onion fly or white rot.

Onion fly This pest can become a menace around the time when the seedlings are transplanted. If there is a history of onion fly in the garden, sprinkle calomel dust up each side of the row while the plants are still in the seedling stage, or dust with BHC.

White rot Calomel dust will also protect against white rot, a white fungal growth at the base of the plant. If this occurs, destroy infected plants and do not grow leeks there again for several years.

Harvesting and storing

Leeks are dug as required and present no storage problem. If severe frost threatens it pays to dig up a few leeks and keep them in the garden shed with the stems covered. An alternative method is to surround a few plants with peat or short litter (composted manure). This will absorb most of the frost and make it possible to dig up the leeks even when the surrounding ground is frozen.

Leeks will continue to grow from the time of planting to the onset of winter. The rate slows down with the arrival of colder weather, although some growth may still be made in mild periods. In mid to late spring (March to April) there is a surge of new growth that culminates in the formation of seed heads. Any plants still left in the ground at the end of spring (late April) should be lifted. These can be stored for a few weeks in a shady corner of the garden, with a little soil over the roots and the blanched stems covered to exclude light.

When digging, make sure that the spade is thrust well down, or the bottom of the leek may be chopped off. The leek makes a mass of fibrous roots, and these help to break up heavy soil.

RECOMMENDED VARIETIES

GARLIC
Best Italian Standard variety, readily available, prolific and easy to grow.
Jumbo Recent variety that can be grown from seed to maturity in about 18 months.

LEEKS
The Lyon (also known as Prizetaker) Popular early variety with long stems and mild flavour.
Marble Pillar Early variety with long white stems.
Musselburgh Mid-season variety, has long, thick stems and broad leaves.
Winter Crop One of the hardiest of the late-cropping leeks.

Onions used to have a reputation of being difficult to cultivate, but modern varieties offer types to suit most conditions so no gardener need be without them. Even so, the right preparation is still essential.

ONIONS
from sets and seeds

Onions do best in a medium to heavy loam; although lighter soils will produce good crops, the bulbs may be smaller.

Prepare the plot early so that winter frost and rain will settle the soil naturally; be sure your digging is completed by mid winter (December). Dig in as much manure and compost as possible, leave the ground rough and finish off with a dusting of lime.

In early or mid spring (February or March) when the soil is dry enough, break down the lumps with a cultivator and a rake. Tread it firmly to a fine tilth. There is a certain artistry and a lot of satisfaction in making a good onion bed.

You can grow onions in the same site year after year – *providing there is no soil-borne disease present*. To do so encourages a rich, fertile soil to build up over succeeding years.

Sowing
Onions will start to form bulbs about late summer (July), irrespective of when the seeds are sown. A late sowing will not mean late bulbing, but smaller bulbs. In general therefore, the earlier the seeds are sown, the larger the bulbs.

Grow onions in rich soil (far right) to produce beautiful golden bulbs like the Rijnsburger Yellow Globe (above)

Outdoor sowings can be made from early to late spring (February to April) whenever the ground is suitable, with a target date of mid spring (March) if possible. Sow the seeds thinly and evenly in drills 13mm ($\frac{1}{2}$ in) deep and 25–30cm (10–12 in) apart.

Sowing in autumn (August to October) gives the plants a longer time of growth and as autumn sowings come to maturity earlier than spring ones, the bulbs can be lifted early in the following autumn (August) while drying-off conditions are still favourable. If you do not time the sowing carefully the plants may get too far advanced by spring and go to seed.

The best sowing date for your area can be determined only by trial and error but, as a rough guide, you should reckon on the beginning of autumn (first week in August) for colder regions; one to two weeks later (mid August) for milder areas; and three to five weeks later (end of August or first week in September) for the more favourable climatic regions. Later sowings will need the protection of cloches throughout winter.

Planting onion sets

Growing onions from sets is an especially popular method in less favourable climates. An onion set is a small onion in an arrested state of development; when replanted it grows to full size. Some years ago sets were viewed with suspicion because of their tendency to go to seed, but with today's varieties this is less likely to happen. Some seedsmen are now combating the problem by storing the sets in a high temperature for several weeks. This kills the embryo flower-bud without harming the set.

Experience has shown that only a small percentage of treated sets go to seed, so they are worth the extra cost.

Plant onion sets towards late spring (March–April) in rows 30cm (12 in) apart allowing 10–15cm (4–6 in) between the bulbs (the closer planting will give bulbs large enough for kitchen use). Draw a drill just deep enough to cover the sets. It is sometimes recommended that the tips should show above the soil, but many gardeners prefer to cover them as this stops birds from pulling them out again.

Care of plants

Hoe the soil lightly so that the roots are not disturbed. Keep autumn-sown plants weeded as long as possible or they may be so choked by spring that rescuing them could prove tedious and difficult.

Watering will help in a dry spell, but stop once the bulbs have formed and the tops (leaves) start to topple. The tops fall over when the bulbs begin to ripen as the supply of sap to the leaves is cut off. You can hasten the process by bending the tops with the back of a rake, but do be careful or the leaves may get bruised or broken. You would do better to let the tops go over naturally.

Ease up gently with fork before lifting

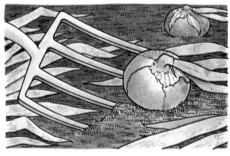

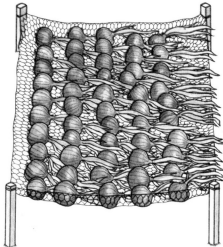

Before storing spread onions out on a bed of wire netting (above) with their roots facing south so that they receive the maximum amount of sun.
Onions are ready for lifting and drying off when their tops fall over (left)

Large onions

If you prefer large onions you will need a greenhouse that can be heated to 10°C (50°F). Make a start in late winter (January), sowing two or three seeds thinly every 4cm ($1\frac{1}{2}$ in) in trays of J. I. No 1 seed compost and thin to the strongest plant.

Harden them off before planting out in late spring (April). The plants must be 20–30cm (8–12 in) apart, with 30–40cm (12–15 in) between each row.

Plant onion sets in shallow drills

Shuffle along drill to cover with earth

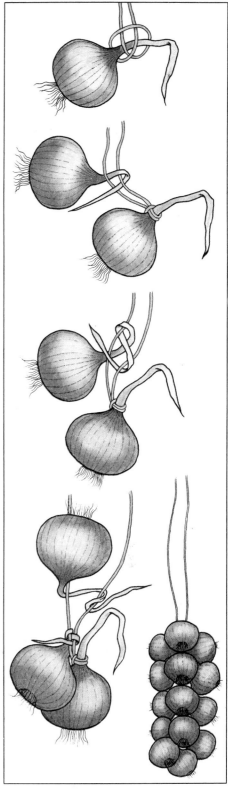

Pickling onions (top) need neither rich soil nor thinning out. For storing choose one of the long-keeping varieties such as Bedfordshire Champion (above)

Harvesting and storing

Beware at this stage of thinking that all the important work is behind you! More onion crops are ruined by poor harvesting and storing than by any other cause. They are ready to harvest when the leaves have turned yellow and the scales of the bulbs are brown. Ease them gently loose with a fork, pull them up and spread them out to dry.

Before storing make sure the bulbs are thoroughly dried off: leave them out in the open, turning them occasionally; place them in an empty frame, or on a path or wire netting suspended above the soil. An excellent drying method is to cover the bulbs with cloches, leaving the ends open to allow the wind to blow right through.

When the tops feel papery and the brown scales on the bulbs can be rubbed off, the onions are ready for storing. Put them in shallow boxes – tomato trays on legs (available from a greengrocer) are ideal as the air can circulate around them. Onions must be stored in a dry, airy place. They will stand some frost, but should be brought indoors during severe weather.

Making an onion string

A space-saving and popular idea is to string the onions together and hang them up instead of storing them away. Take a length of rope or cord and tie a large onion to one end. Using this as an anchor, secure the rest round the rope, building up from the bottom. Hang the completed onion string in a shed, garage or on a sunny wall.

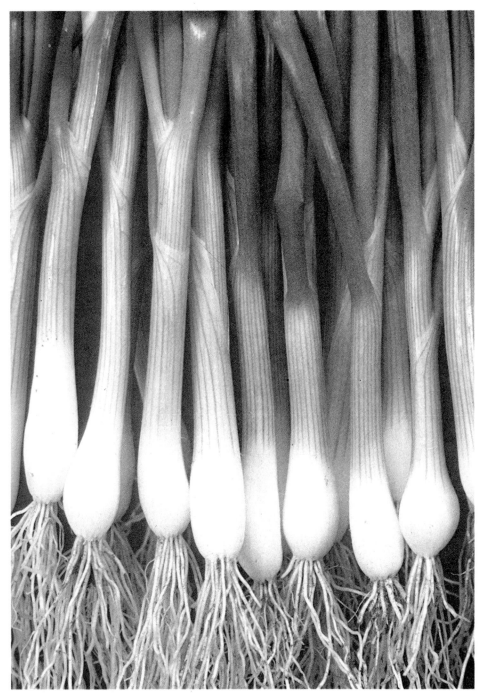

White Lisbon (above) is one of the most popular spring onion varieties. For a constant supply sow 'little and often' throughout the spring and summer

Salad and pickling onions
Salad onions can be sown successively from mid spring to mid summer (March to June). You can sow the seeds more thickly than for 'keeping' onions, and the rows need be only 15cm (6 in) apart. The plants are pulled while still green, starting when they are about pencil thickness. In dry periods water them well before pulling, and firm any plants that are left to grow on.

Thinnings from autumn and spring sowings of your keeping onions can also be used.

Pickling onions are easy to grow and they don't need rich soil. Sow the seeds thickly in a drill about 15cm (6 in) wide during late spring (April); no thinning is required. Harvest the bulbs in late summer (July).

Other types
There are several other kinds of onion which, although not so popular, are interesting to grow.

Welsh onion Forms a small, brownish, flat base; its stock can be raised from seeds sown in early or mid spring (February or March). Use the stems for salad onions. Keep a few clumps to plant again; split them up and replant in spring or autumn.

Japanese bunching onion Grows from seeds sown in late spring (April) and reaches full size in its second year. Like the Welsh specimen, use its shoots and leaves for salads and replant the clumps.

Everlasting onion Sow in spring or autumn. It is similar in habit to the Welsh and Japanese onions. Unfortunately it isn't widely distributed and might be difficult to obtain other than through catalogues of specialist growers.

Pests and diseases
It is as well to be forewarned of the likely attacks on your cherished plants.

Onion fly is the major hazard. It lays eggs at the base of the plants during early and mid summer (May and June) and the grubs burrow into the soil and attack the immature bulbs. Affected plants turn yellow, then collapse; they must be pulled up and burned. Make sure no larvae are left in the soil. The best safeguard is to apply calomel dust on each side of the rows when the plants are still at the 'crook' stage (before the seedlings have straightened up) and again about ten days later.

The pests are more active in light soils and with spring sowings. Autumn-sown bulbs and onion sets, although not immune, are less vulnerable to an attack.

White rot Fungus disease that causes the leaves of the plant to turn yellow and die. Roots rot and the base of the bulb is covered with a white mould. There is no cure and diseased plants must be burned.

Downy mildew Leaves die from the tips down and are covered with a fine, fluffy growth. It is also incurable, so burn any sick plants.

RECOMMENDED VARIETIES

For early and spring sowings
Ailsa Craig; Bedfordshire Champion; Blood Red.

For autumn sowings
Solidity; Reliance; Express Yellow.

Onion sets
Untreated: Stuttgarter Giant; Sturon. Treated: Rijnsburger Wijbo (formerly called Giant Fen Globe).

Salad onions
White Lisbon

Pickling onions
Paris Silverskin; The Queen; Cocktail.

SHALLOTS

The shallot is a smaller member of the onion family. Gourmet cooks often substitute it for onions and it is widely used for pickling.

There is an old gardening tradition that shallots should be planted on the shortest day and harvested on the longest. This seldom occurs in practice, but it is an indication of the hardiness of this vegetable. The more usual times of planting are early or mid spring (February or March), but there is no reason why the bulbs should not be planted earlier than this if weather conditions permit.

Preparing the ground

A medium loam is the best soil for shallots but they will do well in heavier soils provided the drainage is good. Although not quite so demanding in their soil requirements as onions, they do like a good soil. If you are planting in early or mid spring (February or March), prepare the site in autumn as soon as the autumn-maturing crops have been gathered. Dig in some manure or compost and leave the soil rough. If you cannot prepare the site quite so early as this, only well-rotted manure or compost should be used.

Sowing and planting

Shallots can be grown from seed but few seedsmen list this item. Sow in mid spring (March) in drills 13mm ($\frac{1}{2}$ in) deep and 30cm (12 in) apart; then thin the seedlings to 15cm (6 in) apart. Bulbs produced by this method should not be saved for replanting as they will go to seed.

The other method of propagation, and that followed by nearly all gardeners, is to plant selected bulbs 20cm (8 in) apart with 30cm (12 in) between the rows. These bulbs may be purchased from most seedsmen during the planting season; alternatively, you may find that friends or neighbours have some to spare. These bulbs come from a non-flowering type of shallot, although occasional flowering shoots may be sent up (especially in a hot, dry season). If flowering shoots appear, pinch them out.

Bulbs of this type may be selected and reselected from year to year; simply pick out some medium-sized bulbs that are quite firm and of good shape and colour, and put them on one side when the crop is sorted for use.

It is sometimes recommended that shallots should be pushed into the soil until only their tips are showing, but this is not the best method of planting. Pushing them in will often leave them sitting on a hard pan of soil and the roots, in trying to penetrate this hard layer, will tend to push the bulbs upwards.

A much better way is to take out a little hole with the tip of a trowel and sit the bulb in the hollow. Pull the soil back until just the shoulders and tip of the bulb are showing.

Tending the plants

Birds can be a menace to the newly-planted bulbs by pecking the tips and pulling them out again. Blackbirds seem to be particularly guilty. Whether it is curiosity or devilment on their part is hard to say. You can, however, outwit them by stretching black cotton (positioned a few centimetres above the bulbs) between sticks. Pea guards placed over the bulbs also give excellent protection. Once the tips show green the bulbs have rooted and the danger is over.

During the summer keep the plants free from weeds but do not hoe too close to the bulbs. When the clusters of bulbs have formed and are approaching maturity, draw a little soil away from them with your fingers to aid ripening.

Lifting and drying

The time to lift the bulbs is when the foliage has yellowed, a process that begins at the leaf tips. This may tie in with the longest day, if the weather has been hot and dry, but in many seasons may be two or three weeks later.

Ease the clusters of bulbs with a fork before pulling them out. Do not split

Left: Dutch Yellow shallots, slightly larger than the red varieties, will often keep for up to 12 months

131

Left: (top) ease the clusters of bulbs with a fork and leave them in clumps to dry; (bottom) spicy and sweet Giant Red is a heavy cropper

them up at this stage but leave them in clumps to dry.

In a dry season drying the bulbs presents no problems. They can be left on the soil surface and turned occasionally. If the weather is wet or showery the roots are liable to take hold of the soil again. To prevent this, remove them to a hard path, or anywhere outdoors where they will not be in contact with the soil. One useful method is to put a few cloches over them, leaving the ends open so that the wind can blow through.

Storing the bulbs

When the clusters are quite dry they can be broken up. Check each bulb for any sign of disease and don't store any that are diseased. Correct storage of the bulbs is important. On no account should they be stored in bags (except net ones) or in deep boxes, because they will heat up and go bad. Spread them out thinly in a light, cool place. The shallow tomato trays with a leg at each corner, that can be bought from local greengrocers, make excellent containers for onions and shallots. In good storage conditions the bulbs will keep sound for eight or nine months.

Pests and diseases

Shallots may sometimes be attacked by the onion fly or by onion white rot disease, but such attacks are not common. For the most part they are easy to grow and trouble free.

Onion fly This pest lays its eggs at the base of the plant during early and mid summer (May and June) and the grubs burrow into the soil and attack the immature bulbs. Affected plants turn yellow and then collapse. Pull them up and burn them, making sure there are no larvae left in the soil. The best safeguard is to apply calomel dust on each side of the rows.

White rot Fungus disease that causes the leaves of the plants to turn yellow and die. Roots rot and the base of the bulb is covered with a white mould. There is no cure and diseased plants must be burned.

RECOMMENDED VARIETIES

Giant Red Mild, spicy and sweet; crops heavily and stores well.
Dutch Yellow Slightly larger than the red shallot; will often keep for nearly a year.

PERENNIALS

ASPARAGUS

Asparagus has a large, fibrous root system and needs plenty of room. It is perennial, and takes several years before it comes into full production.
To maintain a regular supply during the cutting season you will need at least twenty-five plants – the minimum number, incidentally, that many growers will supply. This makes it difficult to fit an asparagus bed into a small vegetable plot, but the small grower is not ruled out entirely. It is possible to compromise and be satisfied with a dozen plants in a single row.

Asparagus is easy to grow once its permanent bed has been well prepared.

Other than thorough preparation there are several factors you should consider before committing yourself to growing it. First, with this crop, you cannot expect a rapid return for your time, money and effort. Two or three years must elapse before it produces tender stalks that are ready to eat. Furthermore, if you are expecting to move house in the near future then your successor will be the one to benefit from your asparagus bed, just as it is beginning to give a good yield.

Finally, asparagus is space-consuming. For an average family you will need a minimum of 25 plants, planted 45cm (18 in) apart, in rows 90cm (3 ft) apart.

However, there is no reason why you shouldn't grow one or two other quick-maturing crops between the stalks. A few Tom Thumb lettuce, for instance, or a sprinkling of radish can be sown and harvested without interfering with the growth of the asparagus plants.

If none of these considerations deter you, then your asparagus bed will be a worthwhile investment that can continue to yield for 20 years or more.

Choosing the site
The soil of an asparagus bed must be rich but, within reason, it can vary from fairly heavy to quite light. It should also be a soil that does not dry out too easily, nor must it hold excessive water and become waterlogged in winter. In fact, regardless of soil type, it is always best to grow asparagus on a slightly raised bed. The bed should receive as much sun as possible and it should be sheltered from very strong winds.

Preparing the ground
A light-to-medium loam in which the roots can spread freely is best for asparagus, but fine crops can be grown in heavier soils providing the drainage is good. If drainage is poor dig the plot over, digging in as much well-rotted manure or compost as possible, and then raise the bed with about 30cm (12 in) of good topsoil. On light to medium soils double dig the site incorporating as much manure or compost as you can spare. Gardeners living near the sea can use seaweed, as this is excellent for asparagus.

Prepare a strip 3m (10 ft) wide so that the spreading roots will be able to find plenty of food. The site should be an open, sunny one with, if possible, some shelter from the prevailing wind.

Asparagus may be grown either on the flat, in rows 60cm (24 in) apart, or in ridges, 1·2m (4 ft) apart. Many people prefer ridging as it gives a greater length of blanched stem and makes cutting easier. Three rows on the flat or two rows in ridges is the usual arrangement, with 45cm (18 in) between plants.

*Left: shoots develop ferny stems in summer
Below: a grand crop of sticks will reward work and patience with the asparagus bed*

Raising or buying plants

You can either raise plants from seed or buy them as one- or two-year-old plants from nurserymen or specialist growers. Don't buy three-year-old plants; their longer roots take too long to re-establish themselves.

Sow the seeds in late spring (April) in drills 5cm (2 in) deep and 38cm (15 in) apart. The seeds will germinate more quickly if they are soaked in water overnight before sowing. When the seedlings are about 15cm (6 in) high thin them to stand 30cm (12 in) apart.

Asparagus produces both male and female plants; the females are easy to identify as they bear the berries that contain the seeds. It is generally considered that the males – having to expend no energy on reproducing – give the heaviest crop. However, as the ratio of males to females is about equal it is very difficult, unless you grow a large number of plants, to select all males. It is more important to make sure that the best plants of either sex are saved for growing on. Strong, healthy plants will be easier to pick out in the second season.

As to variety, Connover's Colossal is an excellent choice, producing an early crop of thick, succulent stalks

Transplanting the crowns

Whether your plants are raised from seed or bought, the planting procedure is the same. Plant out in late spring (April). Take out trenches 30cm (12 in) wide and 30cm (12 in) deep, then return enough soil into the trench to make a ridge about 25cm (9 in) in height. The roots of asparagus are long and spidery and the best method of planting is to sit the plants on the ridge with the roots trailing down each side. It is most important to remember that the roots must never be allowed to dry out. Do not lift them, or unpack them (if bought in) until you are ready to plant them, and fill in the trench as each plant is put in. Try to have the ground prepared beforehand so that they can be unpacked and planted as soon as they arrive. The crowns, when planted, should be about 8–10cm (3–4 in) below the soil surface.

Tending growing plants

No sticks should be cut during the year after planting; leave the plants to make their fern (leaves) unchecked. If you are growing the plants in two rows then you can grow a catch crop of lettuces, radishes, young roots or French beans in that first season. In the autumn, when the fern has yellowed, cut it down to leave about 2–3cm (1 in) of stem and clear away

and burn the cut foliage to help minimize any pest or disease problems. Remove all weeds by pricking the soil over, *lightly*, with a fork, then mulch the bed with manure or compost. In mid spring (March) rake the bed clean and then apply a good, general fertilizer at about 70–100g per sq m (2–3 oz per sq yd).

In the second year after planting, if two-year-old crowns were used, you can cut a few spears (stems) but limit the number to three or four from each plant. In the third season (when the plants will be four or five years old) you can cut them over a period of about a month. After this, the bed will be in full production.

To grow the plants by the ridge method, dig out a shallow trench from between the two rows after the autumn

clean-up, and heap it up over the crowns to form a ridge. In mid spring (March) after applying the dressing of spring fertilizer, fork the ridges over lightly and then mound them up again with a hoe. When you have finished cutting, level the ridges out again.

The maintenance of an established bed then falls into the same routine of cutting off the foliage and mulching in autumn, followed by a fertilizer dressing in the spring. A 'bonus' that asparagus appreciates once it is established is a yearly dressing in late spring and early summer (late April or May) of agricultural salt at around 70g per sq m (2 oz per sq yd).

If the weather is dry in late summer and early autumn (July and August) then you must keep the bed well watered as it is

Below: dig trench 30cm (12 in) deep and wide, then form ridge 25cm (9 in) high. Rest asparagus crown on top, spread out roots and cover to original soil level

Above: to cut asparagus sticks, use a sharp, narrow-bladed knife. Follow the stem down through soil and cut neatly about 8–10cm (3–4 in) below soil level

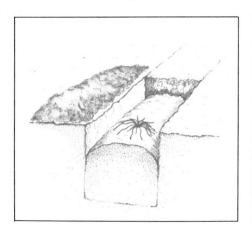

RECOMMENDED VARIETIES

Connover's Colossal Probably the best-known variety; early and reliable with thick, succulent spears.
Martha Washington Tender, delicious and a prolific cropper; has some resistance to asparagus rust.
Brocks Imperial (F.1 hybrid) Early and vigorous, producing large crops of uniformly thick spears.
Suttons Perfection A reliable, standard variety available as two-year-old roots.

during this period that the plants have to produce their ferny foliage which provides the crowns with food for the following season.

It does the crowns no good if the fern stalks are blown about in high winds, so some form of staking is usually necessary. One good way of doing this is to push in bamboo canes at intervals, and then run string around and between them to support the ferns.

Harvesting the spears

The cutting period for an established bed runs from late spring to mid summer (April to June), varying a little according to district and season. A good general rule is to cut for eight weeks after you start cutting. Resist any temptation to prolong the cutting season for another week or two as this will have an adverse effect on the following year's crop. The time to begin cutting is when the first spears are 8–10cm (3–4 in) above soil level. Emerging spears may sometimes be damaged by a late spring frost, but you can guard against this by spreading a little short litter, such as bracken or straw, evenly over the bed.

Cutting asparagus

You can buy a special asparagus saw for cutting, but this is not necessary unless your crop is very large. A narrow-bladed kitchen knife is the next best choice. The cutting must be done with great care or other shoots, still below ground, may be damaged. Sever the sticks about 8–10cm (3–4 in) below soil level. It is at this stage that the ridge system comes into its own, for it is much easier to follow a selected shoot down if it is on a ridge and you can gently draw the soil away.

Cut all the spears as they appear and then grade them according to thickness for cooking. Any surplus can be frozen for later use. Spears less than 6mm ($\frac{1}{4}$ in) in thickness are known as sprue. These are useful in soups.

Pests and diseases

Asparagus is prone to one or two pests and diseases. Good hygiene, in particular the cutting and burning of old, yellowed ferns, is one of the best preventive methods.
Asparagus beetle The main pest of asparagus is the asparagus beetle. The grey larvae of this little creature is particularly destructive in its attacks on the stem and fern during late summer and early autumn (July and August). Examine the ferns from time to time and, if you find the pests, treat with derris dust. A second application, 10–14 days later, will kill any grubs that have emerged from the eggs

since the first dusting.
Asparagus fly This insect lays her eggs in late spring and early summer (April and May) on the young shoots. The yellowish-white maggots tunnel into the shoots, causing them to wilt. Cut out all affected

Below: one new shoot of Asparagus officinalis *appearing during summer among the older stems*

shoots and burn them. Fortunately this pest is not so common as the beetle.
Asparagus rust A fungus disease called asparagus rust appears on the stems and foliage of the plants from late summer (July) onwards. This takes the form of small reddish pustules that turn darker as the season advances. Dusting the foliage with flowers of sulphur will help to keep the fungus at bay.

RHUBARB

Rhubarb is too often relegated to some out-of-the-way corner of the vegetable garden and then forgotten. Yet, given a good start and a little care, it will crop heavily and regularly over a long period.

Four rhubarb plants should be enough for the average family and six for a large one. There are two methods of establishing a rhubarb bed: one is to buy the planting crowns and the other is to raise your own roots from seed. If time is not important, growing from seed is cheaper and not difficult, but planting crowns gives a quicker return.

Preparing the soil

Rhubarb prefers a sunny, open site. It will grow in most soils but does better in a soil that is rich and light. As it occupies the ground for a long time (a good bed should crop for at least ten years) it makes sense to give it a good start. Begin by taking out a trench 90cm (3 ft) wide and a spade's depth, and then break up the subsoil. Before returning the topsoil, fork in some well-rotted manure or compost – about a bucket load to each plant. This should be done several weeks in advance of planting so that the soil has time to settle.

Planting or sowing

You can buy crowns from market stalls or nurserymen during the planting season. Choose roots that have at least one good bud or crown. The best planting time is early winter (November) followed by early to mid spring (February or March).

Sow seed outdoors in mid to late spring (late March or April) in drills 2–3cm (1 in) deep and 38cm (15 in) apart. Thin the plants to stand 15cm (6 in) apart and then let them grow on. It may be possible, by the end of the summer, to see which are the best roots to retain when thinning, but a better selection can be made if the plants are left for another season. You can then pull stalks from the rejected plants before they are discarded; don't pull any from the chosen roots.

In early winter (November) lift the roots carefully and replant them firmly 90cm (3 ft) apart, so that the topmost bud is just about 5cm (2 in) below the level of the surrounding soil.

Pulling the stalks

No stalks should be pulled in the first year after planting. In early autumn (August) the stalks yellow and die down naturally, and the goodness in them is returned to the crowns. By pulling too soon you delay

Champagne Early has a fine flavour

*Above left: give a good mulch in autumn
Above: cover crowns with removable box
or bin to force. Above right: yellow
leaves of forced rhubarb contrast with
those of a normal crop (left)*

the build-up of a good crown with strong buds. In the second season after planting you can pull some (but not too many) of the stalks.

Cut off any seed-heads that push their way up through the leaves (and put them on the compost heap) as the production of seed weakens the plants. Stop pulling rhubarb after mid summer (end of June). If you then want stalks for jam, take one or two from each plant. Always leave some stalks to feed the crowns for the following year.

When pulling rhubarb, slide a hand down the stem as far as possible and then detach the stalk with a quick, outward twist. One peculiarity of this plant, that should not be forgotten, is that while the stalks are edible the leaves should never be eaten as they contain oxalic acid and are poisonous.

Tending the plants
In autumn rake off the withered leaves and mulch the area with some good compost or manure. The goodness from this will be absorbed into the soil with beneficial results. Repeat this dressing annually to help keep the bed in the best possible condition.

When crowns produce only a succession of thin stalks it is a sign that the roots need lifting and dividing. Fork them out, chop them up with a sharp spade and select only the strongest, outlying crowns for replanting. Only divide one or two roots at a time to make sure there is no break in the supply of stalks.

Forcing rhubarb
Rhubarb 'forcing' means persuading it to produce stalks before its normal season. There are two ways of doing this. For the first method you will need a greenhouse with some heating; a temperature of 10°C (50°F) is high enough. Dig up strong-growing crowns in late autumn and early winter (October and November) and leave them on the open ground so that the roots are exposed to the weather. In mid or late winter (December or January) take them into the greenhouse and plant them closely together in the soil border, or under the staging or in a deep box. If using boxes, put the crowns on a few centimetres of good soil and then cover them completely with more of the same soil.

There are two important points to remember with this type of forcing. The soil around the crowns must be kept moist, and they must be forced in the dark. Black polythene makes a useful screening material. If you are using boxes it is a simple matter to invert one box over another.

The disadvantage of this method is that, after forcing, the crowns are exhausted and are of no further use. Therefore you must either buy crowns specially for forcing, or take up valuable space in order to grow extra crowns for the purpose. But as rhubarb freezes well there is no longer the same need to take this trouble in order to have rhubarb early in the year.

The second, and easier, way is to force the crowns *in situ* in the garden by covering selected roots with bottomless boxes, buckets or tubs. An old dustbin, with the bottom knocked out and the lid used as a cover, is ideal for this purpose. The point in having a removable cover is that it enables the crowns to be inspected without disturbing the box or bin. You can gain a little extra warmth by heaping strawy manure or decaying leaves around the bin. Alternatively, fill the bin loosely with hay or straw.

This practice, although giving later stalks than the greenhouse method, has the advantage that the crowns are not seriously harmed. Providing the same roots are not used for forcing each year, they soon recover. The simplest method of all (still giving stalks earlier than from unprotected roots) is to cover the roots in mid winter (December) with 30cm (12 in) of straw. You can leave the straw in place, after the rhubarb has emerged, where it will rot down to form humus.

Pests and diseases
The only calamity likely to affect rhubarb is crown rot. This bacterial disease causes rotting of the terminal bud, and may extend right back to the rootstock. Dig up and burn affected plants.

RECOMMENDED VARIETIES
Victoria Long, cherry-red stalks of excellent quality and flavour.
Champagne Early Fine-flavoured variety with long, bright scarlet stalks.
Glaskin's Perpetual Grows well from seed and produces a good yield over a long period.
Holstein Bloodred Vigorous grower and prolific cropper with juicy, dark red stalks.

ROOT-CROPS

BEETROOT AND LEAF BEET

The first tender, succulent young roots of beetroot are one of the joys of the vegetable gardener's year. Furthermore it is a root which most people can grow without difficulty.

There are three types of beetroot – the globe beet (which is the most popular), the intermediate or cylindrical beet and the long beet. Although the long beet is still grown commercially and for exhibition, it has been superseded to a great extent by the other two kinds. For early sowings always use the globe beet. The intermediate beet is bigger but it grows more slowly, so it is more suitable for maincrop use.

Sowing the seed clusters
Beetroot is unusual in that each 'seed' is really a capsule containing several seeds. Extra care should be taken, therefore, to sow thinly. You can sow early crops in a continuous row, but where the maincrop and late sowings are concerned, it is better to sow one or two seed clusters at 10cm (4 in) intervals and then thin to the strongest plant. The drills should be 2–3cm (1 in) deep and 30cm (12 in) apart.

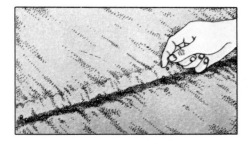

Sow seed capsules thinly at intervals

Early sowings
For an early crop, sow in early spring (February) in a cold frame or under cloches. A barn cloche will take three rows, 23cm (9 in) apart. Outdoor sowings can begin after the middle of spring (after mid March). Although the beetroot is a biennial plant, forming a root in its first year and seed in the second, it can telescope this process if sown early, and throw up seed stalks in the first year. Gardeners describe this as 'bolting'. For these early sowings, therefore, choose a variety with some resistance to bolting.

Maincrop sowings
Do not sow maincrop beetroot too early – towards the end of early summer (mid May to early June) is a good time. If you

are sowing in late summer (July), go back to using the small, globe beet as these are the quickest to mature, providing the summer is not too hot and the autumn mild. They will give tender young roots for use in late autumn and early winter (October and November).

Long beetroot need a deep, fertile soil, free from stones. They should be thinned to 23cm (9 in) apart with 38–45cm (15–18 in) between the rows.

Tending beetroot
In periods of drought give the beetroot a good soaking of water to keep them

growing. Dry weather tends to affect the eating quality of the roots; it is also one cause of the plants 'bolting'.

Be very careful when hoeing beetroot; once the leaves have begun to hide the roots do not hoe too close to the rows. A tiny nick at this stage will turn into an ugly crack later on; so if need be, hand weed around the plants.

Harvesting and storing
Beetroot are ready for pulling as soon as they are big enough to use, and some thinning of the earliest sowings can be done in this way. However, it always pays

to do a little preliminary thinning as soon as the plants are big enough to handle. Beetroot is relatively hardy but can be injured by severe frost, and it is wise to lift the roots by about the end of autumn (end of October). The foliage shows the approach of maturity by beginning to lose its bright, fresh colour.

Ease the roots up with a fork and rub off any soil adhering to them. Take great care, when digging up long beet, so that the roots are not damaged. Twist off the tops about 5cm (2 in) from the crown. Long beetroot have a much greater tendency to 'bleed' when cut than the other kinds; to prevent this always twist off their tops.

Sort the roots through, putting on one side any that are cracked or damaged for immediate use, and store the remainder in boxes of peat, sand or soil – a thin layer of roots followed by a layer of the medium, until the box is full. The medium should be just damp enough to stop the roots from shrivelling. An alternative method is to make a little clamp (as you do for carrots) in the garden.

Other types of beetroot

In addition to the ordinary beetroot there are several leaf beets that make excellent vegetables. Here the process is reversed, for it is the leaves which are used and not the roots. All the leaf beets throw up flowering stems in their second year. Let these run up (but not to seeding point), then chop them up and put them on the compost heap.

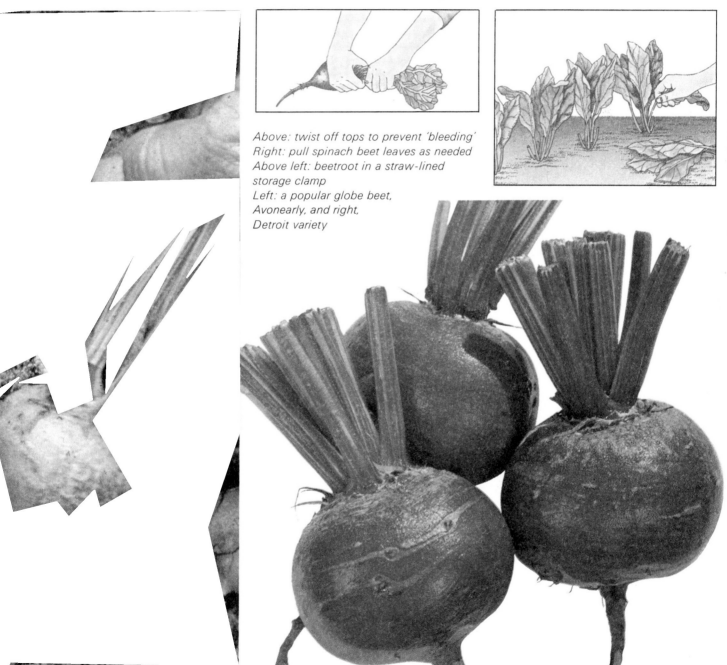

Above: twist off tops to prevent 'bleeding'
Right: pull spinach beet leaves as needed
Above left: beetroot in a straw-lined storage clamp
Left: a popular globe beet, Avonearly, and right, Detroit variety

Spinach beet Probably the best known of the spinach beets and a substitute for spinach. It also appears in the catalogues as Perpetual Spinach. The roots, when at their peak, produce lots of thick, fleshy leaves which you can boil like spinach, but without boiling them down nearly so much. To harvest, take a few leaves from each plant; fresh leaves will grow in their place.

Sow spinach beet in mid or late spring (March or April) in rows 2–3cm (1 in) deep and 38–45cm (15–18 in) apart. Thin the plants to 23cm (9 in). They require no other attention, except for hoeing and watering in dry weather. A good row of spinach beet will give pickings for a year; but if you make a sowing in early autumn (August), this will give plenty of young leaves for picking in the spring. The advantage of an early autumn (August) sowing, where space is at a premium, is that you can use it as a follow-on crop to some of the earlier vegetables.

Seakale beet or Swiss chard The plant produces large fleshy leaves with a broad white mid-rib. This is a dual-purpose vegetable, for in addition to using the leaves as spinach, the broad mid-ribs can be cut out, chopped in pieces and used as a substitute for seakale *Crambe maritima*, which is grown for its tender shoots that must be forced.

Sowing times and distances, and cultivation are the same as for spinach beet, and the early autumn sowing is particularly useful where space is a problem. The seed is usually listed as seakale beet or Swiss chard, but there is now an F.1 hybrid called Vintage Green, which is said to be more vigorous and prolific. Spinach beet and seakale beet (Swiss chard) are both forms of *Beta vulgaris cicla*, but the latter provides leaves as well as mid-rib shoots for eating.

Ruby chard An ornamental form of Swiss chard with long, bright red stalks and crumpled leaves and can be cooked in the same way as seakale beet. Sowing and cultivation are as for seakale beet.

Below: Boltardy, a magnificent example of a globe beetroot
Bottom: two forms of Swiss chard, seakale beet (left) and ruby chard (right)

Pests and diseases
Blackfly and boron deficiency can be a problem when growing beetroot.
Blackfly Keep a close watch for this insect and spray with derris at the first sign of trouble.
Boron deficiency Causes the heart leaves to turn black, and black spots appear inside the roots. If you have encountered this trouble before, take preventive action by watering the plants with a foliar feed containing trace elements.

RECOMMENDED VARIETIES

GLOBE BEETROOT
Boltardy (resistant to bolting)
Avonearly (resistant to bolting)
Early Bunch (resistant to bolting)
Crimson Globe
Burpee's Golden (for leaves and roots)
Snowhite
Detroit Little Ball (late sowings)

INTERMEDIATE BEETROOT
Cylindra
Formanova

LONG BEETROOT
Cheltenham Green Top
Long Blood Red

SEAKALE BEET/SWISS CHARD
Vintage Green (F.1 hybrid)

CARROTS

Carrots are a highly nutritious vegetable, a rich source of vitamin A. By making successional sowings and storing carefully you can have a supply for most of the year. Furthermore, they are a crop that yields a high return from a small area.

In length carrots may be short, intermediate or long. In shape they may be round, cylindrical with a blunt end (known as stump-rooted or short-horn), or tapering. From a harvesting point of view they fall roughly into four groups: early round; early stump-rooted (picked young in bunches); intermediate and long. The intermediate and long carrots are grown for storing and using during the winter months; they may either be stump-rooted or tapering.

If space in the garden is at a premium it may be necessary to drop intermediate and long (maincrop) varieties from the cropping programme and concentrate on 'bunching' carrots—young carrots from the early stump-rooted varieties.

Soil requirements
The ideal carrot soil is a light but deep loam which does not dry out too quickly. Such soils are found naturally in various parts of the country, although they are not widespread. Fortunately, carrots will do reasonably well in most soils, with the exception of sticky clays and very light soils. In heavy loams they may split in wet weather, and in shallow soils only the stump-rooted varieties are suitable. In stony soil they may become misshapen or the roots may fork.

Fresh manure is not suitable for carrots as it may also cause forking roots, but you can use well-rotted manure or compost if it is dug or forked in a week or two before sowing. The tap root (main root) of a carrot should be able to go straight down into a soil where the food values are evenly distributed; a site previously well-manured and cultivated for a crop like potatoes is ideal. Before sowing rake in a balanced fertilizer, such as Growmore, at 70g per sq m (2 oz per sq yd).

Sowing under glass
If a heated frame is available, sow round or stump-rooted carrots in late winter (January). It is better to delay sowing in a cold frame or under cloches until early spring (mid-February). Make up a bed, about 23cm (9 in) deep, of prepared soil in the frame and sow the seeds thinly in rows 15cm (6 in) apart. The soil should be a good, riddled loam with some coarse garden sand and peat added. (The John Innes formula of 7 parts loam, 3 parts peat and 2 parts sand is a good guide.)

If using one of the modern glass-to-ground frames, fork over the bed, removing any large stones, and add some well-moistened peat and the balanced fertilizer. For sowing under cloches, prepare the soil strip in the same way. A large barn cloche 58cm (23 in) wide will take four rows of carrots sown 15cm (6 in) apart or five rows sown at 10cm (4 in) apart. Prepare the soil in good time so that you can put down the cloches three or four weeks before sowing. This will warm up the soil and give the crop a better start.

Below: easing up carrots with fork before lifting. Below left: prime examples of stump-rooted Chantenay Red Cored

143

Outdoor sowings

Sow (thinly) outdoors from mid spring (mid March) until late summer (mid July). Make the intermediate maincrop sowings in early summer (May or early June). It used to be recommended to sow considerably earlier than these times, but it has been found that later sowings are more likely to escape the carrot fly.

Long carrots should be sown by early summer (mid May); so limit late spring (April) sowings to small sowings of the early stump-rooted varieties which can be harvested quickly before the long varieties go in. Stump-rooted varieties can be used again in late summer (July) to give tender young roots for pulling in autumn. For outdoor sowings, allow 20–23cm (8–9 in) between rows for early short-horn varieties and 25–30cm (10–12 in) for maincrops.

Block method Another way of growing carrots is to sow a block of six rows only 8–10cm (3–4 in) apart. If sowing more than one block put a 60cm (2 ft) wide path between blocks. Plants kept in rows are easier to weed. The seeds in the blocks can be sown broadcast but this means more hand-weeding. Eventually the foliage takes over and stops further weeds from growing. An old table knife, heated and then bent over at the end, makes a useful tool for hoeing such narrow rows. The block method is space-saving and gives a heavier crop over a given area, but the individual roots may be a little smaller.

Thinning the seedlings

Theoretically you should sow carrots so thinly that no thinning out is necessary. But as this is hardly practical, just aim to sow as thinly as possible.

While some thinning can be left until the pulled roots are big enough to use, always make a preliminary thinning to 2–5cm (1–2 in). Thin maincrops to stand 8–10cm (3–4 in) apart, and the late summer (July) sowings to 5–8cm (2–3 in). Do this as soon as the plants are big enough to handle. With the late summer (July) sowings it is essential to thin the plants as early as possible or they will not have time to make usable roots.

In dry weather water the rows well before thinning. Afterwards, always firm the soil back with your feet and water again. Never leave thinnings lying around as they may attract the carrot fly. Drop them into a bucket as they are pulled out and put them on the compost heap. Do

Top: round carrots are particularly good on shallow soils. Left: cylindrical Early Nantes is excellent for the first spring sowings in frames or under cloches

not make early pullings from the maincrop rows as this also helps the carrot fly by leaving uncovered soil in which eggs can be laid; leave the roots in until harvest time comes round.

Lifting and storing
Lift and store maincrop carrots for the winter months. Although in theory carrots are hardy enough to spend the winter outdoors, in practice it is better to dig them up. Slug damage may occur during mild periods and heavy rains can cause cracking if they are left in the ground too long.

Lift the roots in late autumn or early winter (the end of October). By that time the foliage will have lost its rich green and turned a dull colour. Carefully ease up the roots with a fork before pulling them out, and rub off any soil. Cut the tops off

Cover them with a layer of hay, straw, dried bracken or any dry litter which will not rot, and cover this, in turn, with about 10–15cm (4–6 in) of soil, leaving a wisp of the covering material sticking out of the top as an air vent to prevent the carrots going off. A heavier soil covering is not necessary. Although slight frost will not harm the carrots if it penetrates into the clamp, it is wise to leave them undisturbed until the frost has gone. In mid spring (March) push off the soil covering or the roots will rapidly make new growth. Rub off any new shoots that may have formed, and transfer the carrots to a box for use.

Pests and ailments
The foliage of healthy, growing carrots should be a rich, lustrous green. If it loses this richness, suspect either greenfly or carrot fly.

of spraying. Weathered soot (soot from house chimneys which has been stored under cover for about six months) is also a help in keeping the fly away and has a slight nitrogenous value. Although later sowings often escape the flies, they are not immune.

Bright sunlight Sometimes causes greening of the roots at the shoulders (just below the leaf stems). Although this is not a serious ailment, it does detract from their appearance. Prevent this problem by drawing a little soil up over the tops of the roots if they are exposed. Where carrots are grown close together the leaves will give adequate protection.

Below: for indoor storage, pack carrots head to tail between layers of dry sand
Bottom: carrots can be stored outdoors in a clamp made of straw and soil

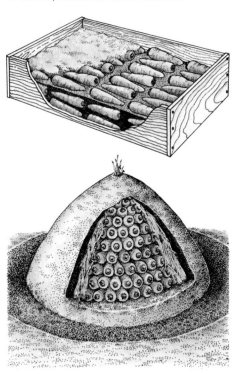

New Red Intermediate, a very long and pointed carrot, is good for winter storing

about 13mm ($\frac{1}{2}$ in) from the crown. Put aside for first use any carrots which are split or damaged.

The sound roots can be stored in one of two ways. For storage in a garage or shed, take a wooden box and put a layer of sand, peat or reasonably dry soil in the bottom. Follow this with a layer of carrots packed head to tail. Alternate layers of covering and carrots until the box is full. The covering medium prevents the roots from shrivelling.

To store carrots outdoors, keep them in a little clamp. Pack the carrots in a conical heap with the roots pointing inward.

Greenfly The delicate, ferny foliage is liable to be attacked by these pests (aphides), but they can be prevented if the crop is sprayed with derris.

Carrot fly Appears any time from late spring to mid summer (April to June) and lays eggs in the soil close to the roots. As the maggots hatch and attack the roots, the foliage first takes on a reddish tinge and then turns yellow. The little cracks and tunnels made in the roots are often enlarged by slugs and wireworms until the vegetables are of little value. Prevent carrot fly by dusting the seed-drills with an insecticide such as BHC before the seeds are sown, or by spraying the young plants with a trichlorphon-based insecticide. Do not eat the vegetables within three weeks

RECOMMENDED VARIETIES

EARLY ROUND
Parisian Rondo

EARLY STUMP-ROOTED (SHORT-HORN)
Amsterdam Forcing
Early Horn
Early Nantes

MAINCROP SHORT
James' Intermediate
Chantenay Red Cored
Autumn King

MAINCROP LONG
St Valery
New Red Intermediate

PARSNIPS

Parsnips are a hardy root crop and easy to grow – an ideal vegetable for the beginner. The only important point to remember is that they require a long growing season.

Parsnips do best in deep, loamy soil (shallow, stony ground is suitable only for the stump-rooted varieties). Grow them on ground that was well-manured for a previous crop; fresh manure can cause the roots to fork. If your soil is not already limed, rake in a dressing of garden lime at 70g sq m (2 oz per sq yd).

When to sow
Start sowing in early to mid spring (February to March), when the soil is easily worked to a fine tilth. You can sow as late as mid to late spring (mid April) and still get good-sized roots.

Make shallow drills (furrows) with a hoe or side of a rake, 2·5cm (1 in) deep and 40cm (15 in) apart, and sow a few seeds at 15cm (6 in) intervals.

Parsnip seeds are very light, so choose a calm day for sowing. (Alternatively you can use pelleted seeds.) They are slow to germinate, and the best way to keep weeds under control is to sow a few fast-germinating radish seeds between each parsnip station (cluster of seeds). When the radishes are large enough for eating, pull them up and hoe the soil.

Parsnip seeds soon lose their viability (ability to germinate), and any left over from a packet should be thrown away.

Smooth, long-rooted Tender and True parsnips (right), show a marked resistance to canker. Equally smooth is the stump-rooted variety (below)

Tending and harvesting
Once the seeds are sown all you have to do is keep the plants free from weeds until their foliage meets. Autumn frost cuts down the foliage but does not harm the roots: in fact, unlike some crops, parsnips taste even better when they have been frosted.

Leave the roots in the ground in winter and dig them up as required. If severe weather threatens, lift a few roots and keep them in a box of sand or dry soil in a shed or garage, so that you have a supply if the ground becomes frozen.

The end of the harvesting season is mid spring (March), when new growth is seen. Dig up all remaining roots at this time before they become woody.

Parsnips are generally free from pests, but there is an incurable disease known as parsnip canker, which is encouraged by cold, damp soil. The symptoms are cracks on the shoulder of the root, followed by brown patches and, in severe cases, rotting of the crown. A wet autumn after a dry spell encourages canker to develop in the root.

Later-sown crops are not so liable to suffer an attack, and once the trouble has been encountered, the next year's seeds should not be sown before late spring (April): use a canker-resistant variety.

RECOMMENDED VARIETIES
Improved Hollow Crown Long, well-shaped roots.
Tender and True Long, smooth roots.
Offenham Stump-rooted, with broad shoulders.
The Student Intermediate roots of good quality.
Avonresister Small, conical roots. This variety has some resistance to parsnip canker.

RADISHES

The humble radish ought to be the easiest of all vegetables to grow. Germination is usually good and the growing time is short. In practice, however, many gardeners confess to disappointments. The failure usually lies in two simple and easily-corrected faults—sowing too deeply and too thickly.

There are two sorts of radish—the popular summer kind and the less-well-known winter radish.

Radishes prefer a light-to-medium, fertile loam; they do not like cold, wet soils. The best radishes are those that are grown quickly. The summer radishes are better known, and if it takes them more than six weeks to reach the pulling stage they will usually be 'woody' (tough and stringy) rather than 'hot'.

A soil that was manured for the previous crop is the best choice. If there is some good, well-rotted compost available it can be pricked into the top few centimetres of soil. It is a good plan to mix this with equal parts of a good brand of moistened peat, to keep the soil damp.

SUMMER RADISHES

The summer varieties may be round, oval or long. For early forcing and growing under cloches the round varieties are to be preferred. Where successional sowings are to be made it is not economical to buy the seed in small packets. Buy in larger packets or by the 28g (1 oz). Nowadays, several seedsmen offer packets of mixed radish seeds. These are a good buy for the main sowings as they prolong the period of pulling.

How to sow

Make small, successional sowings to avoid having too many come ready at

Three recommended varieties for summer: quick-growing Scarlet Globe (above left) has crisp, delicately-flavoured flesh; sweet-tasting Icicle (right) – seen with globe-shaped Sparkler – is also quick growing and crisp; and king-sized Red Prince (above) is a juicy, tasty newcomer

once, for the roots should be pulled when they are at their best. Radishes are the ideal intercrop and should never need to have ground reserved especially for them. They can be grown between rows of peas or beans, on the sides of celery trenches, or in the spaces reserved for brassicas; anywhere, in fact, where there is a patch of ground that will not be needed for the next six to eight weeks.

Radishes are also useful as 'markers'. If a few seeds are trickled along the drill when slow-growing crops such as parsnips, onions or parsley are sown, the radishes will come through first, thus enabling you to identify the rows and hoe between them before the other seedlings are through.

Sowings can begin in early spring (February) in frames or under cloches, or in mid spring (March) outdoors. Where lettuces have been sown under cloches, a single line of radishes may be sown

between the rows of lettuce. These will be cleared before the lettuce need all the room available.

Successional sowings outdoors can be made at 10–14 day intervals. From late summer until mid autumn (late June until early September) make the sowings, if possible, in the lee of taller subjects such as peas or beans so that the radishes will have some shade for part of the day.

Except for single rows under cloches, do not sow the seeds in a v-shaped drill; instead sow thinly in a broad band about 15cm (6 in) wide. Make the sowing on the soil surface and then rake thoroughly with a rake or cultivator. This will put

Flea beetle This pest eats holes in the leaves and can decimate a crop if not checked. Prevention is better than cure, so as soon as seedlings are through the soil, dust them with derris. Renew the application if rain washes it off. When the plants are past the seedling stage, the danger is over.

Birds Sparrows particularly may attack the seedlings, but a few strands of black cotton criss-crossed over the rows will be enough to drive them away.

WINTER RADISHES

The winter radishes are not nearly so well known as the summer ones, but they are not difficult to grow and seed is easy enough to obtain as most seedsmen stock the main varieties. There are both round and long types. They are much larger than summer radishes, with roots weighing up to 500g (1 lb) each. They can be used as a vegetable but are generally sliced thinly for use in winter salads.

The seeds should not be sown until late summer (July). This makes them useful as a follow-on crop to some of the earlier sowings. Sow the seeds thinly in drills 13mm ($\frac{1}{2}$ in) deep and 25cm (10 in) apart, and when the plants are large enough to handle, thin them to stand 20cm (8 in) apart. Keep the plants clean by hoeing and weeding and see that they do not lack water during dry periods.

The roots will be ready for use from late autumn (October) onwards. They will store well in boxes of dry sand or soil in a little clamp, but in light-to-medium loams they can be left in the ground to be dug as required. In severe weather cover the roots with a little straw or litter, to prevent them deteriorating.

most of the seeds just beneath the soil surface, which is deep enough.

Thinning and tending
If any thinning is necessary, do it as soon as the plants are big enough to handle. Ideally one plant to every 6 sq cm (1 sq in) is enough. It is not customary to weed radishes as the crop is on the ground for such a short time. Generally speaking, each radish patch can be pulled over three or four times. Any plants that are left after this will have failed to develop properly or will be too tough, so hoe them up with the weeds and put them on the compost heap.

Two recommended varieties for winter: Black Spanish, available in both round (above left) and long (above) forms, and China Rose (top). Like all winter radishes, they are much larger than summer varieties and can be used as vegetable or salad

Radishes should never be allowed to dry out, especially on light soils; in dry periods give them plenty of water to keep them moving.

Pests and diseases
Flea beetle and birds are the main enemies of the radish grower.

RECOMMENDED VARIETIES

SUMMER RADISHES

Cherry Belle Globe-shaped and scarlet; good for forcing under cloches.
French Breakfast Red with white tips; a long radish and one of the best known.
Icicle Long, all-white radish.
Scarlet Globe Early and crisp.
Red Prince Recent introduction, two or three times the usual size.
Yellow Gold Egg-shaped, yellow radish with white flesh.

WINTER RADISHES

China Rose Oval root, about 15cm (6 in) in length; rose-coloured with white flesh.
Black Spanish Black skin and white flesh; available in both round and long forms.
Mino Early Japanese introduction with white flesh and a mild flavour.

SALSIFY, SCORZONERA AND HAMBURG PARSLEY

Salsify, scorzonera and Hamburg parsley are three lesser-known root vegetables but they are not difficult to grow and worth trying for a change. Their general cultivation is the same in each case.

Prepare the site for salsify, scorzonera and Hamburg parsley by digging and manuring it in the autumn. If this is not possible, try to choose a strip that was manured for the preceding crop. Fresh manure should not be used as it may cause the roots to split and fork. Stony soils can have the same effect. A light to medium, fertile loam, with a good depth of fine soil, is ideal.

However, by using the 'crowbar method' it is possible to produce fine-quality roots in less suitable soils. To do this you make holes with a crowbar 30–45cm (12–18 in) deep and 7–10cm (3–4 in) wide at the top, and fill them with a good compost such as the J.I. No 3 or a home-made mixture on similar lines. Tamp the soil down lightly and then sow a few seeds in the centre of each hole. When the seedlings are through, thin to the strongest plant. The holes should be 25cm (9 in) apart. Good, strong roots can be obtained by this method, even in heavy soils.

Cultivation of all three root vegetables consists mainly of hoeing and weeding. Should the weather become very dry, a good watering followed by a mulch of peat or compost will help the plants to keep going. None of these vegetables is much troubled by pests or diseases.

Salsify, scorzonera and Hamburg parsley can all be lifted as required, but it does pay to dig up and store a few roots if a period of severe frost seems likely. It is during such periods, when other vegetables may be difficult to gather, that these roots are most appreciated. The alternative, if storage space is at a premium, is to spread some peat or short litter between the rows. This will 'turn away' most of the frost and make it possible to dig some of the roots even though the surrounding soil is frozen hard.

SALSIFY

This root is also known as the 'vegetable oyster' as the flavours are thought to be similar. The plant is a biennial with narrow, grey-green leaves and a cream-coloured root.

Previous page, above: salsify crop, well established after two months' growth; and below: salsify Mammoth — the roots are delicious boiled or fried

Above: Scorzonera Russian Giant deserves to be better known. The roots (below) have a delicate flavour and after lifting they can be stored in sand or soil

Sow in mid or late spring (March or April) in drills 2–3cm (1 in) deep and 30–38cm (12–15 in) apart. Thin the plants, when large enough to handle, to 10cm (4 in) apart and later take out every other plant.

Harvesting is from late autumn (October) onwards. The roots can be stored in a box, with alternate layers of roots and sand or soil, but in most soils there is no necessity to lift them and they will be fresher if lifted as required.

In lifting the roots take care not to damage them or they will 'bleed'. Should any be damaged use them as soon as possible and do not attempt to store them. The flesh of salsify soon discolours when exposed to the open air. To prevent this, rub lemon juice on the cut surfaces.

If all the roots have not been used by the spring those that are left in the ground will produce tender new growths. These green shoots are known as 'chards', and they can be cut and cooked when they are about 15cm (6 in) in length. The shoots can be used green, or they may be blanched and used like the chicons of chicory.

SCORZONERA

These roots are often linked with salsify and in some regions are known as 'black salsify', but the plant is a perennial and not a biennial. It has narrow, pointed strap-like leaves and long, tapering dark-skinned roots with white flesh that are thinner than salsify. In the past the root was used as a medicine as well as for culinary purposes, and it is still said to be good for the digestion.

Do not peel the roots; when they have been steamed or boiled you can remove the skin quite easily.

Sow in mid or late spring (March or April) in drills 2–3cm (1 in) deep and 38cm (15 in) apart, and thin the seedlings to stand 20cm (8 in) apart.

Like salsify the roots are used during the autumn and winter and can be stored in boxes of sand or soil. However, they are just as hardy as salsify and it is better to dig them as required. Lift them carefully as the long, thin roots are easily broken. If the roots do not reach a good size in their first season – 5cm (2 in) thick at the top can be considered a good size – leave them down for a second season.

HAMBURG PARSLEY

This root is shorter than those of salsify and scorzonera. It sometimes appears in the seed catalogues as 'turnip-rooted parsley'. In shape and size however the roots are like parsnips but with a much smoother skin. The flavour is distinct and pleasant, somewhere between parsley and celery. You can use the parsley-like foliage for garnishing. In the summer pick a few of the tenderest and youngest leaves to add a new flavour to salads.

Sow the seeds in mid or late spring (March or April) in drills 13mm ($\frac{1}{2}$ in) deep and 38cm (15 in) apart. They will grow quite successfully in partial shade. Hamburg parsley is occasionally attacked by parsnip canker, but this is the exception rather than the rule.

The roots are perfectly hardy and can be dug as required during late autumn and winter (October to January). If peeled they tend to discolour and lose some of their flavour. Because the roots are smoother than parsnips, a good wash and light scrubbing is enough to prepare them for cooking. They can also be used in soups or grated for winter salads.

Above right: use foliage of Hamburg parsley for garnish and in salads
Right: distinctively-flavoured roots of the easy-to-grow Hamburg parsley look like parsnips

RECOMMENDED VARIETIES

SALSIFY
Mammoth The best-known variety.
SCORZONERA
Russian Giant The only variety on general offer.
HAMBURG PARSLEY
Usually appears under the parsley entries of seed catalogues and is listed by name only.

TURNIPS AND SWEDES

Turnips are not difficult to grow, have a long season of use and will thrive in any good garden soil which does not dry out too quickly. Swedes are larger and sweeter than turnips; they are also hardier and store well.

Turnips and swedes all belong to the cabbage (brassica) family and their treatment is very similar.

Turnips are grouped according to whether they are ready for harvesting in spring and summer, or in autumn and winter. The autumn and winter varieties can be stored, but spring and summer varieties (which take about 10 weeks to mature) do not store well.

Spring and summer turnips
If you have a cold frame you can make a sowing of turnips in early spring (February). You will need a soil depth of at least 15cm (6 in). A sowing can also be made under cloches – one row for tent cloches and three rows, 25cm (9 in) apart, under barn cloches.

Start outdoor sowings from mid to late spring (mid March) in rows 13mm ($\frac{1}{2}$ in) deep and 30cm (12 in) apart. Sow the seeds thinly along the drill, or else in clusters 15cm (6 in) apart. In either case, thin the plants to some 15cm (6 in) apart. Make successional sowings throughout early summer (May) to mature in late summer and early autumn (July and August). These sowings may suffer if the

Right: Green-top white turnip
Below left: Purple Top swede, one of the most popular varieties

weather is hot and dry as turnips dislike such conditions. It is, therefore, a good plan to site these sowings in the lee of a taller crop; this will give turnips some shade for at least part of the day. Water well in a dry spell. The summer turnips, especially, need to be 'kept moving'; if they take too long to mature they tend to become stringy or woody.

Autumn and winter turnips
Sow autumn and winter varieties in mid summer (June) in drills 13mm ($\frac{1}{2}$ in) deep and 38cm (15 in) apart. These can be grown as a follow-on crop in the ground vacated by the first peas or potatoes. Thin the plants to 20cm (8 in) apart. These varieties take a little longer to mature and will be ready from mid autumn (September) onwards. About the end of autumn (late October) lift any roots that are left and store them in boxes of sand or soil, or in a little clamp in the garden. Leave about 2–3cm (1 in) of stalk on top of the turnip and shorten the roots a little – but do not trim them right back.

Turnip greens
Late varieties of turnip can also be sown in early or mid autumn (August or September) to provide turnip tops for use in the early spring. These turnip greens are rich in iron. For the production of tops, sow the seeds thinly in a continuous row and do not thin them. Allow 30cm (12 in) between the rows.

Pests and diseases
Flea beetle and a condition resulting from boron deficiency are the main enemies.
Flea beetle This attacks the seedlings as soon as they have formed their first leaves. It is often referred to, rather

vaguely, as 'the fly'. A severe attack can cause a row of seedlings to disappear overnight. Do not wait for trouble; as soon as seedlings appear, dust the rows with derris and repeat the application if rain washes the dust off. The danger is over once the plants are through the seedling stage.
Boron deficiency Occasionally turnips may suffer from boron deficiency, a condition which shows itself in a brown rot when the roots are cut open. The remedy is to apply borax; only a tiny quantity is needed – about 2g per sq m (1 oz per 20 sq yd). To obtain an even distribution, mix it with sand.

SWEDES
Swedes are milder and hardier than turnips. Sow the seeds thinly in early or mid summer (May or June), in drills 13mm ($\frac{1}{2}$ in) deep and 40cm (15 in) apart. Thin out to 20cm (8 in) apart.

They are hardy enough to remain outdoors all winter and can be lifted as required. Any remaining in the ground by spring will also produce edible tops.

RECOMMENDED VARIETIES

TURNIPS
Early (spring and summer)
Model White
Early Six Weeks
Snowball
Tokyo Cross (F.1 hybrid)
Late (autumn and winter)
Golden Ball
Manchester Market
Green-top White

SWEDES
Purple Top
Chignecto (resistant to club root)

SALAD AND
FORCING CROPS

AUBERGINES AND SWEET PEPPERS

When in fruit aubergines and sweet peppers are ornamental as well as useful. They are often looked upon as 'luxury' vegetables, too difficult for the average gardener to grow. This is unfortunate, for while they do need glass protection (at least for part of their lives) they are no harder to cultivate than tomatoes, and in milder districts it is possible to grow them outdoors.

The aubergine is also known as the eggplant because the fruits of one variety are white and look like goose eggs. In some catalogues it is listed under this name. The fruits of the more common varieties are purple and may be oblong or oval in shape. They can be sliced and fried, or stuffed like marrows. The capsicum genus includes sweet peppers, the fruits of which can be eaten when unripe and green, or when they have ripened to red or yellow.

Growing from seed
Unlike tomatoes, that are freely available at planting time, the plants of aubergines and sweet peppers are not often to be found, and you will almost certainly have to raise your own. If you are the owner of a greenhouse with some heat, then this is not a difficult process, as the seeds will germinate in a temperature of around 18°C (64°F).

A start can be made in early or mid spring (February or March), according to the facilities available and depending on how the plants are to be grown on afterwards. For instance there is no point in starting too early unless you are growing the plants on in a greenhouse. For planting in frames or under cloches mid spring (March) is early enough to sow, and where an outdoor crop is planned, delay the sowing until late spring (mid April).

Sow the seeds in seed trays filled with J.I. seed compost or in a good, soilless medium, spacing them about 2–3cm (1 in) apart. When the seedlings have formed the first true leaves, prick them out into 9cm (3½ in) pots and grow them on, making sure they have plenty of light. Should you have to delay the final planting, do not let the plants become pot-bound and stand still; move them on into 12cm (5 in) pots.

If you do not have a greenhouse you can still raise a few plants on a warm,

Above right: the large fruits of the vigorous Moneymaker, ready for picking
Right: fine, well-developed examples of Long Purple – delicious when stuffed
Far right: Slice-Rite, a heavy cropper

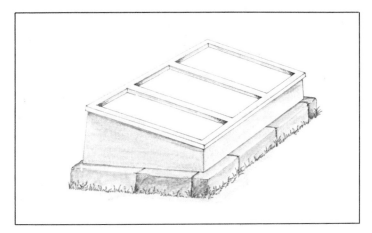

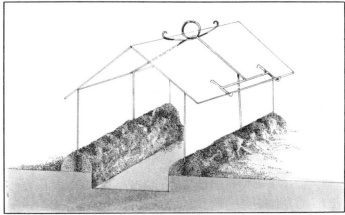

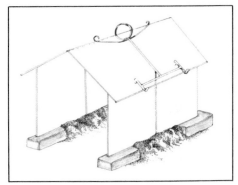

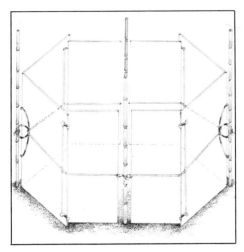

Above left: frame raised on blocks to take tall plants; above right: barn cloche over a trench gives extra space; left: another simple solution – a cloche on bricks with gaps earthed up; below left: cloches can also be stood on end

sunny windowsill. Sow the seeds in a seed tray and then prick them out into separate pots. Keep the pots close to the light and remember to turn them daily so that the plants grow evenly.

Growing on in the greenhouse

In the greenhouse, aubergines and sweet peppers may be planted directly into the soilbed, or you can grow them in pots on the staging. A good plant may reach about 75cm (30 in) in height. A few weeks before planting into the soilbed, fork in some well-rotted compost or manure. When planted out, aubergines should be 60cm (24 in) apart and sweet peppers 45cm (18 in).

For growing in pots use J.I. No 3 or one of the soilless mediums. Should good,

well-rotted compost be available, mix some of this in at a rate of about one part in four. For aubergines the final move should be into 23 or 25 cm (9 or 10 in) pots; sweet peppers will fruit in 18 or 20cm (7 or 8 in) pots.

Frames and cloches

If you are using a frame it is more than likely that you will have been growing an early crop of lettuces or young root vegetables in it. If so, no other preparation will be required. Otherwise make up a mixture as described above.

Similarly, with cloche cultivation, if the ground has already been prepared for a previous crop then no other treatment is necessary. Otherwise fork some compost into the top 15cm (6 in) of soil.

For an outdoor crop choose the sunniest and most sheltered position possible. The foot of a south-facing wall, where the heat is reflected back onto the plants, is always a good choice. Remember that the soil at the base of a wall dries out quickly and water accordingly.

Other suitable places are the corner of a sunny patio where the plants can be grown in pots or tubs, or a conservatory or garden room.

Raising the headroom

One problem that may be encountered is what to do if the plants outgrow the accommodation provided. The old-fashioned type of frame with a sliding light is usually too shallow for aubergines and sweet peppers. You can, of course, use it to protect the plants in the early stages and remove the light when the leaves touch the glass, or you can raise the frame on bricks or concrete blocks.

The newer, all-glass frames are more suitable for these taller crops. Some are span-roofed, which gives welcome additional height in the centre. Special adaptors to raise the height can be bought for large barn cloches such as the Chase type; you can raise them on bricks or blocks. Fewer bricks will be needed if you place them at the corners of the cloches; soil can be drawn up to fill the gaps between the bricks.

Another method of gaining headroom is to set the plants out in a shallow trench. Make the trench some 15cm (6 in) narrower than the width of the frame or cloches. Do not make the trench too deep – about 8cm (3 in) is enough – or the plants will have to make do with the poorer soil below. Place the excavated soil along the edges of the trench to gain another few centimetres of height.

As a final resort, if the plants are still outgrowing their headroom, take off the cloches and stand them on end around the plants. But do remember to anchor them to the ground or a summer gale may badly damage your crop.

Tending growing plants

When the aubergine plants are about 15cm (6 in) high, pinch out the growing point. This makes the plants bush out and produce fruit-bearing laterals.

The same treatment can be given to the sweet peppers but is not always necessary as the plants generally break naturally. A single cane should be used to keep the plants upright.

Keep the plants clean and see that they never dry out. Once the first fruits have set, feed at fortnightly intervals with liquid manure. Remember that the soil must be moist when liquid feed is given; liquid manure should not be applied to dry soil. In dry spells, therefore, it will be necessary to water first. If you are also growing tomatoes you can use your tomato fertilizer for the aubergines and sweet peppers as well.

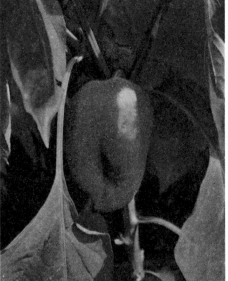

Sweet peppers planted out – red indicates maturity. Two early fruiters are Canape (top right) and New Ace (right) both good for growing outdoors

Pests and diseases
Both of these vegetables are usually free from pests or diseases, the red spider mite being a possible exception.

Red spider mite These little creatures, that live by sucking the sap from the undersides of the leaves, like dry conditions and dislike water. Mottled leaves, that may later turn brown and fall off, denote their presence. Control can be achieved with liquid derris or malathion insecticide. Spraying with clear, tepid water, night and morning, will also help.

Ripening and harvesting
As the fruits of sweet peppers can be used when still green you can begin picking as soon as the fruits are large enough, or else leave them to turn red and develop a stronger flavour; the colder nights of mid to late autumn (late September) will eventually bring growth to a halt.

Pick off the first few flowers that appear, as this will encourage a heavier crop later on in the season.

With aubergines the fruits must be allowed to ripen. This stage is reached once the fruits are glossy and fully coloured. To obtain fruits of a good size, limit each plant to four or five fruits. When these have set, pinch out later fruits as they appear.

CELERY AND CELERIAC

Celery is not one of the easiest vegetables to grow, but it is very rewarding. Home-grown sticks – grown well – are far superior to anything that you can buy.

Celery needs a sunny open position, a rich soil and plenty of water. Very light soils and heavy clays are not suitable unless you try to improve them.

Types of celery

There are several different types of celery that you can grow. Trench celery gives the best sticks but needs plenty of room and attention. Self-blanching celery is easier to grow and, with the introduction of improved varieties, is now nearly as good in quality and flavour. Celeriac is the easiest of all to grow, though probably the least known. It produces a turnip-like, celery-flavoured root that can be grated into salads or boiled as a vegetable.

When and how to sow

The plants of all types can be raised from seed. Start them early as they need a long period of growth. Sow trench celery and celeriac in mid spring (early March) and self-blanching celery in mid to late spring (late March). A greenhouse with some heat is a distinct advantage, especially for trench celery, but plants can be raised from seed sown in a seed pan placed in the sunny window of a warm room. If this method is used it is advisable to start in the early spring (second half of February). Sow the seeds in J.I. seed compost or one of the soilless composts. Growth in the initial stages is slow.

When the seedlings are large enough to handle, prick them off into boxes, spacing them 5cm (2 in) apart all ways, and put them close to the light. If you are putting the trays in a cold frame, provide plenty of ventilation. Gradually harden off the plants in readiness for planting out in early or mid summer (late May or June).

Buying plants

If you do not have the time or the facilities for raising your own plants, buy them at planting time from nurserymen or market stalls. Most of the plants offered will be trench celery. Some self-blanching celery plants can be found but you will rarely see celeriac plants on sale.

When buying plants, choose those that are a healthy green and not too large.

Trench celery

Trench celery comes in white-, pink- or red-stemmed varieties. The white is not quite so hardy as the pink or red and is generally picked first.

Prepare the trench in early or mid spring (February or March) so that the soil has time to settle. Dig out a trench 38cm (15 in) wide for a single row, or 45cm (18 in) wide for a double row, and shovel out the loose soil. Break up the bottom of the trench with a fork and then put in a layer of well-rotted manure or good compost. Do not return all the top-soil at this stage; leave about 8–10cm (3–4 in) of the trench open. (The surplus soil can be spread along the sides of the trench and used to grow a catch-crop – such as lettuce, radish or spring onion.) To give room for earthing-up, leave about 60cm (24 in) on either side of the trench.

Weathered soot (soot that has been stored in the open for at least six months) is excellent for celery. If this is available incorporate it with the soil as the trench is filled up again.

The plants are ready for planting in the trench when they are about 15cm (6 in) high. Use a trowel for planting and space plants and rows 25cm (10 in) apart. If you are growing a double row, the plants in the two rows should be opposite each other as this makes earthing-up easier.

To dig up the sticks, remove the bank of soil at one end and follow the stems down to the root; then thrust the spade well down under it and lever the stick out.

It is a good plan to mark the site of the celery trench with sticks, and to choose a follow-on crop for the next season that will make good use of the enriched soil. A row of cauliflowers is a good choice.

Self-blanching celery

Self-blanching celery does not need earthing-up, and plants of these varieties should be planted on the flat, with 20cm (8 in) between plants and rows. Make short rows so that a block of plants is formed. As the plants grow they will exclude the light from each other, except for the plants on the outside. A simple method of blanching these is to peg boards upright around the block and fill in any gaps between the boards and the plants with straw, bracken, sawdust, or some similar 'short litter'.

A box frame that may have been used for an earlier crop makes an excellent container for self-blanching celery.

Tending growing plants

Cultivation during the growing period (until earthing-up) is the same for all types of celery. Keep the plants free from weeds and see that they never lack water.

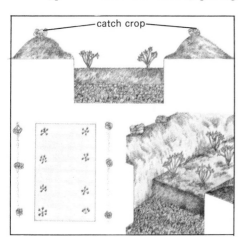

Trench celery in the early stages of growth allows for a catch crop as well

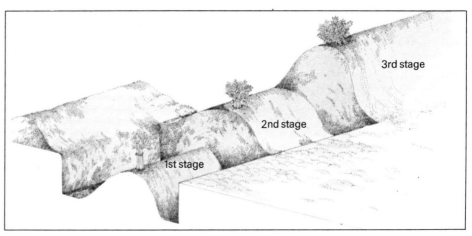

Above: the three stages of earthing-up; leave about two weeks between each one

Right: use overlapping cardboard 'collars' as an alternative method to earthing-up

During late summer and early autumn (July and August) a fortnightly application of liquid manure will help to push the plants along. Soot water, made by stirring a handful or two of soot into each can of water, is also good and has the advantage that slugs dislike it.

Earthing-up

Earthing-up should begin towards mid autumn (the end of August). Choose a dry day for this when the soil is friable. First, remove any suckers from the base of the plants and any small, outer leaves that would be buried. Draw the stems together at the top and hold them firmly with one hand. Then dig out soil from the sides of the trench and bank it up against the stems. As it is difficult to use a spade with one hand, a trowel or hand fork may be used instead. Cover the stems to about a third of their length.

Repeat the process about a fortnight later, this time taking the soil two-thirds of the way up the sticks, and after another two weeks finish off by banking the soil up to the top of the plants so that only the tips are showing. Finish off the bank by patting it smooth with the back of a spade so that surplus water will run off. Three or four weeks after the final earthing the sticks will be ready for use.

At each stage of earthing take care that soil does not fall into the hearts of the plants, or they may rot. One way of preventing this is to tie the stems loosely at the top. Another is to wrap strong paper or cardboard around them before earthing. Corrugated cardboard, with the smooth side against the stems, makes an excellent medium. Ordinary newspaper is not suitable as it will rot before the sticks are ready to use. Using a barrier of this nature also helps to foil the slugs.

In mid to late winter (end of December), if frost threatens, cover the tops

Above: trench celery Giant White shows final depth of soil after earthing-up

Below: Golden Self-blanching should be grown close together to exclude light

of the plants along the ridge with some protective straw or litter.

Trench celery without earthing
An alternative method of growing trench celery (useful on heavy soils where the drainage is poor) is to grow the plants on the flat and dispense with earthing-up, using cardboard collars instead. Overlap the edges of each collar and fill the space between the top of the collar and the tips of the leaves with peat so that light is totally excluded.

Growing celeriac
Celeriac is grown on the flat and does not need blanching. Raise plants from seed as for trench celery in mid spring (March) – with heat, if possible.

When planting, allow 30cm (12 in) between plants and 45cm (18 in) between rows. Planting should be done in early summer (late May). As the roots swell, draw the soil away from them so that the swollen root stands out. Should suckers appear, follow them down to their source of origin and cut them off. In late autumn (October) draw soil up over the roots to protect them from frost.

The roots can be left in the ground all winter, to be used as required; but in heavy soils it is better to lift and store them. Cut off the outer leaves but leave the little tuft in the centre. The roots store well in boxes of sand or dry soil.

Pests and diseases
Celery is subject to several pests and diseases, notably slugs, celery fly maggots and celery leaf spot fungus disease.
Slugs These are the main enemy of the celery family, and every effort should be made to keep them at bay. During the growing season sprinkle slug pellets among the plants or water them with a liquid slug repellant. Renew the slug pellets just before earthing-up.
Celery fly maggots The small white maggots of the celery fly burrow into the leaf tissues leaving blistery trails. At the first sign of trouble, spray with malathion. Remove and burn badly-affected leaves. A very light dusting with weathered soot at fortnightly intervals will often serve to keep the fly away. This should be done in the early morning when the dew is still on the plants.
Celery leaf spot This fungus disease takes the form of small, brown patches with black specks. It spreads rapidly and can be fatal to the plants. Pick off and burn all affected leaves. Spraying with Bordeaux mixture or zineb in the early stages of growth is a good safeguard. If, however the seed has been bought from a reliable source it will have been treated against this disease and there should be no trouble. For this reason surplus celery seed should never be used in the kitchen.

Celeriac variety Globus is easy to grow and gives a fine celery-like flavour

RECOMMENDED VARIETIES

CELERY – trench
Giant White Excellent variety of white celery producing good-quality plants.
White Ice Very flavoursome variety; crisp and almost stringless.
Clayworth Prize Pink Pale pink in colour and has a very sweet flavour.
Giant Pink Produces very long, heavy, pale pink sticks of excellent flavour.
Giant Red Makes robust growth and solid stems; very dark red in colour.

CELERY – self-blanching
Golden Self-blanching Very early variety; economical to grow and excellent for cooking; has solid, golden-yellow hearts with a nutty flavour.
Lathom Self-blanching Highly resistant to bolting; produces stringless sticks of outstanding flavour.
American Green A green celery that is grown in the same way as self-blanching; pale green, crisp, fine-flavoured stems.

CELERIAC
Globus Fine-flavoured roots that are excellent for cooking.
Marble Ball Large, globular roots that produce few sideshoots; fine flavour.

CHICORY AND SEAKALE

Chicory and seakale, although not related, have certain 'cultivation points' in common. Both produce tender, edible young shoots that must be blanched in darkness to prevent them developing a bitter flavour and both can be forced to provide winter crops.

CHICORY

Chicory is a perennial plant but is usually treated as a biennial. The root that it forms in its first season is forced into growth during the winter and early spring. The leaves of the blanched new growths are tightly folded and look rather like small, creamy-white cos lettuce. These new growths are called chicons. They can either be eaten raw in winter salads or used as a cooked vegetable.

A light-to-medium loam is the best soil for chicory, but the plants will succeed in heavier soils. Fresh manure is neither necessary nor advisable as it probably still contains toxic elements that may damage the roots. A soil that was well manured for the previous crop is ideal. Supplement this, before sowing the seeds, with a feed of general fertilizer at some 70g per sq m (2 oz per sq yd).

Sowing and thinning

Sow the seeds in early to mid summer (late May) in drills 13mm ($\frac{1}{2}$ in) deep and 38cm (15 in) apart. If sown too early the plants have a tendency to produce flowers in the first season at the expense of forming roots. When the seedlings are large enough to handle, thin them to 25cm (9 in) apart. Cultivation during the summer months is simply a matter of keeping the plants clean by regular hoeing and weeding.

Storing the roots

In late autumn or early winter (October or November), as the foliage is dying down, lift the roots carefully and store them in a cool, frost-proof place until needed for forcing. One method that saves space indoors is to pack the roots close together in a trench, leaving the foliage intact. Cover the roots with extra soil to keep out the frost.

How to force

To prepare the roots for forcing, cut off the foliage about 2–3cm (1 in) from the crown, taking care not to damage the growing tip, trim off any sideshoots and then shorten the roots to a uniform length of about 20cm (8 in), by cutting the tips.

There are several ways of forcing the roots, but whichever one you choose, it is essential that the chicons should be formed in complete darkness. One method is to use deep boxes and pack the roots upright in moist peat. Then cover them with a 17cm (7 in) deep layer of dry sand, light, sifted soil or more peat. Alternatively you can pack them in 25cm (10 in) pots, invert a second pot over the first one, and cover the drainage hole with a piece of slate to keep out the light. Then place the boxes or pots in a heated greenhouse or take them indoors; a temperature of about 10°C (50°F) is enough to induce growth.

Another method of producing chicons is to force the plants *in situ*, although this method will give you a later crop. The simplest way of doing this is to cut off the foliage and then earth up the roots to a depth of about 17cm (7 in). Alternatively put boards down on either side of the row and peg them upright. Fill in the space between the boards with leaves, peat or sifted soil. In severe weather give extra protection by covering the rows of chicory plants with straw or short litter.

Cutting the chicons

When the points of the chicons protrude through their covering (usually after about one month) they are ready for cutting. Remove the covering with care so

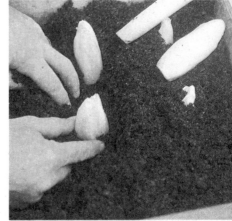

as not to damage the tender young growth, and then cut the chicon off just above the crown.

SEAKALE

Seakale is also a perennial plant and, as the roots crop for a number of years, needs a semi-permanent site. It likes a rich soil and a sunny spot. Prepare the site in autumn or winter by digging in as much manure or good compost as possible, and finish off, 2–3 months later, with a dressing of lime at 70g per sq m (2 oz per

Below left: Witloof chicory – the leaves can be used like spinach in the summer
Bottom, far left: forcing chicory in peat and cutting the forced chicons
Below: Seakale Lily White has very white, sweet shoots
Bottom: preparing seakale root cuttings, and picking a forced crop

sq yd). Seaweed, if you can get it, is an excellent manure for seakale. You can raise the plants either from seeds or root cuttings.

Growing from seed

Seed is the cheapest method of raising plants but it will take you a year longer to produce a plant that is vigorous enough for forcing.

Sow in mid or late spring (March or April) in drills 13mm ($\frac{1}{2}$ in) deep and 30cm (12 in) apart. Thin the plants to stand 15cm (6 in) apart and then leave them until the following mid spring (March). Choose the best plants for transplanting; plant them in their permanent positions in rows 60cm (24 in) apart, with 60cm (24 in) between the plants.

See that the plants do not lack water during the summer months, and in mid summer (June) give a dressing of agricul-

tural salt at about 35g per sq m (1 oz per sq yd). If flowering shoots should appear, cut them out.

Method of forcing

In autumn, when the foliage has died down, the roots are ready for forcing. If you want an early crop then lift them and force them indoors. Pack them close together in boxes or pots in the same way as for chicory, but do not cover the crowns. Simply invert another box or pot over them to keep out the light. A temperature of about 10°C (50°F) is enough to bring them on. Cut and eat the blanched shoots when they are about 20cm (8 in) in length. After forcing in this manner the roots should be discarded.

The easiest method is to force the plants *in situ* by covering them with special seakale pots, large plant pots, boxes or discarded buckets in much the same way as rhubarb. To generate a little more heat, pile leaves or strawy manure around the covering pots or boxes. This method of forcing does not harm the roots. When the last blanched growths have been cut in the spring, cover the crowns with leaves or a little compost and then prick over the soil with a fork.

Propagation from cuttings

If you already have seakale in the garden, then you can take cuttings from the side roots that form on the main roots. These side roots are called thongs. Choose the thongs that are straight and about the thickness of a pencil and cut them into 15cm (6 in) lengths. Cut the top of the root straight across and the bottom slantwise; this solves the difficulty of knowing whether you've planted them right way up.

If the thongs are taken from roots lifted for forcing, tie them in a bundle (making sure to label them) and keep them in sand or soil until planting time in mid spring (March). Plant them with the crowns about 5cm (2 in) below the soil surface.

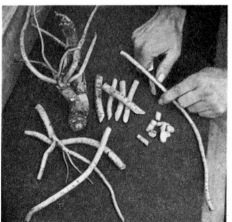

RECOMMENDED VARIETIES

CHICORY
Witloof (or Brussels) Very popular variety with large, tight, crisp heads.
Red Verona Produces pink-tipped chicons.
Sugar Loaf An excellent variety that is becoming more widely-known.

SEAKALE
Lily White The only variety in general use; produces tender, sweet shoots.

CUCUMBERS AND GHERKINS

There are three ways of growing cucumbers in the vegetable garden – in frames, under large barn cloches, and out in the open. Cucumbers like a rich soil, and for best results some soil preparation is necessary. Although the type of soil is less important than the quality, a good, medium loam is the best choice.

Where a cool greenhouse is available there is no difficulty in raising your own plants. Fill several 9cm (3½ in) pots with a good compost – J.I. No 1 or a soilless compost – and put one or two seeds on edge 13mm (½ in) deep in the soil. If two seeds sprout, remove the weaker one.

Late spring (April) will be soon enough for this sowing, as the weather will not be sufficiently warm enough to put the plants in the frame until early summer (mid May). If the pots fill with roots before conditions are suitable for transplanting, pot them on.

Gardeners without a greenhouse can still raise their own plants by keeping the pots on the sunny windowsill of a warm room. Once the seedlings are through the soil, turn the pots daily so that the plants grow upright and evenly.

How to transplant

Although cucumbers can be transplanted successfully, they do not like root distur-bance and transplanting must always be done with care. For this reason, use peat or fibre pots as they can be planted out intact and will break up in the soil. Keep the soil moist until the pot has disintegrated, for if the pot dries out the roots of the plant cannot break through.

Growing in frames

Frames which have been used to grow early vegetables usually become vacant in early to mid summer (late May or early June) and will then be ready to take cucumbers. If manure was put into the frame at the beginning of the season, no more will be needed; if not, remove the soil, put in some well-rotted manure, good compost, or old rotted turfs and replace the soil. A layer of manure or compost 15cm (6 in) deep, topped by 10–15cm (4–6 in) of soil, is about right.

Burpee, the outdoor, ridge cucumber

A frame with a single light (sliding top) will take one plant; a double light will take two. Plant the cucumber in the centre of each light, and when it has made six leaves, pinch out the growing point. Allow two shoots to form and, when these have six leaves, stop them (pinch them out) in the same way. Each shoot should break into two, giving four in all. Train these four shoots into the corners of the frame and stop them when they arrive.

Sideshoots or laterals grow next, and the fruits will form on these. Quite often the plants will produce more laterals than are needed, so some judicious thinning of the weaker shoots may be required to prevent overcrowding.

When the flowers appear, the male ones should be pinched out, as they encourage production of seeds in the fruits produced by the females. Female flowers are easy to identify as there is a minute cucumber behind each one. Some modern varieties of cucumber produce only female flowers. When fruits have set, stop each lateral one leaf beyond the fruit.

Watering and spraying in frames
Never put cucumber plants in a hollow where water can gather around the stem, as this may cause collar rot (rotting at the base of the stem). It is better to plant them on a slight mound where water will drain away from the stem. A good method of watering is to sink two 13cm (5 in) pots about half their depth into the soil, one on either side of the plant stem and about 30cm (12 in) away from it, and then water into the pots. Keep a small can in one corner of the frame so that the water will be the same temperature as the frame.

Cucumbers like a moist, humid atmosphere so encourage this by syringeing the plants twice a day with tepid water.

Growing in cloches
Cucumbers can also be grown successfully under large barn cloches. There are two ways of preparing the site. One is to dig out a trench along the cloche run, 60cm (24 in) wide and a spade's depth. Loosen the subsoil with a fork, then put in a good layer of manure or well-rotted compost, before returning the soil.

The second method, more economical of manure, is to prepare stations 90cm (3 ft) apart. Dig out holes 45–60cm (18–24 in) square, and about 30cm (12 in) deep, and half fill these with manure or compost. Tread this down firmly before returning the soil. In heavy soils it is better to replace the excavated soil with a good potting compost. Mark each station with a stick. This method can also be used for glass-to-ground frames.

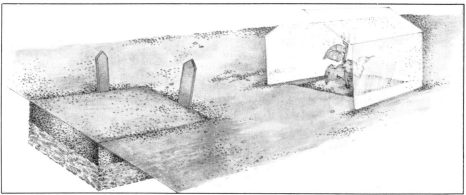

Top: cucumber seed on edge, planted 13mm ($\frac{1}{2}$ in) deep in potting compost, and a frame cucumber planted on a slight mound, with two 13cm (5 in) pots sunk to half their depth into the soil on either side to assist watering; above: under barn cloches, set in stations 30cm (12 in) deep, half-filled with manure and topped up with soil

Cultivation under cloches is the same as for frames except that the plants are stopped only once. The two shoots which form are then trained in either direction along the cloche row.

Cucumbers dislike strong sunlight, and some protection should be given to frame and cloche crops. This can be done by flecking the glass with a coloured solution, preferably white, or draping something over the glass that will break the sun's glare without cutting out too much light (old lace curtains are ideal).

Purchasing plants
If you have to buy cucumber plants, choose them with care. Select dark green, short-jointed plants, and avoid any that are light in colour, lanky or have thin stems. These will have been forced along too quickly. Your best plan is to find a good local nurseryman, or an amateur grower who has a few plants to spare.

Growing ridge cucumbers
Outdoor cucumbers are also known as ridge cucumbers, from the time when market gardeners grew large quantities of them on specially-prepared ridges. For the gardener who needs only a few plants, it is much easier to prepare stations 75cm (2½ ft) apart, in the same way as you cater for cloche plants.

If the plants have not been raised in

Apple-Shaped, a prolific cucumber strain

advance, you can sow seeds directly into the soil towards the end of early summer (late May). Push in three seeds, on edge, about 13mm ($\frac{1}{2}$ in) down and 8cm (3 in) apart, and then thin to the strongest plant.

If the nights are cold when the seedlings come through, protect them with a single cloche or a jam jar. Screens of lath and polythene, about 60cm (24 in) high are easy to make and give good shelter from cold winds. Stop the plants when they have made six leaves, to encourage the production of laterals, and keep them well supplied with water. Do not remove male flowers from ridge cucumbers, as this variety needs to be pollinated to produce fruit.

In an average summer, ridge cucumbers can be a worthwhile crop. In recent years improved varieties have appeared; these have thicker fruits that are a little shorter and have a rougher skin than frame varieties.

Japanese climbing cucumbers
Another group of outdoor cucumbers is the Japanese climbing type. By tying them in carefully, you can train them to climb up a fence or trellis.

Pests and diseases
Red spider mite and cucumber mosaic virus are the main enemies of the cucumber.

Red spider mite This pest sucks the sap from the leaves, giving them a mottled, and later a rusty, appearance. Cut off and burn badly affected leaves. Fortunately, the mite dislikes water and regular syringeing will help keep it away. Red spider mites rarely attack outdoor plants.

Cucumber mosaic virus A serious disease of cucumbers is the cucumber mosaic virus. Affected plants turn yellow, wilt and then die. Unfortunately, there is no cure. The virus is spread by aphides, and keeping the greenfly population down by spraying regularly with an insecticide such as derris or malathion is the best safeguard against the disease. Pull up and burn any infected plants as soon as they are seen.

Growing gherkins
The cultivation of gherkins, the little pickling cucumbers, is the same as for ridge cucumbers. Gherkins crop prolifically so one or two plants will produce enough for the average household. Cut the fruits when they are 5–8cm (2–3 in) long, and examine the plants every few days, as the fruits form quickly.

La reine, female-flowering cucumber

ENDIVE AND CORN SALAD
useful winter salad crops

These vegetables, once neglected but now increasingly in demand, can be a valuable addition to the salad bowl at a time when lettuce is scarce; corn salad, for example, is said to be best eaten with game.

Endive and corn salad can be grown in their own right but it is more common to find them used as a substitute for lettuce, especially during the autumn and winter months when good lettuces are at a premium. The leaves of corn salad are used in the green state but endive, which is allied to the chicory family, is bitter and needs blanching before it is eaten. Neither crop is difficult to grow and it is surprising that salad lovers, in particular, do not make more use of them.

ENDIVE
In appearance, endive is like a rather loose-leaved lettuce. There are two types of endive – the curled-leaved, that is generally preferred for summer use, and the plain-leaved or Batavian. The Batavian is a little hardier than the curled and is more suitable for winter use.

Endive prefers a light to medium soil but will grow in heavier soils that have plenty of humus and are well drained. A soil that was well manured for the previous crop is always a good choice. Nitrogenous fertilizers should not be used as they tend to promote lush growth that may lead to heart rot during the autumn and winter months.

Successional sowing
The plants take about three months to reach full size and may be sown from late spring to early autumn (April to early August). Where they are intended as a substitute for lettuce, the best time for sowing is during the late summer (late June to end of July).

The seeds should be sown thinly in drills about 13mm ($\frac{1}{2}$ in) deep and 30–38cm (12–15 in) apart. When the seedlings are big enough to handle, thin them to stand 30cm (12 in) apart. If you want a second row, it is a good plan to thin the plants to 15cm (6 in) and then, a week or two later, take out every other plant to form a second row. This row of transplants will form a natural succession to the earlier row. Move the plants carefully, taking a good ball of soil with each plant, so that the check to growth is reduced to a minimum. Transplanted endive, moved carelessly, are apt to run up to seed.

Protecting your crop
Keep the plants clean by hoeing and weeding, and see that they never lack water. With the advent of colder weather in late autumn some form of protection is advisable. Endive will stand some frost, but not severe frost unless given the protection of frames or cloches. Straw or short litter worked in amongst the plants is a help, but cloches of some kind are undoubtedly the best method of defence.

Blanching
A simple method of blanching is to draw the outer leaves of the endive up over its heart and gently tie them together about 10cm (4 in) from the top. This gives a blanched heart, although it wastes the outer leaves. An alternative method, and a much better one, is to cover the whole plant with a box or large flowerpot. If you use pots, remember to cover the drainage holes. The leaves of the selected plants must be completely dry before blanching begins, or the hearts will rot – another good reason for using cloches.

The time it takes to obtain a good blanch varies with the season. In early autumn it may be only one or two weeks; later on, probably three weeks or four. Inspect the plants from time to time and, as soon as they are fully blanched, cut them for use. Cover only a few plants each week; it is a mistake to blanch too many at once as they will not remain in good condition for many days after being blanched. In their green state they should stand for several weeks.

CORN SALAD
There is a wild form of this plant that grazing sheep are fond of and this has given it an alternative name of 'lamb's lettuce'. The cultivated type has larger and more succulent leaves.

Previous page: Batavian
Green plain-leaved
endive, an excellent
lettuce-substitute for
autumn and winter
months
Above: Green Curled
endive needs to be
blanched before eating
Right: corn salad, or
'lamb's lettuce', needs no
manuring but likes a
sunny, sheltered position

This plant is hardier than endive and will grow in most soils that are in good condition. A sunny, sheltered position is best. Fresh manure is neither necessary nor advisable – a soil manured for the previous crop will suit it well enough.

Sowing and cropping
For an early crop, a sowing can be made in mid spring (March). The main sowings should not be made until early autumn (August) and can continue at fortnightly intervals until the end of mid autumn (September). This makes it a useful follow-on crop to earlier vegetables. These sowings will give pickings in autumn and winter, the time when they will be most valued.

Sow the seeds thinly in drills 13mm ($\frac{1}{2}$ in) deep and 15cm (6 in) apart. No special care is needed apart from attention to watering; the plants should not be allowed to dry out.

There are two methods of gathering the leaves. One is to pull up the entire plant and cut off the root; the other is to pick over the plants like spinach and cut off tufts of leaves as you want them. The second method is slower but has the advantage of giving a regular supply of tender young leaves. If you follow this method, do not take more than half the leaves from any plant at one picking.

Protecting your crop
Although corn salad is hardy, a better and cleaner crop will result if you cover the plants with cloches during late autumn and early winter (October and November). A barn cloche will cover four rows. If you can't get cloches, protect the plants during severe weather with a *light* covering of straw. Remove this when milder weather returns.

Both endive and corn salad are liable to be attacked by slugs. A few slug pellets, scattered at intervals between the rows, will deal with this problem. Slugs apart, the plants are generally free from pests and diseases that afflict salad crops.

RECOMMENDED VARIETIES
ENDIVE
Green Curled For first use.
Batavian Green Plain-leaved and a little hardier than the curled.
Winter Lettuce-leaved Has large leaves and stands well.

CORN SALAD
Verte de Cambrai Round, succulent leaves.
Large-leaved Italian Hardy, with large leaves.
Large-leaved English Similar to above.

LETTUCE

As lettuce is a main ingredient of many salads, its importance can scarcely be over-emphasized. Fortunately it is so easy to grow that the real skill comes in having a steady supply for the table over as many months as possible and not just a glut in mid summer.

Lettuce are not particularly fussy about their soil requirements – except that the earth must be well drained. They will grow quite happily between rows of slower-maturing plants. Whilst the surrounding soil must never be allowed to dry out, it is equally dangerous for it to become waterlogged. Cold, damp soils are not conducive to rapid growth and should be improved by the addition of sand and peat to lighten them. Light, dry soils can have their water-holding capacity increased by adding peat or other organic materials, such as manure.

Main types
With lettuce, perhaps more than with most vegetables, it is important to sow the right varieties at the right time. An understanding of the three main types is essential in order to have a steady supply over as long a period as possible. The **cabbage head** group can be subdivided into two classes: flat or smooth, that grow over a long period; and crisp or crinkled, that are mainly for summer cropping.

Cos This is a tall, pointed variety of which there are two kinds – large and intermediate. The cos is generally a summer crop that can be overwintered. While they are not nearly so popular as the cabbage lettuce, cos deserve to be more widely grown, and the intermediate ones are certainly gaining in popularity.

Loose-leaved This type does not make a heart, but produces a succession of tender leaves which can be picked as required. It has the advantage of standing well in hot weather.

Successional sowing
The aim of every salad-lover growing his own lettuce is to have a steady succession for as many months of the year as possible. This is easy to achieve on paper but much more difficult to accomplish in practise. Successional sowings, however carefully planned, have a habit of taking different times to mature according to different weather conditions – and these, unfortunately, are outside your control.

There are two ways of planning for succession. One is to make successional sowings of the *same* variety; the other is to sow two *different* varieties at the same time. Sometimes a combination of both methods will give the best results. If, for example, a flat lettuce is sown at the same time as a crisp variety, a succession

Row upon row of the beautiful pale-leaved Suzan, a smooth cabbage variety. Sow them under glass in autumn for transplanting early in the winter. The first of the crop will be ready for the table by late spring

is almost assured because, on average, the crisp varieties take longer to mature.

Transplanting is another aid to succession: transplanted plants, however carefully moved, are bound to be checked (slowed up) and so will take longer to mature than those left undisturbed.

In order to avoid having too many lettuces ready at once, the golden rule is to make small sowings at frequent intervals from mid to late spring (March to April), and transplant from these until mid summer (June). These sowings will be under glass. In summer months it is better to sow *in situ* (directly into the soil) and thin out, throwing away unwanted seedlings. This is because plants that are transplanted during this period are more liable to go to seed.

Growing under glass

The use of glass will help to extend the season at both ends. Few people will want to heat a greenhouse specially for growing lettuce, but where heat is needed for other plants, a few can be grown in deep boxes or in 13cm or 15cm (5 or 6 in) pots on the staging. Lack of daylight in winter is the main obstacle, and only the specially-bred varieties should be grown.

Heated frames Where heat is provided through a soil-warming cable buried a few centimetres below the surface, a frame is much more economical than a heated greenhouse, and can be used for growing lettuce – at a minimum temperature of 10–13°C (50–55°F) – during the winter. (A transformer will be needed to reduce the voltage, for safety reasons, and it cannot be too strongly emphasized that the equipment must be installed by a qualified electrician.)

Cold greenhouses These, and especially the glass-to-ground type (which traps all the available winter light and heat), are a boon to lettuce-growers as seeds sown in late summer can be planted out inside the greenhouse from late autumn to early winter (October to November).

Alternatively you can sow *outdoors* and bring the seedlings under glass at planting time. The lettuce will be ready for cutting from mid spring to early summer (March to May). Any plants that may be in the way if you have tomatoes ready for transplanting can be pulled up and used first.

Cold frames These are useful for providing an early crop, especially the metal types with glass all round. Seedlings that have been started under glass during the winter as already described, can be planted in the soil bed and the frames then put over them.

The older type of frame with sliding

Three crisp, sweet lettuce that are sown outdoors for summer and autumn salads. Webb's Wonderful (above) and Lobjoit's Green Cos (below right) last well in hot, dry weather. Little Gem (right) is also known as Sugar Cos

lights (glass lids) generally requires a soil bed to be made up inside it, so that the soil level is raised and the plants are reasonably close to the glass.

Growing under cloches

The simplest method of growing lettuce under glass is to use cloches. The tent-shaped (inverted 'V') cloches will cover a single row (or two of a small variety) while barn cloches (shaped like miniature greenhouses), cover three rows. Glass is preferable, but there are various plastic and polythene cloches available that are satisfactory provided they can be securely anchored and are not in too exposed a position.

Sow the seeds directly into the soil – which will have warmed up a little if you place the cloches in position a week or two before sowing. Sow as thinly as possible, in drills about 12mm (½ in) deep. Thin out or transplant the young plants as soon as they are about 10cm (3–4 in) high. Subsequent cultivation consists simply of keeping the surrounding soil clear by weeding and hoeing, but you must take care not to damage the roots which lie just below the surface. It is also a good idea to give a liquid feed every

ten days while they are actively growing.

Lettuce do best in an open, sunny position, but some shade is an advantage for those maturing during the hottest months, so put them in the lea of a row of runner beans or other tall plants.

General pests

The main pests to guard against are slugs, birds and aphides. Slug bait will help to keep them down and spraying with a good insecticide will control the greenfly. It is wise to spray occasionally before the hearts have formed, even if no greenfly can be seen, as it is impossible to get at them once the lettuce begin to 'heart up'.

Watch out for birds as they can soon ruin a promising crop, sparrows being especially notorious for this. The old method of using black cotton (not thread) is still effective. Simply push in sticks at intervals and then run the cotton from stick to stick, just clear of the plants. A

Unrivalled (left) and Tom Thumb (above left) can be sown 'little and often' for cutting from spring to autumn

touch of the cotton on a bird's wings is enough to send it winging away. Or you can try proprietary bird repellents.

Main diseases

The two main diseases are mosaic disease and grey mould (*botrytis cinerea*). Mosaic shows up as stunted growth and a yellow mottling of the leaves. It is a virus spread by aphides and once plants are attacked there is no cure, which is another good reason for early spraying against aphides.

Grey mould is much more widespread and serious. Affected plants wilt and then collapse. If a collapsed plant is pulled up you will find that the stem has turned brown and rotted at soil level. Although there is no cure at this stage, some measure of control is possible by spraying the fungicide Benlate at the first sign of trouble.

Grey mould is generally a disease of plants grown under glass or cloches and is rarely encountered outdoors. This gives us a valuable clue to its prevention – adequate ventilation. Where plants under

RECOMMENDED VARIETIES

Type	Variety	When to sow	When to transplant	When to cut	How to grow
smooth cabbage	Kwiek	early autumn	late autumn	mid winter to early spring	heated greenhouse or frame
	Premier Suzan	mid autumn	early winter	late spring to mid summer	cold frames, cold greenhouses or cloches
	Imperial	early autumn	thin out instead	early summer to mid summer	outdoors
	Tom Thumb	early spring and early autumn	thin out instead	early summer, and late autumn to early winter	outdoors; good under cloches
	Unrivalled All The Year Round	mid spring to early summer	late spring to mid summer	mid summer to early autumn	outdoors
crisp cabbage	Webb's Wonderful Avoncrisp	mid spring to early summer	late spring to mid summer	late summer to mid autumn	outdoors
large cos	Lobjoits Green Paris White	mid spring to late summer	late spring to mid summer	late summer to mid autumn	outdoors
intermediate cos	Little Gem (also listed as Sugar Cos)	mid spring to late summer	late spring to mid summer	mid summer to mid autumn	outdoors; good under cloches
	Winter Density	mid autumn	early winter, or thin out instead	late spring to mid summer	under cloches
loose-leaved	Salad Bowl	mid spring to early summer	thin out instead	mid summer to mid autumn	pick leaves as required

Key to seasons
early spring (February)	early summer (May)	early autumn (August)	early winter (November)
mid spring (March)	mid summer (June)	mid autumn (September)	mid winter (December)
late spring (April)	late summer (July)	late autumn (October)	late winter (January)

glass are given plenty of ventilation, grey mould should not be a problem. Open up frames in all but the severest weather; leave a slight gap between cloches, and where there is a ventilating pane, close it only in hard weather. Lettuce are much tougher than is generally supposed.

Another safeguard against grey mould is good hygiene. Yellow leaves, or any lying flat on the soil, should be removed, and any affected plants disposed of at once. Keep the plants free from weeds, with a good circulation of air round them.

Care of plants

When it is necessary to water lettuce in frames or greenhouses, do so early in the morning so that the soil has time to dry out before nightfall. Water the soil *between* the plants and keep it off the leaves as much as possible. There should be no need to water those under cloches during the winter, as enough water will seep in from the soil at the sides.

Outdoor varieties Most of these need about 30cm sq (12 in sq) in which to mature, but under glass this can be reduced to 23cm sq (9 in sq) so that the optimum use is made of the glass. The variety Tom Thumb is small, quick-maturing and needs only 15cm sq (6 in sq). It makes a useful crop for both early and late sowings.

Imperial is one of several varieties which can winter outdoors in a sheltered spot for maturing in early spring. These varieties will survive an average winter, though they may not come through a severe one. The increasing use of cloches, however, means that these 'winter' varieties are of less importance now, and they are being replaced by more tender ones.

Cutting time

Cabbage lettuce should be firm when pressed gently at the top of the heart; test a cos by pressing at the tip – never squeezing from the sides. With your early spring crop, it is a good plan to plant at 13–15cm (5–6 in) intervals and then to cut every other lettuce when the row begins to look crowded. These surplus plants, although not properly hearted, will be welcome, and mean an earlier start to the season.

One final point: nothing equals home-grown lettuce for freshness and flavour, but do cut them when they are at their best. Avoid the heat of the day, when they are limp and flaccid, and cut them in the early morning or late evening.

The loose curly leaves of Salad Bowl are picked individually as required

MUSTARD, CRESS, BEAN SPROUTS

Mustard and cress are traditionally grown together. White mustard is the kind grown for salads; cress can be either plain or curled. There is also American or land cress – a perennial that tastes like watercress. Newer crops such as alfalfa and adzuki beans and mung beans can provide a similar crisp ingredient for salads or be used as a cooked vegetable.

Mustard, cress and bean sprouts are all good crops for stimulating the interest of children in growing things, as they like something that grows quickly and can then be eaten.

MUSTARD AND CRESS
Packets of mustard and cress will be found among the vegetable seeds in shops and stores, but this is an expensive way of buying them. Buy 30g (1 oz) packets from a seedsman or, if you intend to make successional sowings throughout spring and summer, buy a still larger packet. Always use fresh seeds; old seed oddments may give poor germination results.

If mustard and cress are needed together, sow the mustard three or four days later, as it grows more quickly.

Growing and harvesting
As these crops are eaten in the seed-leaf stage a rich soil is not necessary. The J.I. No 1 compost is good enough. If you grew tomatoes or cucumbers in the previous season, the spent compost from these crops will make a first-rate medium for mustard and cress.

To grow, fill a seed tray with the growing medium and press it down with a block of wood until the surface is firm and level and about 13mm ($\frac{1}{2}$ in) below the top of the tray. Sow the seeds evenly and thickly. Do not cover them with soil – simply press them into the medium with the flat piece of wood. Water them in well with a fine spray, or immerse the tray in water until the soil surface turns dark as

the water comes through. If the seeds are given a good watering to begin with, no more should be needed until after germination. Cover the trays with brown paper until the young shoots appear.

The main difficulty in growing mustard and cress is that the seedlings tend to bring up their seed cases and particles of soil with them. These cling to the stems and leaves and make the end-product gritty. One way of preventing this is to cover the growing medium with a layer of silver sand and press the seeds into it. Another method is to cut a piece of hessian, the size of the inside of the tray, and lay this over the seeds. Keep the hessian damp until the seeds are through. The hessian will hold the seed cases and soil in place while allowing the shoots to push through. When the seedlings are about 2–3cm (1 in) in height, carefully remove the hessian and leave them to grow on.

Mustard and cress can also be grown on moist absorbent paper (such as blotting paper or kitchen paper).

Cut the seedlings when they are about 5–8cm (2–3 in) in height with a pair of sharp scissors that will cut cleanly, then empty the tray on to the compost heap and refill with new soil.

AMERICAN LAND CRESS
This cress can be grown in ordinary garden soil and prefers a north-facing or semi-shaded position where the soil will remain moist. It needs plenty of water and should never be allowed to dry out.

The plants are quite hardy and take about 8–10 weeks to mature from seed. If they should prove difficult to establish from a spring sowing, try again at the

beginning of autumn (early August). Thin the plants to about 10cm (4 in) apart and keep them free from weeds at all times. Pinching out the growing points will help keep up a steady supply of leaves.

If you sow the seeds in a block, rather than in rows, the plants can be covered in autumn with a cold frame or cloches, and the season of picking will be prolonged.

Far left: mustard (larger leaves at rear) and cress traditionally go together
Below left: American land cress likes a moist, shady spot in which to grow
Above: bean sprouts – or mung bean – are ready for eating after 4–6 days' growth

BEAN SPROUTS
Recent years have seen the introduction of several crops producing shoots that can be used either in salads or as a vegetable. First to arrive, and still the most popular, was the mung bean. The seeds of this bean can be sprouted indoors on strips of flannel or sheets of kitchen paper kept moist.

Two more recent additions are alfalfa, with a flavour similar to garden peas, and the adzuki bean. It is usually recommended that these be grown by the 'jar' method. Place a measure of seed in an ordinary jam-jar (or similar jar) and then cover it with a piece of muslin kept in place by an elastic band. Fill the jar with water, shake well and drain off again. Repeat this procedure night and morning until the sprouts are ready for use – in about 4–6 days.

One advantage of these seeds is that they can be sprouted at any time of the year. Full instructions are given on the packets or in an accompanying leaflet.

SPINACH AND SPINACH SUBSTITUTES

Spinach is an excellent 'food value' vegetable, rich in vitamins A, B1, B2, and C. It also contains useful quantities of calcium, protein and iron. For spinach lovers there are also several other leaf vegetables – perpetual spinach, New Zealand spinach and Good King Henry – that have a similar flavour.

SUMMER SPINACH

The round-seeded or summer spinach can be sown from mid spring through mid summer (March to the end of June) and is 'in pick' 8–10 weeks after sowing. It needs a fertile soil with good, moisture-retaining properties. On light or hungry soils the plants will soon go to seed.

If the ground is being prepared especially for this crop, dig in some manure or good compost during the winter months. Some well-dampened peat may also be incorporated and will help to keep the soil moist. In many cases, however, spinach can be used as an intercrop; for example, it can be grown between rows of peas or dwarf beans.

Sowings maturing during the summer will benefit from a little shade for part of the day. Good sites for these sowings are between rows of tall peas or in the lee of a row of runner beans.

Sow the seeds thinly in drills 2–3cm (1 in) deep and 30cm (12 in) apart. As soon as the seedlings are big enough to handle, thin them to stand 15cm (6 in) apart. When the plants have grown until they touch each other, take out every other plant and use them in the kitchen.

Regular hoeing will keep the weeds down by creating a loose, dry, layer of earth that acts as a mulch. Water during dry spells; do not allow the plants to dry out or they will go to seed.

Picking can begin as soon as the leaves are large enough. Cut the leaves off close to the stem, taking a few from each plant.

Even well-grown plants of summer spinach will not crop for long, and to keep up a regular supply it is necessary to make successional sowings every two or three weeks.

WINTER SPINACH

The prickly, or winter, spinach – 'prickly' applies to the seeds, not the plants – is sown in early to mid autumn (August to September) for use during the winter

172

months. It makes a good follow-on crop to some of the earlier sowings. Before sowing, rake in a general fertilizer at 70g per sq m (2 oz per sq yd). An open site with some shelter from cold winds is preferable. Sow the seeds in drills 2–3cm (1 in) deep and 30cm (12 in) apart. Thin the seedlings to stand 23cm (9 in) apart. If the soil is dry at the time of sowing, water the drills well beforehand. Once established there should be no watering problem as the normal rainfall of an average autumn and winter will be enough for their needs.

Although the plants are hardy they give a better and cleaner crop if some protection can be given, ideally with cloches, during the winter months. Straw or short litter tucked around the plants is one way of doing this.

Picking is the same as for summer spinach, the largest leaves being taken first; but pick rather more sparingly as leaf production in the winter months is slower. In early spring a dressing of nitrochalk at 35g per sq m (1 oz per sq yd) will help the plants along, by increasing production of leafy growth which in turn will help to give you earlier spinach pickings.

SPINACH SUBSTITUTES
In addition to 'true' spinach there are several spinach-type vegetables that have a similar flavour. All are very little troubled by pests and diseases.

Perpetual spinach This is another name for spinach beet (which was included in the section on leaf beets, page 142). The leaves of spinach beet are thicker and fleshier than those of the true spinach and are preferred by many people for this reason.

Sow in drills 2–3cm (1 in) deep and 38–45cm (15–18 in) apart, and thin the plants to stand 23cm (9 in) apart. Sow in late spring (April) for summer use and in early autumn (August) for winter use. If the winter row can be cloched, a heavier and cleaner crop will result. Pick the leaves as they become large enough and never let any leaves grow on until they become tough, or the production of new leaves will be hindered.

New Zealand spinach This half-hardy annual thrives best in a light to medium soil and in a sunny position. Unlike summer spinach it will tolerate hot, dry conditions without running to seed. It has a low, spreading habit and needs plenty of room. Allow 90cm (3 ft) between the plants.

For an early crop, sow in mid spring (March) under glass and prick the seedlings off into 9cm (3½ in) pots, ready for planting out towards mid summer

Above left: Viking, a comparatively new summer spinach variety
Below left: low-growing New Zealand spinach thrives in hot, dry conditions
Below: versatile Good King Henry, another spinach substitute, that can also replace broccoli on the menu

(late May). Alternatively, sow *in situ* in late spring (April) and cover with cloches until the risk of frost has gone. If protection cannot be given, delay sowing until early summer (mid May). The seeds are hard and should be soaked overnight before sowing.

Keep the plants watered in dry spells, and pinch back the shoots to encourage the production of more leaf-bearing sideshoots. The dark green, triangular leaves are smaller than those of summer spinach but picking is done in the same way (by taking individual leaves). Plants bear freely until cut down by frost.

Good King Henry This is a hardy, perennial plant, not widely known outside its native English county of Lincolnshire. It is a useful, dual-purpose plant; in the spring shoots are produced from the leaf axils and these can be cut and cooked like spring broccoli. Later the large triangular leaves can be used as a substitute for spinach.

The plants can be propagated by division or from seeds sown in late spring or early summer (April or May) in drills 30cm (12 in) apart. Soak the seeds overnight before sowing. When the seedlings are large enough, thin them to stand 30cm (12 in) apart.

Because the plant is a perennial and needs to build up its reserves for the following season, shoots should not be taken later than mid summer (June), but leaves can be removed until early autumn (August).

RECOMMENDED VARIETIES
SUMMER SPINACH
Sigmaleaf Large-leaved, round-seeded variety; can also be sown in autumn for overwintering.
King of Denmark Large, round, dark green leaves.
Longstanding Round Quick-growing with dark leaves; the standard summer variety.
Viking Excellent recently-introduced variety with dark green leaves.

WINTER SPINACH
Greenmarket Large, dark green leaves.
Longstanding Prickly Very hardy; the standard winter variety.

SPINACH SUBSTITUTES
Perpetual spinach or spinach beet (No named varieties). Has succulent spinach-type leaves.
New Zealand spinach (No named varieties). Plants have low, creeping habit and soft, thick fleshy leaves.
Good King Henry (No named varieties); useful substitute for spinach or broccoli.

SWEET CORN

Many gardeners mistakenly believe that sweet corn is a luxury crop too difficult for the average gardener, or that it can only be grown in very mild climates. In reality sweet corn is no harder to grow than outdoor tomatoes.

There are two important points to keep in mind when growing sweet corn, or corn-on-the-cob as it is also known. First, the plants will not withstand frost and cannot be planted out until the risk of frost is past. Secondly, the plants do not like being transplanted and should always be moved with care.

A sunny site is essential, with shelter from cold winds if possible. Cold, wet soils are unsuitable because they take too long to warm up, but any other good garden soil will do. Do not use fresh manure as it may induce leaf growth at the expense of the cobs. Soil that was well manured for a previous crop is ideal and will only need the addition of a general fertilizer at the rate of 70 g per sq m (2 oz per sq yd).

Sowing methods

There are three ways of growing this delicious vegetable. If you possess a cold greenhouse or cold frame you can start in late spring (mid April) by sowing two seeds in an 8 cm (3 in) pot. Pull the weaker one out if both germinate. If you use trays they must be 15cm (6 in) deep, but because of the problems with transplanting it is better to use pots.

Peat or fibre pots are good; because you can then plant out, pot and all, into the soil with the minimum disturbance of the roots. Be sure to keep the pots moist after planting so that they will rot down and allow the young roots to grow through into the soil. Slit each pot up one side and remove the bottom. If you use plastic or clay pots, water the plants well before moving them and tap the sides of the pots gently so that the soil ball slips out easily. Transplant in early summer (mid May) if the plants are going out under cloches; otherwise, wait a week or two longer.

Another, and possibly better, method is to sow the seeds directly into the soil under barn cloches in late spring or early summer (late April or early May). Draw out two drills 40cm (15 in) apart and 5cm (2 in) deep, and sow three seeds every 30cm (12 in) along the row. Leave two plants at each station. De-cloche the plants around mid summer (mid June).

The third way is to sow the seeds directly into the open ground towards mid summer (end of May), using the same sowing distances as for cloches. If you have no glass at all you can gain valuable time by starting a dozen or so plants in pots on a sunny windowsill.

Aids to fertilization

Sweet corn is an attractive and interesting plant, as it carries both male and female parts on the same stem. The male tassels at the top of the plant are the pollen bearers. When the pollen is shed it falls onto the female silks—the tufts of fine hairs at the end of each immature cob.

To assist good fertilization, set out the plants in blocks rather than in long rows. An excellent technique is to have two short rows of plants covered by cloches; then sow or plant another two rows between the cloches. The outdoor rows will mature later, but they will get quite a lot of shelter from the outlying cloches. Pollen is usually distributed by the wind, but in calm periods it helps if the plants are tapped gently about mid-day.

Tending the growing plants

Do not hoe too deeply or too closely to the growing plants, as they are not deep rooting and there is a danger of breaking the surface roots. Water the plants in dry periods, and mulch with compost, peat or spent mushroom manure to help conserve moisture. Sweet corn is a crop that

Right: fully-ripe, golden corn ready for cooking and eating. Below: corn growing under cloches with tops removed to air them in dry, sunny weather. Below right: cob still covered by sheath. Far right: very young cob with sheath removed

benefits from foliar feeding (being fed through the leaves), so spray at two-week intervals until the cobs have formed: each plant usually produces two cobs—sometimes more.

Unless the plants are in a very sheltered position you will have to stake them. Extra support can be given by drawing a little soil round the base of each plant. Staking each plant is time-consuming: a better method is to drive in a stake or strong cane at the ends of each row, with perhaps a light cane in between, and then run garden wire from cane to cane and all round the block. It is then simple to tie each plant to the wire.

Sweet corn plants are generally pest and disease free, though in an indifferent summer there may be trouble with poor fertilization and some of the grains may fail to swell. Tapping the plants at midday, as suggested, will help to prevent this.

Harvesting the cobs

Part of the art of growing sweet corn lies in knowing when it is ready for picking. Apart from the natural plumpness of a ripe cob, a reliable sign is that as the cob matures the silks turn brown and dry. Also, there is often a slight cracking of the sheath against the silk.

The grains of corn are enclosed in a leafy sheath which can be gently parted so that you can look at them. In a ripe cob they will be a rich yellow. The final test of ripeness is to pierce one of the grains with a thumb nail. If the liquid that comes out is pale and watery, then the cob is not ready. Close the sheath and leave it to ripen a little longer. When the liquid is rich and creamy the cob is at its best and must be picked at once before it becomes mealy and unpalatable.

Pick the cob by cutting it off with a knife or breaking it off with a sharp, downward twist. When all the cobs have been gathered chop up the plants and put them to rot on the compost heap.

Once picked, the cobs should be cooked and eaten as soon as possible, as they deteriorate rapidly .

TOMATOES
sowing and planting indoors and out

It is the aim of almost every gardener to grow his own tomatoes.
Thanks to the great deal of progress that has been made in recent years in breeding new varieties, it is now possible for the amateur to achieve a really good crop – with or without a greenhouse.

When growing tomatoes under glass, beware of starting off your tomato seeds too early. Plants which suffer a check from too low a temperature take a long time to recover. It is the *night* temperature of the greenhouse that is most important. A constant 18–21°C (65–70°F) is necessary to start the seeds off, with a follow-on minimum night temperature of about 12°C (54°F).

From late mid spring (the second half of March) or, with insufficient heating facilities, a few weeks later, you can sow seeds in a box of John Innes Potting Compost No 1 (J.I. No 1) or one of the soilless composts. Space the seeds 4cm (1½ in) apart, and cover them with a light sprinkling of compost. Water gently with a fine rose on the watering can, and keep the compost moist but not over-wet.

When the seedlings have made their first pair of true leaves (after the little seed leaves) pot them up into 9 cm (3½ in) pots containing J.I. No 2 or a similar mixture.

Ripe, heavy trusses of delicious tomatoes reward you for your weeks of loving care

Transplanting the young plants

The plants will be ready for transplanting into their final quarters when they are about 20–25cm (8–10 in) high, probably from early summer (early to mid May) onwards. If they are to be grown on staging they will need to be put into 25cm (10 in) pots.

The best results are generally obtained from plants in a 'glass-to-ground' greenhouse. Here the tomatoes can be planted directly into the soil bed, which should be enriched with good compost or well-rotted manure. It is important to dig in the compost or manure in good time, so that the soil can settle before the tomatoes have to be planted.

If you have no heating at all, it is better to buy the plants from a good nurseryman. Look for plants that are short-jointed, well-grown and a rich dark colour.

Transplant the young shoots carefully into the prepared bed, so that the soil ball is just below the soil level, and water them well, using a fine rose on the watering can. They should be spaced some 40–45cm (15–18 in) apart.

Giving support

Instead of an individual cane for each plant, a good alternative method of supporting them is to run a wire from end to end of the greenhouse above the plants and just below the roof. Strong, galvanized wire hooks are pushed into the soil close to each plant and a length of stout garden string is fastened to the hook at one end and the wire at the other. It is then a simple matter, as the plant grows, to give the string an occasional twist round the stem.

Support tomato plants by tying to canes (below), or by twisting string from wire hooks to a horizontal line (below right)

Growing by ring-culture

The drawback to planting directly into the greenhouse soil bed is that the soil soon becomes 'sick' (unhealthy in gardening terms), with the resultant risk of

Lining for ring-culture bed and cross-section of plants in bottomless pots, one plant in earlier stage of growth

disease affecting your tomatoes. To avoid this, the soil bed should be dug out to a spade's depth every couple of years and then filled up with new soil.

However, a less arduous way round the problem is to grow your tomatoes by the ring-culture method. Remove the soil to a depth of 15cm (6 in) and replace with pea-gravel, weathered ashes, or peat: gravel is the longest lasting. If a strong polythene sheet is laid across the bottom and up the sides of the trench before the aggregate is put in, moisture will be retained and less watering will be required.

Bottomless pots (usually sold as ring-culture pots), which can be bought from any good seedsman, are placed on the aggregate and filled with J.I. No 3, or a similar mixture; the tomato plants are then planted out into them. The object in ring-culture is to encourage the plants to form two sets of roots—one in the pot for feeding and the other in the aggregate below the pot for supplying water.

Once the plants are growing strongly

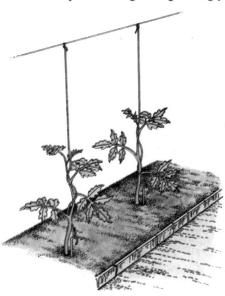

and have sent out roots into the aggregate, watering in the pots should cease, except when feeds are given. If the aggregate is kept moist the plants will take up all their water from below. By using this method, contact with soil-borne diseases is eliminated.

Using 'Gro-bags'

A third method is to grow your tomatoes in the new 'Gro-bags'. These are bags of specially-prepared growing medium which are simply laid on the greenhouse soil or staging. The tomatoes are planted directly into the bags through pre-marked openings, and the only chore then is to keep the medium in the bags watered.

The cordon method

Practically all greenhouse tomatoes are grown by this artificial method that restricts all the growth to one main stem. All tomatoes, if left to themselves, will produce sideshoots that will grow on to make additional stems on which fruit can be borne. These sideshoots come from the leaf axils where the leaves join the stem. By adopting the cordon method the plant is kept from sprawling, and produces earlier and better fruits. Pinch out the sideshoots between finger and thumb as soon as they appear.

GROWING OUTDOORS

Here you have three methods of growing and three different types of plant: the *cordon* type (already described), the *dwarf* and the *bush* tomato. The dwarf tomato is a distinct type which breaks (forms sideshoots) naturally to form several stems. In the bush tomato the stems are more numerous and more pliable and the low-growing plants form a small bush. Neither dwarf nor bush tomato is suitable for greenhouse culture.

In the cold frame

If you have the old type of cold frame, with a sliding light (glass lid), it can be used to start off a few plants. Allow about 30cm (12 in) between the plants when putting them in. Provide a good enriched soil, as for the greenhouse soil bed, and cover with the light until the plants are touching the glass. Plant them in early summer (mid May) and if the nights are cold, or frost is expected, be prepared to cover the glass with old sacks, matting, or anything else that will prevent heat loss—but remember to remove the covering in the morning.

You must also be sure to ventilate the frame on sunny days; even early summer sun can 'toast' the plants badly when it is shining through glass. Remember, however, to close it again in the evening.

When the tops start touching the glass, remove the light and support the plants. You have given them a good start and every week saved is of vital importance when growing outdoor tomatoes.

For the newer types of garden frame, which have more headroom, the dwarf or bush varieties are better, and it may be possible to keep them covered throughout their growth, although adequate ventilation must still be provided if weather conditions demand it.

Under cloches

The bush and dwarf tomatoes are also ideal for growing under barn-shaped cloches. Decide on the strip of soil to be covered and prepare it well in advance. It should be 'in good heart' (that is, a good fertile soil) but not too enriched or the plants will produce plenty of foliage at the

Barn cloches standing on end, anchored by canes tied to the handles, protect young tomato plants growing outdoors

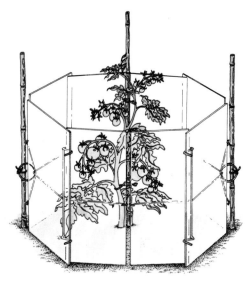

expense of fruits. Old bonfire ash makes an excellent dressing for outdoor tomatoes and should be worked into the soil as the strip is prepared. If no ash is available, sulphate of potash at about 35g per sq m (1 oz per sq yd) will help to promote strong flower and fruit production. Incidentally, if the strip has been really well prepared, additional feeding during the growing period should not be necessary. Put the plants out in early summer (the second half of May), allowing about 30–45cm (12–18 in) between plants, according to the vigour of the variety, and cover with the cloches.

If the plants outgrow the available headroom, remove the cloches carefully and stand them *on end* round the plants. Secure a cane to the handle of each cloche and into the soil so that it cannot be blown over. Later, when the weight of fruit pulls the plants down, the cloches can be put over them again to assist ripening. At the same time, cover the ground under the fruit trusses with straw or polythene to prevent any contact with the soil.

Growing without glass

While many thousands of tomato plants are sold each year for planting outdoors, they are nearly all cordon varieties. Very few nurserymen offer dwarf or bush varieties as young plants. This means that if you want to grow them, you must raise them from seed. If you have neither greenhouse nor frame, you can still get results by sowing the seeds in a pot or seed tray placed in the window of a warm kitchen and then following the method already outlined. When the seedlings are ready, set out the number you require into

9cm (3½ in) pots and keep them in the window, turning the pots each day so that growth is even. Gradually harden them off by moving them to an unheated room and then to a sheltered sunny position outdoors during the day (but bring them in each evening), before planting them out into their final positions.

For plants which have to grow and fruit without any glass protection at all, choose the sunniest and most sheltered spot available. A border facing south, backed by a house wall or close-woven fence, is ideal. Another good site, often overlooked, is the corner of a sunny patio which will accommodate a few plants in large pots or tubs. If the plants have to be grown right out in the open, some shelter can be given by putting in short stakes on the north side and fastening old sacking or sheets of plastic to them. Make sure, however, that this barrier is quite firm and that there is no danger of it blowing down onto the plants.

While all three types can be grown outdoors, the cordon varieties are usually preferred. Because the growing season for outdoor tomatoes is relatively short, it is usually accepted that a plant cannot be expected to set more than five trusses of fruit with any hope of ripening them. So when the stem has reached two leaves beyond the fifth truss, pinch out the growing point with your finger and thumb. You can also use the ring-culture method for growing tomatoes outdoors.

Later in the Course we will be telling you how to look after the plants while they are growing, as well as giving guidance on problems likely to be encountered and hints on how to ripen up the fruits.

The first section on tomatoes concentrated on sowing the seeds and transplanting, both in the greenhouse and outside in the garden. Now follow their care through to ripening and harvesting.

TOMATOES
growing and ripening

When your tomato plants are growing strongly, your main tasks are weeding, training and watering. The little onion hoe is the best weeding tool to use for the soil of the greenhouse border (and in frames and under cloches), but hoe only lightly or you may damage the roots.

Training and supporting
Keep cordon plants to one stem by nipping out the sideshoots which form in the axils of the leaves (where the leaf joins the stem). Do remember that sideshoots come from the *axils* of the leaves and fruiting trusses from the stem *between* the leaves.

Nip out the sideshoots as soon as they appear; this lessens the danger of damage to the plants. If you are a smoker with nicotine-stained fingers, wash your hands thoroughly before doing this job or else use a pocket knife. Tomatoes are highly susceptible to nicotine virus, and this can be transmitted from your fingers.

As the plants grow, continue to tie them to their stakes at regular intervals to keep them upright, or twist the supporting string gently round them.

Dwarf tomatoes need little or no training. They produce sideshoots naturally, on which the fruit is borne. An easy way of supporting the plants is to fasten each one to a short stake with a single tie; then run a string, in and out of the plants, from stake to stake.

Bush tomato stems also divide naturally, but their sideshoots are more numerous and more pliable. Stakes are not needed, but when the fruits are swelling their weight will pull the sideshoots to soil level. So put down some slug bait and then slide straw, hay, peat or black polythene under the fruits to keep them clear of the soil.

Some bush plants tend to produce more foliage than is required, particularly if they are on good soil. About early autumn (the middle of August) go through them and cut out stems which are just flowering as they will not give sizeable fruits before the end of the season. By removing these surplus stems you give the plants more light and air.

Plenty of water
Watering always poses something of a problem. There are no hard and fast rules, but for greenhouse tomatoes there are

broad guidelines. When you transplant, give the plants a good watering; after that water only sparingly until new roots begin to form and new growth is seen. From then on increase the supply as the plants grow. When they are mature it is almost impossible to overwater, and in hot weather it may be necessary to water them twice a day.

With plants in frames or under cloches let nature help. Push down the frame lights, or remove the ventilating panes of the cloches when rain is imminent. Plants under cloches will draw much of the water they need from the sides of the cloches where rain has run down into the soil.

Avoid too dry an atmosphere in the greenhouse. Damp down the path and staging and spray the plants with clear water night and morning to keep the air moist. See that ventilation is adequate; in hot weather leave a ventilator a little way open all through the night.

Heat is more important than sunshine to tomatoes once the fruits start ripening

Setting and feeding
When the plants are flowering, encourage the fruits to set by gently tapping the supporting canes or strings about the middle of the day to help distribute the pollen. With dwarf or bush plants this treatment is not necessary.

Don't start feeding until the first fruits have begun to swell. Use a good, proprietary liquid fertilizer and follow the manufacturer's instructions exactly. If you prepared the tomato bed well, then dwarf and bush tomatoes should not need feeding; bush plants in particular will tend to produce lush foliage at the expense of fruit if given too rich a diet.

Ripening the fruit
As the sun begins to lose strength and the nights turn colder, ripening inevitably

179

slows down. If you have a cool greenhouse, and you have any form of heating, turn it on at night towards mid autumn (late August and September) so that the remaining fruits will ripen. Where you started off the plants in a frame and then grew them on as cordons, cut the strings holding the plants to their supports, remove the canes and then lay the plants down gently onto clean straw or black polythene. Follow the same procedure with plants that outgrew their cloches. Put the frame lights or the cloches back in place, and the fruits will continue to ripen throughout late autumn (October).

Pick all the fruits which have no protection at all by the end of mid autumn (September) and ripen them indoors. Putting the fruit in a sunny window is not the best way of ripening them; neither is it

Below: give fruiting bush plants more light and air by trimming surplus stems

Below: fruits may split if you allow the soil to dry out and then water it heavily

necessary to denude the plants of their leaves in order to expose the fruits to the sun. Leaves should not be taken off unless they have yellowed naturally or are diseased. Both practices spring from the mistaken belief that sunshine is essential for ripening tomatoes; it is not. Providing the temperature is high enough tomatoes will ripen without sunshine. It is quite a common occurrence to find ripe fruit hidden beneath the leafy foliage of a bush tomato plant.

To ripen tomatoes indoors, put them in a basket, cover them with a piece of cloth and keep them in a warm kitchen. Another good way, particularly with the greener fruits, is to put them on layers of cotton wool in a drawer in a warm living room. Any fruits from greenhouse, frames or cloches which have not ripened by the end of autumn (late October) can also be brought in and treated this way.

Pests and diseases
The modern tomato is a highly-developed plant and as such is subject to various diseases – most of them occurring in the fruiting stage. However, if you raise and tend your plants carefully, you should be able to harvest a healthy crop without difficulty. The list which follows are the more common troubles that can occur.

Potato blight (so called because it commonly affects potatoes). Affected plants show brownish-black patches on the fruits which quickly go rotten. There is no cure but the disease may be contained if you pick off the leaves and fruits as soon as you see signs appearing. You can help prevent it by spraying with a suitable fungicide towards the end of mid summer

To finish ripening outdoor cordons, lay the plants down on a bed of clean straw

(end of June), with a second spraying a fortnight later. Keep potatoes and tomatoes as far apart as possible to avoid contamination. Blight is generally confined to outdoor plants but may appear in frames or under cloches.

Leaf mould This is a serious disease of greenhouse tomatoes. The symptoms are a greyish mould on the underside of the leaves with yellow patches on the upper surface. Remove and burn affected leaves and spray with a systemic fungicide. A stagnant atmosphere, especially at night, is the cause and adequate ventilation is the best safeguard. The disease is more prevalent in some areas than in others; if you know it to be troublesome in your district, spray with the fungicide in mid summer and again in late summer (June and July) as a precautionary measure. The variety Supercross (F.1 hybrid) and some strains of Eurocross are immune to this disease.

Blossom-end rot Generally a greenhouse disease in which the end of the tomato opposite the stalk becomes blackish-brown and shrunken and finally rots. There is no cure. The cause is irregular and faulty watering.

Greenback This is not a disease but a condition. Affected fruits have a hard, yellow patch which refuses to ripen. It may be caused by too much sun, or lack of potash. Eurocross and Alicante are among several modern varieties which are resistant to greenback.

Split fruits Caused by letting the plants get dry and then watering heavily. The fruits cannot absorb the water fast enough and the skin ruptures. It ought not to occur in a greenhouse where watering can be controlled, but it is sometimes difficult to prevent outdoors when periods of drought are followed by heavy rains unless you water regularly during dry spells.

Leaf curl When the leaves curl upwards this is generally a sign that the plants are receiving too much nitrogen. Occasionally it may be caused by minute quantities of spray from a selective weedkiller. Tomatoes are especially vulnerable to these and the greatest care must be taken when using them anywhere near tomato plants.

Red spider mite This tiny creature can be a nuisance under glass, though it is not usually a problem outdoors. It is encouraged by a dry atmosphere. The mites feed on the underside of the leaves which become mottled and may turn yellow. Spray or dust with malathion to control them. The mites dislike water, so regular spraying will discourage them from taking up residence.

TUBERS

POTATOES
preparing to grow

Potatoes are the most important crop in many vegetable gardens. In the first of this three-part section we cover the preparation of soil for growing potatoes, buying seed tubers and sprouting them, and recommend some varieties.

Potatoes fit well into a three-year crop plan, so you can give them one-third of the kitchen garden or allotment. But do not be tempted to exceed this area, for if potatoes are grown too often on the same plot of ground it is liable to suffer from 'potato sickness'. Few vegetables benefit more from crop rotation than the potato.

Types of potato
Potato varieties can be divided roughly into four groups: first-early, second-early, early-maincrop and late – but there are no hard and fast dividing lines between these groups. Some catalogues list only three groups, putting the first-earlies and second-earlies together.

First-early and second-early potatoes are simply those varieties that form their tubers early and so are most suitable for early lifting. These are usually dug up while the haulms are green, but they can also be used when they are ripe and the tops have died. Most early varieties do not crop as heavily as the later ones.

The tubers of early-maincrops or lates can also be used while the haulms are still green, but it is rather wasteful to use them in this way as they will give a much better crop if left to mature.

In a small garden it is generally best to cut out later varieties for storing and concentrate on a few rows of earlies for summer use, because these 'new' potatoes have the best flavour and come at a time when shop prices are high.

Soil requirements
Potatoes will grow in most soils, but the ideal is a medium loam that will not dry out too quickly and is still loose enough for the tubers to grow in. Heavy clays and very light soils are the least suitable, but you can improve these by digging in well-rotted manure or compost so that your soil is in a good, fertile condition.

All potato plots will benefit from adding manure or well-rotted compost during winter digging but, if manure is in short supply, give it to the brassicas (especially brussels sprouts, cauliflowers and broccoli) and follow these with potatoes. Potatoes usually do well after greens.

Some varieties are more suited to certain soils than others. When moving into a new area it is always a good plan to consult local gardeners as to the best varieties to grow.

Above left: potato flowers are followed by small green fruits that are poisonous. The seeds they carry are not worth saving as they do not grow true to type
Left: crop from one root of Arran Pilot

Seed potatoes

Potatoes are propagated by planting selected tubers of the previous year's crop. These are known as seed potatoes, but this is really a misnomer as the tubers are not the seed of the potato. The true seed is contained in the little 'potato apples', about the size of small tomatoes, that form on the haulms. The seed cannot be relied upon to breed true and is not of much use to the gardener, although it is valuable to the plant breeders in their search for new and better varieties. The production of these potato apples varies widely with different varieties and in different seasons.

A tuber, on the other hand, is reliable and always grows true to type. In theory

Tubers selected for next year's seed should be put in a shallow box and left outside to harden for two weeks
Right: second-earlies Pentland Beauty
Below right: red-skinned Desirée

there is nothing to prevent a gardener using his own home-grown tubers year after year, but in practice this does not work because the potato is subject to virus diseases that are spread mainly by greenfly. These diseases cause a rapid deterioration of the stock.

Certified stock

In the seed-growing areas of the British Isles (mainly in Scotland and Ireland), potatoes are grown in fields that are too exposed or at too high an altitude for the greenfly to live. These crops are inspected by Ministry of Agriculture officials who certify that the plants are healthy and true to type, and the number of the certificate given is then quoted on all the quantities, however small, that are sold from that particular crop.

Certified seed is generally known as 'new' seed and you should order it as early as possible, although the tubers may not be available until late winter or early spring (January or February).

'Once-grown' seed

New seed is expensive and many gardeners like to make it go as far as possible by growing it on for a second year. The tubers selected for the second crop are then described as 'once-grown'. Where only a few potatoes are grown it is better to buy new seed each year, but a compromise can be made by growing half new seed and half once-grown. This

practice is reasonably safe with the earlies, that are dug up before the greenfly can do too much damage, but is more risky with maincrop varieties that are ready later in the year.

Pick out seed tubers as the crop is dug up, taking them from the best roots only. Never save tubers from weak plants. Choose tubers about the size of a hen's egg, or a little smaller and put them in a

183

shallow box. Leave the box outside until the skins of the tubers have been toughened and greened by the sun; if you suspect the presence of greenfly, spray the tubers with a good insecticide. Store them in a light, cool and frost-proof place until you are ready to chit them up.

Chitting potatoes

Before you plant the tubers in spring, chit them (set them up to sprout). To sprout the tubers, tilt a box (such as a shallow, wooden tomato box) up at one end and stand the tubers upright in it with the rose end uppermost. The rose end of a potato is the end containing the eyes from which the sprouts grow.

Cardboard egg boxes or trays are also excellent for chitting. There is no need to tilt these as the potatoes are held upright in their individual compartments. Fill in any spaces with crumpled newspaper.

This practice of sprouting the tubers has two advantages. By producing sturdy shoots 2–4cm (1–1½ in) long it cuts down on growing time, as sprouted tubers come through the soil much sooner. It also enables dud tubers to be picked out and discarded. Once-grown seed chits earlier than new seed and can be set up by mid to late winter (end of December). New seed should be set up as soon as it is received.

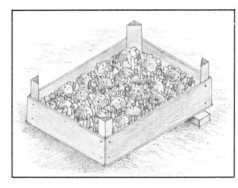

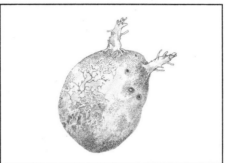

RECOMMENDED VARIETIES

FIRST-EARLIES
Foremost White-skinned and oval.
Pentland Javelin White-fleshed and oval.
Pentland Jewel White and round.
Arran Pilot White and kidney-shaped.

SECOND-EARLIES
Home Guard White and oval.
Pentland Beauty White with pink markings and oval.

EARLY-MAINCROPS
King Edward VII White with pink eyes and kidney-shaped.
Majestic White and kidney-shaped.
Desirée Red-skinned and kidney-shaped.

LATES
Pentland Crown White and oval.
Golden Wonder Russet-skinned and kidney-shaped with white flesh.

Top: to chit up, stand potatoes on end in tilted shallow tray, 'rose' end up, and fill in gaps with crumpled newspaper. When tuber shoots are 2–4cm (1–1½ in) long, they are ready for planting out Above and left: late variety Pentland Crown is oval-shaped, with white flesh

POTATOES
planting and tending

We have now covered preparation of the soil and buying and sprouting seed tubers. The next stage in the proceedings is to tell you how to plant, hoe and earth-up your potatoes, and also how to cope with frost and pests and diseases. Later on we deal with harvesting and storing your potato crop.

Planting times and distances for potatoes vary with variety. Plant first-early and second-early varieties in mid and late spring (March and April) and early-maincrop and late varieties in late spring and early summer (April and May), or even into mid summer (June). Give earlies 25–30cm (10–12 in) between the tubers and 60cm (24 in) between the rows. Early-maincrop and late potatoes should have 38cm (15 in) between the tubers and 68–75cm (27–30 in) between the rows.

If the seed tubers are new Scottish or Irish stock some of them may be rather large. Provided there is at least one good sprout on each half, these can be cut lengthwise down the centre. Don't cut the tubers until you are ready to plant.

Methods of planting
The trench method is one of the most popular ways of planting potatoes. Put a garden line down across the plot and draw it tight. Keeping the back of the spade up against the line, 'chip' out a trench 10–15cm (4–6 in) deep. Plant the tubers in the bottom of the trench, taking care that the sprouts are not knocked off. Then move the line over the required distance (depending on variety) to mark out the next trench. As the second trench is taken out, throw the soil forward to fill in the first trench, and so on.

Another method is to make the planting holes with a trowel. This way you can vary the size of each hole to suit the size of the tuber. In addition you create minimum disturbance of the soil – an important point if manure or greenstuff has recently been dug in.

In the 'lazy bed' method of planting, place the tubers just below soil level so that they stand upright. Then, using a draw hoe, draw the soil over them from either side to form a ridge. This method is of value on heavy soils where the drainage is not too good, as any surplus water that may lie at the bottom of the ridges will then be below the level of the potatoes.

A more modern method is to plant the tubers just inside the soil and cover them with a sheet of black polythene 60cm (24 in) wide. Slit the polythene just above each tuber so that the sprouts can push through. To keep the polythene in place put stones or soil along the edges. The tubers form under the sheet, or just inside the soil. You can pick out the largest tubers for first use by freeing and lifting each side of the sheet in turn.

There is no saving of time by this method but it does cut out hoeing and earthing-up.

Pots and cold frames
If you have a greenhouse with some heat you can grow pots of potatoes on the greenhouse staging. Half-fill some 20cm (8 in) pots with good soil or compost and plant one tuber in each. Add more soil as the plants grow. When a plant has made a good soil ball and is forming tubers, it is quite easy to tap it out of the pot, pick off the largest tubers and then slip the roots back in the pot again.

You can also plant tubers in a cold frame in early or mid spring (February or early March). Ventilate them freely during the day and replace the light at night until the plants have reached the glass.

Protection from frost
Large barn cloches are good for protecting an early row of potatoes. If there is a ventilating pane, take it out so that the plants are not forced too quickly, but replace it at night if there is any danger of frost. The haulms of potatoes are easily damaged by frost. Shoots that are just emerging from the soil can be covered again by drawing soil over them if frost threatens, but this cannot be done once leaves have formed. Sheets of newspaper, kept in place with clods of earth, serve quite well.

If the young plants are blackened by frost, do not assume that they have died; new shoots will soon form. The crop will be later, of course, and in many cases may not be quite so heavy.

Hoeing and earthing-up
Hoe the plants when the rosettes of leaves have formed, but do it as lightly as possible so that the underground stolons (the shoots on which the tubers form) are not cut off.

Earthing-up takes place when the plants are 15–20cm (6–8 in) tall, and consists of drawing soil from between the

Four ways to plant potatoes. Below left: in trenches 10–15cm (4–6 in) deep; below: in individual holes, causing less soil disturbance; overleaf: by 'lazy bed' method – especially suitable for water-retaining soils; and right: covering with black polythene to save earthing-up

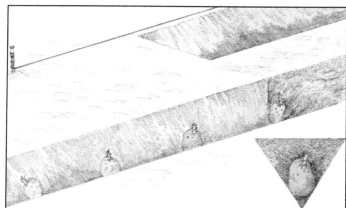

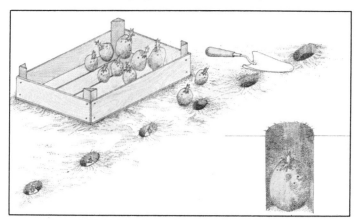

Above: two young plants suffering from potato blight. Right: cover plants with newspaper if there is danger of frost

rows to make a ridge. This prevents the tubers from pushing through into the sunlight. Tubers greened by the sun cannot be eaten.

To earth-up, stand between two rows of potatoes and, with a draw hoe, reach out over the plants and draw the soil up and under the lower leaves with a steady hand. Then turn round the end of a row to earth-up the other side. Repeat until all rows have been earthed-up on both sides. It makes for easier earthing if you first loosen the soil between the rows by forking it over.

Pests and diseases

The most frequently-encountered enemies of the potato are potato blight, common scab and potato eelworm.

Potato blight In mid and late summer (late June and early July) spray the plant with a fungicide such as Bordeaux mixture as a safeguard against potato blight. This is a fungus disease that spreads quickly in damp, humid conditions, and its presence is revealed by dark brown blotches on the leaves and the rapid deterioration of the haulms. Any sudden collapse of the foliage should always be viewed with suspicion. If this happens, cut off the haulms about 30cm (12 in) above the soil, remove them from the plot and burn them. This will prevent the blight spores from getting into the soil and infecting the tubers. The tubers may then be left in the soil for a couple of weeks to ripen off.

Common scab Another trouble that may be encountered is common scab; this is caused by a minute soil organism. The trouble is only skin deep and does not affect the eating or keeping qualities of the tubers. It is usually worse in light, hungry soils. Some good compost or grass mowings, placed in the bottom of the trench at planting time, will help to give clean tubers.

Potato eelworm This pest can be a serious problem. The tiny eelworms, too small to be seen by the naked eye, attack the plant stems and roots. Stunted plants with thin stems are an indication of their presence. The only cure is to starve them out by not growing potatoes on infected ground for several seasons. A three- or four-yearly crop rotation is a good deterrent.

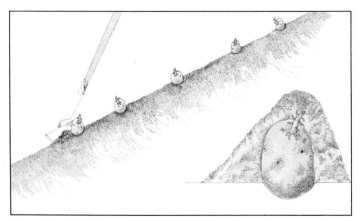

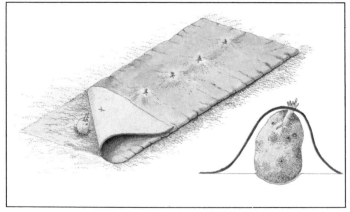

HARVESTING AND STORING POTATOES

The cultivation of the potato has now been described in some detail. Here we explain how to harvest and store this all-important vegetable, to enable you to get the best results.

It is usually the late varieties of potato that are grown for winter use and storage, but if the early ones have not been used up before the haulms have died off there is no reason why these, too, should not be stored. Most earlies, when ripe, will keep until mid winter (late December) at least.

Signs of maturity
The first sign of approaching maturity is a yellow tinge in the lower leaves of the haulms. This is followed by a gradual browning of the leaves and stems, until finally the haulms wither and die.

A change also takes place in the tuber. The skin of a 'new' (that is, immature) potato can be removed easily, whereas that on a ripe tuber is firm; once the skins have 'set', the crop is ready for lifting.

Lifting the tubers
To lift the crop, use either a digging fork (that is, one with square tines) or a potato fork (flat tines). Stand facing the row to be lifted, and thrust the fork in at the *side* of the ridge, not across it, otherwise some of the tubers will be pierced with the tines. Put the fork in at an angle so that when thrust well down, the tines are below the root; then lift the root cleanly and throw it forward. Shake off the dead haulm, and spread the potatoes out so that they are all on the soil surface. Before moving on to the next root, fork carefully through the area to bring up any tubers that remain.

Lift the crop on a dry day, if possible, so that the potatoes can be left out for an hour or two to dry. The soil will then come off them more easily. Rub off as much of it as possible when picking the potatoes up, and sort them into two grades – the eating or 'ware' potatoes, and those too small for use. Never leave the little ones lying about on the soil as they are apt to turn up again later as 'self-sets', producing new potato plants. Any tubers that have been speared by the fork should be placed on one side and used first.

Checking for disease
The ware potatoes can be put into sacks or boxes, or piled up in a heap on the soil.

After lifting, potatoes should be left to dry out for a couple of hours. This makes the removal of soil much easier

If heaped, they must be covered with the dead haulms or some other litter that will exclude light, to prevent them turning green. Leave the tubers for two or three weeks, before sorting through them all over again.

The purpose of this interim period is to give any diseased tubers a chance to show themselves. If the potatoes were stored away immediately after lifting, and not re-examined, any diseased tubers would continue to go bad, and could spread disease through the bag or heap.

Disease shows as a pinky-brownish patch on the skin. It is not difficult to see on white tubers, but may prove more difficult on coloured ones. If in doubt, scratch the skin with a finger-nail to see whether the discoloration goes right into the tuber.

How to store
Sound tubers can now be stored for the winter in a cool, dark, frost-proof place. These three conditions are not always easy to meet indoors. A cool pantry, or an unheated spare bedroom or boxroom, would be suitable, or a brick garage –

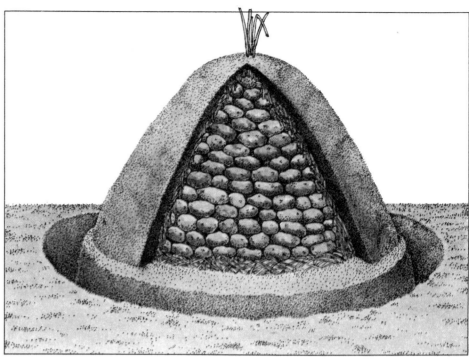

Above: drying off the harvested crop
Right: an outdoor clamp not only saves indoor storage space – the tubers will remain firmer than if in bags
Below right: it is essential to remove any shoots that appear on stored tubers

provided the door is not left open in frosty weather. Wooden sheds are seldom frost-proof, but will serve if extra covering can be put over the tubers during severe frost.

Boxes and sacks If the tubers are stored in boxes, the top of each box must be covered to exclude light. Hessian potato sacks, once so common, are now difficult to obtain and have given way to paper sacks, that can be bought from most large stores. Polythene sacks are not suitable, as a certain amount of light can penetrate and moisture can build up inside.

Outdoor clamp Where the crop consists of more than a couple of sacks, storage space can be saved by making an outdoor clamp (see diagram). This provides ideal conditions, and keeps the potatoes firmer than if they are stored in bags.

To make a clamp, level the soil and tread it firm. Put down a layer of straw to make a bed for the tubers, and pile them up on this. Pack them neatly so that the sides of the clamp are as steep and level as possible. The heap can be round or rectangular, but for average quantities a conical shape is more usual. Then cover the potatoes with a layer of straw (or hay or dried bracken) about 15cm (6 in) in thickness.

The next step is to mark out a circle approximately 25cm (10 in) from the straw. Thrust the spade in all the way round the circle, and dig out the soil beyond it, piling it up on the platform between the mark and the straw. Keep the same depth of soil all the way up. Fill in cracks and hollows with loose soil from the bottom of the trench, and finish by patting the soil smooth with the back of

the spade. Subsoil should not be used, so if necessary extend the trench outwards.

To begin with, leave a wisp of straw sticking out at the top of the clamp. With the onset of colder weather, pull this out and fill in the hole. During spells of severe frost, straw or litter spread over the clamp will give added protection; the most vulnerable parts, of course, are those facing north and east.

Inspect the clamp at intervals to make sure that rats or mice have not found it. If

there are tell-tale holes, fill them in and set traps for the culprits, making sure that these are safe for domestic pets.

If it is necessary to open the clamp during the winter months, make sure that it is adequately sealed up again, and never try to open it while frost is about.

Towards late spring (end of March), get the potatoes out of the clamp and rub off the sprouts. Any tubers that have been stored indoors should also be de-sprouted in the same way.

CARE AND CULTIVATION

INTENSIVE CULTIVATION OF VEGETABLES

Most gardeners would like to get a 'quart into a pint pot' – particularly where the vegetable plot is concerned. Generally speaking, the smaller the plot the more important it is to obtain the maximum yield from it. To do this, there are certain guide-lines and methods to be kept in mind.

One of the most important factors in intensive cultivation of vegetables is the fertility of the soil. To crop a strip of ground intensively year after year it must be built up to, and maintained in, a high state of fertility. The other main ingredient of intensive cultivation is careful planning. There is no need for an elaborate crop plan, but you should know, well in advance, what you want to plant, and when.

Maintaining soil fertility
When any part of the soil becomes vacant in autumn or winter, dig and manure it as soon as possible. Put all suitable waste material into a compost heap so that it can be returned to the soil. Mulch with peat or compost during the summer months, not only to conserve moisture but so as to add to the humus content of the soil when the mulch is dug in. In the spring, or when follow-on crops are planted during the summer, apply a general fertilizer at the rate of 70g per sq m (2 oz per sq yd).

Aim to get a quick turnaround of crops whenever possible so that valuable space is not left lying idle any longer than is necessary. This is particularly important during the summer months. Do not dig deeply during this period; keep the moist soil down below where it will do most good, and simply prick the topsoil over with a fork to a depth of 8–10cm (3–4 in). Rake the soil down again at once before it has time to dry out.

Choosing vegetables and varieties
Care is needed in the choice of crops to be grown and the selection of varieties. While the choice will depend, to some extent, on what each household likes, it is wise to go for those crops that are expensive to buy and those that soon lose their freshness when gathered (often the two are synonymous).

Sweet corn, tomatoes, salad crops, French beans, peas and young roots of beetroot and carrots are all good choices for intensive cropping. Late potatoes take up too much room, but a row of first-earlies is always worthwhile, especially when they are really early and ready when shop prices are still high. When choosing brassicas avoid the larger cabbages and grow smaller ones like Greyhound (pointed) and Vienna Babyhead (round). Brussels sprouts take up too much room, unless you pick a dwarf variety; you may prefer to grow a row of sprouting broccoli or its delicious autumn counterpart, calabrese.

Choose early varieties for the first sowings and then use them again in late summer when the growing time is short. Let the accent be on varieties that mature quickly, even though they may be smaller, and do not hesitate to sacrifice the tail-end of one crop if, by so doing, there will be time to plant another.

Intercropping and double-cropping
There are two practices that are of special value to the holder of a smaller vegetable plot – intercropping and double-cropping.

Intercropping is the growing of a quick-maturing crop between the rows of a slower one. A good example is spinach between rows of dwarf peas and lettuces planted between rows of French beans. Radishes, that need only three or four weeks in which to mature, can always be grown as an intercrop. Another method of intercropping, often overlooked, involves sowing or planting the intercrop first. If, for example, you sow lettuces or carrots in rows 45cm (18 in) apart instead of the customary 30cm (12 in), you can then plant a row of dwarf cabbages between them in mid summer (June). Provided you keep the basic principles of intercropping in mind – that the intercrop should be harvested before the second crop needs all the room – you can devise many variations on this theme.

In double-cropping the second crop is not sown or planted until you have gathered the first. Examples of this method are brassicas or leeks after early potatoes, or lettuces or roots after a first sowing of peas.

Cutting down on spacing
A further point to consider in intensive cultivation is the amount of room to be given between plants and rows. Every plant should have enough room in which to mature, but no more. Carrots 5cm (2 in) in diameter and beetroot 8cm (3in) in diameter are large enough for general use. Lettuces, that are normally given 30cm (12 in), can be restricted to 25cm (10 in) without any harm being done, while smaller varieties will head at 15cm (6 in). Thinning should be done early so that unwanted seedlings are not competing for food and air.

In recent years the 'block' system has become quite popular; several rows are sown quite close together. A wider space between one block and the next serves as a path. Five rows of carrots, for example, with 15cm (6 in) between rows, followed by a path 45cm (18 in) wide, take up less room than five rows at the customary spacing of 30cm (12 in), and weed growth is also less.

Using cloches
In any system of intensive cultivation cloches are a great help. Try to acquire enough to cover at least one row of vegetables. The value of cloches in warming up the soil in spring and bringing on early crops is well known; less appreciated is their worth in extending the season into autumn and winter. They often make it possible to harvest two crops in a season, and can give partial protection to three or more. As an example, you can sow lettuces in early spring (February) in soil pre-warmed by the cloches. These can be de-cloched in late spring (April); the cloches are then moved to cover a row of early French beans. After the risk of frost has gone in mid summer (early June) you can put tomatoes out under cloches. At the end of the year use them to finish off lettuces sown in late summer to early autumn (July to August).

Right: suggested cropping plan for a plot 9 x 4·5m (30 x 15 ft). Row spacing is drawn to scale but not row length, so the plot appears elongated. Some inter-crops are sown before the main crops; for instance, kohlrabi, turnips and carrots go in before late peas. Space has been left for two courgette plants, started in warmth, at the end of the sweet corn rows, lending added interest to the plot

Intensive cultivation of vegetables

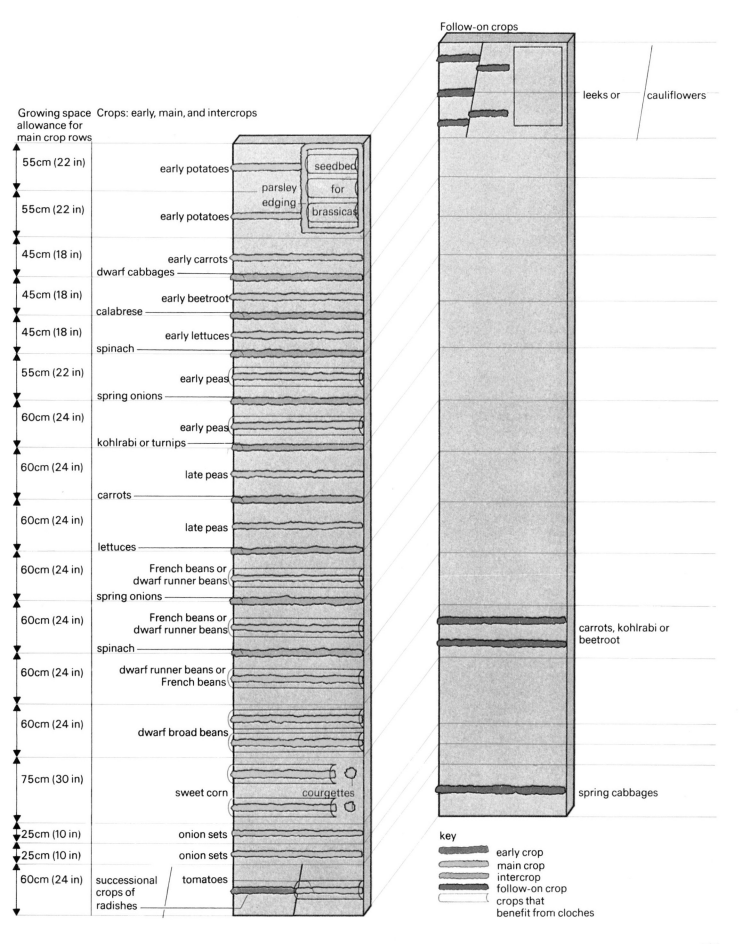

Follow-on crops

leeks or / cauliflowers

Growing space allowance for main crop rows

Crops: early, main, and intercrops

Growing space	Crops
55cm (22 in)	early potatoes
55cm (22 in)	early potatoes
45cm (18 in)	early carrots / dwarf cabbages
45cm (18 in)	early beetroot / calabrese
45cm (18 in)	early lettuces / spinach
55cm (22 in)	early peas / spring onions
60cm (24 in)	early peas / kohlrabi or turnips
60cm (24 in)	late peas / carrots
60cm (24 in)	late peas / lettuces
60cm (24 in)	French beans or dwarf runner beans / spring onions
60cm (24 in)	French beans or dwarf runner beans / spinach
60cm (24 in)	dwarf runner beans or French beans
60cm (24 in)	dwarf broad beans
75cm (30 in)	sweet corn / courgettes
25cm (10 in)	onion sets
25cm (10 in)	onion sets
60cm (24 in)	successional crops of radishes / tomatoes

parsley edging

seedbed for brassicas

carrots, kohlrabi or beetroot

spring cabbages

key

early crop
main crop
intercrop
follow-on crop
crops that benefit from cloches

191

SMALL-SPACE VEGETABLE CROPPING

A small garden need not be a barrier to the growing of vegetable crops. Methods of crop-spacing, involving calculation of the exact amount of room required for vegetables to mature to eatable size, mean that you can grow enough to supply the kitchen throughout the year.

Old gardening manuals indicate that gardeners of bygone days had an enviable amount of space at their disposal. Carrots, for instance, could be thinned to 15cm (6 in), beetroot to 20cm (8 in), parsnips to 25cm (10 in) and swedes to 30cm (12 in). Today, with gardens becoming ever smaller, it is important to make the fullest use of vegetable space. Crops must have enough room to mature, but no more. The problem is to decide exactly how much is enough.

Determining correct spacing

There are several points that must be taken into account in finding a successful solution to this problem. The first one is that you must not fall into the trap of giving the plants insufficient room.

Space is always needed for adequate cleaning and cultivation of a crop; weeds rob the plants of food, light and air, and it is also difficult for the gardener to move freely among rows of plants that are less than 25–30cm (10–12 in) apart, except in the case of the strip method of cultivation that is explained later. Some crops require special methods of cultivation; potatoes, for example, need earthing-up and it is difficult to do this with a row spacing less than 60cm (24 in). This distance can be reduced to 55cm (22 in) with early varieties, where large tubers are not so important and the ridges need not be so well formed. Leeks also come into this category since they can be grown in rows 30cm (12 in) apart, but actually need a minimum of 38cm (15 in) if they are to be earthed-up a little to obtain a greater length of blanched stem.

Give some thought as well to the size of vegetables you require. Those for exhibition will naturally need more room than those for the kitchen. This is not to say that exhibition specimens cannot be eaten – they can – but a housewife needing a medium-sized onion for a stew will not look kindly on one weighing a few kilograms. It is now accepted that small

roots have a better flavour than large ones. Generally speaking, the larger a root becomes the more likely it is to coarsen in texture. This size is something that can be controlled by spacing. Carrots for pulling young need not be more than 4cm (1½ in) in diameter, and can therefore be thinned to that distance, while main-

crop ones for storing will be large enough at 8–10cm (3–4 in). A beetroot or turnip 10cm (4 in) in diameter is big enough for most needs, while the massive parsnip of former years can be replaced by a couple of roots at half the space – 13cm (5 in). Swedes will be large enough if thinned to 15–20cm (6–8 in).

The size of your family is yet another point that needs to be considered. Today families are generally smaller, and it would seem that the era of the giant marrow and the outsize cabbage has gone. The trend in the newer varieties of cabbage, for instance, is towards smaller, compact ones with few outer leaves, that are more suitable for smaller families; while larger cabbages may serve for several meals they soon lose their freshness when cut open.

Below: summer cabbage Primata, a small ball-headed variety

Left: vegetable plot at Wisley showing maximum use of available space

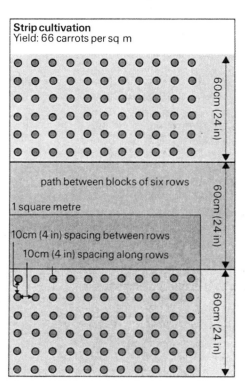

Strip cultivation
Yield: 66 carrots per sq m

path between blocks of six rows

1 square metre

10cm (4 in) spacing between rows

10cm (4 in) spacing along rows

60cm (24 in)
60cm (24 in)
60cm (24 in)

Particular spacings

The size of cauliflowers is governed largely by the richness of the soil and the amount of space they are given. If you want 'mini' cauliflowers for a small family, the answer is to plant them closer together so that smaller curds will form. For this purpose the usual spacing of 60cm (24 in) between plants and rows can safely be reduced to 45cm (18 in).

With peas the general rule is that the distance between the rows should ap-

Below: dwarf broad bean The Sutton grows to a height of 30cm (12 in)

Below: strip cultivation of carrots can more than double your yield

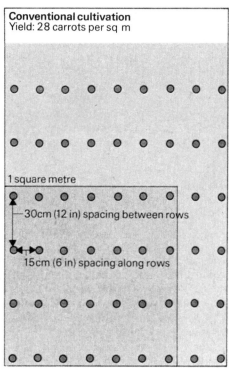

Conventional cultivation
Yield: 28 carrots per sq m

1 square metre

30cm (12 in) spacing between rows

15cm (6 in) spacing along rows

proximate to the height of the peas. Dwarf varieties 45–60cm (18–24 in) high do well enough with a row spacing of 45cm (18 in). Another method worth trying is to sow three rows, spacing them only 30cm (12 in) apart. They will fill the space and help to hold each other up, and you can pick them by reaching over the rows from either side.

Not much can be done to reduce the normal area for runner beans, especially if they are climbing, but you can grow French beans in a double row, this being a particularly good method if you need only two rows. Space the seeds at 15cm (6 in) with 30cm (12 in) between the rows.

The dwarf broad bean is a most useful vegetable, needing a spacing of 25–30cm (10–12 in) between plants and 30cm (12 in) between rows. Three rows, as suggested for peas, gives a worthwhile sowing, resulting in a crop that can be picked over for several weeks.

The new varieties of brussels sprouts tend to produce tight, medium-sized sprouts suitable for freezing. The older varieties have always been a problem in the small garden as they need 60–75cm (2–2½ ft) of space all round. The varieties Early Half Tall and Peer Gynt (F.1 hybrid) are only of medium height and will crop at 53cm (21 in) between plants and rows.

Strip cultivation

Some research has already been done on this problem of vegetable spacings, and the work is continuing. One method to come out of the research is the strip system of cultivation, that is of particular value for the growing of carrots, but can also be adapted for other roots and for onions.

Briefly, the system is to sow a number of rows close together, with 45–60cm (18–24 in) paths between the strips. For example, six rows of carrots can be given only 10cm (4 in) between the rows, instead of the customary 30cm (12 in). Hoeing with a small onion hoe and weeding can be done from the paths on either side of the strip. One advantage of this method is that after the seedling stage the foliage forms an even carpet that effectively cuts out weeds.

Within the limits of your own soil and site there are minimum distances at which each vegetable will produce a satisfactory crop. To get full production it is worthwhile trying to find these distances, there being plenty of scope for every gardener to experiment for himself. Careful planning in the initial stages and the right choice of varieties are the first steps towards success.

THE IMPORTANCE OF TYPE AND VARIETY

The importance of a good working knowledge of the types and varieties of vegetables available cannot be stressed too much. If you are to make full use of the area you have set aside for food growing, it is essential that you choose wisely.

Fortunately knowledge of which types and varieties of vegetables to choose can be obtained through the pages of an up-to-date seed catalogue. The modern seed catalogue may justly be described as the seedsman's shop window, and nowadays it is an extensive window. Moreover even in these days of increasing costs, the catalogue is free and any seed firm of repute will be pleased to send you one.

Careful study of a good seed catalogue always repays the time involved and will prove of absorbing interest. It also helps to avoid mistakes in selection and planning. As it can be done in an armchair, in front of a glowing fire, there can be few more pleasurable forms of gardening.

Using a seed catalogue
'But why' you may be thinking 'should one go to the trouble of ordering direct from a seed firm when so many shops and stores sell seeds during the spring months?' One answer to this is that the seeds displayed in shops and stores are usually the most popular varieties of standard vegetables. New introductions and unusual vegetables are not generally found there. Another point is that this is purely a serve-yourself service and the assistant at the cash desk will not be an expert on seeds.

If you need help in assessing the merits of different varieties it is better to study a good seed catalogue and then send in an order, or buy from a recognized seed-shop or garden centre where you can seek expert help. It is worth remembering, too, that a good seed catalogue does not only describe the different varieties; it often gives useful tips on sowing and growing them as well.

Seed catalogue terminology
Gardeners are accustomed to talking, rather loosely, about types and kinds of vegetable, and about varieties, strains and hybrids. A newcomer to vegetable gardening often finds these terms rather confusing. 'Types' and 'kinds' really

mean the same thing. The broad bean is a type or kind of vegetable; so is a lettuce or carrot. Varieties are selections within the kinds or types; Bunyard's Exhibition is a variety of broad bean, Webb's Wonderful is a variety of lettuce and Early Nantes is a variety of carrot.

A strain is a particular selection of seeds within a variety. When we speak of a good strain or a pure strain we mean that the seeds will always produce plants that are true to the characteristics of that variety. A poor strain, on the other hand, means that those characteristics are less evident than they should be.

You will notice, when reading your catalogue, that some varieties have 'F.1' after the varietal name. This is the accepted symbol for an F.1 hybrid. To produce these, two parent plants with desirable characteristics are selected. These are then inbred (fertilized with their own pollen) until the special qualities are fixed. The two varieties are then crossed and their progeny becomes a first cross (F.1) hybrid. The special qualities of these hybrids are usually increased vigour, better quality, improved colouring and a marked uniformity of size. As the pro-

duction of these hybrids is more expensive than that of ordinary seeds, they naturally cost more, but they are well worth the expense.

Breeding varieties
Plant breeding and plant selection is going on all the time. Plant breeders do not make their crossings haphazardly (hoping for something to turn up) but with a definite goal in mind. Their main objectives are: first, to breed plants for a particular purpose; second, to breed plants for a particular season; third, to breed plants for a particular microclimate, site or type of soil.

One of the main groups of vegetables bred for a particular purpose are those that are grown for freezing. For instance the newer varieties of brussels sprouts give sprouts that are tight, of good colour and of medium size. This is what the commercial grower needs in order to satisfy the demands of the frozen food firms. Acres of sprouts, and other greens are now grown for this purpose alone. Similarly, slim carrots that can be tinned whole are now being produced for the canning firms.

Plants bred for a particular season include the early and late varieties. By reducing the time taken for some vegetables to mature, the plant breeder has produced some varieties that will crop earlier than others. There are also varieties with special characteristics of hardiness, resistance to frost or mildew, or with some degree of self-protection (as with cauliflowers) that are suitable for late use. Incidentally, the reason why early varieties of some vegetables are often recommended for follow-on crops that will mature late in the season is because, with their shorter growing period, they are eminently suitable for use when the days are getting shorter.

whether you have the time and the staking materials for the taller peas and the tallest runner beans. Again, is your garden very exposed? If so, the dwarf varieties of peas, beans and sprouts will merit your attention. If your aim is to grow early crops you will have to make sure that you have the right varieties.

All this may seem to be just commonsense, and to a large extent it is, but it is surprising how often these points are overlooked.

A good seed catalogue classifies early and late varieties, tall and dwarf, hardy or not so hardy. Most of them now show, with an asterisk or similar symbol, the varieties that are suitable for freezing.

take the two peas Early Onward and Onward. The first is an early cropper and the second a maincrop variety. By sowing them at the same time, or within a week of each other, a succession will be assured. The same thing applies if the lettuce Hilde (early) and Webb's Wonderful (maincrop) are sown together. The alternative, using the second method, would be to make successional sowings of Early Onward and Hilde.

With some vegetables it is a definite advantage to make small, successional sowings. It is easy to get too many radishes or too many lettuces at one time. Sowing single rows at intervals is much better than sowing several rows together

Above left: Early Nantes carrots are ideal for early or maincrop sowings
Above: Exhibition Longpod, a broad bean that may win you show prizes
Right: if you want a cut-and-come-again lettuce, try Salad Bowl

The third group includes plants for warm areas and for frames and cloches, plants for the colder parts of the country, dwarf varieties for exposed sites and roots suitable for shallow soils – such as stump-rooted carrots and globe beetroot.

Making your selection
It is true, of course, that most of the new or improved varieties are designed for the commercial grower, but indirectly they also help the home gardener, for many of them will appear in the retail catalogues.

You can now see why the selection of your vegetables should not just be a matter of picking up the odd packet of seeds here and there, but the result of a carefully thought-out appraisal of your needs. You must know what your soil is like and what it is capable of producing. You will also need to assess your available time and materials: for instance,

Planning succession of crops
All of us, space permitting, want to keep up a steady supply of vegetables. On paper it is not difficult to work out a succession of, say, lettuces that will last throughout the summer months; in practice it will prove much more difficult as the vagaries of climate can play havoc with the most carefully thought-out plan. A cold start in the spring, followed by a sudden spell of hot weather, will sometimes run two sowings into one.

There are two methods of trying to obtain a succession; one is to use different varieties that mature at different times, and the other is to make successional sowings of the same variety (about three weeks should be allowed between sowings). This second method is the cheaper one, especially if you buy a large packet of seeds in the first place.

As an illustration of the first method

and ending up with a glut. With cabbages and cauliflowers it is a good plan to sow the seeds in two batches. This will give at least two plantings–more if larger plants are put out first– with a corresponding staggering of the harvest period.

Selections for other purposes
Where the vegetables are required for a particular season or purpose (for example, late cauliflowers, spring cabbages or plants to stand through the winter) it is essential to choose the right varieties. The catalogue will state plainly which are the late cauliflowers, which cabbages should be sown in autumn for cutting in the spring, and which varieties are best for surviving the rigours of winter. Many catalogues also have some kind of symbol to indicate the varieties most suitable for frame and cloche use.

EASY-CARE VEGETABLES

There must be many people who, for one reason or another, are prevented from giving as much time to their gardens as they would like. Growing vegetables may seem to need a great deal of time, but there is a good range of basic vegetables that can be grown without too much attention.

One way that you can save some time is to sow as many crops as possible *in situ* and so cut out transplanting. This will mean some loss of the earliest crops, but that cannot be helped. Lettuces, for example, are hardier than is generally supposed and can be sown outdoors from mid spring (March) onwards. Courgettes can be sown in early summer (May) where they are to fruit.

Small cabbages of the pointed or ball-headed types can be sown *in situ*. Simply sow a few seeds at intervals of 30cm (12 in) along the drill, and then thin the seedlings to the strongest plant. Kales can also be sown in this way.

This practice of station sowing can be used for other crops and does cut down the time needed for thinning and weeding as a little onion hoe can be used between the plants. Most root vegetables can be grown in this way, and so can lettuces. Pelleted seeds are useful for this type of sowing.

In the case of lettuce and radishes the packets of mixed seeds now offered by most seedsmen are labour saving, giving longer cropping periods per sowing.

Early potatoes
Save time and energy when growing early potatoes by cutting out earthing-up. Earthing is done to prevent the tubers from pushing through the soil into the sunlight, which makes them green and inedible. However, as earlies are dug up in an immature state and before the tubers have reached full size, earthing-up is not as essential as it is for the later varieties.

Easy peas and beans
Staking is a time-consuming business; avoid it by growing only dwarf varieties. The dwarf pea has been with us for many years and there are some good varieties that only need 45–60cm (18–24 in) in height. Dwarf varieties of broad beans need very little support – a few twiggy sticks pushed in among them will keep them from falling over. French beans, too, need only a few twiggy sticks to keep them upright.

The easiest way of growing runner beans is to sow the variety Kelvedon Marvel in drills 5cm (2 in) deep and 90cm (3 ft) apart, allowing 23cm (9 in) between the seeds. The plants will run along the ground to form a continuous row. Any runners that seem likely to stray across into the next row should be pinched back. To pick the beans, simply lift up first one side of the row and then the other. Some gardeners disapprove of this method, pointing out that pods that touch the soil may be mud-splashed in heavy rains and will not be straight. But as the pods have to be washed and cut up before they are eaten, neither point is of much importance. Slug damage of the lowest pods may occur, but slug bait can be put down to keep these pests at bay.

Tomatoes and celery
Because of the time needed to tie them in and pinch out sideshoots, outdoor tomatoes may not seem feasible. The answer is to grow only the bush varieties, which break naturally and need no tying, unless it is one tie to a central cane. When the weight of the fruits begins to pull the stems down, slip black polythene or short litter under the fruits to keep them clear of the soil.

Trench celery is labour-intensive and has to be ruled out, but the self-blanching varieties are a good substitute. Planted in blocks 20cm (8 in) between the plants they soon fill up the space allotted to them and weeds are crowded out. Boards, pegged round the outside of the block, will

Bush tomatoes like Pixie don't need to have their lateral shoots pinched out

exclude light from the plants on the edges, or soil may be drawn up to them.

Simple substitutes
Instead of celery you could grow celeriac. This turnip-rooted form of celery is planted out in flat ground and does not need earthing-up.

Another good 'substitute' vegetable is spinach beet. The true spinach has a comparatively short life and successional sowings are needed to keep up a supply. Two sowings of spinach beet – in the spring for summer use and in early autumn (August) for winter use – will give pickings over a long period.

Other 'easy-care' vegetables
There are other crops worth mentioning in this labour-saving context. Rhubarb, apart from the initial effort of making the bed, does not require much attention. A clean-up of the old leaves each autumn, followed by a dressing of good compost or manure, will keep it going for years.

Onion sets and shallots, once planted, need only regular hoeing along the rows to keep the crop weed-free. Leeks make a good follow-on crop to early vegetables and can stay in the ground all winter; for the gardener too busy to raise his own plants from seed, there is usually no difficulty in buying plants from a reputable nursery or garden centre at the appropriate time.

Kohl rabi is easy to grow and stands drought better than turnips. It can be station-sown *in situ*. In appearance it is rather like a sprouting broccoli and the root – which is really the swollen stem – is formed above ground. The swede may also be station-sown and does not ask for any special treatment. All these vegetables have already been described in depth in their respective sections.

Whether or not to water
One question that can be a real problem is whether to water or not. Watering is a tedious and time-consuming chore, especially in drought periods when hose-pipes are banned. It is some consolation to know that, in general, dwarf varieties of vegetables suffer less from lack of water than the taller ones. The best advice that can be given is that if watering cannot be kept going, it should never be started. Leaving the plants to forage for themselves will do them less harm, in the long run, than starting to water and then having to stop.

COMMON VEGETABLE DISEASES

The vegetable grower, taking time off to peruse his favourite gardening books, can suddenly encounter in their pages a horrific array of plant diseases. But the reality is less dreadful. Many gardeners meet few, if any, of these diseases and most of them can, if the right steps are taken, be cured, controlled or prevented, provided they are caught in time.

One of the most important factors in preventing the spread or recurrence of diseases of vegetables is the practice of good crop rotation. Many diseases, in particular virus ones, have resting bodies that lie dormant in the soil until the next growing season. If the same vegetable, or a close relative, is being grown again then the disease will launch a fresh attack. Hence the importance of crop rotation: diseases 'resting' in the soil are encouraged to die out rather than build up strength.

There is another gardening 'rule' that is vital to the checking of disease spread: never compost diseased material. Just because a plant is dead does not mean that the disease is also dead. So destroy all diseased plants – preferably by burning them – to prevent contamination.

Plant-disease organisms are, in general, very specific in their activity, each tending to be restricted to a small group of closely-related plants. Cucumber mildew, for instance, only attacks cucumbers, marrows and other members of the cucurbit family. Consequently, although there are exceptions to this rule, it is helpful to discuss vegetable diseases on a crop basis.

Potatoes

The best-known disease of this crop is potato blight, that blackens the leaves and can lead to rotting of the tubers. To control this disease, spray at the first sign of attack with a copper fungicide and follow this with two or three repeat treatments at 14-day intervals. Finally cut off, remove and burn the haulm 7–10 days before lifting the crop in order to prevent infection of the tubers.

Virus diseases are another major cause of crop reduction. These infections are detected by the yellow mottling, rolling or crinkling of the foliage. Much the best insurance against virus diseases is to buy fresh certified seed potatoes each year.

Common scab is another widely-spread disease. This produces blemishes on the surface of the tubers but otherwise has no ill effects. Incorporating plenty of bulky organic matter into the drill at planting time reduces the incidence of common scab. It is also important not to lime the soil before planting potatoes as lime favours the disease.

Tomatoes

Potato blight is a major disease of outdoor tomatoes; it not only damages the leaves but also causes a black rot of the fruits. Here again the use of regular sprays with a copper fungicide is recommended to prevent this.

Various soil-borne fungi can cause damping off of seedlings and foot rots of older plants. Foot rot is a very general term used to describe various diseases, all due to fungi of one sort or another, that reveal themselves as a blackening and rotting of the plants.

One of these soil-borne fungi, *Phytophthora parasitica*, is also responsible for buck-eye rot of the fruits. This takes the form of dark patches, with darker concentric rings, at the end of the fruit opposite to the stalk. Watering the soil with Cheshunt compound or captan fungicide is the best way of guarding against these diseases. Another fruit blemish, that is similar to buck-eye rot but has no concentric rings, is called blossom-end rot. This trouble, however, is not caused by disease but is produced by water shortages at an earlier stage of development.

As with potatoes, tomatoes can also be infected by a variety of virus diseases that cause leaf discoloration and growth distortion. There is no cure for these diseases, but they can often be prevented by controlling the aphides that frequently transmit the infection.

In a hot dry summer, leaf mould disease may be a nuisance. The leaves develop yellow patches on the upper surface and a brownish mould beneath. The best remedy is to spray at regular 10–14 day intervals with a copper fungicide, used according to manufacturer's instructions.

Peas

Garden peas are subject to attack by various soil organisms, both at the time of germination and in the later growth

Below, far left: potato tuber rotted with blight disease
Below left: tomato with buck-eye rot
Below: yellow and brown discoloration of tomato foliage indicates leaf mould

stages. Some protection against these diseases can be obtained by the use of captan-based seed dressings, but it is still necessary to practise crop rotation.

Attacks by powdery mildew (that appears as a white powdery covering on leaves and stems) are common in dry summers, particularly on late crops. Anti-mildew sprays (like dinocap) will help to combat this disease; you should also pull out and burn infected plants as soon as they have finished cropping, otherwise they act as sources of infection for later-planted rows.

Broad beans
Chocolate spot is the commonest disease of this crop. It shows up as chocolate-coloured spots on the leaves and pods and as dark stripes on the stems. At the first sign of attack the plants should be sprayed with copper fungicide and then repeat sprays given at intervals of 14 days. Broad beans are most susceptible to attack when grown in waterlogged conditions, so getting the soil into good condition before sowing the seed reduces the risk of infection.

Runner beans and French beans
These are other crops in which root and foot rots can be troublesome. So here again the use of seed dressings, coupled with crop rotation, is to be recommended.

Brassicas
Club root, which causes thickening and distortion of the roots, is the commonest and most serious disease of brassicas. The soil-borne organism responsible for club root thrives on acid conditions, so the first step is to apply a heavy dressing of lime. Crop rotation should also be practised. Finally it is essential to apply 4 per cent calomel (mercurous chloride) dust to the seed drill and to the planting holes. Indeed, seedlings should not be raised in infected soil. Instead they should be grown in sterile growing compost.

Grey mould (botrytis), downy mildew (that shows as white fungal growth under the leaves, although its disease-carrying bodies rest in the soil), white blister (white pustules with a silvery sheen appearing on leaves and stems) and various leaf-spotting diseases occur from time to time, but these diseases generally do not have serious effects on cropping. The best approach here is to remove and destroy all infected leaves.

Swedes and turnips
Swedes and turnips can be attacked by the diseases listed under brassicas. They may also be attacked by powdery mildew, but

this disease does not usually have very serious effects. In addition the roots can be attacked by various root rots. Dry rot shows itself by sunken, cankerous areas appearing on the side of the root. Soft rot may enter through these wounds or where mechanical damage has taken place. This turns the roots to a slimy mass, often leaving the skin almost intact. Black rot turns the flesh of the root dark brown or black. There are no specific control measures for these root diseases, but any infected plants that are discovered should be removed and destroyed.

Parsnips
Parsnips are remarkably free from disease. They may, however, be attacked by downy mildew, powdery mildew and leaf spot. Fortunately these diseases have little effect on the crop.

Canker (sometimes called 'rust') can, however, be very damaging to the roots. This disease first appears as reddish-brown marks on the top of the root. Later it can lead to a general rot. The easy answer in this case is to sow canker-resistant varieties such as Avonresister.

Carrots
Disease is not usually a problem with growing carrots, but serious rots can develop in storage. So it is essential to select only sound roots for storage and to avoid storing the carrots in excessively wet conditions. One disease that is easily recognized at lifting is violet root rot, that shows as a web of violet-coloured fungal threads on the outside of the root.

Freshly-lifted infected roots are edible peeled, but liable to rot when stored.

Onions

Downy mildew of onions can be a serious problem in wet seasons. The first sign of attack is the appearance of light-coloured spots on the leaves. These then enlarge and the affected leaves topple over and shrivel. This disease can have serious effects on the crop yield, so the plant should be sprayed with a general fungicide (such as zineb) at the first sign of attack and repeat treatments given at 7–10 day intervals. It is also important to collect and burn any infected leaves in order to reduce the carry-over of disease.

Another common disease of onions is white rot, that is generally favoured by cool conditions. This disease can be detected by the leaves yellowing and wilting even when there is plenty of soil moisture. If affected plants are closely examined it will be seen that there is a white fluffy fungal growth at the base of

the bulbs. This cottony growth later gives rise to small, black, dot-like sclerotia that are the resting bodies of the fungus. These sclerotia fall off into the soil and are then spread around by subsequent cultivations to provide a source of infection in later years. At present there is no cure for infected plants nor is it easy to disinfect the soil. So, once the disease has appeared in an onion bed, the only answer is to practise long-term crop rotation.

Leeks

Leeks can be attacked by the onion diseases already mentioned. In addition they are subject to attacks by rust disease, which appears as yellow or orange spots. Any leaves showing infection spots should be removed immediately and burned. A programme of regular sprays with a general fungicide should be initiated to protect the plants from further attacks.

Another important disease of leeks is white tip, caused by the fungus *Phy-*

tophthora porri. Normally this disease is restricted to the tips of the leaves, which die and turn white, but it can also affect the edges of the leaves.

At the first sign of the disease the plants should be sprayed with a copper fungicide and repeat applications given at intervals of 14 days during the winter.

Shallots

Shallots are normally very free from disease though they can, on occasion, be attacked by diseases that affect onions.

Lettuce

Outdoor lettuce is normally fairly resistant to disease attack. In overcrowded beds, however, the plants can become infected with a downy mildew. Affected leaves turn patchy yellow and the fungus can be seen on the underside as mealy-looking spots. Since this disease is usually confined to the outer leaves it does little real damage, though heavy infections can spoil the look of the heads. The answer to this disease on outdoor lettuce is to use wide spacings to ensure free air movements around the plants.

Sclerotina disease, which is also called drop, may develop on lettuce in warm weather. The attack begins at ground level, producing a white, fluffy fungal growth that then spreads over the plant, causing it to collapse. Later the fungus produces its small, black, resting bodies (sclerotia) that contaminate the soil. It is therefore important to remove and burn any infected plants as quickly as possible.

Grey mould (botrytis), only occasionally encountered outdoors although very prevalent in the greenhouse, can cause the plants to wilt completely and the leaves to become covered with grey furry mould; spraying regularly with benomyl or thiram will assist in preventing and controlling the disease.

Marrows and cucumbers

Marrows, cucumbers and other cucurbits are all liable to attack by a powdery mildew (cucumber mildew) that can seriously check their growth. This disease can be controlled by spraying with an anti-mildew fungicide. Infection by mosaic virus is also a common problem with cucurbits. This type of virus is readily recognized by the presence of small, puckered leaves showing yellow mottling. Any young plants with these symptoms should be dug up and burnt as they will not produce worthwhile crops. Established plants that become infected in the later growth stages can, however, be left to grow on, but destroy them after the crop is harvested.

Above left: leek attacked by rust disease
Left: roots of brassica thickened and distorted by club root
Below left: carrots suffering from violet root rot
Below: onions infected with white rot
Below right: lettuce stem rotted by grey mould
Right: lettuce leaf infected with mildew

COMMON VEGETABLE PESTS

Success in vegetable growing is measured by the yield of healthy, succulent produce. Crops that are ravaged by insects not only yield less but are also much less appetizing. Sensible and effective pest control, therefore, plays an important role in vegetable gardening.

Pests can, and do, attack vegetables at all stages of growth – from seed germination right through to cropping time. Constant vigilance is needed to guard against this type of damage, and some understanding of the nature of plant pests and the timing of their attacks is helpful in planning effective countermeasures.

Seedling pests
Seedlings are liable to attack by soil-borne pests from the moment germination begins. These are the unseen killers that are the main cause of gaps in seed rows or even total failure of the sowing. Insurance against these pests is cheaply and easily obtained by the use of a combined insecticide/fungicide seed dressing. Alternatively, HCH (formerly known as BHC), diazinon or bromophos powders can be dusted into the open seed drills at sowing time.

Root flies
The larvae of cabbage-root fly and carrot fly are common and damaging pests. The female lays her eggs on the soil surface close to the developing seedling and the grubs then burrow down to feed on the root or bulb. In the early stages there are no obvious signs of damage and it is only when the plants are beyond recovery that the extent of the attack becomes apparent. So here again it is important to take preventative action by applying bromophos, diazinon or HCH around the bases of the young plants. As a wise precaution, make a second application about three weeks after the first, to insure against repeat attacks. Carrot fly can also attack parsnips so this crop, too, should be treated in the same way.

Flea beetles
These tiny beetles live in the soil and are most active at night. Consequently they are not too easily spotted. The damage they cause is, however, only too obvious as the young leaves of the seedlings become pitted with small, round holes. This damage greatly reduces seedling vigour and can lead to the death of the

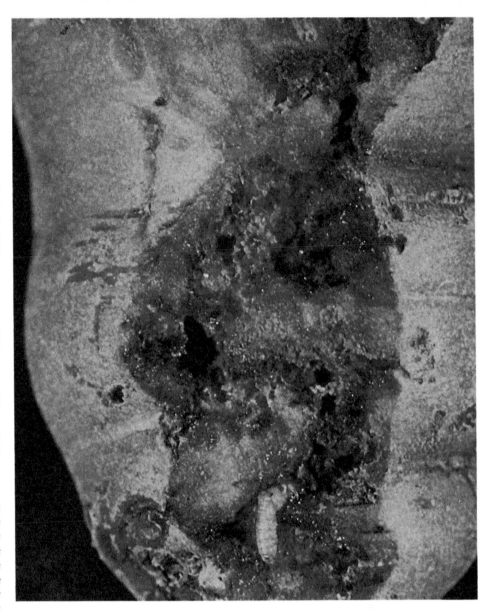

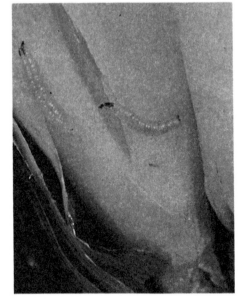

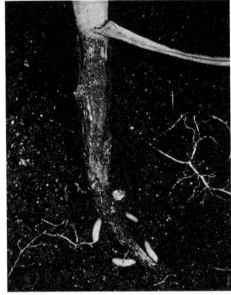

*Left: three examples
of plants suffering attack
from root-fly larvae –
(top) carrot root fly,
(bottom left) onion fly
and (bottom right)
cabbage-root fly
Right: pea moth maggots
can quickly bore their
way into developing
pods
Below: radishes and
turnips are especially
susceptible to the
ravages of flea beetles
Bottom: pea and bean
weevils bite tell-tale
semi-circular notches out
of the leaf margins*

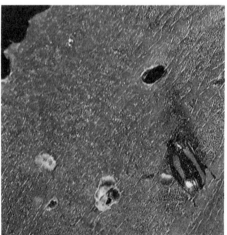

Slugs

Slugs and snails can do enormous damage in the vegetable garden to both seedlings and mature plants. Not only do they gnaw at the stems at soil level but they can also climb and eat the foliage. Most species of slugs and snails are readily killed by spreading slug pellets on the soil around the threatened plants. This treatment, however, is not effective against the keeled slug that is so damaging to potato tubers. This small, dark-coloured slug spends all its life in the soil and is not attracted to the poisoned bait. The only way of reducing crop damage from this pest is to restrict potato plantings to early varieties that are less prone to attack.

Caterpillars and maggots

If these larval forms of butterflies, moths and flies are not controlled they can cause a lot of damage to vegetable crops. Leaf-eating caterpillars of the cabbage white butterfly and other species rapidly make all kinds of brassica crops inedible. Not only do they eat their way into the heads of the vegetables but they also foul the leaves with their green excrement. So it is important to deal with these pests at the first sign of attack. Make regular checks on the undersides of the leaves for clusters of yellow or orange eggs. Any clusters that are found should be rubbed off and the plants given a thorough spraying with a general insecticide. This will deal with any eggs that have been missed and will also give short-term protection against further attacks. Since attacks by these pests can go on over a fairly long period, be vigilant throughout the summer.

Large drab-coloured caterpillars, called cutworms, that live in the surface layer of the soil, can be very damaging to lettuce and other salad crops. Cutworms eat through the plant stems at soil level and the first indication of their presence is when the stems are completely severed and the attacked plants wilt. Cutworms can be controlled by using a spray-strength solution of HCH, diazinon or pirimiphos-methyl as a heavy soil drench along the crop rows.

The young grubs of the pea moth bore their way into the developing pods, infesting the peas and making them inedible. These pests can only be controlled in the short period between the eggs being laid and the entry of the grub into the pod. So spray the plants at early blossoming and then give a repeat spray about a fortnight later.

White blisters on the leaves of celery plants indicate an attack by celery fly. The adult females lay eggs on the underside of the leaves and the young grubs quickly

plants. Luckily these pests are readily controlled with an HCH dust. Radishes, turnips, cabbages and other brassicas are vulnerable to attack.

Pea and bean weevils

These small, beetle-like insects live in the soil and commonly feed at night on the foliage of peas and broad beans, biting semi-circular notches out of the leaf margins. Plants damaged by these pests are not killed, but their cropping potential is reduced. So it is well worthwhile to spray both the plants and the surrounding soil with a general garden insecticide at the first sign of attack.

tunnel into the leaf tissue. They then continue to feed inside the leaf, thus producing the characteristic white blisters. Protective spraying with a general insecticide is one way of dealing with these pests. Established infections, however, can only be eliminated by the use of chemicals such as pirimiphos-methyl that can penetrate the leaf tissue and kill off the grubs within the blisters.

Aphides

Aphides can be very troublesome pests since they not only weaken the plants by sucking the sap but can also transmit virus diseases. Blackfly, for instance, are major pests on all types of beans since they damage the flowers and reduce the set of pods. The traditional method of dealing with blackfly of broad beans is to pinch out the growing tips at the first sign of infestation. A more modern approach is to spray with a systemic aphicide such as menazon. Greenfly and blackfly sprays should also be used on runner beans and on French beans where it is not practicable to pinch out the growing tips.

Greenfly can attack most vegetable crops but are particularly damaging on lettuce and carrots. Here again the application of a good greenfly killer should be made at the first sign of attack. Brassica crops are subject to attack by grey aphides that quickly build up into massive infestations. So regular inspections coupled with prompt and thorough spray treatments are necessary to ensure clean, healthy crops.

Most types of aphides are readily seen and easily recognized. Root aphides, however, which live in the soil and attack plant roots (lettuce are particularly vulnerable), are generally not noticed till infested plants wilt and die. When these are lifted it will be seen that the roots are covered with a greyish, 'cottony' mass of aphides. Should this type of infestation be observed then it is a good idea to apply a heavy solid drench with a general insecticide before making further sowings.

Whitefly

In recent years, cabbage whitefly has become a major pest of all types of brassicas. Like aphides, whitefly weaken the plants by sucking the sap. They also foul the plants with sticky excretions of honeydew that favours the development of disfiguring sooty moulds. Unfortunately whitefly are rather difficult to control because of their complicated life cycle. Crawling larvae hatch out of eggs that are laid on the leaves. These larvae pass through several growth stages before changing into pupae from which new

Above: bean that has become heavily infested by blackfly, the bean's major adversary
Left: lettuce root aphides are not often spotted until plants wilt and die

adults hatch out. Only the winged adults are susceptible to most general insecticides, so a minimum of three sprays at 3–4 day intervals is necessary in order to deal with emerging adults that continue to develop from the resistant larval stages. Bioresmethrin, resmethrin and pirimiphos-methyl, however, do have some effect on the larval stages and so products containing these insecticides are to be preferred for whitefly control.

Use of pesticides

Some gardeners are afraid to use pesticides on edible crops because they consider that these treatments may leave harmful residues. But in the development of garden chemicals, several years of intensive research are carried out to ensure their safety in use. For instance, it must be firmly established that the chemicals quickly break down into harmless substances following their application to plants. The speed with which this happens varies with different chemicals so it is important to read the directions for use on the product label. These clearly state what interval must be left between the last spray application and the harvesting of the crop. Provided that this instruction is obeyed there is no risk of the crop being contaminated.

A GLOSSARY OF KITCHEN GARDEN TERMS

Like most other specialists, gardeners have their own words and phrases to describe certain things. Here we list the most common kitchen garden terms, giving a simple explanation in each case.

The following selection of terms is given in alphabetical order for easy reference.

Acid and alkaline An acid soil is one that is deficient in lime, and an alkaline soil one that has enough lime. The degree of acidity or alkalinity is measured by something known as the pH scale – below pH 7 being acid and above it, alkaline. Most vegetables do well in a soil that is slightly alkaline.

Aphides A general term embracing greenfly, blackfly, whitefly and the grey cabbage aphid.

Blanching The practice of excluding light from the stems and/or leaves of a vegetable, usually to improve the flavour. Celery, chicory, leeks and endive all need blanching in this way.

Blind A 'blind' plant is one without a growing point, sometimes the case among the brassicas. As these plants will never make anything except outside leaves, they should be thrown away as soon as you find them.

Bolting Vegetables that run up to seed before their time are said to 'bolt'. This sometimes happens with lettuce, particularly after transplanting in a dry period, and also affects beetroot and carrots, especially when beetroot are sown early. The most common cause is a check to growth.

Brassicas The generic term for greens and brussels sprouts. Swedes, turnips, kohl rabi and radishes are also members of the brassica family.

Buttoning A term applied to cauliflowers when the curd begins to open out while it is still quite small. It is usually caused by the growth of the plant being checked in some way.

Catch-crop Another word for intercrop. Any crop that can be grown quickly between the rows of a slower crop.

Clamp A heap of potatoes or roots covered with straw and then a layer of soil, for winter storage.

Clove A segment of a bulb, often used in connection with shallots or garlic.

Compost Manure made by the rotting of waste vegetable matter. The word is also used to describe a particular medium for seed sowing or potting – for example, the John Innes composts.

Cordon A method of training fruit, especially apples and pears, that keeps plants to a single stem. A cordon-grown tomato, for example, is one that has the sideshoots pinched out as they form.

Curd The head of a cauliflower.

Dibber A steel-pointed stick, about 30cm (12 in) long, with a box- or T-handle, used for making holes for plants when they are transplanted.

Drawn A plant is said to be 'drawn' when it has been brought on too quickly. The result is a spindly, pale-coloured plant. Avoid these when buying young tomato, celery or brassica plants.

Drill A narrow furrow, made with the corner of a hoe, into which seeds are scattered or sown at intervals.

Earthing-up Drawing soil up to a plant, as with potatoes to prevent greening of the tubers, or with celery and leeks for blanching. Earthing-up may also be done to stabilize plants and give them a better root hold.

Eye The growth bud of a potato tuber.

F.1 hybrid A first cross of two plants that have been inbred to 'fix' certain desirable characteristics. In vegetables, F.1 hybrids are usually of better colour and shape than non-hybrids, and are also more uniform in size.

Foliar feed Feeding a plant through the leaves by spraying or watering with a proprietary solution. This is of value for leafy crops such as brussels sprouts or sweet corn.

Green manuring Growing a crop such as rape or mustard to dig into the soil to improve the humus content.

Haulm The top growth of plants, particularly when used in connection with potatoes or peas.

Humus The dark, residual material of decayed vegetable matter or animal manures. It is of particular value in all soils as it improves both the structure and water-holding properties.

'In good heart' A gardener speaks of a soil being 'in good heart' when it is a rich, fertile loam, well supplied with humus. The opposite terms are 'poor' or 'hungry'.

In situ Sowing seeds where the plants are to remain, as distinct from sowing in a box or nursery bed (for transplanting).

Intercrop Same as catch crop.

Light The sliding lid of a garden frame.

Liquid manure This can be made by putting some manure in a hessian bag and suspending it in a tub of water. Leave for several days, and then stir it well, diluting it until it is the colour of weak tea. Proprietary liquid manures may also be bought and should be used according to the instructions on the bottle.

Loam Ideal garden soil – neither too clayey nor too sandy.

Mulch A layer of compost, lawn-mowings, peat, sawdust, well-rotted manure or black polythene put down between rows of vegetables. The objects are to conserve moisture and to smother weeds. Always water soil thoroughly before putting down a mulch, and do not push it right up to the plants – leave a slight gap so that rain can get in.

Root run The area taken up by the roots of a plant.

Set A small, immature bulb – an onion, for example – that is planted to grow on.

Previous page: lettuce that have bolted
Right: spraying a foliar feed over the leaves of a crop of sweet corn
Below: humus content of soil is improved if green manure is dug in during autumn

Spit A spade's depth of soil. To dig 'one spit deep' is to turn the soil over to the depth of the spade.

Stopping Halting the growth of a plant by pinching out the growing point. This is done with tomatoes when the plants have set as many trusses of fruit as are likely to ripen, and also with marrow, cucumber and melon to make the plants produce flowering sideshoots on which fruits will form in due course.

Strain A particular selection of a variety, often referred to as a 'good strain' or a 're-selected strain'.

Tilth Soil worked down to receive a crop. 'A fine tilth' is a soil that has been raked down fine and even.

Tine The prong of a fork, rake or cultivator.

Top dressing An application of well-rotted compost, or a fertilizer that is spread on the soil surface, either before or after planting. This may be lightly pricked into the soil with a fork, or can be hoed in during normal cultivation.

Variety A selection – produced either naturally, or more often by breeding – of any kind of fruit or vegetable.

SECTION II

GARDENING UNDER GLASS

INTRODUCTION

If, not so long ago, someone had predicted that greenhouse gardening would become one of the top hobbies, it would have been met with as much scorn as the idea of man on the moon once was – yet this is just what has happened.

The vagaries of the weather have finally impressed upon the home gardener the many advantages of using protected cultivation, whether a small cloche, frame, or full size greenhouse. Each can have its own individual and special applications.

Although in the past wise gardeners may have employed cloches or a frame or two, and perhaps have yearned for a greenhouse, a structure of any considerable size was not very easily acquired. This was owing to the unavailability of suitable designs, erection difficulties, and especially to financial problems. Today, with the mass production of simply erected, prefabricated greenhouses and the introduction of plastics, and with firms springing up everywhere to supply them at reasonable cost, a greenhouse in every home garden will soon be accepted as part of the routine of life – along with the television, refrigerator, and car.

The rise of greenhouse gardening as a hobby is not really difficult to understand. A gardener entering the world of the greenhouse encounters a land of enchantment, fascination, and delight. The Victorians appreciated this fully and those who could afford them would not be without their conservatories, which were sometimes very spacious and grand indeed. For them, fuel costs, its supply, and enough servants to look after the work, were no problem, and most prominent households had their 'tropical paradise'. The years following the Victorian age saw a decline in greenhouse gardening, and it was for a long time still regarded as an expensive, rather 'highbrow' hobby. However, the more recent 'boom' has again made the idea of a conservatory feasible – this time for most people. It's now more modest in most cases, and takes the form of a sun lounge, garden room, or home extension, as well as the more conventional glass, lean-to greenhouse. These structures often tend to become the favourite parts of the home because of the restful and relaxing effect an environment of plants and greenery can have.

By keeping a greenhouse frost free or slightly heated in winter you can enjoy growing plants from almost the world over. You can look forward to as much colour in winter as in summer, and you can have a wealth of pot plants and cut flowers for the home. Aesthetic considerations aside, there are many culinary pleasures too: fresh salads the year round, luscious fruits such as grapes, melons, figs, and nectarines, and earlier or better vegetable plants for the kitchen garden. If you think heating may overburden your budget, there are numerous uses for an unheated greenhouse. It can be regarded as a covered garden in which to grow to perfection, unblemished by the weather, most outdoor hardy plants.

A greenhouse, frame, or cloches, can greatly influence household costs. Both food and decorative plants for rooms or garden are hardly cheap. Any structure enabling you to grow your own, soon pays for itself.

A greenhouse or a few frames can make an enormous difference to your outdoor garden. You can enjoy the new varieties and seed novelties introduced each year, and protect and save your more tender garden plants over winter. Today, a frame or small greenhouse used for bedding plant production only, will quickly recover its cost. Many superb house plants, and pot plants for gifts, can be raised for a matter of pence, yet they are extremely expensive to buy in florists.

An often overlooked aspect of greenhouse gardening is its value as an ideal hobby for the disabled, infirm, or not-so-young. It is frequently pleasant to have weather protection for ourselves as well as our plants. Flower show enthusiasts and floral art lovers will also find the greenhouse has much to offer.

In this book we have tried to collect together practical information derived from past experience as well as from modern trends, discoveries, and inventions. This should help beginners to start right as well as being of interest to 'old hands'. We have also tried to sweep away some cobwebs in the form of incorrect or outdated customs. Green shading which is quite wrong, and growing in unhygienic hit-or-miss potting composts using unsterilized animal manures, are just two examples of practices still difficult to persuade gardeners to abandon. In other ways as well, modern research and development, and the work of plant breeders, has made growing much easier for the greenhouse gardener and we have tried to emphasize these. The FI hybrids or new selections of many plants are much stronger and more vigorous than old varieties, and there are also better and universally safer pesticides. A combination of where the advantages of two of these benefits can be seized, for example, is in the case of cucumbers and tomatoes. Both can now be grown very successfully together in the same greenhouse. Foliar feeding using vitamins and plant hormones, and systemic pesticides, which can attack pests from inside the plant's tissues, are two more very useful modern aids.

Cloche and frame gardening is a little 'art' of its own, one that can be fun as well as useful, embracing the production of flowers the year round as well as edible crops. The subject is well covered by this volume, although often omitted in books on general greenhouse gardening.

We also look into the future by including sections on the use of artificial light. There is much yet to be discovered in this field and it gives the ordinary home grower a chance to research and perhaps add to scientific knowledge of how plants react to light. The subject is really in its infancy, and as well as having applications under glass it is possible to apply the techniques to growing rooms or chambers, and places where natural light cannot normally penetrate. Another special section deals with conservatories and garden rooms now rapidly becoming eagerly sought after as features of modern homes. Fancy shapes are rarely desirable for the utilitarian greenhouse and it is wise to stick to conventional squares and rectangles. The conservatory or garden room, however, lends itself to many exciting possible architectural designs which could be exploited more frequently.

You don't have to be an experienced outdoor gardener to embark on greenhouse gardening. Remember that greenhouses can be erected on paving or asphalt, in yards, and even on flat roofs and balconies, where there may be no soil for miles. A greenhouse with no ground soil is, in some ways, an advantage – it eliminates the temptation to use it! Except where the greenhouse is portable as already mentioned, the ground soil in a permanent greenhouse can lead to trouble if grown in. Its use is a common beginner's mistake. The lure of the ground soil is of course greater if you have been used to outdoor gardening. Under cover, soil may give good results the first year and then soon deteriorate. This is called 'soil sickness': a vague term denoting a build up of unbalanced fertilizer salts, waste products from plants and other chemical substances, and possibly pests and disease organisms. Outdoors a plot intensively cultivated can get 'sick' too, hence the practice of rotation, but the effect is delayed by washing out by rains, the action of frost and the sterilizing effect of ultra violet light from the sun (which does not penetrate glass), and natural pest and disease predators. In any case, far more reliable and certain results are obtained by growing in containers of one or other of the specially designed potting composts, and sowing seeds in proper seed composts.

Dirty water such as collected from gutters or stored in filthy open tanks and butts, must not be used for irrigation – this is a frequent common mistake! What is the point of employing clean sterilized seed and potting composts if you do. Clean tap water is much safer even if it is limey. Dirty rainwater can be a 'soup' of infection.

A frequent mistake is to buy a greenhouse that ultimately proves too small. The more capacious the greenhouse the easier it is to maintain a steady environment. In a tiny greenhouse, for example, the temperature can fluctuate alarmingly with changes in the sun's power during the day. Plants rarely enjoy this. Reasonable room also makes working easier and more comfortable, and there is more scope for growing and arranging plants.

A final hint, left last so that it remains well remembered, is to pay great care to summer shading and ventilation. Study this section of this book well. Far too many beginners lose a whole greenhouse of plants in a matter of hours because shading is overlooked and vents are left closed on a sunny day. When this happens the temperature absolutely rockets up, and even tropical plants can get boiled or baked to death.

This book should give the beginner an excellent introduction to the possibilities and scope of greenhouse gardening as well as useful practical basic advice. It is especially hoped that the book will inspire the desire to adventure further and perhaps to specialize as well.

FRAMES AND CLOCHES

CHOOSING FRAMES AND CLOCHES

A frame – or two – costs little to buy, or make yourself, and can be fitted into most gardens. Nearly everything you grow in a greenhouse can also be grown in frames, allowing for the restrictions in height and size.
Even if you have a greenhouse, frames can take over much of the work to leave more space for decorative plants and those demanding full greenhouse height.

First you must decide whether to buy a ready-made frame or make one yourself from a frame kit of glass-to-ground design with timber or metal sections. An all-glass frame is suitable unless you want extra warmth for propagation, or for growing cucumbers or melons.

Lids, known as 'lights', can be bought separately and you can place these over your own timber or brick-built sides, or even set one over a pit dug in the ground, adding to it as required. The lights can be easily stored away in the summer, when not in use.

Modern frames are often fitted with sliding glass sides, to give access or for added ventilation, and lights that slide aside as well as lift up so that they can be removed completely for easy working.

Choice of material
Aluminium alloy framework has many advantages: it is long-lasting, requires no maintenance and, being lightweight, is ideal for moving about. If you prefer timber, choose wood that is noted for its weather resistance, because frame sides are likely to come into contact with damp soil for long periods. Avoid soft woods treated with creosote as the vapour continues to be harmful to plants for some time. Green Cuprinol is suitable, but before using any other preservative check the maker's literature to be sure that it is safe for plants.

Plastic, instead of glass, for garden frames is light, easily portable and

A large glass-to-ground frame, with aluminium-alloy framework, being used to house trays of seedlings and plants waiting to be transplanted

obviously advisable where small children are using the garden. From a gardener's point of view, however, glass has many advantages (see the section on choosing a greenhouse on page 222). You must use glass if the frame is to be heated, and would be advised to do so in windy areas as plastic can blow away.

Siting the frame
If you use a frame as an adjunct to your greenhouse (and it has vertical sides), you can push the frame close up to one side. This helps to reduce warmth loss from both the greenhouse and the frame.

If using a frame for greenhouse and pot plants, put it in a shady place – against the north side of your greenhouse is ideal. But most vegetable crops, and those alpines which you may be housing

in frames when not in flower, prefer a bright, open position.

With many frames it is often convenient to set them back-to-back, or alongside each other in rows. To obtain more height, stand your frame on a base of bricks or concrete blocks, or place it over a pit (providing you make sure that water does not collect in it).

Electric soil-warming cables

Frames do not have to be 'cold'; you can heat a large one with a small paraffin lamp provided you take great care to see that there is always ventilation. But installing electric soil-warming cables is by far the best method. Lay them in loops across the floor of the frame, making sure that they do not touch each other. Place a little sand on top and keep it moist: this will hold the cables in place and conduct the warmth more uniformly. Use only about 2–3cm (1 in) of sand, then a thermostat can be installed above the sand level to control the frame's temperature.

If you need extra warmth (as for pot plants) run cables round the frame sides as well. With glass-sided frames, fasten the cables to wooden battens with cleats and thrust the battens into the ground.

If you are growing plants to be rooted into a deep layer of compost (such as salad crops, cucumbers and melons) site the warming cables near the bottom of the compost. In this case a thermostat of the rod type should be thrust into the compost. Temperature can also be controlled manually or by a time switch. The considerable bulk of compost will hold warmth over the periods when the electricity is off.

Wattage depends on the size and purpose of your frame; decide after you have consulted the suppliers of such equipment.

You can use small heated frames inside the greenhouse for high-temperature propagation, or for housing a small collection of low-growing tropical plants. An aluminium framework, glass sides and top, and 2–3cm (1 in) or so of sand over the cable, are recommended. The wattage required is usually about 20W per 1000 sq cm (20W per sq ft) of frame floor, and a thermostat is essential.

Frame cultivation

If possible, avoid using soil. Instead, line a trough or pit with polythene sheeting, slitted here and there for drainage, and fill it with a proprietary potting compost. You can grow excellent, high-quality salad and other crops with little risk from pests or diseases.

Where you are moving pots or other

Above left: timber-sided frame, with glass lights, shelters bedding plants prior to planting out. Above: rows of barn cloches protect lettuce that are almost ready for cropping

containers in and out, firm the floor and cover it with polythene, over which is spread coarse sand or shingle. If you keep this damp, it will moisten the air in the frame; the polythene will help to keep out soil pests.

Grow house plants, and pot plants like cineraria, calceolaria, primula and cyclamen, in frames until the decorative stage when they are ready to transfer to the house, conservatory or greenhouse. Use frames to raise bedding plants and for many forms of propagation from cutting and seed. You will also find them especially useful for crops like lettuce, radish, beet and carrots that you want in the kitchen even before winter is over.

Keep plants like dormant fuchsias, chrysanthemums and pelargoniums (that are used for summer garden or greenhouse decoration) in frames during the winter when they often look far from attractive. Store dormant tubers and bulbs there to leave the greenhouse less cluttered. Some crops, like strawberries and violets, lend themselves particularly to frame culture.

Keep glass frames (and cloches) as clean as possible to admit maximum light and discourage plant pests and diseases. Remove any mud splashes by careful use of a hose, if necessary.

CLOCHES

Early cloches were of glass and often held together by clumsy wires that were difficult to manipulate. Modern designs are simpler and often make use of plastics, which are very suitable for this purpose as cloches are frequently used only for weather protection, high temperatures being rarely necessary.

Select your type

There are tent, barn and т-shaped cloches, and a flat-topped 'utility' one. These are usually held together by special metal or plastic clips. Some cloches can be opened for ventilation or for watering, others have perforated tops to allow the rain to enter. Plastic ones with a cellular structure give greater warmth retention.

You can make simple and effective tunnels, ideal for protecting rows of vegetables, by sandwiching lengths of polythene between wire arches at intervals along the row, or by aligning ordinary cloches end-to-end. Anchor your plastic ones carefully in windy areas as they can easily blow away; use stones, bricks, wooden or metal pegs, or some special cloche fitments.

Cloches are most useful from autumn to late spring for providing protection from excessive wet and cold. Set them in place to dry and warm the soil before you dig and fertilize it, in preparation for sowing or planting.

Cloche cultivation

Use individual cloches for protecting isolated tender plants (such as fuchsia) in beds and borders, and protect groups of hardy and half-hardy annuals until they become established. You can also root cuttings directly into the ground of a nursery bed if you use cloches to cover them.

Many flowers grown for cutting benefit from cloche protection, especially low-growing bulbs in pots or bowls. Other favourite cloche flower crops are anemones, hellebore (Christmas rose), lily of the valley, violet and polyanthus. You can harden off bedding plants under cloches if frame space is not available. Also use them to protect sweet peas in the early stages.

In the vegetable garden, cloches give you year-round cropping. If you plan carefully you can move them from one

Top: tunnel cloches of polythene sheeting are versatile. They can be cut to any length, depending on whether you want to cover one plant or a whole row. Above: corrugated plastic cloches are used here to cover strawberry plants; being lightweight these cloches need to be anchored against the wind with wire hoops. End pieces can be added to give the plants greater protection

crop to another as needed, thus putting a limited number to maximum use.

Working with cloches

You do not need to remove cloches for watering; the water that drains off them will seep into the soil provided that it has been well prepared. It should be porous and moisture-retaining, but well-drained. Work in plenty of humus-forming material, like peat or rotted garden compost. To avoid the wind rushing through your cloche tunnels, block the ends. This also applies to individual cloches used as miniature greenhouses to cover single, or small groups of, plants. When the weather permits ventilation, move the cloches along to leave a small gap between each one and remove the ends of tunnels.

Leave plenty of room between rows for comfortable access and keep the soil along the sides of the cloche rows well hoed to allow water retention. Soluble fertilizers can also be applied along the outside edges of the cloches.

Store glass cloches, and plastic tent and barn types, on their ends and stacked inside each other. For this purpose put down some clean boards (or lay a section of concrete) in a corner of the vegetable plot, and cover it with roofing felt for glass cloches.

HOW TO MAKE A COLD FRAME

The cold frame, measuring 1350 by 915 mm (4 ft 5 in by 3 ft), is big enough to satisfy the most enthusiastic gardener. Our instructions can easily be adapted to different dimensions according to the size you want in your garden

If you haven't yet reached the greenhouse stage with your gardening, what better than a cold frame to give you a taste for growing your own vegetables and flowers from seed? And if you have a greenhouse, how are you going to cope with all those seedlings in it waiting to be hardened off if you don't have a cold frame? In any case, you will be needing as much space as possible in the greenhouse for your growing plants as spring merges into summer.

Like most good things in life, a well-made frame is not cheap, so you can save money by making it yourself.

Tools
steel measuring tape
set square and pencil
panel saw
tenon saw
hammer
bradawl
medium screwdriver
hand or electric drill with 4mm ($\frac{3}{16}$ in) and 3mm ($\frac{1}{8}$ in) bits
plane

Materials
timber (as cutting list)
110g ($\frac{1}{4}$lb) 25mm (1 in) plated panel pins (general nailing)
110g ($\frac{1}{4}$ lb) 40mm (1$\frac{1}{2}$ in) plated panel pins (general nailing)
twelve 40mm (1$\frac{1}{2}$ in) No.8 countersunk brass or plated wood screws (top frame)
twenty-two 30mm (1$\frac{1}{4}$ in) No.8 countersunk brass or plated wood screws (joint reinforcing)
eight 50mm (2 in) No.10 roundhead brass or plated wood screws (final assembly)
2 handles (top frame)
2 sheets horticultural glass 610mm (24 in) square
2 sheets horticultural glass 610 × 305mm (24 × 12 in)
waterproof wood glue
1 litre (2 pints) horticultural wood preservative

TIMBER CUTTING LIST

PART	QTY	NAME	SECTION	LENGTH
A	2	edge stop	25×15mm (1×½ in)	615mm (24½ in)
B	2	top frame rear	50×30mm (2×1¼ in)	1320mm (52 in)
C	3	top frame ends; centre strut	50×30mm (2×1¼ in)	915mm (36 in)
D	4	glass ledge	25×15mm (1×½ in)	810mm (32 in)
E	1	rear panel top	19×150mm (¾×6 in)	1325mm (52¼ in)
F	4	front and rear panels	19×150mm (¾×6 in)	1325mm (52¼ in)
G	4	side panels	19×150mm (¾×6 in)	865mm (34 in)
H	2	side panels top	19×150mm (¾×6 in)	865mm (34 in)
I	3	vertical battens	30×30mm (1¼×1¼ in)	380mm (15 in)
J	2	vertical battens	50×30mm (2×1¼ in)	265mm (10½ in)
K	2	runners	30×30mm (1¼×1¼ in)	785mm (31 in)
L	2	vertical battens	50×30mm (2×1¼ in)	380mm (15 in)
M	3	vertical battens	30×30mm (1¼×1¼ in)	265mm (10½ in)
N	2	capping timbers	25×15mm (1×½ in)	290mm (11½ in)
O	2	capping timbers	25×15mm (1×½ in)	405mm (16 in)
P	1	stop (not shown)	25×15mm (1×½ in)	150mm (6 in)

(see working drawing on next page)

Construction

First of all, check that the space in your garden allows for a frame of our dimensions and, if necessary, adapt the measurements to the area you have before buying the materials. Then estimate the cost from our Materials and Timber cutting lists so that you have an idea of the total outlay. It is as well to check the current prices with your local timber yard or do-it-yourself stockist.

The cold frame illustrated has been specially designed for home construction using simple wood-working joints only. The finished job, however, presents a spacious and rugged structure capable of giving many years of service.

The timber sections specified in the cutting list are standard stock sizes kept by most timber yards, but if you experience any difficulty in obtaining a particular size, then the next available larger size may be used provided that the necessary dimensional adjustments are made to the various parts.

For ease of construction and to make the frame completely portable, it is built as five separate assemblies. The main frame consists of front, back and two sides, each assembled as a panel and then fixed together with wood screws at the corners. The sides, being slightly higher than the front and back, form a recess into which the glazed top frame is dropped. Runners (part 'K') are fitted to the inner side of the end members (see left-hand inset in the drawing on the next page) and these allow the top to slide back for interior ventilation or for working inside the main frame.

The unit shown is designed around standard sized sheets of horticultural glass to avoid the need or expense of specially cut glass sizes. The design may, however, be re-sized to suit individual needs simply by amending the lengths of the panels affected.

Whether building to the sizes shown or to amended sizes, it is as well to work so that one panel is completed before the next is made, and in the order shown. This should help to ensure that any variations in timber sections or sizes are automatically catered for as work proceeds. Waterproof wood glue is recommended for all permanent joints to ensure a rigid structure.

The instructions given provide a frame measuring 1350 × 915mm (4 ft 5 in × 3 ft), standing 430mm (1 ft 5 in) high at the back, coming down to 330mm (1 ft 1 in) at the front. Before starting work, be sure to read through the following stages of construction.

Stage 1 – glazed top

Cut parts 'C' to length and then notch the ends (see drawing) to present a snug fit to parts 'B'. Use a tenon saw to cut the notches. Cut parts 'B' to length, remembering to allow for any variations in sectional timber sizes. Assemble the frame by screwing parts 'B' to parts 'C', after drilling pilot holes for the screws.

Taking measurements direct from the assembled frame, cut parts 'A' and 'D' to length and glue and nail them in position. Parts 'A' provide an edge stop for the glass, and parts 'D' a ledge upon which the glass rests.

Stage 2 – front and rear panels

Parts 'E' and 'F' must be approximately 6mm ($\frac{1}{4}$ in) longer than the overall length of the completed top frame to allow this to run smoothly between the side members, so before cutting these parts check the length (parts 'B') of the top frame. Now reduce the depth of part 'E' by cutting a 15mm ($\frac{1}{2}$ in) strip from the top edge to provide clearance for the sliding top frame, using a panel saw.

Cut parts 'I' and 'M' to length. These parts form the vertical jointing battens for the main cladding, parts 'E' and 'F', and are fixed centrally and at either end of the front and rear panels. Study the right-hand inset section on the drawing and note that the side pieces must be set back sufficiently to accommodate parts 'J' and 'L' of the end panels. Use a piece of the timber from which these parts will be cut to determine this distance. Assemble the front and rear panels by glueing and nailing to the battens 'I' and 'M', then reinforce each butt joint with a 30mm ($1\frac{1}{4}$ in) screw.

Stage 3 – side panels

It is vital when building the side panels to be sure to make an opposite 'pair' and not two identical pieces.

Cut parts 'G' and 'H' to length and note that these should be approximately 50mm (2 in) shorter than the overall length of the side pieces (parts 'C') of the top frame. Mark an angled line to parts 'H', allowing the full 150mm (6 in) width of the board at the higher back edge and reducing to 30mm ($1\frac{1}{4}$ in) for the lower front edge. Cut to the line – remembering to make a pair.

Assemble the side frames by glueing and nailing, then reinforce each joint with a 30mm ($1\frac{1}{4}$ in) wood screw. Note that parts 'L' and 'J' must overhang the sides 'G' and 'H' by approximately 15mm ($\frac{1}{2}$ in) to provide a fixing point for the capping timbers, parts 'O' and 'N' (see right hand inset section). Add the top

frame runners (parts 'K') and then trim the tops of parts 'L' and 'J' flush to 'K'. Finally add the capping timbers, parts 'O' and 'N', by glueing and nailing.

Stage 4 – final assembly

Drill two 4mm ($\frac{3}{16}$ in) holes to parts 'I' and 'M' as clearance holes for the 50mm (2 in) main assembly wood screws (see drawing). Hold the frames firmly together and, using a bradawl through the holes, bore pilot holes in parts 'J' and 'L' for the screw threads. Fix the frames together, but do not apply glue to the joints; in this way the assembly can be easily dismantled for re-siting.

Try the sliding frame and plane it as necessary to achieve a neat sliding fit. Part 'P' (not illustrated) is then fitted as a 'stop' under the central part 'C' to butt against part 'M' when the frame is fully closed.

At this stage the assembly must be dismantled and given a thorough soaking with a horticultural-type wood preservative. When the preservative has dried, the handles should be added (see drawing) and the glazing fitted and secured by panel pins. To do this, lay the glass in position and with the hammer head lying sideways on the glass, gently tap the pins halfway into the timber frame.

Rest the frame on a row of loose-laid bricks, thus providing a neat finish and also helping to preserve the woodwork by keeping it clear of damp earth.

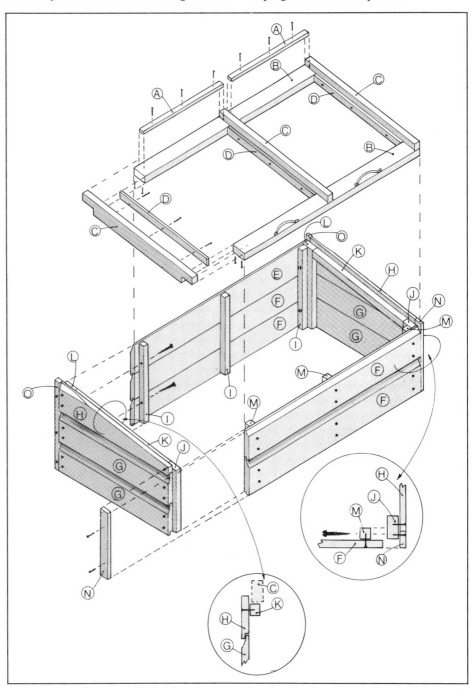

USING CLOCHES IN THE VEGETABLE GARDEN

The value of cloches lies not only in the sunshine they draw and the warmth they generate beneath them, but also in their ability to shield crops from cold winds – particularly in winter and early spring – and give protection against birds. Here we describe the main types available today before going on to look at the use of cloches throughout the year and at the crops that benefit.

Good cloches are not cheap to buy, but their cost should be reckoned against the number of years they can be expected to last and the value of the crops they will protect. When this is done, a row of cloches will be seen to be a very good investment indeed.

The main types

In recent years, glass cloches have lost ground, in terms of popularity, to the newer polythene and plastics models, but glass is still the most durable. At one time, packs of these cloches were on offer, but today it is customary to buy the fittings and glass separately. The obvious disadvantage of this type is that glass breaks, but with care and experience breakages can be kept to the minimum.

The most usual types of glass cloche are the 'tent' and the 'barns'. The first has two sheets of glass 60 × 30cm (24 × 12 in); the low barn has two sheets 60 × 30cm and two sheets 60 × 15cm, and the large barn is made up of four 60 × 30cm sheets. The latter are big enough to protect tomatoes, melons, sweet peppers, cucumbers and aubergines, at least for part of their growth.

Polythene cloches are usually of tent or tunnel design, and need to be firmly anchored so that the wind cannot carry them away. Plastics designs come in many different forms. A useful one is corrugated, bent to a half-circle and secured with hoops pushed into the soil. These cloches can be stacked flat when not in use, so taking up little space.

Some of the different types of glass, polythene and plastics cloches are also illustrated on page 212.

How to use them

In French, the word 'cloche' means 'bell', and the earliest cloches were, in fact, bell-shaped. They were used for striking cuttings or for protecting individual plants. Later, the 'continuous' cloche was invented, with open ends so that a number of them could be used together to make a row or 'run'.

Some cloches can still be used individually to protect particular crops

Open-topped, tunnel-shaped cloches not only make watering easier, they also make it more effective, the narrow base width concentrating water around the roots

such as a newly-planted cucumber or marrow. Single cloches can also be used for raising brassica seedlings. A low barn will take five rows 10cm (4 in) apart, and if the seedlings are thinned to 5cm (2 in) a single cloche will cover about 60 plants.

Whether used singly or as a run, the ends should always be closed with pieces of board or glass to avoid the creation of a wind tunnel. However, an exact fit is not necessarily essential.

Weeding and ventilation
The modern barn cloche has a detachable pane that makes weeding possible without removing the whole cloche; this pane can also be adjusted for ventilation purposes. Where this refinement is not available, ventilation can be given by leaving a slight gap between the cloches.

Watering
Watering is not the problem you might

Above left: a run of tent cloches in situ over newly-planted seed
Left: ventilation panels can be removed from barn cloches in warmer weather
Below: pots sunk into the soil will allow water to seep sideways beneath the cloche to nourish plant roots

expect, being necessary in spring and summer only. To get at plants growing in the centre, the cloche can be removed completely or the ventilating panel taken out, while for side rows watering can be done *over* the cloche: water runs down the side sections and into the soil, from where it seeps sideways beneath the cloche.

A good method of watering such plants as tomato, cucumber and melon is to sink plant pots about half their depth into the soil, approximately 15cm (6 in) from the plant stem, and then water into the pots.

The need for watering will be less if the ground is prepared well in advance – this should be kept in mind where a sequence of cloche crops is planned. If the soil is dug and manured in autumn or winter, it will retain moisture much better than a hastily-prepared site in spring. Failing this, fork in some good compost or well-moistened peat to the top layer of soil.

Layout
Where cloches are to be switched from one crop to another, a lot of effort can be saved if the strips are reasonably close together. Glass barn cloches, in particular, are heavy and moving them from one end of the garden to the other involves time and effort. Careful planning can cut this down.

De-cloching
Unless the weather suddenly becomes very warm, de-cloching of crops should be done gradually. Begin by removing the ventilating pane altogether or spacing the cloches a little farther apart. The next stage is to remove the cloches completely in the daytime, replacing them for one or two nights until the plants have become accustomed to the changed conditions.

Storage
With the possible exception of large barns, cloches are not usually required during summer months. Unused cloches should not be left lying about on the garden, for more breakages happen then than when they are in regular use. Those that are easily dismantled should be taken down and stored away. Tent and barn cloches can be stood on end and stacked one inside the other in a vacant corner or alongside a path.

Before using them in the autumn, give the cloches a wash so that the maximum amount of light is available to the protected crops, and to lessen the chances of harbouring pests and diseases.

Right: two types of barn cloche – the four-part (above) and the three-part model (below) with one ventilation panel

CROPS FOR CLOCHES

Previously we described the main types of cloche available, and also provided weeding, watering and ventilation details. Here we outline the range of crops that benefit from the protection afforded by cloches, giving the sowing or planting season in each case.

The gardener who has a run of cloches at his disposal will get off to a good start in the spring, for a crop with cloche protection for most or all of its growth will mature up to three weeks earlier than an unprotected one. This means that in many cases the same sowing strip can be used again – later in the year – for a different crop. Dwarf peas, for example, if sown under cloches around mid spring (middle of March), will be ready for picking in mid summer (June); as soon as they have been cleared, plant cabbage or cauliflower, or sow carrots or beetroot for pulling young in the autumn.

Spring and summer sowings
If you have any cloches to spare in late winter (January), put these in place and leave them for about a month to dry out and warm up the soil – this pre-warming is an important facet of cloche cultivation. Then, in early spring (February), you can sow lettuce, carrots, peas or broad beans there.

Another crop that benefits from growing under cloches in the spring is new potatoes. Tubers planted in mid spring (March), if already sprouting, will be through the soil well before the last frosts, and cloches will prevent damage. Give potatoes plenty of air during the daytime but close up the cloches at night. If the haulms are drawn up too quickly they will flop over when the plants are de-cloched.

By about late spring (middle of April) you can cover runner beans, dwarf French beans, or sweet corn, all these being sown *in situ*. This will give you about a month's start on the same crops sown without protection.

From early to mid summer (middle of May to early June) – according to district – tomatoes, sweet peppers, aubergines, cucumbers, marrows and outdoor melons will be ready for planting out under cloches. The cucumbers, cantaloupe melons, and some dwarf varieties of tomato can be covered throughout their growth if large barns are used, but smaller cloches are helpful for temporary protection. Even if you keep these tender

crops under cover for just the first few weeks after planting, it will be worthwhile, for this is a critical period – especially if the nights are still cool.

Continuing protection
When the plants are pushing at the roofs of the cloches, it is time to de-cloche, but a respite can be obtained for another week or two if the cloches are raised up on bricks.

In the case of cordon tomatoes, you can give continued protection by carefully tipping the cloches on end and standing them around the plants. Ideally, two cloches should be allocated to each plant, but if your supply won't run to this, use one cloche and leave the plant open on the south side. The cloches help to keep the plants upright; they also allow rainfall to reach the plants naturally, and enable you to pick the crop without first having to move the cloches. Do make sure, though, that each cloche is securely fastened to a cane pushed into the soil, or else a summer storm could bring disaster.

Lettuce (above) will benefit from cloche protection in early spring

It is not always realized that cloches can extend the season at *both* ends. Late summer (July) sowings of beetroot, carrots, turnips and lettuce, if cloched in mid autumn (September), will continue to grow until early winter (November). The little lettuce Tom Thumb can be sown as late as early autumn (August) and still mature by early winter (November), provided you cloche it.

Ripening tomatoes
Cloches can be used for ripening tomatoes in the autumn. The weight of fruit growing on dwarf varieties pulls the laterals down. Flowering shoots continue to form, mostly at the top of the plants, but by mid autumn (early September) it will be too late for these to make anything and you can cut them out. You can then replace the cloches over the plants. Where the tomatoes have been grown as cordons, cut them from the supporting

canes, lay them carefully on a bed of straw or black polythene, and cover them with cloches. Ripening will then continue well into late autumn (October).

Drying off bulbs
Cloches are also useful for drying off onion, shallot and garlic bulbs. Spread them out in a narrow band just less than the width of the cloches, and cover. This gives the bulbs the full benefit of the sun, while keeping the rain out. Leave the ends of the cloches open so that the wind can blow through.

Autumn and winter sowings
All your cloches should be occupied throughout the autumn and winter. Lettuce of the Suzan type can be sown in mid autumn (September) and cloched a month or so later. Thin them to about 5cm (2 in) when they are large enough to handle, and thin them again around early spring (February) to 13–15cm (5–6 in). These thinnings can be transplanted. In late spring (April) take out every other plant for use and leave the others to heart up properly. For an overwintering cos lettuce, try Winter Density. To keep botrytis at bay, give ventilation in all but the coldest weather.

Both endive and corn salad will give better and cleaner crops if they are given cloche protection, and this is also true of spinach beet. A sowing of round peas – Feltham First is a good choice – can be made in late autumn (October), and one of broad beans in early winter (November). All these overwinter successfully.

If you have had difficulty growing spring cabbage, it is worth trying it under cloches, for these give complete protection against marauding wood pigeons.

A year's programme
There are many variations on the cloche theme that you can try out for yourself, but here is one suggestion for a run of large barn cloches throughout the year:
Mid autumn (September) – sow Premier or Suzan lettuce. A barn cloche will take three rows 20cm (8 in) apart.
Late autumn (October) – cover.
Late spring (middle of April) – de-cloche. Sow two rows of dwarf beans 30cm (12 in) apart, and cover at once.
Early summer to late autumn (end of May to October) – cover dwarf tomatoes, sweet peppers, cucumbers or melons.

Tent cloches (above left), and the ventilation panels of barn models (left), can be removed from dwarf French beans during the day in early summer
Far left: drying off shallot bulbs

ORGANIZING AND EQUIPPING THE GREENHOUSE

CHOOSING A GREENHOUSE

Greenhouses come in all shapes and sizes – and today no garden need be without one, however small, for there are many simple and easy-to-erect models as well as more elaborate and decorative ones.

The acquisition of a greenhouse opens up an exciting new area of gardening, where you don't have to worry about extremes of weather or damage from cold, wind or excessive rain. You can regulate the amount of water your plants receive and, because fertilizers are not washed away by rain, you can feed them correctly.

Temperature and ventilation can be adjusted and, by applying shading, even the light may be altered to suit plant preferences. Pests and diseases are easier to combat and the plants are protected from damage by birds and small animals.

Which type?
Most greenhouse styles offer the choice of a glass-to-ground or a base-wall design. The glass-to-ground type allows very efficient use of space for growing. When staging is fitted, there is enough light beneath for the accommodation of a varied selection of plants. The all-glass house is also ideal for tall subjects like tomatoes and chrysanthemums. By arranging your space carefully you can grow many different kinds of plants together. For example, you can grow tomatoes along the south side, followed by chrysanthemums – putting the pots on the floor. Your staging can then run along the north side, providing a surface on which to grow a variety of pot plants, with some space below for plants that like a certain amount of shade (as do many house plants). On the end wall you can train climbers bearing either beautiful flowers, or edible crops like cucumbers.

But for some purposes a greenhouse with a base wall of brick, concrete or timber boards (usually called a 'plant house') is preferable. Plants liking deep shade can be grown below the staging. This design is more economical to heat artificially and therefore is preferable when the greenhouse does not get much sun. It is also a good choice where high temperatures have to be maintained for propagation or for tropical plants (many of which do not demand much light). Greenhouses with a base wall at one side and glass-to-ground at the other are also available. These should be oriented east-to-west with the base to the north.

Planning ahead
Before buying your greenhouse, make sure that you are not infringing any rules or regulations by erecting it in your garden. If you are a tenant you should seek your landlord's permission; should you move, you can take the greenhouse with you. If you are a freeholder and wish to have a permanent structure (like a lean-to against the house wall) you will almost certainly require planning permission from your local council.

You must also do some advance thinking about the foundations of the greenhouse. You can lay old railway sleepers or concrete footings, or build a low, cemented brick wall on which the greenhouse can be free-standing or screwed into position. Do have a path of concrete, brick or paving stones down the centre of the house, for dry feet and clean working.

The best positions
Freestanding, rectangular greenhouses get most benefit from the sun if you orientate them east-to-west, with the long sides facing north and south. The 'high south wall' greenhouse *must*, in fact, lie this way to catch as much winter light and sun as possible. Staging, if used, should run along the north side.

With a lean-to, you may have no choice in the siting, but what you grow in it will depend on which way it faces. An east- or west-facing lean-to is usually fairly versatile since it gets some sun and some shade. If north-facing it will be very shady and is best devoted to pot plants (such as cinerareas, cyclamen, primulas and calceolarias) and house plants for permanent decoration. A south-facing lean-to can become very hot in summer and, unless you want to install shading, you should choose sun-loving plants like cacti and succulents.

Types of material
You should consider the cost of subsequent maintenance as against initial outlay when choosing your materials.

Glass or plastic? Glass has the unique property of capturing and retaining solar warmth. It also holds artificial warmth better. Polythene has a limited life and for long-term use a rigid plastic (like Novolux) is the wisest choice. Plastic surfaces are easily scratched by wind-blown dust and grit, causing dirt to become ingrained and a loss of transparency over a period of years. Plastic also becomes brittle with weathering and may disintegrate.

However, plastic is advisable if the site is likely to be the target for children's games or hooligans out to break glass, or where quick erection or portability is desirable, or where temporary weather protection is all that's necessary. Moulded fibreglass greenhouses are also available, but tend to be expensive and the fittings have to be free-standing.

Aluminium frames Aluminium alloy (often white-coated) is now tending to replace timber for the frame as it has many advantages. It is lightweight yet very strong, and prefabricated structures are easily bolted together. Sophisticated glazing, using plastic cushioning strips and clips instead of messy putty, means that the greenhouse can easily be taken apart for moving. There is no fear of rot, warp or trouble from wood-boring in-

A 'vertical-sided 'barn' or 'span' model (far left) with timbered base walls on three sides. The 'Dutch light' house (left) is always a glass-to-ground structure; it has sloping glass walls which are designed to trap the sun's rays.
A 'lean-to' (below) can be set against a garden or house wall, where it can double as a conservatory or home extension

sects, or need for maintenance, like painting or treating timber.

Timber frames These may look better in a period-style garden. Select one of the more weather-resistant timbers such as cedar, teak or oak, but remember that all timber needs painting or treating with a wood restorer or preservative from time to time.

Providing shade
If your greenhouse receives plenty of sun you will need shading in the summer.

Slatted blinds, run on rails over the exterior of the roof, are efficient but costly. They also have to be made to fit. Interior blinds are far less efficient in reducing temperature, since the sun's heat-producing rays have already entered the greenhouse, though they do help to prevent direct scorch.

The simplest and cheapest effective method of shading here is with an electrostatic shading paint that is not washed off by rain but can easily be removed by wiping with a dry duster. You apply and remove it like a blind.

All year round ventilation
Ventilators are usually fitted in the roof and sometimes in the sides as well, reducing excess heat in summer and controlling humidity at all times.

Types of heating
It makes sense to heat your greenhouse, if only to keep out frost, since this greatly widens its usefulness. Your heating need not be costly if you don't waste it.

Oil heaters Both oil and paraffin are easy to store and portable heaters are particularly valuable as supplementary heating

in periods of extreme cold or during power cuts. Use paraffin heaters that are specially designed for greenhouses; the blue-flame design is best.

Electricity is trouble-free and gives accurate temperature control, but it can be expensive if used wastefully. Fan heating is very effective providing the fan and heat output are controlled together (preferably with a separate, rod-type thermostat); avoid a heater with a continuously-running fan. Ventilation becomes almost unnecessary with this system, and if you line your greenhouse with polythene to form a kind of double glazing you can cut fuel consumption by up to half.

Convector heaters and electrically-heated pipes are also efficient when used together with an accurate thermostat.

Natural gas There are special greenhouse heaters using natural gas, with good thermostatic control. They can also be adapted to work from bottle gas, though this makes them more expensive to run.

Natural gas, oil and paraffin, when burned, all produce carbon dioxide and water vapour. The carbon dioxide is beneficial to plants, but the water vapour can be a nuisance in winter when you will do better to keep the greenhouse dry. You will need some ventilation to keep down humidity and supply air for the fuel to burn, but this cold air does mean that some of the heat is lost.

Other types of heating Solid fuel (with the heat distributed by hot water pipes) and oil-fired boilers are still relatively cheap methods of heating. Hot water pipes, linked to a boiler, maintain high temperatures but are costly to install.

Heated propagators You will need some form of heated propagator so that you can germinate seeds without heating the whole greenhouse to a high temperature. Electrically-heated models are simple and cheap to run.

Automatic watering
There is a wide choice of equipment here. The water can be fed to the plants by overhead sprays, trickle-feed pipelines, by capillary sand benches or capillary matting. In the case of capillary watering, the sand or matting under the pots is kept constantly moist by whatever automatic system is installed.

Artificial lighting
A paraffin lamp will give you enough light in the evenings for most jobs, but if the greenhouse has an electricity supply you can install either a lamp-holder and lamp bulb or a fluorescent tube.

ERECTING AND SITING A GREENHOUSE

To be the owner of a successful greenhouse, you need to spend at least as much time and thought on where to site it as on which type to choose. Equally, attention to detail when laying foundations and erecting the structure will amply reward the extra time spent.

In most cases it is wise to choose an open position for the greenhouse where it will get as much sunshine as possible. This generally means that you should try to position the unit with one of the longest sides facing south. It is a simple matter to shade the glass when you want to reduce light entry, but it is difficult to increase light without the trouble and expense of artificial lighting.

Remember that, in winter, nearly all plants will enjoy plenty of sunlight – even summer shade-lovers. Winter sunlight also means plenty of free warmth and your heating costs will be reduced.

Shady and windy sites
Avoid, where possible, a site that is near large trees (especially evergreens). Falling branches may break the glass, and spreading roots may upset the foundations. Falling leaves and exuded gums from some species dirty the glass, and you may also find that the roof is covered with bird droppings. Evergreens cast shade all year round, and many trees harbour numerous pests and diseases that can attack greenhouse plants and crops.

Small shrubs and trees are not usually a menace; these can even be planted (far enough away so that they do not cast shade) to act as windbreaks in windy areas. Strong, cold winds, usually from the north and east, can add greatly to the fuel bill. Other suitable windbreaks are fences, walls and hedges – as long as they are not too high.

Low ground and hollows
When choosing a site for your greenhouse, look carefully at the ground contours of your garden. In all cases where the site is at the foot of a hill there is a danger of frost pockets forming. Cold, frosty air can run off a slope almost like water, and surround a greenhouse that is set in a hollow. Where no other site is available, a low brick wall can help to deflect icy air currents.

In hollows and on low ground, water may collect or the ground may become very damp. These conditions are particularly unhealthy in winter when the greenhouse should be as dry as possible.

Sites near the house
Many people put their greenhouse at the far end of the garden – some distance from the house. There is often no good reason why it should be tucked away out of sight. Modern structures are rarely 'eyesores' and some designs are very attractive, especially when filled with decorative plants. There are many advantages in having the greenhouse within close reach of the house. Both water and electricity can be run to the greenhouse easily. Electricity, even if you don't want it for heating, may be needed for automatic aids or lighting; you may also wish to run natural gas from the house.

When the greenhouse is to be heated by solid fuel or paraffin, remember that the fuel will have to be carried to the greenhouse and, in the case of solid fuel, the ash carried away – yet another reason for avoiding remote sites. If you don't want to see a greenhouse from the windows of your home, you can always screen it with low shrubs or small ornamental trees.

In some cases greenhouses can be heated economically by an extension of the same central heating system used in your home. In this case the greenhouse should, preferably, come into contact with the house wall, and a lean-to is usually the best design. Where high temperatures are required it is always an advantage if the greenhouse can be set against a house wall, or a south-facing garden wall. Such a wall usually absorbs warmth from the sun during the day and radiates it at night, thus saving fuel and acting as a kind of free storage heater.

Laying the foundations
Most modern, prefabricated, amateur greenhouses are easy to erect single-handed, though with the larger sizes you may need assistance. The ground must always be firm and level, so laying a shallow foundation (by digging a trench and filling it with a fluid concrete mix that finds its own level) is often a wise move. However, some greenhouse manufacturers recommend their own base plinths

and the small additional cost of these is well worth while. Some designs do not need elaborate foundations but are secured by 'ground anchors'. A separate hole is dug for each anchor and the framework is then bolted onto these before the glazing is put in.

Brick or concrete base walls, if required, are best constructed by a professional builder – unless you are reasonably expert in this sort of work. Greenhouse manufacturers always provide a detailed groundplan of the structure, so follow this closely when putting in foundations or base walls.

When erecting your greenhouse, use a spirit level and plumb line to make frequent checks on levels and verticals.

Fitting the glazing
Stand glass panes in a dry, covered place until you are ready to use them. If they get wet they are very difficult to separate and you risk breaking them. Glazing is best done when the weather is not too cold or your fingers may be too numb for careful handling. Do any metal or timber painting before the glass is put in. If you are using putty, only put it below the glass as a bed for the panes – not over the top as well, as in ordinary domestic glazing.

Plastic greenhouses
Be especially careful, when erecting and siting plastic greenhouses, to avoid possible wind damage. The suppliers usually issue special anchoring instructions and recommendations. When plastic is to be fastened to a timber framework, don't use creosote preservatives on the wood. Some plastics will become weakened by contact and all will be severely discoloured, making the greenhouse most unsightly. Moreover, creosote fumes are harmful to plants. For the same reason creosote should not be used on any timbers in close contact with plants in a confined area – such as in greenhouses or frames. Instead use one of the proprietary horticultural timber preservatives on the market.

Tending the site
The surroundings of your greenhouse should be kept tidy and weed-free. Weeds will harbour many troublesome pests; for example nearby stinging nettles may bring you an infestation of whitefly.

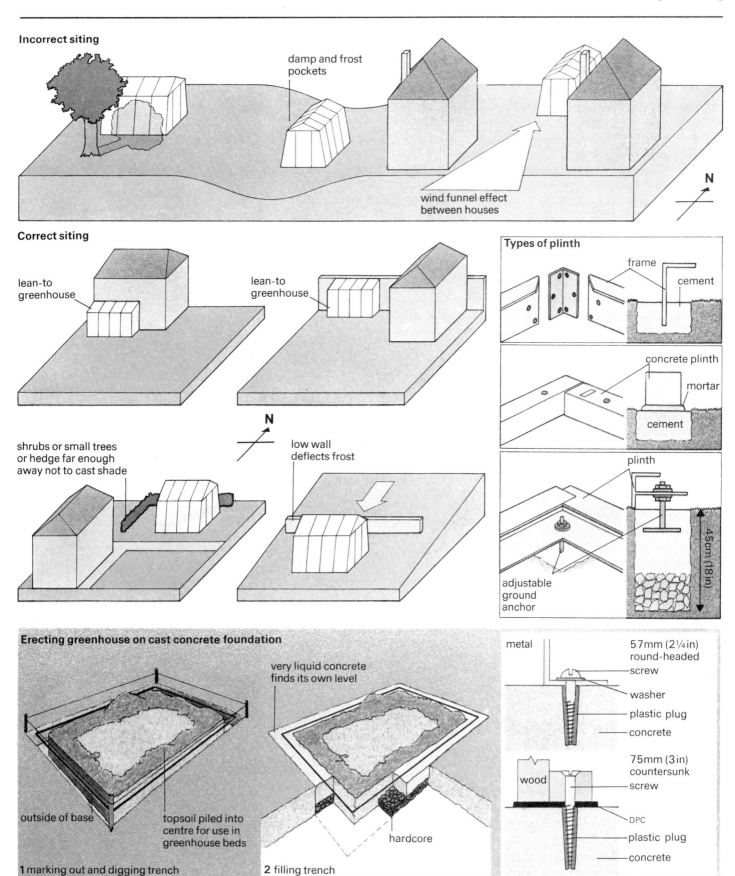

Incorrect siting

damp and frost pockets

wind funnel effect between houses

N

Correct siting

lean-to greenhouse

lean-to greenhouse

N

shrubs or small trees or hedge far enough away not to cast shade

low wall deflects frost

Types of plinth

frame

cement

concrete plinth

mortar

cement

plinth

adjustable ground anchor

45cm (18in)

Erecting greenhouse on cast concrete foundation

very liquid concrete finds its own level

outside of base

topsoil piled into centre for use in greenhouse beds

hardcore

1 marking out and digging trench

2 filling trench

metal

57mm (2¼in) round-headed screw

washer

plastic plug

concrete

75mm (3in) countersunk screw

wood

DPC

plastic plug

concrete

Top: avoid shade, damp, frost and wind – enemies of the greenhouse
Centre left: use house or garden walls for economical lean-to greenhouses; make use of low-growing shrubs or low walls to help protect against wind and frost

Bottom left: dig trench on a firm, level spot, remembering to place soil in centre for future use. Concrete over hardcore provides a solid base for the greenhouse that can be anchored with the right type of plugs and screws (bottom right)

Centre right: ready-made base plinths in in metal or concrete need only very very simple foundations, and are easy for the amateur to put together. The adjustable ground anchor system requires a solid concrete base

BASIC EQUIPMENT FOR THE GREENHOUSE

When you buy a greenhouse the price usually covers only the structure. All other items – sometimes even the ventilators – have to be bought as 'extras'. But this does allow you considerable choice of interior and exterior fittings. There are also many tools and gadgets available, in a variety of designs and price levels. Some of these are essential basic equipment and others can be bought as you need them for particular jobs.

In many greenhouses staging and shelving will be found useful at some time or other. Staging is often thought of as a permanent fixture but it need not be so. There are some small units now available that can be easily assembled and dismantled, moved about from place to place in the greenhouse, and extended to increase staging space if required. This form of staging makes the greenhouse very versatile and is specially useful in a glass-to-ground structure where a wide variety of plants of different heights can be grown and viewed.

Staging materials
Probably the most important aspect of your staging is the top surface. For most purposes a solid surface, strewn with some kind of moisture-retaining material, is the best surface for the warmer months. In winter it is an advantage if the staging top is of an 'open' nature to allow for air circulation around plants and, in warmed greenhouses, the distribution of heat; for this, slatted staging is suitable. However it is not common practice to change your staging according to the seasons, nor is it necessary. If you install open-type staging, it is a simple matter to cover it with polythene or asbestos sheeting, and then in mid spring (March) to cover this with a layer of moist shingle or other moisture-retaining material. You can then remove it all in mid autumn (September). This process helps considerably to maintain air humidity.

Instead of the conventional timber slats modern staging, particularly when constructed from metal angle strips, often has a top surface of wire or plastic mesh.

A really solid, substantial staging, made from bricks or concrete has an advantage worth noting in these days of fuel economy. Where a greenhouse receives a good amount of sunshine during the day, the bricks and concrete will store heat and evolve (radiate) it during the night. Sometimes enough warmth will be given out to keep the greenhouse frost free, and it will certainly be enough to keep the temperature more even. It is particularly valuable where rather high temperatures are being maintained for propagation or for growing sub-tropical plants, and where a relatively high warmth and humidity are needed all year round.

Portable shelves
Shelving is always useful – even more so if it is portable. Depending on how the basic greenhouse structure is designed it can be fitted to the sides or suspended from the roof – or both. If buying the brackets and the shelving material separately, then thick plate glass shelves are worth considering instead of the conventional planking or slats. Glass is a good choice if your greenhouse is very crowded as it allows more light to reach the plants below. Strips of strong plate glass can sometimes be purchased relatively cheaply as off-cuts from scrap.

Below left: staging – **1** *and* **2***, metal frames with open wood tops, and* **3***, wire mesh stretched over wood frame, allow good air circulation, while the more solid combinations in* **4** *retain heat*
Below: shelving – **1** *suspended by metal straps from roof;* **2** *fixed with an angle bracket;* **3** *bolted-on aluminium type*

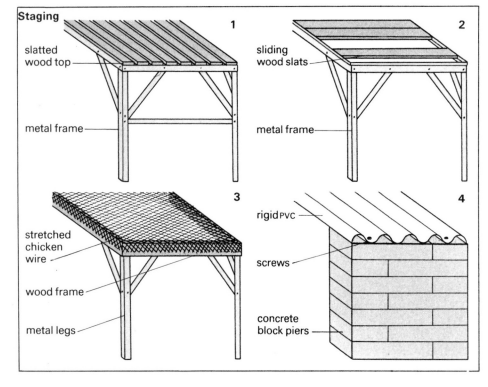

Staging

1 — slatted wood top, metal frame
2 — sliding wood slats, metal frame
3 — stretched chicken wire, wood frame, metal legs
4 — rigid PVC, screws, concrete block piers

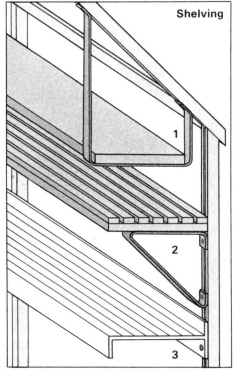

Shelving — 1, 2, 3

Types of thermometer

Thermometers are absolutely indispensable to proper greenhouse management. You will need at least one maximum and minimum thermometer in the greenhouse interior. Others may be useful for interior or exterior frames and outside the greenhouse. In all cases do buy a quality instrument, as this will give you accurate readings and last far longer than a cheap one. Tiny temperature indicators show the highest and lowest temperatures that have been reached; these are usually set with a magnet supplied with the instrument. Designs are now made that can be gravity set, and there are also pushbutton types. You may also want a frost forecast thermometer; this is a kind of hygrometer (for measuring humidity) but it has a scale indicating the possible chance of frost. Advance warning will enable you to check heating equipment, close vents and so on.

Watering and spraying equipment

Even if you intend to install automatic watering, a watering can will be useful at some time, even if only for applying liquid feeds. Choose one with a spout that will easily reach to the back of the staging and one that's not too heavy for you to lift when it is full. Some designs have extendible spouts. If your greenhouse is fitted with a water tap, then you can use a watering lance that is controlled by a finger-operated valve. Get one with a nozzle that will deliver a fine spray for damping down, as well as a normal flow.

Ideally, you should also buy two hand sprayers. One should have a fairly large capacity for damping down or spraying foliage with water, and for applying pesticides. Another small sprayer, holding about 500cc (1 pt), is useful for treating the odd plant (when it is not necessary to make up a vast amount of pesticide). Don't forget that foliar feeds can also be applied with sprayers. A special feature to look for when buying a sprayer is a nozzle that can be directed upwards as well as downwards, and that will reach between the plants easily. This will ensure thorough coverage of the undersides of leaves when spraying pesticides; most pests first congregate under the foliage. The pump-up or pneumatic type of sprayer is convenient and economical.

Potting benches

A very useful piece of equipment is a portable potting bench. This is a tray with one side missing that can be placed on the staging when needed. Use it for mixing compost, sowing, pricking out and potting jobs, and store it out of the way when not in use. You can easily make a bench using a sheet of aluminium (available from most do-it-yourself shops, often as off-cuts). Bend three of the edges upwards with pliers to prevent compost being pushed off the sides and back. Aluminium is one of the best materials to use because it is easy to clean and sterilize and is resistant to the hard wear caused by trowelling, cutting operations, and mixing. It is also lightweight and easily made into the shape you want.

Plastic and clay flowerpots

Keep a selection of flowerpots to hand. Plastic is easy to clean, but a few clay pots (if you can get them) are handy from time to time – some plants prefer them. The most useful sizes to keep in store for a wide range of pot plants are 8 or 9cm (3 or $3\frac{1}{2}$ in) and 13cm (5 in).

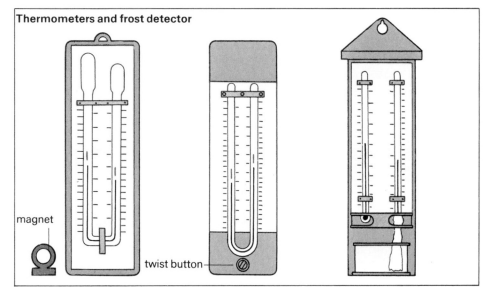

Thermometers and frost detector

magnet

twist button

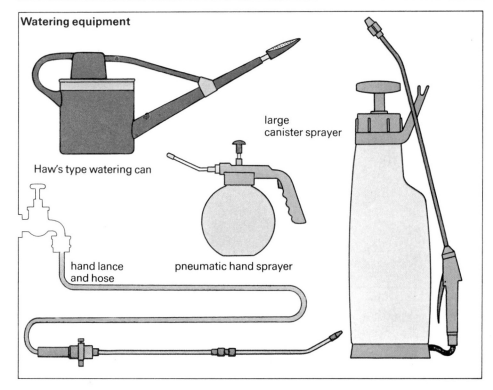

Watering equipment

Haw's type watering can

hand lance and hose

large canister sprayer

pneumatic hand sprayer

Above left: two different types of thermometer, with magnet or twist-button setting, and frost detector (similar to a hygrometer) to help give you valuable warning of a cold snap
Left: some of the basic equipment to cope with different watering needs

SHADING THE GREENHOUSE

Don't leave attention to shading until it is too late. You will find that correct shading, ventilation and damping down, are essential in the greenhouse for the cultivation of strong and vigorous plants.

Excessively high temperature in summer, coupled with lack of shading, is a common cause of failure among beginners in greenhouse and frame gardening. There is also still much misunderstanding about the subject, even where professional gardeners are concerned.

It is an advantage to site a greenhouse in an open sunny position, because this gives much free warmth in winter but, because of the heat-trapping effect of glass, shading will invariably be required in summer. Often it may be necessary much earlier than this during sunny periods, when temperatures can be sent rocketing, even in spring (February or March). Plants that are not used to bright sunlight and warmth, having just been through the winter, may wilt. The numerous greenhouse plants that flower in spring, such as cineraria, calceolaria and primula, will last much longer if kept shaded and cool. Seed sowings will also need shading at this time.

In summer an unshaded greenhouse, especially one that is badly ventilated and watered, may become an oven. Temperatures over 50°C (120°F) can be easily reached and even tropical plants will be shrivelled by the end of a day. Plastic greenhouses should be less of a problem in summer, because the solar heat is not trapped to such a great extent as with glass, but shading will still be necessary.

How much light?

A knowledge of the light requirements of the plants you grow is essential. In a mixed greenhouse the plants can then be placed accordingly. Deep-shade lovers, like many sub-tropical and house foliage plants, can go under the staging. Those preferring less can be sited in the natural shade of taller plants on the staging or under climbers. Plants demanding maximum light can go on shelves or under parts of the roof left unshaded or only slightly shaded during summer.

The effect of too much light and sun will be seen as bleached foliage, which in severe cases can become literally scorched brown. The plants will wilt, and if you have been watering them from above there may be brown spotting of the leaves. Droplets of water act as minute lenses, focusing the sun's rays and causing these burned spots. Plants with hairy or furry foliage are particularly prone to this kind of damage because the water droplets are supported just above the leaf surface and the focus is then much better. Plants commonly affected are saintpaulia, gloxinia, smithiantha, and others of the gesneria family with hairy leaves.

High temperature dangers

Greenhouse fruits, such as the tomato, can become blistered by excessive sunlight. Brown to grey watery 'scald' marks appear on the fruits. In the case of tomatoes high temperature is a frequent cause of failure, and shading is nearly always important during the ripening stage. At temperatures over about 32°C (80°F) the red pigment of the tomato fails

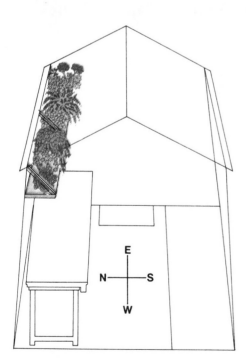

By placing your plants in different positions in the greenhouse, you can suit all their requirements for warmth and light. Small heat- and light-loving plants, such as Columnea gloriosa, *will do well if placed on a high shelf*

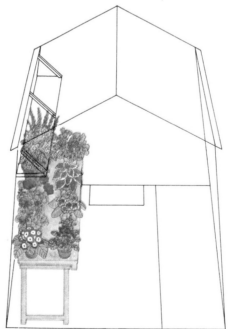

Larger heat- and light-loving plants can be placed on the staging. Plants which will thrive in this position, and provide an attractive display, include gloxinias, regal and zonal pelargoniums, primulas, cinerarias, calceolarias and hydrangeas

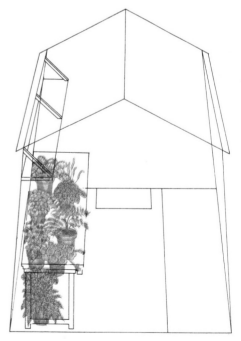

Some plants, especially many foliage plants, prefer shade; and those with variegated leaves, such as Tradescantia virginiana, *can lose their colour if left in bright sunlight. The best place to keep them is underneath the staging*

to form properly and the yellow persists. In addition there may be numerous other ripening faults, such as 'greenback', where the fruit is unevenly ripe and patched with red and yellow or green. Ventilation and white shading should be used to keep down temperatures during hot sunny weather.

The necessity of shading

Once the sun's rays have penetrated the glass or plastic lights of a greenhouse or frame, a part of them is converted into heat after striking the interior. This heat cannot readily pass back through the glass and so is 'trapped' inside. It is obvious therefore that for shading to be most efficient it must stop the sun's rays before they penetrate the glass. Exterior blinds are very effective, but remember that they also will absorb heat from the sun; so that this heat is not transferred to the glass or plastic roof the blinds should be a few inches above it. This will allow air to circulate and carry away heat.

Well-designed greenhouse blinds rest on runners and generally the slatted type of blind is best. These can be made of timber or of bamboo, and have to be made specially for your greenhouse and to the measurements you give the makers; they are lowered or raised by cords in the conventional manner. It is also possible for the blinds to be photo-electrically controlled, giving automatic operation.

Slatted blinds will of course let some direct sunlight pass through, but this light does not remain in one spot for long, owing to the sun's movement across the sky. Hessian or plastic sheeting and other materials are also sometimes used as blinds, but are very easily blown away.

In recent years interior blinds have come onto the market. These types are convenient because they stay clean and are not in danger of blowing away. However, they are of little use in keeping down temperature.

Shading paints

For very many years shading paints, applied to the exterior glass, have been used as a cheap method of shading during summer. Various mixtures of flour, whiting, glue and chalk have been suggested – often messy and even damaging to structures. Serious accidents have occurred, such as putting an arm through the glass when trying to scrape off such mixtures at the end of the season. Proprietary preparations of this kind were often tinted green, and even some modern methods of shading still employ the colour green.

Research both in Britain and in Holland has shown that white is the best colour, as it reflects back a much wider range of the sun's spectrum. Green actually absorbs much solar energy (indeed, this is the principle of photosynthesis of plants) and so a green-shaded greenhouse becomes considerably hotter than a white-shaded one. Plants also seem to grow better in a white-shaded house and there is a better rendering of flower and foliage colours as well as more sturdy growth. Remember that the shade cast by green leaves, such as in a wood or under shrubs, is not the same as that cast by a green-painted glass roof.

A remarkable modern invention is an electrostatic type of shading paint, which is marketed under the name of 'Coolglass'. This is specially formulated to reflect back as much of the sun's heat as possible but to let useful rays through. It can be sprayed or brushed onto the glass and diluted to give any degree of shade needed. It has the curious property of staying firmly on the glass even during heavy rain, yet being easily wiped off with a dry duster. This type of shading has given very good results with crops like tomatoes, cucumbers, fuchsias, begonias, carnations, orchids, chrysanthemums, foliage plants, and most frame crops.

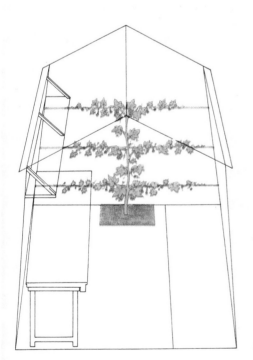

An end wall is a good site for climbing plants. The east wall is the best place, in this greenhouse, for a cucumber vine. It likes a draught-free position – well away from the door – and plenty of heat and light without being in direct sun

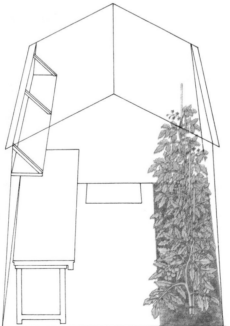

Some plants, like tomatoes, need plenty of heat and sun. The ideal place for them is along the south side of the greenhouse. However, even sun-loving plants need shading on very hot days when excessive temperatures can scorch their foliage

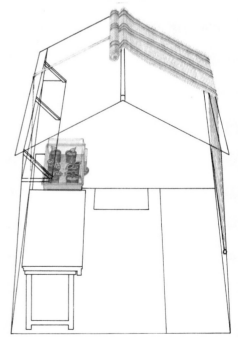

Two important pieces of greenhouse equipment concerning heat and light; a propagator, for providing the high temperatures needed by cuttings and germinating seeds, and an exterior blind for the most effective shading

AUTOMATIC WATERING IN THE GREENHOUSE

The majority of home gardeners have to leave their greenhouse to itself during the day and most people have to be absent from the garden now and then. It is on these occasions that watering can become a real problem, especially if the summer happens to be very hot and sunny. Automatic watering can solve this.

Apart from the problems of absence, automatic watering will be invaluable if you have lots of plants to look after. Moreover, it generally keeps plants constantly moist and encourages the humidity essential to healthy growth. This eliminates the chore of damping-down, and avoids extreme changes between dry and waterlogged soils or compost. Erratic watering is the cause of many troubles like dropping of buds and flowers, and cracked fruit in tomatoes.

The first attempts at automatic watering were usually improvised wicks – textile lamp wicks or blotting paper, with one end dipped into a tank or bucket, and the other end in the soil around the plant roots. Such arrangements usually have the disconcerting habit of drying up, or ceasing to work, as soon as your back is turned. Alternatively they may flood the plants.

Watering through sand
The first really successful system was introduced by the National Institute of Agricultural Engineering and is called the capillary sand bench. This system relies on the capillary action of water rising through any fine material like textile fibres or sand, but the water is always below the level of the plants and there is no risk of flooding. The plants are potted in plastic pots, with large drainage holes, that are kept clear of any obstruction. The pots are then stood on staging spread with a few centimetres of sand, preferably of what builders call 'washed grit'. The pots are pressed down firmly, so that the sand comes into direct contact with the compost in the pots through the drainage holes. The sand is kept constantly moist, by any one of several methods, and the compost in the plant pots will then take up moisture as

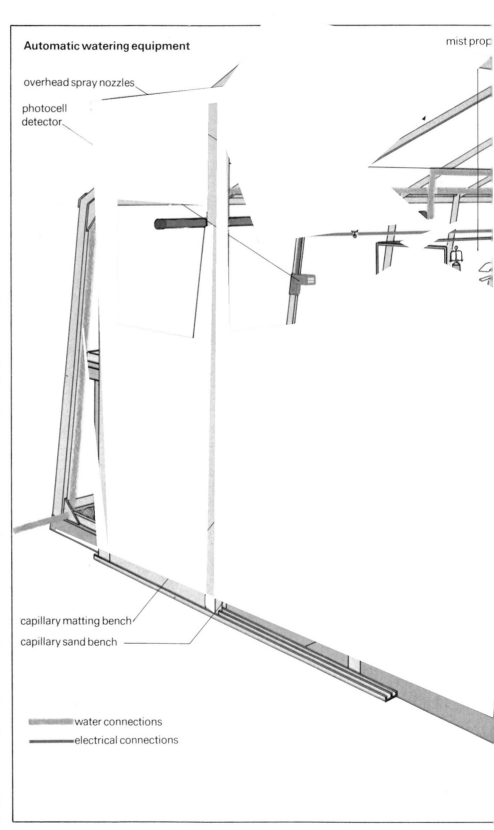

Automatic watering equipment

mist prop

overhead spray nozzles

photocell detector

capillary matting bench

capillary sand bench

water connections
electrical connections

required. The amount taken up will vary automatically with the needs of the plant and temperature and humidity conditions – provided the sand layer is always well supplied with water. One other important condition is that the potting compost must be nicely moist when potting, otherwise there will be no flow between the moist sand and the compost.

Regulating the level

Originally an ordinary ball valve cistern was used to provide a constant water level for the sand layer, a perforated plastic pipe being connected to the cistern and running the length of the sand bench. You can make such an arrangement yourself, but proprietary equipment specially designed for this purpose can be bought.

This is usually in the form of units that can be connected together as you require to extend the system. Instead of ball valves, neat little plastic float valves are available, with full instructions for installation. The sand has to be spread on plastic sheeting if ordinary slatted greenhouse staging is used for the bench, and the water level has to be just below the sand. The water is led into the sand by means of glass fibre or plastic wicks several centimetres wide. A good way to convey water along a considerable length of staging is to run plastic guttering against the edge; the gutter is kept constantly filled with water by means of the float valve connected to the mains or a tank, and the wicks are laid in the sand and dipped in the gutter at intervals along the bench.

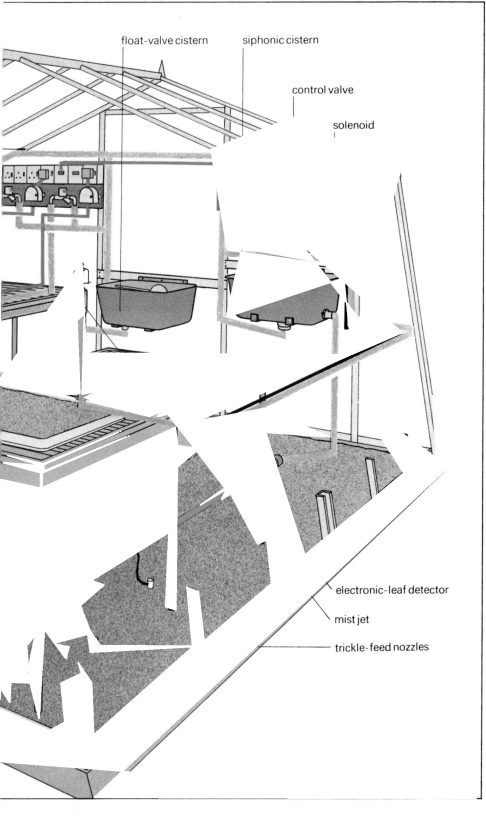

float-valve cistern siphonic cistern

control valve

solenoid

electronic-leaf detector

mist jet

trickle-feed nozzles

Capillary sand bench: compost in plastic pots takes up moisture from sand bed

Plastic matting

A modern development instead of sand is a special kind of plastic porous matting. This is lightweight and very convenient to use. It can be cut and tailored to fit any shape of staging and even cleaned in a washing machine at the end of the season. It can be spread on polythene sheeting laid over the staging, and the edge dipped in a run of guttering as already described.

All capillary materials, such as sand, vermiculite, plastic matting, glass wool wicks, and so on, must be thoroughly moistened when being set up, otherwise the flow of water by capillary action may not start.

A neat little arrangement for simple distribution of water semi-automatically, which has now been in use for some years, is the siphon system. This has a small plastic tank fed with a drip feed valve connected to the mains or other source of

Above: plastic float valve cistern attached to wall at far end provides constant water level for sand layer in upper bench
Below: lower bench is supplied with water from auxiliary cistern at its own level

water supply. The valve is a sensitive one and by hand adjustment the rate at which the tank fills can be regulated. When full the tank siphons its water into plastic piping fitted with nozzles at intervals. These can be set over pots or along rows of plants, or along a sand or plastic matting capillary bench if desired. Of course with this arrangement you have first to experiment with the filling rate and adjust the amount of water according to the plants' needs or the area to be watered. Various other proprietary systems using trickle-feed pipe lines and nozzles have also been introduced.

Electricity
Electrically-controlled systems are, as you would expect, extremely accurate and efficient. Water flow in this case is governed by a water valve operated by electromagnet, and the water can be fed to nozzles or spray jets.

Two methods are now used to control the electromagnetic valve. The first is called an 'electronic leaf'. There are several designs, but they basically estimate the drying rate of a surface and switch the valve on and off accordingly. The second is an important innovation using a photoelectric cell to estimate the solar energy reaching the greenhouse. An electronic circuit then controls the valve to issue the right 'dose' of water. At night or during very dull weather no water, or very little, will be given. On a bright sunny day, however, the photocell will 'instruct' the valve to water at frequent intervals. This photoelectric system can be adapted to almost any kind of watering – capillary bench, trickle-feed nozzles or overhead spray. It can also be used for mist propagation and when connected to mist jets can be further used for automatic damping-down. A selection of application methods can be controlled by one photo-electric cell if desired, and the system is as automatic as you can get. Once set up it requires virtually no attention.

Slimes and algae
With all automatic watering there is usually trouble sooner or later from slimes and algae. Good light encourages their growth, so remember never to use transparent plastic tubing to convey water. Unused areas of sand benches can be covered with black polythene. Fortunately, there are now products available, such as Algofen, that will keep water systems free from slimes and algae. This has been cleared as safe by the Ministry of Agriculture and can be used freely *according to label instructions* even where there are edible crops.

CONTROLLING CONDITIONS
IN THE GREENHOUSE

VENTILATION AND HUMIDITY IN THE GREENHOUSE

One of the advantages of growing plants in a greenhouse is that the condition of the atmosphere can be controlled. Unfortunately many beginners seem to give this little consideration. Here we explain how best to regulate the circulation and humidity of the air in your greenhouse.

The vital constituents of the air – carbon dioxide, oxygen, water vapour and nitrogen – are visible. The old saying 'out of sight, out of mind' applies! Yet air should be considered a 'fertilizer' because it is essential as a plant food. In photosynthesis, carbon dioxide (CO_2) in the atmosphere is used by plants, in the presence of water and light, to make starches, sugars and celluloses, and many other chemicals of which they are composed. Oxygen is also used and exchanged, and some plants – such as the pea family – make use of certain beneficial bacteria in their root nodules to take in nitrogen directly. Normally nitrogen is taken up only as nitrates from the soil.

The humidity of the air, the moisture it contains, is also unseen – but its presence becomes apparent when drops form as condensation on the greenhouse structure. A high humidity can be bad in winter and good in summer, so this also has to be controlled.

Adjustment of ventilators

Make sure that there are plenty of ventilators in the greenhouse structure. There is no need to be afraid of having too many, since you don't have to use them all at the same time. Although there should be a generous number they must fit tightly: ventilation does not have to mean *draughts*. Many times in the winter the vents may have to be kept closed, and even a small icy draught will counteract any benefits a heater may give. Sliding doors, now commonly fitted to greenhouses, are useful for extra ventilation in summer. They can be adjusted easily and will not slam. Both side and roof ventilators should be fitted, preferably on both sides of the greenhouse. This enables them to be opened on the side away from the prevailing wind. Where to position

side vents is a matter of some controversy. Often there may be little choice, especially if the greenhouse has a base wall. However, in summer, vents set as low as possible will give good air circulation, since hot air rises rapidly and draws cool in from below.

Adjustment of ventilation will affect both temperature and humidity. Apart from the obvious cooling effect of the air change, a flow of air increases evaporation of water from the greenhouse. When water evaporates it absorbs energy, in the form of heat, from the surroundings. If the greenhouse interior is well damped down and watered in summer this will have a further cooling action. On the other hand, a fast flow of air may hasten evaporation excessively and you will have to be constantly watering to keep the air moist and the plants from drying out. Ventilation must therefore be given in moderation, and the amount you give will depend on the type of plants you grow and the outside weather conditions.

Humidity

In summer most plants prefer a moist atmosphere since this reduces the rate at which they lose moisture from their leaves – the process called transpiration. This, in turn, lessens the rate at which the roots dry out, and so the plants are able to absorb nutrients through their roots more easily. A moist atmosphere in summer also discourages red spider mite, a very common pest when the air is hot and dry.

In winter the aim is quite different – every attempt must be made to keep down humidity. In most home greenhouses the rule is, the drier the air, the better. When conditions are cool, perhaps cold, and daylight poor, many fungoid diseases flourish when the air is humid. These include moulds, mildews, and fungi causing stem and storage organ rots (of bulbs, corms, tubers, and the like). Ventilation again becomes very important, but many beginners are reluctant to give it. However, there are many winter days in Britain when the outside air is well above freezing, and you can then ventilate freely. Again, much depends on the plants you are growing, but in most home greenhouses a temperature higher than

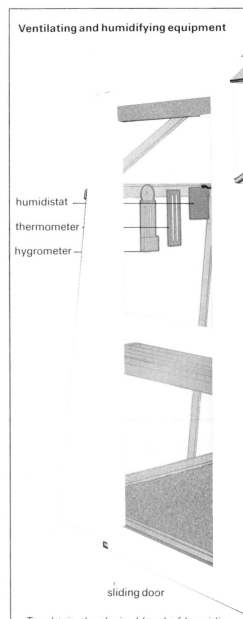

Ventilating and humidifying equipment

humidistat
thermometer
hygrometer

sliding door

To obtain the desired level of humidity in the greenhouse you can install a thermostatically-controlled fan to remove hot air. In addition, a humidifier, controlled by a humidistat, will dampen the air when humidity is low

For adequate ventilation at all times it is advisable to have automatic roof ventilators that will open or close, depending on the temperature within the greenhouse

5–8°C (40–45°F) is rarely necessary.

In winter the air is further kept dry by *not* damping down and by watering, sparingly, only those plants that are still growing. Dormant plants should require no water at all. Staging that is kept moist automatically in summer, or covered with moist peat or grit to maintain humidity, must be allowed to go dry.

Use of heaters

Paraffin wick heaters are very popular and are probably the most widely used method of warming a greenhouse. Unfortunately, they are also frequently associated with winter plant troubles attributed to fumes. Typical symptoms are browning of leaf edges, leaf shrivelling, and scorched spots. Often this is caused by oxygen starvation, due again to lack of ventilation. Oil must have oxygen to burn properly. If a greenhouse is tightly sealed, with an oil heater burning, the time will come when the air becomes short of oxygen. The oil will not burn properly so that oil vapour and other results of incomplete combustion – harmful to plants – are produced. Where oil heaters

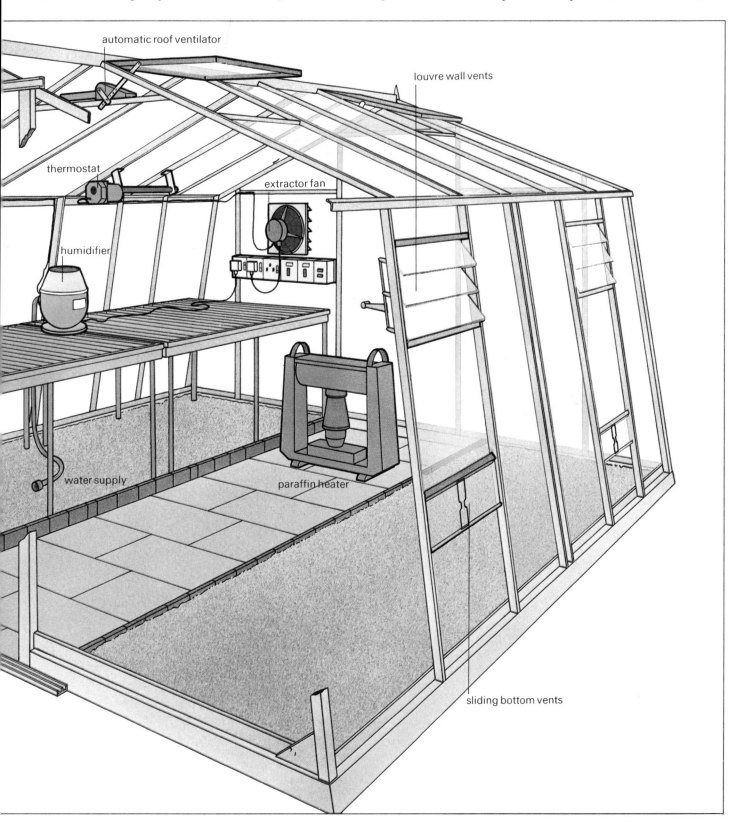

automatic roof ventilator

louvre wall vents

thermostat

extractor fan

humidifier

water supply

paraffin heater

sliding bottom vents

Above: easy to fit automatic roof, or side ventilator works on a special unit filled with a mineral that expands or contracts with temperature changes, activating a push rod to lift the vent
Below: fix extractor fan, controlled by rod thermostat, high up to remove hottest air, and if placing thermostat high up, set it to allow for temperature difference between plant level and its height

are used there must *always* be some ventilation, however cold the weather. Because oil forms its own volume of water, as water vapour, when it burns. This contributes to humidity and is another reason for carefully checking your ventilation.

Condensation

When the weather is cold some condensation is normal and indeed inevitable. If there is so much that drips form everywhere and the glass (or plastic) is coated with droplets, ventilation is seriously at fault. You are also probably overwatering. Plastic greenhouses are particularly affected by condensation because the water forms droplets instead of a film as it does on glass. The droplets interfere with light entry so that plants may become pale and weak. Efficient ventilation is the answer, together with reduction in quantity of water applied.

Watering

In summer it is a good idea to water early in the morning. This keeps up humidity during the day and there is adequate moisture for the plants at their time of greatest need – during bright daylight when photosynthesis is most rapid and plants are growing quickly. In the night there is little growth and little water requirement. Moreover, a high humidity during the cool of the night can encourage diseases like grey mould even in summer, something you may often see in tomato houses. High daytime humidity is good for tomatoes, aiding pollination.

Fan ventilation is now popular in greenhouses in summer owing to the ease with which it can be operated by a thermostatic control. It is wise to have some form of automatic humidification in conjunction with fan ventilation, prevent rapid drying out of the house. Over on the next page we tell you more about humidity and the most desirable levels according to the plants grown, how to use a wet and dry bulb hygrometer to help measure the changing levels of humidity in your own greenhouse; automatic humidifiers described on page 230 help cut down manual watering.

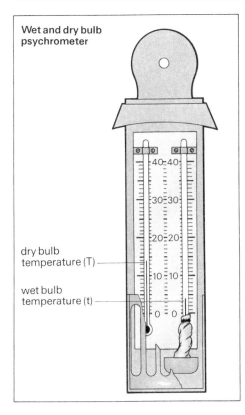

Wet and dry bulb
psychrometer

dry bulb
temperature (T)

wet bulb
temperature (t)

Above: two examples of a wet and dry bulb psychrometer. The diagram on the left shows the greenhouse type, while the one on the right, protected by louvred screens against the elements, is one you might spot in public parks or seaside places
Below: damp down greenhouse paths regularly during hot, dry spells; this helps to contain evaporation in the surrounding atmosphere

The temperatures recorded on the dry bulb thermometer (referred to as T) and the wet bulb thermometer (t) are noted, and by reference to tables supplied with the instrument, the relative humidity of the air can be found. The relative humidity, called RH for short, is the measure usually used. An RH of, say, 60 per cent – a roughly 'normal' figure, means that the air contains 60 per cent of the water that it is possible for it to hold at the temperature when the reading is taken.

The direct-reading hygrometer is simply a dial calibrated in RH, and usually also has sections marked 'dry', 'normal' and 'moist'. It works by the expansion and contraction of a special fibre that moves a needle on the scale, but the instruments are rarely accurate at the extreme ends. Fortunately for the greenhouse this does not matter. For most purposes, readings from about 35 to 50 can be considered 'dry', 50 to about 70 as 'normal', and 70 to 85 as 'moist'. In summer the RH should generally be kept not below about 70 per cent and in winter not below about 50 per cent. This is because the humidity level must relate to the outdoor temperature.

Regulating humidity

By siting plants carefully in the greenhouse it is possible to provide a single plant (or a small group) with its own microclimate. Trays of moist sand placed near, or on, an automatic capillary watering bench, will give localized moist air. Plants needing drier conditions can be put on shelves, near vents or on slatted staging. In summer many of the sub-tropical species can be freely sprayed with a fine mist of water to moisten the foliage thoroughly. The water should be clean and lime-free; if the mains tap water is limey, use clean rainwater instead so that the leaves do not become marked with lime deposits. In summer nearly all plants, whatever their nature, will benefit if you damp down the floor and staging from time to time. How much damping down you do depends on the humidity requirements of your plants.

Most forms of automatic watering will also keep up humidity automatically. Special automatic humidifiers are obtainable and usually consist of a fan blowing air over a spray of water, this operation being controlled by a special switch that is sensitive to air moisture. The photo-electric method of automatic watering can also be adapted to control humidity by being connected to misting jets that damp down the floor or staging.

For hot-water pipes, and similar types of heat radiator, simple water reservoirs with wicks can be fitted (as is done with domestic radiators). But when the heating is in operation in winter it is often desirable to keep humidity down. For the same reason the 'humidity' trays fitted to some older designs of paraffin oil heater should rarely be used.

ESTIMATING GREENHOUSE HEATING NEEDS

Before buying heating equipment for the greenhouse it is essential that you know roughly how much heat is necessary to maintain the temperature at the desired level during cold weather. To this end, you must first calculate the rate of heat loss.

Heating greenhouses is still a very misunderstood subject and much of the equipment available is far from perfect. It is not unusual for beginners to buy heaters that are quite unable to cope during severe cold spells. What may seem a financial saving on equipment and fuel can lead to a great deal of waste.

Once you have calculated how much heat the plants in your greenhouse will need during the coldest spells, you can decide whether or not a heater is necessary, and – if it is – you can work out an approximate figure for fuel consumption. However, even the most expensive fuels need not be a serious burden in the average small greenhouse.

When assessing heating requirements, there is an important basic point that should be borne in mind: the higher the temperature in the greenhouse compared with that outside, the faster heat will be lost – and the faster your heater will have to develop heat to maintain the temperature you want.

Clearly, you must aim for the lowest necessary temperature for fuel economy, and take all precautions to avoid waste. Heating equipment should distribute heat evenly, so that no part of the greenhouse structure is raised to an unnecessarily high temperature. Many beginners tend to have excessive levels in winter, whereas nearly all the common popular greenhouse plants are perfectly happy with about 4–7°C (40–45°F).

Assessing heat loss

To find out approximately how much heat your heater will need to produce, you must first get an idea of how fast your greenhouse will lose heat when the temperature outside is at its lowest, and that inside at the desirable minimum. Armed with this knowledge, you can choose equipment with the output to balance the loss; only if the outside temperature continues to drop (as in a very severe winter) may some form of extra heating be needed.

Construction materials like glass, wood and brick have widely different thermal conductivities and rates of heat loss. The area of these materials, and the heat loss through the floor, are additional factors to take into account.

Summing up, to calculate how much heat your greenhouse will lose at any desired interior minimum temperature, when the temperature outside is at its lowest, you need to know the following points:

1 The desired interior minimum temperature.
2 The expected exterior minimum.
3 The area of construction materials.
4 The area of the ground covered.

Let us assume that **1** is 7°C (45°F) and that **2** is −7°C (20°F) which is a good few degrees of frost. Various methods of calculation can be used to estimate heat loss, using factors to take into account the thermal conductivity of the different construction materials. However, they

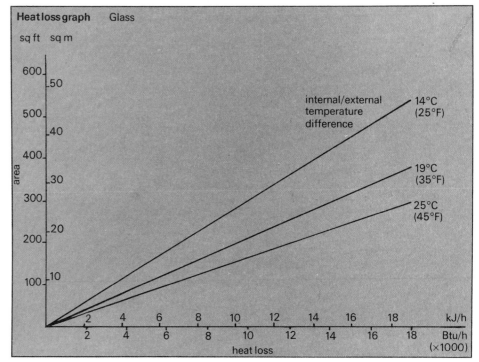

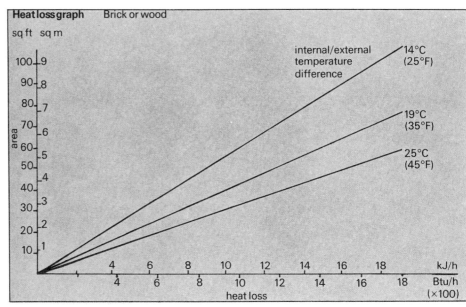

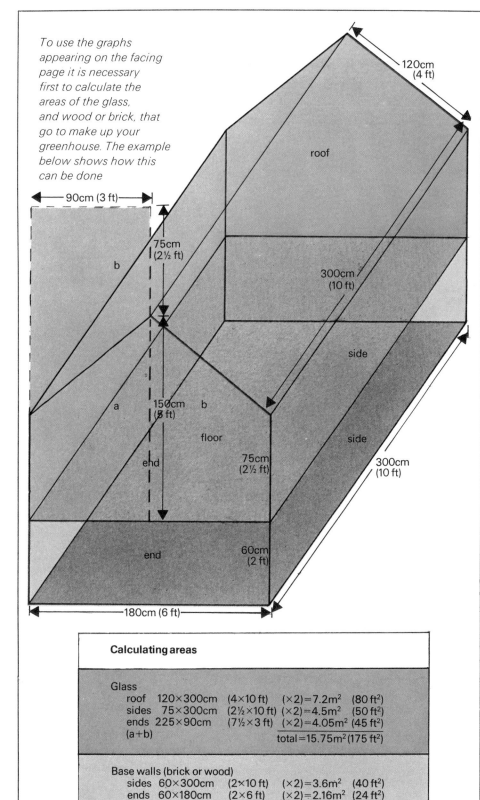

120cm (4 ft)

roof

90cm (3 ft)

75cm (2½ ft)

300cm (10 ft)

b

side

300cm (10 ft)

a

150cm (5 ft)

b

floor

side

end

75cm (2½ ft)

end

60cm (2 ft)

180cm (6 ft)

Calculating areas

Glass
roof	120×300cm	(4×10 ft)	(×2)=7.2m² (80 ft²)
sides	75×300cm	(2½×10 ft)	(×2)=4.5m² (50 ft²)
ends	225×90cm	(7½×3 ft)	(×2)=4.05m² (45 ft²)
(a+b)			total=15.75m² (175 ft²)

Base walls (brick or wood)
sides	60×300cm	(2×10 ft)	(×2)=3.6m² (40 ft²)
ends	60×180cm	(2×6 ft)	(×2)=2.16m² (24 ft²)
			total=5.76m² (64 ft²)

Floor
	180×300cm	(6×10 ft)=5.4m²	(60 ft²)

The graphs to the left enable you to discover the maximum heat loss rate that your greenhouse is likely to experience during the winter – and thereby choose heating equipment of the appropriate output. As well as the more likely temperature difference of 14°C, graphs are also included for 19°C and 25°C (25°F, 35°F and 45°F)

are often lengthy and complicated. Here, we give a method involving simple graphs that are based on figures already worked out for indoor/outdoor temperature differences of 14°C (25°F), ie 7°C inside and −7°C outside; 19°C (35°F); and 25°C (45°F).

The graphs give an estimate of the heat lost from glass, and brick or wood (that are more or less the same in this respect), for any section of the greenhouse. There is no need for a graph for heat lost through the floor, since this is near enough 100 × its area in sq m (10 × the area in sq ft), the figure obtained being kilojoules, or British thermal units, per hour (kJ/h or Btu/h). All good-quality heating equipment should be rated in terms of these units – don't buy any unless this is specified by the manufacturer. The area of glazing bars can be ignored, being quite small in comparison with the main areas of construction materials.

An estimate to within about 950 kJ/h (900 Btu/h) is good enough – equal to about 250 watts in electrical terms. Any figure of kJ/h can be converted to watts by dividing by 3·6 (3·4 in case of Btu/h).

Take the example of an average-sized greenhouse of 1·8   3m (6 × 10 ft), with a wooden base wall, glass sides and roof, to explain the calculation.

By referring to the graphs, we find the following:

For glass, 15·75 sq m (175 sq ft) equals about 6100 kJ/h (5800 Btu/h).

For brick or wood, 5·76 sq m (64 sq ft) equals about 1100 kJ/h (1050 Btu/h).

For the floor, 5·4 sq m × 120 (60 sq ft × 10) equals 650 kJ/h (600 Btu/h).

This gives a final total of 7850 kJ/h (7450 Btu/h).

From this it is seen that if there is about 7°C (12°F) of frost outside (−7°C or 20°F), to keep the temperature at 7°C (45°F) inside, a heater giving about 7800 kJ/h (7500 Btu/h) must be installed. If this figure is divided by 3·6 (3·4), we get about 2·2 Kw for an electric heater: a 2 Kw or, to be safe, 2½ Kw electric heater should therefore be installed.

Although these graphs assume the popular 7°C (45°F) minimum, and the average 7°C (12°F) of frost, it should be realized that most plants will be quite safe should the temperature in the greenhouse fall for short spells to merely frost-free.

Provided the heating equipment has some form of thermostatic control, no heat should be wasted if the equipment is overrated. In fact, it is wise to err on the side of equipment that when turned on full, gives a higher heat output than necessary, rather than risk an underestimate.

GREENHOUSE HEATING SYSTEMS

Having explained how to estimate the heating requirements of your greenhouse, here we look at various ways of producing that heat.

The wrong choice of greenhouse heating equipment can mean high fuel bills, so make sure you pick the right methods for your particular needs.

Paraffin wick heaters

The most widely-used form of heater seems to be the paraffin wick type. This is convenient and portable but the necessity for manual control can lead to fuel being wasted. In recent years attempts have been made to automate combustion, but the designs are prone to fume and still need further improvement. Another disadvantage of this thermostatic type of heater is that it continues to give off considerable heat and consume much paraffin *after* it has been turned off.

Many very small heaters are sold, but often they are quite incapable of providing enough warmth, so always check the kilowatt (or Btu) output, and also the paraffin capacity. If a heater is to provide enough warmth it will have to burn adequate paraffin, for you cannot get heat from nothing.

It is important to choose a heater that is designed for the greenhouse, as some domestic types give off fumes that can harm plant life. Generally, the 'blue flame' type of heater can be recommended where a good growing temperature needs to be maintained. With this type, extra air can get to the wick – promoting more efficient combustion – and there is little or no fuming.

A paraffin heater should preferably have hot-air tubes to distribute the warmth more efficiently, otherwise a current of warm air will rise directly upwards and be cooled by contact with the greenhouse roof. This means that a considerable amount of heat is lost before the warm air gets a chance to circulate properly. This rule, incidentally, applies to other forms of greenhouse heater as well, so always try to distribute the heat evenly around the house.

Other constructional features to look for include a stainless steel lamp chimney, a copper tank (that will not rust and leak), and a reservoir of reasonable size so that filling is not a chore. Some designs are fitted with a humidity water trough, but this is both unnecessary and undesirable.

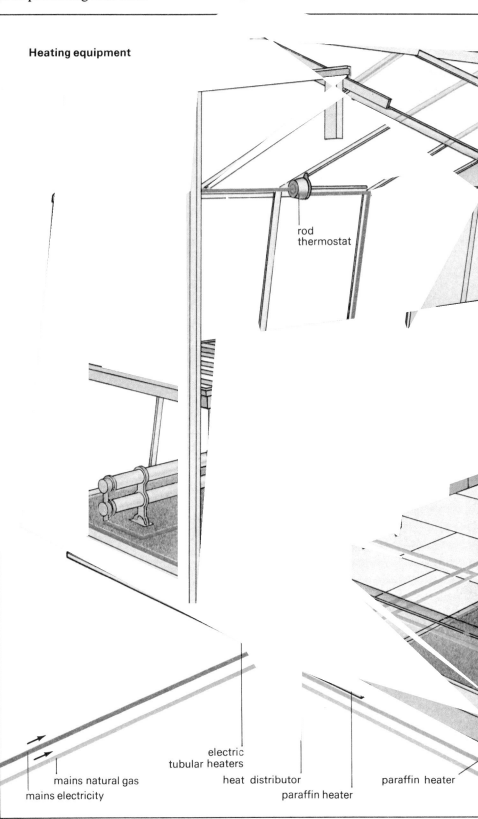

Heating equipment

rod thermostat

electric tubular heaters

heat distributor

mains natural gas

mains electricity

paraffin heater

paraffin heater

Combustion of paraffin produces too much water vapour as it is, without adding to humidity by filling a water trough. If a trough is fitted, leave it empty.

An especially useful feature is that some designs can be kept topped-up automatically with paraffin from a large drum, thus enabling them to burn for long periods without attention.

Paraffin wick heaters can be used in greenhouses with a floor area of about 1.8×3.7m (6×12 ft), but in this case the maximum-output heater is usually necessary, or else two or more heaters, depending on temperature requirements. Where high temperatures are needed it is better to choose some other form of heating equipment.

Natural gas
This has now become a popular fuel, but for the type of heater where combustion products are released into the greenhouse, you should exercise the same care over ventilation as in the case of paraffin lamps – otherwise you will have trouble with condensation and unsatisfactory combustion of the fuel.

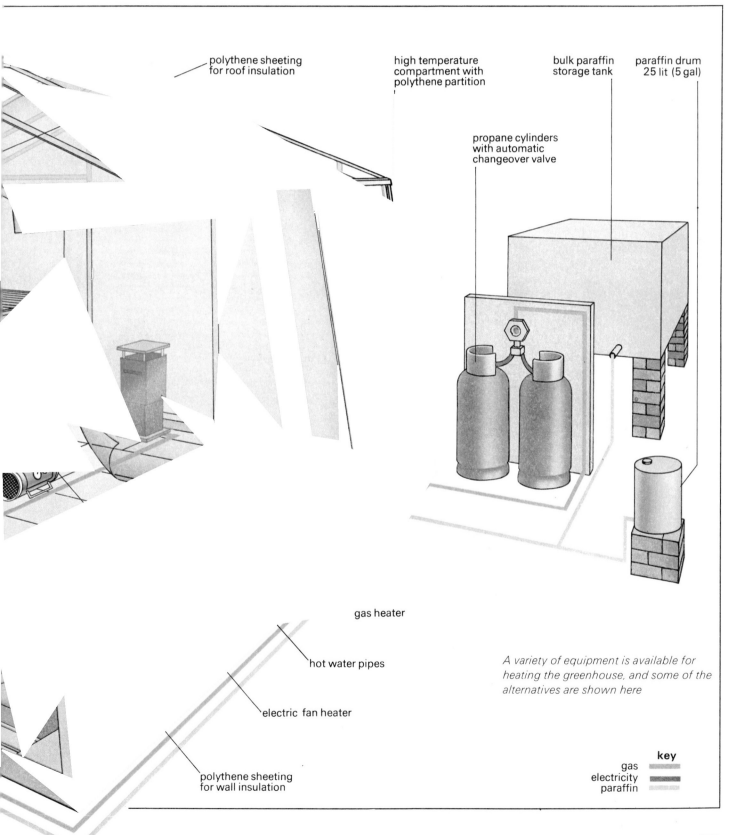

polythene sheeting
for roof insulation

high temperature
compartment with
polythene partition

bulk paraffin
storage tank

paraffin drum
25 lit (5 gal)

propane cylinders
with automatic
changeover valve

gas heater

hot water pipes

electric fan heater

polythene sheeting
for wall insulation

A variety of equipment is available for heating the greenhouse, and some of the alternatives are shown here

key
gas
electricity
paraffin

With natural gas there is better thermostatic control, hence less waste of fuel. Where it is impossible to run a piped main, a bottled source can be used, though this tends to be expensive. Continuous burning can be achieved by using a pair of bottles with an automatic changeover valve that comes into operation when one bottle is empty.

Hot water pipes

These were one of the first forms of greenhouse heating, but unless high temperatures are required or the greenhouse is very large – exceeding the average amateur size – installation and running can be expensive. Water pipes hold heat for a long time and are difficult to control accurately by thermostat. At high temperatures heat exchange is more rapid and control better.

Modern equipment is designed for easy installation and maintenance. Hot water pipes are an especially practical proposition when the fuel used is the same as that employed for domestic heating, for bulk buying at a cheaper rate is then possible.

Although solid fuel is the cheapest for hot water pipe heating, liquid and gaseous fuels are more easily and accurately controlled by thermostat.

It is important to have as generous a run of pipes as possible, and preferable to convey the heat around three sides of the greenhouse.

Don't put the pipes too near the glass – you may find it best to run them along each side of a central pathway.

Electricity

This need not be expensive unless wastefully employed – as in the case of using an immersion heater to warm hot water pipes. Electricity is most economical when heaters with a low heat capacity – and hence immediate response to thermostatic control – are used to distribute the warmth. It has the advantage of not giving off water vapour, that could otherwise cause trouble in winter months.

The most suitable appliances are fan heaters, tubular heaters, and convectors.

Fan heaters These should have the fan and heating element switched on together by a separate, rod-type thermostat. Moving air will quickly transfer the warmth from the heater to the greenhouse sides. Once these are warmed, it is best to let the air remain relatively still.

A rod thermostat between the power point and the heater will give more sensitive temperature control – provided the heater's own thermostat is on its highest setting.

Tubular heaters These are designed to hold little heat and are hollow inside.

They should be spread out around the greenhouse and not all banked in one or two positions.

Convectors These are best put under staging if possible so that the rising warm air is better distributed.

Never let any one small area of the greenhouse structure become hotter than really necessary. The greater the heat gradient between the inside and the outside, the faster heat will be lost.

Dividing into compartments

A greenhouse can be divided into compartments of different temperature with advantage. A permanent partition with a door, or a temporary polythene one, can be used. An extra warm section should preferably be a middle one – or the end farthest from the door. Lining a greenhouse with polythene can cut heat loss by up to 40 per cent – if done correctly. Allow some 13–25mm ($\frac{1}{2}$–1 in) of static air between the polythene and the glass.

Retaining heat through insulation

The value of double glazing has been appreciated for some years. However, the sealed-glass variety used domestically is expensive and impractical for greenhouses. Extra glass panes added to the inside have also proved far from convenient because condensation and dirt get behind them in a very short time, and frequent cleaning is not easy when a greenhouse is full of plants. Polythene sheeting is much easier to manage, and can be put up in autumn and left for the winter months only; it is simple to take down, roll up and store for the summer.

The insulation effect of polythene is quite dramatic. At least 40 per cent can be cut from the normal heat loss figure – and this means a corresponding reduction of fuel bills. Lining is especially suited to greenhouses with electric fan heaters or other 'dry' forms of equipment. Where paraffin or gas is burnt – and there is no flue – condensation may be a problem, for considerable water vapour is produced during combustion. In all cases, however, the vents should be separately lined so that they can be opened to permit generous and free ventilation whenever the weather permits.

Remember that the sun is a valuable source of free heat, so any insulation arrangements you may put into operation should not obscure light longer than necessary. Only a little winter sunlight will shoot up greenhouse temperatures even when it's well below freezing outside.

Left: old carpeting put on greenhouse roof at night conserves heat when cold

EFFECTS OF LIGHT ON PLANT GROWTH

The first part of this section on the use of artificial light examines the principles behind the effects of light on plant growth. We go on to deal with the techniques and equipment for growing plants with artificial light that can be adapted from commercial practice for use in the home or greenhouse.

Below: a colourful group of popular house plants thriving under the beneficial influence of a Grolux tube

Most gardeners are familiar with seed potatoes that have been chitted up in the light – the sprouts are sturdy and blue-green in colour. Now compare these with potato sprouts that have been stored for several months in a sack in a dark corner of a shed. They are etiolated – pale and sometimes up to 15cm (6 in) in length. This is a very clear example of what happens to plants when they are deprived of natural light.

Unfortunately the problem of making up a plant's light deficiencies cannot necessarily be solved by simply suspending an ordinary light bulb over it. The reaction of different species and varieties of plants to light is very complex – no two species react in the same way; some plants prefer full sun while others like shade

(sometimes even heavy shade) and some flower in summer while others flower in spring, autumn or even winter, each one adapting itself to particular environmental needs and conditions.

Before you can use artificial light intelligently with the object of supplementing daylight and assisting plant growth, you will need more precise knowledge of the principles of light and the effects of light on plant growth. You will then also be able to appreciate why some sources of artificial light are better than others.

The effect of latitude
The difference between the amount of solar light radiation (sun's energy reaching the Earth) that is received in summer

and winter is due largely to latitude. The farther from the equator your garden lies the lower the amount of radiation it receives. In Britain, even in the extreme south of England, the sun never rises more than 15 degrees above the horizon in mid winter (December); as it then has to penetrate a much thicker layer of the Earth's atmosphere its power is reduced. In fact the total solar energy supplied in a winter month may be only 10 per cent of that experienced in a summer month.

In addition to the effect produced by latitude there are also local conditions to take into account. Cloud cover, for instance, which can vary over quite a short distance, and industrial pollution, can be important factors in reducing solar radiation. Taking the average figures for the British Isles as a whole, there is not sufficient natural light (not enough daylight hours) to grow many plants effectively between late autumn and mid spring (October and March).

Early experiments

In the late 1940s W. J. C. Lawrence of the John Innes Institute noted that serious light deficiencies existed during the winter months and he started using artificial light on tomato seedlings, not only to produce better plants but to shorten the time between pricking out and planting. Although the results were rewarding, the cost of the lamps used at the time (high pressure mercury) did not convince growers that the expense was worthwhile.

Since that time more efficient lamps have been produced, commercial growing

rooms introduced and the technique of inducing plants (chrysanthemums in particular) to flower throughout the year has become established practice.

Principle of light

Any source of radiation – whether the sun or an artificial radiator (lamp or heater, for example) – emits a certain amount of energy consisting of electromagnetic vibrations (such as visible light, radio waves or gamma rays). The wave motion of these vibrations has a constant speed but the length of the waves may vary, and it is the length of the waves that determines what kind of energy is produced. Some wavelengths – the relatively narrow waveband between 380nm and 780nm (one nm, or nanometer, is one millionth of a millimeter) – are visible to the human eye. It is this visible part of the spectrum that is called light.

Below 380nm comes ultra-violet radiation; this causes the skin to tan and can be dangerous to plants. Above 780nm is infra-red radiation (heat).

Within the visible spectrum the wave length of the radiation determines the colour of light. As the wavelength increases you see the following sequence

Right: map showing the average means of daily duration of bright sunshine (in hours) in Great Britain
Below: diagram showing how energy level decreases with increasing wavelength

of colours – violet, indigo, blue, green, yellow, orange and red. 'Beyond' red is far-red – partly outside the visible spectrum but important to plants. For convenience the spectrum can be simplified into four spectral divisions: blue 400–500nm, green 500–600nm, red 600–700nm and far-red 700–750nm.

Light can be considered not only as a wave motion but also as a flow of light particles. Each of these light particles represents a certain amount of energy that depends upon the wavelength

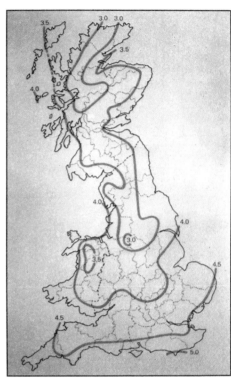

(shown by colour) of the type of light; the shorter the wavelength the higher the amount of energy per light particle. Thus a blue light particle contains a greater amount of energy than a red one.

Plants react to light in three ways: to the intensity of light, to the duration of light and to the colour of light. Each of these reactions will now be considered in greater detail.

Light and photosynthesis

The energy necessary for plant growth is almost all derived from the radiant energy that is absorbed by the parts of the plant growing above ground. The carbon required by the plant for food and for cell structure is derived from the carbon dioxide in the air. Photosynthesis is the process by which light energy is used to reduce this carbon dioxide to sugars that can later be converted to a variety of different structural and food materials. Photosynthesis is dependent on the particular pigments (the chlorophylls)

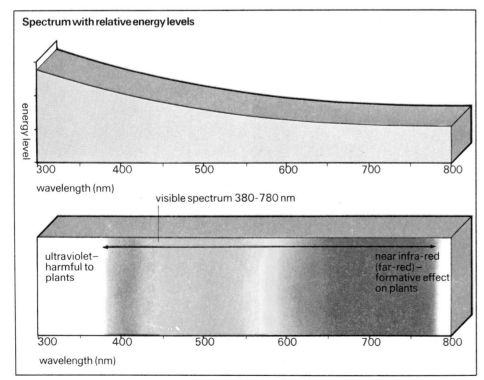

Spectrum with relative energy levels

energy level

wavelength (nm)
300 400 500 600 700 800

visible spectrum 380-780 nm

ultraviolet – harmful to plants

near infra-red (far-red) – formative effect on plants

wavelength (nm)
300 400 500 600 700 800

end of the day, or using them for a short period during the middle of the night – known commonly as night-break.

Only relatively low illuminance levels are needed to achieve the desired effect, the actual level depending on the type of plant concerned. Simple tungsten-filament lamps (domestic light bulbs) are generally used. You need not be too fussy about the arrangement of the lamps over the growing area so long as it provides the required illuminance as evenly and cheaply as possible. Generally a minimum of 50–100 lx is considered adequate.

Light and photomorphogenesis

The rate at which photosynthesis can take place depends on the number of suitable light energy particles received. Red light contains more light energy particles per unit of energy than any other suitable wavelength. From this it could be assumed that a pure-red light source would be the most beneficial for good plant growth. But there are other light requirements (in addition to photosynthesis) that must be taken into account if the plant is to develop satisfactorily. As well as red light (about 660nm), blue light (about 450nm) and far-red light (about 735nm) also exert controlling influences on plant development; this is known as photomorphogenesis – the effect of different light wavelengths on plant growth. Plants grown entirely in blue light have a suppressed, hard, dark appearance and are inclined to 'rosette', while those grown in red light tend to be softer, and suffer some degree of stem elongation. Red light can also suppress the elongation or etiolation that occurs in darkness, but far-red light cannot. Thus the effect of light on vegetative growth (stems and leaves) is complex. This, then, is the reason why the careful choice of a light source for growing plants in the greenhouse – or the house – is so important.

Right lamps for the light

Suitable lamps for artificial illumination are expensive and it would be unfortunate if you chose the wrong lamp for the lighting technique you had in mind. Photosynthesis, photoperiodism and photomorphogenesis are only three, albeit extremely important, factors to be taken into consideration. There are others, such as temperature, size of greenhouse, bench or bed widths, height of roof above the growing area, and number, type and stage of development (seedling or mature stage) of the plants and the proximity of other plants in the growing area. These aspects will now be covered in more detail.

that produce the basic colour of the green leaves. Chlorophylls absorb mainly blue and red light; green is largely reflected.

Not all the light available to a plant is absorbed by the leaf; a proportion of it is reflected at the leaf surface and some light is transmitted through the leaf without being absorbed.

Allowing for this wastage, for photosynthesis to take place a great deal of light must fall on the leaf surface. Although this is likely to happen in summer, in winter the amount of sunlight available to greenhouse plants is greatly reduced.

In commercial practice the aim is to maintain between 5,000 and 10,000 lx (the amount of light falling on an area one metre square is measured in lx or lux). This will be dealt with in more detail in the following sections when we look at different kinds of lamps and their uses.

Light and photoperiodism

Photoperiodism is the effect of day-length on plant development. It has been known for more than 50 years that the flowering habits of some plants depend on the relative length of day and night and that these habits vary widely from one kind of plant to another.

This knowledge has led to a broad classification of plants into three groups. First there are those that will only flower (or will flower more readily) when the

Above: mixed varieties of year-round pot chrysanthemums – those in flower on the right received supplementary artificial light, the others did not

daily period of light exceeds a certain critical minimum; these are known as 'long-day' plants. In the second group are those that will flower only when the day-length is less than that critical minimum – 'short-day' plants. The third group contains plants that flower equally readily in any day-length – 'day-neutral' plants.

The position for individual plant species, however, cannot be stated quite so simply. Some plants require a certain day-length for bud initiation and a different period for flower development (short-day/long-day plants or long-day/short day plants). In others, sensitivity to day-length varies with temperature. The effects of relative day-length on flowering behaviour first drew attention to the phenomenon of photoperiodism and it is in the control of flowering that artificial lighting techniques have so far been used most successfully.

Sufficiently long photoperiods can be provided during naturally short days by using artificial light to shorten the night. This can be done by switching lights on at dusk to lengthen the day or turning them on for a few hours before dawn to produce the same effect at the opposite

USING ARTIFICIAL LIGHT IN THE GREENHOUSE

Having seen how plants react to light the next step is to make use of this knowledge to determine how much irradiation greenhouse plants need and the most effective ways of providing it.

The commercial grower uses light to grow plants to a certain stage in the quickest possible time. He is, therefore, prepared to meet the cost of providing the high level of irradiance (the energy emitted by the lamp – including light) and temperatures necessary to give him optimum growth response. Furthermore he grows, in many cases, tens of thousands of plants at a time, which enables him to install the lamps in blocks at least four lamps square – making a minimum of 16 lamps. He can also double-batch – treat two batches of plants at the same time by moving the lamps every 12 hours from one batch to the other.

The grower uses artificial light to start plants early; for example he will propagate tomatoes in the middle of winter ready for planting out in the greenhouse from late winter to mid spring (early January to mid March), while cucumbers are planted out before this and lettuce are cropped from late autumn to mid spring (October right through to March). He also uses light to extend daylight – by turning the lamps on at dusk or before dawn, in the middle of the night or from dusk to dawn.

Home greenhouse uses

The amateur gardener may be interested in these techniques but will also want to provide extra light during dull winter days to ensure that plants (such as saintpaulia, or other houseplants) continue growing and flowering during the months when the average natural light is not strong enough to promote normal plant development.

The amateur gardener, therefore, does not need to be too concerned about the commercial growers' exacting growing conditions. You can, however, use artificial light effectively by starting later in the season, say at the beginning of spring (early to mid February), so that once the propagating stage has been completed the plants can be set out in their growing positions at a time of the year when natural light is improving and outside

Isolux diagram
2400mm (8ft) 125W lamp
Height: 400mm (16in)

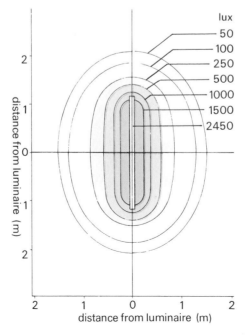

lux
50
100
250
500
1000
1500
2450

distance from luminaire (m)

distance from luminaire (m)

Above: the area under the greenhouse staging can be made use of by installing supplementary lighting that is mounted under the bench
Left: diagram showing the illuminance distribution from a 125W fluorescent tube

temperatures are rising, and when it won't be too costly to maintain a minimum temperature of 13°C (55°F) throughout the night.

However, during the period from seed germination to planting out you will have to keep temperatures up to around 18°C (65°F) during the day, dropping down to 16°C (60°F) at night. To heat the whole greenhouse to these temperatures would be very expensive, but fortunately there are ways of keeping the heating bills under control. The first step is to reduce the heat losses from the house to the outside air. A 250-gauge polyethylene sheet attached to the inside of the glazing bars will effectively save up to 40 per cent heat loss. Next, as only a few plants will be irradiated, use a plastic curtain (500-gauge polyethylene) to partition off the propagating area. This area must have some means of ventilation, but if the greenhouse has fan ventilation do not include it in the propagating area – a single roof vent should be adequate for this. You can, however, use a small fan to circulate air among the young plants, and help deter grey mould (botrytis). But if you are already using a fan heater to boost the air temperature, then an additional fan will not be necessary to provide ventilation.

Uniform illuminance
Before choosing and installing one of the lamps readily available, there is one more factor that needs to be considered – the evenness of illuminance that the lamp provides. How this evenness varies can be seen from isolux diagrams; an isolux is a line joining equal levels of illuminance. These figures vary appreciably according to the type of lamp and luminaire (reflector) used. The diagram (left) shows the illuminance distribution from one 2400mm (8 ft) 125 watt fluorescent tube mounted at a height of 400mm (16 in). Observe that the lines are more or less oval and that the illuminance falls more rapidly as the distance from the lamp increases. As commercial growers must have illuminance that is as even as possible across the growing area (to ensure uniform plant growth), the aim is to provide an illuminance within 10 per cent plus or minus of the recommended illuminance. For example: if an illuminance of 5000 lx is stipulated then the illuminance across the growing area should not be more than 5500 lx or less than 4500 lx; the latter illuminance level is generally referred to as the cut-off figure.

It can be clearly seen that the cut-off for a fluorescent tube is only a few centimetres, so to irradiate an area more than

150mm (6 in) in width it will be necessary to use two or more tubes. You can see that immediately under the lamp the illuminance is 2450 lx but at a distance of 1m (3¼ ft) on either side it has fallen to about 200 lx – less than one-tenth. Note also that the light output at each end of the tube drops by nearly one half (to 1250 lx), so you could not expect the same plant response beneath the area 150mm (6 in) wide at either end where the illuminance is less, as you would from the remaining 2130mm (7 ft) length of tube.

To take an example: supposing you wish to provide 2450 lx at plant level with two 2400mm (8 ft) tubes fixed 400mm (16 in) above the growing area, it would then be necessary to install the tubes approximately 300mm (12 in) apart – the distance being measured from the centre line of each lamp. If you then decided to increase the illuminance to 5000 lx, the distance from the centre line of each lamp would be reduced to 50mm (2 in).

Advantages of fluorescent tubes
Despite the apparent complications in setting up a lighting installation with fluorescent tubes, this light source has several advantages. First, being a linear source of light, an even illuminance can be expected over the growing area. Secondly, fluorescent tubes need very little headroom compared with mercury and sodium discharge lamps and so are ideal for the modern small greenhouse, where the height of the eaves level above the bench is only 760mm (2½ ft), and also for use under the staging.

As a general rule the area under greenhouse benches is too dark during the winter months for the majority of plants to grow normally, even if temperatures higher than 7°C (45°F) are maintained. However, two fluorescent tubes under a 760mm (2½ ft) high bench will transform this normally unproductive area into one that will grow many plants, even in the middle of winter. But extra precautions

Diagrams showing the arrangement of 125W tubes to give illuminances of 11000 and 8000 lx at various different heights above the greenhouse staging

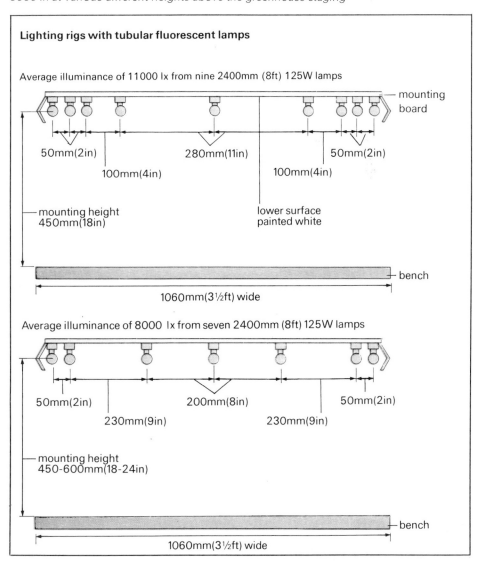

Lighting rigs with tubular fluorescent lamps

Average illuminance of 11000 lx from nine 2400mm (8ft) 125W lamps

mounting board

50mm(2in)   280mm(11in)   50mm(2in)
100mm(4in)   100mm(4in)

mounting height 450mm(18in)

lower surface painted white

bench

1060mm(3½ft) wide

Average illuminance of 8000 lx from seven 2400mm (8ft) 125W lamps

50mm(2in)   200mm(8in)   50mm(2in)
230mm(9in)   230mm(9in)

mounting height 450-600mm(18-24in)

bench

1060mm(3½ft) wide

will be needed to ensure all the electrical fittings under the bench are protected from water seeping through from the bench above.

The third advantage of the fluorescent tube is that it radiates much less heat than would mercury and sodium discharge lamps used to irradiate the same amount of bench area.

Other kinds of lamp

To appreciate the advantages of the fluorescent lamp, compare it with other available sources of artificial light, for instance the MBFR/U (mercury fluorescent reflector), SOX (low pressure sodium) and SON (high pressure sodium) lamps.

The first to consider is the 400 watt MBFR/U. Instead of the light being distributed evenly along a 2400mm (8 ft) length, as in the case of a 125 watt fluorescent tube, it is concentrated at the bottom of a lamp that has a diameter of only 180mm (7 in). Unlike the oval isolux of the fluorescent tube, the MBFR/U isolux are circular. Again the illuminance falls off rapidly so that to cover any sort of area at all a minimum of two lamps would be required; to achieve the ideal, you would need four lamps, which would emit heat equal to that of a 1720 watt electric fire (1600 watts from the lamps and another 120 watts being generated by the control gear). Two lamps would effectively cover an area of 1250 × 760mm (4 ft 2 in × 2½ ft). To overcome any problems with cut-off near the edges of the bench where plants will not be receiving the desired amount of light, these plants can be changed over – with those in the centre of the bench – halfway through the irradiation period. This also applies to SOX and SON lamps. Two lamps should successfully irradiate the average small greenhouse bench 760mm (2½ ft) wide if they are installed over the bench centre line. Four lamps would be required to cover a bench 1070mm (3½ ft) wide, the centre of the lamps being suspended 150mm (6 in) from each bench edge. Similar results can be expected from the 310 watt SONR (high pressure sodium reflector lamp) in comparable conditions.

The 180 watt SOX lamp is a linear source. The lamp is very efficient and will produce an illuminance of 6000 lx when hung 1200mm (4 ft) above the growing area. The lamp's cut-off point is again marked, in fact light output falls appreciably towards each end of the tube; nevertheless two lamps should effectively irradiate a bench 1070mm (3½ ft) long, 760mm (2½ ft) wide. Again, due to the narrow cut-off, it is necessary to install the lamps parallel to the centre line of the

bench, and suspended about 150mm (6 in) in from each edge of the bench.

The 400 watt SON/T (high pressure sodium tubular lamp) with the Camplex luminaire produces a quite different isolux pattern. In this case 'tubular' indicates the fact that although the lamp is tubular in shape it is only 338mm (13 in) long, so it can be considered to produce a spot light source. The lamp is usually suspended horizontally and, with the luminaire, produces a dumb-bell shaped isolux pattern.

This is an efficient light source that even at a height of 1500mm (4 ft 11 in) gives an illuminance of 4500 lx at bench level. However, the cut-off is quite marked, there being a 25 per cent fall in illuminance at 500mm (19½ in) from a point immediately below the centre of the lamp. Compared with the other types of lamp the 400 watt SON/T produces a very high illuminance (45,000 lumens at 2000 hours) so this lamp should be suspended 1500mm (4 ft 11 in) above the growing area, which would make it impractical for the small greenhouse unless the plants being irradiated were positioned on the floor. One lamp of this type should be

sufficient for most gardeners' requirements.

Protecting other plants

Plants have a tendency to grow towards a strong light. As an example, if you were to place a plant on a south-facing window-ledge you would observe that after a period of time the stems would be bending over towards the light. This property is known as phototropism. In a small greenhouse or, in fact, in any greenhouse where plants are grown in the vicinity of a powerful lamp, phototropism will occur, especially during winter months. To prevent this it is advisable to hang a sheet of aluminium foil between the lamp and the plants being grown in natural light only.

Similar precautions should be taken when long-day treatment is given in one section of the greenhouse, as even this low level of overspill (less than 50 lx) could have an adverse effect on the untreated plants. You can imagine what would happen if the light from lamps used for plants receiving long-day treatment was to spill over to plants that you wanted kept in short days.

Left: this type of fluorescent tube lighting can be used to maximum effect because one batch of plants can be moved and replaced by another Below: 400W SON/T lamps in a commercial setting

GROWING PLANTS WITH ARTIFICIAL LIGHT

In the preceding pages we have shown that both the amount and the colour of light influence plant growth and development. We have also discussed various methods of installing lamps.
Now we explain the techniques used for growing popular greenhouse plants under artificial light.

Many plants raised in greenhouses can benefit from extended day lighting and/or supplementary lighting. Supplementary lighting is the use of artificial light to supplement poor natural light during winter months. The object is to encourage plants to start into growth sooner and come into crop or flower earlier.

Night-break lighting provides an additional period of light in the hours of darkness. This often proves an economical way of lengthening the plant's day hours. Times given for night-break lighting are centred around 1.00 am.

The following paragraphs discuss a wide range of plants, from tomatoes to antirrhinums.

Tomatoes
Tomatoes need a minimum night temperature of 13°C (55°F). They also need plenty of light, and in the early months of the year natural light is not strong enough to produce sturdy, well-developed plants. So under normal cool house conditions of 7°C (45°F) it is not possible to start picking until mid summer (June). By then shop prices will have fallen and the effort and expense in producing the crop may seem hardly worthwhile. The ideal, therefore, is to use artificial light to start them cropping earlier.

Sow the seeds in pans in early spring or even late winter (February or January), and germinate in a temperature of 21°C (70°F) – an electric propagator provides the right conditions. As soon as the seeds are large enough to handle, prick out into 9cm (3½ in) pots and grow on under artificial light. The total average illuminance should be 10,000 lx so, as only about 12 plants will be needed in the average gardener's greenhouse, a 400 watt MBFR/U lamp mounted 970mm (3 ft 2 in) above the plants should be adequate. Two 1500mm (5 ft), 65 watt warm white fluorescent tubes, each of them mounted 380mm (15 in) above the plants, would

Above: check that night-break lighting will not disturb your neighbours

also be effective. Three weeks' irradiation can be sufficient; during mid spring (March) the lamps can be turned off on clear sunny days. Tomato plants should never be irradiated longer than 16 hours each day or growth and flowering may be retarded. You can start before early spring (mid February) but you would then have to maintain a continued minimum night temperature of 13°C (55°F) after the propagating period.

Aubergines and sweet peppers
These vegetables can be grown out of doors during a warm summer but cropping may be disappointing. For better results start them early, perhaps in a propagator in early spring (February), and treat them as you would tomatoes. You can cut your running costs by irradiating the young plants at the same time as the tomatoes.

Lettuce
Lettuce is a major commercial green-house crop during the winter months, but under normal light conditions it may take six weeks or more before the young plants are ready for planting out in the greenhouse border or heated frame. To speed things up sow pelleted seed individually in 5cm (2 in) pots with a peat-based seed compost and germinate them in a temperature of 10°C (50°F). If you irradiate the seedlings 24 hours a day for 14 days immediately after germination, planting out time can be advanced by up to four weeks. In this way you can grow and clear a lettuce crop before the border is needed for tomatoes. An illuminance of 5000 lx is adequate. If, however, you have problems in blacking out your greenhouse at night so as to avoid disturbing neighbours, irradiate for 12 hours daily at 10,000 lx.

Bulbs
Daffodils and other narcissi, hyacinths,

Above: these fine calceolaria show the benefit of supplementary light
Right: the larger cucumber plant, grown in supplementary light, is well in advance of one grown in natural days

specially treated for forcing) are used. successive batches can, with a careful selection of varieties, be forced to provide a continuous supply from mid winter to late spring (December to April). For tulips 18°C (64°F) should be the aim until buds are showing, then drop to 16°C (61°F) until flowering. Keep hyacinths in the dark for the first 1–7 days depending on the variety. Temperatures need to be higher than for narcissi or tulips; start off with 24°C (75°F) and then, when colour shows, drop to 18°C (64°F). Hyacinths need a relatively high humidity, but still follow the general watering rule for all bulb flower crops – restrict it to just enough to ensure good, firm growth.

If you have space under the greenhouse bench, then you can force them there, provided you exclude daylight with black polyethylene sheeting. Keep up temperature by means of a small fan heater if necessary, and pay careful attention to

tulips and crocuses can be forced successfully under 40 watt general service lamps installed on a frame on the basis of 2·5 lamps per square metre or yard.

As the foliage and flower-stalks increase in height so the frame is raised accordingly. Completely darkened sheds and cellars are adequate for forcing as long as you can maintain a temperature of not less than 16°C (61°F). Store the bulbs in boxes in mid to late autumn (late September) and stand them in a cool place outdoors, such as by the north side of the house or wall, and covered with 15cm (6 in) of straw or 10cm (4 in) of moist peat. Make sure the straw and peat are kept moist. Towards mid winter (end of November) when the shoots are about 6·5cm (2½ in) long the bulbs will be ready for forcing.

Daffodils and other narcissi need 16°C (61°F) and if pre-cooled bulbs (bulbs

ventilation. The daily lighting period can be restricted to 12 hours and this can be done at night to economize on heating.

Chrysanthemums
Although considerable success has been achieved in producing good quality blooms during the winter months, those being produced between late winter and mid spring (January and March) were inferior to those flowering in or before mid winter (December). As a result of research, growers are now using supplementary lighting as well as the normal night-break techniques, to maintain bloom quality throughout the winter. For the purpose of all-year-round production, chrysanthemum varieties are divided into response groups: for example a 10-week variety is one that requires only 10 weeks from commencement of short days (when night-break lighting is finished)

Illuminance requirements for various plant species

Plant species	Illuminance lx (MBFR/U)	Irradiation period	Irradiation time per 24 hours in hours	Purpose and further details
Aechmea fasciata (urn plant)	2000	early winter to early spring	8–10 (night-break)	promoting vegetative growth of seedlings
Antirrhinum majus (snapdragon)	4000	for 4–5 weeks after appearance (sown early winter)	day-lengthening to 16	flower advancement by approx 4 weeks
Aphelandra	367	early winter to early spring	6–8 (night-break)	promoting vegetative growth; at higher irradiance levels also earlier flowering
Begonia Elatior	67	late autumn to late spring	8 (day-lengthening)	suppressing bud formation; more and earlier cuttings
Begonia Lorraine	33–67	in winter; for 40 days after taking leaf cuttings	8 (day-lengthening)	preventing flower-bud initiation; improved sprouting
Begonia rex	100	from the end of mid autumn	8 (night-break) mid winter 2 (night-break) autumn and spring	improving vegetative growth of young plants; better foliage
Begonia semperflorens	2000	mid winter to early spring	10 (night-break)	improving vegetative growth and earlier flowering
Bulbs: tulip, daffodil and other narcissi, crocus	1000	mid winter to early spring	12 (no daylight)	flower forcing
hyacinth	1667	mid winter to early spring	12 (no daylight)	flower forcing
Calceolaria hybrid	333	after flower-bud initiation	4–5 (day-lengthening) 8 (night-break)	acceleration of flowering
Callistephus chinensis (China aster)	733	from mid autumn	8 (night-break)	stem elongation and flowering advancement (to mid spring)
Campanula isophylla (bellflower)	333–667	early winter to mid spring; for some weeks after stopping	8 (night-break)	flowering in spring instead of summer; more cuttings
Carnation (dianthus)	433	middle of late winter to end of early spring	all night	increasing flower crops
	433	early autumn to late spring	6–12 (night-break)	extending flowering time
Chrysanthemum	300	in winter	day-lengthening to 16	year-round cultivation; to prevent bud initiation in winter critical day length: 14·5 hr
	100	third week of early autumn to late spring	night-break (from 2–5 each night depending on time of year)	year-round cultivation; to prevent bud initiation in winter critical day length: 14·5 hr
	833	early autumn to late spring	7 (night-break)	stock plants; to promote vegetative growth for cuttings
Cineraria (or Senecio) cruentus	367	after flower-bud initiation, for about 2·5 months	9 (night-break)	flower advancement by 2–4 weeks in a period of 2·5 months
Cyclamen persicum	2000	early winter to early spring	8–9 (night-break)	promoting vegetative growth of seedlings
Dahlia	1333	in winter	2 (night-break)	flowering advancement
Euphorbia fulgens (scarlet plume)	67	early autumn to late winter; for 5–7 weeks	8 (night-break)	earlier flower crops critical day length: 12 hr
Euphorbia pulcherrima (poinsettia)	100	from the beginning of late autumn; for 2–3 weeks	2–3 (night-break)	retarding flower initiation (eg till mid to late winter)
Euphorbia (splendens) milii (crown of thorns)	367	late autumn to late spring	4 (night-break)	improving vegetative growth; year-round flower production
Ferns	2000	early winter to early spring	10 supplementary during the day	improving vegetative growth
Fuchsia	400	mid to late autumn	4 (night-break)	flowering promotion

Illuminance requirements for various plant species

Plant species	Illuminance lx (MBFR/U)	Irradiation period	Irradiation time per 24 hours in hours	Purpose and further details
Gerbera	2000	early winter to early spring until 2 weeks after planting out	15 supplementary during the day	improving vegetative growth of young plants
	2000	next 6 weeks	6 supplementary during the day	improving vegetative growth of young plants
Kalanchoe	1333	late winter to mid spring	10–12 supplementary during the day	early crop
	3333–6667	late winter to mid spring	10–12 supplementary during the day	improving vegetative growth
	333–667	from late autumn	8 (night-break)	flower retarding
Lilium (lily)	3333–6667	mid winter to mid spring	day-lengthening to 12	promoting bud initiation by day-lengthening
Matthiola incana Column (stock)	4000	late winter to early spring; until planting out	16 supplementary during the day	flower initiation
	2000	late winter to early spring until planting out	8 (night-break)	improving vegetative growth
Regal pelargonium	133–200	from mid winter, after flower-bud initiation	2–4 (night-break)	earlier flowering
Saintpaulia (African violet)	2000	in winter	day-lengthening to 16	improving and advancing flower production
	6667 (beneath greenhouse benches)	in winter	24 (no daylight)	improving and advancing flower production
Saxifraga cotyledon	133	middle of early spring; for 3 weeks	3–4 (night-break)	flowering advancement (1–4 weeks)
Sinningia speciosa (gloxinia)	2000–3333	early winter to early spring	8 supplementary during the day	improving vegetative growth of seedlings
Stephanotis floribunda (Madagascar jasmine)	267–400	mid autumn to mid winter	day-lengthening to 14	second flower crop in autumn and winter
Strawberry	117 (cyclic; 15 min/hr) or 67 (continuous)	from middle of late winter; for 40 nights	8–9 (night-break)	earlier and larger crop by flower promotion
Vriesea splendens (flaming sword)	2000	early winter to early spring	8 supplementary during the day	improving vegetative growth seedlings

The Gardener's Seasons

early spring	(February)	early autumn	(August)
mid spring	(March)	mid autumn	(September)
late spring	(April)	late autumn	(October)
early summer	(May)	early winter	(November)
mid summer	(June)	mid winter	(December)
late summer	(July)	late winter	(January)

to flowering. The night-break lighting is used between early autumn and late spring (August and April) to prevent premature flower-bud development and encourage vegetative growth, and varies from two hours each night in early autumn (August) to five hours in mid winter (December). As the first two weeks of short days are critical, so far as quantity of daylight is concerned, it is necessary to supplement this with artificial light between the beginning of winter (November) and the end of early spring (February). For this purpose 400 watt MBFR/U or warm white fluorescent lamps are used to produce 7200 lx, which will be enough to give gratifying results.

Saintpaulia (African violet)

So long as temperatures can be maintained at 18–21°C (64–70°F) these plants will grow normally under the greenhouse bench. Two 1500mm (5 ft), 80 watt warm white fluorescent lamps 380mm (15 in) above the plants will be adequate for a space 760mm (2½ ft) wide and 1400mm (4½ ft) long. The daily lighting period should be 12–14 hours.

Antirrhinums

Special greenhouse forcing varieties should be used. Sow between late autumn and early winter (October and early November). Plants are grown in a temperature of 10°C (50°F) and high temperatures should be avoided. Make quite sure you remove all sideshoots. In a propagating case or under mist with a bottom heat of 21–24°C (70–75°F) germination should take place after three days. Five days later the seedlings can be placed under a 400 watt MBFR/U lamp or warm white fluorescent tubes from 1700 hours to 0700 hours. This lighting should be switched off after about two weeks. This period of long days will enable you to have an early show of flowers.

PLANTS IN THE GREENHOUSE

STOCKING THE GREENHOUSE WITH PLANTS

When you buy and erect your first greenhouse it will look depressingly bare, and you may wonder how you will ever fill it with plants, Do not despair, however; bear in mind that most greenhouse gardeners eventually find themselves at the other extreme and cry out for more room.

Don't be too impatient to fill your greenhouse. Take your time about selecting plants, and choose those that will be happy together (sharing the same, or very similar, conditions of light, temperature and humidity) and suited to the environment created by your particular greenhouse and site.

If you want some quick colour you can always grow annuals from seed while planning your long-term plant selections.

Mixing and matching plants
There are a number of growing routines that you can adopt using groups or successions of popular plants. For example, you may want to use the greenhouse for raising bedding plants early in the year, followed by tomatoes and then chrysanthemums. Alternatively, you might want to specialize in vegetables such as cucumbers, melons or climbing French beans, or in flowers such as carnations or orchids. Any other plants must then be chosen to fit in with these.

Your scope for mixing plants is very wide since, by positioning them carefully, you can largely satisfy their individual requirements. For instance, you can shade the glass immediately above plants needing deep shade or else put them under the staging. Put plants demanding plenty of light as near the glass as possible and well away from others that might cast shade. Stand plants preferring high humidity on moist shingle, and keep those that like drier air on slatted staging.

Trouble arises, however, when you try to put together plants with widely differing demands, such as mixing tropicals, sub-tropicals, alpines, succulents, semi-aquatics, sun or shade lovers and hardy plants. Of course there are always a few examples of these groups that seem more tolerant of conditions that are abnormal to the group as a whole. For example *Aphelandra squarrosa* (zebra plant) is from warm parts of Brazil, yet it can be acclimatized to a quite cool

greenhouse. Numerous succulents also make themselves at home in fairly moist conditions.

Using the whole greenhouse
When stocking your greenhouse, you must also remember that plants have many different habits of growth. It is not only their height that varies; they may become bushy, grow erect, trail or hang, climb, or be capable of being trained into standards or other shapes. It is by exploiting the many different and exciting shapes of plants that a really attractive greenhouse is created.

The greenhouse should be able to cope with these variations, if you arrange to have shelving that can be set at different heights and make provision for pots or baskets to hang from the roof – remembering that such containers can be very heavy when filled with moist compost. You can also install staging of various heights and leave parts of the greenhouse clear so that plants can be grown from floor level to the full house height. For climbers, wires or plastic netting fastened to one side (particularly in a lean-to) may give you further scope.

All-year-round interest
You should be able to plan your greenhouse so that there is as much 'going on' in winter as in high summer. Plants like cinerarias, calceolaria, primula, browallia, schizanthus and annuals such as salpiglossis will give colour from late winter to late spring (January to April), especially if batches of seed are sown in succession. Remember that variety may greatly influence the time of flowering and by choosing several varieties you may enjoy the same type of flower for a longer period. For example most of the compact-growing cinerarias will flower early, perhaps even in mid winter (December), while the large, exhibition kinds usually flower much later in spring. The same can be said for calceolarias, of which the newer F.1 hybrids are remarkably quick-flowering. In the case of bulbs, too, there are specially-prepared kinds that you can force gently for early flowers, keeping their untreated counterparts for later blooms.

In the decorative greenhouse or conservatory evergreens will provide attractive foliage through winter, but select

them carefully to avoid creating too much shade. This is especially important when choosing and siting evergreen climbers.

Better house plants
The present-day range of house plants provides many exciting evergreens and some gloriously exotic foliage. Although popularly described as 'house plants' they often do far better in the greenhouse because of its higher humidity. However, these house plants must always be selected with their minimum temperature requirement in mind. Avoid buying those needing more warmth during the winter. Unfortunately many come onto the market in mid to late winter (late December) and they may have been standing in chilly, draughty florists' shops for some time. These plants take some weeks to show the effect of such treatment, so don't be surprised if they suddenly wilt or drop their foliage after being transferred to your greenhouse.

Acquiring healthy plants
Be critical about accepting plants and cuttings from other gardeners. These may have been passed on because the originals were rampant and weedy. Many poor-flowering impatiens (busy Lizzy) are acquired this way. It is better to wait for plants of which you know the botanical origin, and the variety and name. Remember that there are many specialist growers who sell only healthy plants that are correctly named. These are the people from whom to buy plants like orchids, carnations, alpines, begonias, streptocarpus, achimenes, pelargoniums, fuchsias, virus-free fruit (including strawberries), cacti and other succulents, bulbs and other storage organs, and the many other popular favourites for growing under glass.

Growing from seed
All greenhouse gardeners should make themselves familiar with the techniques of growing from seed. Numerous delightful and uncommon plants can be obtained this way. As well as the good selection of popular greenhouse plants that you can order from the general seedsmen, there are rare and unusual plant seeds to be obtained from specialist seedsmen.

Many house plants can also be raised from seed, including palms and cacti.

SEED SOWING AND PRICKING OUT

Many different plants are raised from seed sown in containers in a greenhouse: summer bedding plants, flowering pot plants, and vegetables like tomatoes, lettuce, celery, cucumbers and marrows. But the techniques of sowing and subsequent care are similar.

Late winter and spring is the main period for most sowings; more precise timing is usually given on the seed packets. A heated greenhouse, or a propagator, is necessary for germination (that is, starting seeds into life).

Seed trays and pots
Seed trays, approximately 5–6cm (2–2½ in) deep, are available in either wood or plastic. Plastic ones last for many years,

if well looked after, and are easy to clean. Hygienic conditions are important if you are to raise healthy seedlings, so clean the seed trays thoroughly before use.

For very small quantities of seed use plastic pots 9 or 13cm (3½ or 5 in) in diameter. These are also recommended for very large individual seeds, such as marrows and cucumbers. Again, wash all pots carefully before use.

Types of compost
Garden soil is not a very suitable medium in which to grow seedlings as it is full of weed seeds and harmful organisms, and it may not provide the correct conditions required by the seed for successful germination. Instead, buy one of the ready-mixed seed-sowing composts, the most popular being John Innes Seed Compost,

consisting of loam, peat, sand, superphosphate and ground chalk.

Alternatively there are many brands of seed compost which consist only of peat with added fertilizers; these are known as 'soilless' composts because they do not contain loam. When using soilless compost you have to be especially careful with watering, for if it dries out it can be difficult to moisten again; over-watering may saturate it and cause the seeds to rot. With a little care, however, soilless compost gives excellent results.

Building in drainage
Be sure that surplus water is able to drain from all containers. When using John Innes composts it is essential to

Pricking out seedlings with a dibber

Place a layer of crocks in the bottom of flower pots to provide drainage

place a layer of crocks (broken clay flower pots or stones) at least 13mm ($\frac{1}{2}$ in) deep over the bottom of the pot. Cover the crocks with a little roughage, such as rough peat. If you use seed trays, crocks are not needed, just cover the drainage slits with some roughage.

Soilless compost can be used without any crocking – unless it is going in clay flower pots, in which case you must cover the large hole at the bottom with crocks.

Once you have arranged the drainage material add the compost to about 13mm ($\frac{1}{2}$ in) below the top of the tray or pot, to allow room for watering. Firm it gently all over with your fingertips, paying particular attention to the sides, ends and corners of seed trays. Make sure that the surface is level by pressing gently with a flat piece of wood that just fits into the tray or pot. Soilless compost should not be pressed hard but merely shaken down by tapping the container on a hard surface or lightly firming with the wood.

Very tiny seeds (like lobelia and begonia) should be sown on a fine surface. So before pressing down, sieve a layer of compost over the surface using a very small-mesh sieve. Alternatively you can sprinkle a thin layer of silver sand over the compost before sowing. Do not use builder's sand as this contains materials toxic to plants.

Water the compost lightly, using a fine rose on the watering can, before you sow.

Sowing the seeds

Seeds must be sown thinly and evenly otherwise the seedlings will be overcrowded and you will find it difficult to separate them during pricking out (transplanting). They will also have thin, weak stems and be prone to diseases like 'damping off'.

Small seed is usually sown broadcast

(scattered) over the surface of the compost. Take a small quantity of seed in the palm of one hand – just sufficient to sow a tray or pot. Hold your hand about 30cm (12 in) above the container and move it to and fro over the surface, at the same time tapping it with the other hand to release the seeds slowly. If you move your hand first backwards and forwards and then side to side this will help to spread the seeds evenly. You may find it easier to hold the seeds in a piece of paper, instead of in your hand.

It is difficult to sow very small seeds evenly, some being as fine as dust, but if you mix them with soft, dry, silver sand (using 1 part seeds to 1 part sand) this helps to bulk them up and makes them easier to handle.

Large seeds, which are easily handled, can be 'space-sown' – that is placed individually, and at regular intervals, on the surface of the compost. Tomato seed, for instance, can be treated in this way.

Very large seeds, such as cucumbers, peas and various beans, are best sown at two per 9cm ($3\frac{1}{2}$ in) pot. If you use

1 *Cover drainage materials with compost, firming it gently with the fingertips*

3 *Scatter a little seed into tray by tapping it gently from your open hand*

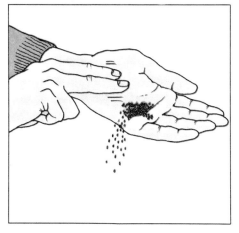

peat pots, they can later be planted, complete with young plant, into the final pot or open ground. When they have germinated, remove the weaker seedling, leaving the stronger one to grow on.

Pelleted seeds

This term describes seeds that are individually covered with a layer of clay which is often mixed with some plant foods. They are easily handled and can be space-sown in boxes or pots. The compost around pelleted seeds must remain moist as it is moisture which breaks down the coating and allows the seeds to germinate.

After sowing

Seeds should be covered with a layer of compost equal to the diameter of the seed. It is best to sieve compost over them, using a fine-mesh sieve. However, do not cover very small or dust-like seeds with compost as they will probably fail to germinate.

If you use John Innes or another loam-

2 *Level the surface of the compost by pressing with a flat piece of wood*

4 *With large seeds, sow two in a small pot and remove the weaker seedling*

1 *Sieve compost over seeds;* 2 *Stand tray in water till surface looks moist.* 3 *Use a dibber to lift seedlings and transfer them to a new tray, where they will have room to grow on*

containing compost the seeds should then be watered, either using a very fine rose on the watering can or by standing the containers in a tray of water until the surface becomes moist. (This latter method is not advisable for loam-less composts as they tend to float; moisten them well before sowing the seed.) Allow the containers to drain before placing them in the greenhouse.

A good, or even better, alternative to plain water is a solution of Cheshunt Compound, made up according to the directions on the tin. This is a fungicide which prevents diseases such as damping off attacking seedlings.

Aids to germination
Place the pots or trays either on a bench in a warm greenhouse or in an electrically-heated propagator. Most seeds need a temperature of 15°–18°C (60–65°F) for good germination. The containers can be covered with a sheet of glass that, in turn, is covered with brown paper to prevent the sun's warmth drying out the compost. Turn the glass over each day to prevent excess condensation building up on the inside. Water the compost whenever its surface starts to become dry. As soon as germination commences remove the covering of glass and paper, for the seedlings then require as much light as

possible if they are to grow into strong, healthy plants.

Pricking out
Once the seedlings are large enough to handle easily prick them out into trays or boxes to give them enough room to grow. Generally, standard-size plastic or wooden seed trays are used that are 6cm (2½ in) deep; there is no need to put drainage material in the base. The trays are filled with compost in the way described for seed-sowing, again leaving space for watering. A suitable compost would be John Innes Potting Compost No. 1 which can be bought ready-mixed. It consists of loam, peat, coarse sand, John Innes base fertilizer and ground chalk. Alternatively, use one of the soil-less potting composts that contains peat, or peat and sand, plus fertilizers. Make sure the compost is moist before you start pricking out.

You will need a dibber for this job – either a pencil or a piece of wood of similar shape. With this lift a few seedlings at a time from the box or pot, taking care not to damage the roots. Handle the seedlings by the seed leaves – the first pair of leaves formed. Never hold them by the stems which are easily damaged at this stage.

Spacing out
The number of seedlings per standard-size box will vary slightly according to their vigour. Generally 40 per box is a good spacing (5 rows of 8). For less vigorous plants you could increase this to 54 per box (6 rows of 9).

Mark out the position of the seedlings with the dibber before commencing, ensuring equal spacing each way. Next

make a hole, with the dibber, which should be deep enough to allow the roots to drop straight down. Place the seedling in the hole so that the seed leaves are at soil level, and then firm it in by pressing the soil gently against it with the dibber.

If only a few seeds have been sown in pots each seedling could be pricked out into an individual 7cm (3 in) pot. But if you have single seedlings, such as marrows, already started in 9cm (3½ in) pots, these will not need to be moved.

After pricking out, water in the seedlings (with a fine rose on the watering can) preferably using Cheshunt Compound. Then place them on the greenhouse bench or on a shelf near to the glass, as maximum light is essential. Continue to water whenever the soil surface appears dry.

Windowsill propagation
If you do not have a greenhouse, heated frame, or propagator, you can still raise seedlings in the house. Ideally the germination conditions should be as similar as possible to those which are recommended for greenhouse cultivation. Windowsills are the best places for raising seeds, and if they are wide ones you can use standard-size seed trays.

However it is usually possible to fit a few pots onto the narrowest of windowsills. For best results use trays or pots that are fitted with propagator tops. The temperature on the sill must not drop below the average room temperature and south- or west-facing sills are obviously best.

Make sure the seedlings are never deprived of daylight or allowed to get cold at night. Never draw the curtains across between the plants and the warm room air on cold nights, if necessary bring them into the room. Finally, to maintain strong and even growth, turn all pots and trays around every day.

Use a pot with a propagator top when starting off seedlings on a windowsill

POTTING OFF AND POTTING ON

The basic terms used in potting are 'potting off', when young rooted cuttings or seedlings are moved from trays into pots, and 'potting on', when the more advanced plants are transferred to bigger pots.

Nowadays plastic pots are generally used in preference to clay, but whichever type you have ensure that they are clean and dry before using them.

POTTING OFF

As soon as cuttings have developed a good root system they should be carefully lifted from their trays and put into individual pots about 7·5–9cm (3–3½ in) in diameter. When seedlings are large

Before placing a pot-bound plant in its new pot, carefully remove old drainage crocks from the base of the rootball

enough to handle easily they can be treated in the same way (as an alternative to pricking out into trays).

For this first potting, use a fairly weak compost, such as J.I. No 1, or an equivalent soilless type consisting of loam, peat, coarse sand, John Innes base fertilizer and ground chalk.

Allowing for drainage

Drainage material is not necessary in plastic pots as the holes are devised so that the compost does not leak. Furthermore, there is a trend towards using less

drainage material in the bottom of small clay pots. When there are some drainage holes provided, place a few crocks (pieces of broken clay pots or stones) over the drainage holes and cover with a thin layer of roughage such as coarse peat or partially-rotted leaf mould. If you are using soilless compost, crocks or drainage materials are not normally necessary. Place a layer of compost over the drainage material and firm lightly with your fingers.

Transferring the plants

Hold the rooted cuttings or seedlings in the centre of the pot, with the roots well spread out, and trickle compost all around until it is slightly higher than the rim of the pot. Give the pot a sharp tap on the bench to settle the compost well down and lightly firm all round with your fingers. Make sure the compost is pushed right down to the bottom.

Some soilless composts, however, require little or no firming, so check the manufacturer's instructions first.

Remember to leave about 13mm (½ in) between the surface of the soil and the rim of the pot to allow room for watering.

After potting off, water the plants thoroughly, using a fine rose on the watering can, to settle them in further. Then they can be returned to the bench.

POTTING ON

Plants need potting on to prevent them becoming 'pot-bound' (when the roots are packed very tightly in the pot). If this happens the plants will suffer from lack of food, growth will be poor and they will dry out very rapidly and require frequent watering.

However, it is worthwhile noting that some plants, such as pelargoniums, are more floriferous (bear more flowers) when slightly pot-bound.

Plants should be moved to the next size of pot, for instance from a 9cm (3½ in) to a 13cm (5 in), from a 13cm (5 in) to a 15cm (6 in) and so on. The reason for moving only to the next size pot is that plants dislike a large volume of soil around their roots because they cannot absorb water from all of it and, therefore, it is liable to remain wet. This can result in root rot and the possible death of the plant. Small moves allow plants to put out new roots quickly.

Composts and drainage

Richer composts (those containing more plant foods) are generally used for potting on. If you prefer the John Innes type, then use No 2, which contains twice as much fertilizer and chalk as No 1. Some plants (for example chrysanthemums,

*To pot on a pot-bound plant: **1** place crocks and drainage material in bottom of larger pot, then carefully remove plant from old pot; **2** half-fill new pot with compost; **3** hold plant in centre of pot, add more compost to within 2cm (½ in) of rim; **4** firm all round plant*

tomatoes and strawberries for fruiting under glass) like an even richer compost, such as J.I. No 3 – particularly when they are moved into their final size of pot).

Drainage material, as described under potting off, is generally advisable when using soil composts in pots that are 13cm (5 in) or larger. A layer of crocks about 2–3cm (1 in) deep should be sufficient, plus roughage.

Repotting the plant

Remove the plant from its pot by turning it upside-down and tapping the rim of the pot on the edge of a bench. The rootball should then slide out intact. On no account disturb this ball of roots and soil, but remove old crocks, if any, from the base. Scrape off any moss or weeds on the surface with an old wooden plant label or similar object.

Place enough soil in the new pot so that, when the plant is placed on it, the top of the rootball is about 13mm (½ in) from the top of the pot. This will allow for a light covering of compost with room for subsequent watering. Firm the compost lightly with your fingers and then stand the plant in the centre of the

new pot. Trickle fresh compost all round the rootball until you reach the top of the pot. Give the pot a sharp tap on the bench to get the compost well down and firm it all round.

If you are using soilless composts, follow the maker's instructions for firming. You will probably need to add more compost to reach the desired height. Finally, water in the plants, using a fine rose on the watering can.

Potting on is best done when plants are growing actively in spring and summer – or in the autumn, although growth will then be slowing down. Plants potted in spring and summer will quickly root into the new compost because of the warmer weather.

RAISING ANNUALS FOR THE GARDEN

There are several advantages to raising your own bedding plants in the greenhouse, apart from the obvious one of saving money. Every year leading seedsmen offer a splendid range of seeds for popular and less common bedding plants, together with new varieties and introductions, and also F.1 hybrids that have greater vigour than ordinary strains.

When you grow your own plants from seed you have better control of their quality and timing. Bought plants are often damaged through overcrowding in their seed trays, or through having been kept in them too long before you are able to plant them out. Sometimes, also, they have not been hardened off properly.

All these disadvantages can be avoided when you raise your own plants in pots; this helps enormously when bedding out since there is less root damage and the plants grow away faster.

When to sow
Most of the favourite bedding plants can be sown in the greenhouse from about mid to late spring (March to April). Some, however (such as fibrous-rooted begonia and antirrhinum) are slow-growing and these should be sown as early as late winter (January), otherwise they may not be ready for reasonably early display. On the other hand, avoid unnecessary early sowing, or you will waste greenhouse space and heat; you may also spoil the plants if bedding out has to be delayed because the weather is too cold. Fast growers, like tagetes (marigolds), can be left until the very last.

In some cases it is a good idea to sow seeds from a packet over a period of time, and not all at once – especially when the quantity of seed is generous. Having several batches of seedlings in various stages of development means you will be able to enjoy a long flowering period.

Sowing techniques
How you sow can be varied to suit the cost, quantity and the size of the seed. Large seeds that are easy to handle (like zinnia) and that may also be expensive (as in the case of F.1 hybrids), should be sown individually in small pots. Finer seed can be sown in a tray or pan; prick out the seedlings into more trays when they are large enough to handle. If seed is cheap and very fine it can be mixed with a little silver sand, to reduce the density of distribution, and sown directly into seed trays. Instead of pricking out you can then thin the seedlings by pulling out the excess and discarding them. This may sound wasteful, but it saves considerably on time – also a valuable commodity.

For germinating seeds use a sterilized seed compost such as the John Innes Seed Compost or one of the many proprietary composts. See that it is nicely moist – but not wet – before sowing. A useful rule is to cover the seed with its own depth of compost. Very fine or dust-like seed, however, should not be covered. Many failures are due to deep sowing, to water-logged compost or (always fatal) to compost that is allowed to dry out after sowing and during germination.

Nowadays plastic seed trays are available; these are clean and easy to use. The standard size is 35 by 25cm (14 by 9 in) but smaller ones are useful as germination trays for the propagator.

Germinating the seeds
After sowing cover the seed containers with glass and then a sheet of brown paper, newspaper or translucent white paper. Or you can slip the tray into a polythene bag, to help to retain moisture.

Some form of propagator will be most helpful for germinating the seeds. For bedding plants high temperatures are not only not necessary, but quite undesirable. Too much heat will force the seedlings and they will become spindly, pale and weak. A temperature range of 7–18°C (45–65°F) is adequate for most parts; the lower temperatures will suit the more hardy plants (like antirrhinums) and the higher will be needed for more tender subjects like zinnias. But if you propose using a propagator for other greenhouse work then get one that can be 'turned up' for more warmth when required. Generally an electric propagator is convenient and, if fitted with a thermostat, is economical and allows of easy temperature control. There are also inexpensive, small electric propagators for warming only one or two seed trays, and designs that are heated by paraffin oil lamp. Many people manage to germinate the odd trays of seeds in their homes on the windowsill of a warm room. If you have a warm greenhouse used for warm house plants, you can also use it for seed germination. It will, however, be too

Newspaper provides a cheap and handy cover to shade seedlings. It is often better placed under the glass

warm – and probably too dark – a place for the seedlings to grow on happily.

Germination time may vary from a couple of days to about three weeks depending on the type of seed, and temperature – don't be tempted to hasten germination by using unnecessarily high temperatures. Make a daily check to see whether germination has occurred. Remove the container's cover when the first seedlings are through so that more light can penetrate. Exposure to bright sunshine in the early stages is, however, harmful and may result in scorching of the tiny seedlings, so put the container in a shady corner.

Pricking out seedlings
Pricking out should always be done as soon as possible – as soon as the seedlings are big enough to handle easily. In the case of very tiny seedlings, such as lobelia, small groups can be 'patched out' since it is impossible to separate them.

When pricking out, be generous with your spacing. Commercial growers often overfill their seed trays; the roots become entangled and suffer from the disturbance caused when the young plants are divided for planting out. After pricking out it is a sensible precaution to water in the seedlings with a Cheshunt compound (used according to maker's instructions). This will help prevent damping-off disease – a serious menace to seedlings. This fungus disease attacks the stems at compost-surface level and the seedlings then topple over. It occurs mainly where greenhouse hygiene has been neglected and will spread very rapidly unless promptly checked.

Hardening-off and bedding out
All bedding plants must be given a period of gradual acclimatization to the open air before planting out. This is called hardening-off and frames are especially useful for the process. In the greenhouse

Plants should be watered while hardening off in a frame – the last stage before planting out

itself move the seed trays, gradually, to cooler spots. Then about three weeks before you plan to bed them out, move the trays to frames outside. Open the frame lights a little more each few days as the three-week period passes until, finally, they are fully exposed day and night. For the first week or so you may have to close the frames at night depending on weather conditions. Do not bed plants out until all danger of frost has passed.

If you have used peat pots, or pots of similar organic composition, for raising some of your bedding plants, do remember to keep them well watered after bedding out. Plants in these pots are intended to be planted pot and all to avoid root disturbance, but they will not rot down to allow the roots to grow out unless kept quite moist.

PLANTS FOR UNHEATED GREENHOUSES

Too many people deprive themselves of the pleasure of owning a greenhouse by thinking of the cost of heating it during the winter. But you can enjoy enormous benefits from protected cultivation without providing any additional heat. There is a wide range of plants that need only shelter from wind, excessive rain, frost or extreme cold, to give finer results and earlier crops or flowers than if grown in the open. Indeed, these plants will not do well in a greenhouse that is too warm – and so an unheated one is ideal.

This section on plants for unheated greenhouses looks at what types of greenhouses are suitable and suggests some plants that can be grown from seed and from bulbs to provide a display of colour all year round.

The degree of hardiness of the plants you can grow will vary according to the severity of winters normally experienced in the part of the country in which you live. In mild areas, for example, comparatively tender plants will survive quite easily. In colder regions you may have to be more cautious in your selection.

Below: tagetes germinate in natural warmth

Suitable greenhouses

To make the most of free warmth from the sun the unheated greenhouse should let in as much light as possible. A glass house will trap more warmth than a plastic one, but if you propose to grow only hardy plants then this will not be so important. Remember, however, that any extra free warmth may be useful for gentle forcing and early growth, even if the plants are completely cold-resistant. An all-glass (glass-to-ground) greenhouse will capture much natural warmth, and so will a lean-to structure set against a south-facing wall. In some cases such a lean-to will remain frost-free overnight as the rear wall can store warmth during the day and radiate it at night.

Don't choose a site shaded by buildings or trees if you are erecting a cold greenhouse. Nor should you put the house in a hollow or at the foot of a slope or hill; these sites are often frost pockets. Wet or waterlogged ground is also best avoided since plants in a cold greenhouse dislike an excessively humid atmosphere in winter, and are more prone to attack by fungus diseases.

Spring sowings

Probably very few home greenhouse owners use heating from about late spring (April) onwards. In spring a glass greenhouse will usually become sufficiently warm naturally to germinate most bedding plants, tomatoes and more exotic summer fruits like melons. These can be grown on to give useful summer and autumn cropping. Without warmth, or perhaps with just a small heated propagator, most of the more hardy and

Delicate annuals can give spectacular displays with the protection of a cold greenhouse. Below: Salpiglossis sinuata. Bottom: schizanthus, the butterfly flower

Left: double-flowered petunias
Above and above right: achimenes, native
of Central America, and Tecophilaea
cyanocrocus, *the Chilean blue crocus*

quick-growing bedding plants can be raised. Tagetes (African and French marigolds) are extremely easy plants, and you can leave the sowing until quite late. Avoid slow developers that prefer congenial warmth (such as fibrous-rooted bedding begonias). But the slow growers like antirrhinum will do well since they are perfectly hardy and can be started as early as late winter (January).

Summer and autumn displays
During the summer and autumn the greenhouse can become a wonderland of colour for only the price of a few packets of seeds germinated from late spring to early summer (April to May) without artificial warmth. Outstanding for its colourful blooms is salpiglossis; stop the plants at the seedling stage (when a few centimetres high) to promote bushy growth. Pot on into 13cm (5 in) pots.

The new compact strains of schizanthus are also easy to grow and showy, and need no stopping or training. Many

of the more choice garden bedding plants, especially F.1 hybrids, make splendid pot plants. F.1 hybrids of zinnias are spectacular when given weather protection, and you can produce magnificent columns of blooms if you grow the large-flowered antirrhinum as single spikes by removing all sideshoots.

The cold greenhouse is ideal for protecting delicate or double flowers that are prone to weather damage and summer winds and rains. Double petunias do very well, provided there is maximum light, and some varieties will fill the house with a clove-like scent that you won't notice outdoors. The recently-introduced variety of hibiscus Southern Belle, with its enormous, but papery-thin, flowers, is almost certain to be spoilt outdoors but will be seen in its full glory with greenhouse protection. Sow it in a warm place indoors and move the young plants to the greenhouse in about early summer (late April or May). From then on they make rapid growth and the plants will need 25cm (10 in) pots as a minimum size for their final homes.

Bulbs for summer and autumn
For summer and autumn display many bulbs or similar storage organs can be started in spring. These include begonia, gloxinia, achimenes, polianthes (tuberose), hippeastrum, the glory lily, gloriosa (which, contrary to many warnings, can be started late and still flower well), canna (of which the best for the small greenhouse is the variety Lucifer – the

earlier you start these the better), smithiantha and many lilies and nerines.

With nerines, use the named greenhouse varieties that are potted on in early autumn (August). Storage organs of most greenhouse plants that flower from summer to autumn can be stored dry over winter in a frost-proof place in the home, and started into growth again in the following year.

Winter and spring displays
Of special importance for the winter-to-spring display are hardy bulbs. An unheated greenhouse is the ideal place for them; and you will be amazed at how much more beautiful many of them are than you had previously realized. They usually flower much earlier under protected conditions and the flowers will often be more noticeably scented and unblemished. Choose unusual varieties with double or more delicate flowers.

As well as the popular hyacinths, daffodils and narcissi, grow a selection of the smaller, dainty bulbs generously grouped in bowls or pans. Such collections could include allium, babiana, bulbocodium, chionodoxa, eranthis (winter aconite), erythronium, fritillaria, galanthus (snowdrop), leucocoryne, leucojum (snowflake), muscari (grape hyacinth, of which there are some especially fine forms), puschkinia (striped squill), scilla (squill), tecophilaea and urginea.

Crocus, alone, can be had in an astonishing range of varieties and species from which you can choose a selection to flower over a long period. And under glass the birds cannot tear them to shreds. Tulips grown in pots provide a glorious display, especially the double varieties.

There are numerous other spring-flowering plants notable for colour. Polyanthus make fine pot plants and are easy to grow from seed. Coloured (and completely hardy) strains of primrose are now available and are particularly good for pots.

GREENHOUSE PLANTS FOR HANGING BASKETS

Hanging baskets, suspended from the roof, are an excellent answer to the eternal problem of dwindling shelf space in the greenhouse. And, in fact, many plants are seen at their best displayed in this way.

Do make sure, first of all, that your greenhouse roof will support the weight of your hanging baskets; remember that, after watering, a container may be very heavy. Hanging containers, and the type of plants put in them, should also be chosen in proportion to the size of the greenhouse and the height of the roof. Baskets over 25cm (10 in) in diameter are rarely suitable for the average $3 \times 2 \cdot 4$m (10×8 ft) home greenhouse, especially when the roof is rather low.

Plastic-covered wire baskets are now readily available, also some non-drip designs. And for some plants, particularly

orchids, wooden baskets made from hardwood timber slats (usually teak) make pleasing containers.

Be sure to hang them where you can water and tend to them easily, and where the drips will not fall on other plants.

Preparing the basket
Mesh baskets look much more attractive if lined with sphagnum moss with the mossy side facing out. Over this place a few pieces of polythene before filling up with potting compost. The polythene will prevent water draining too fast and compost drying out rapidly, but make a

few slits in it to prevent waterlogging. In some cases a plastic lining should not be used – as with plants liking well-aerated compost (such as orchids and columneas) or when you want plants (usually bulbs) to grow out of the basket side through the moss itself.

Plants from seed

When it comes to filling the basket there are, for a start, several suitable plants that can be raised successfully from seed. Red or blue pendulous lobelias and *Thunbergia alata* (black-eyed Susan) are quick, easy and inexpensive to raise this way.

Above: cascading white blooms of Campanula isophylla *Alba*
Left: well-cared-for trailing lobelias can completely smother their container
Far left: massed planting to bring a welcoming splash of doorway colour, includes ivy-leaved pelargoniums, tagetes, alyssum and petunias

Thunbergia alata is really a climber, but you can use it effectively in baskets if you encourage the stems downwards by stapling them to the underneath of the basket as they grow. Easy from seed, too, is the lovely *Campanula fragilis* (not to be confused with the well-known *C. isophylla* that is similar but can only be grown from cuttings). However, *C. fragilis* will take about two years from seed to reach a size that will give a good display.

A little-known exotic lobelia with very large flowers that are a delightful shade of blue is *Lobelia tenuior*. It is, however, a little tender and is best not used for baskets that will be put outside during summer.

A charming foliage plant to grow from seed as an annual is *Cardiospermum halicacabum* (balloon vine). This, like thunbergia, is a climber, but it hangs well from suspended containers. Its small, graceful, vine-like leaves make an interesting change from the often-used *Asparagus sprengeri*. An additional attraction of the balloon vine is that it produces dainty, pale green, inflated seed capsules like those of physalis (Chinese lantern).

Striking flowers and foliage

One of the most impressive foliage plants for baskets is *Cissus discolor*, but it has the disadvantage of being deciduous in the average cool greenhouse. The foliage is gloriously coloured and marked and the plant should be given a container of its own. Well grown, it will hang down almost to the floor. In a cool greenhouse be careful to keep it on the dry side over winter.

Another good choice for baskets are columneas, although they need a winter minimum temperature of 10°C (50°F). According to species, columneas may have velvety or shiny foliage; but the flowers are all usually tubular and in showy shades of orange. Columneas are often a little 'difficult' since they demand a high humidity combined with a congenial temperature all year round. They also need an open compost made from fibrous peat and moss.

Among the best and (deservedly) most popular of basket plants are the ivy-leaved pelargoniums. As well as interesting foliage these plants have long-lasting flowers; these are produced freely from early summer (May) in the greenhouse, often continuing into the winter in frost-free conditions. There are many named varieties with single and double flowers in a wide range of colours. It is best to plant about three well-rooted cuttings to each 25cm (10 in) basket, but if plants have been saved and grown on from previous years only one may be needed.

Of similar merit are fuchsias, although the flowers tend to come periodically or may be delayed, and the blossoms can be spoiled by bad weather if put outside. When choosing fuchsias try to get varieties especially suited to hanging; you will usually find this information in the growers' catalogues. Varieties with extra long and large blooms, like Pink Flamingo and Mrs Rundle, and those derived from *Fuchsia triphylla* that have cascading clusters of long, tubular flowers usually in shades of rich salmon pink, look especially pleasing when viewed from below.

A similar effect is given by the pendulous begonias. These have quaint, tassel-like flowers in a selection of colours. Some bear masses of flowers

shaped like their large-flowered counter-parts, only these are small and pendulous. Various types can be found described in the back pages of 'major' seed catalogues where bulbs and other storage organs are listed. Although you get much quicker results from tubers, you can also grow them from seed, but this must be sown early in the year if you are to enjoy a long display throughout the summer.

Bulbs and tubers

Attractive bulbs for planting from early to mid autumn (August to September) are lachenalia (Cape cowslip) of which the best for baskets is *Lachenalia bulbifera*, usually listed in catalogues as *Lachenalia pendula*. Plant the bulbs through the sphagnum moss of the basket, omitting any plastic lining. You will need about 8cm (3 in) of space between each bulb; plant a few in the top of the basket as well. In the cool greenhouse a basket so planted will become a 'ball' of tubular flowers coloured red, yellow and purple, from mid winter (December) onwards.

An exciting tuber to plant from mid spring (March) onwards is *Gloriosa rothschildiana* (glory lily). This is a climber, but can be most impressive if encouraged to hang over a suspended

Above left: a gay, mixed basket, with pelargonium, lobelia and tagetes
Above right: quaint, tassel-like flowers of the eye-catching pendulous begonia
Below: cross-section of a basket showing placement of sphagnum moss, polythene and compost

sphagnum moss

potting compost   polythene

basket. Three tubers to each 25cm (10 in) basket give the best effect. The brilliant red and yellow flowers are like reflexed lilies. This is a plant best confined to the greenhouse since it is liable to damage if put outside.

Plants for small baskets

Excellent for small baskets or similar hanging containers, and easy for the cool greenhouse is *Rhipsalidopsis (Schlumbergera) gaertneri* (Easter cactus) that flowers in spring. Flowering from about mid winter to early spring (December to February) is the Christmas cactus *Schlumbergera × buckleyi* with magenta-coloured flowers. *S. truncata* (crab cactus) comes in several colours, and is also winter flowering. All have a pendulous habit and quaint flowers shaped like Chinese pagodas. Cuttings root very rapidly and are often easy to beg from friends.

Good for small containers, too, is the dainty *Streptocarpus saxorum* (Cape primrose) with small velvety foliage and flowers like a miniature form of the giant-flowered, well-known hybrids. The stems are reddish and the blooms a violet colour. A winter minimum temperature of about 10°C (50°F) is needed.

BULBS FOR WINTER FLOWERING

Early bulbs can bring added colour to your home in winter. Order them in early autumn (August), to plant in bowls or pots indoors or in the greenhouse in mid autumn (September).

Bulbs, corms and tubers that are generally grown in pots for early flowering are hyacinths, daffodils (narcissi), tulips, crocuses and cyclamen.

Choosing your bulbs

Always buy top-size bulbs for flowering indoors; you will get more and better blooms from these, and they are well worth the small extra cost. Top-size daffodils will have two or three 'noses' or growing points per bulb. Hyacinths are measured by their circumference, in centimetres, around the widest part of the bulb, and the top-size variety measure approximately 18–19cm (7–7½ in). 'Prepared' hyacinth bulbs, which give blooms about mid winter (December) are usually 16–17cm (6–6½ in) in circumference.

These 'prepared' bulbs grow much more quickly than untreated bulbs and flower in time for Christmas in Britain. The bulbs are refrigerated by the suppliers, a process that speeds up the period before flowering, but you must plant them as soon as possible after purchase. If not, the effect will wear off and they will then bloom later – probably in late winter (January).

Top-size tulips can also be recommended for planting in bowls: these measure about 12–14cm (4½–5½ in) in circumference. Crocuses should be no smaller than 7–9cm (2½–3½ in) round.

Inspect the bulbs before you buy them – or immediately upon receipt if you are buying from a mail order firm – to ensure

Far left: fragrant Cyclamen persicum
Left: tulips and hyacinths in wooden tub
Below left: Narcissus bulbicodium *Hamilton*
Below: Crocus chrysanthus *Advance*
Bottom: Crocus tomasinianus *Ruby Giant*

that they are not soft or infected with mould. Bulbs should feel firm to the touch and quite heavy in relation to their size. Bulbs that feel soft or very light are undoubtedly rotting inside and will neither flower nor grow properly.

There are many varieties of hyacinths, daffodils, tulips and crocuses – choose those that appeal to you. The Roman hyacinths are the earliest to come into flower, apart from the treated varieties. The narcissi varieties Paper White and Grand Soleil d'Or are extremely attractive for indoor planting arrangements, and the large-flowered Dutch crocuses, together with dwarf early single and double tulips can also be highly recommended for winter flowering in the home.

Materials for planting

You can buy special bowls for bulbs from garden centres and shops. The usual growing medium to use with these is bulb fibre, also easily obtainable from your garden suppliers. This is basically peat combined with a mixture of crushed charcoal and oyster shell. You can also grow your bulbs in ordinary plastic or clay flowerpots, provided you first cover the drainage holes with a layer of crocks topped with a thin layer of roughage. Use a conventional potting compost in pots, such as J.I. No 1, or a loamless (soilless) compost. They must be moist before use.

How to plant

Now to the method of planting the bulbs. First place a layer of fibre or compost in the bottom of the container and firm it lightly with your fingers. Then stand the bulbs on the growing medium, ensuring that their tips are level, or just above, the rim of the container. Then place the compost or fibre between and around them and lightly firm it with your fingers. After planting, the upper third of hyacinth bulbs should remain exposed and the noses of daffodils and crocuses must be visible. Plant your bulbs close together for the best flower display but do not let them touch each other. For example a 15cm (6 in) diameter bowl will hold two or three hyacinths, one daffodil, five tulips, or eight crocuses; and a 30cm (12 in) diameter bowl will contain seven to nine hyacinths, six to seven daffodils, twelve tulips or sixteen crocuses. These estimates are for top-sized bulbs.

Caring for your bulbs

After planting, place the bowls in complete darkness in a cool place – a cellar is ideal. Many people bury the bowls about 15cm (6 in) deep in a bed of ashes or sand in a cool part of the garden. Or you can put each container into a black polythene bag and place it in a cool, shady part of the garden. Try to keep the temperature below 9°C (48°F) at this stage.

Leave the bulbs in these conditions for a period of six to eight weeks (during which time roots will develop) until they start to produce shoots. Daffodils, hyacinths and tulips should be brought back into the light when their shoots are 2–3cm (1 in) long, and crocuses when they have 13mm ($\frac{1}{2}$ in) high shoots.

Above: while roots are developing you can store bowl in black polythene bag and place in cool, shady part of garden

To start with, place the bowls in subdued light, then, after a week, transfer them to full light and a temperature of 10°C (50°F). The temperature should not be higher than this until the flower-buds are well formed, at which time you can increase the temperature to 15°C (60°F).

Keep the compost or fibre moist at all times. Do not over-water bowls; remember that they have no drainage holes in the base, and so the fibre could become saturated. If this should happen, carefully stand the bowl on its side until the surplus water has drained away.

It should not be necessary to stake the flower-stems but if these do become top heavy, insert two or three canes and encircle them.

When the bulbs have finished flowering, stand them in a cold frame or a sheltered spot out of doors to complete their growth. Water and feed them until the leaves have completely died down. Then remove the bulbs, clean and dry them and store in a cool dry place until planting time in the autumn. You must not grow them indoors again, but you can plant them in the garden where they will make a good display during spring of the following year.

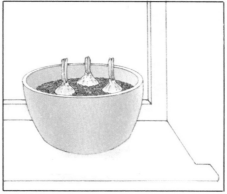

To prepare bulbs for indoor use, above: set bulbs in layer of peat fibre; above right: place more fibre over and around bulbs, and firm this down lightly; below: bury bowl for eight weeks in bed of ashes in cool part of garden; below right: dig up bowl and place for one week on windowsill in subdued light

GROWING CACTI AND SUCCULENTS

Cacti and succulents add an exotic note to every collection of greenhouse and indoor plants.
Once known as the 'Cinderellas of the plant world', their popularity
is now assured. With a little care they can be induced to grow well and produce flowers of
astonishing variety and colouring. Here we look at the different types of cacti and how
they can be grown successfully.

Succulents are plants that have evolved with the ability to store water in their leaves, bodies and roots to enable them to survive periods of drought. They are more common than most people realize – in fact, most countries in the world have some form of succulent plant in their native flora. Even in Britain, sempervivum (houseleek) and sedum (stonecrop) are quite often seen even though the climate does not seem to warrant succulent growth.

One of the largest families in the succulent flora is the CACTACEAE, or cactus family. Cacti differ from succulents in having areoles from which their spines grow and from which, in many cases, the flowers are produced. These areoles look rather like small felt pin cushions; the spination of the other succulent plants resembles thorns.

It is believed that both cacti and other succulents originated from a common source before the continents of Africa and America parted in the continental drift many millions of years ago. Today cacti are native to North and South America, but succulents, though mainly indigenous to Africa, can be found growing native in many other parts of the world.

Types of cacti

There are two completely different types of cacti: the epiphytes and the so-called 'desert' cacti. Both groups require separate forms of cultivation as their habitat is so different.

The epiphytes (or 'jungle' cacti) that include such well-known plants as schlumbergera (formerly zygocactus), the Christmas and Easter cacti, epiphyllum, rhipsalis and so on, are flat-stemmed plants growing in the tropical rain forests of Central America. They do not live on the ground but on the branches of forest trees, in crevices and joints that have accumulated leaf mould and bird droppings. Their stems and roots obtain moisture from rain and they are continually shaded from the tropical sunshine by overhanging branches.

The second type is the so-called 'desert' cactus; the name is slightly misleading as the true habitat of these plants is not desert but a form of heathland with grass and small shrubs. They are native to North and South America but seem to adapt well in other places; too well in some cases – as in Queensland, Australia, where the opuntia (prickly pear) invaded vast areas of farmland and defeated all efforts at eradication until its natural predator, the caterpillar of the cactoblastis moth, was imported. These cacti inhabit areas of little rainfall but have

Serried ranks of cacti bristling with protective spines (previous page) or a mixed group of succulents (opposite) form a unique display. Below: opuntia (prickly pear) with seed pods. Bottom: schlumbergera, an attractive jungle cactus

powers to absorb water when it is available and retain it for future use when times are dry and hard. Sometimes they can absorb moisture from morning mists through their stems and spines.

General cultivation
In Britain most cacti are grown in greenhouses or garden frames, as the winters are too damp and humidity causes the plants to rot if they are planted outdoors. Cacti will withstand a habitat that has very cold, but dry, nights and winters, but cannot survive a damp, cold atmosphere.

Some gardeners still use clay pots for growing cacti, but most have now changed over to plastic, as these are lighter on the greenhouse staging and easier to keep clean, especially for exhibition purposes. Also, plants in plastic pots do not require watering so often.

Whereas the 'desert' cacti will grow well in full sun provided there is sufficient ventilation, epiphytes, being 'forest' cacti, require shading from sun from early summer to mid autumn (May to September), and can only be grown on top of the greenhouse staging during the winter months. Evidence of sunburn shows as red pigmentation on the stems; affected plants should be shaded at once. Never stand the pot in a container of water as they cannot tolerate bog-like conditions.

How much water?
How much water to give and how often to water are key questions with this group of plants, and it is difficult to give an easy answer. Common sense plays a great part here: if it is hot and sunny, plants growing under glass require a great deal of water. Those growing in clay pots may need water each evening. Be careful when

Cacti and succulents grown indoors should be treated as ordinary house plants; they will require watering during the winter (especially if there is central heating) otherwise they will dehydrate. Also if they are kept on a windowsill, and there is frost, bring them into the room, inside the curtains; cacti and succulents will not withstand damp frosts. A quite large plant will go to pulp overnight and is a heartbreaking sight next morning when the curtains are drawn back.

How much heat?
Cacti and succulents require heat during the winter, but remember that they hate a stagnant, stale atmosphere because it causes fungus and rot. So even during the winter provide the plants with some fresh air on a sunny day.

If you heat by paraffin, remember that for every 5 lit (1 gal) you burn, the same amount of water vapour is produced. Even so, many people find heating by this method satisfactory, providing that the appliance is well maintained, and not in a draught. It is very sad to see a collection covered in black, oily soot where a stove has flared. This is also very difficult to remove and it takes years for the plants to grow out of the effects.

Electricity is clean and easy, but unfortunately very expensive. Under-soil cables are very good, but costly to run and install for a complete collection; this method is favoured for seed-raising and for the propagation section, where plants are put to root. Fan-heaters create a very dry heat, so spraying will have to be done occasionally during the winter when it is sunny or the plants become dehydrated. With a special type of electric water heater that gives off steam when it boils, spraying is not required. Should there be a power failure for any reason, a certain amount of heat will be retained in the pipework, providing the power cut does not go on for too long.

Gas heating for the greenhouse is becoming very popular but be sure that you can obtain spare parts should anything go wrong. Laying a gas supply to the greenhouse could prove to be costly if it is any distance from the house, especially if it necessitates taking up cement paths as well.

Lining your greenhouse with sheet polythene provides a form of double glazing during the winter, and cuts down heating costs appreciably. If you do decide to fit this, make sure that the sheets are overlapped in such a way that the condensation will not drip onto your plants and cause rot, but run down safely out of harm's way.

Composts used for growing cacti and succulents must be particularly porous, such as J.I. No 2 or 3, to which you should add some very sharp sand, grit, or broken brick to ensure good drainage. This is very important, especially when growing in plastic containers. The pot size should be as large as the diameter of the plant with its spines plus a further 13mm ($\frac{1}{2}$ in) all round. The epiphytic cacti will require the addition of humus to the potting compost in the form of leaf mould, peat or well-rotted manure, and again the soil must always be well drained.

watering not to leave any droplets on the crowns of the plants, as this could cause scorching when the sun comes out, and badly damage a plant; this is one reason for watering in the evenings and not during the day. If the weather is overcast or damp the plants will not require much water. Desert cacti rest during the winter months and need very little water then, although overhead spraying from time to time can be beneficial. Some succulents can grow in the winter and rest in summer, and it is as well to know the plant's habits and treat it accordingly.

GROWING CARNATIONS IN THE GREENHOUSE

Perpetual-flowering carnations of the size and quality sold in florists' shops are not easy for the beginner to grow successfully, but once you have mastered the right conditions for them in your own greenhouse, you will be well rewarded by the magnificent shape and varied colours of these show blooms. Here we look at aspects of the cultivation of perpetual-flowering carnations, including propagation by cuttings taken from your own plants, and list some of the most attractive varieties available today.

Greenhouse carnations of the kind seen in florists' shops are called perpetual-flowering carnations, and are the product of over a century of breeding in France, Britain and the United States. The Sim varieties, introduced just after World War II, are still by far the most popular, and should continue to dominate the world's markets as long as they are carefully protected from pests and diseases, and as long as research into methods of producing virus-free stocks continues. They originate from a scarlet self carnation, William Sim, that became a phenomenal market variety and produced sports in almost every other colour known in carnations, as well as innumerable new varieties.

Greenhouse requirements

The amateur gardener's greenhouse cannot compare with the huge structures of commercial growers, yet very successful results are produced, in spite of the drawbacks of fluctuation in temperature and humidity and the fact that plants often have to be left without attention for most of the day.

Heating Your greenhouse must allow the plants maximum light at all seasons, as well as full ventilation from the roof and both sides. To keep up flower production in winter, do not allow the night temperature to fall below 16°C (61°F). If this is too expensive, compromise by heating your greenhouse sufficiently to maintain a temperature of about 5°C (40°F) to keep out the frost. By this method some flowers can be obtained for about three-quarters of the year. Electric heating is cleaner and more convenient than any other method, and economical in that it can be controlled by a thermostat, power being consumed only as necessary. Fan heating is probably the most popular method of electric heating used in domestic greenhouses, and it is economical to install. The fan can generally be used independently of the heater, and is very handy to promote air circulation in the summer.

Above: carnations in a commercial greenhouse are supported by a wire grid. Red-edged Skyline (top), Laddie Sim (pink), Joker (crimson), William Sim (scarlet) and Yellow Dusty
Right: corset the bud with an elastic band to stop the calyx from splitting

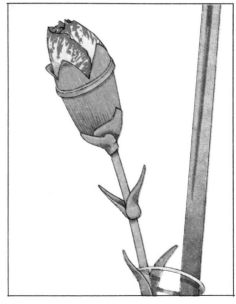

Staging This is simple to erect; make a base of breezeblocks and crossing timbers to support lengths of corrugated asbestos or galvanized iron. Cover the galvanized iron with polythene for protection, then put on a layer of pea shingle. Keep the staging low because some varieties, the Sim types in particular, eventually grow taller than the people who grow them. Young plants are obviously shorter than older ones, so keep them on the lighter side of the greenhouse.

Care and cultivation

The best time to buy plants that are 'stopped and broken' is mid spring (March). These have sideshoots and are bushy (as distinct from rooted cuttings that do not have side growths). They are taken out of the 8cm (3 in) pots they are grown in before being despatched for sale, or can be bought in small peat pots.

Potting Before you start potting, make sure that the roots of the young plants are moist. If they are not, immerse the rootball in water until the bubbles of air stop rising. Use 15–18cm (6–7 in) clay or plastic pots, with J.I. potting compost No 2. Push three or four canes into the compost and tie twine round them, to keep the growths within bounds. Alternatively, use circular wire supports that clip on to a central cane. Water newly potted plants only when they are growing strongly. Over-watering is the commonest cause of failure, so keeping the plants on the dry side usually improves them. The roots are very easily drowned.

Start feeding the plants about a month after potting, and repeat once every two weeks thereafter. Use any soluble fertilizer that has equal parts of nitrogen and potash, following the manufacturer's instructions for application. If the plants do not appear healthy for any reason, withhold fertilizer.

Disbudding and shading Flower-buds appear about two months after potting. Most growers disbud, leaving only the crown bud on each stem. This is usually corseted with a small elastic band to prevent the calyx from splitting when the flower expands. To disbud, hold the stem near the bud with one hand, and pull the bud and its stalk sideways with the other.

Lightly shade the greenhouse before the flowers unfold, to prevent scorching from strong sunlight. Coolglass is most effective for this, and can easily be rubbed from the glass with a dry rag or brush when it is no longer required.

Autumn and winter blooming It is always a problem to decide whether to leave the flowers on display in the greenhouse or to take them indoors to beautify the house. If you take the latter course you can encourage flowers to bloom in the greenhouse right through to late autumn (October). After this time it is advisable to remove any buds that appear, so that the plants can rest and recuperate – unless you are prepared to maintain a constant temperature of about 10–16°C (50–61°F). Buds that look promising in late autumn (October) almost always damp off in winter if there is insufficient heat to dry the atmosphere. The plants require very little water during winter, but demand more the following spring when they begin to flower for their second season. Stop feeding during winter if you are not maintaining a high temperature, except perhaps for an occasional high potash feed, as a kind of tonic.

Propagation from cuttings

Perpetual carnations can be grown on for a third year, but they require so much attention that it is better to start again with new young plants that you can produce from your own cuttings. Take axillary side growths off the plant during early or mid spring (February or March), by pulling them out sideways (as with disbudding). If the cuttings have not broken out cleanly, remove the lowest pair of leaves and trim the stem across, with a razor blade, just below a joint.

Set the cuttings firmly in pots or trays in a half peat, half sharp sand mixture, and spaced about 4cm (1½ in) apart. Hormone rooting powder is useful to speed up the rooting process, and it is also helpful if you can heat the trays from the bottom with soil-warming cables. The cuttings take three or four weeks to form roots; after this lift them carefully and put them into 8cm (3 in) pots, using J.I. No 1 or a proprietary soilless compost.

Keep young potted plants out of cold draughts and water them sparingly until they begin to make new growth. After a month or so the rooted cuttings should have about ten pairs of leaves – sufficient growth for them to be stopped. Do this when the plants are turgid so that you can make a clean break. Hold the plant firmly in one hand and snap the top of the plant clean out with the other, leaving about six pairs of leaves. Do not be tempted to use the top piece as a cutting as it would make a very poor plant. Provided the stopped plants do not receive any serious checks, they should begin to produce axillary growths or sideshoots that, after a few weeks growth, turn the rooted cutting into a stopped and broken plant, like the ones you bought at the beginning.

Pests and diseases

The most serious pest attacking greenhouse carnations is the red spider mite, a sure killer if it is not dealt with quickly. The pest is a mite, not a spider, but it is so-called because it spins a web to protect its eggs. The mites are not easily seen with the naked eye, but are readily visible through a magnifying glass. They vary in colour from yellow and orange to red, and can usually be found on the underside of the leaf. Here, covered with their web, the hatching mites are protected from contact insecticides. The mites cause great damage by sucking the sap of the plants, and they multiply so rapidly than an infestation can occur before you have noticed their presence. The sap-sucking debilitates the plants to such an extent that they become lifeless, brittle, strawy in appearance and eventually ruined.

Azobenzene smokes are useful as a measure against the mites, if your greenhouse can be sealed effectively against loss of smoke. Use the smokes twice in about ten days to catch the in-between hatching period. Organo-phosphorus compound sprays such as demeton-s-methyl and dimethoate are also effective against the mites because of their systemic action.

Other pests that attack carnations are thrips, caterpillars and greenfly. Greenfly are not just a nuisance but a menace. They suck the plants' sap and can transmit viruses from diseased plants to healthy ones. They, and the other pests, can be controlled with standard insecticidal sprays, used according to the manufacturer's instructions.

Some varieties to choose

There are a great many different varieties available today, with new ones continually appearing. Those listed below are of short to medium height unless described otherwise.

Bailey's Masterpiece	crimson self.
Deep Purple	unique purple colour.
Fragrant Ann	white self, the most popular of all.
G. J. Sim	light red with white stripes; tall.
Golden Rain	clear, canary yellow.
Joker	large crimson blooms that are deeply serrated.
Laddie Sim	salmon-pink, does not fade.
Lavender Rose	lavender-pink, with strong stems.
Paris	light salmon self.
Red-edged Skyline	orange-apricot, striped and edged with red.
Rose Splendour	cerise self.
Tangerine Sim	brilliant cerise self.
William Sim	scarlet; the forerunner of all the Sim types.
Yasmina	light purple with a paler edge.
Yellow Dusty	yellow self; tall.
Zanzibar	French grey, suffused cerise and maroon.

PROPAGATING AND STORING CHRYSANTHEMUMS

Chrysanthemums that have been propagated with care and grown on well should produce good quality blooms that will make a fine display in the garden or greenhouse. Here we detail propagation procedures and consider the cultivation of late-flowering types.

Stock selection of chrysanthemums is carried out by retaining for propagation the plants that have produced the best blooms in the previous season. Cuttings for propagation are taken from a 'stool' – the root of an old plant with a portion of the old stem and surrounding young shoots – that has been lifted and stored at the end of the growing season.

HOW TO PROPAGATE

Both early- and late-flowering chrysanthemums are propagated from cuttings of basal shoots taken from stools that have been stored in a cold frame.

Lifting and storing stools

Leave the stools of the early-flowering types of chrysanthemum in the garden until the beginning of early winter (November). This provides a period of time during which the temperature occasionally falls below 4·5°C (40°F) – a cooling period that is necessary before plants can produce flowers.

Cut the main stems down to 15cm (6 in), then lift the stools carefully with a fork and wash off the soil with water that

has had a little disinfectant such as Jeyes fluid added, to remove any pests. Remove all the leaves and cut down all green growth. Box the stools up into clean containers to a level no deeper than the original soil mark, in J.I. No 1 or a mixture of equal parts of loam, peat and grit. Water the stools well in to settle the compost. Make sure they are labelled correctly and try to keep to one cultivar per tray. Place these trays somewhere dry and frost-free, such as a cold frame, where there is plenty of light and air. Probably no more water will be needed until the trays go into the greenhouse in late winter (January). Keep an eye on them until then so that you can deal with any diseases such as mildew or botrytis that may appear; if they do, dust with flowers of sulphur or captan.

During early and mid winter (November and December) the late-flowering chrysanthemums will be coming into full bloom in the greenhouse. As they mature, mark the plants that produce the best blooms and use them for future propagation in the same way.

Taking cuttings

In late winter (January) start to propagate plants for the new season. The late-flowering types should come first, particularly the large exhibition cultivars and those that require early stopping.

Prepare a rooting compost of J.I. No 1 or a mixture of equal parts of peat, loam and coarse grit, or any soilless compost. Water the stools well the day before you wish to take the cuttings, so that they have time to plump up. Depending on the number to be rooted, insert about six cuttings round the edge of an 8cm (3 in) pot. If you use a standard seed-tray, the compost should be about 5cm (2 in) deep. Firm it with a board, then sprinkle a layer of sharp sand on the surface, and space cuttings 4–5cm (1½–2 in) apart each way.

Snap off a new basal shoot from the stool, just below a leaf joint, to form a cutting about 4–5cm (1½–2 in) long. It is optional whether you remove the two bottom leaves as the cuttings will root well either way. Dip the bottom 13mm (½ in) of the stem into a hormone rooting powder, and make a hole 20mm (¾ in) deep in the compost with a dibber the size of an ordinary pencil. Place the cutting in it and firm gently right up to the stem. Some of the sand sprinkled onto the surface of the compost will fall to the bottom of the hole, creating drainage that helps to prevent decay. Water the cuttings well in using a fine rose.

Keep the cuttings in the greenhouse until they have rooted. The time taken for

Lift each stool carefully, label it, then store it in a clean container (above)
Good propagation will result in fine display blooms such as Princess (left)

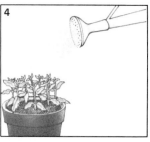
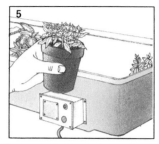

Above: to propagate chrysanthemums from cuttings, dip the stem of each shoot into a proprietary hormone rooting powder, 1, insert it into the compost using a small dibber, 2, firm gently round the stem, 3, and water the cutting well in with a fine spray, 4.
Place containers in a bottom-heated propagator, 5, or individual polythene bag, 6, until the cuttings have rooted firmly

rooting will depend on the conditions provided. In a propagator with a bottom heat of about 16°C (61°F) and an air temperature above 4·5–7°C (40–45°F) they should root in about two weeks, but on an open bench with a general temperature of 10°C (50°F) they will take a week or so longer. The cuttings can be rooted without heat when the risk of frost is over, but they take longer and the delay also affects the timing of blooms.

You can continue propagating until mid spring (early March); the late-flowering varieties should root during late winter and early spring, and the early-flowering during early and mid spring.

Growing on

As soon as cuttings of both early- and late-flowering chrysanthemums have rooted, remove them from the heat to a cold frame. They need slow and steady growth in a cool place to produce short, sturdy plants with big root systems. Some growers plant cuttings of early-flowering chrysanthemums directly from the rooting tray into a 10–15cm (4–6 in) deep layer of compost on top of a 15cm (6 in) bed of weathered clinker or ashes. Others prefer 10cm (4 in) deep trays or a succession of pots up to 13–15cm (5–6 in). All these methods have proved satisfactory, so each grower should adopt the system that will suit the facilities available to him or her.

Late-flowering plants, however, must be transferred from their rooting quarters into a succession of pots, starting with an 8cm (3 in) pot and moving on as the root system develops to a final pot size of 20, 23 or 25cm (8, 9 or 10 in). Grown in this way, they can easily be transferred back

Yvonne Arnaud (above); Anna Marie (left)

weather warms up during spring. During late spring (April), give the plants more air; by the end of the month the lights can be removed from the frames permanently. Replace them temporarily if a heavy rainstorm threatens.

LATE-FLOWERING TYPES

Late-flowering chrysanthemums are put out to stand in the open garden after being potted on twice, but they must be brought back into the greenhouse to flower in late autumn and winter.

Potting-on

In mid spring (March), the young plants that have been grown in 8cm (3 in) pots must be moved into larger pots to accommodate the developing root system. A compost containing a stronger mixture of fertilizer is necessary – J.I. No 2 is most suitable, or you can use an equivalent soilless compost. Before potting, decide on the type of compost you intend to use for the final potting. If you choose a soilless mixture, then the second potting should consist of similar material.

Use a 13cm (5 in) pot for the second potting, then return the plants to the cold frame, ensuring that there is a space of 5–8cm (2–3 in) between each pot to allow for leaf development. Leave the frame lights off at all times unless heavy rain, hailstorms or frost threaten – all such hazards are possible in late spring (April). The chrysanthemum is not a tender plant, and it would survive the hazards referred to, but the growing point could be damaged and the timing of growth and flower development affected.

Final potting

The final potting is the most important of all. The plant will remain in this pot from early or mid summer (mid May or early June) until it flowers in mid winter (November), or even later in some cases. You will need a selection of 20–25cm (8–10 in) pots because some plants make more vigorous growth than others and therefore require more space. J.I. No 3 is suitable for most cultivars, but if you are using a soilless compost, follow the recommendations for use given by the manufacturer.

Put some crocks or pebbles at the bottom of the pot to provide drainage, then place a 2–3cm (1 in) layer of peat on top. Partly fill the remainder of the pot with compost and firm gently with a rammer. Finally, put in a handful of loose compost, on which you can rest the plant taken from the 13cm (5 in) pot. Place the plant in the pot, ensuring that you have left about 5cm (2 in) of space down from

from the open garden into the greenhouse towards the end of mid autumn (September), so that they will come into flower during early and mid winter (November and December).

When you move the rooted cuttings into the cold frame, ensure that they have as much light and air as possible. Leave the frame lights off whenever the weather permits, and when they are on keep them raised a little at all times, unless there is a risk of frost. During early spring (February), frost usually occurs at night, so cover the frame lights with sacks or pieces of old carpet. Water sparingly – just enough to keep the plants going. A strong root-system will develop from plants that have to forage a little for moisture. When the plants are settled in the frame, spray with a good insecticide such as malathion or a systemic insecticide containing gamma HCH (BHC) and menazon, as a control against pest attack – leaf-miner flies and aphides become active as the

the rim for future top dressing. Fill in around the plant and firm well, using the rammer. Insert a cane on each side of the plant and secure it with soft string. Stand the pots close together when you have completed potting so that moisture is conserved. If possible, withhold water for 10–14 days after potting, to encourage the roots to move into the new compost. An overhead spray in the evening should prevent undue flagging.

Preparing a standing-out ground
Prepare a level site, in full sun if possible, for the late-flowering chrysanthemums to stand throughout the summer. The aim is to give each plant as much room as possible. Stand them in rows, preferably on an ash base; each pot should also stand on a slate or tile to keep out worms.

Drive strong posts into the ground at the end of each row, and stretch wires between them at 45 and 105cm (18 in and 3½ ft) high. Fasten the wires to the canes, to keep the plants from being blown over. This advice may sound unnecessary on a quiet day in midsummer, when the plants are only 75cm (2½ ft) high, but it is quite another matter in early autumn (August) when they are 1·5m (5 ft) or more tall.

Watering procedure is similar to that recommended for the early-flowering varieties (Week 88). An overhead spray on warm evenings usually suffices, but during dry spells water more heavily, giving a really good soaking. With pot-grown plants, watering should generally be more frequent than with the early varieties that are planted in the ground. Because of this extra watering, a certain amount of food is leached through the pot. About six weeks after the final potting, therefore, it is necessary to feed the plants. Dry and liquid fertilizers both give good results, as does a mixture of both. If you use dry fertilizers, give a pinch every other day. With liquid fertilizers, better results can frequently be obtained by applying little and often rather than a full dose every ten days, so dilute the feed to a quarter strength and use it at alternate waterings.

Top dressing
In late summer (the end of July), roots will appear on the surface of the compost. When this occurs, apply about 13mm (½ in) of top dressing made up of the final potting compost – either soil-based or soilless – that you used before. A further top dressing will be necessary about three weeks later.

As with the early-flowering varieties, decide how many blooms you want to grow and restrict the laterals accordingly.

If you are growing for show purposes, restrict them as follows: large and medium exhibition – one or two laterals; exhibition incurved and decoratives – three laterals; large singles – four or five; and medium singles – five or six. Apart from the large exhibition type, these will all carry a larger crop of smaller blooms when being grown for cut flower uses.

Securing the buds and housing
At the beginning of early autumn (August), the first buds will start to appear on late-flowering chrysanthemums – the large exhibition type first. If possible, these should be comfortably secured towards the end of early autumn (by the third week of August). Buds on the incurved and decorative types will appear from early to mid autumn (the end of August to September). Once the buds are secured and growing well, remove any surplus laterals, always selecting those with the weakest bud. Continue feeding on alternate days until the calyx breaks and the buds begin to show colour. Then gradually reduce the feed over the next few weeks.

Prepare your greenhouse for late-flowering chrysanthemums by washing down the glass and framework and fumigating inside to clear away any pests.

Pamela – an early-flowering spray chrysanthemum – is ideal for cutting

As soon as the buds show colour, and before the frost comes, remove all dead leaves and weeds around the plants, wash the outside of the pots, and spray over and under the leaves with an insecticide such as gamma HCH (BHC) and menazon to kill any pests, and a fungicide such as benomyl to rid the plants of any disease. Then bring the plants into the greenhouse and position them in their winter stations. Leave doors and ventilators fully open for as long as possible to enable the plants to become acclimatized to the change of environment.

After bringing in all the plants it is advisable to fumigate the greenhouse occasionally – this should help to keep your chrysanthemums free from pests and diseases. Always keep a buoyant atmosphere in the greenhouse. High temperatures are not necessary – just enough heat to keep the air moving and to maintain a temperature of 10°C (50°F) is all that is required. A fan-heater is most suitable and will provide both warmth and air movement. Your chrysanthemums should then bloom well throughout the dreary months of early and mid winter (November and December).

MAKING AN ORCHID COLLECTION

Here we introduce some orchids for beginners, and others that are suitable for hot greenhouses, and give hints on buying and starting a collection. We will then be going on to cover aspects of cultivation.

When a potential orchid-grower takes a look round at the range of orchids offered by orchid nurseries it is all too easy to become bewildered by the sheer number of plants available, all with completely different descriptions. It is therefore advisable to visit an orchid nursery and make a first choice with expert assistance. If an orchid nursery is not within easy reach, order direct from one that offers beginners' collections, or visit one or two of the many orchid shows held throughout the country. Chelsea Flower Show is a good place to start as it always has a large section devoted to orchids. In addition there are many reliable books available, with illustrations to help the beginner understand the long lists of names quoted in catalogues.

Orchids for beginners

Hybridization has created easily-grown orchids of great variety and beauty.

Cymbidiums The most widely grown orchid plants are the cymbidium hybrids. The blooms are used extensively for cut flowers, and they can often be seen in florists' shop windows. These are quite large-growing plants, with pseudo-bulbs and long, narrow leaves. Their flowering season extends throughout the winter and spring months. The flower spikes are produced from the base of the leading bulb during the summer, and grow steadily until they reach a height of 90cm–1.2m (3–4 ft). They can carry an average of 12 large, colourful blooms that will last in perfection for a good ten weeks. These long-lasting qualities, together with their ease of flowering, make this group the most popular in cultivation today. The colours found among the cymbidiums range from pure white, through many delicate shades of pink and yellow, to the stronger reds, bronzes and greens, all with contrasting-coloured lips. Where room permits a large collection of these gives a wonderful show of colour for nine months of the year.

Cymbidiums have all been hybridized from a mere handful of original wild species coming mostly from India and Burma. From the earliest days of hybridization, new varieties have always created a good deal of excitement and as generation after generation of hybrids have been bred so the size, shape and colour of the plants has become larger, rounder and more exotic. One specialized line of breeding has produced cymbidiums in miniature form, the plants and flowers being half the size of the standards. These varieties are often more acceptable for the smaller greenhouse. Today the species are seldom seen in collections, the hybrids having surpassed them in every way, and the latest always being the most eagerly sought after.

Odontoglossums Next to the cymbidiums, and second in line for popularity are the beautiful odontoglossums and their allies. Like the cymbidiums, the odontoglossums have been interbred for many generations and will cross-pollinate with several closely-related genera. These crossings have given the odontoglossums added colour and new shapes, and they and their allies now cover a very wide range of different types. Many 'meristem' plants (that is, those propagated by a particular method) are available, in every colour of the rainbow, with an endless array of intricate patterns and markings on the petals and lip.

The odontoglossums are smaller-growing than the cymbidiums and are bulbous, with less foliage. They are continuous-growing, with their flowering season spread throughout the year. The plants will bloom upon completion of their bulbs, that is approximately every nine months, but they do not always produce their flowers at the same time each year. The blooms will last for eight to ten weeks, depending on the time of year: not quite so long during the summer as the winter.

The original odontoglossum species are high altitude plants, growing at great heights in the Andes. In some cases they grow almost on the snow-line, at heights of up to 1800m (6000 ft). At this altitude they are subjected to nightly frosts that do them no harm. Therefore they like very cool conditions under cultivation, and if a greenhouse becomes overheated during the summer, they will do better if placed outdoors in a suitably shady position.

Cattleyas Where slightly warmer conditions are available, you can try the large, glossy 'chocolate box' cattleyas. Here again we have a large group of plants, highly bred and intercrossed with their closest relatives. The largest and most flamboyant are the result of careful, selected breeding. Their huge blooms, up to six at a time, have a colour range from pure white, through many shades of yellow, to pink and rich mauve. Mostly the lip is large, rounded and much frilled around the edges.

Although considered a little too large for today's cut-flower requirements, they are the most exotic of plants to grow for pleasure. The blooms will last approximately two to three weeks and they flower in either spring or autumn. Often, a well-grown plant can be encouraged to bloom twice in one year. The best types available are often meristem plants.

The cattleyas and their allies are bulbous, their bulbs being long and club-

Above: two paphiopedilum or 'slipper' orchids, showing how varied the shape of the petals and 'pouch' can be
Left: vanda hybrids like this brilliantly-coloured specimen can bloom twice in one year and like a hot greenhouse

shaped. One, or sometimes two, thick leaves are carried by each of the bulbs, which flower from their tips. The young buds are protected by a sheath, through which they grow to eventual flowering.

'Slipper' orchids The well-known 'slipper' orchids include yet another large and varied group of orchids that differ from all other forms by their pouch-like lip. These plants are generally modest in size, without pseudo-bulbs, and produce a number of lateral growths. The species is usually found growing on grasslands, or on rocky outcrops with very little soil, the roots keeping just beneath the humus. The foliage can be plain green in colour, or mottled and marbled in attractive patterns. The undersides of the leaves are often a dark purple.

The species are widely grown and have different flowering seasons. The winter varieties are in bloom by mid winter (December), and carry a single bloom on a slender stem. These will last for eight weeks or more on the plant, and the larger the plant the more flower stems it will produce in one season. The spring-flowering varieties quickly follow the winter ones, and these in turn are followed by the summer- and autumn-flowering types. It is possible to grow nothing but the delicate paphiopedilums and have some in flower all the year round. The species vary greatly one from the other, and contain among them many combinations of colour – brown, green, purple, yellow, red, as well as white, all in numerous variations. The white and yellow varieties belong to a group of stemless paphiopedilums that are plants of small stature and have the most delightful of flowers sitting just above the

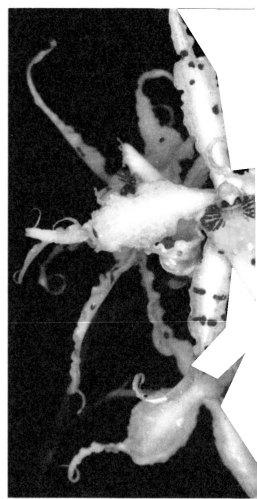

foliage. Closely related to the paphiopedilums are the phragmipediums, a small genus noted for the few species that have long, trailing, ribbon-like petals. These lateral petals will extend while the flower is opening, growing 2–3cm (1 in) a day until they attain a length of over 45cm (18 in). Taking these petals between finger and thumb and extending them at full length creates a flower 90cm (3 ft) or so across, surely the largest flower in the world!

The paphiopedilums and phragmipediums have steadfastly remained well at the top of the popularity list, and although many fine hybrids are grown today, the true species are still widely grown and admired for their graceful, handsome flowers.

Hot greenhouse orchids

If you have a hot greenhouse, there is a completely different range of orchids that is easy to grow with sufficient heat.

Phalaenopsis This reigns supreme among hothouse orchids. Commonly known as 'moth' orchids because of the spread of their pure white petals, they are monopodial in habit, but do not attain any great height. A standard-sized plant will

Phalaenopsis are expensive plants to raise from seed, mainly owing to the high temperatures they require, but the grower is amply rewarded by long, drooping sprays of delicate and beautiful flowers. The flowers are large and circular and will last for many weeks; when it has finished flowering, a flower spike will often grow again from its length, producing even more flowers. A large, mature plant that has been well grown is almost continuously in bloom. Phalaenopsis hybrids have no set time for flowering and can be in bloom at any time of the year.

Vandas The vandas are a further group of sun-loving, hot-growing orchids that are monopodial in habit, with some varieties growing to a height of 1·2–1·5m (4–5 ft). However, the average flowering size is about 25–30cm (9–12 in) tall. Long aerial roots sometimes accompany the growth of these most attractive plants. Their flowering season is variable, and they are capable of blooming twice in one year. The flower spikes come from the axils of the leaves and carry up to a dozen large, long-lasting blooms.

There are many colourful species to be found among the vandas, and these are grown as much as the plentiful hybrids. This group also produces the beautiful blue colour so rare in orchids, and one species in particular, *Vanda caerulea*, is the parent of the many blue hybrids now available. The best of these is *Vanda Rothschildiana*, that is greatly sought after for its unusual colour. Other colours scattered among the vandas include pink, yellow and brown. The flowers are generally spotted, veined or tessellated. New hybrids are continuously being raised from seed, bringing in other genera closely related to increase the colour variations still further.

Above: Odontoglossum cirrhosum *comes from Ecuador and likes cool conditions*
Left: the unusual Dendrobium stratiotes *is from the tropical forests of Asia*
Right: attractive cymbidium orchid with strongly contrasting lip markings

carry up to six large, broad leaves, that are thick and fleshy, compensating the plant for its lack of pseudo-bulbs. They are often grown on pieces of wood and have a downward habit, at the same time producing the typical orchid aerial roots, flattened and silvery on the outside. Orchids that are grown on wood very soon adhere to it ·with these strong, clinging roots; within a few months supporting ties can be removed and the plant becomes self-supporting.

The foliage on some of the phalaenopsis species is beautifully marked and mottled with light and dark grey-green spots. The undersides of these leaves may be purple, making a most handsome-looking plant, even when it is not in flower. The colours of phalaenopsis are somewhat restricted to white and pink, but there are a few yellow ones that have been recently introduced, as well as some very fine reds and mauves.

A selection of species

So far we have mentioned most of the popular genera among orchids, dwelling on the types that are being greatly hybridized. There remain many species that are grown for their individual beauty and appeal, and that are ideal for the amateur grower who has only limited space available. The following species have been chosen for their compact habit of growth, ease of culture and free-flowering habit. All are cool-growing and recommended for the beginner, being showy and interesting and are sure to whet the appetite and encourage the new grower to seek further knowledge of these fascinating plants.

Brassia verrucosa The 'spider' orchid. It has large flowers on gracefully-arching sprays. Sepals and petals are long and narrow, green-spotted with brown. From Honduras.

Coelogyne ochracea Sweet-scented sprays of small, delightful flowers. It is snow-white, the lip marked with yellow and orange. Spring-flowering. From India.

Cymbidium devonianum Miniature flowers, reddish-green on long, pendant sprays, with a dull purple lip. Early spring-flowering. From India.

Dendrobium infundibulum Large, pure white flowers, in clusters from the top of the bulb, with a deep yellow stain at the throat. Early summer-flowering. From India.

Dendrobium nobile Attractive rose-pink and white flowers, the length of the cane, with a white lip and a large, deep maroon blotch in the centre. From India.

Encyclia cochleata Upright spray of curious dark-green and dark-purple flowers with lip held uppermost. Common name is 'cockle-shell' orchid. Blooms for long periods during spring and summer. Comes from Honduras and Guatemala.

Laelia anceps Tall flower spikes that average four blooms. Large, showy and delicate mauve with lip richly-coloured and marked yellow in the throat. Autumn-to winter-flowering. From Mexico.

Lycaste cruenta Bright golden-yellow flowers. Three-cornered in appearance. Single, fragrant blooms. Spring-flowering. From Guatemala.

Odontoglossum grande 'Tiger' orchid. Large, richly-coloured flowers in yellow with chestnut-brown bars and a shell-shaped lip in creamy-yellow and brown. Autumn-flowering. From Guatemala.

Paphiopedilum hirsutissimum Large single bloom, very long-lasting. Petals pale green tapering to bold pink, heavily dotted with purple. Pouch, light green. Spring-flowering. From India.

Above: Dendrobium infundibulum *is from India and forms clusters of white flowers*
Left: Lycasta cruenta *is spring-flowering and comes from Guatemala*
Far left: two phalaenopsis orchids, often known as 'moth' orchids because of the spread of their pure white petals
Below: delicately-coloured Cattleya saskelliana *comes from Venezuela*

ORCHID CARE AND CULTIVATION

Here we deal with all aspects of orchid cultivation including indoor culture, and tell you how to make the most of these fascinating and beautiful plants.

Orchids under cultivation can be divided into three groups according to their temperature requirements. These comprise the cool, the intermediate and the hot growing types. The cool house orchids, that are more generally grown and usually recommended for the beginner, require a winter minimum night temperature of 10°C (50°F). This will rise by at least 5°C (10°F) during the daytime. Summer night-time temperatures will be approximately 3°C (5°F) higher, but be sure to keep daytime temperatures down to a maximum of 24°C (75°F).

Intermediate house orchids require temperatures at least 3°C (5°F) higher than the cool, while in the hot house, plants succeed well with a minimum night temperature of 18°C (65°F) winter and summer, and a correspondingly high daytime temperature.

It therefore follows that a cool greenhouse will require artificial heating during the autumn and winter months (end of September to early May), depending on the outside weather conditions. In the intermediate, and especially in the hot section, artificial heating will be required all the year round.

Ventilation and shading

Temperatures inside the greenhouse are controlled by ventilation and shading. Ventilation is most important to orchids, and fresh air, without a draught, should be applied at all times. During the winter, with cold, dull days and little or no sun, it may be possible only to open one ventilator just a crack for an hour or so. This will be sufficient to freshen up the air inside without causing a drop in temperature. During the summer months fresh air can be applied to the cool house almost permanently. It is far better to leave the ventilators open all night during very warm spells of weather than to allow the temperature to rise in the early morning before opening the ventilators. You must be a little more careful, however, in applying fresh air in the hotter houses, where a drop in temperature could be harmful. Small electric fans can work wonders in a small greenhouse, and will keep the air continually on the move

without altering the required temperature. They can be used with equal advantage throughout the year, and are an important asset for people who have to be away from home all day. Automatic ventilators can be brought into play whenever required, taking much of the worry out of growing greenhouse orchids.

Orchids enjoy light, but cannot stand the direct burning sun that penetrates the glass during the summer months. However, take advantage of any bright sunny days that occur from mid autumn to early spring (September to February) to give the orchids full light without fear of burning. From mid spring (March) onwards and throughout the summer months, use some form of shading in the greenhouse. The ideal form of shading is roller blinds that can be attached to the outside of the glass, with a 25cm (9 in) gap between the blinds and the glass to allow for a cooling air flow. They can be rolled up and down as required, allowing the plants maximum light on sunless days. Apart from preventing scorching of the plants, the shading also assists in keeping the temperature down in summer. It may also be necessary to shade the glass with white paint that reflects the light.

Humidity and damping down

Humidity is perhaps the most important single factor in orchid culture. Remember that the plants thrive where humidity is naturally high, and they have evolved as epiphytes living more or less on nothing but humidity. The orchid greenhouse must therefore be damped down daily, until the floors, staging, and all parts of the house are thoroughly soaked. In the summer damp down two or three times daily, and spray the plants overhead once a day. Do this towards late afternoon, or when the sun is just passing over the greenhouse. Providing all foliage is dry by nightfall, the plants will enjoy their daily spraying. During the winter months damping down will probably be necessary only once a day, or every two days, depending upon the immediate weather conditions. The aim should always be to balance the temperature with the humidity. When the temperature is low on cold

winter days, the humidity must also be low, and when the temperature is at its maximum on hot summer days, there should be maximum humidity to balance.

Don't spray overhead during the winter as the water is cold and will remain on the foliage too long before drying up, leading to the appearance of damp marks. Soft-leaved plants such as the lycastes and also the paphiopedilums and phalaenopsis should not be sprayed at any time, since they are particularly prone to damp spots on the foliage. They do, however, require a humid atmosphere around them.

Damping down is carried out to create the humid growing conditions that orchids enjoy, but should not be confused with the actual watering of the plants: this is a separate routine procedure. Water with a spouted can, flooding the surface once or twice to wet the compost thoroughly. This should drain away immediately. Watering of orchids is carried out according to their growing cycle. During the summer months the orchids are growing at the maximum, new bulbs are being made and the plants are in their period of peak energy. This means they will consume copious supplies of water. The ideal is to maintain the compost in a constantly moist condition. Allowing the compost to become bone dry for any period will slow growth, while the other extreme of soaking it to the extent that it eventually becomes sodden, will lead to souring and loss of the plant roots.

During this summer growing period the orchids can also take limited amounts of artificial food; this can be in the form of a liquid food diluted and sprayed over the foliage, or given directly through the compost at regular 10-day intervals. Feeding should be gradually lessened towards the autumn and discontinued throughout the winter.

Rest periods

Many orchids rest during the winter months, when little or no activity is going on within the plants. They can be likened in this respect to an animal that hibernates for the winter after spending the summer storing food within itself to carry it safely through the winter sleep. A resting plant is in a similar state, having spent the summer making up bulbs that contain sufficient moisture to carry it through the winter. The roots stop growing and taking in moisture. Many orchids will spend the winter months in

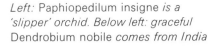

Left: Paphiopedilum insigne *is a 'slipper' orchid. Below left: graceful* Dendrobium nobile *comes from India*

Below: perfectly-shaped specimen of Odontonia amphea *Vanguard, a popular and striking meristem hybrid orchid*

this dormant state, their bulbs remaining hard and plump without the assistance of extra water.

It does not follow, however, that all orchids rest, and this can be clearly seen by observing the plants themselves. By autumn some orchids have completed their pseudo-bulbs, but the bulbless types do not rest, and must therefore be kept moist throughout the winter. The bulbous types may, at this time, shed some or all of their foliage (the first indication of their coming dormant period). Provided there are no signs of new growth, the plant is, to all appearances, commencing its rest. From this time on the plants need no water and can stand in the full light. It may be an advantage to move them from the staging to a shelf close to the glass, where they can enjoy maximum light.

Those orchids that do not rest for the winter usually slow down their growth, but otherwise they require the same attention as during the summer. Continue watering, to keep the plants evenly moist – though at longer intervals as they will take longer to dry out. These continuous-growing plants lose a percentage of their foliage at the beginning of winter, but at the same time new growth will appear from the base of the latest completed bulb, and this will continue to grow throughout the winter. To withhold water from a growing plant will result in a much smaller bulb being made by the end of the season. The bulbs should progress in size until they reach maturity. If they become smaller year by year, it is clear that the conditions provided do not suit them.

The resting plants should retain plump bulbs while they are in their dormant state. If any undue shrivelling takes place, water the plants thoroughly once and the bulbs will plump up again in a very short time. At any time after late winter (January), watch the resting orchids for signs of new growth. Once this happens, it is clear the plants have woken up and are on the move again. When the new growth is about 5–10cm (2–4 in) high (smaller on dwarf plants) the new roots will appear. Begin watering again at this stage; the new roots just being made will need all the moisture they can get, but be careful to avoid over-watering.

Flowering cycles

It has been seen that orchids flower at different times of the year, and therefore at different periods of their growing cycle. Some orchids bloom during their resting period while others produce spikes when in full growth. Therefore the flowering-time need not necessarily be taken into consideration when deciding whether or not to water. A plant that blooms during its resting period has retained sufficient energy in its bulbs to support the growth and flowering of the spike without the assistance of extra water. Plants that flower during their growing season usually do so from the new growth when very young, and only after flowering do the new roots appear, so again the older bulbs support the new growth and flower spike. Watering should be quite straightforward if you watch your plants instead of the calendar, and make sure to water growing plants only.

Orchids should bloom annually quite naturally after a good growing season. If they fail to do so, the culture is at fault. A well-grown, contented plant will bloom without any further assistance from the grower. This, basically, is the art of orchid culture, and every grower strives to bloom every plant in their collection at least once a year.

Potting and repotting

When it comes to potting orchids, bear in mind that the vast majority of those grown in greenhouses are epiphytic by nature. A good basic compost for all orchids is fine bark chippings, either used by itself or mixed with a small percentage of sphagnum peat or sphagnum moss. This provides a good, open, well-drained compost that does not deteriorate quickly and through which the orchids can push their roots with ease. Either plastic or clay pots can be used, but you will find that with such an open compost clay pots will dry the plants out very much quicker. Most growers today use plastic pots.

An orchid plant is in need of repotting when the leading bulb or growth has reached the rim of the pot and there is no room for any further bulbs to be made within it. It also requires repotting if the roots have become so numerous that they have pushed the plant up above the rim.

The showy Vanda sanderiana *originally came from the Philippines and is often considered to be the finest of all orchids.*

In any case, you should repot orchids every year, choosing a pot large enough to allow for a further season's growth. Remove the plant from its old pot, shake the old compost from the roots or clean it out from between the thick rootball. Trim the roots if they are very long, and remove any dead ones.

Orchids are propagated by removing the oldest bulbs from the back portion of the plants. Provided these are firm and not too old, they can be potted up on their own, and will most likely begin new growth within six weeks or so. Any number of leafless back bulbs can be removed from a plant, provided it is left with at least three strong bulbs to maintain its flowering size. The slightly-reduced plant will probably fit back into its original pot. Place the last remaining bulb towards the rim of the pot and leave maximum room for growth to the front of the plant.

Good drainage is important for all orchids, so place a layer of broken crockery at the bottom of the pot. Put the plant into its new position, keeping the base of the new growth level with the pot rim. Fill in the compost all round and push down with the fingertips until the surface is slightly below the rim of the pot. This will allow for future watering and prevent the compost from being washed over the edge.

Indoor culture
The cultivation of orchids in the home is becoming increasingly popular. In spite of certain difficulties over conditions, you can encourage orchids to thrive indoors if you understand what requirements are necessary. Standing a plant over a hot radiator or in the centre of an ill-lit room gives it no incentive to grow and only spells disaster. Much more thought must be given to growing orchids indoors, and you will only be successful if you can maintain the all-important growing environment that they need. If you have a large, south-facing bay window available where house plants thrive, there is a good chance that some orchids will do well there also. The best type of orchids to select are those that can do with less humidity and that generally rest for part of the year. One or two examples are *Odontoglossum grande*, with large, striking flowers of rich yellow and chestnut; *Laelia gouldiana*, with large, brightly-coloured flowers of mauve; *Dendrobium nobile*, with clusters of pink and white flowers; *Coelogyne ochracea*, with small sprays of fragrant white and yellow flowers; and *Paphiopedilum insigne*, with long-lasting bronze and green flowers.

By far the best and most certain way of growing orchids in the home is to put them in a mini indoor greenhouse or orchid case. These are now generally available, including ones that have been designed specially for orchids. They provide heat, light and ventilation, giving a permanently controlled microclimate in which the orchids can thrive, with minimal cost, throughout the year. Ferns and foliage plants can be added to create a good-looking showcase for permanent display.

Propagation by meristem culture
Many seedlings can be grown from a single pod taken from a hybrid. When these finally reach flowering size (a process that takes approximately four years), no two plants ever produce identical blooms, each one being an individual.

Only the best quality plants produced

Above: meristem culture – seedlings grown on agar under sterile conditions – with temperature and humidity gauges

are taken on for meristem culture. This is a method of mass propagation of a single clone or plant. It is a highly-organized technique (mainly practised by commercial growers with cymbidiums) that involves taking the youngest growth from the plant and removing from its centre the nucleus of growing cells that is the meristem tip. No larger than a pinhead, this small embryo is cultured in the same way as the seed; from this minute piece of tissue any number of identical 'carbon copies' can be successfully produced. This

process takes a further three to four years before the plants will be of flowering size. These orchids will always be referred to as 'meristems'.

The grower now has two choices. He may prefer to purchase unflowered seedlings of unknown expectancy, with the excitement of flowering them for the first time and hoping for one outstanding variety, or he can obtain proven meristem-cultured plants, knowing exactly what he is buying. This latter choice is preferable when buying for the cut flower market since you can obtain exactly what the florists require.

The orchid seed pod is produced by crossing two selected flowers. It takes up to nine months to ripen on the plant. The pod, heavily laden with literally millions of incredibly small seeds, is ready for sowing when splits begin to appear along the edges. The seed is sown in sterile flasks on a special growing medium (obtainable from a specialist nursery) that includes various salts and sugars for the nourishment of the seed. The young plants thrive in these sterile conditions and after 12 months they are strong enough to be taken from the flasks and potted up. From this stage on they are repotted at regular intervals until they reach flowering size.

SCENTED FLOWERS FOR THE GREENHOUSE

Many flowers are famous for their scent, and it is not difficult to fill a greenhouse full of fragrance. We include others here that become more sweet-smelling under greenhouse or conservatory conditions.

When growing flowers for their scent it is important to choose your varieties carefully. Many flowers, usually thought of as sweet-smelling, such as lilies and freesias, also have varieties that are completely scentless.

Fragrant lilies

Among the easiest plants to grow are the bulbs and other storage organs. Lilies immediately spring to mind, but most of those that make the best pot plants are not particularly scented. But certain lilies can be temperamental outdoors and by growing them indoors under glass you may get more reliable results – and more perfume. Also some of the new hybrid lilies are expensive and you may prefer to give them protection. However, when cultivated this way the plants do tend to grow tall and will need staking.

One of the most powerfully-scented lilies is *L. auratum* (goldband lily). The variety *L. a. platyphyllum* has very large, beautiful flowers and a strong stem. The various forms of *L. speciosum* are also good for the greenhouse. They have charming flowers with reflexed petals in carmine and red shades as well as white. Their height varies from about 90cm–1·5m (3–5 ft). *L. japonicum* (bamboo lily) is of neat habit and makes fine pot plants when grouped in threes in 18cm (7 in) pots. It has fragrant, pinky, trumpet flowers and rarely exceeds 90cm (3 ft) in height.

Tuberose and Peruvian daffodil

Polianthes tuberosa (tuberose) has been an important plant in the manufacture of perfume. For pots a good choice is the variety The Pearl with its attractive spikes of double white flowers. It is, however, an untidy plant and is best grown as three bulbs to each 18cm (7 in) pot. Plant the large, elongated bulbs with their tops well protruding from the surface of the compost. You can force the bulbs in gentle warmth to flower at almost any time of year, but spring is the easiest time to get them to flower. After flowering,

Above: delicate-flowered freesia may not always be scented. To be sure, buy corms of a named variety
Left: strongly-perfumed Lilium auratum *bears striking bloom up to 30cm (12 in) across in early to mid autumn (August to September)*

expose the bulbs to as much sunlight as possible. This seems to 'ripen' them and they are more likely to flower again the following year.

Provided you buy the largest possible bulbs, *Hymenocallis narcissiflora* (Peruvian daffodil) is easy to grow and very impressive. The variety usually sold is *H. n.* Advance. This has a tall, strong stem that bears several large, spidery, white flowers with a structure similar to the daffodil (they belong to the same family) but sweetly scented. If potted in spring, flowering will continue during summer. Plant one bulb in each 18cm (7 in) pot.

Cyclamen and freesia

At one time the cyclamen also gave its name to many fancy perfumes. Like so many plants where there have been attempts to breed larger flowers, the scent has often become faint or lost altogether. Even so, there are still strongly-scented strains such as Sweet-scented Mixed. The flowers are not so large as the giant-flowered forms, but the scent is strong and the range of colours delightful. The Puppet strain of cyclamen are also strongly fragrant. These are pleasing miniatures that can be grown in very small pots.

The freesia is another plant that may or may not be scented. Flowers grown from seed or from corms of obscure origin may have no fragrance at all. The strain Van Staaveren, however, has a lovely perfume and can be sown in mid winter (late December) for summer flowers and in late spring to mid summer (April to June) for flowers in autumn and winter. About

seven seeds to each 13cm (5 in) pot will make a good group of bloom for decoration. They also make fine cut flowers.

Certain freesia varieties available as corms also have a fine fragrance – for example Snow Queen, Blue Banner and Golden Melody. In addition, these all have very large, beautiful flowers.

Scented flowers from seed

Several very fragrant plants can be raised quickly from seed. The lovely *Calonyction aculeatum* (moonflower) is one that is not well known. It opens its large, white, convolvulus-like flowers in the evening and fills the air with scent. Although perennial, it is easy to raise as an annual and it will climb up a few bamboo canes or can be trained on a wall support.

Exacum affine is best grown as several seedlings per 13cm (5 in) pot. The blue flowers are small but have a strong, spicy scent, providing you take care to choose a scented strain of seed.

Several types of stock make good pot plants or can be used for cutting in winter. The strain Giant Brilliant Column produces handsome spikes of exhibition blooms and some of them are excellent for cutting. For exhibition, remove all sideshoots and allow one central spike only to develop. Beauty of Nice is also a favourite with flower arrangers. For winter cut flowers, sow the seed from late summer to early autumn (July to August). For the large double flowers get the Hansens 100 per cent double strains and prick out only those seedlings with light green leaves; these are the ones that give the double flowers.

Sweet-smelling climbers

There are three perennial greenhouse climbers outstanding for both beautiful flowers and perfume. The easiest is *Jasminum polyanthum*, which is happy with a winter minimum temperature of about 4–7°C (40–45°F). It can be kept within bounds by drastic pruning, but it tends to become rampant and is ideal for covering a large expanse of wall, for example in a lean-to. It becomes covered with masses of white flowers from about early spring (February) onwards (depending on temperature) and its scent is very strong. Not difficult, but needing more overall warmth for healthy growth, is *Stephanotis floribunda* (Madagascar jasmine), which has clusters of white tubular flowers during summer, and *Hoya carnosa*, with its umbels of pink-to-white starry flowers from mid summer to mid autumn (June to September).

Carnations and gardenias

Of the specialists' flowers, carnations are probably the most renowned for scent – but again the variety is very important. Consult the catalogue of a specialist grower of perpetual-flowering types; varieties with good scent will be so described.

Gardenias have tended to go out of fashion. This may be because they often need a fairly high level of greenhouse heating, at least during part of their development, and now that fuel is so expensive fewer people want to grow them. Unless you can give a winter minimum of about 13°C (55°F) it is better to avoid them.

Cold greenhouse flowers

For cold greenhouses, roses in pots should not be forgotten for early fragrant blooms, and, of course, many of the favourite spring-flowering bulbs (such as narcissus and hyacinth) are also highly fragrant. In addition, there are scented shrubs like daphne – the best for the greenhouse being *Daphne odora* that has strongly citrus-scented, pale purplish flowers in winter.

Stephanotis floribunda *(Madagascar jasmine) climbs up to 3m (10 ft) high*

SCENTED FOLIAGE PLANTS

Plants with scented foliage are not often noted for their showy flowers, but the leaves are usually attractive. Grown under glass, the fragrance from the leaves is generally even more pronounced, especially when the temperature rises, and the air of the greenhouse can become filled with their scent.

In most cases you can release the fragrant essential oils from the leaves of plants with scented foliage by gently pressing (or sometimes crushing) a leaf between the fingers.

Hardy plants with scented foliage
A number of the plants are almost hardy, some may even be perfectly hardy in sheltered parts of the country. This makes them a good choice for a cold or unheated greenhouse or conservatory. Popular as a house plant in recent years is *Eucalyptus globulus* (Tasmanian blue gum). This will eventually become far too large for pots, but in mild regions it can thrive outdoors. The leaves on young plants up to about three years old are roundish. Mature foliage is elongated. When crushed, the foliage emits the familiar smell of eucalyptus, but the scent is more 'flowery' and pleasant than the oil you buy from the chemist when you have a cold. The plants are easily raised from seed sown in early spring (February).

In mild areas *Choisya ternata*, sometimes called Mexican orange blossom, is hardy. In colder regions it may be successful if given a sheltered spot. It makes a good evergreen for large pots in cold greenhouses (provided you give it room to spread), or it can be grown as a wall shrub. The foliage is a glossy light green, giving out a strong citrus smell when bruised. Clusters of small, attractive and fragrant white flowers are also produced from time to time during the year, often continuing well into winter in a cold greenhouse. Small container-grown plants are usually available from good garden centres.

A few alpine species (such as the alpine species of artemisia) have scented foliage, and there are various reasonably-compact or low-growing aromatic herbs that, with frost protection, may also serve a useful purpose by providing leaves to flavour cooking during the winter.

Above left: erect-growing Myrtus communis. *Left: many pelargoniums have strongly scented leaves*

Above: Eucalyptus globulus *(Tasmanian blue gum) is an excellent choice for unheated greenhouse or conservatory*

Sweet-smelling myrtles

Excellent for a cold greenhouse are the various species and varieties of myrtle. *Myrtus communis* (common myrtle), can be grown but it needs a tub or a large pot and may become too big for a small greenhouse. It is erect in habit and the white blossom is delightfully fragrant; the rarer double form is especially attractive. Where space is lacking the compact variety *M.c.* Tarentina is useful. It bears pink buds that open to creamy-white flowers from early to mid autumn (August to September).

Especially suited to a greenhouse, too, are *M. bullata* and *M. ugni*. Both can be kept to below about 110cm (3½ ft). The former is a splendid foliage plant and is sometimes sold as a house plant. It has bronze-coloured puckered foliage of waxy texture, giving it the common name of puckered-leaf myrtle. Large white flowers are followed by red berries. *M. ugni* is the edible myrtle having pink, bell-shaped flowers and dark red fruit rather like the strawberry in flavour. It is neat and compact in growth.

For a cold conservatory with plenty of height there are two lovely myrtles. *M. apiculata* (Chilean tree myrtle) needs at least 2·5m (8 ft) of height. The form *M. a.* Glanleam Gold is very striking, having dark green foliage with golden-yellow margins.

M. lechleriana also needs plenty of height – at least 1·8m (6 ft) to display itself properly. The white flowers, borne in spring, are deliciously scented and the young growth has a bronze tint.

Lemon-scented leaves

Lippia citriodora, lemon-scented verbena, often called aloysia, can easily be grown in 20–25cm (8–10 in) pots in a cold greenhouse. The leaves emit a powerful lemon scent when crushed, but the shrub is deciduous. Panicles of small, mauve tubular flowers appear in early autumn (August). The shrub is easy to keep 'within bounds' and will withstand quite drastic pruning – best done in late spring (April).

Another plant giving a powerful lemon scent when the foliage is crushed or gently pressed between the fingers is *Eucalyptus citriodora* (lemon-scented gum). However, this species is suited only to reasonably warm conditions. Raise it from seed sown in spring in a warm propagating case and it will grow on slowly during the summer. In autumn you must put it in a warm greenhouse or on a warm windowsill in the home. The leaves are a pleasing olive green and slightly hairy. The minimum winter temperature it needs is about 10°C (50°F), preferably higher, and you should be sure to maintain a fair humidity. It can be kept for several years quite happily in a 13cm (5 in) pot before you will need to repot it, or replace the plant altogether.

Fragrant-leaved pelargoniums

The most popular of all scented-leaved plants are the pelargoniums. There are numerous pungent-smelling varieties and species and others that have a specific scent such as rose, lemon, mint or a fruity smell. The shape of the foliage is very variable and they often make good house plants although the flowers are rarely showy. *P. crispum* Catford Belle and *P.c.* Mabel Cirey have lemon-scented leaves and good flowers. *P. crispum minor* (finger bowl geranium) has very tiny leaves and a scent that is fragrant and lemony, rather like citronella. *P. citriodorum* Prince of Orange grows to be a fairly large plant with white flowers. *P. quercifolium* has an unusual scent – a mixture of pine and lime. It has 'oak-leaf' foliage and a somewhat creeping habit.

Pelargonium capitatum (attar of roses) has attractive foliage that is strongly rose-scented. The variety *P. denticulatum* (fern leaf) is so named because of its ferny leaf-shape. It has a fairly strong rose scent and also very small white flowers.

P. denticulatum tomentosum has a powerful mint scent and *P. tomentosum* a peppermint-like perfume. Both have rather hairy foliage.

Among the fruit-scented types, *P. fragrans* has a pleasing, piney-nutmeg smell and *P. odoratissimum* resembles apples. *P. grossularoides* has an apricot-rose perfume, while *P.g.* Lady Plymouth has attractive variegated foliage and a peppery lemon scent.

GREENHOUSE CLIMBERS

A few climbers in the greenhouse will greatly enhance its appearance. Choose from plants that are small and compact and can be fitted into the tiniest space, or from others that will cover a large area. Some will grow quickly from seed, some are annuals, and some become steadily more beautiful as the years pass.

The description 'climber' is often loosely used to include plants that could more properly be called wall shrubs – plants that are unable to support themselves by tendrils or by twining. Special provision has to be made for supporting them and training them into the required shape. Nearly all climbers, however, will need some support; very few can be left to ramble without some artificial means to hold them in position.

Root restriction

A common characteristic of climbers is that they tend to be rampant and rather too vigorous. Left to themselves (and perhaps given too much food and water) they may become a tangle of stems and foliage, producing little in the way of flowers. This is especially true of perennials that are planted in a border of ground soil in the greenhouse or given excessively large pots.

The first cultural hint, therefore, is to use relatively small pots or containers, or restrict root spread in the ground by planting in a plunged clay pot or placing slates, tiles, bricks or asbestos sheeting around the sides of the planting hole when it is made. For most annuals an ordinary flowerpot 13–25cm (5–10 in) in diameter is satisfactory – depending on the expected (or required) ultimate size of the plant.

Selecting the support

When it comes to supporting, training and displaying the plants there are a number of points to be considered. Often the nature of the plant will suggest the best method, while in other cases there may already be a support in existence for which you need to choose a suitable climber; for example you may wish to cover a lean-to greenhouse wall or a roof-supporting column, pillar or post.

If you intend to plant permanent wall

Vigorous Ipomoea tricolor *Heavenly Blue (left, above) and* Cobaea scandens *(left) will both flower in the year of planting*

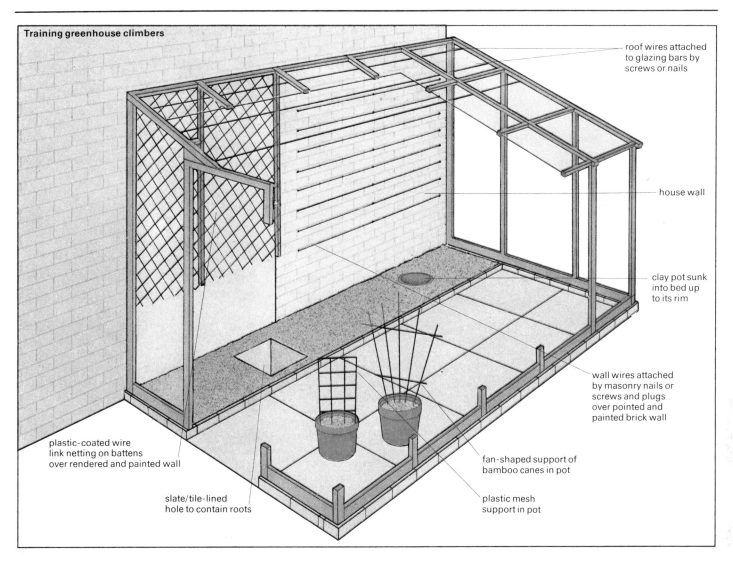

Training greenhouse climbers

roof wires attached to glazing bars by screws or nails

house wall

clay pot sunk into bed up to its rim

wall wires attached by masonry nails or screws and plugs over pointed and painted brick wall

fan-shaped support of bamboo canes in pot

plastic mesh support in pot

slate/tile-lined hole to contain roots

plastic-coated wire link netting on battens over rendered and painted wall

shrubs or climbers, then first pay some attention to the wall itself. A brick wall, or similar rough surface, is best rendered to give a smooth finish, filling in all holes so that there are no crevices where pests or diseases may accumulate. A coat of white vinyl emulsion or exterior paint will give a background that is both hygienic and pleasing.

To give wall support, attach wires to masonry nails driven into the wall or to screws fixed with plugs. Or you can use plastic-coated wire netting or mesh (obtainable in white for white walls) fastened to a wall or other part of the greenhouse structure. Plastic mesh without wire reinforcement is also sold for the support of climbers, but is less advisable for long-term use, as some plastics become brittle with age (especially in a sunny greenhouse) and may then collapse under the increasing weight of a growing climber. For a similar reason perishable materials like string or canes should be avoided for perennial climbers.

If you want your climber to grow up into the greenhouse roof, train it along wires stretched from end to end of the building, fastened to the glazing bars. For very small climbers, and particularly annuals, bamboo canes are suitable. You can usually insert several in the pot and arrange them like the spines of a fan. Small plastic mesh supports, intended for inserting in the flowerpots of house plants, are also convenient. For fastening stems to supports, a number of 'patent' plant ties are sold in garden shops. These are neat and secure and most can easily be moved from place to place.

Quick-flowering climbers

Several delightful climbers will flower in the first year of sowing and planting. *Ipomoea tricolor (rubro-caerulea)*, better known as morning glory, has long been prized for its glorious, large, blue, convolvulus-like blooms borne freely each morning but fading by early afternoon. In recent years varieties with new colours have been introduced, such as the blue and white striped Flying Saucers, the mauve Wedding Bells and the deep, rose-coloured Early Call that also has very long-lasting flowers. Sow seed in a warm propagator in mid spring (March) and

transfer single seedlings to 13cm (5 in) pots or several to larger pots. Well-grown plants will reach about 1·8m (6 ft) high in one year and become smothered with bloom.

Similar in height and vigour is *Cobaea scandens* (cup and saucer plant) – so called because of the flower shape. The flowers are deep violet, but a rare white form is said to exist. Another fast-grower is *Eccremocarpus scaber* (Chilean glory flower). Provided it is sown early it will flower the same year, and it is hardy in sheltered places in mild areas although not often a long-lived perennial. It bears masses of showy, vivid orange flowers.

Some people like to grow sweet peas under glass especially for cutting, but not all varieties are suitable. Choose types that flower in late autumn to early winter (October–November) and Cuthbertson varieties. With care the large-flowered Spencer varieties can flower well, but rarely before late spring (April). In all cases there is a tendency for buds to drop and a greenhouse with good light is vital to success. All plants must be stopped at the seedling stage.

Extremely easy (even for children) to grow, is the lovely little climber *Thunbergia alata* (black-eyed Susan). Even the small seedlings are impatient to flower and at this stage the best bright orange colours with jet black eyes can be selected for growing on. Inferior colours can be discarded if desired. Growth will only reach 1m (3 ft) or so and there is usually room for this climber in the smallest greenhouse.

Exotic climbers

Striking and exotic, and much easier to grow than most gardening books imply, is *Gloriosa rothschildiana* (glory lily). This is grown from a long tuber that can be planted late on in spring (April) when the warmer weather keeps up the greenhouse temperature. Pot so that the blunt, roundish end is at the centre of an 18cm (7 in) pot. It is from here that the roots and shoots will grow. Just cover the tuber with potting compost; it does not matter if the pointed end protrudes above after placing the tuber longways. The plant will support itself by tendrils formed at the end of the leaves but will nearly always need further assistance from the grower. The flowers are like reflexed lilies, with bright crimson and yellow flowers from summer to autumn. Over winter store them, completely dry, with the pots on their sides. Usually at least two new tubers will be formed and can be separated when replanting at the appropriate time the following year.

Some climbers are best bought as small plants (usually rooted cuttings) from a garden centre, nursery or gardening shop. Being perennial they may take several years to reach full flowering size but, like most climbers and wall shrubs, are a wonderful sight when in bloom. Bougainvillea is among the most showy and colourful. In this case it is the bracts and not the flowers that make the long-lasting display. There are a number of named hybrids of *Bougainvillea × buttiana*, and *B. glabra* is also popular. The colours range from orange to mauve shades and even young plants will cover themselves with bracts. Bougainvilleas can be trained as wall shrubs or the stems led up along wires in the greenhouse roof when the plants have reached sufficient height. A winter minimum of about 10°C (50°F) is advisable for best results. Pruning should be done in early spring (February) by cutting out all weak growth and cutting back to keep the desired shape.

Scented climbers

A very vigorous but popular jasmine for the greenhouse is *Jasminum polyanthum*.

Left: Bougainvillea
glabra, *covered
with long-lasting
bracts; below left:
fragrant-flowered*
Hoya carnosa; *below:
bell-shaped
flowers of* Abutilon
megapotamicum
Right: the beautiful
Lapageria rosea

A superb fragrant climber is *Stephanotis floribunda*, sometimes sold as a house plant trained around a wire hoop. In the greenhouse it will grow up into the roof and the waxy white tubular flowers, delightful because of their scent, will hang down in clusters. This climber likes a rather humid atmosphere and a winter minimum of about 10°C (50°F). It will survive lower temperatures if kept on the dry side during the cold months. *Hoya carnosa* also likes a fair degree of humidity. It is sweetly scented and has umbels of pinkish, starry flowers. The foliage is evergreen and there is a form with cream-margined leaves, greatly enhancing its beauty. Although surviving winter at about 7°F (45°F), best results are obtained if 10–13°C (50–55°F) can be maintained. It does well in shade and little pruning is required. Both stephanotis and hoya greatly benefit if you spray them with tepid water from time to time during summer.

Other popular climbers

A very beautiful evergreen climber for a greenhouse just kept free from frost is *Lapageria rosea* (Chilean bell-flower). Large, red tubular flowers of waxy texture are borne during autumn. It is a good choice for a shady greenhouse, even a north-facing conservatory or lean-to. The plants need little pruning and are happy in 25cm (10 in) pots. Pink and white forms are sometimes available but are not common.

An easy wall shrub for a frost-free conservatory is *Plumbago capensis*. This has either blue or white phlox-like flowers from spring to autumn. Pruned sparingly it will reach a height of at least 3.5m (12 ft) and looks most impressive if a blue and a white form are grown together and allowed to intermingle. When flowering is over, prune back all growth by about two-thirds.

Abutilon megapotamicum is a quaint, almost hardy climber with dainty red and yellow lantern-like flowers borne from spring to autumn. It is a good choice for a pillar or roof-supporting column, and demands little attention. Popular, but not a very wise selection for the greenhouse is *Passiflora caerulea*, the common passion flower – which is, in any case, perfectly hardy. Far better for under glass is the species *P. quadrangularis* (granadilla), with much larger, exotic flowers, and other warmth-loving species when available. These need 10°C (50°F) in winter and moderate humidity. They are best trained along wires and if you don't let the shoots become too long, then the flowers can be kept reasonably low.

It has creamy-white flowers during late winter (January) and is extremely powerfully scented. To prevent rampant growth the roots are best restricted by growing in 25cm (10 in) pots. Do not be afraid to prune or cut back at almost any time, otherwise this climber can smother everything. It is ideal if you have a large area to cover but when strictly controlled is also suitable for a small greenhouse. A winter minimum temperature of about 7°C (45°F) is adequate.

HOW TO USE A
SHADY GREENHOUSE

There is no doubt that the ideal site for a greenhouse is one in full sun. You can shade easily enough, but it is not so simple to provide light of solar intensity. The sun is also an important source of free heat in winter. Nevertheless, you can still put a shady greenhouse site to excellent use.

Town dwellers, in particular, often have little choice but to put their greenhouses in the shade. Small town gardens are frequently overshadowed by walls or other buildings. But don't let this discourage you; it merely means you will have to choose your plants with care and common sense.

There is a wide range of greenhouse plants for which shade can be a great advantage (if not vital), at least during their flowering period. And if you already have a sunny-sited greenhouse and are contemplating erecting an extra one, you may consider deliberately putting it in a shady place. For example, a north-facing conservatory built as a lean-to against your house may not be ideal as a suntrap but it will be excellent for displaying most of your favourite pot plants for a large part of the year.

If you wish to put a shady greenhouse to use in winter, remember that it will cost more to heat than one that traps the sun's warmth. If you cannot provide artificial heat, choose hardy (or almost hardy) shade-tolerant plants.

Enough warmth to keep out frost will greatly extend your range. Although a little extra warmth does not necessarily mean more scope in terms of colourful and decorative plants, it does mean that you can grow some less common and more exotic species.

Exotic hardy plants
Where there is no heat at all, create an impression of tropical warmth with foliage plants like *Fatsia japonica* and the various hardy palms. These will thrive in

There is a wide range of flowering plants suitable for shady greenhouses. Above right: evergreen climber Lapageria rosea albiflora *and (right)* Cyclamen persicum *Far right, above: spring-flowering* Primula × kewensis; *far right:* Fuchsia cordifolia

semi-shade, but not in extreme gloom. Most of the hardy ferns, however, positively enjoy having very little light.

For both attractive evergreen foliage and glorious flowers, the camellias are very important where light is limited.

They will usually flower well as quite young plants in pots as small as 13mm (5 in). When they eventually become too large for the cold greenhouse you can put them out in the garden. Another evergreen (and an indispensible climber for the rear wall of a cold, shady lean-to) is *Lapageria rosea* (Chilean bell-flower). This has shiny foliage and large, tubular, waxy flowers that are usually carmine in colour – less commonly pink. They are borne in early autumn to early winter (August to November).

Most of the hedera (ivies) will tolerate a good deal of shade and there are now many decorative variegated forms that can be used as small pot plants or to cover an expanse of wall. *Hedera canariensis* is particularly pleasing and in cool conditions develops a reddish tint to the green and cream variegated foliage. This ivy is almost hardy, if not entirely so in sheltered places, and so it will grow especially vigorously in a warm greenhouse or room.

Hardy border plants

A number of hardy border plants make good pot subjects for an unheated shady house. Especially suitable are the hardy cyclamen, bergenia (the handsome flowers tend to get damaged outdoors in winter), primulas of various kinds, a number of lilies, trillium (which should be given a leafy compost and will even enjoy deep shade), the long-spurred aquilegias (columbine), Excelsior hybrid digitalis (foxglove) – if there's height for them to grow to about 1·5m (5 ft) – and hostas (plantain lily) that bear delightful flowers as well as having beautiful foliage. All the hardy spring-flowering bulbs should ideally be given a cold, shady greenhouse for them to display their flowers which will then last much longer, but good light is essential in mid and late winter (December and January) to keep their foliage short and green.

Pot plant displays

A shady, frost-free greenhouse makes an ideal conservatory for the display of nearly all the popular pot plants that are grown to give a mass of colour from mid winter to early summer (December to May). These include cineraria, calceolaria, primulas such as *P. malacoides, P. obconica, P. sinensis* and *P. × kewensis*, autumn-sown schizanthus (butterfly flower), salpiglossis and other annuals, and cyclamen.

If the house is not too shady most of these can also be grown in it from the earliest stages – from seed or storage organs. Where the amount of shade is

considerable, however, it is better to use frames warmed with soil-warming cables. Place them where there is good light for the earlier stages of growing, so that strong, compact plants will develop. Ideally, of course, this is where another greenhouse with an open, sunny position can help enormously.

Flowers for summer and autumn

For summer- and autumn-flowering plants shade is usually vital, and as most of those grown in the home greenhouse will need no extra heat during the summer, a shady greenhouse is the ideal home for them. The 'top' group of shade lovers is the family GESNERIACEAE. This includes saintpaulia (African violet), streptocarpus (Cape primrose), gloxinia, *Rechsteineria leucotricha* (silver song), now commonly grown from seed, the gesneria varieties (that are now classed with the genus rechsteineria), achimenes and smithianthas.

Nearly all the popular foliage plants, with the exception of coleus, also like a fair degree of shade. Shade in summer is particularly essential to most of those now known as house plants, such as foliage begonias, peperomia, pilea, maranta (prayer plant) and calathea. Most of these will be happy under the staging.

Fuchsias will generally do better with some summer shade, more especially to prevent high temperatures that cause the flowers to fall or be short-lived, but the shade must not be too heavy. Regal pelargoniums also benefit from slight shade; it makes the flowers last longer.

Bulbs and vegetables

Many of the summer-to-autumn-flowering bulbs or other storage organs may have to be fairly heavily shaded, both to keep the temperature down and to prevent sun scorching flowers or foliage. The giant-flowered begonias can be severely damaged by excessive light, the flower petals becoming bleached or scorched at the edges. Hippeastrums and lilies may suffer similarly.

Few vegetables will enjoy a shady greenhouse, but if there is warmth it can be used for blanching plants like endive, and for forcing and blanching seakale, chicory and rhubarb. One exception, however, is the mushroom. This does not need light – but darkness is not essential either, as many people suppose.

SALAD CROPS FOR GROWING UNDER GLASS

Anyone with a greenhouse, frame or a few cloches should give serious thought to growing salad crops. They are rich in vitamins and minerals, low in fat content and, usually, in carbohydrates. With weather protection a wide range of these vegetables can be cropped almost all year round

To make the best use of the type of protection you have, and to employ it economically (especially important where heating is employed), give proper consideration to its height. A greenhouse has plenty of headroom and you can use this to advantage by growing tall crops like tomato and cucumber, while low-growing crops can often be grown as catch crops (quick crops grown alongside a main crop) in the remaining space.

You can also adopt the catch-crop technique with frames and cloches; for example, along with lettuce grow even smaller vegetables like radishes, so that no space is wasted.

Tomatoes

Undoubtedly the tomato is the most popular of all salad crops. It does, however, have its fair share of problems. Many of these arise from the practice of growing plants in the ground soil and using crude animal manures or garden compost that has not been properly fermented. These methods introduce innumerable pests and diseases to which tomatoes are very susceptible. Like most crops they also succumb to 'soil sickness' if grown in the same ground year after year. For this reason it is wise for the home grower, with the average-sized greenhouse, to grow the plants in good soil compost in pots at least 25cm (10 in) in diameter, or in a trough made from a frame of timber boards draped with polythene with slits cut for drainage. Growing bags, filled with special tomato compost are now also available. These are placed flat on the floor and holes are then cut in them to take the plants. You can, however, make your own simple and inexpensive compost. Mix three parts of peat with one part of washed grit and add (according to instructions) a proprietary, balanced, complete fertilizer containing magnesium, iron and trace elements.

Erratic watering of tomatoes and

extremes of feeding lead to cracked and split fruit, and often to premature falling of flowers and young fruits. Ring-culture was designed to even out water uptake, but the method is still much misunderstood. The plants are grown in bottomless pots, and you can buy inexpensive fibre cylinders for the purpose. Set the ring on an aggregate consisting of 'ballast'. This is a mixture of coarse, stony pieces (that help support the rings of compost) and fine particles that convey moisture to the rings by capillary action. Keep the aggregate thoroughly moist, but not waterlogged. Apply liquid feeds to the compost in the rings. Alternatively, instead of this aggregate, you can use peat. Discard it at the end of the year (dig it into the outdoor garden) and use fresh peat for the next tomato crop. This way you don't have to dispose of heavy aggregate, nor do you have to clean and

sterilize it for future use. You also avoid the risk of carrying over pests and diseases from one crop to the next.

It is important to put the aggregate down on plastic sheeting so as to prevent the tomato roots entering the ground soil. Do not, in place of aggregate, use ashes or other materials that may contain harmful chemicals, and do not overwater as this can cause root rot.

Although tomatoes can be cropped all the year round, this is an uneconomical practice for most people, owing to the fairly high degree of warmth needed for winter fruiting. The usual method is to sow from early spring (February) onwards, depending on the warmth available (a minimum of 10°C 50°F). If your greenhouse is sited in a sunny position, and warmth can be maintained, you can start sowing in early winter (November). Tomatoes need shading only when the

weather is at its hottest, and to keep temperatures below 27°C (80°F) during ripening – otherwise there may be ripening troubles.

Cucumbers

Similar advice applies to cucumber, which most people find convenient to sow in late spring (April). This is another crop apt to be frequently overwatered; remember, cucumbers are not bog plants! If the roots get too wet they decay, and the young fruits rot and fall. Growing methods can be much the same as for tomatoes, but the plants must be properly trained for the best results. For a small greenhouse, stretch about five wires along the roof some 15–20cm (6–8 in) apart and stand the pots on the staging so that the plants can be grown up underneath the wires. Stop the plants (by taking out the growing tip) when they reach the top wires; then train any lateral shoots along the wires and tie them in. When a flower bearing a little fruit has formed stop (by cutting off) the shoot two leaves further on. Remove all flowers not bearing fruits. These are male flowers and if they are allowed to pollinate the females, they will cause the fruits to become seedy, club-shaped and often bitter. Varieties bearing only female flowers are now obtainable and well worth consideration. Cucumbers need more shade than tomatoes, and this is ideally provided by a coating of white Coolglass on the exterior of the greenhouse.

Sweet Peppers

These peppers, which you may also encounter under their Spanish name of pimiento or generic name of capsicum, are an excellent crop to grow with tomatoes, and they take up less height. You can eat the fruits when green, yellow or red, and you can cook them or use them raw. Modern hybrids are easy to grow and give splendid yields. If possible, sow early – at the same time as your tomatoes, in a similar compost and in 18–20cm (7–8 in) pots. Again, if there is sufficient warmth, sowing can be done in early winter (November) to give pickings by late the

A fine crop of ripe tomatoes (above left) and cucumbers (right) raised under glass

following spring (April). Well-grown plants produce as many as 30 fruits on each, but thinning is usually necessary to prevent overcrowding and distortion of the fruit that may press together when swelling. Otherwise they need little attention apart from watering and feeding as required. Green fruits will ripen to a full red colour after picking if put in a warm place indoors. You can also grow plants outside, keeping them under cloches until summer. Do not uncover them before all danger of frost is past.

Lettuce

Lettuce is most conveniently grown in frames or under cloches, but greenhouses are often devoted to this valuable year-round crop. A cold greenhouse or, for out-of-season production, a frost-free greenhouse, is all that is necessary. Frames can be equipped with electric soil-warming cables or special outdoor cables can be run in the soil under rows of cloches. These are operated from a transformer (that lowers the voltage) so there is no danger if the cables are accidentally cut when working the soil with tools.

It is vital when growing lettuce to choose your varieties with care. Not all are suited to winter culture, and winter types may bolt in summer. Examine the seedsmen's catalogues carefully. The descriptions of the various types explain which are suited to which seasons.

Like tomatoes (and for similar reasons) lettuce are prone to pests and diseases if grown in the ground soil. The most deadly enemy is grey mould (botrytis) a common fungus that attacks most plants living or dead. It is especially serious for lettuce and can wipe out the contents of frames or greenhouses in a few days unless promptly checked. Poor ventilation, allowing an excessive humidity, encourages the fungus that forms a greying, furry covering over the plants and causes them to rot. If you have added decaying manure or vegetable matter to the soil, this will certainly encourage an outbreak. So as a wise precaution, fumigate with TCNB smokes or spray with a fungicide such as Benlate, according to maker's instructions. In winter, when conditions in the greenhouse are best kept drier, it is not advisable to use a spray, so use TCNB smokes. It is not practical to fumigate frames as it is difficult to measure the correct dosage and to disperse the smoke evenly.

You can produce fine crops of lettuce by growing them in pots or troughs of a prepared sterile compost as described for tomatoes. You can also use this compost in frames, taking care to line them first with polythene to avoid contact with the ground soil. Under cloches it is usually convenient to sow lettuce directly into the soil and thin out, but you can, if preferred, raise the plants in seed trays in the greenhouse and transplant them.

Radish and Beetroot

There are several different varieties of radish that are easy to grow as catch crops. Study the catalogues carefully to select suitable types. Some force more easily than others. Radishes are remarkably free from pests and disease, but active surface pests like slugs and cutworms will eat them however 'hot' they may be to our taste. The variety Red Forcing is particularly good for under cover cultivation. Always thin out radish as soon as possible, otherwise the roots never get a chance to grow to their proper size, and their flavour never fully develops.

Globe beetroot make a useful frame crop, and there will usually be room for radish, too, while the beetroot is developing. Sowing can be made in a heated frame from early to mid spring (February to March). Thin to one plant at each sowing point, since the 'seeds' sown are really capsules containing several seeds.

Spring Onions and Carrots

Spring onions, either sown in spring or summer, need only cloche protection. White Lisbon is still a favourite variety.

Carrots are often overlooked as salad vegetables, but young, raw carrots are delicious when grated and seasoned, and are extremely nutritious. Choose the stump-rooted types for frames and cloches; read the catalogue descriptions carefully since not all varieties are happy under cover. Sow in a warmed frame in mid autumn (September) and late winter (January); in a cold frame sow from early spring (February) onwards.

Other Vegetables

Mustard and cress and several other sprouting vegetables like fenugreek, alfalfa, Mung bean and Adzuki bean can be fitted in as catch crops to most heated greenhouses and frames all the year round. They are easy to grow and need no elaborate preparations or compost making, and they are probably the quickest-yielding of all crops. It is only recently that their important food value has been appreciated, and they are a valuable source of protein.

GROWING FRUIT IN THE GREENHOUSE

To make it worthwhile growing most types of dessert fruit under glass, you really need a large greenhouse. However, it need not necessarily be expensive to run, as in many cases little or no artificial heat is required. You may be lucky enough to have an old property whose garden already contains a derelict greenhouse that could be renovated and adapted for the purpose. If you are thinking of installing one specially, a lean-to greenhouse against a south-facing wall is particularly good for fruit-growing.

Among the fruits that can be grown successfully in an unheated or cool greenhouse are peaches, apricots, nectarines, grapes, figs and melons.

Grapes

Interest in grape-growing is developing alongside the increasing popularity of wine-making. A lean-to greenhouse is an excellent home for a vine, though you may have difficulty finding room in it for much else.

Usually the roots of the vines are planted outside in a border alongside the front of the greenhouse. The rods (vine stems) are then passed through a little arch made in the greenhouse base and trained up the side and over the roof. Plant in late winter (January), spacing 1·2m (4 ft) between plants, and cut back the rods if necessary to 45cm (18 in). For a single plant allow two shoots to grow freely during the first year; if you are growing several vines, allow only one shoot on each. With a solitary vine the shoots can be trained horizontally in opposite directions.

Top laterals that form can then be led vertically and all others removed. ·Side growth from verticals should be kept to 60cm (24 in), by pinching off the tips, and removed completely in winter. Also in winter cut back the main leading shoot (or shoots from a solitary vine) to hard wood.

In the second year wires will be needed to support the lateral shoots, and in winter cut back all these laterals to one or two buds. By the third year, you should have a good crop.

In all cases only one bunch of grapes should be allowed to each lateral, and the berries should be thinned to permit those remaining to swell and have room to develop and ripen. No winter heat is necessary, but a minimum of about 10–13°C (50–55°F) during flowering is an advantage. Ventilation must be given freely when possible to avoid trouble with powdery mildew. Consult nurseries for varieties to recommend as suitable for growing under glass.

Peaches, nectarines and apricots

These are ideally suited to a lean-to, and are generally best grown in a border at the foot of the wall and trained against it (preferably as fans), using securely-fastened support wires.

It is essential to obtain varieties suited to indoor culture and on suitable root-stocks. Since the availability of varieties tends to vary from place to place in the country, it is important that a specialist grower should be consulted before you buy; nurseries are usually pleased to advise. Dwarf peaches suitable for pots are sometimes advertised in the horticultural press. Apricots are slightly more difficult to crop well than peaches or nectarines.

Preparation of the soil border and training the vine can be carried out as for plants that are grown out of doors. However, under glass it is more important to keep the plants low-growing and to induce as many base branches as possible. Also pollination under glass may be poor if left to insects that find their way in. To be certain of good pollination it is better to tie a generous tuft of cotton wool to a stick, fluffing it up loosely as much as possible, and then lightly brushing it over the flowers – preferably about midday.

Good ventilation is vital to avoid

You should have a good crop of Black Hamburg grapes three years after planting

excessive temperatures, and damping-down is necessary to keep up the humidity level. Keep all water off the blossoms and off the fruit in the ripening stage, but at other times the foliage will benefit from a spray with water.

Figs

Although often thought of as exotic, good crops of figs are easily possible. The fig is usually best grown in pots since, if given an unrestricted root-run, it can smother everything else in the greenhouse. If planted in a border, the roots should be cased in with sheets of asbestos or slates or similar material. Some varieties can be placed outdoors for the summer if grown in large pots or small tubs. Always keep the plants free from weak or untidy straggly wood. Also, for best quality figs, restrict the fruit to about three per shoot. However, in the greenhouse both the current and the previous year's shoots will yield fruit. During active growth give the plants plenty of water and moderate feeding, preferably using a balanced, soluble feed. Since the roots are restricted this feeding must not be neglected, but neither should it be excessive as this will encourage rampant growth. Avoid high nitrogen feeds as these encourage lush, leafy growth.

Above: good-quality Brown Turkey figs.
Left above: fan-train Moorpark apricots against the greenhouse wall
Below left: melon Blenheim Orange

Melons

For the greenhouse it is best to grow casaba melons – those usually described in the catalogues as indoor melons. The smaller cantaloupes will grow just as well in frames.

Raise them from seed in a warm propagator in mid spring (March). The plants are best grown in large pots on greenhouse staging, using any good potting compost. Supporting wires should be fastened to the side and roof of the house, from end to end, spaced 30cm (12 in) apart. From then on culture is very similar to cucumber regarding training. There is, however, a vital difference and this is that the flowers must be pollinated. To do this first identify the female flowers by the tiny fruit behind them and pollinate by picking a male flower (that has a straight stem and no swelling) and brushing off some of its pollen onto the female flowers.

After pollination you will see the melons soon begin to swell and when it is certain that they are healthy and are continuing to grow, thin them to allow only three or four to mature on each plant. You can buy special nets to support the large, heavy fruits.

The finest flavour and aroma only comes from properly ripe fruit. The end farthest from the stalk should then be slightly soft to the touch if gently pressed with the finger. During ripening it is best to reduce watering and increase ventilation. Slight shading should be given during exceptionally bright, hot weather.

RECOMMENDED VARIETIES

PEACHES
Duke of York White-fleshed; ripens in late summer (mid July).
Hale's Early White-fleshed; ripens at the end of summer (late July).

NECTARINES
Early Rivers White-fleshed; ripens at the end of summer (late July).
Lord Napier White-fleshed; ripens in early autumn (early August).

APRICOTS
Moorpark Large, fine-flavoured fruit; deep yellow skins flushed with red; ripens in late summer to early autumn (mid July to early August).

GRAPES
Black Hamburg For cold or heated greenhouses; produces large bunches of large, fine-flavoured, black fruit.
Royal Muscadine For cold or heated greenhouses; amber-coloured, muscat-flavoured grapes.

FIGS
Brown Turkey Hardy variety, fruiting in mid autumn (early September); large, sweet, brownish-purple fruit.

MELONS
Superlative Succulent, medium-sized fruit.
Hero of Lockinge White flesh; fine flavour.
King George Richly-flavoured with orange flesh.
Emerald Gem Thick green succulent flesh with excellent flavour.

WATERING AND FEEDING GREENHOUSE PLANTS

Even today, when modern scientific knowledge should be making the issues clear, greenhouse gardeners find themselves frustrated by numerous incorrect and illogical recommendations on the subject of feeding and watering plants. Some of these are nothing more than primitive customs that have not yet been abandoned in favour of common sense.

Most pot plant failures are caused by overwatering and, to a lesser extent, by overfeeding.

WATERING

Your first important step is to learn the difference between dry, moist and water-logged soil or compost. Moist conditions should be your aim. If the soil or compost feels moist to the touch, adheres slightly to the fingers but does not ooze free water when pressed, then it is moist. However, do not press hard when testing as this can lead to the soil becoming compacted.

How much water?

The water requirements of a plant vary – often from one day to the next. For instance when the weather is cool or dull (and also in winter when growth slows down) they need far less water – sometimes hardly any if they are dormant. When, as during summer, they have warmth and lots of light, they drink enormous quantities by comparison.

The needs of a plant are also governed by its size and vigour, and whether it is flowering, fruiting or growing vigorously. For these reasons you cannot give fixed doses of water to a plant all year round. The question 'how much water should I give my plant?' cannot be answered by a

Previous page: colourful staging displays result from correct care of plants
Below: symptoms of overwatering – brown edges on the leaves of a pot primula

simple sentence. You must take into account the time of year, the nature of the plant and the prevailing conditions, and then decide.

When in doubt err on the side of less rather than more water. Most plants are able to survive drought to some degree and the symptoms of slight wilting are not serious; they will soon recover when watered. Excess water has a far more serious and insidious effect. The main symptoms are usually slow, sickly growth, yellowing foliage and wilting. But by this time the roots may be in an advanced state of rot, and it may be too late to save the plant by reducing watering. Note that wilting can be a symptom of both overwatering and underwatering, so test the compost.

Desert and water-loving plants

You must, of course, consider the nature of each plant and its natural habitat. But, strangely enough, this is not always a reliable guide for providing the best artificial conditions, for in the wild plants often have to struggle to survive. Many cacti and other succulents, for example, will grow vigorously if given far more water than they would get growing naturally.

On the other hand, aquatic plants need an abundance of water all year round. Not many of these are cultivated as pot plants, but if you are growing them they must be kept standing in water so that the potting compost is always wet.

Waterlogged soils

A waterlogged soil or compost is usually badly aerated. This encourages species of bacteria and fungi that cause rotting of plant roots. Plants with fleshy roots (like bulbs and tubers) are prone to rot if kept wet during their period of dormancy. But modern potting composts are usually based on peat; this means they will hold plenty of water without actually becoming waterlogged, and can still maintain excellent aeration. For some greenhouse plants (like columneas, orchids, brome-liads and certain palms) plenty of air with moisture is vital. You can help aeration by adding sphagnum moss, charcoal or polystyrene granules to the compost.

Insert moisture-measuring device so that the tip is completely covered by soil

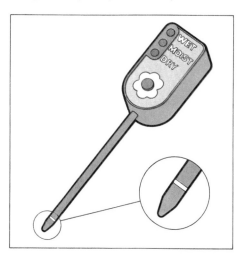

Testing for moisture

Nowadays plastic pots have become very popular. They are convenient and hygienic, being easy to clean. They check evaporation of water, so that plants growing in them need less than in clay pots. The time-honoured method of assessing whether a clay pot needs watering is to tap it with a cotton reel fixed to the end of a cane. If the compost is moist, the pot will emit a dull thud; the sound will be a higher-pitched note if the soil is dry.

Unfortunately this does not work very well with plastic pots, and a better way is to assess the moisture content by feeling the weight of the pot.

Recently, electronic devices have become available that give a rough idea of the water content of compost. They usually consist of a probe which is inserted into the compost, and a meter (or arrangement of tiny neon lights) that indicates the moisture content. With one design the scale is numbered and a booklet is supplied with the meter so that the numbers can be related to the

Rotted roots caused by excessive watering

water on the foliage. The droplets act like lenses to focus the sun's rays on the leaves and may cause burning.

The importance of clean water

Be careful what sort of water you use on your plants. Some people advocate rainwater; if the rainwater is clean, all well and good. Unfortunately it is often collected from roofs and stored in open tanks or butts, which rapidly become stagnant pools of pests, diseases and weed seeds. As you are probably using sterilized potting composts in your greenhouse, it is obviously foolish to water these with dirty rainwater. Mains drinking water is safer – even if it tends to be hard and limey. There are numerous greenhouse plants that object to lime, but they will suffer much more from the dangers inherent in dirty water.

Uneven watering gives split tomato fruits

If you do need soft water for special lime-hating plants, put out clean bowls just after it starts to rain, and store the rainwater in clean, closed vessels. Water that has been boiled for some time and then allowed to cool and settle will also be softer than tap water.

FEEDING

Avoid using animal manures in the greenhouse or for potting composts – unless they are a modern, sterilized, proprietary type. Crude manures can introduce many pests and diseases that can be dangerous to humans as well as to plants. Moreover, they often have few of the nutrients that plants require.

One of the main advantages of manures is that they improve soil texture, but modern seed and potting composts have body built in, usually by the addition of peat. Most pot plants need a higher ratio of nitrogen than plants grown in the soil

outdoors; all proprietary potting composts take this into account. If you use these products, no feeding is needed until the plants are well advanced.

The need for feeding is assessed in much the same way as watering – taking into account the vigour of the plants and the time of year. None is necessary when plants are dormant. But when plants are producing buds, flowers and fruits, some extra feeding is essential. Use a proprietary balanced fertilizer according to the maker's directions. Never give more than is suggested. 'Little and often' is a good feeding rule.

Modern feeding now takes into account the preference of some plants for acid or alkaline soils. In alkaline soils (or composts) iron, magnesium and trace elements essential to plants become 'locked in' and therefore unavailable to the plants.

These nutrients can now be restored in a special form (known as sequestered or chelated) which is easily absorbed. Avoid using hit or miss mixtures or additions of what are known as 'straight' fertilizers that supply only one or two of the basic nutrients (such as sulphate of ammonia or sulphate of potash). Properly formulated feeds for plants like tomatoes, carnations and chrysanthemums that need special nutrient ratios can be bought in proprietary form.

Foliar feeding

You can apply the basic plant nutrients (nitrogen, potassium and phosphorus) as foliar feeds – in specially formulated mixtures. A very recent product of this type includes vitamins and trace elements as well. It is particularly useful for plants that have not yet made an extensive root system, and can also be used as a general plant tonic. Seedlings, newly potted plants and cuttings often react dramatically to such feeds.

Soluble feeds

Plants can only use liquid solutions of nutrients. The quickest-acting are soluble feeds that dissolve readily in water; use these for all short-term, fast-growing plants, such as annuals and biennials. Greenhouse perennials will also benefit from liquid feeds when they are making active growth.

You can also top-dress perennials by mixing a little of a balanced, slow-acting, solid feed (such as John Innes base fertilizer or Growmore) with the top layers of the soil or compost. These will dissolve a little at each watering. Specially formulated proprietary feeds in tablet form are also obtainable.

moisture requirements of different classes of plant. As you gain experience you will find that the 'dry', 'moist' and 'wet' indications on a scale are a perfectly adequate guide.

In spite of these aids, practical experience is the best way to become confident about watering. You will eventually be able to tell all you need to know by feeling the compost with your fingers and by letting the appearance of your plants tell you what they require.

How to water

A common recommendation is to water freely, when you do water, and then leave the plant alone until the pot is almost dry again. This is a helpful guide for some plants – but not all. For example, erratic watering of this kind will not do for tomatoes as it will certainly lead to blossom end rot or cracked fruit; and many ornamental plants (such as fuchsias and begonias) may react by dropping buds or flowers.

Never give so much water that large quantities run from the drainage holes of pots or trays. This will soon carry away any soluble fertilizers in the compost. (A good way to water seed trays or pots is to use a fine-mist sprayer. This will thoroughly penetrate the compost without washing away any nutrients or loosening the seedlings.

During warm weather many plants enjoy an overhead spray. This cleans the foliage and aids plant respiration. Once again you must use your common sense as to how much water to apply. Do not spray open blooms because the tender petals can easily be damaged and brown rot or grey mould may occur. Also, in very sunny greenhouses, avoid getting

USING THE SUB-STAGE AREA IN THE GREENHOUSE

The area under the greenhouse staging can be a very useful place for growing plants – provided it is not already being used to house garden oddments. Just how useful depends largely on the greenhouse design, but with a little planning most of these often-neglected areas can be made very productive.

Never be tempted to use the space under the staging in your greenhouse as a gardening 'glory hole'. Keep some clean bins, bags of compost, clean pots or boxes there by all means, but remember that dirty rubbish will harbour pests and diseases and make cleaning the greenhouse a tedious business.

Plants grown under the staging should not be set directly on the greenhouse floor. Cover the ground with plastic sheeting covered, in turn, with a layer of gravel or coarse sand; alternatively, place the pots on a slatted or mesh stage raised a few centimetres above the ground. This will prevent the plant roots from entering the soil, and also keep soil pests or worms from getting into the drainage holes.

Use common sense when positioning your plants; put those needing most light at the back in the case of a glass-to-ground house, and at the front when the greenhouse has a base wall.

Light areas
Undoubtedly the area under the staging is most versatile in a glass-to-ground greenhouse since it will receive plenty of light. The more light that penetrates the better, since a wider range of plants can then be accommodated. In the Dutch-light type of house, with slightly sloping sides, there is specially good illumination and plants set well back will get almost as much light as plants on the staging top. In all cases light can be increased by using slatted or mesh-topped staging. Some overhead light then usually finds its way through.

Try to prevent plant debris like dead leaves, faded flowers and drips from watering from falling off the plants on the staging onto the plants below; water or organic material left lying on plant foliage for any length of time can cause brown markings or instigate rot and fungoid growth. One way of avoiding this is to stand potted plants in plastic trays that have a layer of coarse gravel

in the bottom; space the trays apart to let light through.

Dark areas
In the case of the base wall type of house the under-stage area will probably be very gloomy. This means you will have to be more selective in what you put there, but for some plants shade can be an advantage – even vital. In a few cases no light at all is wanted, for instance when blanching and forcing vegetables like chicory, rhubarb and endive. For these the area will have to be deliberately blacked out with black polythene. Where there is little light and not enough space to make the area useful for more ordinary plants, you can always grow mushrooms. These do not need light (though there is no need to black out completely) and they are easy to grow in containers filled with special compost that has been spawned by the supplier. Full growing instructions are issued with the containers.

Above: mushrooms like these Agaricus hortensis *are very easy to grow under the staging, because they do not need light. Right: sub-tropical* Calathea mackoyana *is a colourful shade-lover*

Where light is extremely poor, very many ferns will thrive and can be used simply to give decoration to what would otherwise be an uninteresting spot, or to supply cut fronds for floral decoration, or as pot ferns for the house. What type of ferns you can grow depends on the temperature of the greenhouse. It is possible to buy spores of selected varieties of hardy, half-hardy and tender ferns in separate packets, to get initial stock.

Warm greenhouses
If the greenhouse is a warm one or, at least, has a congenial temperature in winter, many exceedingly beautiful and colourful foliage plants of a sub-tropical nature will live happily under the staging

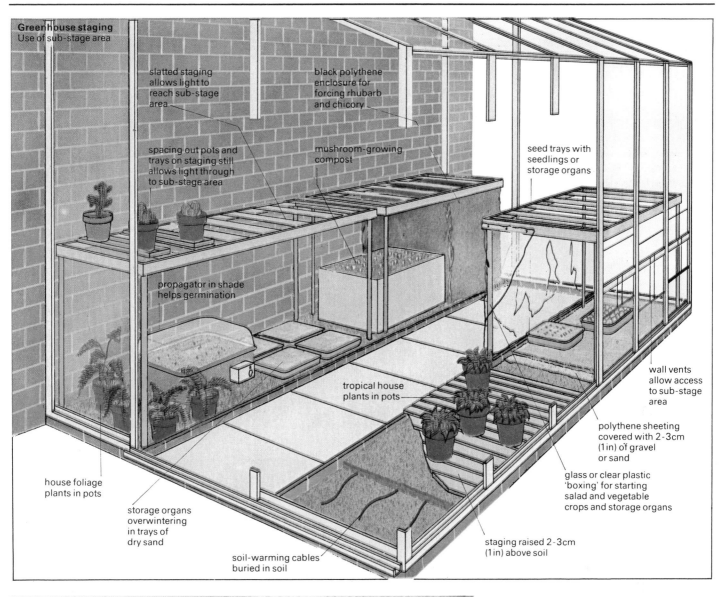

Greenhouse staging
Use of sub-stage area

slatted staging allows light to reach sub-stage area

black polythene enclosure for forcing rhubarb and chicory

spacing out pots and trays on staging still allows light through to sub-stage area

mushroom-growing compost

seed trays with seedlings or storage organs

propagator in shade helps germination

wall vents allow access to sub-stage area

tropical house plants in pots

polythene sheeting covered with 2-3cm (1in) of gravel or sand

house foliage plants in pots

glass or clear plastic 'boxing' for starting salad and vegetable crops and storage organs

storage organs overwintering in trays of dry sand

staging raised 2-3cm (1in) above soil

soil-warming cables buried in soil

– in their natural jungle habitat they would enjoy considerable shade. Suitable plants include maranta (prayer plant), calathea, ctenanthe, foliage begonias, peperomia, *Fittonia argyroneura* and *Dieffenbachia picta* all have exotically marked and coloured leaves. Plants of the GESNERIACEAE family enjoy shade, and most of them have charming foliage and delightful flowers. These include strepto-carpus (Cape primrose), sinningia (gloxinia), saintpaulia (African violet), smithiantha (temple bells), achimenes and *Rechsteineria leucotricha*.

Raising the temperature

You can raise the temperature of the area under the staging easily and cheaply, especially when the greenhouse has a base wall that will help retain warmth. In some cases the space can be 'boxed' or 'cased' with glass or plastic so that temperatures can be elevated quite considerably. The simplest method of heating is to use soil-warming cables.

In a glass-to-ground house useful early salad crops can be raised in soil-warmed beds under the staging – lettuce, beet, radish, carrot and numerous sprouting vegetables including mustard and cress. Later in the year these warmed beds can be used for starting tubers – like dahlias, begonias, sinningia (gloxinia), canna and the like – into growth and also for seed germination. Propagators can be sited under the staging where the shade will be an advantage for most forms of seed germination and for establishing cuttings.

Cold greenhouses
Where there is little or no warmth, the area can be employed for storing dormant plants over the winter and for keeping overwintering storage organs or roots such as dahlias, summer-flowering greenhouse bulbs, chrysanthemum stools and the roots of tender garden plants. Most storage organs are best kept in boxes of clean sand or peat, but many roots have to be prevented from drying out completely during winter and you should make sure you have easy access to them for regular inspection. Some designs of greenhouse have ground-level vents

Above: three sub-stage beauties, (left)
Ctenanthe oppenheimiana tricolor,
(centre) smithiantha and (right)
Aeschynanthus nanus

allowing the under-stage area to be reached from the outside. This can be useful for cultivating salad crops.

Growing-on pot plants
Much of the general growing-on of pot plants can be done under the staging. Popular pot plants like cineraria, calceolaria, primula, polyanthus, cyclamen, coleus and ornamental capsicum can be housed there from the seedling stage to the size when they can be put into their final pots. For many of these plants the diffused light of the under-stage area is a great advantage and even when you move them to the top of the staging for display the glass will need to be shaded. The under-stage area is particularly useful to these plants when they are being grown on during the summer months. Most house plants, too, do not demand full light and can be raised from seed or cuttings under the staging for later removal to the house. Established house

plants can also be given a holiday under the staging from time to time – they will appreciate the humidity.

Raising bedding plants
In the glass-to-ground house the under-stage area is invaluable in late winter to mid spring (January to March) when it is time to raise bedding plants and your greenhouse tends to become very over-crowded. As well as the initial germi-

nation of bedding plants, the trays and boxes can be kept under the staging for a time until the seedlings are well estab-lished. Take care, however, that the area is not too gloomy or the seedlings may become weak and spindly. The idea is to protect the seedlings from sunlight rather than to cast them into deep shade.

Left: exotic green and white foliage of Dieffenbachia picta, *a lover of jungle-like habitat*
Right: Sinningia speciosa, *whose tubers can be started in sub—stage warmed beds*

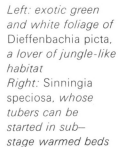

RESTING PLANTS FOR THE WINTER

For very many plants a winter rest is essential for their continued development and success but, in the greenhouse, some plants that would naturally be growing almost all year round can also be kept dormant over the winter to economize on heating and lighting. How you treat plants as they approach their winter rest is extremely important. So, too, is the way you treat them over the winter, and how you care for storage organs like bulbs, corms, tubers and rhizomes.

Many tender plants can survive cold winters in an unheated greenhouse. For instance, many of the summer-flowering bulbs use this cool period to develop embryo flowers and leaves while appearing dormant externally. Others (like tender herbaceous plants and exotic greenhouse perennials), if kept in a dry environment, slow their growth rate right down until they are ready to flourish again in the spring.

Plants with storage organs
Plants that overwinter in the form of storage organs include all the summer-flowering bulbs, tubers such as gloxinia, begonia, and gloriosa, and rhizomes like achimenes, smithiantha (temple bells) and canna. A critical time for these comes after the flowers fade; they then begin to store the foods needed for strong growth in the following year.

In the case of bulbs the entire flower in embryo form is developed inside the bulb, starting after flowering and continuing to form until the foliage begins to wither. So at this time, care with regard to feeding and watering will reward you with a good performance after the plant is started into growth again the following year. Do not chop the foliage off bulbs or tie the leaves in knots as soon as the flowers have faded. Do all you can to keep growth luxuriant and healthy; give frequent liquid feeds, foliar feeds and pesticide sprays to keep the foliage free from pests and to build up the storage organ so that it will grow well the following year. Only when the foliage begins to die down naturally should you gradually reduce watering and feeding. In most cases you can allow the soil in the pots to dry out slowly. Then turn the pots on their sides and store the plants (dry) in

this manner in a frost-free place for the winter period.

With some plants (such as tuberous-rooted begonia and gloxinia) it is better to remove the storage organs and store them in clean, dry sand after removing any adhering potting compost, dead roots and foliage. Drying out as a winter rest, however, is not a general rule. There are cases where storage organs are better kept slowly growing. A typical example is hippeastrum (often wrongly called amaryllis). This is an evergreen bulbous plant that will produce far better blooms if you give it just enough warmth and moisture to maintain the foliage; 5–7°C (40–45°F) is an adequate temperature. Leave plants with brittle tubers or rhizomes (like gloriosa and achimenes) undisturbed, and store them in pots of dry soil on their sides. These plants will have multiplied considerably during the growing season. Wait until it is time to restart them into growth in the spring before splitting or dividing them. If you damage them then they are much more likely to heal quickly, but if the organs are damaged just before the winter rest period there is a greater risk of rot setting in.

Protecting with fungicides
To help reduce the likelihood of rot or fungal attack, it often helps to dip the storage organs in a solution of benomyl and allow them to dry thoroughly before storing. Fungicidal dusts (used according to maker's instructions) can also be beneficial and there are several suitable proprietary products on the market.

Ripening before storing
Some plants, particularly those with bulbs or corms, may not flower well unless they undergo a short ripening process before storage for the winter. Typical of these is polianthes (tuberose); it likes to be given a 'sun bath' so expose it to as much sunshine as the late summer and early autumn (July and August) will provide before immersing it in dry sand for the winter.

Place dahlia tubers in the greenhouse (with their stems pointing downwards) for a few weeks, to allow all sap to drain

Above right: a dusting with fungicide is an aid against rot; right: drain sap from dahlias before storing

before storing in dry peat or sand. Cut back chrysanthemum growth, lift the plants, free the roots from soil and then store them in trays of sterilized potting compost until it is time to restart them in late spring or early summer (April–May).

Herbaceous and pot plants
When herbaceous plants and perennial pot plants in the greenhouse begin to slow down or reach dormancy in autumn, you can prune them back – not too severely – so that they will not take up so much storage room. Most plants with ordinary roots should not be allowed to go completely dry over the winter but, on the other hand, never let them get too moist. Much also depends on winter temperature, and where this is very low – perhaps approaching freezing – keep the plants almost dry. Wet, cold conditions are certain to cause root rot. Tender plants like greenhouse fuchsia, pelargonium and even the more exotic subjects like strelitzia, *Nerium oleander*, maranta (prayer plant) and aphelandra, will usually survive a very cold winter if kept on the dry side. Some, like maranta and other foliage plants, may come through the cold of winter looking the worse for wear, but

new growth rapidly occurs in spring when you recommence watering. Shabby growth can then be removed.

If you grow standard fuchsias, take great care not to rest them to the extent that they die back. Although growth will resume in spring the head could fail and new shoots come from the lower stem.

When whips (the supporting stems of standards) are being grown on from rooted cuttings, they must not be allowed to rest too much. Keep them growing slowly by maintaining adequate temperature and moisture. This applies to all plants grown as standards including abutilon, pelargonium and chrysanthemum (marguerite).

Greenhouse atmosphere in winter

The greenhouse atmosphere is also important to the well-being of resting and overwintering plants. It is vital to avoid excessive humidity, so provide plenty of ventilation whenever weather permits. Home greenhouse owners tend to be afraid to ventilate. Winters in Britain are rarely freezing for long periods and often there are very mild spells. Since most people grow plants needing little more than frost-free conditions there is no reason why ventilation is not possible much of the time.

Special care is needed if you heat the greenhouse with paraffin heaters. Oil produces about its own volume of water on combustion. This leads to much condensation and a very wet atmosphere unless there is adequate ventilation. In such conditions dormant plants are very prone to fungal troubles. The main enemy is grey mould (botrytis) that attacks both dead and living vegetable matter.

It forms a greyish-brown furry mould that, when disturbed, distributes clouds of dust-like spores and so spread the fungus to other plants.

If your paraffin heater is fitted with a humidity trough, do not fill it with water in winter and, of course, never damp down the greenhouse. To help protect resting plants from grey mould in winter a wise routine measure is to fumigate (on a still day) with TCNB smokes. In winter this is better than the use of wet sprays, since it avoids raising humidity.

If you have an automatic watering system, allow it to go dry, or shut it off, for the winter months and water by hand. This will lessen the danger of plants – and air – becoming too moist.

Fumigation protects against grey mould, a common infection in winter

COMMON PESTS AND DISEASES IN THE GREENHOUSE

Although pests and diseases are generally easier to control under glass than in the open, they will multiply and spread more freely unless you make routine checks and take prompt action. In addition, whereas winter in the outdoor garden is a fairly trouble-free time, many common pests and diseases can be troublesome all year round in the greenhouse.

A clean and tidy greenhouse will often deter many pests and diseases. By *not* storing rubbish and garden oddments there, you deprive pests of excellent hiding places, and by throwing away dead foliage and flowers you can discourage fungus diseases such as moulds, mildews and rusts. Make a daily inspection of the underside of the foliage; many pests and diseases make their first appearance here. Discard plants that are sickly for unknown reasons; they can endanger others.

Plants with pale or distorted flowers or foliage (sometimes stunted or mottled, or with striped blooms that fail to open properly) may be suffering from one or other of a number of virus diseases. These diseases can be spread by sap-sucking insects (like greenfly), by knives or scissors, or by your fingers. There is no cure for virus diseases and affected plants are best burned. Tomatoes are especially vulnerable, and ideally grown alone.

Flying pests

Many familiar garden pests invade the greenhouse. Those that fly can enter through the vents. As a good preventive measure, fit screens of muslin to greenhouse vents in summer. This will stop butterflies and moths getting in; the eggs they lay may turn overnight into caterpillars that can do enormous damage before you spot them. Birds can also enter through the vents and may do much damage to plants, besides injuring themselves while trying to escape.

Crawling pests

'Creepy crawlies' may be brought indoors on the bottom of pots that have been standing in the garden. Slugs and snails are easily controlled by the usual baits used outdoors. These pests will often

*Above left: earwigs hide during the day
in cracks and crevices in the greenhouse,
emerging at night to seek out their prey
Left: the aftermath of an earwig attack
on the flower petals of a chrysanthemum
Top: aphides clustered on a rose bud
Above right: the common garden snail,
unless controlled, will climb up glass
walls of a greenhouse and eat seedlings
Above: whitefly sucking sap from a leaf*

may not realize that earwigs are the culprits, and the cause of the damage will remain a mystery. Chrysanthemums need special protection so use BHC dusts liberally. Ant bait is also often effective against earwigs, and can be put in possible hiding places.

Aphides and whitefly

Aphides (or plant lice) are a group of insects that include greenfly and blackfly as well as numerous other closely-related pests that suck plant sap. Few plants are safe from attack, so take routine preventive measures. Systemic pesticides give long-term protection under glass, and there are numerous quick-acting products now sold. Those containing malathion act very quickly, but the old-fashioned liquid derris pesticides are still efficient and very safe.

climb up the glass sides and gain access to pots and trays on the staging. Just one slug or snail can eat a whole tray of small seedlings during the night.

Never stand pots directly on the ground soil of the greenhouse (or outdoors). Stand them on sharp shingle, tile, stone or plastic. This prevents worms entering through the drainage holes. If they do get in, the constant disturbance to the roots will make plants wilt.

Ants have a similar effect, but can be eradicated with a proprietary ant bait; there are several kinds (all very effective) on the market. Woodlice are not, as many believe, harmless to plants and they are especially damaging to seedlings. You will find these pests hiding among greenhouse rubbish. Dusts containing BHC will control them.

Earwigs can hide in the smallest cracks and crevices of the greenhouse structure. There they stay unseen during the day. At night they fly out (it is often not known that they can fly) and eat plants – flowers particularly – leaving the petals holed and ragged. Because they operate at night you

Whitefly has become a serious greenhouse pest. It often infests outdoor weeds, like nettles, and will then be a source of trouble to any nearby greenhouse in summer, and overwinter in greenhouses that are free from frost. In appearance, the fly is minute, with pale grey wings. Like aphides, it sucks sap and also causes leaves and surfaces below them to become sticky with honeydew secretion. This often encourages a growth of black mould which, though not harmful, makes the plants look most unsightly.

Fortunately, a recently-introduced pesticide called resmethrin is particularly effective for whitefly control, and generally useful for other similar pests. Apply it by spraying. Alternatively, malathion and BHC smokes can be used.

Thrips and red spider mite

The tiny thrips cause foliage to become marked with whitish patches that are often encircled by dark specks. To check for their presence, put white paper below the foliage and then shake the leaves. The thrips fall off and you will be able to see them squirming against the white background. Most general pesticides will control thrips; systemics will be absorbed into the plant tissues and remain effective for a long time.

If, during summer, foliage becomes yellow and mottled and tends to fall, suspect a pest called red spider mite. If you look at the undersides of the leaves with a powerful magnifying glass, what you will see (if the pest is present) is a very tiny, mite-like creature and minute round, whitish eggs. In large and severe infestations the mites will show up as many thousands of pale-reddish 'spiders' spinning fine webbing. Since they enjoy hot, dry conditions, you can discourage them by keeping up humidity. Fumigation with azobenzene is very effective, but

Right: the red spider mite will attack foliage, turning it yellow and mouldy
Below: thrips, too, attack foliage but can be controlled by a general pesticide
Below right: the tiny sciarid fly, whose maggot will infest compost unless killed
Bottom: tomato plant, showing the damage caused by sciarid fly maggots

brownish-grey, furry mould which, if disturbed, distributes a cloud of fine 'dust' – the spores that spread the disease. On tomatoes the mould will cause flowers and fruit to drop, and fruit may be marked with small whitish rings with a black speck at the centre. Lettuce and chrysanthemums are especially prone to attack. To check the disease, increase ventilation and, at night, lower the humidity. Benlate sprays and TCNB fumigation are excellent controls and preventives of grey mould.

Using pesticides

Whenever possible, buy pesticides especially designed for greenhouse use. Read the labels carefully because some plants can be damaged by certain pesticides. In certain cases you can simply remove these plants from the greenhouse, or cover them with plastic bags, while other plants are being treated. Follow all safety precautions exactly (especially where edible crops are concerned) and, in the enclosed atmosphere of your greenhouse, take care that you do not inhale any pesticides yourself.

numerous greenhouse plants may be slightly damaged by this treatment, so be sure to check with the maker's label. Liquid extract of derris (not dusts) is a good general control if applied thoroughly.

Sciarid fly

With the now widespread use of peat composts, sciarid fly maggots are becoming increasingly common. These are tiny, whitish, wriggling worms infesting the composts, or the peat spread over staging. There will also be tiny flies about – the 'worms' being their maggots. These maggots can do enormous harm to plant roots, especially seedlings, and may also eat lower parts of stems. Moist conditions

encourage them. Water with a malathion insecticide, but try to keep moisture lower subsequently. The flies must be killed since they are the source of the trouble. Most general insecticides will do this.

Fungus diseases

Two very common diseases caused by fungi are damping-off of seedlings and grey mould. If pricked-out seedlings topple over, it is a sure sign of damping-off. Always water in with Cheshunt compound as a precaution. Damping-off is less prevalent now that modern sterilized composts are used. Grey mould (or botrytis) will attack both living and dead plant tissue. It is usually seen as a

THE MODERN CONSERVATORY

STYLES OF CONSERVATORY

Here we look at some other types of conservatory structures and how you can link them with both house and garden. The following examples illustrate both the traditional and the new in a range of styles that can be suitably adapted to a contemporary setting.

A feature such as a conservatory is something of a hybrid, being neither a free-standing greenhouse nor an integral part of the building. It fulfills both functions in part, acting as an informal living room that can be richly furnished with vegetation.

Long ago conservatories were invariably ornate and usually large, needing a corresponding budget to maintain them in peak condition. Today our style of living has changed and houses are smaller and more intimate. It makes sense therefore to build a conservatory that will not only preserve the form of its parent building but remain within your financial limits as well.

Once you have budgeted you can think about the style and possible position of

Left and previous page: this custom-built conservatory room was designed as a straightforward addition for an owner who wanted a room to use more as a living room-sun lounge than a plant conservatory with the latter's implications of humidity. The simple timber structure follows the lines of the house to provide continuity. Walls are brick-based with bricks carefully selected to match those of the original house wall – now part of the interior

the new feature. The latter will be determined to some extent by the direction of the sun and by the point of access from the house. In general terms however a conservatory will look more at home in a situation where it extends the visual line of a roof, fitting snugly into the angle formed by a projecting wall. This technique has been well exploited in the example shown at left.

White is the traditional colour for interior and exterior painting, but re-

Below and right: architect Stephen Gardiner's glass-walled structure acts as a total contrast to the owner's more conventional red brick house. The informal arrangement of pot plants, climbers and uncut grass softens the dramatic tent-like framework. Although it appears free-standing, the conservatory is in fact connected to the house by a glass-walled walk-through, a solid wood slat ceiling emphasizing its light, open atmosphere

member to use common sense and respect existing colour schemes when making your choice.

Planting is just as important outside the conservatory as inside and provides the ideal link between house and garden. Notice how foliage softens virtually all the examples shown, the walls becoming incidental and the view synonymous with the garden.

We have already emphasized the importance of a well-paved, non-slip floor and it is worth bearing in mind that the choice of a surface does much to influence the mood of the overall composition. Natural

materials such as slate or stone tend to look and feel cool; they are traditional, as many of the fine historical conservatories bear witness, but on the debit side they tend to become slippery unless regularly scrubbed down.

As with any variety of floor paving, make sure that the joints are carefully grouted in the case of tiles, and neatly pointed for brickwork. The stable-type paviors are attractive, but rarely used these days. They are dark blue and the size of bricks, the surface being divided into cubes to give a finished effect not unlike bars of chocolate laid side by side.

Whatever the flooring, make sure that levels are true; with a slight fall there should be a gully available for drainage.

So far we have suggested primarily traditional materials and methods of construction. Since the 1920s there have been striking advances in building technology and this has certainly been echoed in the design of the conservatory's close relation – the greenhouse. It is surprising therefore that so few conservatories take full advantage of such obvious develop-ments as lightweight alloys, geodetic (dome-shaped) construction, and improved glazing techniques. Where conventional ideas are set aside, the results can be not only striking but eminently practical, as shown on the previous page, where the self-contained outside conservatory room is linked to the house by a glass-walled walk-through.

There is no rule that says a conservatory should be at ground level. Many flat-dwellers have no direct access to a garden and here there is obviously scope for a planned conversion that can fulfill a variety of functions.

In the final analysis, should you feel that a modern approach is out of keeping with your own environment, and should you also be able to afford a substantial budget, it might be worth considering a conservatory designed and built by a specialist firm. Here the expertise of craftsmen is brought into play and a superb finished result may be achieved.

Traditional designs can be recreated using up-to-date techniques, thus providing a visually-appropriate structure according to the style of the setting.

If you are lucky enough to own such a conservatory, it is important to handle the situation with sympathy. In other words, the whole setting must be considered as a design exercise. There is nothing worse than a superb building that sits in a poorly-planned area of crazy paving and dwarf walling.

Far left, below: a traditional design that would blend well with most settings, by the conservatory specialists Richardsons of Darlington. It serves equally well as an extra living room or plant conservatory-cum-sun room.

Far left, bottom: built out and at a lower level, this conservatory interior provides plenty of room for a dining or work table area. The 3-tier jardinière with trellised back gives scope for extra plants without taking up valuable floor space

Left, below: there is nothing harsh about this conservatory; its delicate glazing bars and fanlight blend well with the period-style house. Brick paviors and age-old York stone combine with climbers and plants to produce a charming atmosphere Below: the contemporary approach at its best in a two-tone colour scheme with elegant furniture and dramatic plants. This above-ground conservatory room with its view of sky and chimney pots provides a feeling of space rare in the city

THE CONSERVATORY ROOM

You may have an old conservatory in need of renovation or a spare room that you can adapt to the benefit of plants and people alike. Here we present our ideas to show you how to make a charming conservatory room and cultivate plants within.

Little can be done to prevent the disappearance of the larger houses and their accompanying conservatories that are often vast and separate from the main building. They were expensive to keep up in their heyday and the expense of running such places in modern times is formidable.

But the other types of conservatory – annexes to the house and of more modest proportions – are still in evidence and need not share the same fate as their larger counterparts. These smaller buildings, originally conceived in Victorian times, vary greatly both in shape and style. Some still date back to that era and are easily recognized by their highly ornate design, domed roofs, moulded iron gantries and pillars. But with the passage of time styles have changed.

A true conservatory should be more than simply a home for plants, it should also provide an extra living room, a pleasant place for tea, for dinner, for friends, for relaxation – an oasis. So if you have such a spot, why not rescue it from the clutter of old toys, lawn-mowers and bric-à-brac? As long as it's not in such a

state of disrepair that it really defies restoration, there is no excuse for not refurbishing what has become little more than a storage area.

Providing heat

Nowadays heating should not be a problem as long as your conservatory is a half-brick structure, as most of the older types are, and it is built onto the house wall so that frost is unlikely to creep in. Anyhow, efficient paraffin heaters are available today that are very cheap to run and will prevent this.

If you can go to the expense of providing extra warmth, the plant world is at your command, and you will have an enviable display of plants during winter. However, being practical and with your bank balance in mind, we will describe a simple frost-free conservatory.

The basic requirements

Naturally, you could lavish money on the interior design of your conservatory, but all you really need is a water tap and a central paved or non-slip floor on which to arrange your furniture. Tiled floors are expensive and beautiful but may be treacherous when wet.

Open beds around the interior perimeter of the conservatory should be left and are best edged with kerbings or bricks; railway sleepers are a good alternative – all will prevent soil spillage. Include greenhouse staging along one side but do keep the house wall free so that climbing plants can be shown off to full advantage. The borders need to be wide enough – say 90cm (3 ft) – to accommodate a reasonable range of plants for year-round flowering. Always remember that in an ordinary greenhouse the plants are the sole occupants and you the caretaker. In the true conservatory you and your plants share a home.

Problems of space

If space is limited, you may have to forget about borders altogether and grow plants in tubs, but don't be discouraged. Get the largest tubs you can and try to keep to one size. If you're going to paint them, stick to one colour such as plain white; nothing looks worse than a motley assortment of pots, urns and planters in all the colours of the rainbow. Do not compete artificially with the brilliant, natural colour of your plants.

If, on the other hand, you have plenty of room, a small pool built in the centre of the conservatory, with perhaps a fountain playing merrily away, would give a superb focal point. But, as a word of warning, border the pool with a low, wide wall, say 45cm (18 in) high and 23cm (9 in) wide. This should stop children in particular from taking an unexpected bath and save any fish with which you may have stocked your pool from undue alarm. A pool is not advisable if you have small children.

Types of furnishings

Your next adventure will be to choose furniture for the conservatory. The choice is wide and really a matter for your own taste. Upholstered styles, however, must be excluded. Conservatories are of necessity humid and with all the water you're going to be dispensing, stuffed settees or chairs will soon be reduced to little more than culture media for a host of moulds. But you can make a free choice from metal, wood and cane, or plastics.

Tubs and urns come in a vast range of styles, colours and materials. Try to match your tubs with your furniture to get the best effect. Empty wooden tubs and concrete urns are light enough to lift about but filled with 25kg (56 lb) of compost this is no fun. Fibreglass ones, modern or classical reproductions, are light and extremely tough.

Planted-out conservatory room with space for relaxation and entertainment

The positioning of your furniture must depend on how you have laid out your beds and pots. If you have made a central focal point by using a free-standing tree or pool, don't clutter the conservatory. Try placing a bench or settee with its back to one of the borders or putting a low coffee table in front with two chairs on either side. This will enable you to view and enjoy the greater part of the room from one position.

Plants for the conservatory

Having organized your basic structure, don't spend all your money on furnishings before stocking up with plants. When entertaining in your conservatory room you can always import furniture from other rooms for the occasion.

Wall shrubs and climbers

You should now mount the house wall with wires or a trellis since most of the plants for this wall will cling by tendrils, or via twine, or be low-growing shrub types. The border next to the wall can be narrow – 60cm (24 in) in width is ample. But it is best to dig it out to a depth of 45–60cm (18–24 in) and, along with the other borders, fill it with compost such as J.I. No 3. Try to use evergreen climbers as bare stems are out of place in a conservatory where the last thing you want is a feeling of bleakness.

Key to planting plan

1	Jasminum polyanthum	13	Nerium oleander
2	Trachycarpus fortunei	14	Grevillea robusta
3	Jacaranda	15	Salvia leucantha
4	Prostranthera rotundifolia	16	Phoenix canariensis
5	Gerbera jamesonii	17	Nerium oleander
6	Hibiscus rosa-sinensis	18	Rhodochiton atrosanguineum
7	Tibouchina semidecandra	19	Hibiscus rosa-sinensis
8	Protea	20	Bougainvillea
9	Clivia miniata	21	Agave americana
10	Strelitzia reginae		
11	Grevillea rosmarinifolia		
12	Bletilla striata		

Conservatories in corner areas can be laid out with an adaptation of this plan simply by following the diagonal **A–B**.

Conservatory

Plan

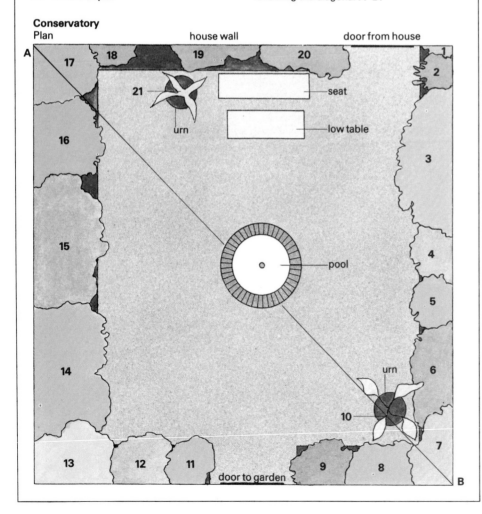

house wall · door from house

A · 17 · 18 · 19 · 20 · 1 · 2

21 · seat · low table · 3

16

15 · pool · 4

5

14 · urn · 6

10 · 7

13 · 12 · 11 · 9 · 8 · B

door to garden

The winter-flowering jasmine *Jasminum polyanthum* is easy, reliable and astonishingly vigorous too. The clusters of starry, heavily banana-scented white flowers will fill the whole place with an exotic perfume from early to mid spring (February to late March). You will rarely see it flower as you will if you grow it like this. It needs plenty of water so don't let it dry out. You should also cut it back severely after flowering, otherwise the whole wall will be taken over.

Left: Plumbago capensis *remains in bloom throughout the summer*
Below: the showy Bougainvillea glabra
Below right: Gloriosa glabra

Albizia lophantha (sometimes known as the pink siris, or Nemu tree) is a lovely shrub when grown against a wall. The finely-divided leaves are attractive in themselves but when the pale lemon, fluffy flowers appear in winter (borne in profusion from December onwards), it is a truly magnificent sight. When seen in the half light or dusk, these flowers possess an almost luminous, ethereal quality. It will grow fast and if you need to prune it remove only the previous year's wood immediately after flowering. Albizia is closely related to acacia and so hates hard pruning and may die back as a result.

Streptosolen jamesonii is a loose-growing shrub that needs support. Orange flowers appear in large clusters from early to late summer (May to July) after which you can prune it. It's a forgiving plant and copes with pruning surgery quite well. Watch out for greenfly though. They seem to be very fond of this plant, and whitefly have been known to cause problems as well. Sprayings of malathion at five-day intervals over a couple of weeks will soon put paid to them.

Plumbago capensis (Cape leadwort) is superb for clothing walls. Its showy heads of light-blue flowers appear throughout most of the summer. *P.c.* Alba is a white form that some people prefer.

Eccremocarpus scaber (Chilean glory flower), a type of climbing plant that becomes woody, is to be recommended. It is a vigorous plant and produces scarlet and yellow flowers throughout the British summer. Do not be afraid to cut it back hard each year. It can become untidy if left to its own devices. A rare yellow form, *E.s.* Lutea, can sometimes be found.

Rhodochiton atrosanguineum (purple bells) is a curious though unspectacular climber that is well worth trying. This quaint plant with slender stems bears drooping, blackish-purple flowers in summer and makes an unusual display.

Passiflora caerulea, the common blue passion flower, should in no circumstances be planted under glass because it is far too vigorous. It grows well on a sunny wall out of doors unless you live in a particularly cold area. It is better to make room for *P. antioquiensis* (or *Tacsonia van-volxemii*), one of the red passion flowers. It will grow and flower well when established and is best trained up the walls and across the roof so that the hanging red flowers can be seen to their best advantage. *P. racemosa*, that has scarlet and purple flowers, is worth establishing. Both require a lot of room, though, and do take a while to settle in before producing flowers.

Another climber that can be shy about coming into flower when young is, surprisingly, one of the honeysuckles, *Lonicera hildebrandiana*. It is far too tender for all but the warmest areas but, where space allows, this giant honey-

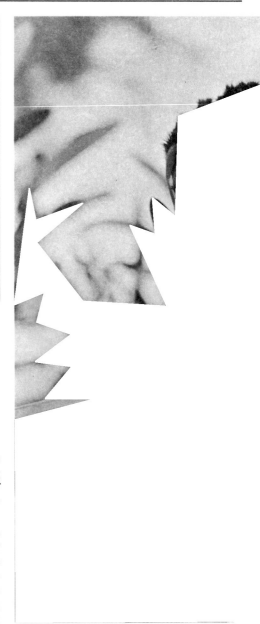

suckle should be grown. Huge, leathery leaves, 15–18cm (6–7 in) long, make the plant seem uncharacteristic of the family. But when you see the 10–15cm (4–6 in) long, creamy-white flowers changing to yellow and occasionally flushed with orange, there is no mistaking it or its truly delightful perfume.

Two climbers you might like to bear in mind that do better out of pots are the *Bougainvillea glabra* and *Gloriosa rothschildiana*. The bougainvillea and its many hybrids with showy bracts of pink, salmon-pink, orange, purple and white, is spectacular in summer. *G. rothschildiana* is a climbing lily that dies back to a tuber each autumn. The reflexed orange and yellow sepals and petals live up to their name of 'glorious'.

Border shrubs and perennials

The borders along the sides of the conservatory can be planted with numerous shrubs and herbaceous plants. Always treat this part of the conservatory as though you were planting a shrub border in the garden, and plan beforehand. The following suggestions will help you to make your choice.

Nerium oleander (oleander) is a large leafy shrub bearing pink, rose-red or white flowers that can be single, semi-double or double. There are also variegated forms that are worth searching for. Always choose a scented variety: some plants offered for sale are unscented and the loss of that heavy, vanilla-like odour is a great pity.

Hibiscus rosa-sinensis comes in such a wide range of colours nowadays that a choice is difficult. Large flowers, both double and single, can be had in deep rose, scarlet, orange, maroon and even yellow. They'll grow into sturdy bushes in

Above left: long-flowering Tibouchina urvilleana *need pruning back in spring*
Above: Clivia miniata, *the Kaffir lily*
Right: Protea nerifolia, *upright in habit, likes full sunlight under glass*
Below right: daisy-like Gerbera jamesonii
Far right: Agave americana Variegata *may take 50 years to reach maturity*

the border and these, together with the oleanders, will probably need pruning after a while. However, do not worry if you prune in mid spring (March) as they will come to no harm.

One shrub you should not be without is *Tibouchina urvilleana* (Brazilian spider flower). It has large, velvety, deep purple flowers right up till early winter (November) and the soft, hairy leaves develop orange tints before falling. Cut it back hard in mid spring (March) to prevent it from dominating a whole border.

You will probably be familiar with that fast-growing plant *Grevillea robusta* (silk bark oak). Where space allows it should certainly be allowed to develop. Apart from its silky, lacinate leaves it can, when old and large enough, produce clusters of bright orange flowers.

The smaller *G. rosmarinifolia* is a cousin that bears no resemblance in size or leaf. It grows to 1·8m (6 ft) and looks almost gorse-like from a distance. The flowers are freely produced even on a young plant and are bright red.

Palms, despite what some people would have us believe, love to have a free root run and you should try *Trachycarpus fortunei* (fan palm) that grows slowly up to 3m (10 ft) or so, *Neanthe bella* (dwarf parlour palm) that rarely exceeds 90cm (3 ft) and the feathery *Phoenix canariensis*. The last will eventually become very large so you will either have

to take an axe to it or have the roof raised. There is, however, a dwarf form, *P. roebelinii*, that grows slowly to 1·8m (6 ft).

Other shrubs that will do well in your border are proteas, with their huge quilled flowers and stiff, upright growth. They require full sunlight to do well and their root systems are much happier in a border than in a pot. Jacarandas are primarily foliage plants with soft, ferny leaves, but given time they will produce clusters of lovely blue flowers.

Prostantheras are not only valuable for

their aromatic foliage but also for the freedom with which they produce their lovely flowers. *P. rotundifolia*, a neat, little shrub that grows to 90cm (3 ft), bears masses of light heliotrope flowers in mid spring (March). *Salvia leucantha* is a far cry from its edible cousin *S. officinalis* (common sage). The stems and undersides of the leaves are thickly white-felted, so too are the flower spikes, but it is the intense magenta flowers seen through this white felt that make the plant unique.

There are other plants besides shrubby ones that will enhance your conservatory. *Gerbera jamesonii* (Barberton daisy) with daisy-like flowers produced almost throughout the year is essential. Modern strains will give many shades of yellow, orange and red. *Clivia miniata*, one of the Kaffir lilies, is a joy in spring. It has umbels of orange and yellow flowers amid its leathery foliage. Orchids are hard to

ignore and one in particular – ideal for conservatory borders – is *Bletilla striata*, the Japanese Geisha orchid. Its small, 4cm (1½ in), flowers are glistening purple and, when given a free undisturbed root run, the plants can produce up to 15 flowers per growth on 60cm (24 in) stems.

In shadier spots all manner of ferns will grow to sizes never possible in pots. *Adiantum cuneatum* Fragrantissimum (maidenhair fern), *Asplenium bulbiferum* (spleenwort) and *Cyrtomium falcatum* (holly fern) are best.

Plants for staging, tubs or urns

If staging is incorporated in the conservatory, you can use this for temporary displays of annuals or plants such as begonia, charm and cascade chrysanthemums, cyclamen, gloxinia and primulas. These, together with forced bulbs, will help to increase the floral display throughout the year.

Some plants are of such architectural value they look better singled out in tubs or urns. *Strelitzia reginae*, the fabulous bird of paradise flower with spikes of blue and orange, is particularly fine. *Agave americana* Variegata, the variegated century plant, is a beauty when large but beware of its vicious spine-tipped leaves.

Zantedeschia (arum lilies) always outgrow their welcome when given freedom so restrict them to a tub where their handsome leaves can best be appreciated. There are yellow and pink forms too.

These are the ones to buy: *Zantedeschia aethiopica*, *Z. albo-maculata* (both white but the latter has spotted leaves), *Z. elliottiana* (yellow with white-spotted leaves) and *Z. rehmannii* (pink arum).

Outdoor planting

Having looked at plants within the conservatory, you must not neglect the world outside. Your new 'room' should not just be part of the house but part of the garden too. Blend them together by training slightly tender shrubs along the outside walls of the conservatory where they will flourish in the protection of the walls. Plant *Callistemon linearis* and *C. citrinus* in a dry, sunny position. These scarlet bottle brushes will provide a riot of colour in summer and their flexuous stems lend themselves admirably to training along a wall.

Acacia verticillata (prickly Moses) is a wonderful plant that hates severe cold but, if trained along a sunny wall, it will astonish you with a show of canary-yellow miniature brushes in late spring (April) and early summer (May).

A single garland of the purple-leaved *Vitis vinifera* Purpurea (Teinturier grape), trained along the guttering on a wire, is very effective. Cut it back hard to prevent light being shut out.

Maintenance and protection

All plants, whether in pots or in the border, will be all the happier for a liquid feed at 10-day intervals in spring and summer. But if your borders are so large as to make this impractical, then a top dressing with a standard fertilizer will do. Make sure none of your plants become dry at the roots and if you can spray overhead daily so much the better.

The more common pests you will encounter and have to deal with include aphides, red spider mites and whitefly. They are all sap-sucking pests that if allowed to multiply will cause serious damage. Red spider only thrives in a dry atmosphere so overhead mistings of water are the best means of protection.

Aphides and whitefly appear at any time and the best way to control them is to use one of the many insecticides available. Always make sure you follow the instructions carefully, otherwise more harm can be caused by pesticide than pest.

So, at its best, the conservatory is an indoor garden, a real link between the house and the outdoor garden, and a living room that can give lasting pleasure, comfort and enjoyment.

Above right: Chamaedorea elegans, *dwarf mountain palm. Right:* Callistemon citrinus

A YEARLY PLANNER
FOR THE
EDIBLE GARDEN

THE EDIBLE GARDEN

Early spring

To check the spread of aphides, start spraying with an insecticide such as BHC or malathion as soon as you see the leaf buds opening. Use the mixture according to the manufacturer's instructions, preferably on calm days so that the spray does not carry too far or blow back into your face. When you have finished wash yourself and your equipment thoroughly.

The strawberry bed
The next job is to clean up the strawberry bed. Cut and compost all dead leaves and any runners that you may have missed last time. Next, weed thoroughly between the rows and plants and follow up with a dressing of sulphate of potash which improves the quality of the fruits and strengthens the plants. (Feeds containing too much nitrogen will induce soft growth which will then be prone to disease and frost damage.)

An excellent way of nurturing strawberries is to provide them with a special polythene 'undersheet'. Use lengths of 150 gauge black polythene and lay them over the whole bed. Where a plant lies beneath the polythene, cut a cross-shaped hole big enough for the plant to pass through. Repeat this procedure all the way down the rows until all the plants are poking through holes and the polythene is neatly tucked in all round them.

You now have a surface layer which will conserve moisture, stop weeds, prevent the fruit from being splashed with wet soil and give protection from slugs.

The food plot
In the vegetable patch, work depends on the weather. If the days are dry, and the soil nice and crumbly, get it ready now for sowing and planting. Rake it over until the surface is as fine as sand, removing stones, twigs and weeds as you go. Finish off with a top dressing of general fertilizer (applied according to manufacturer's instructions), and you are ready to start sowing, providing conditions are right. Our first sowings are of peas and broad beans. These are large seeds and are sown, not in drills (grooves in the earth) like the fine seeds of lettuce and carrots, but in shallow trenches.

Tools for sowing
You will need some basic equipment: a rake, a garden line, packets of seeds and, for later sowings, a swan-necked hoe.

The garden line you can easily make yourself. All you need are two fairly stout pieces of wood, 30cm (12 in) long and about 3cm (1¼ in) in diameter. Through the end of each wooden stake drill a hole wide enough to take a length of strong nylon cord. Knot each end so that it will not pass back through the hole. The length of cord you require depends upon the length of your longest row, plus an extra 3m (10 ft) or so to allow for winding round the pegs and for moving the line, end by end, from one row to the next.

Aligning the rows by the sun
Before you start note which direction is north–south because that is the way in which your rows should run. This is to give each side of the rows an equal ration of sunshine as the sun travels from east to west crossing over them in its path. If the rows run east to west, the north side of the rows will be in permanent shade and the crop on that side will be sparse and slow to mature.

Marking out the trench
When you have decided on the lie of the land, push one end of the garden line into the ground where your row will start. Take the other peg to the far end of the row, push it 15cm (6 in) into the ground and rotate it until the line has been pulled as tight as a violin string. Then push the peg right in.

Sowing peas and broad beans
Peas and beans are sown in rows 45–60cm (18–24 in) apart. The same distance will be left between them and any rows of other, smaller vegetables that are planted on either side of them. Following the line and using a spade, dig a shallow, flat-bottomed trench about 25cm (9 in) wide and 3–5 cm (1–2 in) deep.

Broad beans Here we have a tall variety, Rentpayer, for one row, and a dwarf variety, The Midget, for the second. Place the seeds in 15cm (6 in) apart along one side of the trench and the same distance apart along the other side but with the seeds alternating from side to side. Pop in a few extra at the ends of the rows for filling in gaps later.

After sowing cover the seeds with not more than 3cm (1¼ in) of soil and ham-mer it down with the back of a rake to firm the seeds in. Finally, label the rows carefully with the date of planting and the crop sown.

Peas For this time of year we have chosen Kelvedon Wonder and Early Bird, both early varieties, which will be ready for picking 15–20 days earlier than the main-crop sowings.

Place the peas in their trench so that there is 5–8cm (2–3 in) between each seed, but otherwise get as many seeds in as possible (plus a few extra at the end of each row). Many gardeners are not so painstaking, they scatter the peas thinly in the trench or just throw them in – and sometimes get good crops. But you will probably get more reliable results from placing them carefully. After sowing, cover and firm as for broad beans.

Discouraging mice Before sowing peas bear in mind that mice are very fond of them. They wait a few days until the pea seeds are swollen, soft and tender, then they descend on the row and may leave you with nothing but an empty trench.

Traps baited with cheese may catch some of them, but a far better method is to soak the seeds for an hour or two in a paste made of red lead and paraffin and then sow them immediately.

IN THE PROPAGATOR

As there is now some room in the propagator it is time to make a few more sowings.

Cauliflowers and summer cabbage Start off a few cauliflowers (we suggest the variety Early Snowball) for cutting weeks earlier than those from outdoor sowings. Cauliflowers have a habit of all coming ready at once, and the only way to avoid a glut is to sow several small batches of seeds at different times.

In another pot start some Golden Acre summer cabbage for cutting when shop prices are sky-high.

Leeks for autumn Sow seeds thinly in trays or pots of seed compost and prick them out when they are about 2–3cm (1 in) high.

Early spring: Starting Sweet Peppers

Sweet peppers (capsicums) and celery are expensive to buy but easy to cultivate. Here we explain how to start both these popular vegetables into growth, outline the benefits of successional sowing and plant onions and shallots.

There is confusion as to the difference between the red and the green varieties of peppers. The answer is that both red and green fruits appear on the same plant: green when young, turning red as they age. Pick them when they are young and green to encourage further cropping. The variety we have chosen is Canapé which matures early and has a sweet, mild flavour. Sow the seeds in the propagator in trays or pots of seed compost; I prefer pots so that I can move them outside in early mid summer (early June) when the weather becomes warm.

Celery for salads

Being a half-hardy plant, celery should be sown in the propagator now for planting out in early and mid summer (May and June). As the Edible Garden is not very large we have chosen Golden Self-Blanching which can be planted fairly close together and needs neither earthing up nor blanching collars to produce fine, tender stems. It has a good, nutty flavour and grows easily. Sow the seeds thinly in trays or pots of seed compost in the propagator.

Midsummer lettuce

A few lettuce sown now will be ready for planting out under cloches in about two months' time, and ready for cutting in mid summer when they are scarce and expensive. Sow very thinly in a tray of seed compost. With a little patience you can space them out 5cm (2 in) apart, thereby avoiding having to prick out; lettuce prefer not to be disturbed. If they show any sign of slow growth, before you are ready to plant them out give them a liquid feed and they will respond rapidly. The varieties All the Year Round and Buttercrunch are both reliable and the recent Ilo stands better in hot dry weather than almost any other variety.

Successional sowing

It is best not to rush to sow outdoors as one tends to get better crops from seeds sown in a warm, hospitable soil.

Before we start our main sowings, let us explain the concept of successional sowing, as it plays an important part in avoiding gluts yet giving a steady supply of any particular vegetable.

The usual mistake is to sow too long a row, so that at harvesting time there are many more plants than you can use. With vegetables such as lettuce and radish the answer is to sow a short, or part, row about 1.25–1.75m (4–6 ft) long. When the seedlings of the first row are showing above the soil, sow another short row; continue in this manner right through until midsummer for a fresh and steady supply.

Another way of sowing for succession is by making use of the varying maturing times of different varieties of one vegetable. Early potatoes, for instance, are planted from two to four weeks earlier than maincrop varieties; together the two types will provide you with potatoes from midsummer through to planting time the following year.

Peas can be controlled in the same way. Early peas are followed by the second-early and maincrop varieties so that the rows are ready for picking one after the other. The seemingly odd thing about peas is that for a late sowing you choose an early variety. This is because a pea is classed as early if it matures and 'pods up' quickly; and in order to get a usable crop from a mid summer sowing, the variety that matures earliest is best.

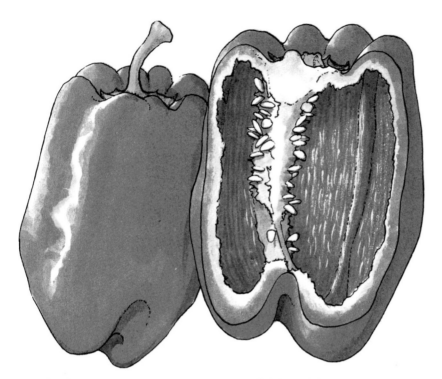

Canapé (F.1 hybrid) is a mild-flavoured and early-maturing sweet pepper that crops heavily. It is hardy enough to be grown outdoors in a sheltered position

Onions from sets

Onion rows can be planted providing there is no frost in the soil and it is dry enough. Nowadays onion 'sets' have almost completely superseded seeds. Choose small sets as they tend to produce better onions – Stuttgarter Giant and Sturon are good yielders. Buy them as soon as they appear in the shops before they become forced into growth by the surrounding temperature. Open the bags or carton and spread them out in a frost-free room or shed.

Digging the onion bed

The first essential is a really rich and fertile soil. So dig a trench, about 30cm (12 in) deep and spread a 15cm (6 in) layer of well-rotted compost in it. On

top of this sprinkle a few handfuls of bonemeal and then turn the soil from the next trench over on top of it. Wear tight-fitting rubber gloves when handling bonemeal; it may well be imported stock which has not been sufficiently heat-sterilized to kill infectious diseases.

Raking and top dressing

Before planting, break down the surface lumps by stamping all over them. Then rake to a fine tilth, removing stones at the same time. Finally, add a top dressing of Fish, blood and bone fertilizer at 70g per sq m (2 oz per sq yd).

Planting the sets

Onion sets have two main advantages over seeds: they don't need thinning and, because they have a head start, they are not so prone to the troubles that can beset young seedlings.

But sets have an annoying habit of popping out of the ground. Birds are usually blamed for this – but they neither eat onions nor use them to line their nests. It seems rather more likely that birds may pull out one or two just for the fun of it, but the main culprits are incorrect planting and over-ambitious worms.

Sets often have a long tail of outer skin which, after planting, gets wet and soft and trails along the ground. The nocturnal worm takes it to be ideal nesting material and tries to pull it down into its burrow. Out comes the set, to be left lying uselessly on its side once the worm realizes its mistake. So cut off the tail before planting.

By incorrect planting we refer to the practice of pushing the sets into the soil rather than placing them on the ground and then piling soil around them. If you push a set in, a hard pad of soil forms underneath the base of the bulbs and the emerging roots have difficulty in getting through it. The result is that the roots push the set out of the ground as they exert pressure on the compacted soil.

The correct way to plant is to draw out a shallow drill 13mm ($\frac{1}{2}$ in) deep. Mark out a row with a line, then put the blade of a swan-necked hoe against it at an angle of 45 degrees with its pointed corner just below soil surface. With both feet on the line to prevent it from 'bellying out', walk slowly backwards along the line. The drill should be reasonably straight and of even depth. Place the sets in it 15–25cm (6–8 in) apart and surround each one with a little soil to keep it upright and in place.

Planting shallots

You can plant shallots from early spring to mid summer (February to June). Plant as for onion sets, but leave more space between rows and bulbs; place them 30cm (12 in) apart. This is because the shallot splits and yields several young bulbs, each of which grows as big as its parent.

IN THE GREENHOUSE

All that the tomato and cucumber seedlings need to keep them growing is plenty of light, warmth and enough water. Keep the compost in the pots moist rather than wet as too much water invites fungus diseases. Place the pots as near to the glass as possible to give the plants all the available daylight. If the glass is dirty, or has become coated with green algal growth, then the amount of light admitted is greatly reduced. So wash the glass regularly with hot, soapy water, but be sure to move the plants well out of the way before you start cleaning.

There is no need to feed the seedlings yet. Potting composts contain enough nutrients to nourish the plants for six to eight weeks, by which time they will have been moved on into larger pots.

Spring Sowings

Early Nantes is a good variety for pulling young

The middle of spring signals the start of furious activity in the Edible Garden. With the right weather conditions, the bulk of your seed sowing can go ahead within the next few weeks.

In a good spring, the soil temperature is high enough to germinate the seeds and the lengthening days ensure that the seedlings have enough daylight to meet their needs. Day length is almost as important as temperature in determining how well plants grow. Experiments indicate that seedlings growing in insufficient light suffer appreciable growth checks from which they seldom fully recover, and if they are vegetables their cropping potential is diminished.

It is, of course, pointless to sow in a cold soil. Unless the minimum germination temperature has been reached the seeds will just lie dormant until they rot. So if the soil feels cold to the touch leave the seeds in their packets. The same applies to wet soil. If conditions are right it should crumble easily under foot and rake to a fine tilth without the teeth of the rake becoming clogged with soil.

But remember that you are the only one who can assess the situation in your garden and decide whether or not to make a start. Choosing the right day can make all the difference between a good and a mediocre crop, but this is something you can learn by experience.

Early potatoes
The first things to go in are the early seed potatoes. Potatoes are listed in three categories: earlies, second earlies and maincrops. The earlies grow quickest and mature first. They are not for lifting and storing, but are intended for immediate eating – as 'new potatoes' – generally from late summer to early autumn (July to August).

We would recommend Ulster Chieftain, which crops heavily in a medium loam and is ready earlier than most other varieties. For light soils choose Arran Pilot, whereas Home Guard will do well on a heavy soil.

Now to buying the 'seed' – which is a small tuber (swollen root) from the previous year's crop. Buy certified stock to be sure that the tubers are free of virus diseases.

For the Edible Garden plot, 3kg (7 lb) of 'seed' should be enough. Examine each tuber to make sure it is healthy and not too soft. If there are shoots already sprouting from the 'eyes' rub off the weak ones with your thumbs, leaving just three or four of the strongest. Some varieties have more eyes than others, and if you leave all the shoots on you will find, at harvesting time, only a small clutch of new potatoes the size of mothballs. Three to four shoots on a tuber will yield, on average, between 15 and 20 good-sized potatoes per root.

If you want a good crop, then a certain amount of planning and soil preparation is necessary. Potatoes dislike shade and stony soils and do not yield well in dry soils because they must have water to swell the tubers. Nor does ground which has been recently limed suit them: they

Arran Pilot – excellent on light soils

may grow reasonably well in it, but their skins will be covered in scabs. However, although these are ugly, they are only skin deep and do not affect the eating qualities of the potato.

Mark out with your garden line, and dig, a trench about 15cm (6 in) deep and 30cm (12 in) wide and place the seed potatoes in it 25cm (9 in) apart. Then dust the soil on each side of the trench with Growmore or Fish, blood and bone fertilizer at around 30–45g per m (1–1½ oz per yd) of row. Put the soil back over the potatoes and firm with the back of the spade. Remember to leave 60cm (24 in) between rows to give the growing plants plenty of room to develop and so that their large leaves will not interfere with the growth of adjoining crops.

Finally, a word of warning: if your garden is infested with small, black, subterranean slugs you will have to take precautionary measures. These common soil pests will destroy your crop. So after you have placed the seed potatoes in their shallow trenches, give them a good soaking with a disinfectant such as Jeyes Fluid, diluted to the recommended strength (as maker's instructions), before putting the soil back over them.

Growing healthy carrots
The next sowing is carrots and the choice of variety depends on your soil. On deep, light soils the varieties with long, tapering roots, like St Valery, give good yields. In most soils, however, the cylindrical roots with rounded ends are more reliable, and make good eating. Try the old favourites Chantenay Red Cored or Nantes Tip Top (both first-class croppers) or the newer F.1 hybrid variety Pioneer. This is very similar to Nantes Tip Top, but being an F.1 hybrid it exhibits all the characteristics of its kind (see box note).

The greatest problem in growing carrots is carrot fly. This is a destructive and widespread pest and, unless controlled, it can ruin a crop. The fly lays its eggs in early summer (May) on or near the surface of the soil in the vicinity of the young carrots. When the eggs hatch the maggots (or larvae) bore their way into the young roots until they are cracked and riddled with holes. Above soil level you will notice carrot fly attack by reddening and yellowing of the leaves which wilt in the sun. If this happens, pull up the roots and burn them.

However, there are various ways of preventing carrot fly from getting a hold. Sprinkle a special insecticide, such as bromophos, into the seed drill immediately after sowing which, it is claimed, will not taint the carrots and is harmless.

If you are apprehensive about using chemical pesticides on food crops, wait until the carrot fly has finished laying its eggs in early summer (May) and then sow immediately afterwards. By using a quick-growing variety, such as Pioneer, you will get a good crop of clean, delicious carrots for lifting in the autumn.

Another way is to fool the fly into believing that you have no carrots in your garden. It is attracted to the young plants by the smell of their leaves, so the plan is to introduce something with a stronger smell into the carrot patch. Either put down a few tin lids or saucers containing creosote or paraffin, or soak thick twine in either fluid and hang it above the rows during the danger period.

There is one further tip for producing good carrots. Never sow the seeds on ground that has been treated with fresh animal manure. If you do the roots will be forked and contorted; sow in soil which was manured the previous year, or which has only received an even dressing of compound fertilizer more recently.

Don't let all these precautions put you off growing this delicious vegetable. Carrots straight from the garden are sweeter and have a better flavour than any others, so they are worth a little extra trouble.

Summer cabbage and cauliflower
After the carrots come the summer cabbages. Here again there is a choice between F.1 hybrids and ordinary varieties. Taking the hybrids first, I can recommend Stonehead with solid, round heads or Hispi which yields large, pointed heads. Of the ordinary kinds I like Golden Acre with round heads as tight as drums and not too big. The cut heads

Early Snowball – ready for summer cutting

F.1 HYBRID
An F.1 hybrid is the first generation offspring, resulting from crossing two good varieties. It possesses all the best features of both parents, coupled with a hybrid vigour peculiar to all first-generation crosses. This gives it a built-in resistance to diseases and earlier maturity, and results in a heavier and more uniform crop than is normally obtained from ordinary varieties.

Seeds of F.1 hybrids are always considerably more expensive than others, but in terms of total crop yield and increased disease resistance they are well worth the extra cost.

average about 1kg (2¼ lb) in weight on a good soil, which is quite enough for a family of four. And being smaller, they can be grown closer together so that you get more cabbages per row.

If you like a large cabbage grow Winningstadt. In a fertile soil this can grow to be really enormous with a pointed, rock-hard head.

Many gardeners sow their summer cabbages in seedbeds and transplant the seedlings into the plot some weeks later. To my mind this is a waste of time and the plants suffer unnecessary root disturbance. The plants will grow, and mature, quicker if the seeds are sown in their final growing place. Sowing *in situ* also reduces the risk of cabbage root fly attack, which is more prevalent in transplanted seedlings.

Golden Acre – fine quality and flavour

For the smaller-headed types sow the seeds very thinly 6mm ($\frac{1}{4}$ in) deep in shallow drills 25–30cm (9–12 in) apart. For the larger kinds space the drills 30–45cm (12–18 in) apart. Sow very thinly and when the seedlings have grown four leaves thin them to the same distances apart as the space between the drills.

Summer cauliflower is one crop which must have a moist, rich soil before it will yield good, large white curds (flower-heads). In a poor soil, where the roots have to search for food and water, it may grow reasonably well but the curds will be mere buttons and hardly worth cutting. For the average garden, the variety All the Year Round is a reliable cropper, or Early Snowball which hearts up a little sooner. Sow as for summer cabbage, in rows 45cm (18 in) apart.

Successional sowings

Make several sowings of spring onions, radish, lettuce and summer spinach between now and the end of summer to ensure a fresh and constant supply.

The spring onion (choose White Lisbon) is one of the few vegetables whose seeds are sown fairly thickly and the seedlings left unthinned. This produces a mini-forest of succulent plants for pulling when they are still young and tender – about 15cm (6 in) tall. You can sow short rows from now until early autumn (August).

Next sow a part row of Lettuce Minetto, and a 'clutch' of Cherry Belle radish seeds in between the ends of the onion rows (or in any odd corner).

Another tasty vegetable for successional sowing from now until late summer (July) is summer spinach of which Long-standing Round comes recommended. Sow thinly in drills 25cm (9 in) apart and thin the seedlings to about 15cm (6 in) apart later on. It is one of the easiest of crops to grow providing, like cauliflowers, it is given plenty of water during dry spells. If left short of moisture at the roots the plants run to seed quickly and the leaves become bitter.

Container-grown strawberries

Those of you who haven't got a strawberry bed are going to regret the omission when summer comes.

It is too late to plant bare-root plants; these must be left until mid to late autumn (September to October) but container-grown plants can be planted right now. These are plants grown from runners rooted into pots the previous summer. In the pots they have made good fibrous root systems that need not be disturbed when transferring them. Simply place two fingers around the neck of the plant, turn the pot upside down and give it a gentle tap with a trowel, and the whole thing will slide out with an unbroken ball of soil.

With the trowel, make a hole big enough to take the rootball with room to spare, put it in and gently firm the soil back round it. When you have finished the top of the rootball should be level with the surrounding soil. Finish off by giving each plant half a handful of general fertilizer and a good watering.

Whether planting a single row or a bed of strawberries remember that the plants will live there for at least three years. Therefore plant them in the richest, best-fed soil in the garden and give them plenty of room to grow into large, bushy plants. Leave a good 60cm (24 in) between rows and 45cm (18 in) between individual plants. Pot-grown plants, planted in the spring, will not yield heavily the first year, but you can expect a few pickings of juicy berries in late summer and a good crop the following year.

Plant strawberries in well-fed soil

Spring: The Seedbed

Once the major spring sowings have been made, the next jobs are weeding and preparing the seedbed, which will provide you with vegetables later in the year, when the first crops are exhausted. Here we show you how to prepare the soil and recommend the best varieties to grow in it.

The purpose of your seedbed is to activate seeds into life, so it must be sited where it will receive all the available sunshine, and its soil must be the richest and finest in the whole garden. The reasons for having a seedbed are two-fold. First, it is the area in the Edible Garden where seeds have the best chance of germinating quickly and successfully. And second, it acts as a kind of plant bank where reserve stocks are kept until they are needed.

The seedbed need not occupy a very large area. The rows may be no more than 90cm (3 ft) long and 15cm (6 in) apart and, as you are unlikely to be growing more than 10 items at a time, it need not be wider than about 1·5m (5 ft).

Preparing the seedbed

How you prepared the soil is vitally important. Seeds need warmth, moisture and air to induce them out of dormancy into life. The sooner they burst their seed coats and form their first small roots and shoots, the faster and stronger they will grow, the better plants they will make, and the heavier the crops they will yield.

Therefore the soil in the seedbed must be fertile. It must also be fine and friable so that the seeds are in close contact with the soil particles and in an environment that rapidly warms up in the sun. So dig it deep and dig in as much well-rotted manure or garden compost as you can lay your hands on.

Then tread the bed (to firm the soil) and rake over the surface repeatedly until the top 2–5cm (1–2 in) is as fine as granulated sugar. Top it with a general fertilizer (such as Fish, blood and bone, or Fish meal) at 70g per sq m (2 oz per sq yd), and leave it to work its own way in.

This is the ideal, which you can readily achieve in gardens blessed with sandy soils or light loams. But you will not find it so easy on heavy clay, which is cold and cloying – the worst possible soil for seed germination. For a heavy clay garden you must prepare a contrived surface.

First dig the soil over thoroughly, add organic matter, then rake it down till the surface is as fine as you can make it. Spread a layer of garden peat 5cm (2 in) thick over the entire surface and sow in the seeds. Peat warms up quickly so the seeds will germinate rapidly, and the roots will soon penetrate into the soil beneath – where the food is.

At the end of the season, when you have finished with the seedbed, fork in the peat. Over the years it will darken and break up the clay into a rich loam.

If you are using this surface-peat method you must water it copiously until the seedlings are well established.

A well-formed brussels sprout plant should have tight, hard 'buttons'. Gather from the base upwards

How and what to sow

The vegetables you sow in the seedbed will be those that are used as 'follow-ons' when the others have been harvested. These are, in the main, vegetables which mature later in the year and are harvested in the late autumn and winter. They are often the most useful crops of all, as they are ready when fresh vegetables are at a premium. They also make use of the ground vacated by earlier crops, such as early peas, broad beans and potatoes.

Vegetables you can sow between mid-spring and early summer (March to late May) are leeks, brussels sprouts, winter cabbage, purple sprouting broccoli, red cabbage and winter cauliflower. With the exception of leeks, they are all members of the cabbage family.

You may be tempted to buy these as ready-grown plants from market stalls and garden centres, or to accept spare plants from kindly neighbours. But by 'importing' plants you run the terrible risk of introducing disease to your previously 'clean' garden, because the soil around the plants' roots may contain spores of the virulent club root disease, which is lethal to the cabbage family. Avoid this dreadful possibility by growing your own plants from seeds – at a fraction of the cost of buying plants.

The sowing procedure is no different from sowing directly into the food plot. In other words sow shallowly, only 6 mm (¼ in) deep, and thinly, then firm the soil back over the seeds.

As each row is sown, label it, not with empty seed packets, but with a metal or plastic tag that will not fade or blow away. If you forget to label you will find, later on, that you can't tell one row of seedlings from another. This will cause problems at planting-out time.

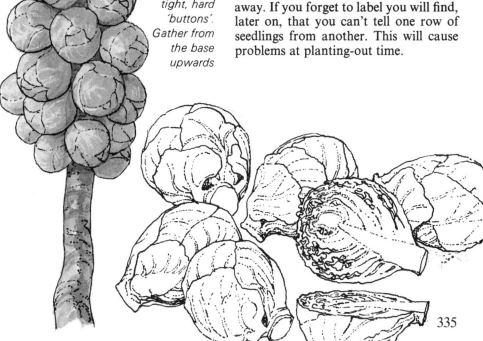

IN THE GREENHOUSE

Dwarf French beans can now be sown in the greenhouse for an early crop in mid summer (June). Flair and Tendergreen are excellent early (stringless) varieties. The most reliable method is to grow the plants in pots.

Use fairly large pots, 25–30cm (10–12 in) in diameter. Put a layer of well-rotted manure or compost, 5cm (2 in) deep, in the bottom and cover it with good, rich soil to within 8cm (3 in) of the rim. On top of this sow six seeds on end and cover them with 2–3cm (1 in) of soil. Sowing them on end reduces the risk of the seeds rotting and seems to hasten germination.

Until the seeds germinate water them carefully and sparingly – just enough to keep the soil moist.

If the celery and pepper seedlings have made four leaves, and if the leek seedlings are about 2–3cm (1 in) high, prick them out singly into 8cm (3 in) peat pots filled with potting compost.

Remember to keep all the growing seedlings watered; the bigger they get the more water they lose through their leaves, and the more they need to replace the loss.

If you look at the soil in the seed trays or pots you may notice a green growth on the surface. This is an alga which in itself is not harmful, but it is inclined to create over-acidity and to slow down growth by excluding air from the seedling roots. With an old kitchen fork gently break up the soil surface.

Finally a few more herbs: hyssop, sweet marjoram, rosemary and winter savory can all be sown in the propagator now for planting out later.

Seedbed varieties

Brussels sprouts Peer Gynt, an early variety ready for picking from late autumn (October) onwards. Fasolt New matures much later, cropping from mid winter to spring (December to February).

Red cabbage Blood Red for shredding and pickling in the autumn (August to October). One well-grown plant will provide enough for 1kg (2 lb) of pickle.

Winter cabbage Christmas Drumhead, a solid head on short plants, ready for cutting from early to late winter (November to January). January King, a good-flavoured roundhead that stands all winter. Ormskirk Late (savoy) has a large crinkly-leaved heart that is at its best from mid winter to mid spring (December to March).

Winter cauliflower Snow's Winter White for late winter and early spring (January and February) cropping. St George, which curds up for mid to late spring (March to April) eating.

Sprouting broccoli Early Purple Sprouting yields a prolific crop of succulent shoots in mid and late spring (March and April) when fresh green vegetables are still scarce.

One of the most rewarding of all vegetables – the more you cut it the more shoots you get – is Green Sprouting (or Calabrese); a delicious vegetable that deserves greater popularity. The central heads are ready in summer and, after cutting, are followed by a plentiful crop of tender shoots which should be peeled before cooking.

Leek Musselburgh has long, thick stems; Marble Pillar, earlier, with long, slender stems of excellent quality. Leeks are hardy enough to be left in the ground all winter (November to March), and remain in top condition right through to mid spring.

Weeding the food plot

In the food plot the bare soil is beginning to disappear – the weeds are on the march. Work your way along the rows of vegetable seedlings pulling out the small weeds before they get established and begin to use up the food intended for the vegetables. It is always easier to remove a young weed than to uproot a big one; also the vegetable seedlings suffer much less root disturbance.

This done, carefully hoe between the rows with a push (or Dutch) hoe. This tool enables you to work walking backwards so that you don't tread over the ground already hoed. Choose a dry, sunny day for the job and leave the uprooted weeds lying on the surface to wither and die and return some goodness to the soil.

Mulching the raspberries

Before the weather starts getting really warm lay a mulch of well-rotted organic material along the ground between the rows of raspberry canes, taking care not to break any new shoots that are just emerging. Put down a layer 8–10cm (3–4 in) deep along each side of the rows. This will feed the plants as they grow, prevent loss of moisture, keep the roots cool in hot weather and protect them from late, hard frosts.

For top-class leeks, sow in a well-prepared seedbed

Late spring: Weeding and Spraying

During the last few weeks of spring when the weeds are shooting up amongst the vegetables, manual or chemical weeding becomes an essential weekly task.
We also show you how to stake broad beans, protect early potatoes, tie in raspberries and thin out young vegetable plants.

Broadly speaking the chemical weedkillers that are used in the Edible Garden can be divided into those that kill through the leaves and those that kill through the roots. Both types are equally effective but their efficiency and usefulness depend on their being used in the right places, at the right times and at the correct strength.

One which we will not be using in the Edible Garden is sodium chlorate – even though it is one of the oldest and most popular of weedkillers. It is an efficient destroyer of plant life, but it does have serious disadvantages. It is fully soluble in water and, when applied to a given area, will spread sideways, endangering other nearby plants. It remains potent in the ground for a considerable time until it is eventually washed out of the soil by rain.

On heavy soils its enduring toxicity makes it unsafe to plant anything for up to a year and even on light, sandy soils the ground must be left fallow for three months or more. So do not use it on the vegetable plot or on the ground around it.

Weedkillers containing simazine are also total root-entering killers but, unlike sodium chlorate, they are not soluble and merely go into suspension when added to water. This means that they do not spread and their destructiveness is confined to the zone of application. You can, therefore, apply them to paths without fear of their toxicity spreading into the food-growing areas.

Then there are the weedkillers containing a chemical called paraquat that revolutionized gardening when it was first introduced. Paraquat kills through the leaves by destroying their internal cell structure and rendering them incapable of sustaining life. It has no effect whatsoever on the soil and is rendered harmless on contact with it. This means that paraquat will only kill what it touches and therefore its application can be accurately controlled. You can use it safely to kill weeds between rows of vegetables providing it does not come into contact with the vegetable leaves.

Unfortunately paraquat can be lethal to humans as well as to plants and you must treat it with great caution. Always wear rubber gloves and wash your face and hands thoroughly when the job is done. Wash the can out, several times, to make sure that all chemical residues are dispersed. You should keep a special watering can for all chemical weedkillers

Dock, thistle, bindweed, deadnettle, speedwell and dandelion – just a few of the weeds that menace your garden

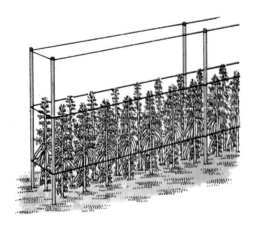
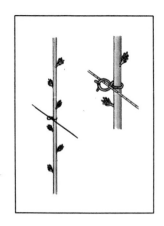

so that you cannot, through error or carelessness, harm your plants with contaminated liquid.

Thinning the seedlings

Some seedlings, such as spring onions, don't need thinning. Also leave carrots unthinned so as not to loosen the soil around them; loose earth makes it very easy for the larvae of carrot fly to bore their way down to the roots. However, the bulbing onions and summer cabbage sown *in situ* need thinning, to give the selected plants plenty of room to grow and develop from an early age.

Thin to the correct distances apart as soon as the seedlings are big enough to handle easily. You can pull out a small-rooted seedling – before it develops a ramifying (spreading) root system and becomes deep-seated – without disturbing its neighbours. Early thinning also causes less growth check. Help to stabilize and protect the transplanted seedlings by drawing a little soil around with a hoe.

Tending and staking broad beans

The double row of broad beans is also growing well, except for one or two gaps where seeds failed to germinate. Fill the gaps with plants taken from the ends of the rows – where you sowed those extra seeds. Starting a few centimetres away from each plant, dig deep down under them and then lift them gently to avoid breaking the roots. Tease them carefully apart and plant them firmly in the gaps. They will not be much disturbed by the move and will soon catch up.

Broad beans are rapid growers; the tall-growing varieties will need supporting to prevent them being blown over. Use 1.2m or 1.5m (4 ft or 5 ft) long canes and, starting at one end of the row, stick them in at 1.8m (6 ft) intervals on each side. Then run lengths of strong twine from end to end, tying it to each stake. Three lengths of twine should be enough – at 30, 90 and 150cm (1, 3 and 5 ft) above the ground. This structure will provide

enough support for the plants at all stages of growth. If your garden is very exposed you may need to criss-cross some twine over the plants for added protection; they will grow up through it.

Protecting the potatoes

Being a half-hardy plant the potato is unable to withstand the least touch of frost, so you must protect the young plants if frost threatens. The common method of covering the emerging leaves with soil is not necessary. The plant has to push its way out again instead of using its leaves to manufacture the food that should be going to the roots to form and swell the young potatoes.

A much simpler way is to take a few sheets of newspaper and throw one over each plant (anchored with a stone) if there is frost in the air. Your garden may look untidy but your potatoes will be protected. But if you miss the weather forecast, or the skies clear in the early morning and frost descends unexpectedly, all is not lost. Get up early and turn the hose on the plants before the sun strikes the leaves. If the sun gets there first the leaves will turn yellow, then brown and finally black. Even so, don't lift the row. Leave it and new growth will emerge from the stems beneath the soil. You will only get about half a crop, and it will take much longer to mature, but at least it will not be a complete loss.

Tying in raspberry canes

In the fruit cage the new raspberry canes will need tying in to their wire supports. Plant ties of paper-covered wire are convenient and inexpensive but you can do the job just as quickly with a ball of garden twine and a sharp knife. Put the ball in your pocket to leave your hands free to hold the loose end of the twine and the knife. Tie in the stems loosely, with the twine forming a figure-of-eight between the stems and the wire. This allows room for the plants to grow without being constricted (see illustration above).

Far left: erect the tall cane support-structure for your broad beans early on as the plants grow very rapidly and soon become top-heavy; once they have fallen over it is not an easy job to get them to stand upright again
Centre left: raspberries also need supporting. Tie stems in loosely to the wire supports so they can grow without hindrance
Top right: useful bees, as well as harmful pests, are affected by insecticides, so spray your apple trees while the flowers are still in bud, and well before bees start pollinating the blossoms

Spraying the apple trees

A number of insect pests which attack apple trees from time to time are at their most vulnerable in late spring. An insecticide spray of BHC or malathion at the tree's 'pink bud' stage will effectively control aphides and capsid bug. If you spray before the flowers open they will not be damaged and there will be no danger of accidentally killing bees while they are 'working' the blossoms.

Remember, as with all garden chemicals, to protect your eyes and skin, and wash yourself and all equipment thoroughly after the job is finished. As an added precaution keep pets away from the area under the trees for a few days.

Spraying with BHC or malathion is not sufficient to conquer woolly aphid, otherwise known as American blight. The fine spray will not penetrate through to the lower layers of the white growth – like cotton wool – that sometimes clothes the branches. The best treatment is to paint the infected parts with a paint brush dipped in tar oil.

Hardening off

Over the next few weeks (early to late April, depending on how mild an area you live in) the lettuce, cauliflower and cabbage seedlings that were sown earlier under glass must be hardened off before you plant them out.

'Hardening off' means giving the plants an acclimatization period before transferring them from the greenhouse to the open ground. Until now the seedlings have been completely protected from the natural elements; they have never encountered wind or low temperatures. To move them from the still, warm air of the greenhouse to the vegetable plot in one move will, at best, give them a rude shock and, at worst, kill them.

Gradually introduce them to the outdoor world by giving them a few days in an intermediate environment.

Using a frame

If you have a garden frame, put the trays and pots of plants into it for about ten days before planting out. The 'light' can be taken off altogether during the day if the weather is warm, sunny and not too windy, but if it is cold and blustery, leave the light on. Prop it open with a block of wood, or a brick, so as to leave a space 15cm (6 in) wide. For the first four or five nights close the light down completely. Later on it can be left open a few centimetres depending on how cold the weather happens to be. Should you strike a patch of hard frost at the outset of hardening off give the plants added protection by throwing a sack or two (or a sheet of heavy gauge polythene) over the frame at night. After hardening off for about 10 to 14 days, the plants will be sturdy enough to withstand outdoor life.

Hardening off under cloches

Glass or plastic cloches are invaluable for hardening off. Place the trays or pots in a straight line on the vegetable patch and put a row of cloches over them. After closing the ends of the row with appropriate end-pieces, leave them for a week. Then remove the cloches and transplant the vegetables into the prepared ground. Cover them again with cloches and seal both ends of the rows. Placing the end-pieces in position is very important: without them the rows of cloches become miniature wind tunnels, creating highly unsuitable conditions for tender plants.

Cloches that are only being used for hardening off can be removed after seven to ten days for use elsewhere. If you want to bring the crop on (force it to maturity days or even weeks earlier than normal) leave the cloches in position until the growing plants need more headroom. With 'tender' plants—such as outdoor cucumbers or runner beans—leave the cloches over them until you are sure that all danger of frost is past.

These are only a few of the uses to which cloches can be put. For those of you who are gardening on a tight budget, a few pounds spent on cloches will provide you with inexpensive heat-retaining, plant-protecting equipment.

Hardening off in the open

If you don't own a frame or cloches you can harden off the plants by taking the trays and pots out of the greenhouse every morning and placing them in a warm, sheltered part of the garden. An ideal place would be at the foot of a south- or west-facing wall, fence or hedge—somewhere where they will catch the sun. At night, take them back into the greenhouse and repeat the out-and-in procedure until you feel they have toughened up enough to stay out overnight. Then leave them outdoors for four or five days and nights and your plants will be sufficiently robust to face the open-air life.

Maincrop potatoes

Out in the vegetable plot it is about time to plant the maincrop potatoes. Use the same method as for the earlies (see page 208) but plant the sets or 'seeds' 30–40cm (12–15 in) apart and feed them more generously. Before replacing the soil, cover them with 8–10cm (3–4 in) of rotted manure or compost and sprinkle over a general compound fertilizer, such as Growmore, at around 60g per m run (2 oz per yd) of row. The more you feed potatoes, the heavier the crop will be.

If, by any chance, you run out of 'seed' before you get to the end of the last row, cut the largest in half with a knife, dust the cut ends with lime and plant the two halves. In fact, if the seed potatoes are on the large side when you go to purchase them, buy less, treat them all this way and save money; the crop will be just as good.

Selecting potato varieties

There are many excellent varieties of maincrop potatoes to choose from. The best course is to try several until you find

Gemini is a tall plant and needs a stout cane to keep it upright. If you prefer a shorter variety that doesn't require staking, sow either Amateur or the more recent Sleaford Abundance. Both are bushy, stocky plants that grow only about 30cm (12 in) or so high and are ideal for exposed sites. Of the two, Sleaford Abundance has the advantage of heavier and earlier cropping. The fruits are medium sized, beautifully red and round and have a sweet, tangy flavour.

To avoid root disturbance and growth check later on, sow two seeds per 8cm (3 in) peat or plastic pot in J.I. No 1 or an equivalent soilless compost. If both seedlings emerge, remove one and let the other grow on. Put the pots where they will receive plenty of light.

Ring-culture tomatoes growing in the greenhouse. The fruit-laden trusses are supported by tying in to bamboo canes

one that suits your soil and your palate.

King Edward is a heavy cropper in fertile, medium to heavy soils, while Arran Banner does well on light soils. Majestic crops heavily and Pentland Crown stores well. Then there is Golden Wonder—perhaps the finest-flavoured of all potatoes.

Tomatoes for outdoors
A few seeds sown now in the propagator will provide you with tomato plants for planting outside by mid summer (June) when, barring freak weather conditions, frost should be over. Given a reasonably good summer and a sunny, sheltered spot in the garden, each plant will yield several pounds of ripe fruit. Any green fruit left at the end of the season makes a delicious green tomato chutney.

If you don't have a vegetable plot you can still grow tomatoes, in a variety of containers, and put them on patios, terraces or anywhere that the plants will get plenty of sun and shelter from strong winds.

Varieties for outdoors
All tomato varieties can be grown out of doors but not all give good crops. However, a number of varieties have been specially bred for outdoor cultivation. They are somewhat hardier than the accepted greenhouse varieties and, in consequence, they grow better and give a higher yield.

Out of the range that we have tried growing in seedsmen's trial grounds, one of the best for form, flavour and fulfilment is the F.1 hybrid Gemini. It also matures and ripens some 10 to 20 days earlier than any other.

IN THE GREENHOUSE
It is time to start preparations for planting the tomatoes in their fruiting positions in the greenhouse.

Ring-culture tomatoes
Our recommendation is that you use the ring-culture method for your tomatoes. It entails a certain amount of initial preparation, but once this is done you will be rewarded by season after season of top quality fruit. The fundamental requirement of successful tomato culture is to grow the plant roots in a sterile medium – peat or aggregate – in a polythene-lined trench. Remember, if you use aggregate as the medium, to begin by removing the soil to a depth of 23cm (9 in) at one end of the greenhouse bed, rising to a depth of 15cm (6 in) at the other end. This slight slope provides gradual drainage. If you are using horticultural peat instead of aggregate, a 10–15cm (4–6 in) layer is sufficient. It needs replacing every three to five years, but it is light and easy to handle and comes in very useful later as top dressing.

Place your bottomless rings 60cm (24 in) apart on the base material, fill them with J.I. No 3 to within 2–3cm (1 in) of their rims, soak them with water and leave them for a week before planting the tomatoes.

There are two reasons why you should not plant immediately. First, it gives the compost time to settle. Secondly, it gives it time to warm up and reach the same temperature as the compost in which the tomatoes are already growing in their small pots. If you plant them as soon as the rings are filled, the plant roots find themselves in a growing medium which is several degrees colder than they are accustomed to. The result is a severe growth check at a critical time, and a subsequent detrimental effect on the earliness and cropping ability of the lower trusses.

Planting in soil
You can plant the tomatoes—60cm (24 in) apart—straight into the greenhouse soil bed. The trouble with this method, however, is that after two or three years the soil becomes 'sick', having accumulated toxic elements that are unfavourable to the crop. You will then have to replace the top 30cm (12 in) of the greenhouse soil bed with fresh sterilized soil.

Late Spring Sowings in the Edible Garden

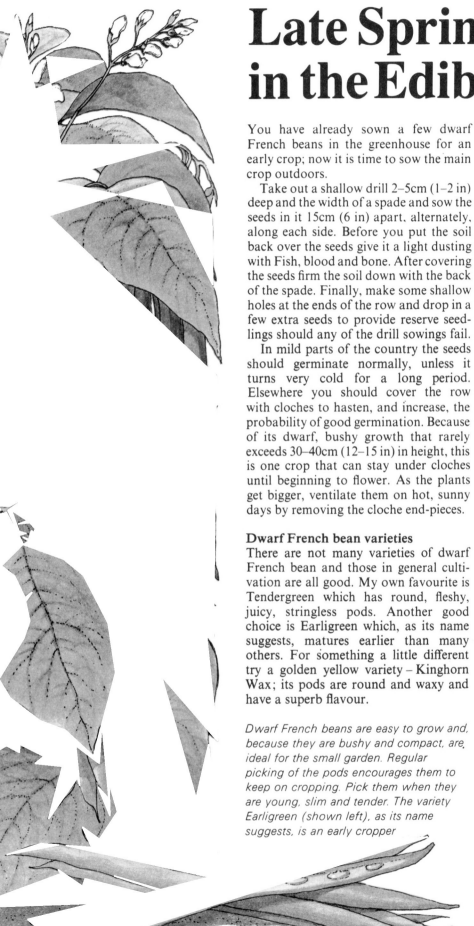

You have already sown a few dwarf French beans in the greenhouse for an early crop; now it is time to sow the main crop outdoors.

Take out a shallow drill 2–5cm (1–2 in) deep and the width of a spade and sow the seeds in it 15cm (6 in) apart, alternately, along each side. Before you put the soil back over the seeds give it a light dusting with Fish, blood and bone. After covering the seeds firm the soil down with the back of the spade. Finally, make some shallow holes at the ends of the row and drop in a few extra seeds to provide reserve seedlings should any of the drill sowings fail.

In mild parts of the country the seeds should germinate normally, unless it turns very cold for a long period. Elsewhere you should cover the row with cloches to hasten, and increase, the probability of good germination. Because of its dwarf, bushy growth that rarely exceeds 30–40cm (12–15 in) in height, this is one crop that can stay under cloches until beginning to flower. As the plants get bigger, ventilate them on hot, sunny days by removing the cloche end-pieces.

Dwarf French bean varieties

There are not many varieties of dwarf French bean and those in general cultivation are all good. My own favourite is Tendergreen which has round, fleshy, juicy, stringless pods. Another good choice is Earligreen which, as its name suggests, matures earlier than many others. For something a little different try a golden yellow variety – Kinghorn Wax; its pods are round and waxy and have a superb flavour.

Dwarf French beans are easy to grow and, because they are bushy and compact, are ideal for the small garden. Regular picking of the pods encourages them to keep on cropping. Pick them when they are young, slim and tender. The variety Earligreen (shown left), as its name suggests, is an early cropper

How to grow haricots

Another type of dwarf French bean is the haricot which you can either eat fresh and green or leave to mature on the plant and then pick for storing as dried beans. A good variety is Carters Granda. Sow the seeds as you would the ordinary dwarf French beans.

Leave any unpicked pods on the plant until they turn brown. Towards the end of the season lift the whole plant out of the soil and hang it, upside down, in an airy shed or garage to dry off completely. When quite dry shell the pods and store the seeds in bottles, tins or boxes for use as required.

Parsnip cultivation

One popular vegetable we have not yet started to grow is the parsnip. It used to be thought that the earlier they were sown the better; but recent experience has proved otherwise.

Parsnips are an easy crop to cultivate, but they are prone to the disfiguring disease known as canker. The best way of avoiding canker is to sow now or even later, rather than in mid spring (March), and to give the rows a light dusting of lime after sowing. There are also one or two canker-resistant varieties now available. One of these is Avonresister, but unfortunately it is a shy seeder (produces little seed) and you may have difficulty buying it. If you can't obtain it, choose instead a long-rooted variety (such as Hollow Crown Improved) and sow from now until early summer (mid May), adding a little lime to help ward off canker.

To sow, take out shallow drills 6mm ($\frac{1}{4}$ in) deep and about 30cm (12 in) apart and sprinkle the seeds in fairly thickly. When the seedlings are large enough to handle easily, thin them out to about 15cm (6 in) apart and draw a little soil around them to prevent them falling over. They require no further attention other than weeding, and are ready for the table in the autumn. Don't lift them until the ground has had a touch or two of frost as only then do they acquire their full flavour and sweetness.

Sowing a patch of parsley

Sow your parsley in a short row or as a clump in the herb bed. It also thrives in tubs and window boxes – or even in an old bucket outside the back door.

For some reason parsley sowing is surrounded by superstition. Some gardeners claim the seeds will only germinate if they are sown when the moon is full, whilst others maintain they only grow if sown on Good Friday. All these mistaken beliefs stem from the fact that the seeds have very hard skins and it takes a lot of moisture, and often considerable time, before they can begin to swell and germinate. Soaking the seeds in water for 48 hours before sowing helps, but then they stick to each other and it becomes extremely difficult to sow them evenly. A method that can be used with considerable success is to sow thinly in a drill 6mm (¼ in) deep and then pour a kettle of boiling water over the seeds before covering them with soil. The hot water softens the seed coat and germination is asssured, although it may take anything from three to six weeks before you see any visible signs of growth.

Windowsill runner beans
Runner beans can be started in warmth several weeks before outdoor sowings can be made. The seeds will germinate if the pots are placed on a sunny windowsill, providing it does not get bitterly cold at night.

IN THE GREENHOUSE
Plant out the cucumber and provide the greenhouse with some kind of shading. In the propagator, start a few early runner beans.

Runner beans
A sowing of runner beans in the propagator now will extend the cropping period by several weeks, and the pods will start forming much earlier.

Runner beans are half-hardy plants; except in mild areas, therefore, you cannot sow them outdoors until well into early summer (the middle of May) at the earliest. This means that they do not begin to yield well until early autumn (August) and only have a short harvest before cold nights and first frosts of autumn finish them off.

But you can lengthen the cropping season by sowing the seeds in warmth some four weeks earlier than you would normally sow outdoors.

Sow the seeds singly, on their ends, and 2–3cm (1 in) deep in 8cm (3 in) pots of seed compost. Until the seedlings break through the surface, keep the compost barely moist; overwatering it (until it is soggy) often rots the seeds before they start to grow.

Germination takes about 10–14 days – sometimes a little longer, depending on room temperature.

Varieties of runner bean
If you like a long-podded bean we suggest the aptly-named variety As Long As Your Arm or the exhibitor's favourite Yardstick. If your preference is for shorter, fatter pods that hang in thick clusters then Cookham Dene, Streamline and Scarlet Emperor are all good choices. If you have previously experienced difficulty in getting the flowers to set pods (a characteristic failing of runner beans, especially in dry sunny summers) we recommend the variety Fry. Its reliability may be partly due to the fact that its flowers are self-pollinating and therefore not dependent on passing insects for cross pollination. It may also be that its white flowers do not tempt sparrows and other birds to peck at them as the red-flowered varieties seem to do. But whatever the reason, it crops well and regularly, has a good flavour and the pods are stringless and freeze well.

If you can't obtain this variety locally you will find it in most seedsmen's catalogues.

Preparing cucumber ring
Cucumber plants grow quickly and your seedling will now be large enough to plant in its final position.

Cucumbers are odd things. Their requirements are at first sight contradictory. On the one hand they like plenty of water around their roots at all times; on the other hand they must have free open drainage. They are also the greediest of all greenhouse crops – you can't overfeed them.

The problem is how to provide them with adequate water without their roots standing in a permanent bath of it. There are several ways of growing them, but most of them are so complicated as to be hardly worthwhile for the cultivation of one solitary cucumber plant.

The most successful method is one used for growing ring-culture tomatoes – in bottomless rings so that they enjoy free drainage, plenty of food and ample water as required.

Half-fill a ring with J.I. No 2 mixed half-and-half with cow dung. If you can't obtain cow dung then rotted garden compost is just as good. Water the ring thoroughly and leave it to stand for a week.

When you come to plant the cucumber you should place the ring in the corner of the greenhouse farthest away from the door because cucumbers hate draughts.

Planting the tomatoes
If you are using the ring-culture method for your greenhouse tomatoes you can now plant them into their well-soaked rings. Put one plant in each ring, then give them a good watering to settle them in. In future only water the base material, never the compost. This encourages the plants to send their roots down into the peat or aggregate.

Shading the greenhouse
Too much direct sunlight beating down on plants under glass is not good for them. Unless your greenhouse is fitted with shading blinds, which can be raised or lowered according to the weather, light shading of the glass panes is advisable.

For this you can either use a weak whitewash (made by mixing a little lime in water) or, preferably, use the proprietary roof-shading paint which you can get from any good garden centre or shop. Don't lay it on too thickly or you will cut out valuable light. The object is to reduce the intensity of direct sunlight to an acceptable level, without detracting from the growth of the plants.

If you don't want to paint the outside of the glass, another way is to hang sheets of newspaper over the bar of a plastic-covered or wire coat-hanger. Suspend the hangers from the roof outside. They can easily be moved to provide shade as and when it is needed.

Late spring: Peas

Spring is now far advanced. Time to erect support for peas, earth up early potatoes, harden off the onions and plant out some of the vegetables that are fully hardened off.

Your row of early peas should now be well through the soil. Take a close look at them, they may require some attention. Young pea seedlings are susceptible to damage by the pea weevil. This insect pest chews neat, semi-circular holes out of the leaf edges and can reduce the total leaf area by as much as a half or more. The smaller the leaf area the less food the plants are able to manufacture for themselves, and in consequence the smaller the crop will be. At the first sign of damage, dust the plants with derris in the early morning when the insects are most active. You will probably have noticed, here and there, some thin, wispy growths that look like small, irregularly-coiled springs. These are the tendrils by which the plants attach themselves to whatever support is available. If no prop is provided they cling to each other in the mistaken belief that they can give ade-quate mutual support. But come a gust of wind, and the weight of filled pods will easily topple them over. Then they will cease flowering and podding long before they should.

Supporting with twigs

In the 'old days' when, even for town dwellers, the countryside was only a short journey away, every gardener would take his knife or bill-hook to the hedgerows and cut bundles of hazel twigs. If you live in or near the country you can still avail yourself of a free supply of these excellent pea-supports, provided you get the local farmer's permission. Stick them in, at 30–45cm (12–18 in) intervals, along each side of the rows, and the peas will find their own way up them. At the end of the season, when you strip the rows and put the yellowing stems and leaves on the compost heap, the twigs will make fine kindling wood—if you still have an open fireplace and are able to burn wood.

Supporting with netting

If you can't get twigs then a simple net structure is the answer, using either

The pea flower, heralding a good harvest

wire or nylon netting, both of which will give several years of faithful service. Wire netting is initially the most expensive but its greater rigidity and stability makes it a worthwhile investment.

When you buy, bear in mind that the total length you require is double the length of the longest row that you are ever

Bushy twigs, gathered from hedgerows and woods, make excellent supports for peas. Stick one in beside each plant

give the soil at the base of the plants a light dusting of lime, which peas like. It also helps to prevent the condition known as root rot, revealed as yellowing of the leaves and stems just above ground level.

Hardening off onions
The onions sown earlier in the greenhouse will, by now, be some 15cm (6 in) tall, and are ready for hardening off (prior to planting out in a week or so) in the cold frame or under cloches. Remember that if you don't own either you can harden them off by putting them out in a sunny place during the day.

Ideally the onion bed should be thoroughly dug and well manured in the autumn. But our plot, prepared in early spring, is nearly ready. All it needs now is a raking over to remove surface stones, followed by a hoeing to annihilate the carpet of small weeds that pop up all over the bare earth.

Summer cabbages and cauliflowers
The cabbages and cauliflowers that have been hardening off can be planted out now. They should be spaced 45cm (18 in) apart with an equal distance between rows. Make holes in the soil with a dibber and plant the vegetables up to their lowest leaves. Firm round each plant carefully, then water them well in.

Planting out lettuce
It is time to plant out any lettuce still hardening off and also to transplant the seedlings from the outdoor sowings. Lettuce do not take kindly to moving. Their roots are small and fibrous and their leaves are comparatively large and delicate. They lose a vast amount of moisture through their leaves, and after transplanting are inclined to become limp and floppy, because the rate of water flow from the roots to leaves has been interrupted and impaired. Unless you can somehow minimize water loss and this incipient wilt, the seedlings will experience a severe growth check. This will frequently result in the plants running to seed before they have made usable hearts.

One way of reducing the risk is to make sure that you always transplant from a wet soil or compost, even if this means watering an hour or so before tackling the job. Furthermore, try to transplant in the later afternoon or evening of a still, cloudy day when water loss from the leaves is at its lowest ebb. After transplanting, give plenty of water every evening at sundown unless it is raining.

Lift the seedlings out of their trays or beds with care. Never pull them out or

likely to grow. You can always fold any surplus wire round the end of the last supporting post, but you can't stretch it out if you have bought too little.

You must also decide whether you will always be content to grow dwarf varieties, which do not exceed 60–75cm (2–2½ ft) in height, or whether you may want to try a row of tall 1·5–2m (5–6 ft) peas, as this will affect the height of the netting. For dwarf varieties buy 8cm (3 in) mesh wire-netting 1m (3 ft) wide and whatever length you need. For tall peas the netting will need to be 2m (6½ ft) wide.

Erecting the netting
When putting up the support structure ask a friend or neighbour to help you. Wire netting, particularly when fresh from a new coil, tends to spring back just as you are ready to put the retaining cane in. This can damage your temper, your person and your young pea seedlings, which may be bruised or even decapitated in the struggle.

Begin by fixing two stout canes or posts about 30cm (12 in) apart at each end of the row, driven well into the ground, so that they can take the weight of the row in full pod without collapsing. Next, staple or tie the end of the coil to one of the end

posts and unwind about 2–2·5m (6–8 ft) of wire down one side of the row. Get your friend to hold the coil while you thread a cane through the mesh from top to bottom and into the soil about 15cm (6 in) away from the pea plant. Carry on down the row, stopping at intervals of 2–5m (6–8 ft) to insert a stabilizing cane. When you reach the end of the row loop the coil around the two end stakes and tie it to both, then proceed up the other side of the row in similar fashion, and finally tie or staple the end of the coil to the last stake.

This two-sided support structure traps the plants inside and compels them to climb up one side or the other. When the row has finished cropping it is a simple matter to part the plants from the wire and roll it up—still attached to the first stake—until it is needed again. You can use strong nylon or polythene plastic netting instead of wire.

In some gardens you will find a single length of netting used in preference to the double-enclosed system. Certainly one length is cheaper than two and easier to erect, but it does not provide as strong a support and several of the plants will grow away from, rather than on to, it.

When the structure is securely fixed,

you will snap the main root system. Put a trowel well under them, prise them up in groups and tease them gently apart, keeping their roots intact with as much soil as possible still clinging to them, and replant them straight away. After they are in, draw a little soil around each one to prevent them from swaying back and forth in the wind and loosening their roots in the soil. Lastly, if your garden is populated with slugs they will make straight for your transplanted lettuce, so put down some slug pellets.

Successional sowings

Sow some more lettuce for a steady supply throughout the summer. Sow a short, part-row, thinly and shallowly and water afterwards if the soil is dry. Put in a pinch of radish seed anywhere vacant, and a row of spring onions.

Earthing up early potatoes

The next job is to give the early potatoes their first earthing. Loosen the soil on each side of the rows with a rake and pull some of it right up to, and around, the emerging stems and leaves. By earthing

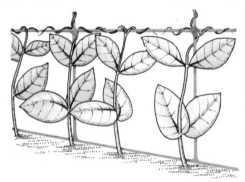

*Above: pea tendrils twining round netting
Below and below right: earthing up
potatoes protects the tubers from being
exposed to light and turning green*

IN THE GREENHOUSE

Tending the dwarf French beans and tomato seedlings and planting out the cucumber into its ring and the peppers into final pots should be done now.

Planting out the cucumber

The time has come to place the cucumber in its ring and the ring on the peat or aggregate bed in a corner of the greenhouse well away from the door. Drench the ring with water daily. The excess will drain away into the soil, aggregate or peat below. As the plant grows, top up the ring with a similar mixture (J.I. No 2 mixed half-and-half with cow dung or well-rotted garden compost) until it comes to within 2–3cm (1 in) of the rim.

Dwarf French beans

Dwarf French bean plants tend to get top heavy as they get bigger, so stick a few bushy, branching twigs into the pots to provide a little support. Start feeding the plants once a fortnight.

Tomato seedlings

If the tomatoes (sown in warmth two weeks ago for planting outdoors later) have germinated, take them out of the propagator. If two seedlings have emerged in any of the pots, take one out and leave the other. Put the pots in the greenhouse, making sure they are in full light, till planting out time.

Potting up peppers

If the peppers are now about 15–25cm (6–9 in) tall then they are ready for their final planting. Plant them singly into 20–25cm (8–10 in) pots of potting compost. By putting them in pots you will be able to move them outside in mid summer (June). They will grow perfectly well in the open if you put the pots against a warm, south-facing wall that will protect them from cold winds.

Put a 90cm (3 ft) cane in each pot to support the plants, water regularly and give them a liquid feed every fortnight from mid summer (June) onwards.

you protect the plants against buffeting winds and ensure that no young tubers are exposed on the soil surface. Potatoes that are uncovered turn green and, if cooked and eaten, can cause stomach upsets. You also kill any weeds growing between the rows when you earth up.

Keeping up the weeding

Watch those weeds; forget about them and they will get the upper hand. Hoe between the rows once a week to get rid of them when they are no more than seedlings. If you leave them to flower and

seed you will have hundreds of weeds flourishing where previously there were only a few.

But hoe with care, for some of the earlier-sown vegetables are growing quite big and many have lateral roots running just below the soil surface. You can, for instance, severely damage the roots of onions and lettuce if you take the hoe right up to the plants. So hoe lightly down the centre of the space between rows and hand-weed the rest.

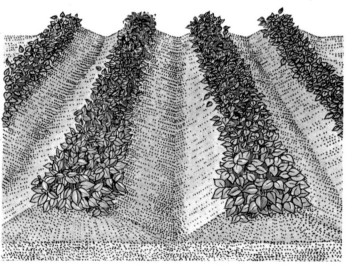

Early summer: Feeding and Watering

Spring has turned to early summer in the Edible Garden. Feeding and watering the vegetables in the food plot are your main concerns. Other jobs include pollinating the greenhouse tomatoes, caring for crops under cloches and runner beans indoors, and planting out the onions.

From now until late summer (July) growth will be at its maximum. For the next ten weeks or so the long hours of daylight and the sun's warmth generate frantic activity within the cell structure of plants. Once mid summer has been reached, and the days begin to shorten again, most of our vegetables, with the exception of those that will mature in winter or next spring, slow down and begin ripening.

Food and water
Take full advantage of the period of optimum growth by giving the plants everything they require. First and foremost they need water. Just as you need a free circulation of blood to provide all parts of your body with food and oxygen, so plants need a plentiful supply of water to transport the essential elements that support their life. Do remember that your plants can only use the plant foods in the soil if they are dissolved in water.

Furthermore a high concentration of inorganic fertilizers in a dry soil can kill, rather than feed, them. The less water there is, the more concentrated the fertilizer solution becomes until it may reach a point where, instead of flowing into the roots it draws liquid out of them and the plants die of dehydration (or, at best, suffer a severe check).

Hoses and sprinklers
During long, dry spells, therefore, give the plants plenty of water. Providing there are no water restrictions in force in your area, use a hosepipe in preference to a watering can. There is nothing worse than giving a parched plant a few drops of water when it needs a good soaking. If the soil is already dry it will itself absorb a considerable volume of water, just to moisten its surface. If you merely fill a watering can full and wave it over your vegetables you will wet the leaves and no more. It is tempting to make one can

do for a whole row, regardless of its length. Plodding back and forth from tap to plot is time-consuming and tiring; this is why a hosepipe (where permitted) is the answer.

Another invaluable piece of watering equipment is an oscillating sprinkler – an attachment which fits on the end of the hose. Depending on the model, and on how you regulate it, it can give your garden a thorough soaking over an area of some 225 sq m (2,500 sq ft). Attach the free end of the hose to the tap, turn it on and leave it to do the watering for you.

Soluble plant foods
Once the soil is saturated, right down to the deepest roots, start giving the vegetables a booster feed. All crops will give a higher yield if they are given a little extra plant food during their period of rapid growth. The best, and easiest, way of doing this is to use soluble feeds. These

are available either as concentrated liquids in bottles or as powders which dissolve readily in water. Of the two the powdered forms are the cheapest, needing only about one teaspoonful to 10 lit (2 gal) of water to give a nutritional solution of the required strength.

The advantages of using a soluble feed are twofold. First, the liquid that falls on the wet soil quickly finds its way down to the roots and is rapidly absorbed into the stems and leaves. Secondly, the liquid that falls on the leaves is taken in through the minute leaf pores, or stomata, and the nutrients become immediately available to the plant. This is called 'foliar feeding' and it is the quickest way there is of getting plants to respond to applied fertilizers.

These liquid feeds must only be regarded as boosters or bonuses. Your main plant feeding programme still entails the proper application of organic

IN THE GREENHOUSE
In order to produce a bumper tomato crop you must make sure that the flowers have set (been pollinated).

Pollinating greenhouse tomatoes
The tomatoes are showing, or are about to show, the first flowers on the bottom trusses. 'Truss' is the term used to describe the cluster of flowers borne on the stem which emerges from the axil of one of the lower leaves. The first truss, the lowest to form on the stem, is always the problem one. Its flowers are almost always reluctant to set.

Before the flower can perform its proper function of developing into a fruit, ripe pollen must drop on to a receptive stigma (the top part of the female flower organ). The pollen then works its way down into the ovary and fertilizes it. Not only must the pollen be ripe, but the conditions for its transference from an anther (the part of the male flower that contains pollen) to a stigma must be favourable. Pollen travels best in warm, humid conditions and worst when the air in the greenhouse is dry and cold. The bottom truss, being low down and near ground level, is sited in the coldest part of the greenhouse because warm air rises and

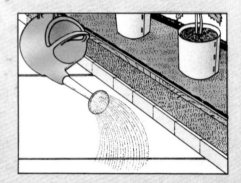

Damp down greenhouse path; humid air helps tomatoes to pollinate

is replaced by colder air. Therefore, in order to get as many of the flowers as possible to set, they need some help. One way is to damp down the path and surrounding ground level area every morning to create a moist atmosphere. At the same time the top ventilator should be opened to keep the atmosphere moving and buoyant. Next, give each plant a few gentle taps to dislodge the pollen and get it airborne.

You may find that you get a better set if you place a sheet of white polythene over the ground beneath the plants to reflect light and warmth upwards onto the trusses. As a last

manures to the soil before planting. These represent the staple diet of the plants; the liquid feeds are supplements applied to give increased yields under intensive cultivation.

Provide your crops with adequate water and ample food, from now until late summer (July) and they will be less liable to run prematurely to seed, and will be bigger, better and tastier as a result.

Caring for cloche crops
Crops under cloches also need water. Being permanently under cover they don't even get the full benefit of natural rainfall. There are one or two self-watering cloches which don't have to be removed in order to water the plants underneath them, but the majority have to be lifted before, and replaced after, watering.

On the other hand the soil under the cloches does not lose water quite as quickly as the soil outside. Much of it condenses on the inside of the glass or plastic and is returned to the soil. So look at the soil under your cloches at regular intervals and weed or water the soil.

Now that the days and nights are warmer you can remove the cloches altogether from most vegetables providing there are no frost warnings. And crops like lettuce, radish and spring onions taste better if they are not forced too much. An early start for seed germination and subsequent weather protection is one thing, but forcing does detract from quality. Lettuce left too long under cloches have a tendency to be limp, loose-hearted and a little leathery. Use the cloches to bring them on by all means, but give them the open air when they are half grown; they will form tighter hearts and have a better flavour. The only crops that still need protection are those that are liable to damage by frost, such as dwarf French beans.

Hardening off leeks
Harden off the leeks for a week or so in a cold frame or under cloches, or introduce them gradually to the elements by putting them outside in a warm spot on sunny days, bringing them in again at night.

Planting out onions
Onions can be awkward vegetables to plant out because they are top heavy at this stage. Their roots consist of no more than one or two white threads attached to the base of a pair of long, lanky, upright leaves. If you try to plant them with their roots just below soil level, they refuse to stand up and are easily dislodged by wind and rain.

Overcome this problem by drawing out a shallow drill 13mm ($\frac{1}{2}$ in) deep with hoe and line. Place the seedlings in it, 15–20cm (6–8 in) apart, with 23cm (9 in) between the drills. With your fingers pull a little soil over the roots, and firm gently, then heap some more soil around each plantlet to keep it firm and upright. Finally soak the whole bed with water to give them every opportunity to re-root quickly.

Windowsill runner beans
If the first leaves have appeared, increase watering and keep the plants near to the window for maximum light.

Pigeon-scaring
Are your vegetables being pecked to tatters by pigeons? If so paint some empty bottles or cans a bright red, push a few 1·2m (4 ft) canes into the ground between the rows and stick the inverted bottles or cans on top of them. It will keep the pigeons away for a year at least, although they may eventually get used to them.

Above: white polythene reflects light
Below: tap flowers to help setting

resort you can always obtain a proprietary tomato setting agent which you apply to the flowers to encourage them to set and form fruit.

To feed soilbed tomatoes pour liquid feed into pots sunk in soil

The higher trusses usually set without trouble providing you damp down regularly and follow a consistent feeding programme to keep the plants growing steadily and strongly.

Feeding greenhouse tomatoes
Begin feeding as soon as the first flower opens on the bottom truss. If you are growing your plants by the ring-culture system, feed into the rings once a week using a liquid fertilizer.

There are, on the market, a variety of branded liquid feeds which are especially formulated to encourage tomato plants to grow and produce fine fruit; all do the job cleanly, efficiently and with the minimum fuss and bother.

If you are growing tomatoes in the greenhouse soil bed, apply the liquid fertilizer once a fortnight all over the bed. In this case the soluble feed supplements the fertilizer forked in before planting. The disadvantage of liquid-feeding the whole bed is that it is impossible to give each plant a controlled amount. It also tends to create over-acidity unless the soil is removed and replaced every year. One way of overcoming the problem is to sink 10cm (4 in) pots, up to their rims, into the soil 30–40cm (12–15 in) away from the base of each plant. Once every two to three weeks fill the pots with a standard liquid feed solution which will gradually percolate through to the roots of the adjacent plants. This method achieves a reasonable control of acidity and means that you don't have to apply fertilizer to the entire bed, so it is less wasteful.

Runner beans
If the seeds have germinated, take the pots out of the propagator and follow the advice given in the section on windowsill runner beans (see above).

Early Summer

Boltardy is less prone to bolting (running to seed) than most other strains of beetroot. This makes it an excellent choice for early sowings. It also has a good texture and fine flavour

We begin to sow beetroot and plant out the leeks that have been hardening off. Work in the greenhouse concentrates on the tomatoes – giving them some support and pinching out their sideshoots.

The ideal soil for beetroot is one that is rich in well-rotted organic matter. If you use fresh manure the beetroot will be forked and misshapen. A good site is one on which potatoes or peas and beans were grown last year and which was heavily manured then.

How to sow
Take a close look at your beetroot seeds. They may be clusters or monogerm type, and sowing methods vary accordingly. If the contents of the packet look like miniature magnetic mines and are about the same size as sweet pea seeds, they are seed clusters. If they are tiny, ordinary-looking seeds they are monogerm – that is, each seed is a single germ that will produce a single plant.

The seed clusters are large enough to be handled individually, so sow them singly 5–8cm (2–3 in) apart in shallow drills. The drills should be 3mm ($\frac{1}{8}$ in) deep and 25cm (9 in) apart. This is called 'station' sowing. After they have germinated the seedlings will appear in clusters; thin them to one per station. The stations themselves will be thinned out once the seedlings are bigger.

Monogerm seeds are sown thinly in the same way as for lettuce and carrots, and the seedlings thinned to the distance recommended on the packet of the variety that you have chosen.

Varieties of beetroot
A recommended variety is Boltardy, which produces nice round roots of first-rate flavour. You can sow it earlier but then the roots tend to get too large and lose some of their sweetness. The best roots are those that are no bigger than billiard balls by harvesting time in mid autumn (September). Your best plan is to sow a row now for pulling young for summer salads and then sow another row or two in early to mid summer (early June) and store them for winter use.

Boltardy has the added advantage of being less prone to bolting in hot, dry weather. Bolting (when plants throw up flower stems and run to seed) renders the roots completely useless. It occurs if the soil is short of plant food or if there isn't enough moisture at the roots.

Two other good varieties are Crimson Globe and Detroit, both of which produce ball-shaped roots of good quality and flavour. For something different try Golden Beet. This unusual beetroot is golden skinned and looks more like a turnip than a beet; nevertheless its flavour is every bit as good as the crimson varieties. There are also a few varieties that grow long roots shaped like thick parsnips, but they need a deep soil to do well and you may find their flavour inferior to the globe varieties.

One splendid beetroot, Housewives' Choice, falls halfway between a long-rooted and a globe type. It is roughly the shape and size of a stump-rooted carrot and its flavour is excellent.

Tending beetroot
Beetroots are easy to grow and are seldom troubled by pests and diseases. But it is vitally important that they do not run short of water at any time during growth. To get good crops of sweet-tasting roots, keep the weeds down and soak the rows with water in dry weather.

Planting out leeks
If the soil in the vegetable plot is dry give it a good soak before starting to plant. Put down your garden line to mark out the row, then make narrow holes 15cm (6 in) deep and 25cm (9 in) apart with a large dibber or a narrow-bladed trowel. Drop one seedling into each hole then, instead of filling it with soil, fill it up with water instead. This will wash some soil round the roots – enough to hold them firm. The rest of the hole will fill itself in naturally with the passing of time.

Harvesting shallots
You should now be seeing the first harvests of the season. The shallots probably now have enough green leaves for a preliminary pulling. These leaves are delicious in salads.

Garden hygiene
Hygiene outdoors in the garden is as important as hygiene in the greenhouse. There is no harm in leaving small weed seedlings lying on the soil to shrivel in the sun, but always put large weeds, lawn

mowings and mounds of leaves on the compost heap. If you leave them lying at the foot of hedges and fences and in odd corners, they become a haven for slugs and snails and a host of other pests.

Water in leeks after transplanting instead of filling in holes with soil

Frost protection
Keep a careful eye on the weather just now. Very often the days are deceptively balmy, giving no hint of the sharp frost that may follow at nightfall. Sheets of newspaper to throw over your potatoes and a few cloches to cover tender plants (such as dwarf French beans) can both prove most useful. If frost threatens, close your frame down tight, opening up again in the morning.

Beans for the Pergola
The runner beans in the Edible Garden were planted at the foot of the pergola, in holes prepared in the same way as the trenches described below.

Preparing the ground
Most vegetables have shallow roots, but runner beans are an exception. To get full value from your row of 'runners' you will have to dig deeply.

If you are planting them in the vegetable plot, put down your garden line and dig out a trench 30cm (12 in) deep. Return to your starting point and dig it 30cm (12 in) deeper; you should then have an excavation 60cm (24 in) deep with earth piled up on both sides. Into the bottom of the trench put a good thick layer of organic matter, such as compost or rotted manure – in fact anything that is not man-made fibre and will rot down. Put the soil that was dug out last (the subsoil) back on top of it, and then add a dusting of bonemeal. Put the rest of the soil back and tread it over well to firm it.

Supporting the beans
With the exception of one or two dwarf varieties (like Hammond's Dwarf Scarlet) runner beans are climbers and need a good support. This is where the pergola comes in useful – failing that use 2·5m (8 ft) bamboo canes or sticks. Put the canes

in now, before sowing, so that the whole structure has a chance to settle down before it has to carry any weight. You will be sowing your beans 30cm (12 in) apart, so you will need twice as many canes as you have space for seeds plus two or three extra ones. That is, one cane or stick on each side at 30cm (12 in) intervals all the way down the row and the extra ones for tying in.

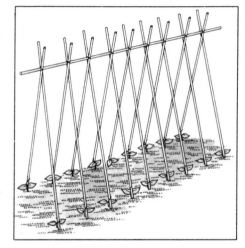

Bean poles make an excellent supporting framework for rows of runner beans

IN THE GREENHOUSE
The tomato plants are getting big enough to need some support. There are two simple and effective ways of doing this. One is to push a stout bamboo cane, 1·8–2·5m (6–8 ft) long, into the soil beside each plant, and then loosely tie the plant to it at 40–45cm (15–18 in) intervals as the plant grows.

Alternatively you can stretch a length of strong wire along the roof of the greenhouse above the row of plants. Next, push a 45cm (18 in) length of strong galvanized wire into the soil beside each plant with the top 10cm (4 in) bent over to form a hook. Then run lengths of tough, nylon cord or garden string between the hooks and the roof wire. As the tomato plant grows you simply twine the cord around the stem.

Cutting out sideshoots
If you look in the joints between the stems and the leaves you will find sideshoots growing. If they are left to

Cut out tomato sideshoots cleanly

sprout the whole plant will almost cease to grow upwards. Instead it becomes an untidy, straggly bush, and its fruiting ability is seriously impaired, so do remove the sideshoots.

Resist the temptation to nip them

off with finger and thumb. Your hands can be the carriers of pests and diseases that may be transferred to the open cuts and infect the whole plant. Also, it is difficult to make a clean cut with finger and thumb. You are more likely to snag the cut and tear into the main stem leaving an open sore which, again, is a receptacle for diseases. To do the job properly get a clean, sharp knife and cut through the sideshoot as near to its point of origin as you can.

Put all the severed sideshoots into a bag or box and take them to the compost heap. Never forget the importance of greenhouse hygiene. Leaving dead plants (or bits of plants) lying about is asking for trouble.

Heating and ventilating
When frost is forecast put a little heat on in the greenhouse. Open the ventilation as soon as possible in the morning to keep air moving and the plants healthy.

Sowing runner beans

Take a trowel, loosen the soil at the foot of each pergola post (or at the foot of each cane) and pop one seed in – about 2–3cm (1 in) deep.

After a seed has been sown at the base of every post, sow a further six or eight seeds by the last post (or at the end of the row) just in case any of the others refuse to germinate; you can use the spares to fill any resulting gaps.

Unfortunately slugs like runner beans. To stop them eating the first small leaves, dust the soil with hydrated lime and spread a few slug pellets at the foot of each plant.

Varieties of runner bean

Yardstick can provide you with prizewinning pods up to 60cm (24 in) in length, and Streamline and Scarlet Emperor both crop well in most seasons, yielding good clusters of shorter, fatter pods. But our first choice would be the recent variety Fry that crops heavily, has a fine flavour and produces stringless beans.

Summer cabbage and cauliflower

Have you thinned the summer cabbage and cauliflowers that were sown in the middle of spring (mid March)? If not they will now be sizeable plants, standing shoulder to shoulder and it is time to give them some breathing space. Thin them to 45cm (18 in) apart and weed the rows at the same time.

Cabbage-root fly

After thinning take precautions to protect the plants from the ravages of the cabbage-root fly. Like the carrot fly it lays its eggs on the surface of the soil around the stems of the seedlings. When the larvae hatch, they burrow their way down to the roots and slowly demolish them. The first visible sign of trouble is the wilting of the plants when the sun is on them. They recover in the evening, but as the attacks get progressively worse, so does the wilting until a point is reached when growth stops altogether.

If you are still unsure of your diagnosis have a look at the leaves; they take on a bluish tinge if the roots are being eaten by the larvae. At this stage there is nothing you can do to save the crop, so pull up all infected plants and burn them.

When you have finished thinning, proceed carefully along the rows, firming the soil around each plant by putting your feet as near to the stems as you can without touching them. The larvae find it difficult to penetrate this hard crust. Furthermore, all members of the cabbage family grow best in a firm, well-trodden soil. Sprinkle a little 4 per cent calomel dust around each stem as a further precaution against the larvae, and finally earth up the plants to give them an even firmer footing.

Cabbage white butterfly

Cabbage-root fly bears no resemblance in appearance or activity to the cabbage white butterfly. The cabbage fly is a dreary, insignificant and somewhat smaller version of the house fly, whereas the cabbage white butterfly is a graceful creature – in spite of its deplorable habits. The green eggs that it lays on the leaves of cabbages and their relatives eventually hatch into voracious green caterpillars. They eat their way steadily through the leaves until only a fine lattice work of veins is left, and the plants are unfit for

Runner beans provide an unusual and attractive covering for the pergola in the Edible Garden

anything but the compost heap.

There are two ways of controlling them. One is to go over the plants once a day, picking off the caterpillars and popping them into a jar of water or weak disinfectant. The other is to spray (or dust) with derris or pyrethrum as soon as you see the first caterpillar. Repeat the treatment at regular intervals until you are certain there are none left.

Planting from the seedbed
Some of the seeds sown in the seedbed in mid to late spring (end of March) are ready for planting out. Start with the red cabbages and a few of the brussels sprouts. There is no need to plant out all the sprouts at once. Leave some of them for a later planting, so that they don't all mature together.

In the Edible Garden one red cabbage was planted at each corner of the east side of the food plot, but if you are planting more, leave 45cm (18 in) between plants and rows. Brussels sprouts will need 60cm (24 in) between plants; plant them in staggered rows 75cm (2½ ft) apart.

Lift a few plants gently out of the seedbed with a trowel and put them immediately – up to their lower leaves – into a bowl or bucket of water. Next put a few spoonfuls of 4 per cent calomel dust in a saucer, slowly add water and stir until it has the consistency of thick cream. Protect the plants against cabbage-root fly by dipping the roots of each one in the paste – and they are ready to plant.

How to plant brassicas
Mark out a row with your garden line. Then pick up a plant in readiness and, with the other hand, thrust your trowel (open side facing you) up to its shoulders in the soil. Don't lift the soil – pull it towards you until you have left a narrow hole just deep enough to take the plant roots. Push the plant in right up to its bottom leaves and take the trowel out. Then thrust the trowel (still with open side facing you) back into the soil, between you and the plant and about 5cm (2 in) away from the newly-planted brassica. Push the trowel back towards the plant. The pressure forces the soil into the hole hard up against the stem and roots to hold them securely. Fill in any remaining depressions and firm around the top with your knuckles. Remember – plant firmly if you want firm, hard cabbage hearts and sprouts.

Sweet corn
Sweet corn, cut from your own garden and cooked immediately, is one of the most delicious vegetables there is. Sow the seeds in rich, well-manured soil. Once they start growing they develop rapidly into quite large plants, so make certain they have an ample supply of food and moisture at the roots.

There is an element of uncertainty in growing sweet corn in Britain. The cobs need a fairly good summer before they will set and ripen. You may find that you only get a worthwhile yield of cobs, on average, two years out of three.

Sweet corn is an exception to most vegetables in that it needs to be grown in block formation. If, for example, you wish to grow twelve plants the usual way is to set them in one straight line; but for sweet corn the layout is a rectangle consisting of four lines of three. For 24 plants it would be a 6 × 4 arrangement, and so on.

The reason lies in the plants themselves. Each plant bears male and female flowers separately and on different parts of the plant. The male flowers emerge right at the topmost tip, whilst the female flowers are borne at the ends of elongated sheaths, sited at intervals in the axils of the leaves along the lower stem. To get cobs to form, ripe pollen from the male flowers must drop onto the receptive female flowers of a plant (the same, or another, plant).

The pollen is not carried from flower to flower by insects. It relies for its transference on air currents. If these currents are too strong the pollen may well be blown away from the waiting female flowers. Growing the plants in block formation reduces the risk of non-pollination, because no matter which way the wind is blowing, some pollen is almost certain to find its way home.

Sow three seeds in 13mm (½ in) deep holes set 45cm (18 in) apart all round and cover each sowing station with an inverted jam jar or cloche.

In about ten weeks time the cobs will start forming, but they will be completely invisible. What you will see are long, torpedo shaped, green sheaths with long, silky threads (called silks) dangling from their tips; these are the female receptacles of the male pollen.

Varieties of sweet corn
For the best chance of success choose an early maturing variety such as Earliking (F.1 hybrid) or, if you live in an area that has a climate similar to that of the northern half of Britain, North Star (F.1 hybrid) which seems to do better in comparatively cold, wet soils and summers.

Thinning parsnips
If the parsnip seedlings are large enough to handle easily, thin them to about 15cm (6 in) apart and draw a little soil round them to prevent them flopping over. They need no further attention, other than weeding, till harvesting time.

Blackfly on beans
Blackfly are particularly troublesome to broad beans and, later on, to dwarf French and runner beans.

The main attack on broad beans comes when the plants are fully grown and in flower. The flies mass on the growing tips like a black plague, but seldom venture farther down. At this time keep a daily eye on the beans and, as soon as you see blackfly settling, nip off about 5–8cm (2–3 in) of the growing tips. It is a messy job, but it does prevent the pest from debilitating the plants; it also hastens the formation of pods so that the crop is ready a little earlier.

Weeding and mulching
Be sure to work regularly at hoeing, to keep the soil between rows clean, and hand weeding between the plants where the hoe cannot reach. If the weather turns hot and dry, put a mulch 2–3cm (1 in) thick of lawn mowings between the rows, providing that the lawn has not been treated with a weedkiller.

Mulches of mowings or moist peat serve a useful purpose. They keep the soil and roots cool in the heat of high summer and reduce the moisture loss. In the long term they also act as an organic fertilizer. The earthworms take them down into the lower reaches of the soil and convert them into valuable plant foods. In short they perform a dual function – as soil insulators and fertilizers.

IN THE GREENHOUSE
If the first dwarf French bean flowers are out, start to feed the plants – once every ten days or so – with a liquid fertilizer that will encourage growth and good cropping.

Marrows and courgettes

If you have ever watched the winner of the 'biggest marrow prize' staggering away with his exhibit from the village show, you may have wondered what becomes of it – and all the others in the prize-winner's garden. There is a limit to the amount of marrow jam or chutney that the average family can eat.

There is no place for such a space-consuming vegetable (that is really a fruit) in the Edible Garden. Instead, choose a kind that takes up less room and yields smaller and tastier marrows.

We recommend the courgette varieties like Zucchini and Golden Zucchini (both F.1 hybrids). These bear prolific crops of small marrows which are at their best, cut and cooked, when about 15cm (6 in) long.

Preparing the ground

In days gone by, when vegetable gardens were much larger, a few marrows would be grown on top of a heap of old manure. The site was ideal, for the manure was rich in plant food and, being of organic matter, never dried out. It provided the marrows with everything that they needed – plenty of food and ample water

at all stages of their growth. Unfortunately this raised-bed system left the impression that marrows should always be grown on humps and hillocks. In ordinary garden soil nothing could be worse. Marrows must have plenty of soil moisture, and if you want good results grow them in shallow pits, not mounds.

The hollows also provide the young plant with a certain amount of protection from the elements. For the first few days of its life it enjoys a favourable micro-climate until it grows up and out of the depression and is better equipped to fend for itself.

Start your marrows in early summer (mid May). First dig out holes 60cm (24 in) square and 45cm (18 in) deep. Into the bottom of each hole put a layer of fresh manure or half-rotted compost, and tread it down until it half fills the hole. Sprinkle a handful of dried blood fertilizer over it and replace and firm the soil.

Sow three or four seeds in the centre of each hole, placing them, on end, about 13mm (½ in) below the surface. If you sow them flat, they have a tendency to rot. After sowing, cover the hole with a cloche, or put a large inverted jam jar over the newly-sown seeds.

Tending the onions

When you planted out the onion seedlings you put a little extra soil around each plantlet to keep it firm and upright. Now pull this soil away, until the bases of the plants are at soil level. It is essential to do this because onions that are planted too deeply tend to grow thick necks and poor, elongated bulbs.

Weeding the food plot

Weeds, as well as cultivated plants, accelerate their rate of growth in the higher temperatures and longer daylight hours of early summer. Unless you are on your guard the vegetable plot can be taken over by them. Hoe regularly between the rows and hand weed to remove those growing up against your vegetables. Well-established weeds are difficult to eradicate and, if you let them flower and seed, you are inviting an even heavier population in the future. What is more, weeds compete with other plants for the fertilizer in the soil – as well as for light and space – so a weedy garden means poorer vegetables.

Supplementary feeding

Few gardeners realize the full potential of

IN THE GREENHOUSE

Feed the tomatoes and cucumbers once a week and make sure they are never short of water.

Tying in tomatoes and cucumber
Remember to tie in the main stems of the tomatoes to their stakes, or twist the supporting strings round them, with every 30cm (12 in) of growth. Cut out the emerging sideshoots as soon as you spot them.

Also tie in the two main stems of the cucumber to stakes regularly.

Cucumber flowers
If you are growing Conqueror or Telegraph, or any similar variety which bears both male and female flowers on the same plant, you will have to pinch out the male ones.

It is quite easy to tell the difference between the sexes. The male flower is borne on a slender stem, whereas the female has a tiny, swollen ovary below it. It is this ovary that will eventually develop into a full-sized cucumber. Being self-fertile the female flower can pollinate itself without the assistance of the male. In fact, if the male is allowed to cross-pollinate the female the cucumbers will taste bitter. So as soon as you can tell one from the other, remove the male flowers before they open and start spreading their pollen.

Those of you who are growing the varieties, like Pepinex, which bear female flowers only, will be spared the trouble of looking for the males and decapitating them.

Cutting out tendrils
Tendrils arise in the joints between stems and leaves of the cucumber plant. They are thin wispy growths that look like small coiled springs. Cut them out because there is no point in letting the plant waste its energies on growing organs which it doesn't need. Left to its own devices the plant would use the tendrils to attach itself to any means of support available.

Pests in the greenhouse
Whitefly may remain undetected in the greenhouse for some time. They are very small and hide away under the leaves of tomato and other plants. But if you brush against the plants and disturb them, they rise in clouds of white dots before resettling to resume their sap-sucking. The remedy is pyrethrum or derris. A spray is preferable to a dust; using an atomized spray you can apply it to the underside of the leaves as well as to the upper surfaces, whereas getting a dust to stick there is virtually impossible.

Smoking out whitefly
A more effective way of dealing with whitefly in the greenhouse is to fumigate with smokes'. These are small cones which look just like fireworks, complete with blue paper. Each smoke cone is designed to treat a fixed area of greenhouse space, so the number of cones you need depends on the size of your house.

To use the cones, first close down all the ventilators to keep the fumes within the house. If there are large cracks or spaces, stuff them with wet cloth or sacking. Place the required number of cones, equally spaced, along the greenhouse path. Light the cone farthest away from the door; then light the others (if any) as you proceed towards the exit. In this way you ensure that you breathe little or none of the fumigant. Close the door tightly and leave for at least two hours.

Some gardeners maintain that the evening is the most effective time to fumigate because the greenhouse can then be kept closed all night. The snag with this method is that, in the complete absence of ventilation, heavy condensation will form on the inside of the glass and this can encourage fungus disease. So fumigate in the morning when the flies are very active and, therefore, very vulnerable.

After two hours, open the house right up and clear it for normal working. A second treatment is essential – 10–14 days after the first fumigation – in order to annihilate the second generation.

Greenhouse greenfly
Greenfly are also a serious problem in the greenhouse. Follow the instructions for eliminating them from the food plot.

A job for marigolds
An old gardening tip is to grow three or four French or African marigolds in the greenhouse. It appears that greenfly and whitefly steer well clear of them as they dislike the pungent smell of the leaves.

their soils, so during the weeks from now until late summer (early–mid July), aim to get more from every piece of ground by applying supplementary feeds. Embark on a regular routine: every weekend for the next six or seven weeks give your vegetables liquid booster feeds (following the manufacturer's recommended strengths). You will be well rewarded for your efforts.

Controlling greenfly
Not only does this time of year bring growth, it also brings greenfly. If the weather favours them (and it usually does) they will descend on your plants in their millions and can do untold harm. Examine the crops in the garden (and in the greenhouse) daily. You will find greenfly lurking on leaves and young stems where they suck the nutritious sap. Left unchecked, their activities will seriously affect growth.

Greenfly multiply at an alarming rate. The first generation gives birth to the second in about ten days – and so they continue until the end of the breeding season. Their natural predators, such as ladybirds and sparrows, help to keep their numbers down, but some assistance from you is required to effect absolute control.

As soon as you see the first signs of greenfly on any plant, spray immediately with pyrethrum or derris. You could use the insecticides in their powder form, but the liquid spray gives a more rapid, and a more effective, kill. The spray or dust will destroy all the greenfly it touches, but will not kill the eggs that have already been laid. So when you have finished, make a note of the date in your diary and reapply the insecticide some 10–14 days later, and yet again in a further 10–14 days. In other words, it is necessary to spray or dust three times at set intervals to clear completely each original infestation.

Summer: In the Strawberry Bed

Strawberries should be producing their first fruits now, but they still need some care and attention. Here we instruct you on how to protect them from fungus diseases and how to root new plants from strawberry runners. We also give advice on preventing blight from attacking your potatoes and tomatoes, and on thinning beetroot, courgettes and sweet corn. In the greenhouse, work centres around the grape vine and the pots of sweet peppers.

Those of you who are living in mild areas may already be enjoying the first of many strawberry harvests – unless the birds found the fruit first. Many birds have a liking for strawberries, so they must be kept away. The 'old-fashioned' way is to put a fairly large jam jar on its side and push the whole bunch of fruit into the jar. It keeps the birds off and hastens ripening as well. But if you have a large bed you will need an enormous number of jars in order to protect each fruiting stem. A more practical method is to cover the plants with small-mesh nylon or polythene netting. Of course, if your strawberries are in a fruit cage, then you have no problem.

Strawberry runners

From the crown of each strawberry plant grow a number of long, wiry, creeping stems. These are called runners and are the means whereby the plants propagate themselves. At one or more points along each runner springs a mini strawberry plant complete with leaves and tiny rootlets. The roots insinuate themselves into the soil, and in no time there is a new strawberry plant growing between the rows.

Putting out these runners consumes the energy of the parent plant. If, therefore, you leave all the runners to grow without control, the parent becomes weakened and its cropping potential is drastically reduced. So unless you need more strawberry plants, cut all the runners right back to base as soon as you see them.

Propagating strawberries

If you do want some more plants, first select the strongest runner from each chosen plant and remove all others. You then have a choice of two methods of propagation. The simplest is to loosen the soil under the plantlet on the runner, push it into the earth and place small stones on the runner, one on each side. The new plant will quickly take root. When it is growing strongly, cut it clear of its runner and then leave it alone till you are ready to transplant it into its fruiting position in mid autumn (September).

A better method, which only takes a little more time and trouble, is to root the plantlets in small pots. Fill some 8 or 10cm (3 or 4 in) clay or plastic pots with potting compost or good rich loam. Sink each one up to its rim in the soil under the plantlets. Then root them as already described. The advantage of this method is that you don't disturb the plant roots when planting out. All you do is cut the runners, lift the pots bodily out of the soil, up-end them, tap the rooted plants out and plant them in their fruiting positions with their rootballs intact.

Fungus diseases

Early summer (May) is usually warm; dry, sunny days are often interspersed with short bursts of wet weather. These are ideal conditions for growth and germination, but they also favour fungus diseases, such as blight and mould. Blight may attack your potatoes and tomatoes; strawberries are susceptible to mould.

Grey mould on strawberries

Moulds come in varying kinds and colours. Grey mould (or botrytis) is particularly troublesome on strawberries. The ripening fruits and their stems become coated with a revolting grey mass and the fruits turn completely rotten. The disease is less likely to strike if you keep the strawberry bed free of weeds and give the plants collars of straw to keep their fruit off the ground. To prevent and check the disease, spray with captan or a systemic fungicide.

Potato blight

The potato is very vulnerable to potato blight. This is the disease that changed the face of Ireland just over a century ago, destroying the staple food of the people and causing a nationwide famine. The disease is caused by a microscopic fungus; unless checked it can destroy whole crops, making the tubers unfit to eat.

The disease first appears as brown blotches on the leaves. These spread to the stems and eventually down to the tubers themselves. Infected potatoes are covered with sunken areas, and underneath the skin the flesh is a reddish-brown. If these symptoms appear on the potatoes in your garden, lift all infected plants immediately, including the roots, and burn them. Do not compost them; they must be burnt because the sickness can be carried in the soil from one year to the next.

Spray all remaining healthy plants with a fungicide such as Bordeaux mixture, or with a liquid copper fungicide. In fact, if early summer (May) has been wet and warm, spray the plants as a precaution, even though they may look healthy.

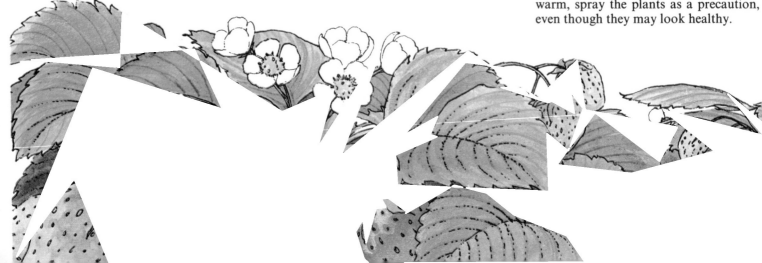

IN THE GREENHOUSE

Make sure the greenhouse has plenty of ventilation, night and day. On hot, sunny days leave the door wide open. Damp the soil and paths every morning and remember to tie in the tomatoes and cucumbers, otherwise their stems will bend and snap under the weight of forming fruit.

Putting the peppers out
It should now be safe to move the pot of sweet peppers out into the open during the day. Place it in a warm sheltered spot and bring it indoors again at the first hint of night chill. After a week of moving it in and out you can leave it outside permanently. If possible, position the pot against a south-facing wall, hedge or fence, the warmest places in the garden. They get the sun all day and, walls particularly, retain enough warmth to keep the chill off the plants in the evening.

Thinning the grapes
For the past few weeks the vine has needed little attention. It is now in full leaf and, like the tomatoes, prefers a moist, airy atmosphere. Water it thoroughly whenever the soil seems at all dry.

The lateral branches will be beginning to fill up with bunches of little grapes. There are, in fact, too many fruits forming for a good-quality crop to be produced. So equip yourself with a small pair of scissors and a step-ladder or stout chair and prepare to thin the bunches. Do not try to do the thinning from ground level – your arms will soon tire and you won't have a good view of what you are doing. Climb up amongst the bunches and carefully snip out all small and over-crowded fruit, so as to leave the remainder with ample space to grow into large, juice-laden grapes. Try not to touch the selected fruit with your fingers to avoid bruising or marking them.

When you have finished, you will have reduced the bunches by about one-third.

Blight-free tomatoes
Tomatoes can be affected by potato blight. For prevention and treatment, see the section on this disease in the food plot.

Hardening off 'outdoor' tomatoes
The tomatoes that were sown in the greenhouse in late spring (April) for planting out in summer are now ready to be hardened off. Put them out in the cold frame or under cloches for about a week. Alternatively, you can put them outside in the open, on warm sunny days, till they have adjusted to life in the garden.

Blight can also strike the tomatoes. This is hardly surprising as tomatoes and potatoes belong to the same plant family (SOLANACEAE). You have only to compare their flowers to see the family resemblance. Only their colour differs, the flowers of the tomato being yellow whereas those of the potatoes are either white or a pinky-blue.

Some potato varieties bear flowers that later produce small, round fruits like miniature tomatoes, only they don't change colour from green to red. New gardeners are often puzzled by the appearance of these green 'moth balls' on their potato plants. Their function is to form true potato seeds. Commercial growers use these seeds in trial grounds where new varieties are produced. Don't eat them – they are poisonous.

If your potatoes show the least sign of blight, give your tomatoes a preventive spray – and vice versa.

Thinning beetroot
If the beetroot seeds you sowed a few weeks ago were the seed-cluster type, then they will now need a preliminary thinning. A number of seedlings will have appeared at each station; remove all but the strongest seedling.

Thinning sweet corn
The sweet corn will also be ready for thinning, having germinated rapidly in the warm, early summer (May) soil. Thin to one seedling per station, if more than one has come through.

Late carrot sowings
As suggested earlier, one of the ways of saving your carrot crop from carrot fly is to sow late; it is now late enough.

Sow a row or two of a stump-rooted variety, such as Chantenay Red Cored or Little Finger. Space the rows 25cm (9 in) apart and sow pelleted seeds rather than ordinary ones. The pellets are seeds coated with a casing material to make them large enough to handle singly.

Place them, 2–3cm (1 in) apart, in very shallow drills that are just deep enough to cover them. After replacing the soil, soak it thoroughly with water and keep it wet until the seedlings come through.

Pelleted seeds need a lot more water than bare seeds because the outer casing must first be moistened until it disintegrates before the seed itself can begin to swell and then germinate. Germination in the warm soil will be rapid and you should see your first seedlings pushing through about two weeks after sowing. Having used pellets there will be no need to thin, and the plants will grow without check to give a good crop for lifting in late autumn (October).

Tending the courgettes
When the courgette seedlings emerge, remove all but the strongest. Also discard the jam jars, if that is what you were using to protect them, but cloches can be left on until you are confident that there is no danger of frost. From germination onwards, make absolutely sure that you keep the plants well watered if there is no rain. Fill the planting hole right up to the rim every time. In a few weeks' time the plants will start flowering and will require more care.

Mid-summer: Celery

There are so many first croppings in mid summer (June) that it is hard to decide which is the most exciting. Potatoes, cabbages, lettuce, spring onions – will all be coming ready for lifting.

However, harvesting isn't the only concern in the garden at this time of year. You must also plant out tomatoes that have been hardening off, and transplant some leeks from the seedbed. And there are more successional sowings to be made – or beetroot, lettuce, summer spinach, radish and broad beans.

Now that all danger of frost is past you can safely plant out the self-blanching celery (sown in warmth) into its final position. The plants will have made good root growth in their peat pots. Water the pots thoroughly then lay down your garden line and put in the plants (pots and all) with 25cm (9 in) between each plant and a similar distance between rows. Then give them a thorough soaking with water and keep them well watered right through the summer. The celery will be ready for eating in mid and late autumn (September and October).

Planting out tomatoes

Those of you who decided, earlier on, to grow tomatoes outdoors, will now have sturdy short-jointed, hardened-off plants ready for planting out. To give them the best possible chance of producing a crop that will ripen even in uncertain summers, choose their position carefully. They must have as much sun as the days can offer and shelter from strong, cold winds. The ideal situation is at the foot of a south-facing wall, hedge or fence. If you are planting them directly into the soil, fork in 70g per sq m (2 oz per sq yd) of a general fertilizer such as Fish meal or Growmore, and give the ground a thorough drenching with water. Allow one or two days for the soil to settle and then put the plants in 60cm (24 in) apart

A fine head of self-blanching celery – plant it out in mid summer for eating in the autumn

and firm the soil well round them. Finish off by giving each one a cane for support later on.

Remember that the soil at the foot of a wall or fence or similar windbreak is usually drier than anywhere else in the garden. This means that your outdoor tomatoes will need just as much watering as those in the greenhouse. They also need regular feeding to give a good crop.

If you are not planting into the garden soil, transfer the plants into 25–30cm (10–12 in) pots, or any similar-sized containers that have drainage holes in the bottom. I have seen excellent crops grown in a variety of containers ranging from smart wooden tubs to old buckets. The container isn't important, it's the contents that matter, and here you have a choice between using a soilless compost, such as J.I. No 3, or a good rich loam from your garden.

Fill each container to within 5cm (2 in) of the rim with the soil or compost. Then, after making a hole with a trowel, put the tomato plant in right up to its lowest pair of leaves. Firm the soil round it, give it a thorough soaking and push in a cane for support. Tie the plant in as it grows. Once planted, the containers can be positioned in the most favourable places.

Growing tomatoes in bags

A recent innovation in outdoor tomato cultivation is the use of special growing bags. These have proved a boon to flat-dwellers and gardeners with limited soil and space. Each bag contains a peat- or bark-based compost suitable for growing a variety of plants, including tomatoes and salad crops.

To use the bag, lay it flat, cut open

the top – following the printed instructions – and plant the tomatoes in the exposed compost. Each bag is big enough to take three or four tomato plants and, providing the compost is kept moist and the plants fed, you can expect a yield of approximately 3–4kg (6–8 lb) of fruit per plant.

At the end of the season, spread the exhausted compost over the food plot where it will serve as an excellent fertilizer and soil conditioner.

Planting out seedbed leeks
Now to the seedbed, where the leeks are waiting to be planted out. For this job you need a dibber with which to make the planting holes; you can either buy or make it. It should be a rounded piece of wood, about 2–3cm (1 in) in diameter and from 30–45cm (12–18 in) long, with a handle at one end and tapering to a point at the other. The handle of an old garden fork, or an old broom handle – cut to length and tapered off, will do if you can fix a handle to one end.

The procedure for transplanting is the same as for planting out the leeks that were sown in the greenhouse. To recap: lift the young leek plants carefully by pushing a trowel deep down under them and levering them up. Shake the soil off and gently tease them apart. Select the strongest and trim off a few centimetres of the leaf tips to prevent them trailing on the ground after planting. Now put down your garden line, and go along it dropping off a leek plant at 25cm (9 in) intervals. Starting at one end of the row, take the dibber and thrust it into the soil. Swivel it to and fro a few times before withdrawing it. You now have a smooth-sided round hole, some 25cm (9 in) deep, into which you drop one leek plant so that its leaf tips are just above soil level. Repeat this process all the way down the line. Then move the line 25cm (9 in) to left or right and plant a second row.

Finally 'puddle' the plants in by filling each hole right up to the brim with water. The water mixes with the soil so that the roots at the bottom of the holes become coated with a kind of thin mud. This enables the plants to re-root very rapidly and they start growing almost immediately. The rest of the hole will fill up gradually with soil as you hoe and weed during the growing season.

Sowing beetroot
At the beginning of early summer (May) you sowed some beetroot for pulling young and sweet for summer salads. Another row or two can be sown now. This

IN THE GREENHOUSE
There should be a treat in store for you any day now – the first greenhouse tomatoes will be ripening.

Tending ripening tomatoes
Look at the tomatoes daily from now on. The moment you see the first fruits on the bottom trusses beginning to change from green to red (or yellow, with the yellow-fruiting varieties), you can pick them. There is no need to wait until they are fully red and ripe. In fact picking partly-ripe tomatoes encourages others to ripen sooner. When picking, snap off the stalk at the first joint (or knuckle) above the fruit so as to leave a short bit of stem attached.

While the plants are in full production, keep up the weekly feeding programme and make sure they never want for water. If you alternately soak the soil and then let it dry right out, your tomatoes will develop blossom end rot. The end farthest from the stalk becomes flattened and turns dark brown or black. If this condition occurs then your plants need more watering at more frequent intervals; and the greenhouse probably needs more shade.

Remember also that it is unnecessary to strip the plants of their leaves in order to let the sun get at the fruit. Ripening depends on the greenhouse temperatures, irrespective of direct sunlight. Removing the leaves, therefore, serves no useful purpose. It just deprives the plants of a valuable part of their own food-manufacturing equipment. Only strip the leaves if they are beginning to show signs of yellowing or disease.

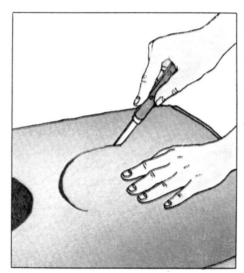

Growing bags have proved a boon to people with limited garden space, particularly for tomatoes and cucumbers

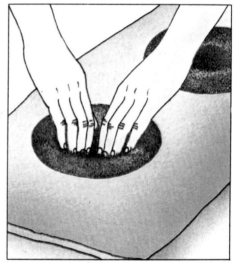

Above left: cut away part of the top
Above: make a hole in the growing medium large enough to take the plant (below)

later sowing will give you beetroot to store for use during the winter. The variety Boltardy is a good choice for sowing at this time being less prone to bolting (running to seed) during hot, dry weather.

Sweet corn
Remove the cloches or jam-jar covers from the sweet corn plants, water them well in dry weather and let them grow on.

Successional sowings
Keep on sowing short rows of lettuce, summer spinach and radish for late crops. There is also still time this month for sowing carrots, early peas and a last row of broad beans to provide welcome crops in mid autumn (September).

Mid-summer: Currants

One of the joys of mid summer (June) is watching the blackcurrant fruits change colour to glossy black.

Picking blackcurrants

Wait until all the fruit on a branch is ripe, and then cut the whole branch off – about three-quarters of the way down. You can take it indoors and strip off and top and tail the fruit at leisure. Doing it this way serves a dual purpose. It makes a tedious fruit-picking job easier, and it also serves to prune the bush at the same time.

Blackcurrants bear this year's fruit on branches that grew last year, so it follows that next year's crop will be carried on new growth made during this year. Cutting off the fruit-laden branches induces the lower buds to shoot and develop into the new branches that will give you next year's crop.

Redcurrants and whitecurrants

Oddly enough, both the red and the white grow quite differently from blackcurrants. They bear their fruit on old wood, so their pruning is a winter job that you can tackle when the time is right. In the meantime, gather the juicy bunches of currants as soon as they are ripe. If the birds are stealing the fruit, cast a garden net over the bushes and leave it in position until all the currants are safely gathered.

New potatoes

In mid spring (March) you planted early potatoes. Since then you have earthed them, protected them from frost, and watched them grow a forest of green leaves – and perhaps even a few flowers.

Make sure you check daily to see whether you have been rewarded by a first clutch of small, white, new potatoes. After some 12 weeks of growth the roots should yield a picking. Don't start by digging up a whole root. First pull the soil away from the side of a root until you expose two or three of the new tubers. If one, or more, of them is as big as a hen's egg, take your fork and start digging up the roots. The first few roots you lift are, in a sense, wasteful; if you left them for another week or two the potatoes would be much bigger – but nobody would deny you this minor extravagance.

Succulent blackcurrants ready for harvesting. Throw a garden net over the bushes if the birds attempt to harvest the fruit for you

To make picking blackcurrants easier, cut the fruiting stems about three-quarters of the way down, then strip off the fruit in comfort. This also serves to prune the bushes

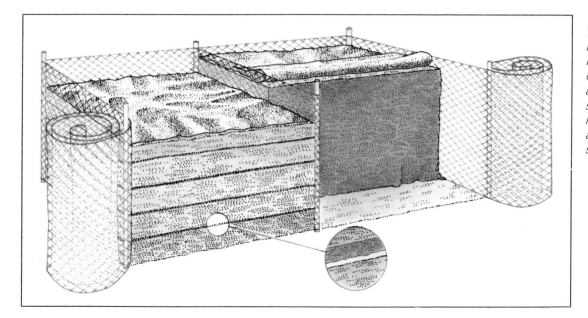

Potato haulms

Don't leave the haulms (leaves and stalks) lying at the side of the row from which the tubers have been lifted. They become havens for slugs, snails and other pests that like to shelter amid rotting plants. Anyway, why waste valuable organic material? The place for the haulms (if they are healthy) is on the compost heap.

The compost heap

There is a mistaken belief that compost heaps are nasty, smelly mounds that attract flies and annoy neighbours. This is not true – if they are properly made and arranged. For your Edible Garden you would do best to make two compost heaps, and site them at the far end of the garden, near the greenhouse. One heap is sealed off and left to 'cook' while the other is in current use.

Materials for composting

Whether you build your own bin or buy one, the construction and maintenance of the compost heap is simple. It will rot down anything of organic origin – that is any material that has lived, whether plant or animal. The only things that will not decompose are man-made fibres.

Do not put on the compost heap anything that is diseased or has been treated with weedkillers. In other words if your lawn has been dressed with a selective weedkiller, the lawn mowings should be disposed of by other means for at least six months after treatment. Similarly, diseased leaves and stems of potatoes, tomatoes and other plants should be burnt, not composted.

But this still leaves a vast amount of waste material for composting. From the garden, over the next few months, you will have potato haulms, beetroot and carrot tops, some useless lettuce and cabbage leaves, and the stems, leaves and roots of peas and beans that have finished cropping. There will also be weekly helpings of grass clippings from untreated lawns. From the kitchen you can use potato peelings, egg shells and tea leaves.

Starting the heap

Begin with a layer of waste material 15cm (6 in) deep. Then sprinkle a proprietary compost accelerator (following maker's instructions) over it. Cover with a 2–3cm (1 in) layer of soil. Repeat these three layers till the bin is full. Check from time to time to see that the heap is moist; water it if it dries out. On the other hand, you don't want the whole heap to get soggy, so cover it with some polythene sheeting. This will also help to keep the heat in and speed up decomposition.

The time it takes for fresh organic waste to change into black, crumbly compost, depends on the prevailing external temperature. On average, the decomposition of an efficiently-organized heap can be completed in about two months in the summer, but will take anything up to six months in the winter. But regardless of time, what you have in the end is a quantity of the very best fertilizer that nature can provide, and it will have cost you practically nothing.

Transplanting brassicas

In the seedbed you have a variety of brassica plants which can be transplanted into the ground that comes vacant as you dig up the potatoes. There are still some brussels sprouts to be moved, as well as savoy cabbage, cauliflowers and purple sprouting broccoli. So after lifting the first potato roots, give the soil a dusting of general fertilizer, such as Fish meal, or Fish, blood and bone, and then tread the ground till it is really firm.

Before planting brassicas always dip the roots in a paste of 4 per cent calomel and, after planting, firm the soil again by treading it hard. Finish off with a really good watering.

Planting brassicas in mid summer (June) has its problems. The weather is often hot and dry. Your planting and transplanting should be done in the late afternoon when the sun is beginning to lose its strength. This will give the plants at least one night in which to start making new roots before their transpiration (water-loss rate) returns to its normal high, summer level the following day. Even so, they will show signs of wilting for a few days if the sun is really strong. Don't worry; this is merely incipient wilt from which the plants will fully recover once their new roots are well established (providing that you water them daily).

After transplanting, put a few slug pellets around each plant as a precautionary measure.

Thinning beetroot

The first sowing of beetroot (if you sowed the seed clusters) should now be 5–8cm (2–3 in) tall and in need of a second thinning – to 15cm (6 in) apart. Beetroot seedlings are inclined to be top-heavy and a strong wind can blow them right out of the ground. To prevent this, draw a little extra soil up around the stems; then water the rows thoroughly.

The Herb Rockery

The herb rockery in our Edible Garden. At the back are the taller plants – papaver (poppy), mint, angelica, fennel, tarragon, anise, dill and sweet cicely. In front of the sweet cicely is garlic, with borage next to it and sorrel in the centre. On the left is a clump of balm, followed by summer savory and chives. In the foreground are basil, parsley, thyme and winter savory, with sage, coriander and marjoram grouped on the right

The herb garden is a very important part of the Edible Garden. In the old 'cottage garden' there were clumps of various herbs dotted here and there and all had their culinary or medical uses. Nowadays medicinal herbs have largely been abandoned in favour of pills and potions. Animals, however, know better. Farmers will tell you that ailing cows and sheep will be found grazing at the foot of ditches where they find a variety of medicinal herbs not present in cultivated pastures.

And although many people regularly employ a few of the herbs when cooking, there are many more – just as flavorsome and easy to grow – that are less well known and little used.

Planting out herbs

One of the most delightful features of the Edible Garden design is the small rockery below the patio which is to be the miniature herb garden.

To start off the herb rockery, we have chosen some of the most useful and easy-to-grow herbs, such as:

Chives, whose grass-like leaves have a mild and pleasant onion flavour.

Garlic, for those who like its distinctive taste.

Marjoram, that will add flavour to both salads and egg dishes.

Mint, which needs to be watched if it is not to take over the whole rockery. Try to

find apple mint (*Mentha rotundifolia*).
Parsley, the most widely grown of all herbs, is not perennial and must be planted afresh each year.
Sage, that is especially good for stuffings.
Thyme, that helps to take away the 'fattiness' of pork dishes.

The first plants to go in are the herbs that were sown in the greenhouse earlier in the spring. You have since hardened them off and they are now ready to be planted in their permanent home.

You could start by putting three plants of thyme in the very front of the rockery. Thyme is a bushy little plant that never grows more than about 30cm (12 in) tall, and it looks most attractive in summer when it is covered with tiny, mauve flowers. Sage is a much bigger plant that can reach over 45cm (18 in) and, as two or three leaves at a time are all that are

needed for flavouring, one plant will probably be enough for your needs. Its grey-green leaves will contrast pleasingly with other plants and its dark, bluish flowers will add a touch of colour to the rockery in summer. The winter savory and marjoram, which have also been hardened off, have attractive flowers too.

Herbs to sow now
In the vacant seedbed you can sow a variety of perennial herbs that will provide you with good, strong plants for transplanting to the herb rockery in mid and late autumn (September and October). Once they are established, they will provide snippets for the kitchen for many years, until they get feeble with age and have to be replaced with new stock. The perennial herbs for present sowing include balm, chives, sweet fennel, lovage, lavender and tarragon (and marjoram, winter savory, hyssop and rosemary, if you haven't yet sown them in warmth).

Sow the seeds thinly and only 3mm ($\frac{1}{8}$ in) deep, in short rows. Remember to label each one, so that you can identify them when they come up. After sowing, soak the bed with water and keep it watered in dry weather to encourage good and rapid germination. The plants can be left unthinned until you are ready to transplant them in the autumn.

Alpine strawberries
Now is the time to sow your alpine strawberries. This is a perennial strawberry that grows into a neat, rounded bush about 15–25 cm (6–9 in) tall and has no runners. The fruit is small (about the size of a forefinger nail) and is produced in abundance all over the plant. It starts fruiting in early summer (May) and continues to crop right through to November unless it is touched by early frosts. You can make an excellent jam with the fruit, and it is also good eaten

Thin out apples by cutting out the crown fruits and any that are overcrowded

raw with sugar and cream.

Sowing swedes
In the main plot make a sowing of swedes for use during the winter months. The comparatively recent variety Chignecto is a good choice, being highly resistant to club root disease. Gardeners often forget that, being a member of the cabbage family, the swede is susceptible to the same pests and diseases as all the brassicas. To sow, put down the garden line, draw out a shallow drill 6mm ($\frac{1}{4}$ in) deep and sow as thinly as possible.

Thinning apple fruits
This is the month of the 'June drop', a term referring to the way some apple trees shed excess fruit. They seem to know how much of a crop they can usefully carry, and get rid of the rest by dropping them off. However, this does not always happen. Now and again the gardener has to lend a hand if he wants a crop of well-shaped, good-sized apples. Take a look at the fruit clusters and, if they appear overcrowded, cut out the 'crown' fruit with a pair of scissors. The crown fruit is the one that has grown from the central flower. It is positioned right at the centre of the cluster and it is slightly bigger than its neighbours. It may look like the best of the bunch but it will often grow out of shape and it does not keep as well as the others. Removing it gives the other apples in the cluster more room and energy to grow to a good size and become round and evenly shaped. At the same time, cut out any fruitlets that are either overcrowding the bunch or look as though they are not going to come to much.

Summer watering
Remember that water is just as important to plants as food in dry weather. In particular, your young marrows and newly-planted celery will need a thorough soaking if it doesn't rain.

Late summer: Gooseberries

Here we give important advice on spraying to ensure a healthy crop of gooseberries and start you thinking about sowing chicory, pollinating the courgettes and staking your dwarf French beans.

In the fruit section of the garden the gooseberries should be ready for picking Most years they will yield a crop of clean, healthy fruit, but even the gooseberry is prone to diseases sometimes. By far the worst problem is American gooseberry mildew. In a bad year this fungus disease (which came to Britain from the United States in the early part of the century) can ruin an entire crop and seriously weaken the bushes. The disease appears as a white powder on the leaves of new shoots and on the fruits themselves. After a while the white areas turn brown and the fruit rots.

Spraying with lime sulphur controls the disease but, unfortunately, many gooseberry varieties are sulphur-shy, and the spray will kill the bushes as well as the disease. Rather than run the risk of applying this fungicide to incompatible varieties you can spray with ordinary washing soda at 250g per 11 litres (8 oz per 2½ gals) of water. Alternatively, spray two or three times at weekly intervals with dinocap. Leave the fruits for a week or two before picking.

One sometimes sees gooseberry bushes completely stripped of their leaves by the caterpillars (which have yellow and black markings) of the gooseberry sawfly; however a heavy dusting with derris soon got rid of them.

Planning ahead
As you learn more about gardening you will soon come to realize that you cannot afford to be so concerned with the present that you have no eye to the future. So while you are enjoying the crops from your summer garden (and this week you may well be cutting the first of the summer cabbage) you should be thinking of your winter larder and how to fill it with fresh vegetables. For instance a sowing of chicory now will provide you with crisp chicons from mid winter to mid spring (December to March).

Sowing chicory
Although chicory is a true perennial it is treated as a biennial in the vegetable garden. Witloof (also called Large Brussels) is an excellent variety. Sow the seeds in shallow drills 6mm (¼ in) deep and 25–30cm (9–12 in) apart. Germination is rapid, and as soon as the seedlings have grown four leaves, thin them to 25cm (9 in) apart.

Pollinating courgettes
By now the courgette plants are well advanced and may be beginning to flower. If you look at the flowers you will notice that there are two different kinds – male and female. The female flower has a slight, elongated swelling beneath it. Before the plants will produce courgettes it is necessary for pollen from the male flower to find its way onto the stigma of the female. In theory, this is the responsibility of passing insects, but they do not always oblige.

To ensure cross-pollination, take a male flower from the plant, strip off the petals and thrust the central, pollen-bearing core into the heart of the female flower. Then discard the male flower and take a fresh one to pollinate the next female – and so on. Don't be discouraged if you can't find any female flowers when the plants start blooming. Courgettes (like other marrows) have a habit of producing a flush of male blossoms for the first week or two, but the females will come – so be ready when they appear.

Care of courgettes
Courgettes are thirsty vegetables, and need plenty of water in dry weather. In dry soils, the fruit refuses to grow, and usually drops off when it is only 2–3cm (1 in) in length. The same thing also happens if the female flower has not been cross-pollinated. The plants are not greatly troubled by pests and diseases, although powdery mildew does sometimes occur in warm, wet seasons. If you see any signs of a whitish powder on the leaves, spray immediately with a colloidal sulphur fungicide.

Staking dwarf French beans
Your dwarf French beans may be beginning to flower. This serves as a reminder that, as soon as the plants begin to carry a crop of pods, they become top-heavy. Give them some support now, before the row is flattened by heavy rain and wind. Push pieces of cane, 60cm (2 ft) long, into the soil on each side of the row at 1·8m (6 ft) intervals. Then run lengths of garden twine between them. It need not be an elaborate structure, just enough to prevent the plants toppling over.

Tending transplanted brassicas
The brassicas that you transferred from the seedbed to the vegetable plot will have recovered from the effects of the move and will be starting to grow again. Encourage them with a little extra feeding, so that they will make as much growth as possible before the days shorten and the weather turns colder. Sprinkle a dessertspoonful of general fertilizer around each plant and then draw up a little soil with a swan-necked hoe. The ridged soil will protect the plants from wind.

Late summer: Raspberries

Late summer (July) will bring you your first raspberry harvests – if you haven't had some already. It is also the time to take steps to be sure that birds, fungus diseases and virus infections don't reach the fruit before you do.
Picking peas and beans are other tasks, and we introduce two lesser-known vegetables to the Edible Garden in the shape of endive and Florence fennel. Both have a distinctive flavour and will make a nutritious addition to any winter diet.

Now is the time to make sure that your ripening raspberries are protected from the birds. If you don't possess a fruit cage, cover them with a garden net. The fruit should be picked when it is dry and soft and red. In contrast to many other fruits, raspberries are picked by pulling the fleshy part away from the conical, white core. It is also worth remembering that the fruiting lateral shoots are brittle and will snap easily unless you support them with one hand while gathering the fruit with the other.

Raspberry beetle
At this time of year watch out for the raspberry beetle. A bad attack can be disastrous and render the entire crop useless. The beetles hibernate in the soil over winter and emerge in early summer (May). They lay their eggs in the very heart of the flowers, and the hatching grubs feed on the ripe fruits around them.

If you suspect the presence of raspberry beetle, spray with derris just as the fruits are beginning to change colour from green to pale pink. The derris will also kill

off any greenfly that may be lurking on the leaves and young shoots.

Diseases of raspberries

Like strawberries, raspberries are prone to the fungus disease botrytis (or grey mould). Should it occur, spray with a systemic fungicide or captan, and thin out the canes in the autumn. Botrytis seldom occurs if the plants have been properly spaced out so that the sun and fresh air can get in between them.

Raspberries can also be afflicted by virus infections, particularly raspberry mosaic. Infected plants show a yellow mottling or spotting on the leaves. For these virus diseases there is no cure. The

plants have to be uprooted and burnt to avoid the spread of the infections to other areas and gardens. Virus infections are carried around by insects, especially greenfly, so the obvious preventive measure is a regular spray with a solution such as derris or malathion.

Sowing endive

We have already sowed chicory for the winter. Now make your winter diet still more interesting and nutritious with a sowing of endive, which looks rather like a very crinkly-leaved lettuce.

Endive is closely related to chicory and like the latter it has to be blanched before its distinctive flavour can be fully appreciated. The greener the leaves, the more bitter the taste, which perhaps accounts for the fact that this vegetable is not so widely used as it might be. Most people first get acquainted with a vegetable when they buy it from a shop. The pity of this is that shop endive has often been exposed to light for too long, and has started to turn green. The only way to savour the true taste of this delicious winter vegetable is to grow your own.

Sow the seeds now in a short drill, 6mm ($\frac{1}{4}$ in) deep in the seedbed. It is absolutely essential that they germinate rapidly otherwise the plants will tend to 'bolt' (go to seed quickly) before they are fit for use. To make sure of quick germination cover the row with cloches and keep the soil well watered. If you haven't got cloches, put a sheet of polythene over the row, with a stone at each corner to hold it down. As soon as the seedlings are large enough to handle, transplant them into their final positions.

Unfortunately endive is not hardy and must be given protection from frost. Furthermore the plants have to be bone dry before you can blanch them. As a rough guide the plants should be fully grown and ready for blanching in about 12–14 weeks from sowing. So from mid-autumn (September) onwards, keep plants permanently covered with cloches.

Well-blanched endive is an excellent substitute for lettuce. The best variety for winter use is Batavian Broad Leaved.

Florence fennel

Another less common vegetable is Florence fennel of finocchio. Although popular in Italy, fennel is seldom seen on sale in Britain outside the big cities, yet it is easy to grow and has a delicious aniseed flavour.

Sow the seeds in shallow drills 30cm (12 in) apart, and when the seedlings are large enough to handle, thin them to about the same distance. When the plants start

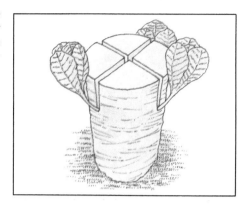

Three baby cabbages growing from a cross-cut made in head of cabbage stalk

flowering, cut them down to about 30–38cm (12–15 in) to encourage new leaves to grow from the crowns. As they begin to mature, their leaf bases swell. You then earth them up to blanch the swollen part of the stems. They will be ready for the table about four weeks after that. The base of the centre stem can be eaten raw like celery or chopped into salads. The outer leaves are tougher and need cooking in salted water until tender.

Cabbages from stalks

You will have cabbages for cutting regularly by now, but what are you doing with the stalks? Most people throw them into the dustbin; wiser ones crush them and put them on the compost heap.

Another productive way of using them is to leave them in the ground and cut a cross in the top of each one about 13mm ($\frac{1}{2}$ in) deep. If you do this you will get anything from two to four baby cabbages growing from the sectional cuts: They are tender and very tasty.

Picking peas and beans

If your peas and beans are podding, check them daily. Pick them as soon as the pods are full. If you leave them they get old and lose their flavour, whereas by picking early and regularly, you get tender vegetables and encourage further cropping.

The Edible Garden is now producing one fruit harvest after another. Prepare for a bumper peach crop by thinning out the bunches of fruit. There is also advice on preventing apple pests and on what supplementary plant foods are suitable to apply in late summer. In the greenhouse it is time to stop the tomatoes and to be on the watch for fungus diseases.

The peach tree, trained against the wall, will need some attention now if you are to get a crop of good-sized fruit. As a guide, one fruit per square metre (yard) of wall space is about right; alternatively, allow just one fruit per short lateral – or two if these sideshoots are very strong. If the tree is carrying more fruit than this, thin them out by removing the smallest. At the same time take a close look at the soil around the tree. Walls tend to deflect rain away from the soil, and there is nothing

worse for a peach tree than dryness at the roots when the fruits are swelling. If you see any signs of dryness, water thoroughly.

Apple pests
There are one or two pests which you should be looking out for on your apple trees. The first is the caterpillar of the tortrix moth, which has the peculiar habit of wriggling backwards if it smells danger from any direction. After hatching out, the pests start by eating the leaves, which they tie together with silken threads. As they get larger they transfer their attentions to the fruit itself, scarring the skin with small pits. The damage to the fruit is superficial, and the apples are perfectly good to eat after peeling. The trouble is that the scarring renders the fruit useless for keeping, and it has to be eaten fresh off the tree. Spray with BHC or derris if you spot leaves stuck together by a silken web.

A more serious pest is the codling

moth. The caterpillars hatch out in late summer (July) and bore their way into the fruit where they are protected from insecticides. So, as a precaution, spray the trees now with derris – particularly if you have previously had this trouble.

Holiday help
During the next few weeks, some of you may be faced with the problem of going on holiday just as many crops are about ready for harvesting. And while you are relaxing in some faraway place your greenhouse may be turning into an oven in the daytime, unless you can recruit the help of friends and neighbours. Find someone who is prepared to spend a few minutes every day watering the plants in the greenhouse and adjusting the ventilation (unless it is automatic).

In return, tell them to help themselves to your lettuce, tomatoes, radishes, peas, broad beans and runner beans. These are the vegetables that will not wait until you

Late summer: Thinning Peach Fruit

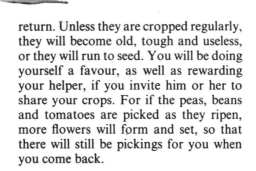

return. Unless they are cropped regularly, they will become old, tough and useless, or they will run to seed. You will be doing yourself a favour, as well as rewarding your helper, if you invite him or her to share your crops. For if the peas, beans and tomatoes are picked as they ripen, more flowers will form and set, so that there will still be pickings for you when you come back.

Late summer feeding
Now that late summer (July) is here there is little point in feeding summer-cropping fruit and vegetables, especially onions and root crops. There should still be ample fertilizer in the soil to meet their decreasing needs. From now onwards these vegetables begin to prepare for their winter rest. They have grown all the leaf they are likely to grow, and the food they have produced and amassed in the leaves starts to trickle down to the roots or leaf bases. Here it is stored, in the form of starch or sugar, to provide us with valuable winter food. The only fertilizer that can now be of any benefit to these crops is a little sulphate of potash – the plant food that helps to ripen soft growth and increases the keeping quality of stored roots and bulbs.

Swede seedlings
Once your swede seedlings are through, watch them very carefully for any signs of flea beetle damage. The beetles eat tiny holes in the leaves and severe attacks can destroy the seedlings completely. To prevent and cure, dust them with derris or gamma-BHC.

IN THE GREENHOUSE
The tomatoes still need regular feeding, but avoid fertilizers with a high nitrogen content. Continued applications of fertilizers rich in nitrogen tend to make the tops of the plants grow thin and spindly. If this is already happening, stop using your regular feed for a couple of weeks and substitute a teaspoonful of sulphate of potash in 9 lit (2 gal) of water.

Stopping tomatoes
A bone of contention between gardeners is whether to stop tomatoes. 'Stopping' means preventing further growth in order to channel the energy of plants into swelling and ripening the fruit already formed. This is done simply by cutting off the growing tip with a clean, sharp knife. It used to be standard practice to 'stop' after eight trusses had formed, and I believe this is still sound advice, if the plants are being grown in a soil bed. On the other hand, if you are growing by the ring-culture method, you don't need to stop them at all.

The ring-culture system directs the maximum amount of liquid fertilizer to where it is most needed — at the roots. In consequence, the richly-fed plants are more capable of producing a heavier crop over a longer period. If you do have a few pounds of green tomatoes at the end of the season, you can always ripen them in the kitchen drawer, or make a delicious chutney from them.

Fungus diseases
Late summer (July) in the greenhouse is also a danger period for the fungus diseases that assail tomatoes and cucumbers. The ones to guard against are brown mould (or cladosporium), grey mould (botrytis) on tomatoes, and foot rot in cucumbers. Grey mould first appears as light-coloured patches on the fruit, and the area around the stalk turns grey in colour. As the disease spreads, a greyish mould forms on the undersides of the leaves, and yellow patches appear on the upper surfaces. Eventually the fruit rots and drops off. The disease frequently enters the plants through any bruised and damaged areas of the stem, and is often a sign that the side shoots have been carelessly pinched out, taking a thin layer of stem tissue with them. To prevent attack, always ventilate the greenhouse freely and remove sideshoots with a sharp knife. Spray with a systemic fungicide as disease symptoms are seen.

Brown mould is a more common trouble. The first signs are pale coloured spots on the upper surfaces of the leaves. These are followed by brown, or brownish-purple patches on the undersides. It is a debilitating disease which so saps the plants' energies that they virtually stop producing. Should it occur, spray with a systemic fungicide or with zineb.

Cucumber foot rot is usually a sign of poor drainage at the roots. Cucumbers hate getting their 'feet' wet, which is why they should always be grown on raised mounds of soil (or by the ring-culture method) rather than on the flat.

The first indication of trouble is a browning of the stem, just above soil level. Unless preventive measures are taken, the stem goes soft and the whole plant wilts and dies. Control it by spraying with Bordeaux mixture.

Early autumn: Blackberries

If you already have some blackberry plants – and would like some more – now is the time to go about it. All you do is bend a shoot over until its tip is touching a patch of soft soil. Push the tip into the ground and put a small stone on top to keep it down. It will root quite quickly, and by planting time (in the autumn) it will have made a nice new plant.

Pruning the fruit trees

A leisurely job for a warm day in late summer (July) is pruning the fruit trees, particularly the espaliers (or cordons if you have them). As far as established bush and standard trees are concerned, the less pruning they receive the better. It has often been said the indiscriminate use of the pruning knife or secateurs has resulted in more fruit being lost than was ever gained. If a bush, or standard, is cropping regularly, and is strong and well-shaped, leave it alone. Do not go in for hard summer pruning. The only trimming a mature tree needs right now is the removal of any branches that are crowding the centre and excluding light and air.

Espaliers and fan-trained pears, however, need a touch of the blade at this time of year. Start now and do it by stages. Spread the work over a four-week period so that you don't weaken the tree by taking too much leaf area away all at once. Shorten all the sideshoots to five leaves from their bases, but leave all leaders unpruned.

Tidying the strawberry bed

In the soft fruit plot, clean up the strawberry bed now that the plants have finished cropping. Remove dead and diseased leaves and, if you have put straw under and around the plants to keep the fruit clean, choose a dry, still day and set fire to it. The fire does not hurt the plants, but merely encourages new leaf growth.

Hoeing the food plot

In the food plot your most valuable asset is your hoe. Late summer (July) has a habit of coming up with short spells of wet weather, which in turn prompts a last growth of weeds to appear. With crops beginning to ripen, the last thing you want is a forest of competitive weeds to keep the sun off them.

Drying shallots

The leaves of the shallots that were planted in mid spring (March) will now be withered and brown, and it is time to lift each 'clutch' of new bulbs. Put a trowel under them, lever upwards and they will part easily from the soil. Then separate the clustered bulbs and look closely at each one. If there are any that are soft and diseased, throw them out. Some may have grown a thick stem, with a seed-head on top. These will not keep, so trim off their stems and roots and take them to the kitchen for immediate use. Leave the remaining healthy, firm bulbs lying on the

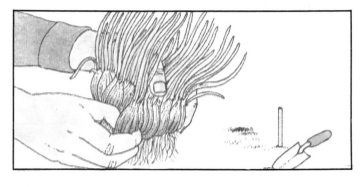
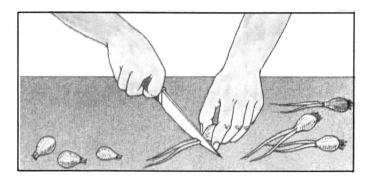
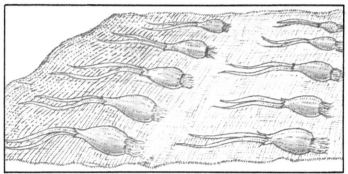
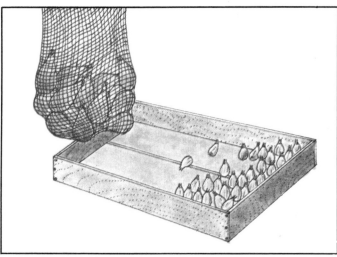

To harvest shallots, first separate bulbs (top, above left) and let them dry out on sacking (above left)
Trim back roots and stems (above right) and store in boxes or net bags (above)

soil to dry, so that their skins will ripen in the sun. But if the weather is wet, don't leave them lying on wet soil. Instead, lay them out on sacks on your path or patio, or on a garden table. They get a good soaking when it rains, but both sacks and bulbs soon dry out in the sun and wind. When they are papery-skinned and dry, trim off the roots right back to the base of the bulb, and cut away the long tail of dry stem. They can then be stored in shallow boxes or put in net bags until required for pickling or cooking.

Late sowings

There is still time, but only just, to sow a last row of lettuce and carrots for the winter. With only a few weeks of growth left, choose varieties that mature quickly. One of the best carrots for this purpose is Little Finger, and Amsterdam Forcing is also very good. All The Year Round lettuce can be sown now and the cos variety Winter Density is another that does not mind late sowing. While you have the garden line and the hoe in your hands, sow a row of parsley for winter use. Being a biennial by nature, spring-sown parsley tends to run to seed in early spring (February to March) whereas a late summer (July) sowing will give plants that remain in prime condition until next year's spring sowing is ready for cutting. If, for some reason, you don't wish to sow another row, you can still enjoy parsley sauce in the winter if you cut some of the

leaves now, hang them in an airy place and then bottle them in an airtight jar when quite dry.

There is no point in sowing summer radish in late summer or early autumn (July or August). Strange as it may seem, the soil is usually too warm for them. They will grow, but will not produce fat, edible roots. However, there is a winter radish that can be sown now. It will produce a crop of roots that you can dig up and use as needed throughout the winter. Black Spanish Round is recommended, with white flesh and black skin (that you peel off) and China Rose – long, cylindrical, with red skin and white flesh.

Sow the seeds in shallow drills spaced 25cm (9 in) apart and thin the seedlings to 15cm (6 in) apart in the rows. They need plenty of water, otherwise the large roots get tough and stringy, and almost too hot to eat. If well grown, the white-fleshed roots are delicious sliced in winter salads.

Pruning the raspberries

If you were fortunate enough to have a good crop of raspberries, make the most of them; use fresh for desserts, make jam or store them in the deep-freeze. Further crops can be harvested later in the year (see page 259).

Now that the plants have finished fruiting you must sort out the young canes from the old and do some pruning. Once a raspberry cane has borne fruit, cut it right out at ground level. Store old canes until next spring, when you can use them to support rows of dwarf peas.

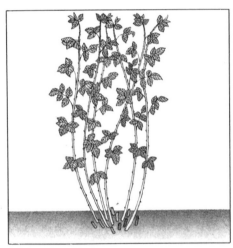

Above: raspberry plant after pruning

Besides cutting out the old canes, also cut out any new ones that are weak and spindly. If the row is more than two years old a certain amount of additional pruning is called for. On good, fertile ground raspberry plants will produce more canes than is good for them. If they are all left to grow and fruit, the plants are weakened and subsequent crops are progressively reduced in both size and quality. So select six to eight of the

strongest, thickest canes from each original plant or 'stool' and ruthlessly cut out all others, giving a better crop of bigger berries and less chance of disease.

Hoeing and mulching

When you have finished pruning, tie the selected new canes securely to the supporting wires. Then run a hoe between them to destroy the weeds, and give them a mulch. In the wild, raspberries inhabit woodland areas, so they will expect to find cool dark soil in our gardens.

Give them, if possible, an 8–10cm (3–4 in) layer of well-rotted manure or garden compost around the roots, or you can use lawn mowings – providing the lawn has not been treated recently with weedkillers. The lawn-trimmings will keep the roots cool and moist for the remainder of the summer, and by spring, worms will have taken the clippings down into their subterranean tunnels and converted them into humus and plant foods.

'Setting' runner beans

In dry weather runner beans have a habit of dropping their flowers before they set. In consequence the crop is sparse and disappointing. There are many theories why this happens. For instance various insects are held to blame. But whatever the reasons experience tells us that two things – watering and feeding – will help prevent this flower drop. By watering I mean thorough watering – turning the hose or sprinkler on the plants until their leaves, flowers and roots are quite soaked. Unless local water regulations forbid it, drench the whole row in the evening when the sun is low in the sky. And once a week apply a good liquid or soluble feed (such as Phostrogen), which plants can absorb through both leaves and roots.

Thinning swede seedlings

When your swede seedlings have grown four leaves, thin to 45—60cm (18—24 in) between plants and rows.

The wise gardener acts today with an eye on tomorrow; so lightly fork your seedbed now in readiness for sowing spring cabbage.

With the help of a passable winter and by choosing the correct varieties, spring cabbages are ready for cutting from late spring (April) onwards. But before you sow, let me offer a word of advice. Spring cabbages can be a nuisance. After a hard winter they take a long time to recover and start growing again. In small gardens they may be occupying the very spot where you intended to sow other crops (onions or carrots, for example) in mid spring (March). What do you do then? Do you wait for them to grow and mature and lose precious sowing time, or do you throw them out? Think carefully before you sow, and measure their worth against the growing area at your disposal and your spring sowing plans.

If you do decide to grow them, choose a reliable variety, like Wheelers' Imperial or Offenham — Flower of Spring, and sow the seeds in a shallow drill in the seedbed any time from now through into early autumn (the middle of August). If the weather is dry, give the ground a good soaking a few days before sowing and keep it well watered until the seedlings are through. As a precaution, dust them with derris to safeguard against flea beetles. The plants will be ready for planting towards late autumn (the end of September).

Unwelcome visitors

A steady stream of fresh vegetables should have come from the fertile soil of your Edible Garden during the last month.

You may find batches of blackfly hiding under the leaves of your runner beans. Left unchecked they suck at the sap and so severely weaken the plants that their cropping potential becomes seriously reduced. To solve that problem, make up a spray of liquid derris and soak the undersides of the leaves. It is no use spraying from above as the pesticide has to come into contact with the blackfly to be effective. If you can, use a long-nozzled sprayer you can push in under the leaves.

Feeding the compost heap

With so many crops maturing now, there is plenty of waste material for the compost heap. Remember that anything that is not diseased and has not been treated with a chemical weedkiller or pesticide represents potential soil fertilizer or mulching material.

Things like potato haulms, rejected outer leaves of lettuces and cabbages, the withering stalks and leaves of peas and beans and carrot tops can be used. You can also use untreated lawn mowings, although they break down faster if they are mixed in with the leaves and stalks rather than dumped in *en masse.*

To recap on the composting procedure: when the layer of waste material is about 15cm (6 in) deep, sprinkle it with a compost accelerator to hasten decomposition and cover it over with a 2—3 cm (1 in) layer of soil. If you are using a compost bin, repeat these three layers till the bin is full. Then pour a large watering can-full of water over it and cover it with a sheet of polythene to keep the heat in.

Supporting brussels sprouts

By now the brussels sprouts will be really sprouting. The tall varieties are shooting up and beginning to look rather top-heavy. Unless they are being grown in a sheltered garden they will need support to prevent them from being blown over. At the very least, strong winds will rock them and loosen their roots. Before this happens, pull earth up around their stems and tie each one to a strong bamboo cane some 120cm (4 ft) in length. Then tread heavily round the plants to firm the soil and promote the formation of a good crop of hard, tight sprouts.

Keep a close eye on your cauliflowers just now. The curds may swell and come ready before you're aware of it. Watch them daily and cut them regularly — preferably early in the morning. If you leave them too long, the tightly-formed curds will run to flower, and then seed, and will be useless for eating.

Cabbages will stand in good condition for a longer period than cauliflowers, but even so they should be harvested in their prime. The test of a good, mature cabbage is its solidity. If it has been well grown in a fertile soil, its centre, or head, should be rock-hard to the touch and its inner heart pure white.

Carrots and beetroot are also ready for pulling, but there is no urgency about these. They will be snug and safe in the ground until well into mid autumn (September). Any roots remaining should then be lifted and stored for the winter.

Bending the onion tops

The onions will now be big enough for immediate use, although many of you will

be growing them for use during the winter months. Onions need a little help if they are to ripen fully and properly. Some books will tell you to bend the necks over to hasten ripening. By this they mean bending the leaves over, just above the bulb, until they are lying flat on the soil. Many gardeners adopt this technique – but it really is not beneficial and could well inflict damage on the onion plants. Bending the leaves while they are still turgid causes bruising and possibly cracking at the bending point, and this is an open invitation for diseases such as onion neck rot to attack the leaf tissues at the point of injury.

The way to prevent this happening is to render the leaves more flaccid, so that they bend over more or less of their own accord. You do this by putting a fork under the onions and lifting them a few centimetres – without actually parting the roots from the soil completely. Although still in contact with the soil, the roots are partially disengaged from their source of moisture and the leaves gradually become limp. In a few days time you will be able to push the leaves over without risking injury to the neck of the bulb. The end result is a healthy onion that will keep in good condition for several months. We shall go into more detail about harvesting and storing onions when the time to do these jobs arrives (see page 312).

Earthing up potatoes
The early potatoes are probably all out of the ground and unless you have any other plans for it, here is the ideal place to plant the spring cabbages – if and when you are ready to grow them.

The maincrop potatoes are still in leaf, and now is a good time to inspect the ground between the rows. Some varieties tend to push their tubers to the surface and a little more earthing-up may be advisable to prevent exposed tubers turning green.

One of the delights of autumn is the sweet crispness of the first ripe apples picked straight off the tree.
Here we tell you how to assess whether your apples are ripe and ready for picking, or whether they need to be left longer on the tree.
Now is also the time to prepare the strawberry bed for planting your strawberry runners.

Most apple varieties become ready to eat in mid and late autumn (September and October), but there are some that are not ripe until early and mid winter (Novem-

Above: when harvesting onions ease the clusters of bulbs with a fork and leave them in clumps to dry.

ber and December) or even later. Two popular eating apples that reach maturity in early autumn (August) are Beauty of Bath and Laxton's Epicure. Both have one thing in common – they are delicious eaten from the branch, or very soon after picking, but if left too long their flesh becomes soft and mealy.

How can you tell whether these, or any other varieties, are ready for picking? It obviously helps if you know the names of the trees you have in your garden and their respective times of maturity. There is a table of 'types and times' in the section dealing about choosing and planting fruit trees. If you know when to expect ripening you can then apply the 'twist test' to the apples on your trees.

The twist ripeness test
The flesh of the apple consists of starch that is gradually converted into sugar as ripening approaches. In eating apples the internal chemical change is accompanied by an outward change of colour, from green to red or yellow. So if your apples look inviting, put your hand under one so

Above: give a second earthing-up to potato plants whose tubers are exposed

that it is resting in your palm, then, very gently, close your fingers around it. Now give it half a turn to the right and a gentle tug. If it comes away easily it is ripe. If it does not, try one or two more; if they also prove reluctant leave them for a few days before trying again.

The same rule applies to cooking apples, except that some stay green even when fully ripe, others change colour from green to yellow, whilst still others are flushed pink or red. But the twist test works for them all. However, there is no reason why a cooker should not be used as soon as it is a good size, whether fully ripe or not, although the less ripe it is the longer it will take to cook and the more sugar it will need in the cooking. Some of the finest varieties of cooking apples – such as Arthur Turner, Early Arthur Turner, Early Victoria and George Neal – ripen in early autumn (August).

Thinning winter radish

If the winter radish seedlings are large enough to handle, thin the seedlings to 15cm (6 in) apart in the rows. Give them plenty of water through the growing season to prevent the roots becoming tough and stringy.

Harvesting sweet corn

Throughout the summer the sweet corn cobs have been growing, hidden from view by their long, green sheaths. As the days go by, the silks gradually darken in colour until they are a dark brown – almost black. This is a sign that the corn is ripening (provided cross-pollination has been successful).

To test for ripeness, peel back a section of the sheath to expose the cob, that should be butter-yellow in colour. If a milky liquid squirts from a kernel when squeezed, then the cobs are not quite ready, so replace the torn pieces of the sheath and wait a few more days. If the inside is as thick as clotted cream then the cobs are ready for cooking.

Once they are ripe, don't leave them too long on the plants or they will become floury and tasteless.

Above: place hand under apple and grip fruit gently. Give half turn: if apple comes away from tree easily it is ripe

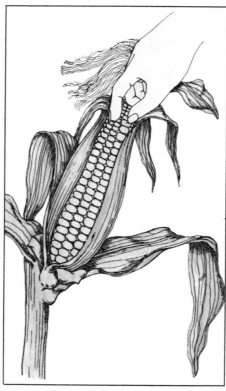

Above: peel back section of sweet corn sheath: if inside of kernel is thick as clotted cream cobs are ready to cook

Florence fennel

If your Florence fennel has started to flower, cut the stems down to about 30–38cm (12–15 in) to encourage new leaves to grow from the crowns.

Strawberries from runners

The most important job in the Edible Garden in early autumn (August) is to make preparations for a bumper crop of strawberries next year. The runners that you 'pegged down' earlier will have

Above: when Florence fennel flowers, trim stems to encourage growth of new leaves

rooted by now, and the sooner you plant them in their final home the better next summer's crop will be.

Preparing the bed

First, however, you must prepare a bed for them. Strawberries spend at least three years in the same piece of ground, so it makes good sense to put the young plants into rich, deep and fertile soil. Ground that has been cleared of broad beans, peas, or early potatoes (as long as you have had no trouble with verticillium wilt, which can also affect strawberries), is excellent for them. These crops were well manured earlier in the year, and the peas and beans have further enriched the soil with the nitrogen from their root nodules. All that you need to do now is to spread some well-rotted manure, or compost, or bone meal at 70g per sq m (2 oz per sq yd) over the ground and fork it into the top 15cm (6 in). Firm the soil by treading over it before planting.

The size of the strawberry bed will depend on your fondness for the fruit, tempered by the amount of space you have available. But whether the bed is large or small your best plan is to put the plants in rows of three, or in multiples of three rows. This is because strawberry plants fruit well the first year, superbly the second year, quite well the third and then they begin to decline. Your objective, therefore, is to allow all the rows to bear fruit for the first two years and then replace a third of the bed progressively with fresh plants every year. By so doing you will have a strawberry bed that never gets old and tired, and always consists of plants in the prime of life.

Planting the runners

When you have prepared the soil, lift the rooted runners, taking care to keep their roots intact and with as much soil as possible attached to them. Discard and burn any young plants that do not look healthy as they may be infected with virus disease. Once this disease takes a hold it can spread rapidly, and you may then have to lift and burn all your plants and start again with new, healthy stock.

Mark out the row with your garden line, and put the plants in 45cm (18 in) apart and allow from 60–90cm (2–3 ft) between the rows, depending on how much room you can afford to give them.

Don't plant too deeply or too shallowly. After planting, the crown of the plant should be level with the surrounding soil. The only immediate attention that the plants are likely to need is plenty of water in dry weather until their roots become thoroughly re-established.

If you don't have your own supply of rooted runners you can buy them from any good garden centre. Alternatively you can get them as pot-grown plants by ordering them by post from a reputable grower. Using a trowel, make a hole big enough to take the plant. Then slide the whole rootball out of the pot, place it in the hole so that the top of the rootball is level with the surrounding soil, and firm the soil back round it.

Check that all bought plants are of

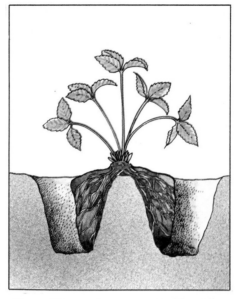

Above: lift strawberry runner with earth still attached to roots, and plant so crown is level with surrounding soil

certified stock, and therefore healthy and free from virus disease.

Varieties of strawberries

The most widely grown strawberry is still Royal Sovereign. This superb variety was raised in Queen Victoria's reign and named in her honour. It crops reasonably well, with pale red fruit of excellent flavour. The main snag is its susceptibility to disease, especially in wet seasons. An early, mid-season variety with a fine flavour is Cambridge Vigour; it also has a higher resistance to disease, and is a prolific cropper on good soils, yielding several pickings of bright crimson fruit every year.

Recent years have seen the in-troduction into Britain of several continental varieties. One of the first was a mid-season variety called Grandee that, it was claimed, was the largest strawberry ever known. The fruit is every bit as good as it was claimed – they are as big as the palm of a hand and have a delicious flavour despite their enormous size. Other continental successes followed, notably another mid-season variety called Tamella, probably the best of all the newcomers, and an excellent late variety named Gento. Tamella produces heavy crops of large, attractive, fine-flavoured berries, while Gento crops well even on limey soils – which strawberries generally dislike.

For a choice of three varieties that will give you sweet juicy fruit over a long period I would recommend Cambridge Vigour, Tamella and Gento.

Once the tops of the onions have bent right over, lift them completely and lay them on their sides, on the soil, to continue ripening. If possible, put them in a sunny place with their 'bottoms' facing south. The next few weeks are vital. If you can ripen the bulbs fully, until their firm flesh is covered with golden, papery scales, they will keep for months.

If the weather turns wet, put the onions somewhere out of the rain, but where the wind and occasional sun can still play on them. A good place is the garage floor – with the doors left open.

Choosing onions for storage

Onions are ready for storing when their skins are dry and golden, and when their leaves and roots are withered and crinkly-dry. To prepare for storing, first examine each bulb, paying particular attention to

the neck and root regions. The good, healthy onion should be firm all over, and there should be no sign of mould. A few bulbs may have small areas of softness and discoloration, that make them useless for storing. The diseased parts will increase in size until the whole bulb is

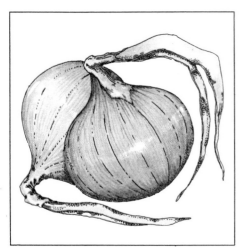

Fully-ripened onion, ready for storing, with papery skin and withered leaves

affected, and it will probably pass the disease on to healthy bulbs as well. If it is badly affected, throw it in the dustbin, but if only a small part shows signs of affliction, cut away the bruised or diseased area and use the remainder quickly in the kitchen for cooking.

String and stocking 'ropes'

The traditional method of storing onions is to make 'ropes' by tying in the necks of the onions to a strong piece of cord about 1·5m (5 ft) long. This will hold 15–20 onions weighing, on average, 112–114g (4–5 oz) each. Hang all the onion ropes made in this way in a cool, dry, airy shed or garage, where frost protection is guaranteed. Stored in this way onions will keep perfectly well until mid to late spring (March to April) of the next year.

Another way of storing onions is to use a few pairs of laddered nylon stockings or tights. Cut off the dried leaves of the onions immediately above the bulbs, and trim off the withered roots. Then pop them down the legs of the stockings, one on top of the other, and hang them up. When an onion is required for the kitchen, cut a hole in the toe, remove the bottom bulb and re-secure the stocking with a rubber band.

Tending runner beans

If you haven't done so already, pinch out the topmost growing tips of the runner beans as they reach the tops of their supporting canes. There is no point in letting the plants waste their energy in growth when they should be concentrating on flowering and podding.

When you have finished pinching out, take a look at the soil between the canes. What you will probably find is a forest of weeds whose roots are depriving the runner beans of nourishment. Pull them up and put them on the compost heap – provided they are not of the pernicious sort, like docks or couch grass; these should be relegated to the dustbin.

IN THE GREENHOUSE

Continue your regular feeding and watering programme for the cucumbers and tomatoes. Give them plenty of ventilation on hot, sunny days, and damp down every morning unless a cloudy day is forecast. If you have more ripe tomatoes than you can eat, make the surplus into tomato sauce or red tomato chutney.

375

Mid-autumn: Crop Rotation Plan

Now we begin the work for mid autumn (September) by explaining the principle of rotating crops so that they receive the greatest possible goodness from the soil while avoiding the risk of soil-borne diseases. We will show you how to plan your rotation programme for the next sowing and planting season. Also, this week, we tackle the sowing of winter spinach.

The middle of autumn (September) is the natural time to look back over the season and assess your successes and failures. Make sure now, whilst most of the crops are still in the ground, that you have a record of where everything is growing (or has been grown), and a few notes on the performance of each kind of vegetable.

The plan on paper is particularly important if you are to sow and plant the respective crops in the right places next year. In other words you should begin to think about crop rotation – a gardening principle that is almost as important as soil fertility. Crop rotation involves grouping certain vegetables together, planting or sowing them in groups and moving the groups around in the vegetable plot in successive years.

Use of soil nutrients
There are two very good reasons for such a plan. The first is that different kinds of vegetables use varying amounts of nitrogen, phosphate and potash. Vegetables that have comparatively large leaf areas use up more nitrogen than others, whilst root crops are hungry for phosphates. Therefore, if you used a general fertilizer at the beginning of the season, some parts of your edible garden will have quantities of residual nutritional elements

left in them. These residues may well be of tremendous value to other groups of vegetables next year.

Furthermore, all members of the pea and bean family have a peculiar characteristic possessed by no other vegetables. The root branches are covered with small, round swellings that, at first glance, can be mistaken for disease distortions. In fact they are normal growths called root nodules. These house large populations of special bacteria that are capable of extracting nitrogen from the air spaces in the soil and converting it into nitrates (valuable fertilizers). Peas and beans, therefore, put nitrogen back into the soil; other crops can benefit from it in due course.

So the best way to dispose of pea and bean plants that have finished cropping is to cut them off at soil level, leaving the roots in the ground, and put only the tops on the compost heap.

Keeping the soil clean
The second reason for adopting a crop rotation system is concerned with insect pests and more especially with fungus diseases. Most of the insect and fungus pests which attack vegetable crops hibernate in the soil over winter. They are able to withstand severe frosts and in the spring a new generation emerges.

Club root disease, which attacks all vegetables of the cabbage family, is a typical example. Even if all plants showing root distortion are pulled up and burnt, some disease spores will remain in the soil. If you plant cabbages or their relatives in the same place next year they will become infected as soon as you put them in. If you move them as far away as possible from the diseased soil, and apply

an appropriate fungicide, they will stand a far better chance of survival.

Three-year rotation plan
For the average edible garden, a three-year crop rotation is the simplest and most effective plan. To begin with, group the vegetables as follows:
1 Root crops – carrots, beetroot, parsnips, potatoes and onions.
2 Peas and beans – broad beans, runner beans, dwarf French beans and peas.
3 Brassicas – cabbage, broccoli, brussels sprouts, kale, cauliflower, turnips and swedes.

There are two apparent anomalies in these groups: onions are not root crops whilst swedes and turnips most certainly are. Onions are included in group **1** because it is a good plan to grow them adjacent to, or in alternate rows with, carrots. The reason is that their respective insect pests (onion fly and carrot fly) are attracted to the plants by smell. By growing the two crops close together the smell from one crop helps to mask the smell of the other and the risk of attack is greatly reduced. Swedes and turnips are admittedly root crops but they are also of the cabbage family and prone to the same pests and diseases. Both, for instance, will get club root disease, so it makes good sense to rotate them with group **3** types.

All remaining vegetables, such as leeks, lettuce, sweet corn, etc, can be grown in the remaining space.

Fertilizer requirements
The last factor that determines the sequence in which the groups move around is linked with their fertilizer requirements. Root crops (such as carrots) grow oddly-shaped roots in freshly

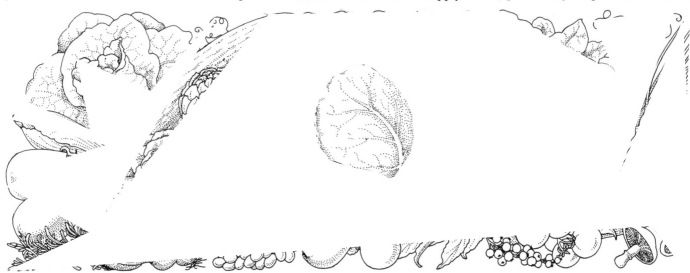

Three-year crop rotation and fertilizer programme

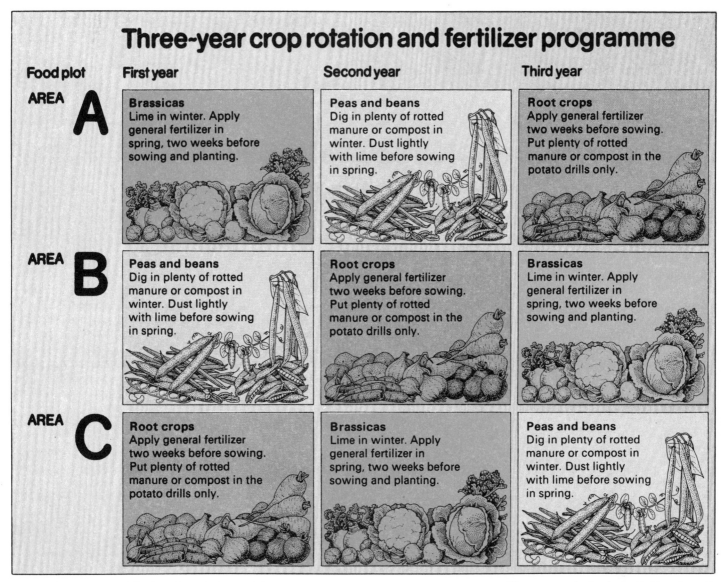

Food plot	First year	Second year	Third year
AREA A	**Brassicas** Lime in winter. Apply general fertilizer in spring, two weeks before sowing and planting.	**Peas and beans** Dig in plenty of rotted manure or compost in winter. Dust lightly with lime before sowing in spring.	**Root crops** Apply general fertilizer two weeks before sowing. Put plenty of rotted manure or compost in the potato drills only.
AREA B	**Peas and beans** Dig in plenty of rotted manure or compost in winter. Dust lightly with lime before sowing in spring.	**Root crops** Apply general fertilizer two weeks before sowing. Put plenty of rotted manure or compost in the potato drills only.	**Brassicas** Lime in winter. Apply general fertilizer in spring, two weeks before sowing and planting.
AREA C	**Root crops** Apply general fertilizer two weeks before sowing. Put plenty of rotted manure or compost in the potato drills only.	**Brassicas** Lime in winter. Apply general fertilizer in spring, two weeks before sowing and planting.	**Peas and beans** Dig in plenty of rotted manure or compost in winter. Dust lightly with lime before sowing in spring.

manured ground and do best in soil that was well manured for a previous crop. They could do no better than follow after the peas and beans in group **2**.

The crop rotation table shows you how the three-year rotation works and which fertilizers to use for the best results.

Winter spinach
Winter spinach is sown in September Longstanding Prickly is an excellent variety, being very hardy. Sow the seeds in shallow drills, 6mm ($\frac{1}{4}$ in) deep and 25cm (9 in) apart; thin seedlings to the same when they have made four leaves.

Choose good, fertile soil that is well drained. In wet gardens sow on a raised bed, or on ridges 50cm (12 in) wide, to prevent the roots becoming waterlogged. Although winter spinach is hardy, leaves fare much better if they are given cloche protection against snow and heavy rain.

Autumn Harvest in the Edible Garden

Beetroot is one of the first root crops to be lifted and stored. An early frost will damage the leaves and a hard one may even get at the roots themselves. In any case there is little point in leaving them in the soil to get tough and stringy. Put a fork under them and lift them right out of the ground. Do it on a dry day when the soil is also fairly dry; it is then a simple matter to rub it off the outer skin. Take all the roots over to the compost heap and screw their leaves off. Then find a wooden box, about 30cm (12 in) deep and put a 2–3cm (1 in) layer of moist peat over the bottom. Place a layer of beetroot over the peat and cover it with more peat. Carry on in this way – a layer of peat and then a layer of beetroot – until the box is full. Put it in a cool, but frostproof shed, cellar or garage and the beetroot will keep in top condition for at least six months. Incidentally, if you didn't try the golden beetroot this year, make a note in your gardening diary to try it next year. They are delicious.

Carrots and parsnips
Later this month it will be the turn of the carrots to go into winter storage. They are hardier than beetroot and you can wait until their leaves begin to lose their lush green colour before lifting them.

Parsnips can be left until late winter (the end of December). Their leaves will die down naturally and the roots are tough enough to withstand hard frosts. In fact the longer they are left in the ground and the more frosts they encounter, the sweeter the cream-coloured flesh.

Beetroot packed carefully between layers of peat will keep for most of the winter

Swedes and turnips
Swedes are as hardy as parsnips and can also be left in the ground. If you still have a few roots in the soil in mid winter (December), and you want them out of the way in order to dig the soil over, then lift them and put them in sacks in a cool, dark place. They will keep well for weeks.

Turnips, although close relatives of swedes, are not hardy. You would be wise to lift them, cut the leaves off and store them in peat. Even so, they do not keep well and are best eaten as soon as possible after lifting.

Earthing-up leeks
Leeks are left *in situ* to be prized out and eaten as and when required. Give them a last earthing-up, then pat down the sides of the ridges with the back of a spade until the soil is quite firm. They will look tidier and the firmed ridges help to disperse excessive rainwater.

Tidying pea and bean rows
As soon as all the peas and beans have finished cropping, take down the supports, strip off the yellowing haulms and (unless they are diseased) throw them on the compost heap. As you can imagine, this grows rapidly at this time of year.

Tie the runner bean canes together in bundles and put them in the garage until next year. Don't leave them in the ground, they look unsightly and they will rot. Pea sticks are not worth keeping. They quickly become brittle with age and are good only for kindling wood. If you used nylon or wire netting for pea supports, tear off clinging bits of vines and leaves, roll it up and store it.

Harvesting the apples
This is the time when many apple varieties become fully ripe. If they are ready for picking, don't delay. Get them off the tree before the wind does it for you and renders the crop useless for keeping. A bruised apple will keep only a few days, and it is such a pity to waste any of this delicious fruit.

Be careful when you are gathering them in; what looks like a wholesome apple from the front may be a wasp-eaten mess on the other side, and the wasp may be still in there, and could sting you. The best remedy for preventing wasps eating chunks out of your fruit is to hang two or three jam jars of sugared water on the branches. The sugar attracts the wasps which then fall in the jars and drown.

We have already prepared beetroot and carrots for winter storage. Now, providing the weather is favourable, lift the rows of maincrop potatoes. The haulms are now dying back, and when they are brown and shrivelled down to soil level, there is no point in leaving the potatoes in the ground. The longer they are left, the greater the danger that they will be eaten by small slugs and other soil pests. Wait for a day when the soil is reasonably dry and the sun is shining before tackling this job. You can use either a spade or a fork; a fork is preferable because it is so easy to slice through some of the tubers with a spade.

Start by putting the fork into the ground a good 60cm (2 ft) away from the centre of the row. Some potato varieties have a tendency to root sideways to a distance of up to 60cm (2 ft) from the main stems. Thrust the fork in as far as it will go, lever it up and throw the soil and roots backwards and over to expose the potato tubers. Lift them out and put them to one side to dry in the sun and air.

Rummage through the soil with your hands to make absolutely certain that you have retrieved all the potatoes. Even marble-sized tubers must be removed or they will be a nuisance next year. The smallest of them will push its shoots up into rows of other things. When all the tubers are out of the ground, leave the potatoes on the surface for a couple of hours at least before you start preparing them for store.

Storing maincrop potatoes

On farms and in large gardens the traditional storage system involved the construction of straw-lined mounds or clamps. Unless you expect to harvest a vast quantity of potatoes, clamps are not worth the trouble. All you need, in order to keep your tubers in good condition, are a few large sacks or paper bags. Whatever you use, it has to be light-proof and it must 'breathe'. Plastic bags are no good because once their necks are tied, the potatoes 'sweat' and may go mouldy or start sprouting. Thick paper bags that will hold a minimum of 25kg (56 lb) are ideal. The brown paper excludes light, thus preventing the potatoes from turning green and useless, and it allows them to breathe.

When the potatoes are dry, rub any clinging soil off with your hands and examine each one for cuts, bruises, holes and diseases. Any that are not perfect, place on one side for immediate use or throw them out. Put the remainder in the sacks, tie the necks and store them in a cool place where they are safe from frost, and rats and mice. Under these conditions the potatoes will keep perfectly well for several months.

Lettuce under cloches

Greenhouse owners are preparing for winter salads now by sowing lettuce (see greenhouse section). If you haven't got a greenhouse you can still enjoy winter lettuce providing you have a few cloches to put over them. The varieties suitable for sowing now under cloches are Arctic King and Valdor. Sow seeds thinly and in shallow drills and thin the seedlings to 25cm (9 in) apart. It is said that you can grow these two varieties without cloches in very mild areas, but it is probably wiser to use cloches wherever you live; otherwise the plants become splattered with wet soil and get very bedraggled.

Spring onions

With winter salads still in mind, it is a good idea to sow some spring onions very soon. For winter pulling, the best variety is White Lisbon Winter Hardy. Sow fairly thinly in drills and leave the seedlings unthinned. With protection, they will be ready in three months or so.

Ripening and storing tomatoes

With the likelihood of frost increasing daily you will have to do something about the green fruit still hanging on the outdoor tomato plants. You can always make green tomato chutney from them, but it would be nice to have a few ripe fruit later on. The way to do it is this: cut off each truss at the main stem, take it indoors and detach all fruits that are fully

grown. To ripen the fruit quickly, place them in the airing cupboard and they will be red in a matter of days. For slower ripening, put them on layers of cotton wool or soft tissue paper in a drawer in a room where the temperature is around 10°C (50°F) – a dressing-table drawer in the bedroom is ideal.

Above: a potato ridge, with tubers exposed and ready for lifting

379

Autumn Digging

Preparation for next year's sowing and planting in the Edible Garden starts now. Autumn is the best time to turn over the food plot as the winter weather is then able to play a large part in breaking down the clods of earth.

The food plot in the Edible Garden is now largely empty, except for a few rows of winter vegetables. The summer crops are over, and most of the root crops are gathered in, leaving only vegetables like winter cabbage, sprouts, leeks, winter broccoli, swedes and parsnips for winter use. Now is the time to dig over this exposed soil. Don't leave it until next week or the week after when it may be raining or even snowing – do it now.

Early to mid autumn (August to September) is the labour-saving time to dig over the garden. For during the winter the frosts will get right into the large clods of earth, split them apart and crumble them to small particles. When you are ready to sow and plant in spring the soil will easily work to a fine tilth.

Feeding the soil
Autumn is also the best time to put 'goodness' back into the earth. Your last season's cropping plan was fairly intensive, and the vegetables drew heavily on the plant foods that they found at their roots. Your feeding programme now will largely determine how good your harvests are next year.

The first job is to spread a good layer, 8–10cm (3–4 in) thick, of well-rotted organic matter over the soil surface. If you have been keeping up your compost heap (or heaps) you should have plenty of suitable material for the purpose. This is what builds up the soil's humus level and restores it to good heart. Lay it on as thickly as you can. Failing compost, try to get some old, well-rotted manure. As a last resort, use one of the processed, concentrated animal manures sold in large bags by garden centres and similar places. Whatever you use, it must be organic. It is pointless digging-in highly-soluble, inorganic fertilizers that will be washed through the soil before the plants need them. Organic manures decompose slowly so their goodness is held in the soil for the plants to use next year.

Spread the 'muck' over the soil and over any weeds that are around. Turn the annual weeds in as you dig; they will rot down to form yet more humus and nutrients. What you must watch out for are the perennial weeds, such as docks, dandelions, daisies, buttercups and plantains. All these have either taproots or bulbous roots and are able to make new growth even when buried quite deep in the ground. Pull these persistent weeds out of the clods of earth and put in the dustbin. When you have finished digging, the area will be covered with rough lumps that the frost can get to work on.

Bay tree cuttings
Bay trees are fairly hardy, but in case the winter is one of hard frosts and biting winds, play safe and bring your potted bay tree into the greenhouse, or at least into the lee of a wall or hedge. It might be wise to take a couple of cuttings, just in case the plant gets damaged or killed by the cold. In any event, the rooted cuttings will come in handy for a village fete or a school coffee morning next year. Choose

Take cuttings of bay tree shoots about 10cm (4 in) long (above), strip off all but top four leaves and plant in pots

young, healthy shoots and cut them off about 10cm (4 in) from the tip and at a point immediately below a node (the slight swelling on the stem from which the leaves arise). Then strip off all but the top four leaves and plant the cuttings 2–3cm (1 in) deep in a 10cm (4 in) pot of good, sieved soil with a few stones at the bottom for drainage. Place the pot on a windowsill indoors that gets little or no direct sun, keep it watered and next summer you will have young, rooted bay trees.

Transplanting spring cabbages
The spring cabbages will have been growing fast in the seedbed and should now be strong plants some 15cm (6 in) high. Plant them into the ground previously occupied by the broad beans. This soil should be ideal for them. It was well enriched with organic matter in the spring and all it needs now is some bonemeal or hoof and horn at 30g per m (1 oz per yd) of each row prior to planting. Spring cabbages do not need a lot of space – in fact a fairly close planting affords the plants mutual protection in hard weather, say 30–45cm (12–18 in) space all round.

Welsh and bunching onions
This week's sowing is Welsh onions. This onion, which originally came from Siberia, not Wales, has a flattish bulb from which emerge, each spring, a number of succulent young growths with a flavour like spring onions. Besides the flavour, its main attribute is its earliness, the young shoots being ready for pulling long before the spring onions or shallots.

Sow the seeds in early or mid spring (February or March). Alternatively find a friend or neighbour who already has a clump in his garden. Before long he will be lifting and splitting it up prior to replanting, and he will be able to give you some of the small bulbs.

Another onion, which is a true perennial and hardy enough to withstand the hardest of winters, is the evergreen bunching onion. The seeds are obtainable from most mail-order seeedsmen and may be sown now, in mid autumn (September), *in situ*. It will give you a few pullings of scallions (onions that do not bulb) next year and plentiful harvests in the years to come.

Covering the endive

If you haven't already covered your endive plants (sown some weeks ago in the summer), do it now. Put cloches over them to protect them from possible early frost. The cloches also help to keep the plants dry, and they must be bone dry before they can be blanched.

With late autumn (October) almost upon us we are about to enter the period when most plants cease growing and 'hibernate' for the winter. All top growth dies back and only the roots remain active. This is the very best time of year to lift and transplant deciduous trees and bushes and perennial fruiting plants. In their dormant state they suffer very little harm from being uprooted and can stay alive for several weeks provided their roots are not allowed to dry out.

Planting hard and soft fruit

The next eight weeks or so are ideal for planting all kinds of hard and soft fruit. Early planting gives the young plants three or four months before their stems and leaves begin to grow. During this period they will be busily forming new root systems below ground, ready to support the new top growth in spring. The other advantage of early planting is that the ground is less likely to be frosty or covered in snow when your plants arrive.

However, should you be unlucky enough to be snowed under, or frosted over, when your plants are delivered, this is what to do. Remove all the wrappings from them and stand their roots in a bucket of water until the ground is fit to work on. If you have ordered so many plants that you haven't enough buckets to hold them all, heel them in. Heeling in simply means taking out trenches about 30cm (12 in) deep and placing the plants in them at an angle of about 45 degrees. Then replace the soil around the roots and firm with the heel of your boot. In their temporary quarters the plants will remain perfectly safe and well for several weeks until the soil is fit for planting. The only thing to remember is not to put frosted soil, or soil mixed with snow, around the roots. Faced with wintry conditions you will have to take out two trenches – one to put the plants into and another to provide unfrozen soil to put around their roots.

Choosing the plants

Buy good plants from a reputable grower. As a rule, poorly-grown fruit trees and bushes with thin, drawn stems and sparse, straggly root systems never do well. If you can, visit a garden centre and select those that are obviously strong and healthy looking. Get the grower to lift them for you and take them straight home for immediate planting. Plants to avoid, even if they look good, are those that are lying around with bare roots exposed to the elements. If there isn't a convenient nursery or garden centre anywhere near, order your requirements from nationally known mail-order growers. Their catalogues are freely advertised in the gardening and weekend press and are well worth sending for. It is vital to place your order as soon as possible. The sooner you do it, the better your chances of receiving the pick of the stock.

When your plants arrive, inspect them carefully. Make sure that the stems haven't been damaged in transit and, even more important, examine the roots. They should be completely wrapped in polythene containing some moisture-retaining material such as moss or wet peat. If they are not, and if they appear dried out, write a letter of complaint at once, demanding your money back or a new order of properly packed plants. Don't stand for any poor quality or bad packing. It is your money and you deserve its full value. What is more, the fruit trees and bushes will spend the rest of their lives in your garden. So start right by planting good stock and they will reward you with years of ripe, delicious fruit.

Blanching endive

There are two simple ways of blanching the endive that you sowed earlier in the summer, and I leave the choice to you. The first is to remove one of your cloches and place a large inverted flowerpot over each exposed plant – covering or plugging the drainage hole to exclude all light. The second method is to drape a sheet of black polythene over the sides and ends of one cloche so that no light can get at the plants underneath. There is no point in blanching more than two or three plants at a time because they should be cut and eaten as soon as blanching is complete. This usually takes anything from one to three weeks, depending on the season.

Blanching Florence fennel

Now that the stems of the Florence fennel are beginning to mature and swell, they also need blanching. In their case pull up a little soil around the stem of each plant to exclude the light from the stems. They will be ready for the table in about four weeks time from now. You can eat the centre stems raw, but the tougher, outer leaves will need cooking.

Early winter: Soft Fruit

The first point to remember. with all soft fruit, is that they are more or less permanent crops. Raspberries and blackcurrants, for instance, are likely to occupy the same piece of ground for at least ten years and probably longer. So it pays to choose a site that suits them, in a part of the garden where their permanence is an asset rather than a hindrance. For example, both raspberries and blackcurrants can be planted as summer hedges. When they are in leaf they effectively screen unsightly compost heaps and they are equally useful as dividers between the flower and vegetable garden.

As soft fruit canes and bushes are long-term residents, it also pays to prepare the ground really well before planting.

Preparing clay soils
If you are gardening on clay, you can grow all the soft fruits successfully provided the soil is reasonably well drained. Your best course is to dig it to a good spade's depth (or two, by double digging) and put in as much well-rotted manure or compost as you have available. Lime is also good for breaking up heavy clay but it must never be used at the same time as organic manures – they counteract one another. In any case. most soft fruits prefer a soil that is slightly on the acid side and lime, being alkaline, has a detrimental effect on their growth.

Your clay-cracking programme, therefore, involves generous quantities of organic material dug in before planting, followed by annual mulches of manure or compost applied around the plants in early or mid spring (February or March).

Sandy soils and loams
If you are gardening on light, sandy soil the treatment is exactly the same as for clay soil but for a different reason. Sandy soils drain very quickly and are unable to hold plant foods for very long. Improving their moisture- and fertilizer-holding capacity involves adding heavy dressings of organic manures to increase their humus content.

Additional spring and summer mulches are vitally important. Provided the lawn has not been treated with a weedkiller for at least six months, put the mowings around the bushes and canes. A good thick mulch does several things. It reduces loss of moisture from the soil by evaporation. It insulates the roots from extremes of temperature – keeping them warm in winter and cool in summer. It also adds to the soil humus content as the earthworms gradually take it down into the ground and convert it into a nutritional, moisture-retentive material. But remember, to be effective, a mulch must always be put on soil that is already moist.

Many gardeners are confused on the subject of horticultural peat: does it help a sandy soil and, if it does, how should it be used? Peat on its own has very little plant food in it. If it is dug into the soil, the bacteria get to work to decompose it into humus. Therefore it is a first-rate soil conditioner and improver but it is not a soil feeder. In fact the soil bacteria use up some valuable nitrogen during the decomposition process, leaving the soil poorer in plant foods than it was before the peat was added. So if you are using peat apply it either as a surface mulch or

spread a general fertilizer over it before digging it in.

The best soils for soft fruit growing are the loams – the soils that are dark, friable and rich in humus. But even these are not inexhaustible and need an annual top dressing of 'organic' fertilizers (such as bonemeal, hoof and horn, or fish, blood and bone) to maintain their fertility.

Choosing the site
In general, soft fruits (and raspberries in particular) hate having their 'feet' standing in water. At the same time their cropping ability is appreciably reduced if their roots are groping for moisture. This is another good reason for building up the humus content of the soil and for mulching in hot, dry weather.

But water shortage problems can often be avoided by careful choice of planting site. Nearly all gardens have a dry end and a moist end. It makes good sense to avoid planting fruit bushes and canes at the top end of a sloping garden where the soil drains quickly and dries out. By the same token it is asking for trouble to put them in at the bottom end where surplus water collects in winter. So choose the planting place carefully, dig it well and add plenty of rich organic fertilizer as you dig. Then the bushes and canes will reward you with an ample supply of top-quality fruit.

Thinning winter spinach
As soon as your winter spinach seedlings have made four leaves, thin them to 25cm (9 in) apart. Remember that the plants fare better if they are given cloche protection against snow and heavy rain.

Preparing for Rasp- berries

Choosing and preparing the site

Raspberries, therefore, can be counted on to grow and give fruit in any part of the garden, provided the soil suits them. Bearing in mind that they will be with you for many years it pays to give them a good start. Select a place where the soil is in no danger of ever being waterlogged. Raspberries hate standing in wet, poorly-drained soil. Their roots literally drown and the plants die off completely. If possible, provide the canes with shelter from strong winds; in summer the fruit-laden sideshoots are prone to snap off in the windy weather that sometimes comes in short bursts in mid and late summer (June and July).

Preparing the soil

Having selected the site, the first job is to give the new canes every encouragement to settle in and make new roots quickly. As raspberries are usually grown in straight rows, a good method is to prepare the ground as if you were sowing or planting runner beans. Dig out a trench 60cm (24 in) wide and about 45cm (18 in) deep. Into the bottom put a layer of well-rotted manure or garden compost, 15–25cm (6–9 in) deep and tread it well down. Next, give the soil on each side of the trench a dusting of bonemeal at 45–60g per m (1½–2 oz per yd) run of row, then replace the soil and firm it by treading. By doing all this now, the soil will have settled down by the time you are ready to plant – towards the end of late autumn (October).

While you are trenching and replacing the soil, watch out for perennial weeds like creeping buttercup, ground elder and couch grass; once the canes are in and growing it will be very difficult to pull up such weeds without damaging the roots of the young raspberries.

Support for the canes

The next job is to erect a support structure. You can do this after planting but it is better to do it before to avoid the danger of trampling on the newly-planted canes as you walk.

One method is to make a fence of strong galvanized wire and stout wooden posts. The posts should be 2m (7 ft) long and, for the average 3·8–4·5m (12–15 ft) row, two should be enough. If your row is longer you will need a post in the middle of the structure as well.

Like the raspberry canes, the posts should give many years of service. To extend their effective lifespan, soak their bases in a solution of 100g of copper sulphate to 5 lit water (1 lb to 5 gal) for two days before putting them in. Then sink the posts into holes 60cm (24 in) deep and fill them in with stones and earth. On light soils, where a solid base is difficult to achieve, strengthen the posts with wood strainers to prevent the posts leaning inwards when they are bearing the full weight of the canes in leaf and fruit.

Run two or three lengths of galvanized wire, evenly spaced, from post to post. If possible, the ends of each length of wire should be attached to straining bolts so that they can be stretched tightly and any subsequent slack taken up.

Choosing your varieties

Aim for a selection of three or four varieties that are strong growers and prolific bearers of sweet fruit. You would be well advised to include at least one autumn-fruiting variety and one or two summer fruiters. There are many excellent varieties to consider, but first choice for your selection should be Glen Clova, Malling Delight and Heritage. These will give you a continuous supply of fresh fruit from late summer (July) to the first hard frosts.

The summer-fruiting variety Glen Clova carries its crop over a long period. The fruit is of first-rate quality and flavour and is excellent for freezing and bottling, and for making jam or for tarts and pies. Malling Delight, another summer-fruiting variety, is a delight both to grow and to eat. It is an exceptionally heavy cropper that has outstripped all others in the British National Fruit Trials and at the Scottish Horticultural Research Institute. Autumn-fruiting raspberries are becoming increasingly popular because they come into bearing later than most other soft fruits. They are also sturdier and shorter in the cane than the summer fruiters and need no supports – except in very windswept gardens. A comparatively new autumn-fruiting variety is Heritage. It is proving to be

Chicory is now ready to dig up. Cut off leaves, place in prepared trench and cover

excellent in every aspect. Its growth is strong and vigorous and it carries a heavy crop of luscious, red berries.

Storing chicory

The chicory that you sowed in mid summer (June) is now ready to be stored until the time comes to force and blanch it in the winter. Chicory has to be blanched – hidden from the light to keep the chicons (edible shoots) white – because exposure to light turns it green and bitter.

The way to store this particular vegetable is to dig a trench 25cm (9 in) wide and 30cm (12 in) deep. Then put the plants in the trench, after first cutting off the foliage which might otherwise rot. Put the soil back over the roots and tread it firmly down to make the trench frost-proof.

In mid winter (December) we shall tell you how to replant the roots in boxes or pots. These then form new shoots which are the chicons that you cut and eat.

Blackcurrants

One of the rewards of growing blackcurrant fruit is that there is no wastage. You can use it for making jams, jellies and pies, or you can bottle or freeze it for the

winter. If you have a very heavy crop, the surplus can be squeezed through a fine-meshed sieve and the juice bottled for use as a refreshing and nourishing drink.

Where to plant

Blackcurrants have the added advantage that, once established, they need very little care and attention. You can plant them almost anywhere providing you give them some shelter. Cold will not kill the bushes, but the flowers open early in either mid or late spring (March or April), and a cutting, frost-laden wind can severely damage them and reduce the crop yield. So try to give them as much weather protection as possible. Then the early insects will be able to pollinate the flowers, thus ensuring a good set of fruit. If you are pushed for space in your garden, you can plant blackcurrant bushes 1·5m (5 ft) apart as a hedge. They have attractive green foliage in summer and produce enough stems to make a reasonable screen when the leaves fall in winter.

Wherever you plant, try to choose a spot where their roots can find water fairly easily. They do not like dry, parched earth; it reduces both the size and production of fruit. In fact, in a dry summer, it pays to give the bushes regular soakings of water as soon as the fruit begins to form.

Choosing the bushes

Bushes can be readily obtained from a garden centre where you can inspect the young plants before you buy them. Look for good, strong specimens with stout stems emerging from an adequate root system. Refuse thin, wispy branches and plants that have a few straggly threads for roots. Even more important is to look closely at the dormant buds along the branches. If the bush is healthy they will be slim and slender; if they are round like small marbles, the bush is suffering from a condition known as 'big-bud'. The buds become the breeding ground of a gall mite. This insect not only damages the bud but, directly or indirectly, causes a virus infection known as 'reversion'. Blackcurrants affected by this incurable disease slowly deteriorate. Their cropping ability declines and they eventually die. So check every single bud on every bush before you buy.

If your established bushes show any signs of big-bud, pick off all the affected buds and burn them. If they are badly diseased, pull up the bush and burn it.

Varieties to choose

If you only have room for three to six bushes, then Laxton's Giant is the variety that we would recommend. It ripens early, from mid to late summer (late June–mid July) and bears large fruit of superb quality that does not drop off as soon as it is ripe – a common fault with many varieties. Wellington xxx is a good mid season variety, producing heavy crops of fruit in late summer (July). Of the end of season varieties, Amos Black (though not a heavy cropper) flowers late, making it a good choice for frosty gardens.

How to plant

Having bought your plants, take them home and put their roots in a bucket of water for a couple of hours before planting. The way you plant will determine how well or badly the bushes grow in years to come. The first rule is to dig a hole wide enough to take the root system fully spread out. Make the hole at least 30cm (12 in) deep. Put in a generous forkload of rotted manure or compost and then fork this into the soil at the foot of the hole. If you cannot get manure, and have no compost, throw in a couple of spades of moist peat laced with a handful or two of bonemeal or a compound organic fertilizer. Now place the bush in the hole, spread its roots out and start replacing the soil around them. When there is enough soil in the hole to hold the bush steady, check on the planting depth.

Blackcurrants are an exception to the golden rule that, when planting most trees and bushes, you should plant them to the soil level mark on the stem – which is the depth to which they were originally planted in the grower's field. But blackcurrant bushes should be planted a few centimetres deeper than the old soil mark so that the lower branches or buds are beneath soil level. This is to encourage the bushes to produce a succession of branching stems from the stool (root clump) that is lying about 10cm (4 in) below the surface of the ground, thus giving a sturdy bush and a greater fruiting area.

Having adjusted the planting depth, replace all the soil and firm it gently with your feet around the stem. As you do this the soil will settle, leaving a slight depression. This acts as a water-retaining hollow and makes watering much easier. If you are planting more than one bush – and you really need six bushes for the average family – allow 1·5m (5 ft) between each one.

When planting is finished, the final touch is to prune each branch back to one

or two buds above soil level. This may seem drastic treatment, but it is necessary to encourage the growth of the maximum number of new shoots that will bear fruit in the following year (some 18 months after autumn planting).

Lifting and storing carrots

If you have not already put your carrots into winter storage, then you should do it now. Put a fork well down under them and throw them onto the soil surface. When you have dug up the whole row, gather them all together and inspect the roots closely. Throw out, or use immediately, all that are diseased or show pest damage. Cut the leaves off the others, just above the root shoulders, and put them on the compost heap. Try not to cut into the flesh of the roots as this will impair their keeping qualities. Then clean all the soil off the roots by hand. Store them in the same way as beetroot – in a wooden box between layers of moist peat. Put the box in a dry, frost-proof place.

Some gardeners leave their carrots in the soil all winter and lift a few as they need them. This may be successful in a mild winter and in a light, sandy, well-drained soil, but, equally, you may lose the crop to slugs or other pests.

British preference

The British eat blackcurrants and more or less ignore the red and white varieties. Yet in North America and on the Continent the red and white are much more in demand. Whitecurrants are especially fine-flavoured and are delicious eaten fresh with sugar and cream. Both types are easy to grow and crop heavily and regularly with the right conditions. The only problem is, birds love them (much more than blackcurrants) and will strip the bushes unless you protect the fruit.

Redcurrants and whitecurrants

In common with blackcurrants, the red and the white need a rich, well-drained soil and moisture at the roots. They will not tolerate wet, heavy soil and equally dislike cold and windy places. Try to give them a site that is fairly sunny, where their flowers and brittle branches are not likely to 'be damaged by late spring gales and hard frosts. Redcurrants and whitecurrants do not make as much new growth every year as do the black-fruited ones and consequently they do not need as much feeding. This does not mean that they should be neglected, but rather that you should give blackcurrants the bulk of your organic fertilizer or compost.

Planting and pruning

Do not plant the bushes quite as deeply as for blackcurrants. The planting hole should be big enough to take the full spread of roots. And when the soil has been replaced and levelled off, the final level should coincide with the nursery soil

mark on the basal stem. In other words you want a single stem emerging from the soil, untrammelled by suckers.

An important difference between blackcurrants and the red and white varieties lies in their fruiting. Blackcurrants bear their fruit almost entirely on the branches that grew the previous year. Redcurrants and whitecurrants, in contrast, fruit on the old wood, so the production of masses of new growth is unnecessary. This means that they will be pruned in quite a different way.

Initially, after planting, the red and the white are not pruned back as hard as blackcurrants. Most of the bushes sold for autumn planting are one year old and will usually have about three branches emerging from a short stem above the root system. After planting, take a pair of sharp secateurs and cut each branch back to three or four buds from the base. Remember to cut just above a bud that faces outwards from the centre, in order to begin to establish a neat bush.

Pest prevention

One of the advantages of redcurrants and whitecurrants is that they are seldom seriously afflicted by pests and diseases. They are not, for instance, attacked by the 'big-bud' mite that can decimate black-currants. Aphides may be a nuisance, but you can control them by spraying with tar oil in mid winter (December) to kill the over-wintering eggs, followed by spraying with derris in summer if a fresh batch of insects appears on the leaves.

Varieties of currants

Our first choice of the whitecurrants is White Versailles. It gives consistently good crops of very sweet fruit. There are more good redcurrant varieties to choose from, but two varieties are outstanding. For an early and reliable cropper I recommend Laxton's No 1 and, for a later crop the American-raised Red Lake.

Where to plant gooseberries

To complete the soft fruit section of our Edible Garden it only remains to put in a few gooseberry bushes. Because the gooseberry is known to be a hardy plant, it is all too often pushed into cold, dreary corners where it does not fruit well. But give a gooseberry bush a fertile soil and it will reward you with a plentiful crop of sweet, juicy fruit that can be almost as large as small plums. So plant them somewhere sheltered from cold, biting winds, where the soil is well-fed and free-draining. In general, gooseberries do not like a heavy clay soil, but one variety, Whinham's Industry, will do well in such conditions.

Planting and pruning

The gooseberry prefers an autumn planting. It starts into growth early in the spring so the earlier it is planted the better its chance of getting a new root system going before the leaves unfurl and growth begins in earnest. As with redcurrants and whitecurrants, gooseberries are grown on a single stem (or leg) so plant them fairly high in the soil – certainly no deeper than the soil mark on the stem. Planting distances are 1·8–2·5m (6–8 ft) apart.

After planting, cut all branches back to about four buds from base, pruning to outward-facing buds.

Varieties of gooseberry

Of the varieties that are readily available, We have chosen four that should meet most requirements. When fully ripe, the berries of Careless are very pale ywllow, oval in shape, sweet and juicy. Leveller, another yellow-fruiting variety, has a first-rate flavour, but it will not tolerate poor growing conditions. Lancashire Lad ripens to a rich red and has tart fruit that is superb for pies and jam. Finally Whinham's Industry (one of the best of all) is a vigorous-growing red variety with fruit that is very sweet when fully ripe.

Standard gooseberries

If you can find them, standard gooseberries are ideal for small gardens. They are grown on bare stems 1·2–1·5m (4–5 ft) tall, with fruiting branches forming a canopy on top. They can be planted between other low-growing plants and their height makes fruit-gathering very much easier.

Planting out the herbs

It was the middle of summer when you sowed various perennial herbs in the seedbed, so they should have developed into a good selection of strong plants. It is time to transfer them to their permanent home in the herb rockery. As when planting anything that will have its roots in the same soil for several years, it pays to invest in thorough preparation. First of all give the soil in the rock 'pockets' a thorough going over with a hand fork and remove every bit of perennial weed. Be particularly careful to fork out all creeping weeds such as couch grass and convolvulus. Any bits left behind will grow again and soon be competing with the herbs for food and light.

When you have cleared the soil and made it friable, add a handful of well-rotted manure or compost and mix it well into the soil. Then plant each herb carefully and firmly, leaving enough space between each one to allow for its eventual full development. Don't forget that what is a tiny thyme plant at present will be a thick clump over 30cm (12 in) across in a year's time.

Protection for vegetables

Those of you who decided in the early autumn (August) to sow spring cabbage should now have sturdy plants growing in the food plot. But they still have the winter months to contend with before they present you with their first harvest in late spring or early summer (end of April or May). Protect them from the worst of the winter weather by lightly forking over the soil between the rows, to a depth of a few centimetres, and giving them a light dusting of sulphate of potash at 35g per sq m (1 oz per sq yd). The potash will harden any remaining soft growth and increase the plants' chances of survival. Other green vegetables can be protected in the same way.

Tall vegetables, like brussels sprouts, may be blown over by strong winds and heavy rain, so make sure each plant is securely staked.

Storing canes and netting

Go round the garden and collect any stakes and canes that are no longer being used. Canes are expensive to buy, and it is senseless to let them deteriorate unnecessarily. Pull them up, clean the wet soil from their bases and tie them in neat bundles of ten or twelve before putting them away in a dry shed or garage. A wise precaution, with hollow canes, is to dip their ends in a bucket of Jeyes Fluid (used according to the manufacturer's instructions) in case earwigs or other pests are lurking inside them.

Netting used for supporting climbers (like peas) should also be brought in for the winter if you have not already done so. Pick off dead leaves and stems and roll it up ready for use next year. Gather up

any cloches that are not in current use; plastic cloches, in particular, are very light and prone to being blown away.

Completing the compost heap

After all the tidying and cleaning up your compost heaps will probably be full to the rim with the remains of the summer's greenery. There is no point in leaving the heaps uncovered any longer. Give them a last and generous sprinkling of compost accelerator, cover them with a layer of soil about 5cm (2 in) deep and put a sheet of heavy-duty polythene (weighted down with stones or bricks) over the top. The polythene will keep warmth in and excessive moisture out.

Winter lettuce

The winter lettuce that was sown in the food plot in mid autumn (September) should now be thinned to 25cm (9 in) apart. Don't throw the thinnings away as they make a delicious salad. Clear away any weeds that could be harbouring slugs and, as an added safeguard, put two or three slug pellets around each plant. Cover the plants with cloches to protect them from frost and to stop them becoming too mud-splashed.

Lifting celery

The celery is best lifted, one root at a time, as required. Fork the root up carefully so as not to damage the stems. Once lifted, if you don't intend to eat it immediately, wrap the stems in clean brown paper. This prevents them from turning green and becoming tough and stringy. Then stand the root in water until needed.

Cuttings from currants

Late autumn to early winter (October to November) is also an opportune time for taking cuttings of currants. They 'take' very easily; prunings left on loose soil will frequently root if accidentally trodden on. To do the job properly, however, cut off 15cm (6 in) lengths from this year's growth (cutting below a leaf bud). Then make v-shaped drills, 10–15cm (4–6 in) deep, in a sheltered spot and put the cuttings in them. Put the soil back round the cuttings and firm it down.

In twelve months' time you should have a good supply of young rooted bushes that are ready to be planted wherever you want them to fruit.

Planting raspberries

A few weeks ago you prepared the ground for the raspberry canes and erected supports for them. Now it is time to put in your chosen varieties. Plant the canes firmly, spreading the roots out and covering them with about 8cm (3 in) of soil. Leave 45cm (18 in) between canes and 1·8m (6 ft) between rows. After planting, cut the canes back to about 30cm (12 in) above soil level if·this has not already been done by the grower.

In spring, two or three new canes will emerge from each old one, and these should be tied in to the support wires as they grow. These are the canes that will bear a crop of fruit in the second year after planting.

The Asparagus Bed

Many gardeners regard asparagus as a luxury crop that has no place in an ordinary vegetable garden. Here we explain what is involved when starting asparagus cultivation and tell you how to prepare the bed and choose the plants.

Asparagus is easy to grow once its permanent bed has been well and truly prepared.

Other than thorough preparation there are several factors you should consider before committing yourself to growing it. First, with this crop, you cannot expect a rapid return for your time, money and effort. Two or three years must elapse before it produces tender stalks that are ready to eat. Furthermore, if you are expecting to move house in the near future then your successor will be the one to benefit from your asparagus bed, just as it is beginning to give a good yield.

Finally, asparagus is space-consuming. For an average family you will need a minimum of 25 plants, planted 45cm (18 in) apart, in rows 90cm (3 ft) apart. However, there is no reason why you shouldn't grow one or two other quick-maturing crops between the stalks. A few Tom Thumb lettuce, for instance, or a sprinkling of radish can be sown and harvested without interfering with the growth of the asparagus plants.

If none of these considerations deter you, then your asparagus bed will be a worthwhile investment that can continue to yield for 20 years or more.

Choosing the site
The soil of an asparagus bed must be rich but, within reason, it can vary from fairly heavy to quite light. It should also be a soil that does not dry out too easily, nor must it hold excessive water and become waterlogged in winter. In fact, regardless of soil type, it is always best to grow asparagus on a slightly raised bed. The bed should receive as much sun as possible and it should be sheltered from very strong winds.

Preparing the ground
For the first time in the Edible Garden you should double dig. Asparagus roots are long, and the more food they find in the depths of the soil the better the crop will be. As double digging (see page 21) proceeds, fork as much well-rotted manure or compost as you can spare into the bottom of the spit. Also dust the top

spit with bonemeal after you have thrown the topsoil forward into the trench.

When digging is finished, leave the surface rough until a week or two before planting time in mid or late spring (late March or early April).

Ordering the plants
Although spring seems a long way away, order your crowns now. Don't be tempted to save a year by buying crowns that are three years old. You will probably find two-year old crowns settle in better

Asparagus plants are unisexual; some of them bear only male flowers and others only female flowers. The male plants are the ones you should grow. These yield an earlier, and much heavier, crop because they devote their energies entirely to growth, so none is wasted on the production of fruits and seed. Fortunately the sexes can be recognized and segregated in the second year of growth from seed, and most of the two-year-old crowns that you buy will be male.

As to variety, Connover's Colossal is an excellent choice, producing an early crop of thick, succulent stalks

How to plant
Soil preparation begins again in mid spring (early March). This is when you form the ridges on which the crowns will be grown. On a dry day, tread the bed to crumble the rough soil. Then take out shallow trenches 90cm (3 ft) apart and form 25cm (9 in) high ridges along the centre of each with the excavated soil.

When the plants arrive it is vitally important that they are kept moist until they are actually in the soil. If they dry out, even for a few minutes, they will die. Asparagus roots are long and spidery. When planting, place the base of the crown on the centre of the ridge with its roots hanging down on each side. Cover them immediately with soil. Place the second crown in position 45cm (18 in) away from the first, and continue in this manner until you fill the trench.

Finally, complete replacement and refirming of the soil and level off with a rake. When you have finished, the tops of the crowns should have about 8–10cm (3–4 in) of soil covering them.

Sowing broad beans
Sow a row of broad beans for an early crop next year. Choose a short-stemmed, tough variety like Aquadulce. Sow them in a warm, sheltered part of the garden.

Asparagus shoots grow into ferny stems

Even in areas where winters are generally mild you must be prepared to give the plants some protection during very cold spells. In colder districts cloche protection is usually a necessity in winter, but any extra work that this makes is offset by the benefits of a really early crop.

Planting trees and shrubs
In early winter (November) there is still time for some last-minute preparation and planting before the onset of winter. The soil is as yet not too cold, and is certainly warm enough for the roots of newly-planted trees and shrubs. But if you don't complete planting during the next few weeks you will lose a year's good growth, for trees, shrubs and perennials planted late in the winter stand much less chance of making new roots before their top growth comes into full production with the arrival of the spring.

Early winter: Planting

Did you know that there is a member of the onion family called the tree onion? It is a perennial that comes up year after year. It has stems about 1m (3–4 ft) tall on top of which grow small bulblets (the onions) roughly the size of onion sets. If you can manage to obtain some, this is the time to put in the small bulbs. Plant them 2–3cm (1 in) deep and 30cm (12 in) apart in a good, rich soil. During their first year the plants concentrate on establishing a firm basal clump. In their second season they will crop well and will then continue to do so for many years. Keep back a few of the bulbs for future planting.

The normal practice, in the second year, is to harvest the bulblets in mid autumn (September) and either pickle them as 'cocktail' onions or use them for flavouring cooked dishes.

In the third year (or thereafter) you can dig up a whole clump in the autumn to reach the larger onion bulbs that have developed beneath the soil. These have an excellent and fairly strong flavour. Keep back two of the bulbs and replant them to provide a continuous supply.

Planting and forcing rhubarb

Another planting for early winter (November) is rhubarb. The crowns are readily available in most good garden centres and shops. There is a mistaken belief that rhubarb will grow anywhere; but if, in two years time, it is going to

produce long, juicy sticks, you must provide it with a good soil that is well-drained but never gets too dry.

Champagne Early is a good variety to grow. It produces long, bright red stalks that are juicy and well-flavoured.

If you already have rhubarb in your garden, bring next year's crop a little nearer by forcing one or two crowns. Lift these and leave them on the soil for the frost to get at the roots. They will come to no harm as this 'frosting' is all part of the forcing process.

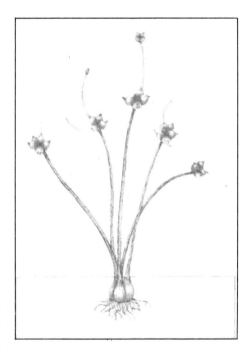

Tree onion, bulbs above and below ground

In mid or late winter (December or January) put them into shallow trays of soil with only the tips showing. Keep the whole tray at a temperature of around 13°C (55°F) and in total darkness (you can cover it with black polythene). The soil should remain just moist. Cut the tender stems when they are 30cm (12 in) or a little longer.

Forcing seakale

If you have seakale growing in the garden, a similar method of forcing can be used. This vegetable, which is a member of the brassica family, will then give you creamy-white, sweet, nutty-flavoured shoots in the winter.

Lift the crowns and cut away the roots to within about 15cm (6 in) of the base of each crown. Plant them 15cm (6 in) apart in large pots containing a mixture of roughly equal parts of soil, sand and peat and put them outside – safe from frost.

Some four or five weeks before you want to plant the shoots bring a pot indoors and force the roots in exactly the same way as for rhubarb.

Caring for asparagus

For the first year of growth let the plants build up their strength for future cropping. Do not be tempted to cut any sticks for eating as this weakens the plants. Give the bed plenty of water in dry spells.

This time next year, in early winter (November), the plants will have died down leaving only a yellowed 'fern' above the soil. At this stage cut all the stems back to about 2–3cm (1 in) above ground level. Clear away the debris and burn it. Push a marker in alongside each crown so that you can see at a glance where they are. Hoe the bed clean of weeds and fork out all those with deep roots, such as docks. Then cover the whole bed with an 8–10cm (3–4 in) layer of well-rotted manure or compost.

In mid spring (early March) top-dress with fish, blood and bone meal at 70–100g per sq m (2–3 oz per sq yd) and lightly fork the soil between the crowns to a depth of no more than 5–8cm (2–3 in).

In the third year after planting two-year-old crowns you can begin to cut, taking only two or three sticks from each plant (and then only if the growth is strong). It will be four or five years before the bed is in full production and well cared for, but then it should remain so for twenty years or more.

Cutting asparagus

Cutting calls for skill, common sense and a long, narrow-bladed, sharp knife. Select the stick you intend to cut and with your hand follow it down below ground to cut it about 10cm (4 in) below soil level. Cutting has to be done very carefully because it is so easy to damage younger, adjacent sticks that are not yet showing above the soil. Leave a few sticks or stems uncut to keep the plant vigorous, and cease cutting altogether after mid summer (the end of June).

IN THE GREENHOUSE

Now, for sowing in the greenhouse – mustard and cress. Now that the summer lettuce is over, mustard and cress makes a useful alternative in sandwiches and salads. Scatter the seeds thinly and evenly onto shallow trays or punnets of soil. Sow more at frequent intervals for a constant supply throughout the winter.

Checking crops in store

Early to mid winter (mid November) is a good time to check over everything you have in store. For instance, gently tip the maincrop potatoes out of their bags onto the garage floor and sift through them to make sure there are no rotten ones. The disease in a single rotten potato, if left unchecked, can spread to all the healthy ones in the bag. At the same time check the apples, carrots, beetroot and anything else that could be spoilt.

Many people believe that grapes are luxuries to be enjoyed only by the wealthy. It is also widely believed that grapes are difficult to grow and need exacting greenhouse conditions. Those of you without a greenhouse, will be pleased to learn that grapes can be grown successfully out of doors in all but the coldest parts of the country.

Try to obtain young pot-grown vines from your local garden centre or shop. When you bring the plants home, water the pots and let them stand to drain for an hour or so before planting.

Two excellent varieties for outdoor cultivation are Black Hamburg and the smaller-fruiting Noir Hâtif de Marseilles.

How and where to plant

Grapes will need some protection from the harshest elements, so plant them in the lee of a south-facing wall or fence. As for soil, any average garden soil will do. In fact it is a mistake to plant grape vines in a rich soil as they will make a lot of soft growth and crop badly. They do, however, appreciate good drainage; and this should usually be no problem against the base of a house wall.

To plant, first tap the rootball out of the pot. Then, with a trowel, make a planting hole and put the plant in, spreading out the bottom roots as you do

so. Firm the soil back in around the roots, water the plant well in and apply a mulch of well-rotted compost.

Supporting the stems

Next you must provide some means of support for the vines when they begin to grow. To get the best results the vines should be held about 2–5cm (1–2 in) away from the wall. The best structure consists of strong wire running between a series of vine-eyes driven into the wall. Vine-eyes are tough nails with circular-holed heads through which wire may be threaded, drawn tight and firmly secured. The distances between the strands of wire and their general direction depends entirely on which way you want your vines to run.

The simplest and best method of cultivation is the single-rod system. By this method a single main stem or rod is encouraged to grow until the required height or length is achieved in four or five years' time. Lateral shoots emerge from the rod every year and it is on these that the bunches of grapes are eventually allowed to develop.

Pruning the vine

After planting cut the stem back to leave no more than four buds. Tie the vine in to its support, and when growth starts in spring choose the strongest shoot for your permanent rod and pinch out the other stems. Cut back all sideshoots that grow from the rod to within 90cm (3 ft) of their point of origin.

In order to build up a strong framework, pruning is vitally important and should be done in mid winter (December) when growth is at a standstill. At this time, after the leaves have fallen, cut back the main rod to wood that is hard and mature, even if it means cutting back to about 25–30cm (9–12 in) from soil level. In addition, cut back all laterals to one bud from the base.

During the second full summer of growth, encourage the vine to grow as

A polythene-covered mound has many advantages for growing strawberries

much as possible. Cut off any flowering shoots to prevent fruit from forming, so that the vine can channel all its energies into extending the rod framework. In addition, pinch out the growing tips of the lateral shoots when they are about 60cm (24 in) long. After leaf-fall in the following mid winter (December), cut back hard these shortened laterals to one bud from the rod and shorten the rod itself to about 90cm (3 ft); this will automatically remove some of the laterals altogether.

In the third year you must again prevent all fruiting by cutting off the flowering shoots. In the third winter shorten the main rod to about 1·8m (6 ft) and cut back laterals as before.

In the fourth year the vine is established and you can begin to enjoy its fruit. In this, and every subsequent year, about early summer (May), stop the laterals at one pair of leaves beyond the bunch of forming grapes; if no grapes are evident stop the laterals at about 60cm (24 in) from the rod. And every winter, after leaf-fall, prune each lateral back to one bud from base until, as the years pass, a gnarled knob of growth spurs is formed.

Given time to develop, your outdoor vine will provide you with good bunches of dessert grapes for many years. But do not expect too much from it; always restrict fruiting (by thinning out the bunches) to one bunch for every 30cm (12 in) of rod. Start by removing poorly formed bunches first, and use vine scissors for the job.

Danish strawberry tip

There is something to be learnt from the Danes when it comes to strawberry cultivation.

Along the breadth of part of a Dane's vegetable plot runs a rounded ridge some 30–38cm (12–15 in) high and some 90cm (3 ft) wide. The whole elongated mound is covered in black polythene through which protrude strawberry plants at 45cm (18 in) intervals. As you will appreciate, by this system the fruit is always dry as all the rain water runs off the sloping sides.

The plants are also protected from slugs and the black polythene serves as a perfect weed control. Good crops of disease and pest-free fruit are harvested on a regular basis. Furthermore, more plants per unit can be grown in an area of level soil because some plants are in effect 'up in the air'. It could well be worth trying this method in your garden next season.

In a garden with limited space the choice of fruit trees is all important. In the average garden there is room, perhaps, for only two (at the most three) apple trees and possibly one pear tree; so it is essential to choose the right varieties and the best forms.

Forms of apple tree
Nearly all fruit trees come in various shapes. The three main forms are bush, half-standard and standard. Even experts differ on which tree form is the best for the small garden but the standard type is probably the most suitable.

A standard apple tree has a bare stem some 1·8m (6 ft) tall with a number of branches emerging from the top. As the tree grows, the branches spread upwards and outwards leaving plenty of room beneath to grow other plants and to tend them unhampered by low branches. In other words, the fruit crop occupies air space, freeing the ground beneath for other things.

A bush fruit tree has branches emerging from a short stem only about 60cm (24 in) high and consequently the lower branches are almost at ground level and they may even touch the ground when they are heavy with fruit.

A half-standard lies somewhere in between the bush and the full standard, with branches emerging from a point about 1·4m (4½ ft) above the ground.

Selecting the rootstock
Having decided which type of tree is best suited to your requirements, then choose your rootstock. Apple varieties do not grow on their own roots. They are grafted on to special rootstocks of varying vigour so that their growth can be controlled to suit the planting site. Some rootstocks restrict growth whilst others are much more 'strong-growing'.

For a fairly compact edible garden make sure you ask your nurseryman (or at your garden centre) for an apple tree grown on M9 or M26 rootstock (or on the slightly larger MM106). If he is not familiar with these terms, take your

custom elsewhere rather than run the risk of buying a tree on an over-vigorous stock. Both M9 and M26 are dwarfing stocks and your tree will grow well, but slowly, to a manageable size. It will also give a good crop in good soil.

Growing trees from pips
The question that puzzles many new gardeners is why go to all the bother of buying apple trees when it is a simple matter to sow a few pips and grow your own. The answer is simple. Pips or, to be more accurate, apple seeds will certainly germinate and will eventually grow into apple trees, but they will be trees of indeterminate and almost certainly indifferent quality. Gardeners who do try this method generally find, after waiting for many years, that all they have is a large tree that produces crops of tiny, very bitter apples.

Choosing varieties
Before buying your tree you must think about the variety you are going to select. If you have room for only one apple tree you will be looking for the seemingly impossible – an apple that will be delicious whether raw or cooked. It is not impossible. The variety James Grieve 'eats straight off the tree' in mid to late autumn (late September) with a juicy, acid-sweet flavour. It also cooks well. Unfortunately it bruises fairly easily and will not keep for any length of time.

Another way of tackling the problem is to plant a 'family tree'. This is a tree bearing three different varieties grafted onto the one rootstock. In most cases the family tree will carry two dessert apple varieties and one cooking apple.

If, however, you have sufficient space in your garden to plant two apple trees – one for eating and one for cooking – my choice would be the dual-purpose James Grieve and the superb 'keeping' cooker Lane's Prince Albert; this variety will give you regular crops of tart, juicy, fine-flavoured apples to use in the kitchen from early winter to early spring (November to February).

You may be wondering why Cox's Orange Pippin hasn't been recommended. In my experience Cox's only does does well in mild areas; it detests cold, heavy soils and crops erratically in colder regions.

In these conditions the late dessert variety Laxton's Superb is far more reliable and its flavour compares favourably with Cox's.

Sowing
For an early to mid winter (November–December) sowing of peas outdoors, choose a round-seeded rather than a wrinkled-seeded variety. Meteor is a very hardy variety (and good on heavy soils); given a sheltered spot it will come through the hard weather safely. In fact peas in general are fairly tough and will withstand a temperature as low as $-11°C$ ($12°F$), but their flowers are less hardy and a sharp frost in mid spring (March) can damage them beyond repair.

Sow your seeds, therefore, in a warm spot in the garden and protect them with cloches when the plants flower in mid to late spring (late March or early April).

Sow the seeds 5cm (2 in) apart in trenches 30cm (12 in) wide and 5cm (2 in) deep, in ground that was well manured for a previous crop – for instance where the onions were grown and then harvested in mid autumn (September). It is better not to use any fertilizer at the time of sowing as the young seedlings should not be making soft top growth but be developing into strong, sturdy plants that can survive harsh winter weather.

Pruning young apple trees
If the standard trees are young, winter pruning 'shapes them up' and controls their future growth. In the case of older trees the pruning serves mainly to tidy them, by cutting out old, dead or diseased branches and by removing ones that may be congesting the centre of the trees and

excluding light and air.

With young, newly-planted trees the pruning is quite severe. Young trees usually have about three long, slender branches. Cut back each of these to an outward-facing bud. In the spring two new branches will grow from beneath the cut. In the following mid winter (December) shorten these branches by half, again cutting to an outward-facing bud. Once more two new lateral branches will develop below each cut, so that in just two years the number of branches has been increased from the original three to twelve, forming an open-cup arrangement.

The tree will then begin to look more like a tree and less like a leggy sapling; your pruning helps to form this canopy of branches and leaves. The tree will then begin to bear fruit.

Pruning established trees
The purpose of pruning is to increase fruit production and improve the quality. Once the tree is well established, continuous hard pruning is unnecessary. Too much of it will induce the growth of new branches and leaves, channelling the energies of the tree away from the production of a good fruit crop.

Root pruning
Sometimes, however, apple trees behave 'contrarily'. Despite correct pruning they produce masses of branches and leaves and bear hardly any fruit. Here drastic measures are called for in the shape of root pruning. When the trees are only a few years old, up to the age of six or seven, the easiest way to prune their roots is to dig the tree up and cut off all thick side roots and the central tap root. Then put the tree back into its hole, push the soil in around the roots and firm it down. Curbing the root system in this way reduces top growth, and then fruit output

will improve.

Older trees need different treatment. To get at their roots, dig out a circular trench, 45cm (18 in) wide, some 45–60cm (18–24 in) away from the base of the tree. As you dig down you will find thick roots that will need to be sawn through. When all the large roots are severed, replace and firm the soil.

Pruning pear trees
Where pear trees are concerned, winter pruning of young trees follows the pattern as described for apples. In the case of older, established trees, never prune if you can avoid it. Never make the mistake of cutting a pear tree hard back even if it is

casting an irritating shadow. It will invariably grow back even more vigorously which may well result in you having to take the drastic action of cutting down that tree.

Planting pear trees
It is not too late to plant pear trees, but the sooner you put them in the better. Remember that the trees should be planted in pairs – the two trees being of different varieties. The reason for this is that, for all practical purposes, pears are not self-fertile and need a cross-pollinator before they will bear fruit. For the average edible garden, Conference is a good variety, that is ready in mid to late Autumn (late September), and William's Bon Chrétien, that ripens in early to mid autumn (towards the end of August).

Spraying fruit trees
There is another job to be tackled this month – all fruit trees and bushes need

spraying with tar oil winter wash. There is a lot of truth in the old saying that one winter spray is worth ten summer ones, and that an application of insecticide in mid winter (December) keeps the trees clear of pests throughout most summers. In the winter the eggs of sap-sucking aphides lie in the cracks and crevices of the bark. So this is the time to spray and kill them before they hatch out and become destructive pests in spring.

Be careful when handling these sprays. Don't let your eyes or skin come into contact with them, and don't inhale them. Wear rubber gloves and cover your nose and mouth with a mask or scarf. Stand on the windward side of the tree so that the spray drifts away from you. Also take care not to spray your neighbours if they are out in their own gardens. Finally, when the job is done, wash any surplus liquid down a drain, rinse out the container several times and wash your face and hands in hot, soapy water.

Tar oil winter wash will also kill mosses and lichens growing on tree trunks and branches, and clear paths and drives of the green algal growth that becomes so slippery when it gets wet.

Blanching chicory
This week you can start to blanch the chicory plants that were sown in mid summer (June) and transferred to a frost-proof trench in late autumn (October).

Lift as many plants as you require for a meal, and cut the leaves off about 2–3cm (1 in) above the crown. Leave them some-where cool and frost-free for a week. Next, cut off any sideshoots, and cut back the root until it is no more than 20cm (8 in) long. Pack the roots on end, in deep pots or boxes of moist peat, and cover them over with a 15cm (6 in) layer of fine grit, sand or sifted soil.

Place the boxes or pots somewhere in darkness, where you can be sure of a constant temperature of 10–13°C (50–55°F). You could, for instance, put them under the greenhouse staging and cover them with a sheet of black poly-thene; or you could put them near the central heating boiler.

The young shoots or 'chicons' are ready when their tips are just peeping through the soil. Cut them immediately above the roots and use them while they are still blanched a pure white. They are delicious served 'au gratin', or added to salads or stuffed with minced meat flavoured with parsley and nutmeg.

Vegetable gardeners have become much more adventurous in recent years. It is now not uncommon to find quite 'exotic' vegetables in food plots and allotments.

For your first year of the Edible Garden we grew, in the main, familiar crops. But next year you might like to be a little more adventurous. There are quite a few rarely-grown, but delicious, vegetables that are not difficult to cultivate.

Asparagus peas
To start with, try a row of asparagus peas. This vegetable is, in fact, no relation to the pea family. The pods look very strange: they are triangular and have three thin, wiry-like outgrowths, while the flowers are reddish-brown and not white like most pea blossoms.

In late spring (April) sow the small seeds 15cm (6 in) apart and 13mm ($\frac{1}{2}$ in) deep in trenches 30cm (12 in) wide. When the seedlings are large enough, thin them to about 30cm (12 in) apart. Asparagus peas make bushy plants so there is no need to support them with netting. But push in a few twiggy sticks here and there to prevent the pea-laden plants toppling over. The pods are cooked whole and have a slight 'tang' of asparagus.

IN THE GREENHOUSE

Dwarf early peas
Buy a packet of dwarf early peas (Early Marvel is a good choice) and about six 25cm (10 in) pots. Put a 5cm (2 in) layer of well-rotted compost or manure in the bottom of each pot and fill up to within 2–3cm (1 in) of the rim with the best soil you can find. Now space out eight seeds on the surface and push each one 2–3cm (1 in) into the soil. Cover them over, firm the soil, water it well and stand the pots on the greenhouse staging near the glass. A temperature of 7–10°C (45–50°F) should be enough for germination.

Cleaning out the greenhouse
The greenhouse is due for its winter 'spring-clean'. Start by getting rid of the withered remains of the tomato crop; these harbour all sorts of pests and diseases, so pull them up and burn them. Then turn your attention to the glass and give it a good wash down with soapy water. The spot where one pane of glass overlaps another is a favourite nesting place for green algae, so gently prize the panes apart and clean out this area with a knife and some Jeyes Fluid disinfectant.

Swill out the whole of the green-house by pouring Jeyes Fluid (diluted according to maker's instructions) over and under the staging, on the path and on the soilbed. It will kill off many lurking or dormant pests. Finally, if you have wooden staging, give it a coating of wood preservative to pre-vent rot. But never use creosote for this job: it vaporizes in warmth and the resulting fumes are deadly to plants.

Lining the greenhouse
One worthwhile tip that you might consider in order to save fuel (and money) is to line your greenhouse with lightweight polythene sheeting to re-duce heat loss.

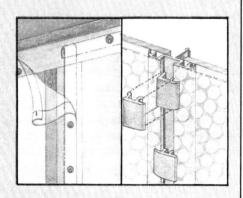

Pin on polythene sheets or use 'bubble' insulation with metal clip and bracket

Sowing leeks

It is time to make a sowing of leeks (a variety such as Marble Pillar), in trays of seed compost. It is well worth starting leeks early to get good thick stems by late summer (July). Sow the seeds thinly in J.I. Compost and transplant the seedlings when they are about 5cm (2 in) tall, into trays of J.I. No 2.

Tomato soilbed

For those of you who do not wish to grow tomatoes by the ring-culture method, now is a good time to prepare the soilbed. The ideal is to spread a good 15cm (6 in) layer of well-rotted compost or manure over the bed and dig it in to a spade's depth. Remember, if you are using manure, that it must be old and well rotted; fresh manure produces rank top growth and seems to restrict root development. After digging, tread the soil to firm it and apply fish, blood and bone fertilizer at 70–100g per sq m (2–3 oz per sq yd).

Sugar peas

Sugar peas, also known as mangetout peas, crop prodigiously in rich, fertile soils. The pods are cooked whole and are very sweet.

Sow the seeds 5–8cm (2–3 in) apart in early summer (May). Sugar peas will need a strong support system (as for ordinary peas) as they grow to about 1·8m (6 ft).

Cabbage and cauliflower

Golden Acre is a good medium size, rounded heart variety which should heart up nicely. Likewise with the cauliflower variety All the Year Round the curds develop quickly once they begin to form. You can keep cauliflowers in good condition for about a week if you dig them up by the roots and hang them, head downwards in a cool, dark place. Alternatively to prevent a glut, it may be worth your while growing winter cauliflowers rather than summer ones. The Australian variety South Pacific is ready for cutting in late autumn (October) for late spring (April) sowings and, in cooler days stands for a considerable time before bolting.

Runner beans

Runner beans tend to be slow to set on the lower stems but then make up very quickly for lost time and produce in quantity.

Of the two varieties, the old faithful Streamline and the more recent variety, Fry (White Stringless), Streamline is ready to pick two weeks earlier. However Fry continue to crop well into the Autumn and come well recommended. The beans are a bit misshapen as a rule but tend to be entirely stringless, succulent and absolutely delicious.

Another noteworthy variety is Cookham Dene. On the trial seed grounds, Cookham Dene outcrops all the other varieties and the beans are of good quality.

Onion sets and seeds

In growing onions there is an important lesson to be learned. If you grow four rows of onions, two from sets and two from seeds, you may find that there is a far higher yield from the seedlings than the sets. The lesson seems to be that sets are the easiest and most convenient way to grow onions but you can increase the yield by as much as 50 per cent if you go to the trouble of sowing a good variety in warmth in late winter (January). Naturally other factors such as the climate (sets are popular in less favourable climates) and the soil type will influence your preference for seeds or sets but it is a point to bear in mind when compiling your seed order for next year.

Plan for Spring

When spring arrives you will be fully occupied with sowing and planting. Work will proceed much faster if your equipment is in order and your seeds have all arrived from the seedsmen.

You should by now (being a far-sighted edible gardener) have your garden and greenhouse almost ready for the activity that spring will bring. If so, your soil will be dug and you will have turned in every available scrap of rotted manure and garden compost. You will have cleaned out your greenhouse and repaired your cloches. You will have washed and sterilized your plant pots and seed trays, discarding those that are cracked and broken beyond repair. And, being really economical, you will have gone round the garden retrieving plastic plant labels and cleaning them with a dash of scouring powder on a damp cloth.

You should also check over your gardening tools; wipe the spade with an oily rag to prevent rust, and it would be a good idea to give the other rust-prone tools (especially the hand fork and trowel) a rub over as well even if they were all done previously in the autumn. Also look at the garden line to make sure that the cord is still strong enough to be pulled taut for drawing out drills in the food plot, without breaking.

Buying in fresh compost

After checking your equipment, start making your shopping list. For seed

EDIBLE GARDEN SELECTIONS

CROP		SUGGESTED VARIETY	COMMENTS
asparagus		Connover's Colossal	start cutting in third year
bean, broad		The Midget	only 30–45cm (12–18 in) tall
		Aquadulce	for a very early crop
		Rentpayer	long pods; heavy cropper
	dwarf French	Tendergreen	stringless, round pods
	runner	Enorma	heavy, early yields; good freezer
		Cookham Dene	long beans; excellent flavour
beetroot		Boltardy	round-rooted; resistant to bolting
		Housewives Choice	long, cylindrical roots
borecole (kale)		Frosty	provides fresh greens in winter
broccoli, sprouting		Early Purple Sprouting	hardy; ready in mid spring
		Green Sprouting (calabrese)	ready in mid autumn
brussels sprout		Peer Gynt (F.1 hybrid)	early and prolific
		Citadel (F.1 hybrid)	for use in mid winter
cabbage, summer		Golden Acre	neat and compact for small gardens
		Hispi (F.1 hybrid)	large, pointed hearts
		Primo	compact, round-headed and reliable
	winter	January King	large heads; very hardy
		Hidena (F.1 hybrid)	very hard heads of good size
	spring	Offenham–Flower of Spring	tried-and-true variety
capsicum (sweet pepper)		Canape (F.1 hybrid)	will crop outdoors in warm, sheltered positions
carrot		St Valery	long, tapering roots
		Pioneer (F.1 hybrid)	heavy cropper; cylindrical roots
		Chantenay Red Cored	excellent, reliable, stump-rooted type
cauliflower (including hearting broccoli)		Canberra	for late autumn cutting
		Early Snowball	invaluable for early use
		Snow's Winter White	a welcome winter vegetable
		St George	ready in mid to late spring
celeriac		Marble Ball	'turnip-rooted' celery; easy to grow
celery		Golden Self-Blanching	needs no earthing
chicory		Whitloof	blanch and use in winter
cress		Double Curled	can be grown all year round
cucumber, outdoor		Burpee Hybrid (F.1 hybrid)	easy to grow; fine flavour
	indoor	Pepinex (F.1 hybrid)	an 'all-female' variety
		Conqueror	good for unheated greenhouses
endive		Batavian Broad Leaved	for winter salads
kohl rabi		White Vienna	root vegetable; nutty flavour
leaf beet		Rhubarb Chard	crops in summer and autumn
		Seakale (Swiss chard)	leaves and midribs are cooked
		Perpetual Spinach (spinach beet)	useful spinach-flavoured winter vegetable; very hardy
leek		Marble Pillar	early and hardy

CROP	SUGGESTED VARIETY	COMMENTS
lettuce	Sugar Cos	very sweet; upright growth
	Ilo	longstanding, smooth cabbage type
	Tom Thumb	small, sweet, crisp head
	Salad Bowl	a 'cut-and-come-again' variety
marrow, trailing	Golden Delicious	prolific and keeps well
	Long Green Trailing	very large; stores well
bush	Zucchini (F.1 hybrid)	cut as 15cm (6 in) long 'courgettes'
	Custard Pie	round, flattened, white marrows
melon	Sweetheart (F.1 hybrid)	will grow in frames and cloches
mustard	Finest White	to grow with cress
onion, spring	White Lisbon	pull for salads
sets	Sturon	heavy yields; large, round bulbs
keeping	Bedfordshire Champion	fine flavour; heavy cropper
	Superba (F.1 hybrid)	large, round bulbs
parsnip	Hollow Crown Improved	sow late to avoid canker
pea, early	Kelvedon Wonder	short-stemmed; very sweet
	Vitalis	one of the heaviest croppers
second-early	Dark-skinned Perfection	to follow Kelvedon Wonder
maincrop	Onward	disease-resistant and reliable
	Dwarf Greensleeves	long, curved pods; fine flavour
potato, early	Arran Pilot	large potato; best for light soils
	Pentland Javelin	white-fleshed; good cropper
maincrop	King Edward VII	old favourite; cooks and stores well
	Golden Wonder	for first-class chips and roast potatoes
radish	Cherry Belle	red, round and sweet
	French Breakfast	long and red; white-tipped
rhubarb	Holstein Bloodred	cut in second year
shallot	Longkeeping Yellow	good for pickling and for salads
spinach, summer	Longstanding Round	keep plants moist to prevent bolting
winter	Longstanding Prickly	use from early winter on
swede	Chignecto	resistant to club root disease
sweet corn	North Star (F.1 hybrid)	the best all-rounder for all districts
tomato, outdoor	Gemini (F.1 hybrid)	for outdoors or under glass
	The Amateur	bush type; good yield and flavour
indoor	Alicante	good flavour; heavy cropper
	Carters Fruit	peels like a peach; delicious flavour
	Davington Epicure (F.1 hybrid)	sweet-flavoured
	Moneymaker	heavy cropper; solid, medium fruit
turnip	Red Top Milan	excellent, early variety

The Gardener's Seasons

early spring	(February)	early summer	(May)	early autumn	(August)	early winter	(November)
mid spring	(March)	mid summer	(June)	mid autumn	(September)	mid winter	(December)
late spring	(April)	late summer	(July)	late autumn	(October)	late winter	(January)

sowing in pots and trays you need a good, sterilized seed compost. Don't be tempted to use last year's compost again; all its goodness will have gone and it is now only fit for adding to the compost heap or throwing on the garden soil. If you are undecided whether to buy the John Innes Seed Compost or one of the soilless ones, I would go for soilless compost. There is very little difference in price and soilless composts are lighter and easier to handle (if instructions are followed) and, by virtue of their high porosity and open texture, they warm up faster in spring – important for good, rapid germination. Furthermore, seedlings tend to grow faster in soilless composts and make bigger and better root systems than they do in the J.I. Seed Compost. Lastly, the J.I. composts are very variable and some bear little resemblance to the original formula laid down by the John Innes Horticultural Institute in the late 1930s.

Ordering seeds

The main item on your list will, of course, be seeds. The sooner you order them the more certain you are of getting your chosen varieties. Seed growers the world over do their utmost to cater for every gardener's needs, but they cannot anticipate the total or partial crop failures that inevitably create seed shortages later in the spring. If you are ordering your seeds from a catalogue, remember to allow for a minimum of 7–14 days for delivery, so place your order at least two weeks before you actually require the seeds for sowing. Bear in mind, also, that your mail order seedsmen may be sold out of a variety that you particularly want and you will not know of his inability to fulfill your entire order until the parcel is delivered. Order in good time, therefore, so that you can get the missing items elsewhere before it is too late to sow. This applies particularly to early-sown crops such as onions and tomatoes.